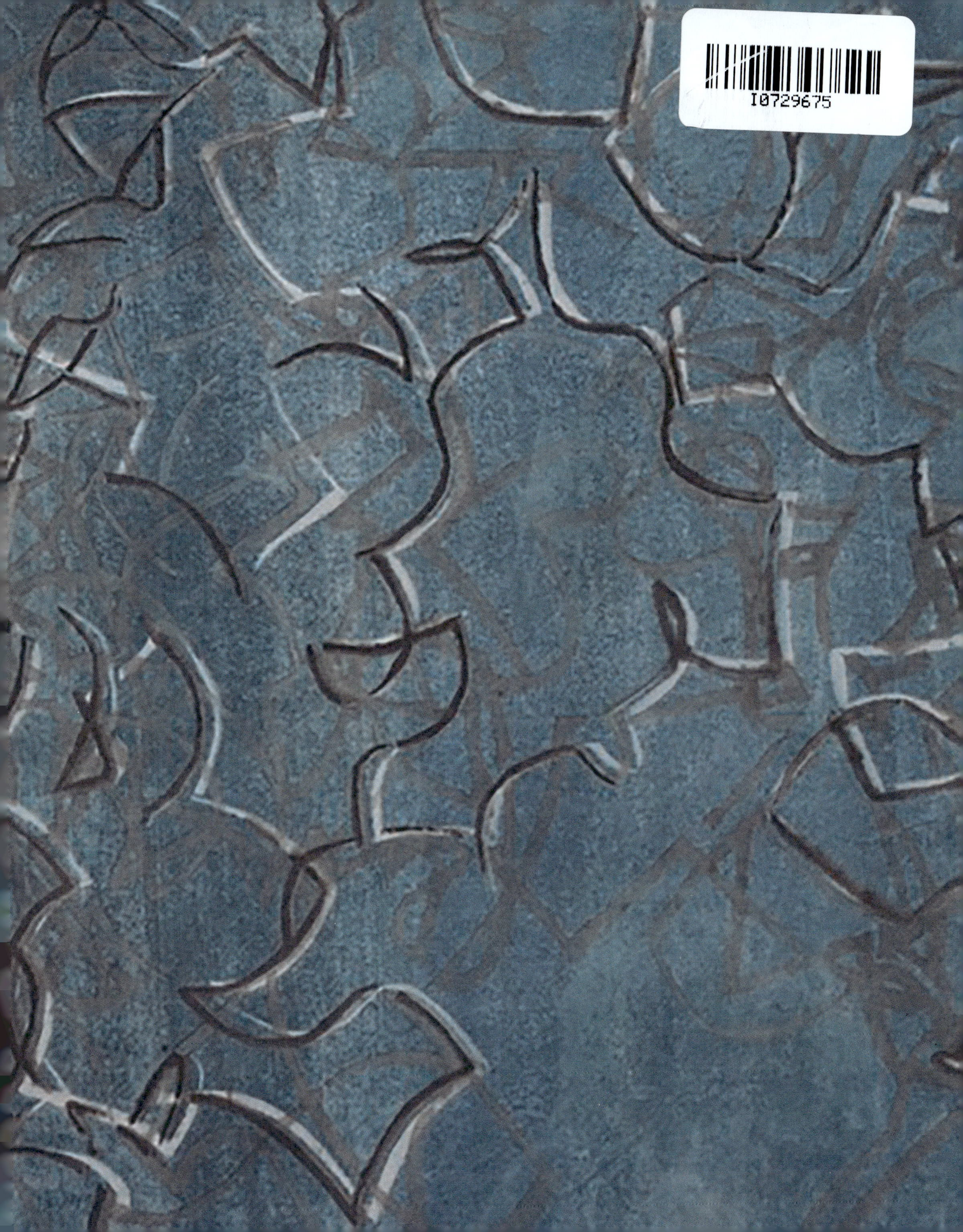

I0729675

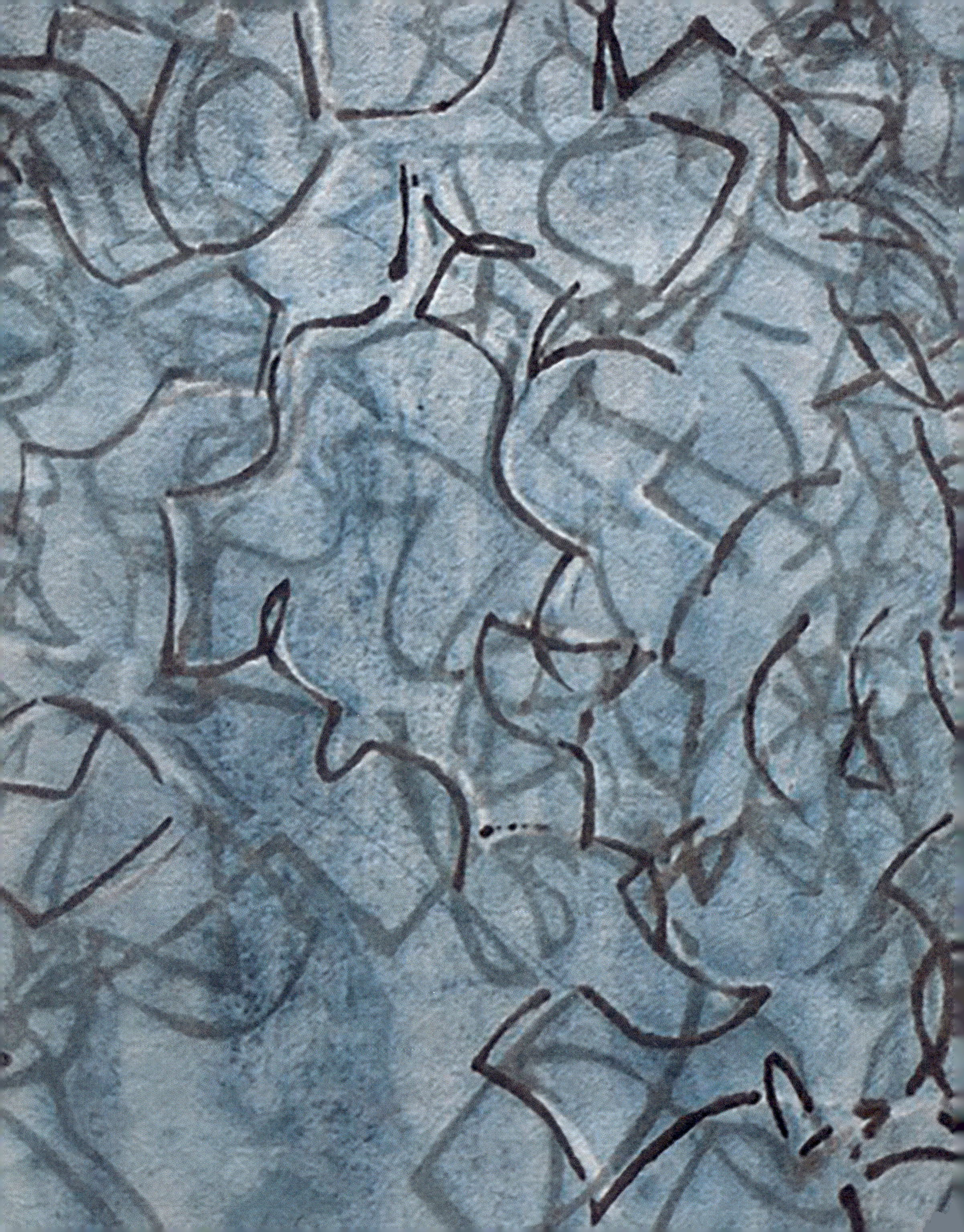

Japanese woodcut

TRADITIONAL
TECHNIQUES AND
CONTEMPORARY
PRACTICE

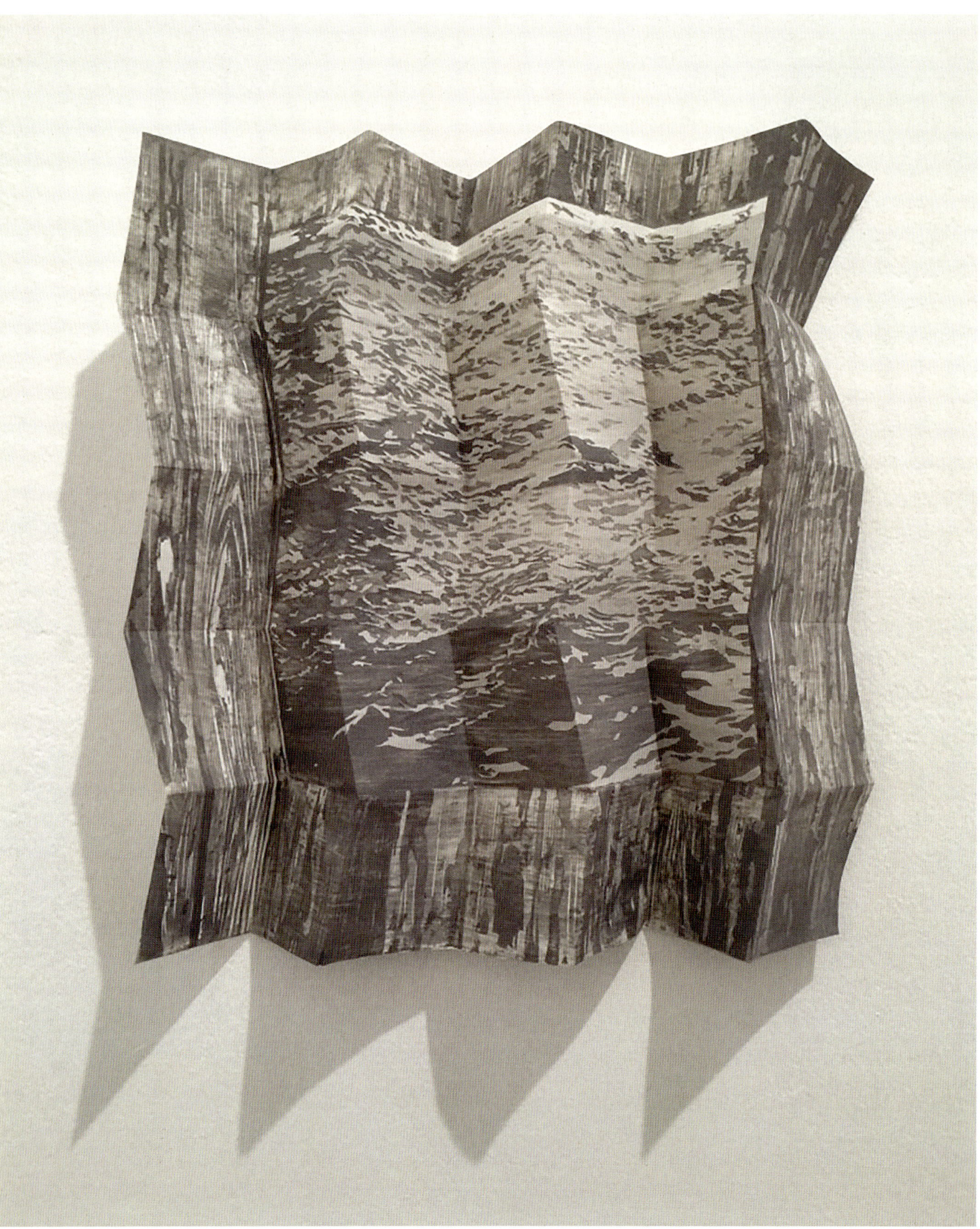

Carol Wilhide Justin

Japanese woodcut

TRADITIONAL TECHNIQUES AND CONTEMPORARY PRACTICE

THE CROWOOD PRESS

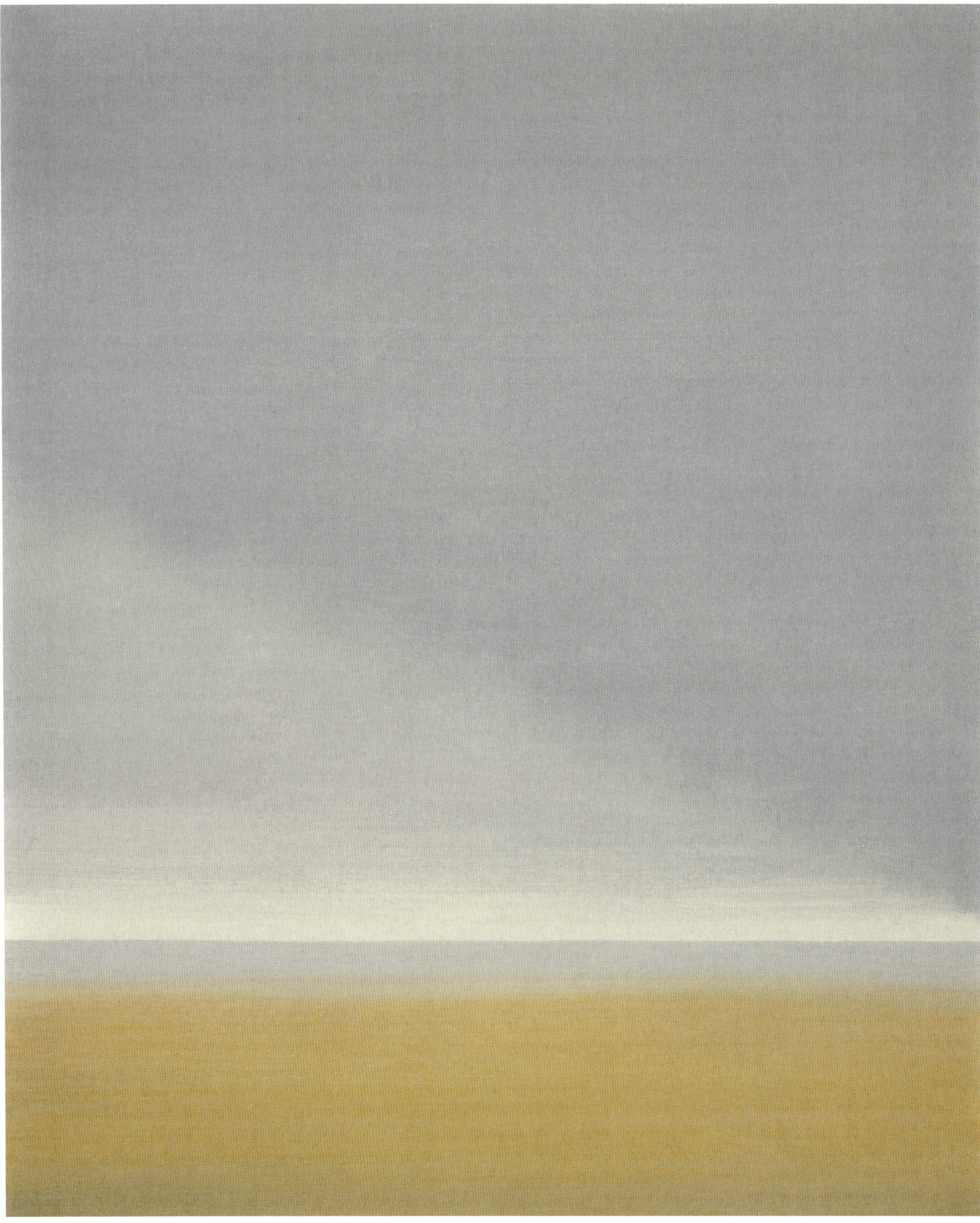

CONTENTS

	Introduction	7
1	A History of Japanese Woodcut	9
2	Materials and Equipment	57
3	Design	91
4	Cutting	105
5	Printing	125
6	Advanced Traditional Printing Techniques	143
7	Printing Large Works	163
8	Contemporary Artists	171
	Glossary	200
	Suppliers	202
	Bibliography	203
	Resources	204
	Artists' Details	205
	Image Credits	206
	Index	207

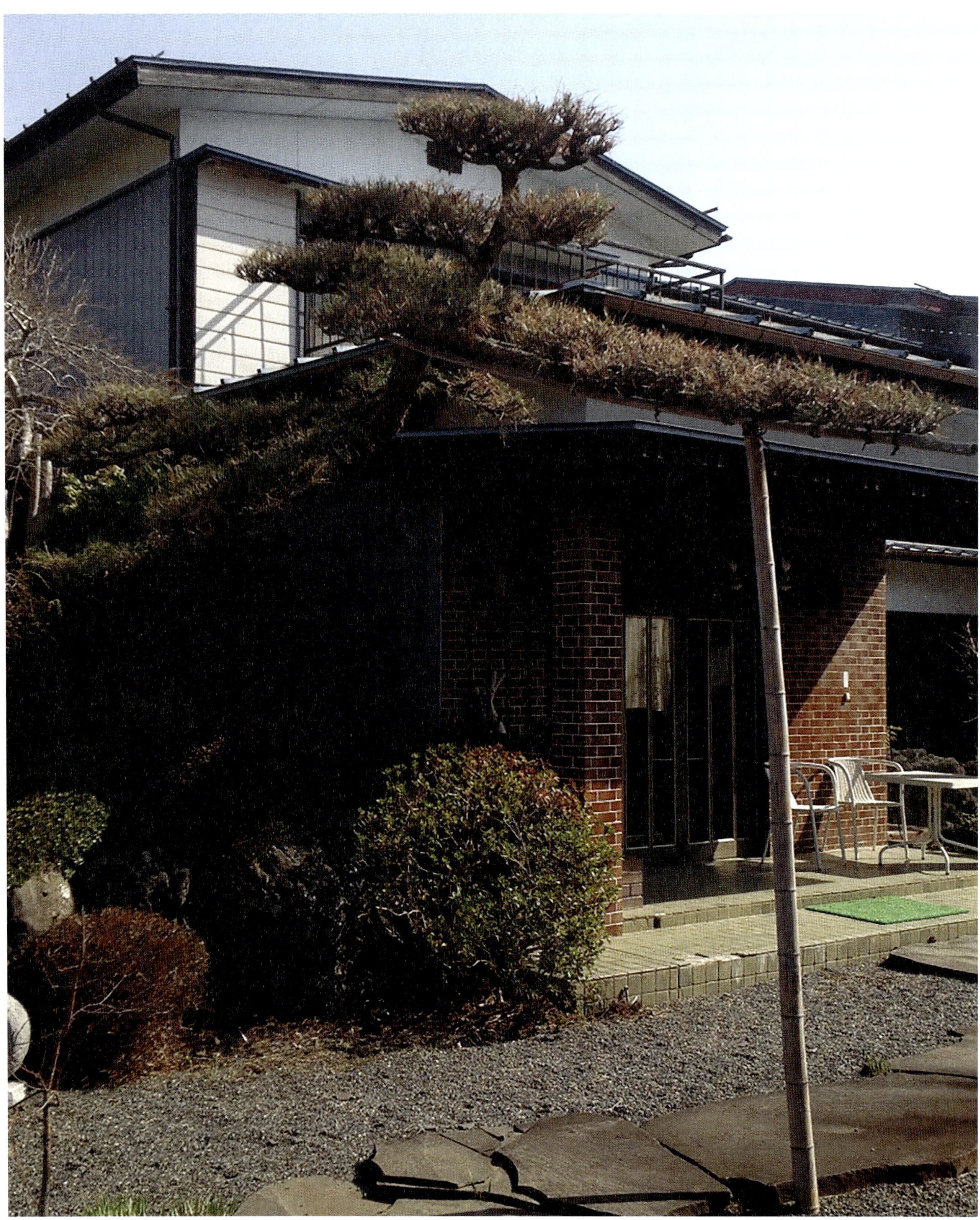

INTRODUCTION

Hokusai's *The Great Wave off Kanagawa* is arguably among the most famous images in the world, but how much do you know about how it was made? Japanese woodcut or Mokuhanga is a traditional multi-coloured woodblock printmaking technique with a long cultural history. The prints of the *ukiyō-e,* translated as Prints of the Floating World, were virtually unknown in the West until the late nineteenth century. They electrified the Impressionist painters in Europe, with their asymmetrical compositions, flat colour and everyday subject matter. You could say that the prints changed the course of modern art.

The beauty of the prints, the luminous colours printed using indigenous dyes, the cursive calligraphic drawn lines, cut with tools whose blades were forged in the same way as samurai swords, the attention to detail and the craftsmanship were second to none.

But it is only in relatively recent years that the technique itself has become acclaimed and practised more widely in the West. Printmakers from across the world are embracing the technique. This is due partly because it is a process that is entirely non-toxic and environmentally friendly, but also allying as it does the certainties of woodcut with the nuance of watercolour, it has opened up a whole new landscape of contemporary printmaking possibilities.

I came to Japanese woodcut entirely by chance. I had a solo exhibition that featured an installation of prints suspended from the ceiling. One day a woman came in and began to handle the prints... I was not particularly pleased, but we got talking and she turned out to be Keiko Kadota who ran the Mokuhanga residency programme in Fujikawaguchiko, Japan. It was set up in order to teach traditional Japanese woodcut to Western printmakers. I applied and travelled to Japan where I encountered the technique of Mokuhanga for the first time and had the privilege of being taught by Japanese *sensei* with the aid of an interpreter. I was there for nearly three months, in a totally immersive environment with five other printmakers from around the world. It has proved to be one of the turning points of my life.

We have become accustomed to inspiring Japanese design and culture in all parts of our daily lives; from Japanese cuisine, manga, anime, fashion, Zen philosophy to of course electronics. Little did I realise when I went to Japan that its architecture also would be deeply familiar to me. My father had built a house in Canada based on the blueprints of Kenzo Tange's showhouse in Japan. It was the first house I ever knew.

On my return from Japan I gained a place on the MA Print Programme at the Royal College of Art enabling me to further embed the technique into my own practice.

I now teach Japanese woodcut to enthusiastic students in London, and this book is informed, in a practical way, by my classes. I also lecture for The Art Society on the subject around the UK and I continue to exhibit my Mokuhanga prints both in the UK and internationally.

◀ The MI-LAB residency building at Fujikawaguchiko, Japan.

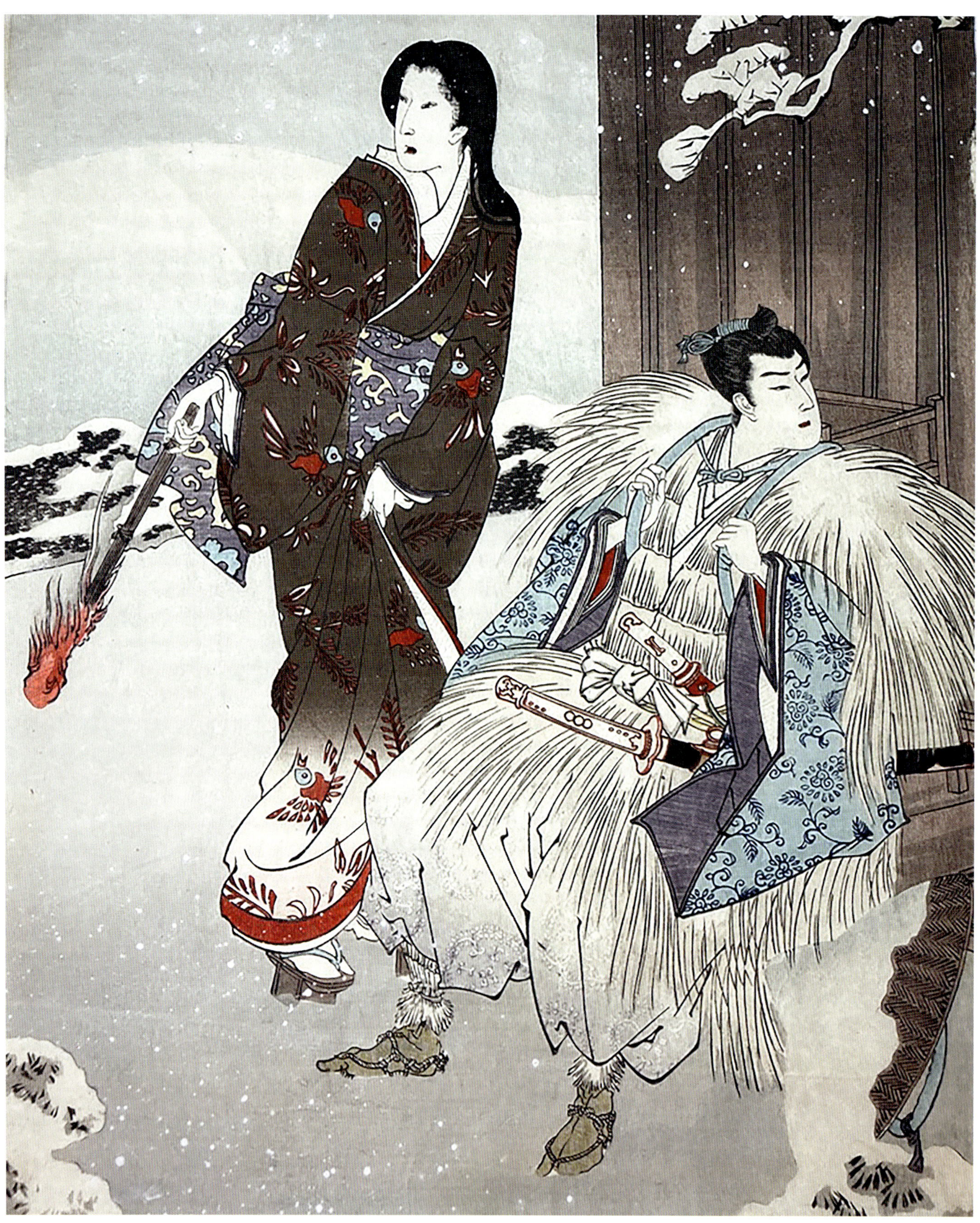

Chapter 1

A HISTORY OF JAPANESE WOODCUT

J apanese woodcut, or Mokuhanga, is a defining element of Japanese culture and national identity. This chapter outlines the key developments and historical context that led to its ultimate refinement, the beautiful, luminous *ukiyō-e* prints that first appeared in the mid eighteenth century.

ORIGINS

The Japanese woodcut tradition dates back well over a thousand years, when the Empress Shotoku commissioned the printing of a million Buddhist *sutras,* or prayers, in 770 CE. These were rolled into scrolls, placed into wooden pagodas and distributed to temples around the country.

The Empress's intention, to convert the Japanese people to Buddhism, is an early instance of the woodcut being used as a vehicle for mass propaganda. Buddhism, woodcut, papermaking and calligraphy were originally all imports from China, but were altered as they were incorporated into Japanese cultural life.

Japanese script developed a more flowing and cursive line than the squarer Chinese characters. To translate Japanese brush calligraphy into a woodcut while retaining the grace of the original required great skill and set in train what was to become a long tradition of highly skilled woodcarving. It is important to remember that these characters were also cut in reverse.

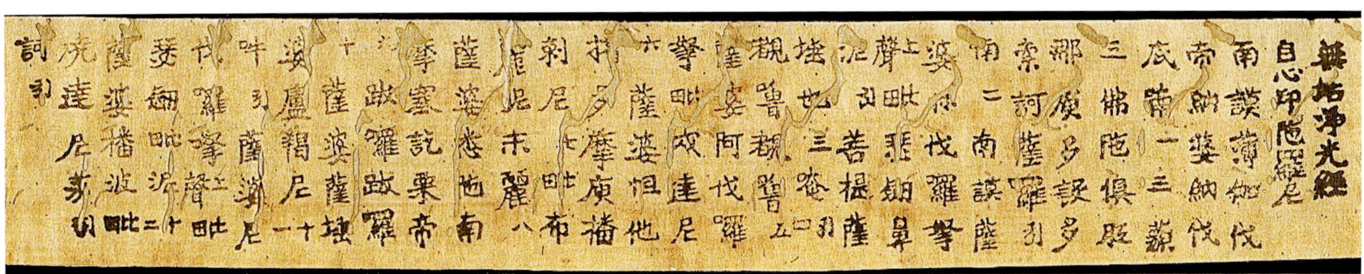

Hyakumanto Dhāranī. The oldest known printed text in Japan from 770 CE. It forms part of a set of one million Buddhist sutras or prayers. The original text was in Sanskrit; this was transliterated into Chinese and then Japanese characters.

◀ *Ukiyō-e* print by unknown artist, part of author's collection.

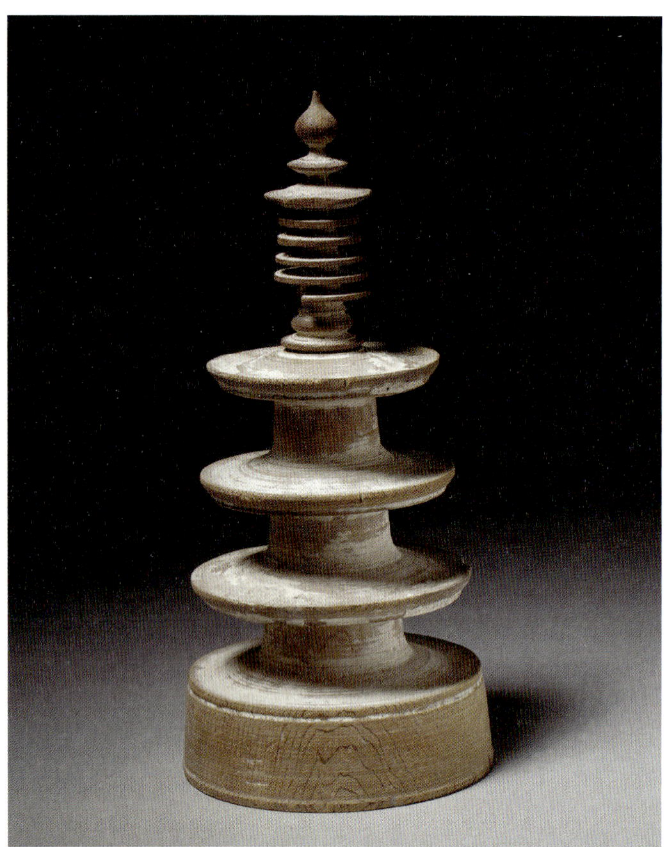

Wooden pagoda. The printed texts were rolled up into small scrolls and placed inside the wood pagodas and distributed to temples across Japan. They were originally painted in white clay.

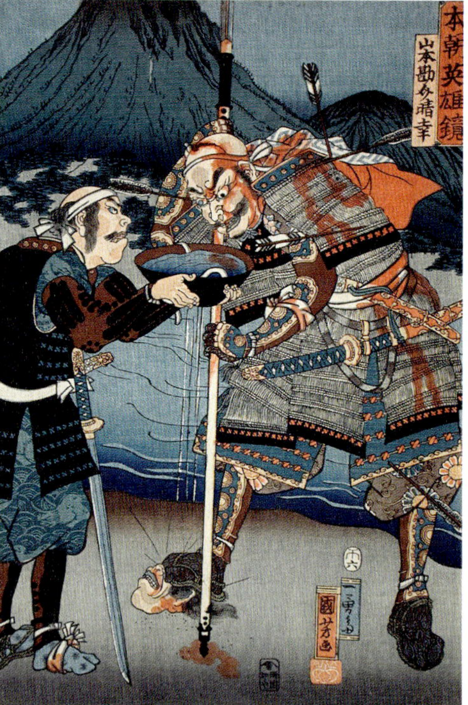

Utagawa Kuniyoshi, 1797–1861. *Yamamoto Kansuke Haruyuki,* from the series 'Mirror of Heroes of Our Country', 1858. Colour woodblock print (34.29 × 20.8cm). The print shows Haruyuki in his dying moments during the fourth battle of Kawanakajima, 1561, one of the great battles of the Sengoku period.

CIVIL WAR

In 1467, Japan descended into a state of devastating civil war, suffering almost continual unrest and outright conflict for approximately the next two centuries.

This so-called 'Sengoku period' coincided with the age of global exploration and colonial expansion by Western powers. The Philippines had been invaded and conquered by the Spanish in 1521. Japan, already weakened and divided by internal strife, was highly vulnerable to invasion. In 1543, Portuguese merchants blown off course landed at the southern tip of Tanegashima, where they quickly established a toehold, founding the port of Nagasaki. Catholic Jesuit soldier priests swiftly followed and began their mission to forcibly convert the local population. Many Japanese were sold as slaves and sent to the West.

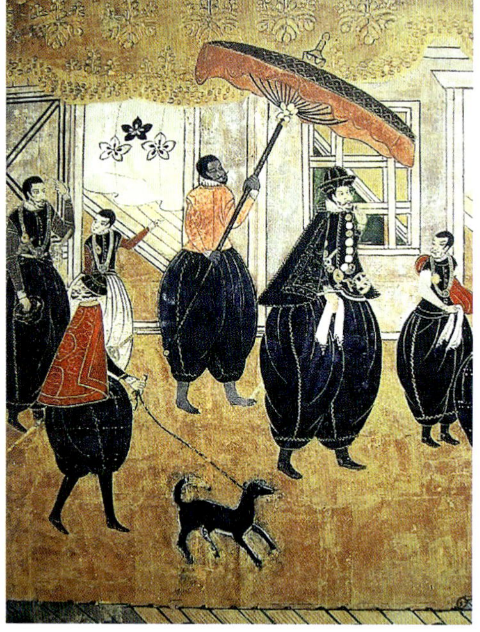

The Portuguese ambassador and his entourage arrive in Japan in 1600. Japanese painting depicting a group of Portuguese *Nanban,* or foreigners, in Japan in the seventeenth century. Unknown painter.

In 1615, the Shōgun Tokugawa Ieyasu defeated the remaining opposition and ended the civil war. Under his Shōgunate, a unified Japan was to remain at peace for nearly 250 years. The Portuguese and the Jesuits were expelled along with Japanese Christian converts.

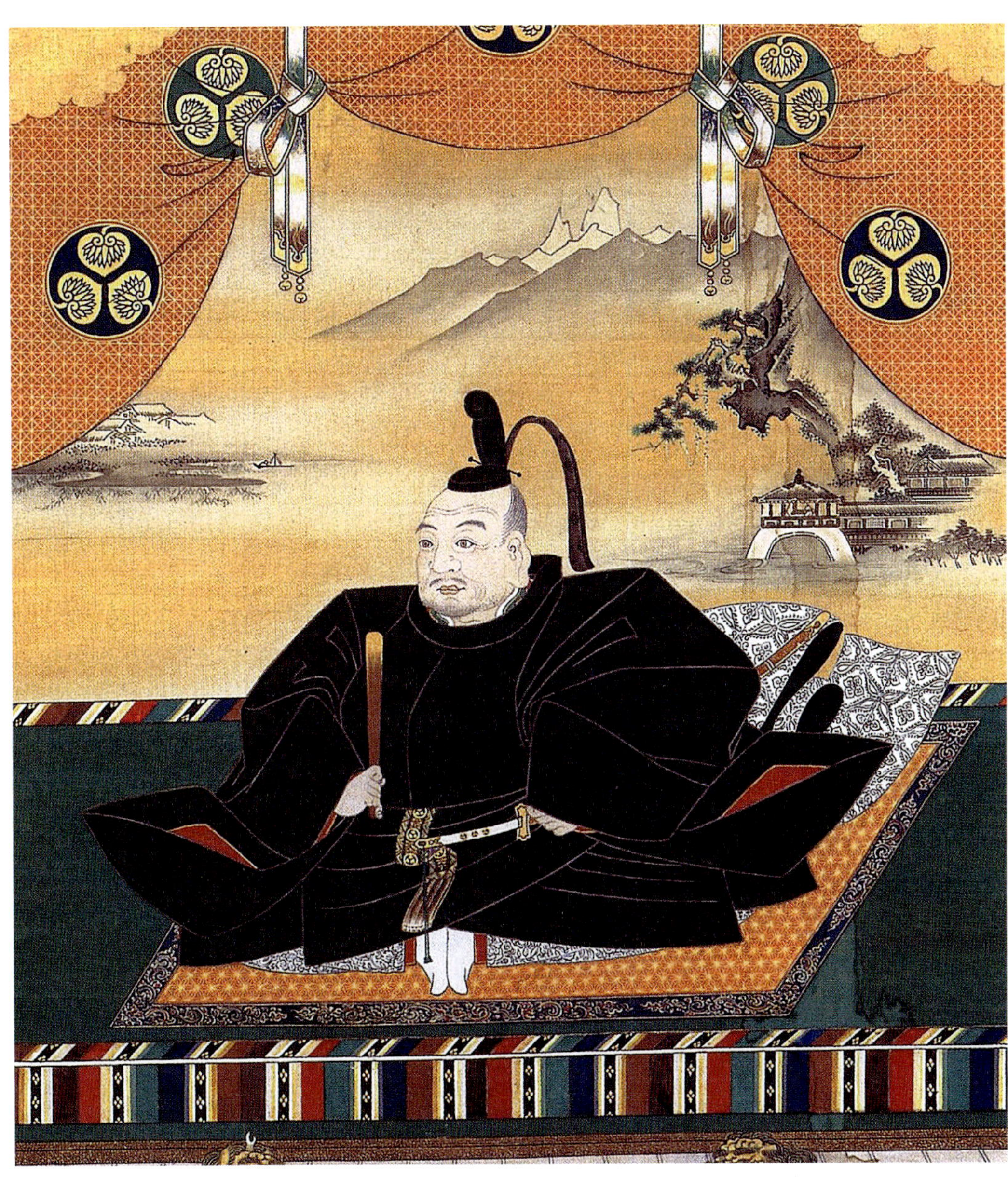

Kanō Tan'yū, 1602–1674. *Portrait of Tokugawa Ieyasu*. Early Edo period.

ISOLATION

After the civil war, Japan's borders were closed. While the *Sakoku*, Japan's long period of isolation (1639–1853), kept the country closed off from the world, it also enabled Japan to flourish undisturbed and grow wealthy. Only ten ships from China, and two from Holland, were allowed to dock per year. The Dutch, permitted because they were Protestant and therefore judged to be less proselytising than the Catholic Spanish, occupied the tiny artificial island of Dejima in Nagasaki harbour ('Exit Island' in Japanese). Nevertheless, a close watch was kept on them; on arrival their belongings were searched for religious tracts and they were not permitted, except on special occasions, to leave for the mainland.

The Dutch traders bought up silks, but especially porcelain, which rapidly became all the rage in Europe. When the demand for these fine ceramics, known as 'white gold', exceeded supply, imitators soon sprang up. Delftware, blue and white tin-glazed earthenware tiles and other products, was the Dutch version. Porcelain manufacture remained a closely guarded secret and unknown in the West until the early eighteenth century when German scientists finally cracked the formula, founding the Meissen factory at Dresden.

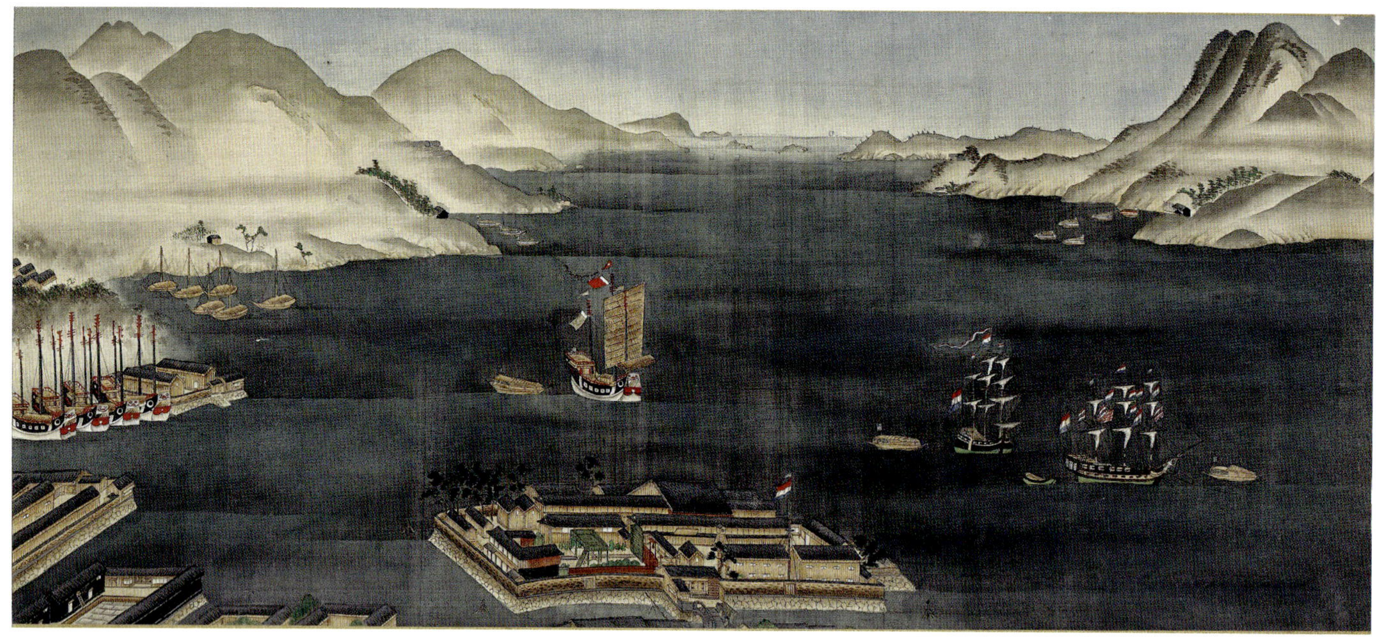

Painting on silk of Japanese and Dutch trade on Dejima (in Nagasaki), 1820. The view includes two Dutch ships and numerous Chinese trading junks.

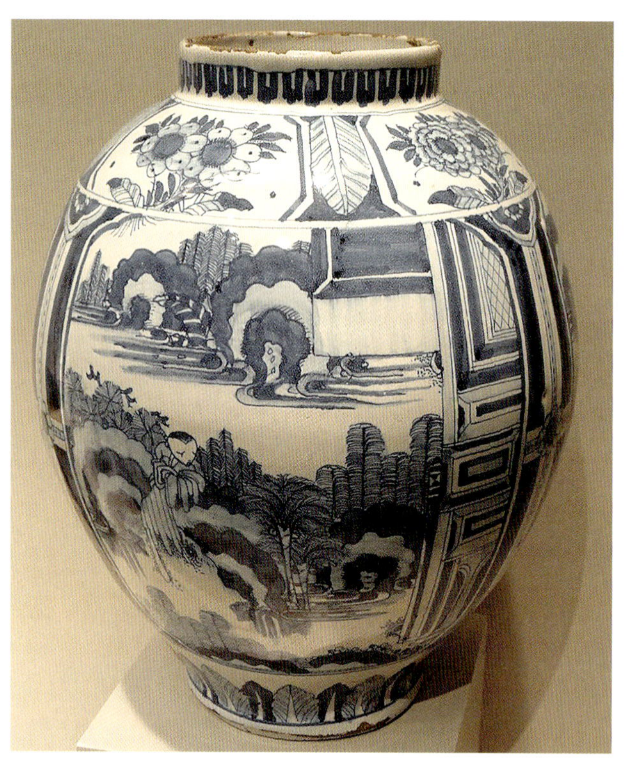

Dutch Delftware vase in a Japanese style, c.1680.

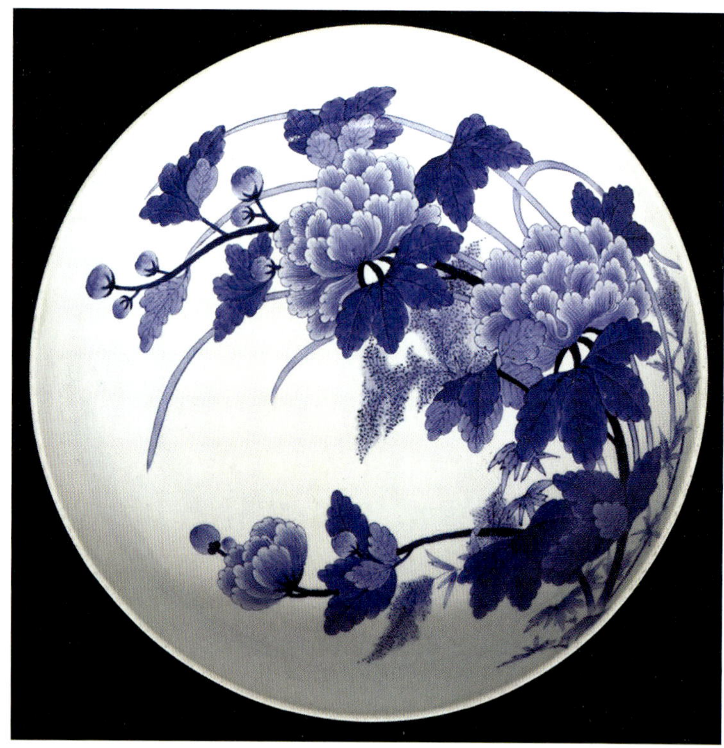

Nabeshima ware bowl, Kyōhō era, 1716–1736.

EDO PERIOD 1603–1868

While the Emperor remained in Kyoto as the ceremonial head of state, the Shōgunate moved the central, administrative and political capital to Edo, the location of Tokugawa Ieyasu's ancestral castle, at that time a small fishing village. Edo (later to become Tokyo) soon developed into a busy city. Here, the court were expected to live for considerable periods of time under the Shōgun's watchful eye.

At this time Japan was a feudal state, governed by strict rules of conduct and manners, where the classes did not mix and travel was strictly controlled. (Given that 70 per cent of Japan is mountainous, travel was difficult anyway.) Artists wishing to become established painters attended the Kano Academy, where guidelines were rigidly enforced about what was considered to be good taste, dictating what the artist could or could not paint. Fine art was largely inspired by Chinese painting and usually displayed at intimate gatherings of the well-educated elite, inaccessible to common people.

Tōyō Sesshū (1420–1506) was a Buddhist monk and one of the great masters of *sumi-e,* or black and white ink painting. He adapted Chinese painting into a more Japanese aesthetic, employing an energetic, calligraphic brushstroke, with subtle tonal variations, giving depth and beauty to his work.

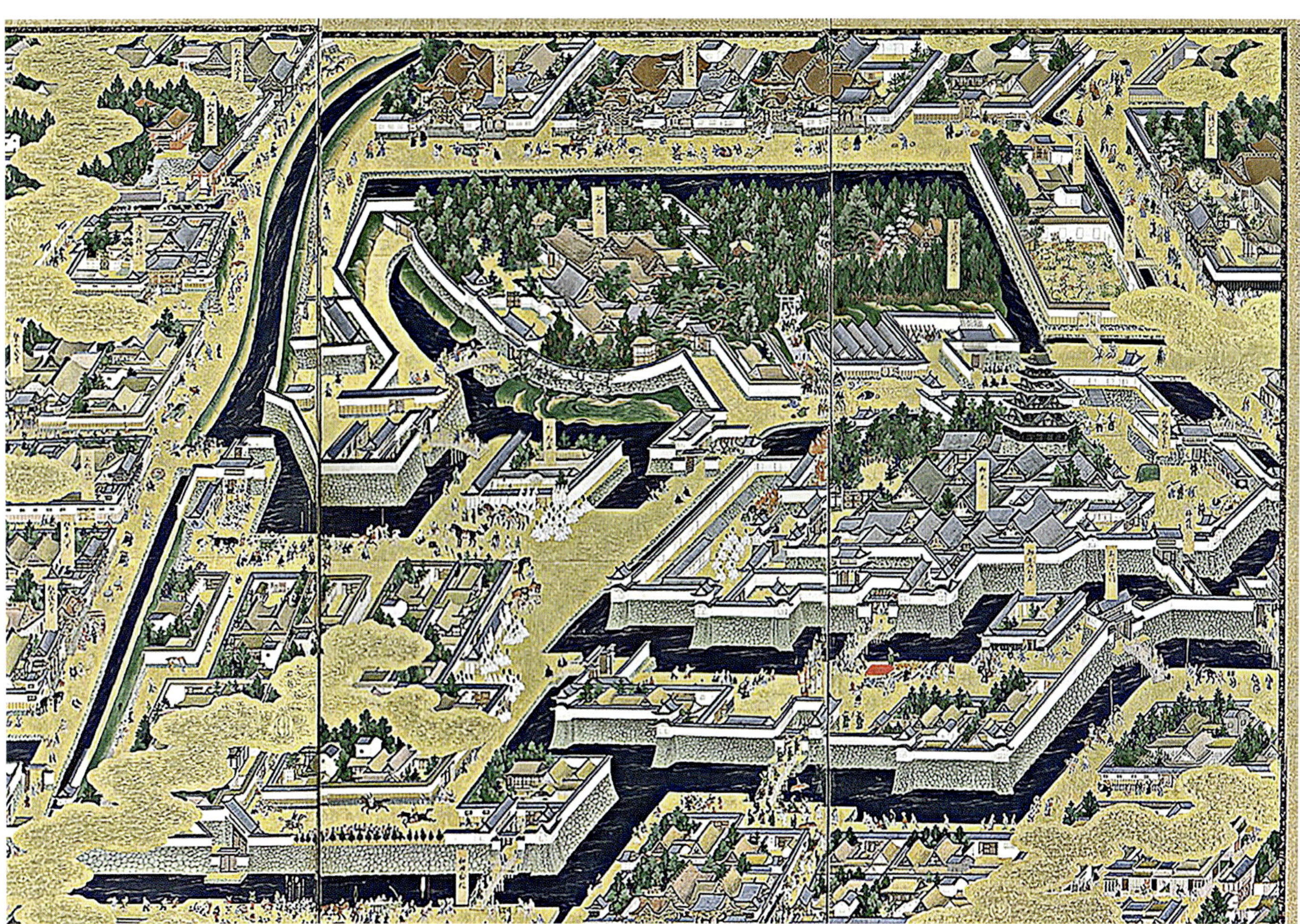

View of Edo (*Edo zu*). Pair of six-panel folding screens (seventeenth century). Artist unknown.

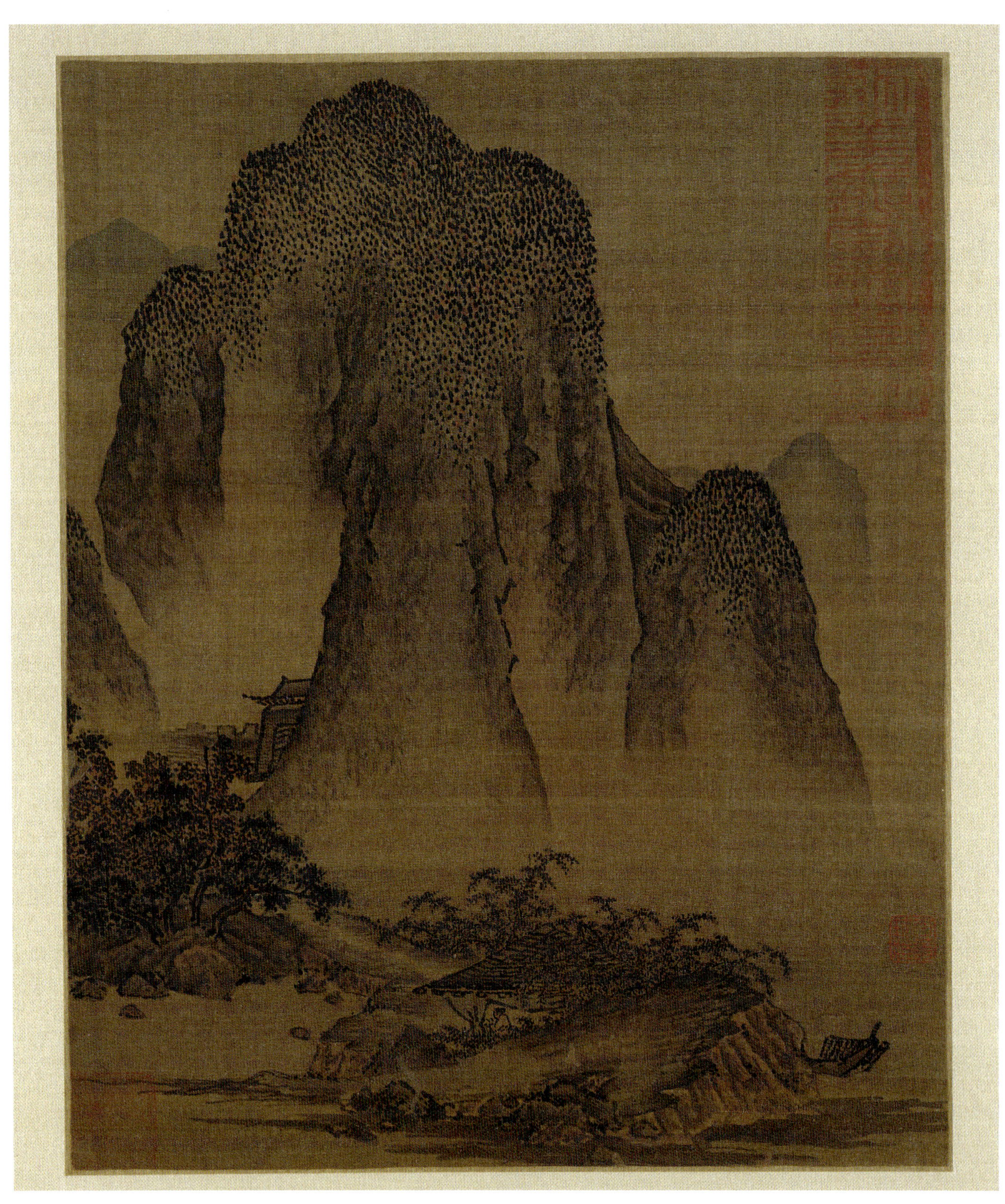

Landscape in the style of Fan Kuan. Chinese Yuan Dynasty (fourteenth century). Album leaf, ink and colour on silk (26.35 × 21.59cm).

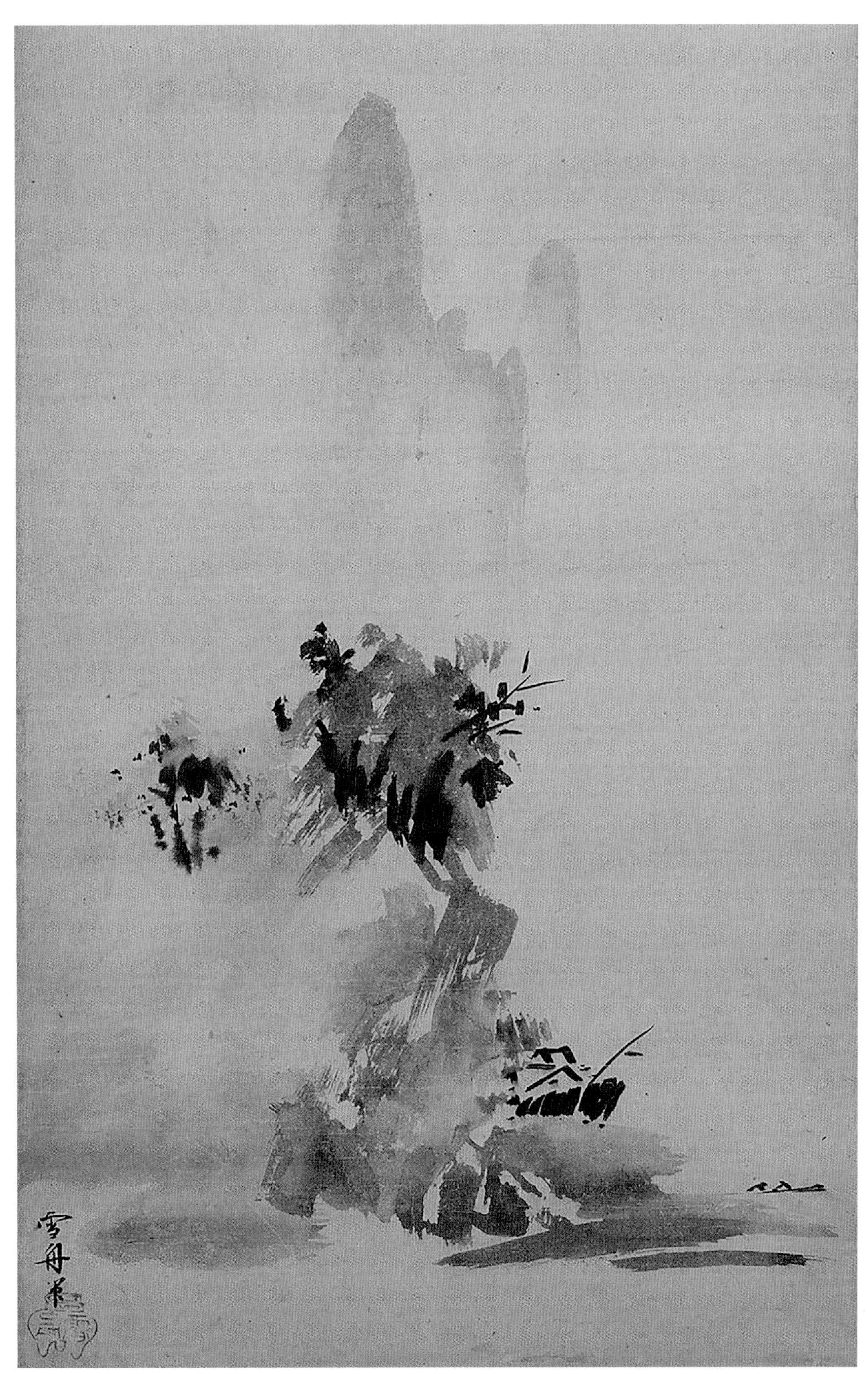

Sesshū Tōyō, 1420–1506. *Haboku-Sansui*, 1495. Splashed ink style landscape (148.6 × 32.7cm, full scroll).

It is interesting to speculate as to whether Rembrandt would have seen Tōyō Sesshū's paintings, as there are striking similarities between the two artists in their way of handling a brush. Both employ the use of fluent, economic and expressive brushwork. It is possible that Rembrandt, as a Dutchman, would potentially have had access to dealers in Japanese artworks and it is known that he printed his etchings on Japanese paper.

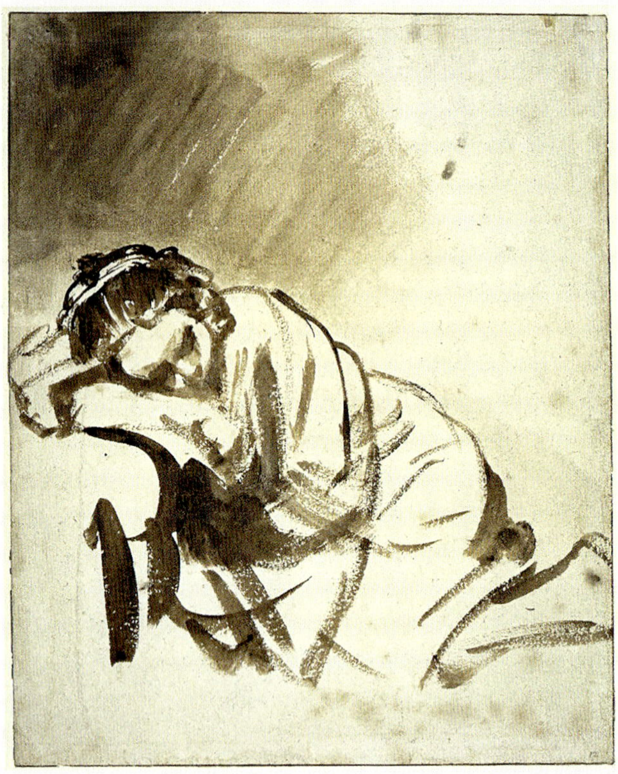

Rembrandt van Rijn, 1606–1669. *A Young Woman Sleeping*, 1654. Brush and brown ink, pen and brown ink, brown wash and white gouache on paper (24.6 × 20.3cm).

POPULAR BOOKS

Ukiyō-e prints, a unique part of Japan's cultural heritage, did not develop from a fine art tradition. Instead, over time, the centuries-long woodcutting tradition developed into book production. The blocks were Japanese wild cherry *sakura*, a hardwood that could deal with multiple printings and at the same time hold the finely cut detailed lines.

Chisels and mallets were used to cut broader sections of the wood. By the late seventeenth century illustrated books known

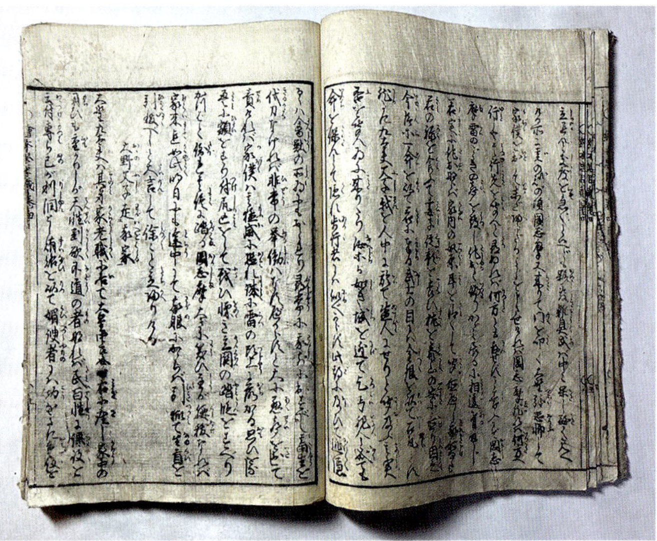

Unknown artist. *Tale of the Forty-Seven Ronin*. E-hon or Japanese picture book, c.1800. Stab-bound library book showing the hand-carved text.

as *e-hon* were being published cheaply for the mass market, and could be borrowed from 'lending libraries' for the price of a bowl of noodles.

There was consequently a high literacy rate, some sources putting it as high as 80 per cent of the male population, double that of the West. The writing and illustrations were cut at the same time (where modern Manga originates).

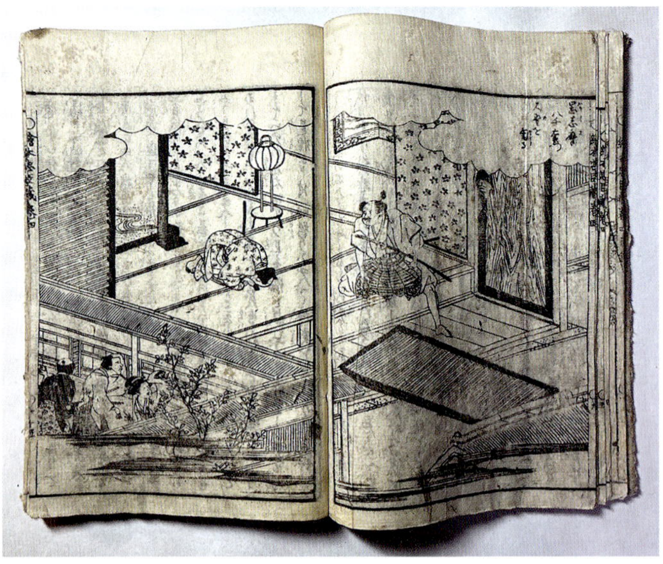

Unknown artist. *Tale of the Forty-Seven Ronin*. E-hon or Japanese picture book, c.1800. Stab-bound library book showing the asymmetrical compositions and fine detail.

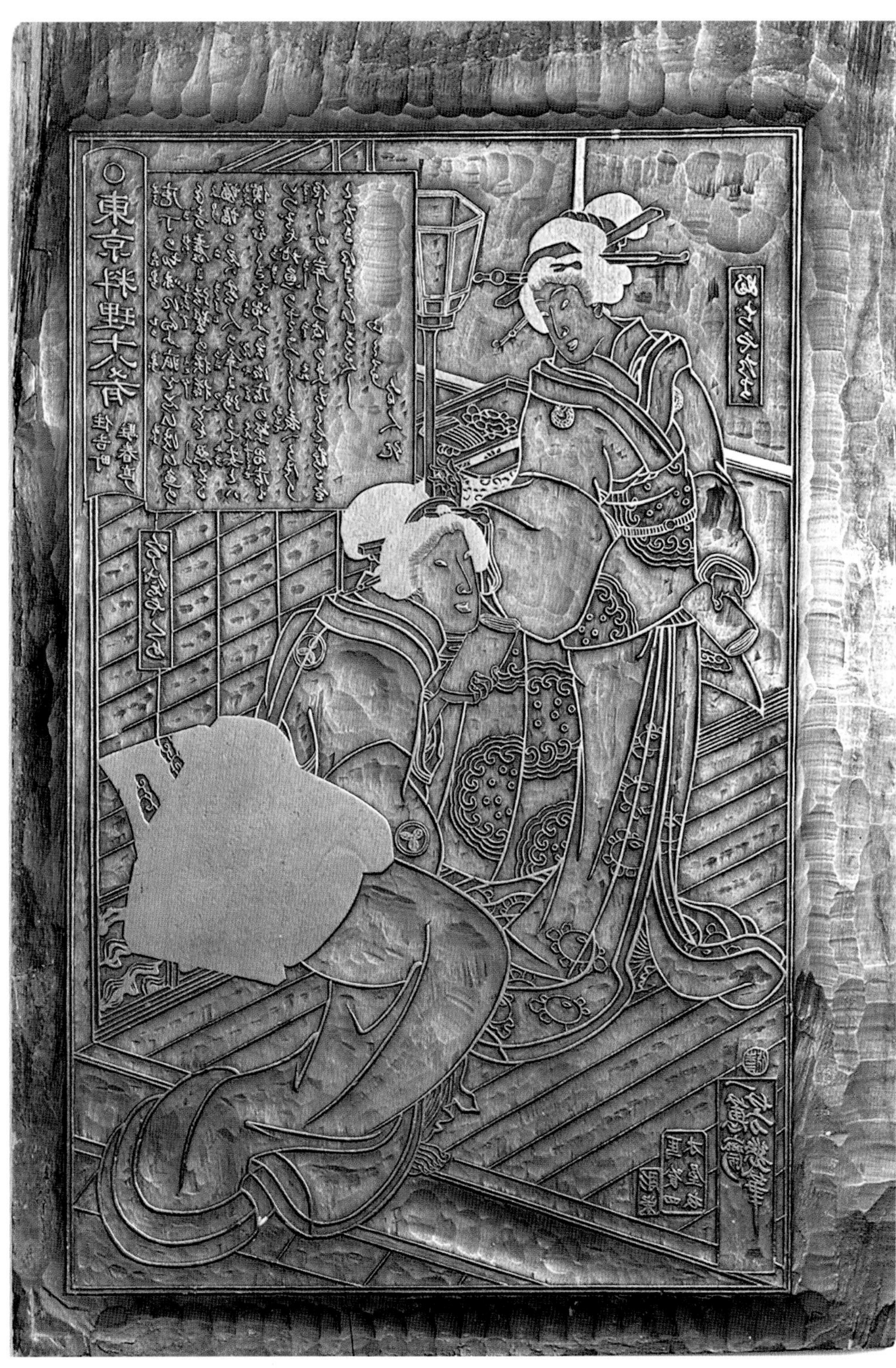

Keyblock for print, Utagawa Yoshiiku, 1862. Sakura (cherrywood) block (10.55 × 15.36cm).

The main publishing houses were located in Osaka, Kyōto and Edo. The style of *ukiyō-e* from each of these centres differed: Osaka *ukiyō-e* mostly portrayed actors of the *kabuki* theatre; in Kyōto printmaking grew from pattern samples for the flourishing textile trade and used softer colours (often mixed with *gofun,* a white pigment made from crushed shells); in Edo the colours tended to be stronger and brighter with the subject matter more urban in nature.

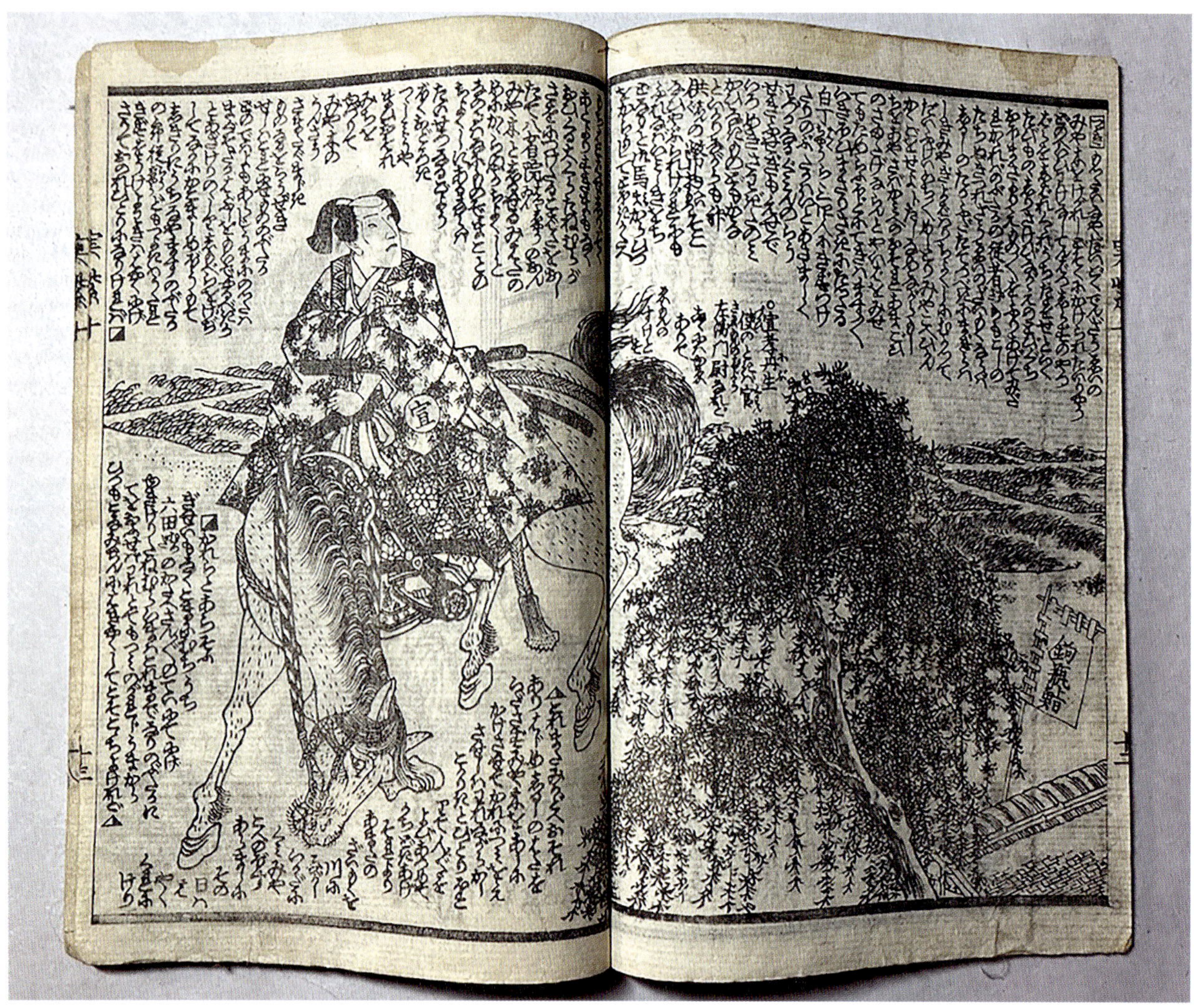

Unknown artist. *E-hon* or Japanese picture book, c.1840. Stab-bound library book showing the text and image cut at the same time.

KENTŌ REGISTRATION

By the early 1700s woodcut illustrations were being sought after as artworks in their own right. Publishers wishing to capitalise on the popularity of their books began to focus on selling individual prints of the black and white illustrations, with artists painstakingly hand-painting them in watercolour to give them extra commercial value. These proved to be very successful, but demand soon outstripped supply and the publishers began to look for a way to step up the production rate.

The artist Suzuki Harunobu is generally accepted as the inventor, in 1765, of the *kentō* registration system. His simple solution to making multi-coloured prints was to have the master carver cut registration notches directly into the key block and each colour separation block. This meant that the printing paper could be slotted into the notches on each colour separation woodblock and the print would be exactly registered on each one.

It was not unknown for as many as 30 different colours to be used per print in this way. This was to revolutionise the way that multi-colour prints could be made and paved the way for the glorious *ukiyō-e* prints to come. It meant that the publishers were able to offer attractive multi-coloured prints inexpensively to the merchant classes, who were eager to buy them.

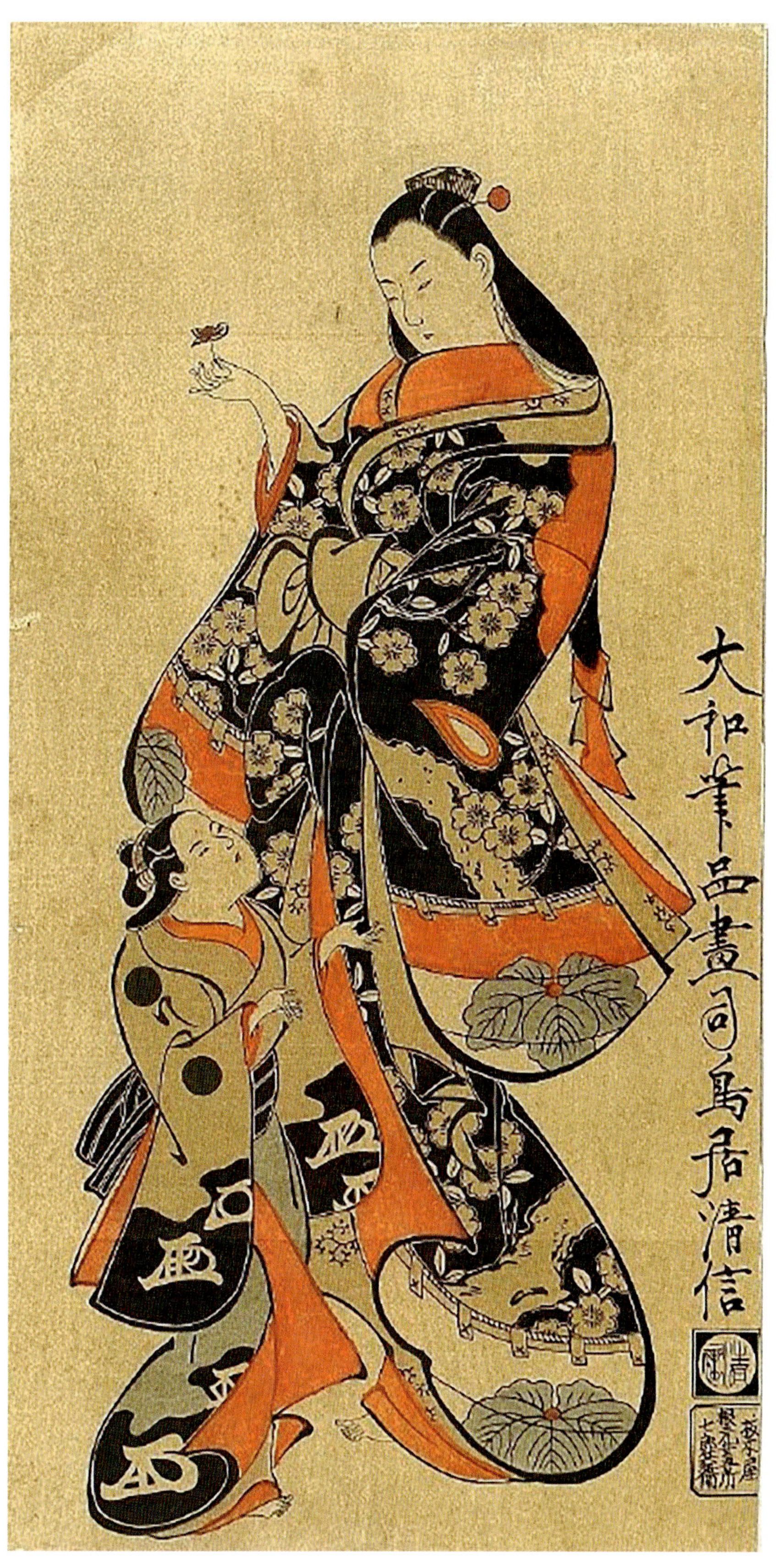

Torii Kiyonobu. *Beauty in a Black Kimono*, c.1710. *Tan-e* hand-coloured print.

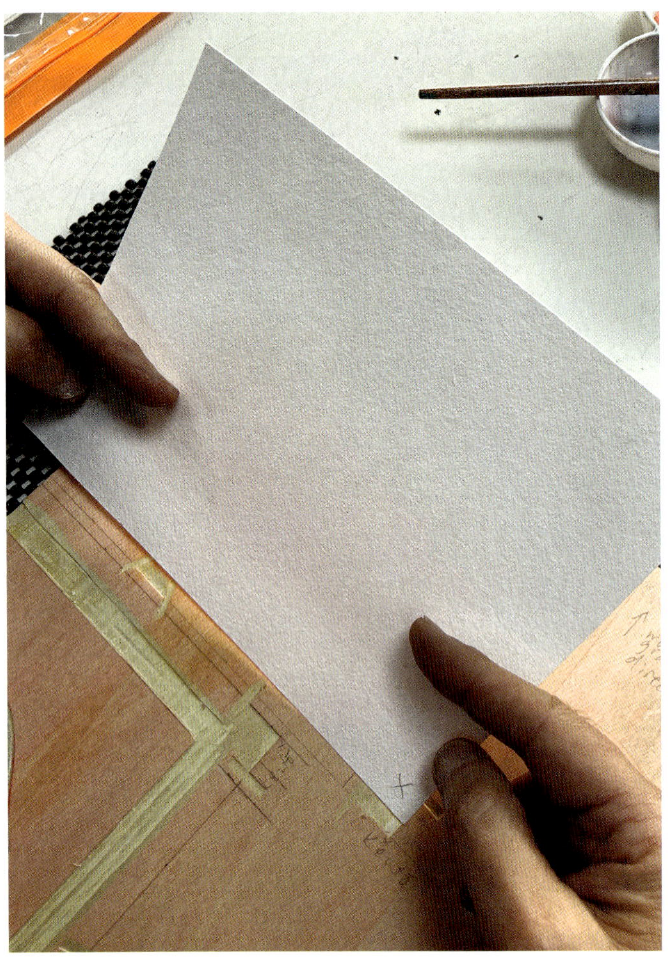

Kentō registration. Showing the printing paper being slotted into the notches cut for the *kagi kentō,* and resting on the *hikitsuke kentō*. This simple device revolutionised the way colour prints could be made.

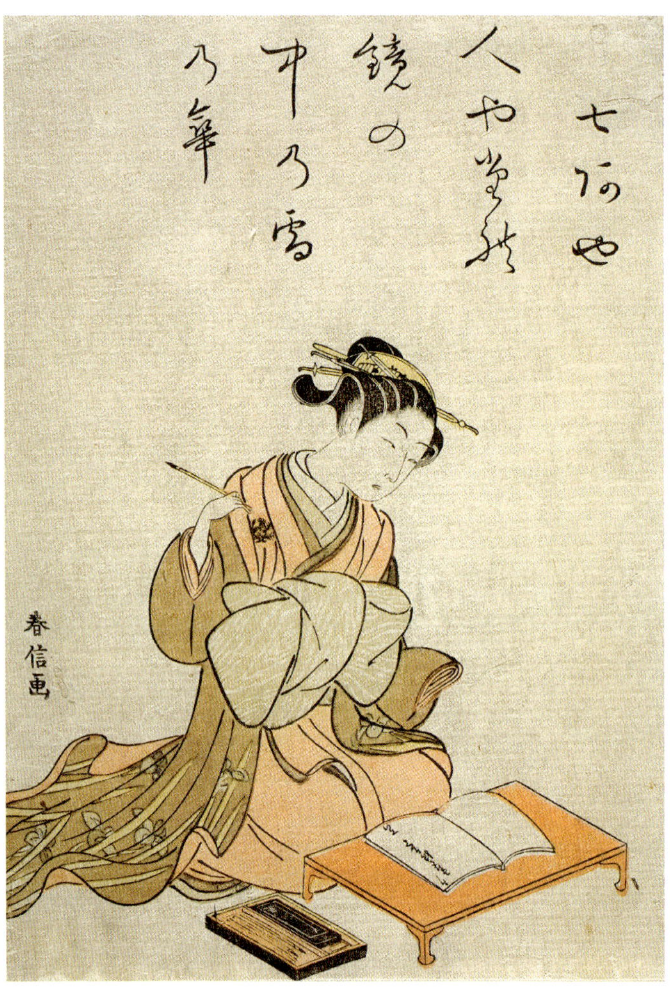

Suzuki Harunobu, 1725–1770. *Courtesan with her Poem*. Colour printed woodblock using *kentō* registration (13.50 × 13.65cm).

CHINESE METHOD

The *kentō* system is unique to Japan. In the Chinese method, two tables were used, the printing paper stacked and clamped on one in alignment with the inked block on the other. The problem with this process was that it required a skilled person to set the paper and block in correct alignment for each printing session. There also needed to be premises to house the tables.

Kentō registration on the other hand was highly portable. The notches would be cut by the most skilled carver in the studio directly into the wood so no calculations were required by the printer. The woodblocks themselves could be transported and printed anywhere, which also gave a greater freedom to the production of prints.

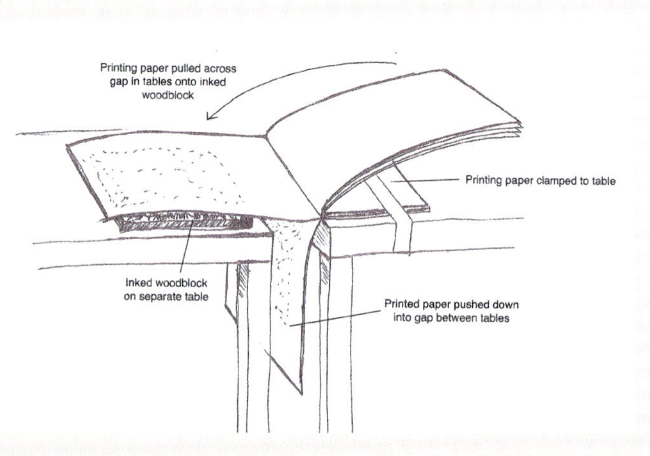

Chinese method of printing using two tables.

UKIYŌ-E

By the mid eighteenth century Edo had a population of around a million people and was the largest city in the world. All the *daimyo* or feudal noblemen and their families were forced to stay at court where the Shōgun could keep an eye on them, virtually held hostage. At this time there was a formal hierarchy in Japanese society: after the Emperor, Shōgun and the aristocracy there were four classes: warriors, farmers, artisans and merchants.

A vast entertainment industry of tea rooms, courtesans, *kabuki* actors and riverside gardens, a cultural demi-monde, consequently sprang up to cater for these bored noblemen, and the merchant classes who supplied these services grew wealthy themselves. These merchants, unable to access the Kano Academy style of fine art, wanted an art form that they

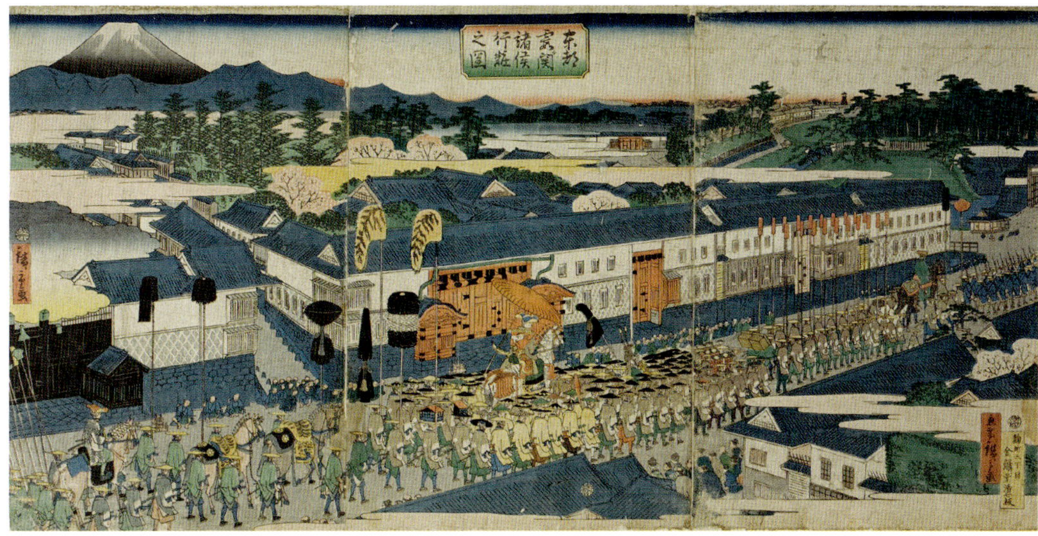

Andō Hiroshige. *Daimyo Procession at Kasumigaseki in Edo.* Colour woodblock print triptych (36.83 × 74.3cm). The Joan Elizabeth Tanney Bequest.

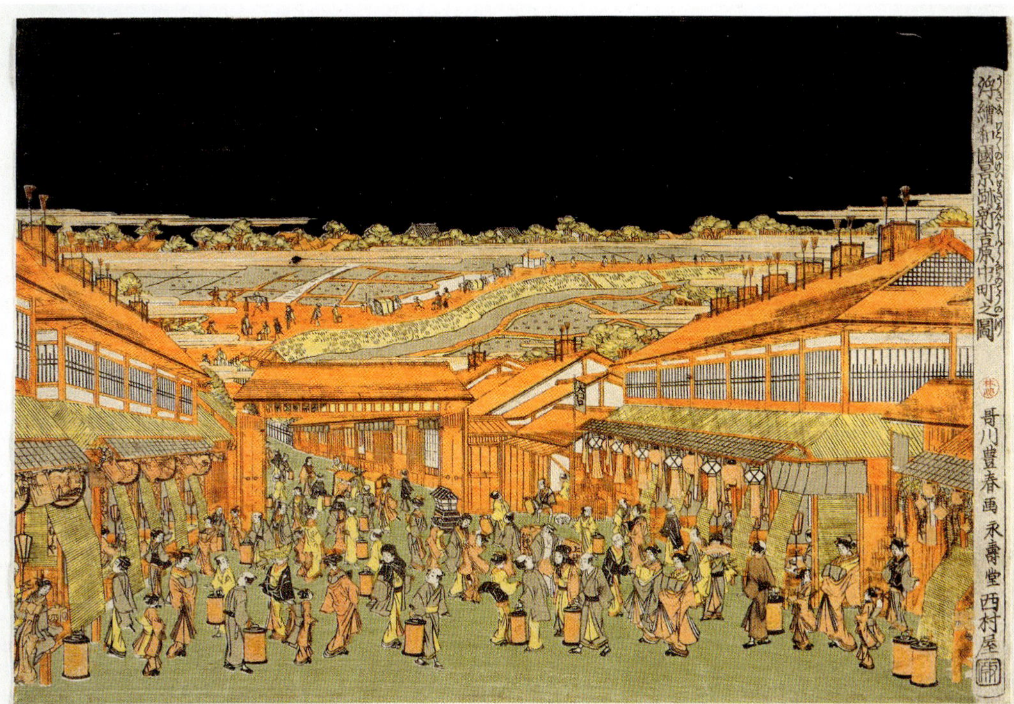

Utagawa Toyoharu, 1735–1814. *Nakano-chō Street in the Shin Yoshiwara Entertainment Quarter,* c.1770. Colour woodblock print (25 × 37.4cm).

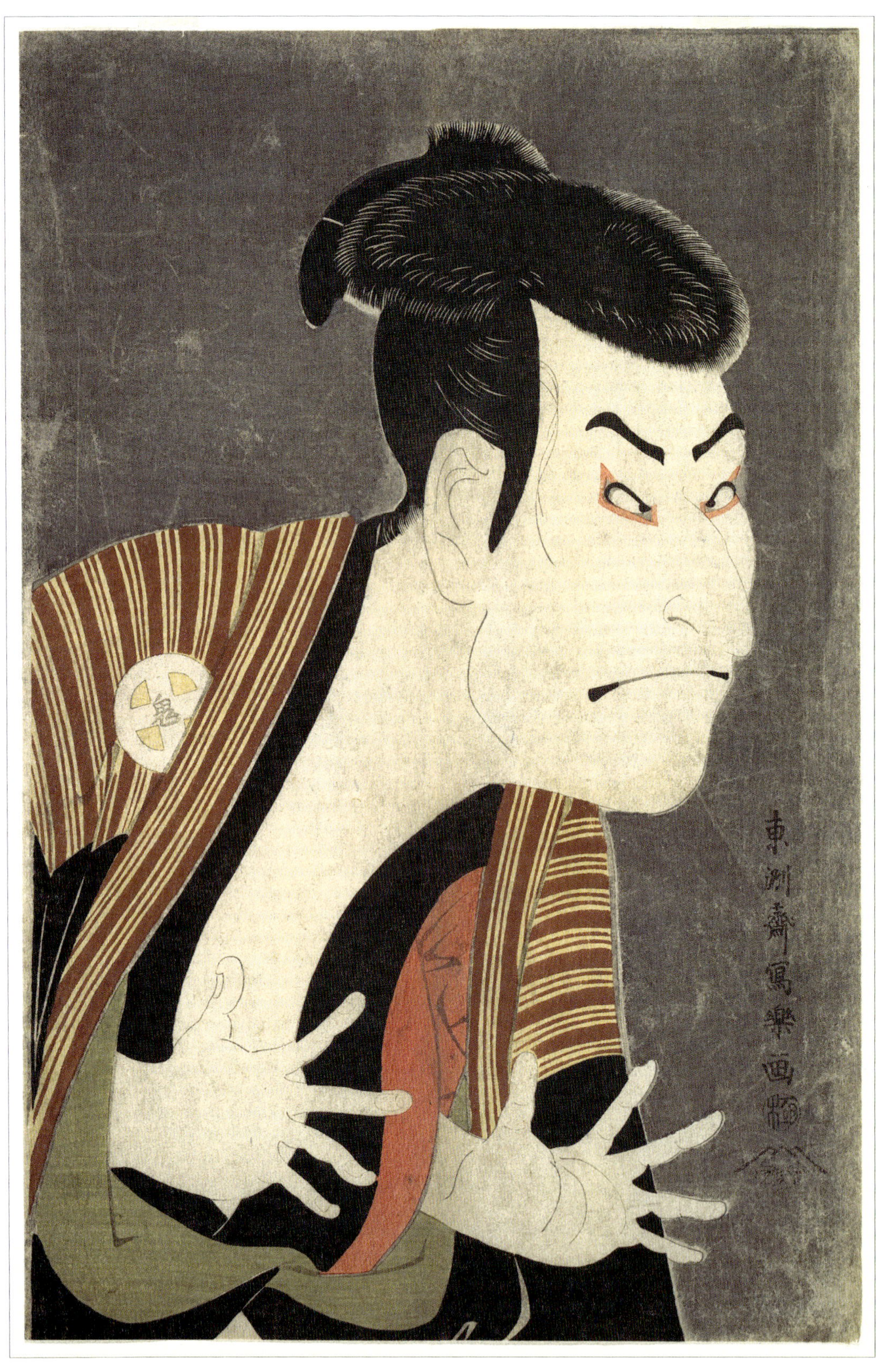

Tōshūsai Sharaku, active 1794–5. *Kabuki Actor Ōtani Onjii as Yakko Edobei*, 1794. Colour woodblock print and white mica (38 × 25cm).

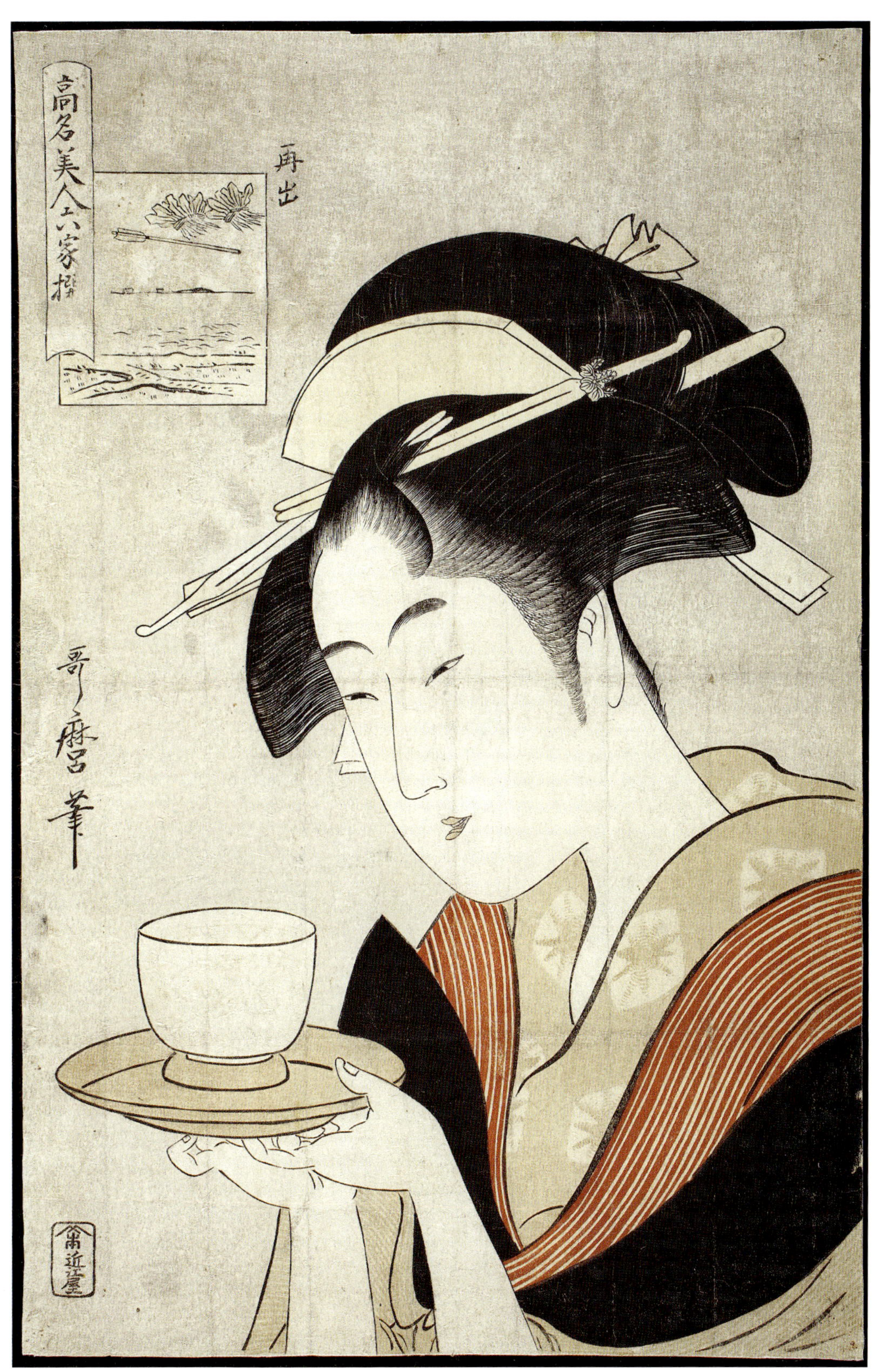

Kitagawa Utamaro, 1753–1806. *Saishutsu Naniwaya Okita*. From the series 'Renowned Beauties Compared to the Six Poetic Immortals', 1795–6. Colour woodblock print (23.8 × 38cm).

could use to decorate their homes, one that reflected their tastes and the vibrant city life that they encountered every day.

The resulting prints, called *ukiyō-e* (translates as 'Pictures of the Floating World') represented a graphic record of popular life. *Ukiyō-e* was a derogatory term given to the art form, as it was seen by the aristocratic class as vulgar. In Buddhism all life is ephemeral and pleasure only fleeting, therefore the only true value in this life was to be found in religious meditation. The prints of courtesans and *kabuki* actors were anything but religious in tone. They were an immediate sensation and wildly popular. They could be bought for a few yen and pasted up like posters on walls, even decorating fire screens. Each season they would be replaced with new prints, the old discarded as ephemera.

HANMOTO SYSTEM

By around 1790 there were around 700 publishers principally active in Osaka, Kyōto and Edo. In the *hanmoto* system the publisher would commission the artist, say Hokusai or Hiroshige, to produce a fine brush line drawing on thin *mino washi* paper, known as the *shita-e.* These drawings were not ostensibly for artistic expression, but marketable commodities owned by the publisher. The subject, format, number of designs, series title and individual print titles would all be agreed in advance including the number of blocks to be used. Prints were made as triptychs or diptychs, less commonly as single sheet prints. Pillar prints or *hanshira-e* were also popular with their tall formats, often sold mounted on decorative paper and wooden rollers, to simulate the expensive hand-painted silk scrolls *kakemono-e* given pride of place in the family home.

From 1791 it was decreed that publication could not go ahead without the censor's approval. The official seal would be stamped onto the drawing itself and this would be cut along with the drawing into the key block, appearing on all of the prints made from the block. The British Museum's 2021 exhibition 'The Book of Everything' showed Hokusai's original drawings for the eponymous book. It is rare to have surviving drawings intended for book production, as usually the drawings would be destroyed in the process of making the key block.

This *shita-e*, or artist's drawing, would be sent to the Mokuhanga studio, where it would be pasted face down onto a wild Japanese cherrywood block *sakura* as a *hanshita*. The thin paper would be rubbed with camelia oil, to make it transparent, so that the details could be seen ready for cutting. The fine

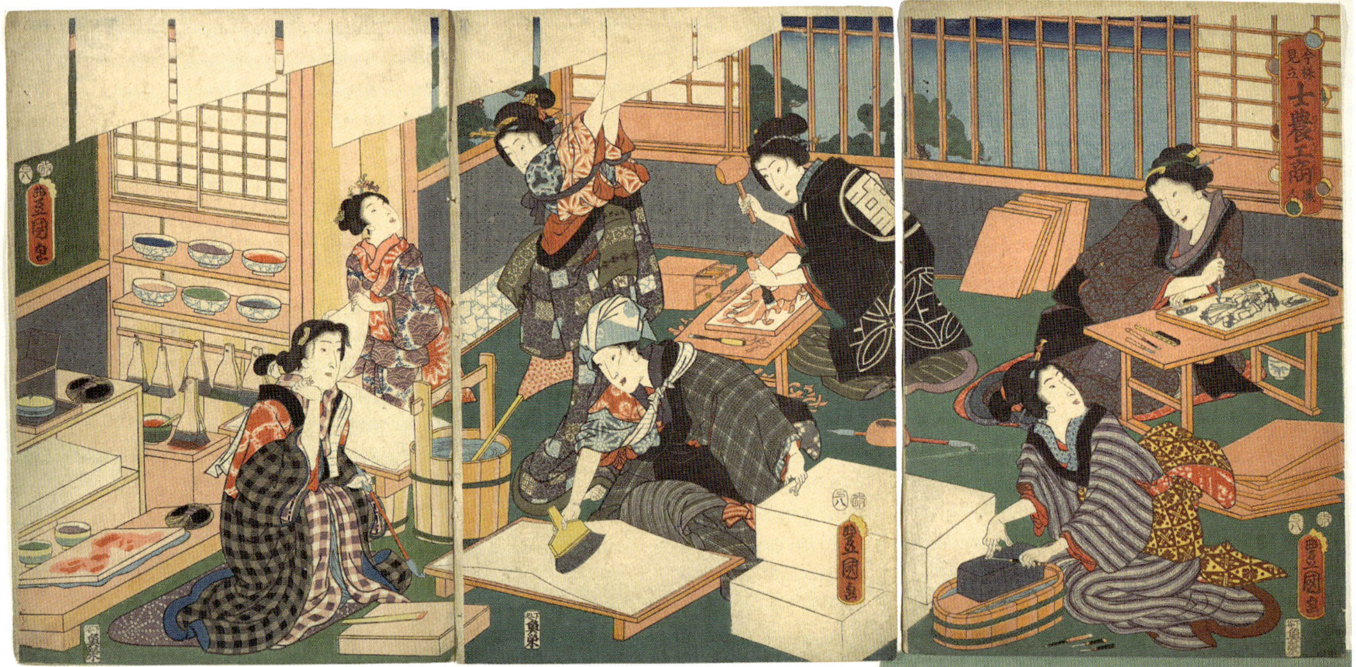

Utagawa Kunisada, 1786–1865. *An Up-to-Date Parody of the Four Classes,* 1857. Colour woodblock triptych (each print measuring 37.8 × 25.7cm).

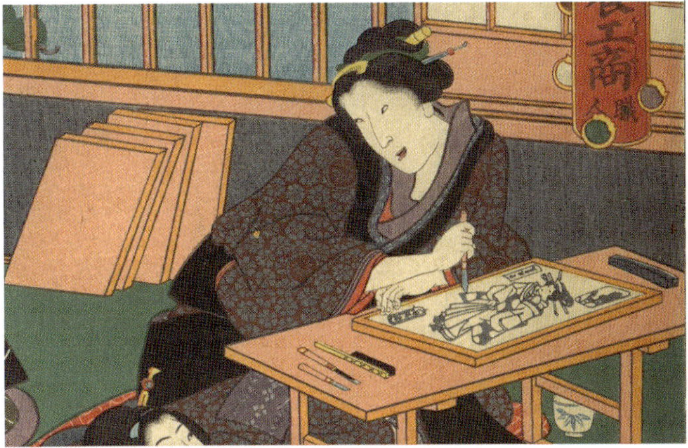

Detail showing the *horishi,* or master carver cutting the key block.

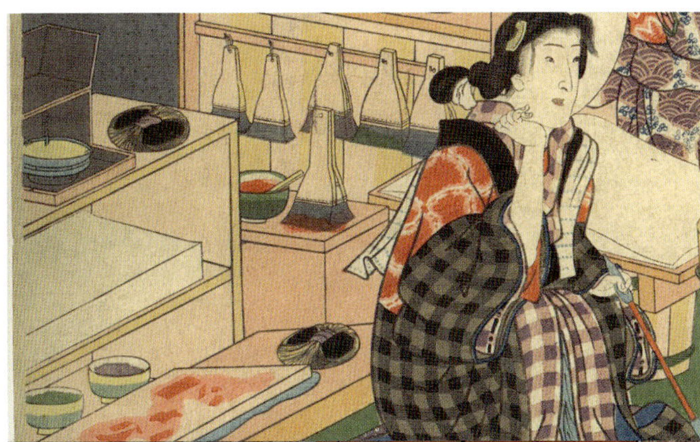

Detail showing the *surishi,* or printer at the *suridai* print table.

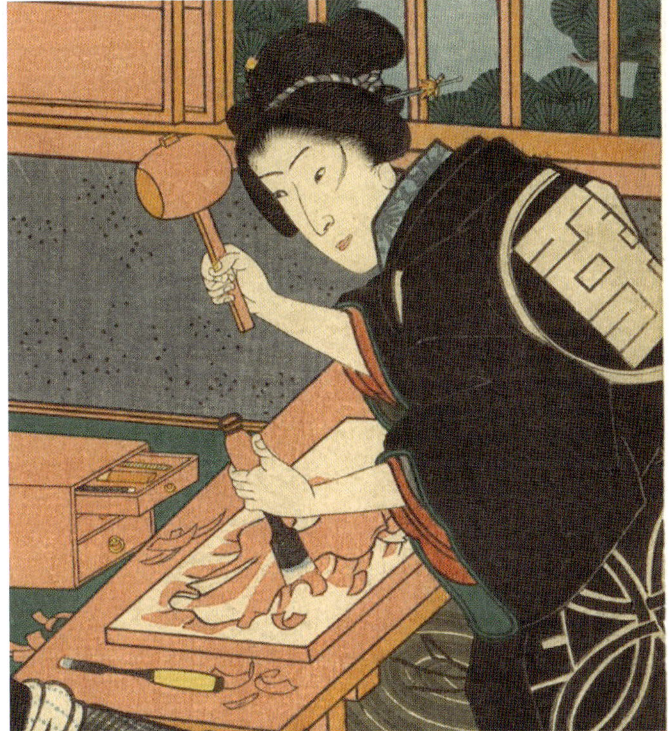

Detail showing the colour blocks being cut with a chisel and mallet.

black outlines would be cut using very sharp tools, through the paper drawing, into the wood by the master carver, the *horishi*.

Then depending on the number of colour separations (and it could be as many as 30), the key block would be printed and the resulting black outline prints in their turn would be pasted down onto the *sakura* blocks, known as *iroita* or colour blocks. At this point the artist would arrive at the studio to oversee the choice of colours and fabric patterns to be printed. The *sakura*

is a very hard wood enabling the retention of very fine raised lines; importantly, because of this hardness many thousands of prints could be printed before the edges would begin to erode, making the blocks very profitable for the publisher. Clearing large areas was done with a chisel and mallet.

The *surishi*, or printer, would work like the others in the studio, seated on a cushion on the floor at a low table, called a *suridai*. The table is angled down away from the printer; this angle helped to avert backache in the lumbar spine. Finely ground pigments mixed with water and *nori* paste were brushed into the block with the *te bake* or hand brush. Dampened *kōzo* paper was slotted into the *kentō* registration notches and the back of the paper would be rubbed down with a *baren*.

CENSORSHIP

When the authorities were alerted to the popularity of *ukiyō-e* prints they were concerned; an artform that was hugely popular and cheap to produce in large quantities had the potential for political sedition or subversion. As a result, after 1791 all *ukiyō-e* prints had to have the stamp of approval from the guild censor to prove that they were apolitical before production could begin.

In 1842 this system was replaced by the *e-nanushi*, or government appointed censor. Prints could depict no aspect of Christianity, no images of the Imperial court, no commentary on the Shōgun's government or the aristocracy, no images of contemporary events or gossip. (*Shunga*, or erotic prints, avoided censorship by printing images in book or album form for private collectors and not for the general public.) The censor's stamp *kiwame*, which translates as 'approved', has been very useful for

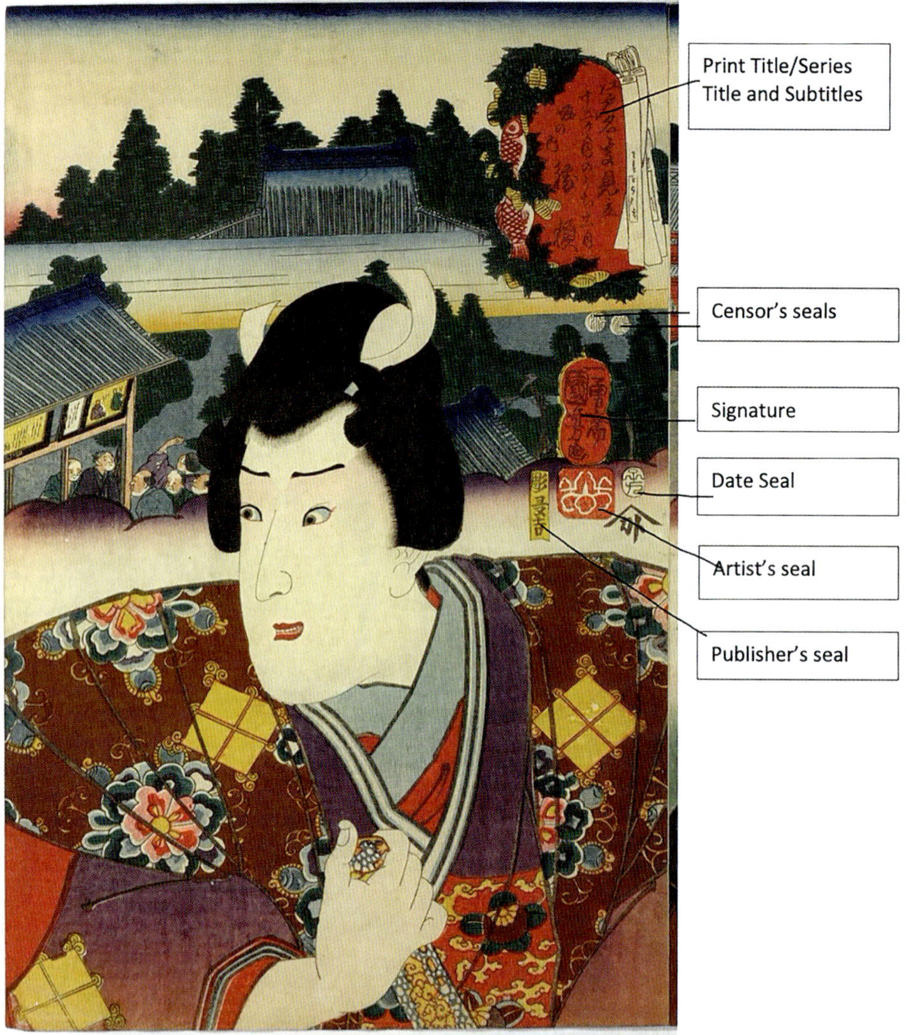

Utagawa Kuniyoshi *Famous Views of Edo Selected for the 12 months 1852*

Reading a *ukiyō-e* print. Prints had to be authorised by the censor, and stamped with a seal before publication.

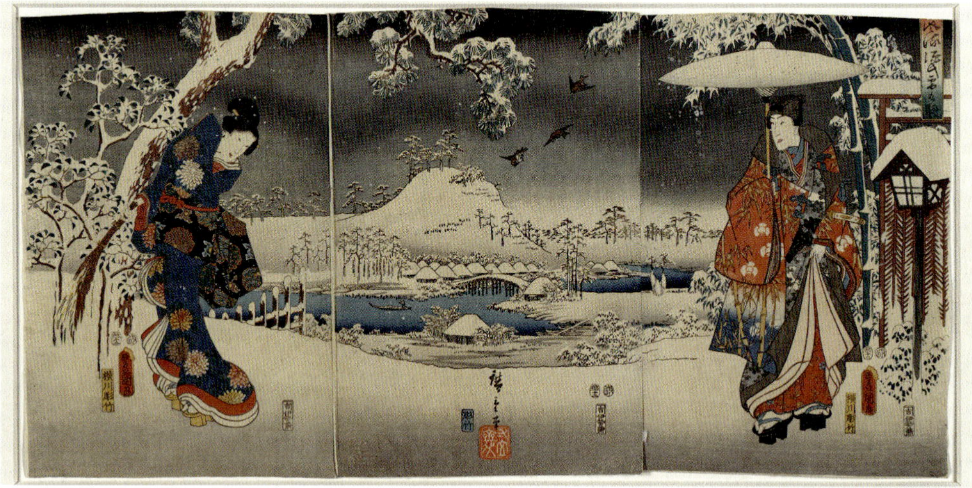

Utagawa Kunisada, 1786–1865. *Tale of Genji,* 1853. Colour woodcut, triptych (36.8 × 76.1 cm). Triptychs were the most common format for *ukiyō-e* prints.

I found a print at an ephemera fair in London that I excitedly recognised as an Utamaro. The stallholder thought that it was a reproduction from a book, but looking at the back of the paper I could see unmistakeable evidence of pigment, showing that it was indeed a real print. I paid £3.00 for it, far less than it was worth, but not nearly as much as it would have been had the print been made in Utamaro's lifetime. Tell-tale indications were that it had no censor stamp that would have given the date, also comparing the colour palette of my print with the authenticated print held in the British Museum collection, there were obvious differences, showing that the colours were not selected by Utamaro in his lifetime, but they are still the indigenous pigments used before 1868. It is an old print but not a valuable one; I love it nevertheless. *Ukiyō-e* prints continue to be made today mainly for the export market.

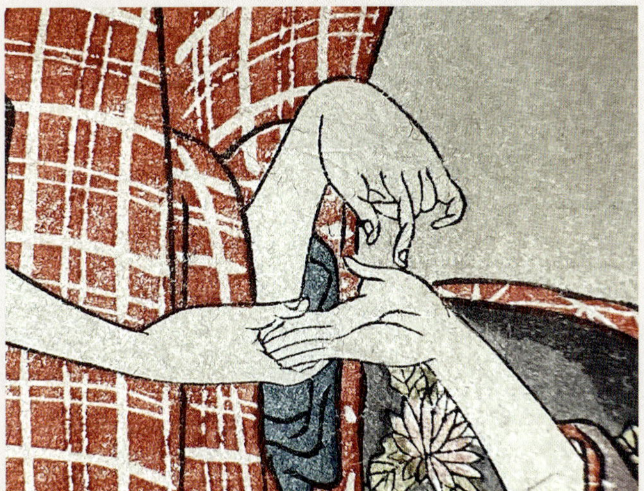

Kitagawa Utamaro, 1753–1806. *Hitsuji no koko,* from the series 'Seiro juni toki tsuzuki', 1790. Detail of the wonderful fine detailing of hands, showing the apprentice reading the palm of the servant.

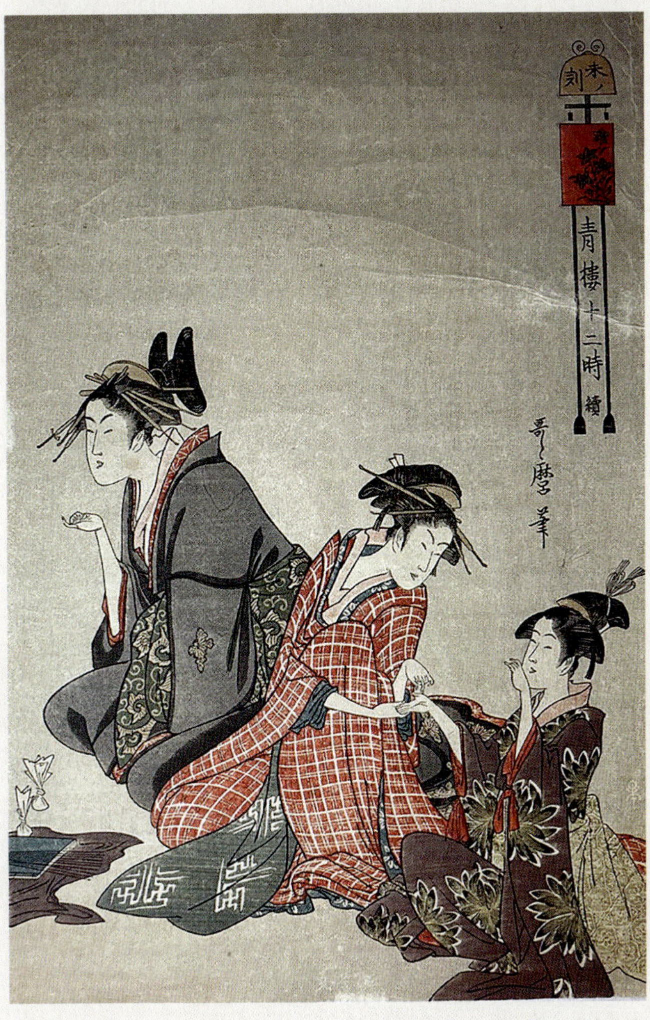

Kitagawa Utamaro, 1753–1806. *Hitsuji no koko, 'The Hour of the Goat' (about 2pm)* from the series 'Seiro juni toki tsuzuki', 1790. Colour woodblock print. This print is however from an unknown but later date.

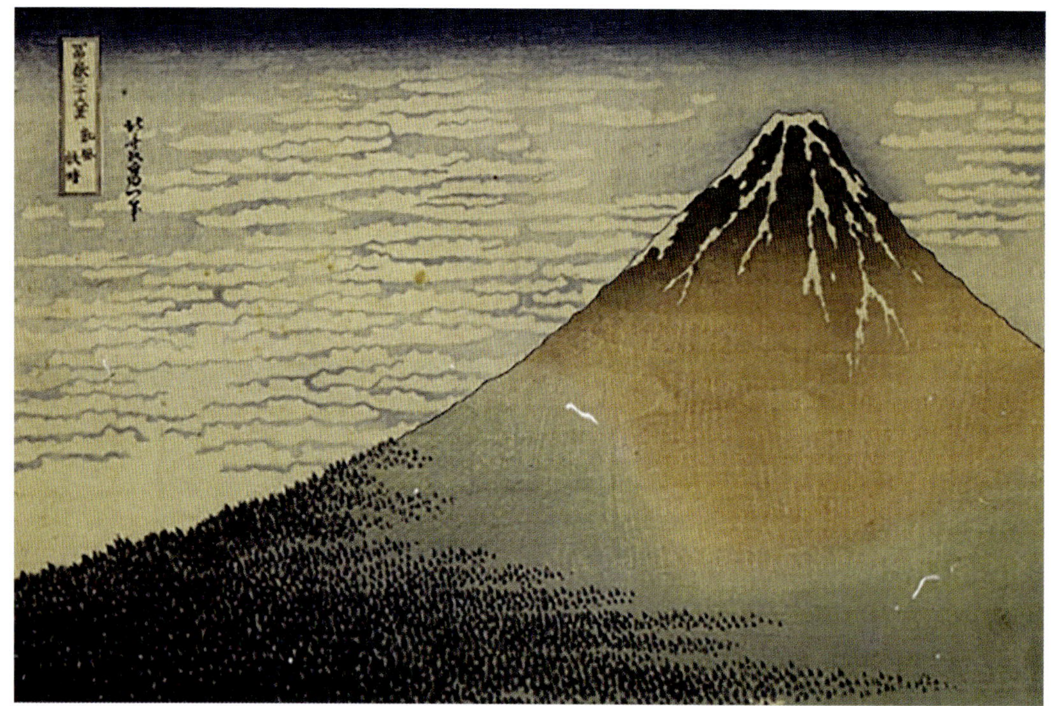

Katsushika Hokusai, 1760–1849. *South Wind, Clear Sky,* c.1830. From the series 'Thirty-six Views of Mount Fuji'. Colour woodcut 26.2 × 38.7cm. This is an early version that was made in Hokusai's lifetime, sometimes called *Pink Fuji.*

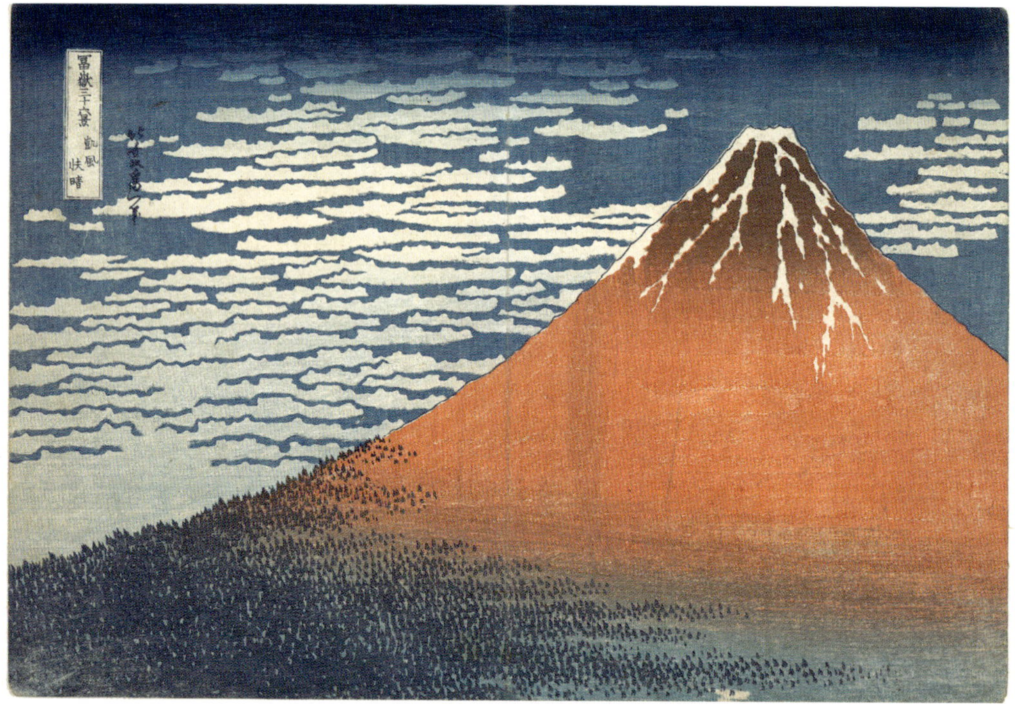

Katsushika Hokusai, 1760–1849. *South Wind, Clear Sky,* also known as *Red Fuji.* From the series 'Thirty-six Views of Mount Fuji'. Colour woodcut (26.2 × 38.7cm). This is another version of the same print, and much more famous.

collectors of *ukiyō-e* prints, as it also included the date: if the print was made during the artist's lifetime this makes the print more valuable. The censor also limited the size of the prints to restrict their visibility and potential implementation as a focus for political unrest. The publishers managed to circumvent restrictions in size to some extent by making prints that were double or triple height, or displayed as triptychs or even polyptychs.

Despite the tight constraints on *ukiyō-e* printmakers there was an unforeseen consequence of the success and popularity of the prints. They did change Japanese society in an unanticipated way: prints were sold for money, making the publishers and merchants cash-wealthy. (Samurai, above the merchant class in status, were at this time still paid for their services in rice.) The cash economy eventually changed the feudal system and propelled Japan into the modern era.

Blocks of the prints by popular artists were a valuable commodity owned by the publisher. Blocks might be remodelled to suit current fashions, or to reflect a change in theatrical casting, even recutting the features of an actor. The blocks were used as collateral for loans or sold for profit. If the prints were not selling well, or if the block began to lose its crisp edges due to overproduction, the block's surface would be planed down and the key block and separations would simply be recut, in this way extending the profitable life of the print run. The block would over time get thinner and thinner until it was too thin to be used; there was very little wastage. The life of an image could last well beyond the artist's lifetime.

At the British Museum's Hokusai Exhibition of 2017, 'Beyond the Great Wave', there was a surprising example of this. Hokusai's *Fine Wind, Clear Sky* made during his lifetime, with colours selected by him to show the delicate light of dawn touching Mount Fuji, was translated after his death into the graphic print known as 'Red Fuji', famous around the world, but not perhaps the nuanced print that Hokusai intended.

UKIYŌ-E ARTISTS

The golden era of *ukiyo-e* lasted for about a century from 1765–1868. The details of many of the earliest *ukiyo-e* practitioners are unknown due to the ephemeral nature of the prints and the low social status of the artists.

Students would be apprenticed at an early age and the right to incorporate the studio name into their own was a privilege to be earned. They would eat and sleep at the studio, learning all the menial tasks such as sweeping the floor, fetching and carrying, before embarking on tool sharpening, paper dampening, *dosa* preparing (brushing size onto the paper), pigment grinding and only then would they start cutting wood. Calligraphy was taught at the same time as drawing, using the same brushes and *sumi* ink.

There were strict hierarchies within the carving process: at the bottom the novices would start on kimono patterns; hands and feet, face and hairline would be for more experienced carvers, with the master carver in charge of the all-important key block and *kentō* registration.

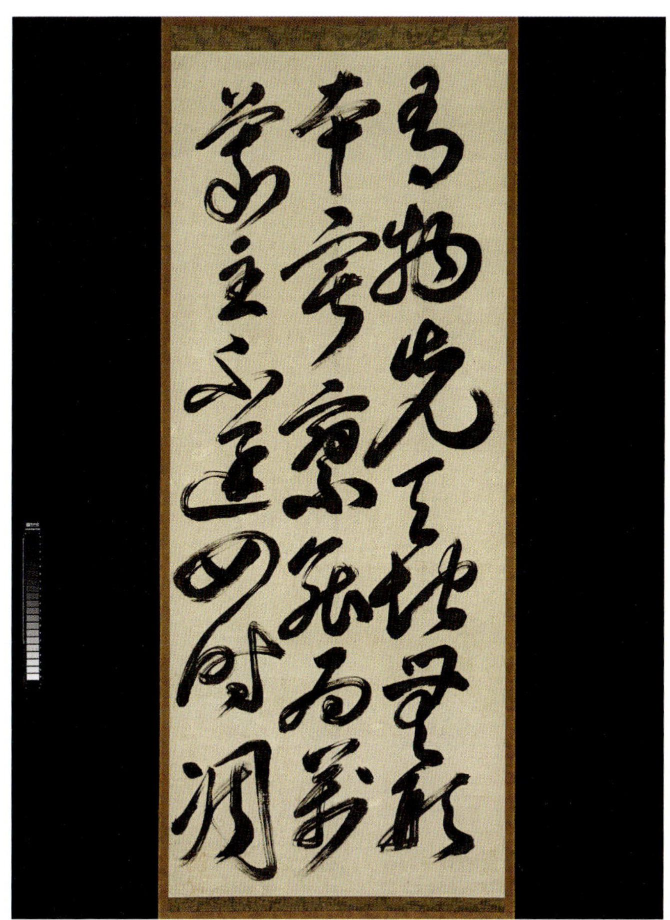

Bankei Yōtaku, 1622–1693. A *Gatha* (Contemplative Verse) by Fu Daishi. Hanging scroll, ink on paper (126 × 51.8cm).

Most artists aspired to run their own studio, or inherit their master's studio on his death. Rather surprisingly, printing was often seen as a lesser accomplishment, often carried out by itinerant workers and not necessarily in the main studio, with the exception of *bokashi* printing (graduated shading) that was accorded to the most skilled printer.

Okumura Masanobu 1686–1764

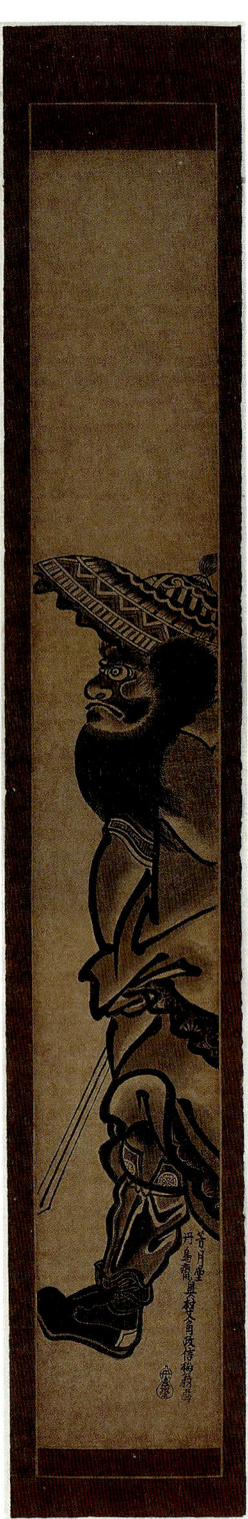

Okumura Masanobu, 1686–1764. *Shōki zu (Shōki Striding)* c.1741. Colour woodcut (69.2 × 10.1cm).

Masanobu was born and worked his whole life in Edo. He started his career as a painter and book illustrator, notably *The Tale of Genji*, and then took the unusual step of abandoning his publisher, setting up his own wholesale business, *Okumura-ya*. His trademark style was called *urushi-e*, where thick lines were printed with brass powder, dusted onto the ink to make a lacquer effect.

He was said to have been the inventor of the *hashira-e* or pillar prints (70 × 12cm), that were in vogue in the mid eighteenth century. They came to be used to decorate the interior supporting beams of the traditional Japanese house. It is thought that Masanobu had been experimenting with the more usual hanging scroll picture format, where two pieces of cherrywood were joined together. Apparently, Masanobu used wood of an inferior quality, that split when dampened and so rather than waste the wood, he cut them lengthwise making a long, thin matrix. The compositional possibilities of this unusual format gave rise to the most interesting prints, where figures appear to be walking off the picture plane.

Suzuki Harunobu 1724–1770

Harunobu was born into a samurai family, probably in Kyoto. Unlike other *ukiyō*-e artists he kept his family name rather than taking the name of the artist's studio. He was an innovator, using cherrywood for his prints instead of the catalpa that had been used before. He also printed with thicker inks, to give a more opaque effect, moving *ukiyō-e* away from being a mere facsimile of watercolour painting. Most importantly, however, in 1765 he instigated the *kentō* registration system, where notches were cut into the print block itself, so that printing became a simple matter of sliding the paper into the cut depressions. This made registration simple and quick to achieve and therefore many more colours could be employed for a single print. His prints were known as *nishiki-e*, or brocade pictures, for their use of many bright colours and they heralded the start of the golden era of *ukiyō-e* (1765–1868).

Kitagawa Utamaro 1753–1806

Utamaro was born Kitagawa Nebsuyoshi in the Musashi province and after his father's death he moved to Edo, where he was apprenticed to Sekien, the townscape painter. He produced illustrations for poems and plays under the name Toyoaki.

In 1780 he moved into the house of the leading publisher of the day, Tsutaya Jūzaburō, and changed his name to Utamaro.

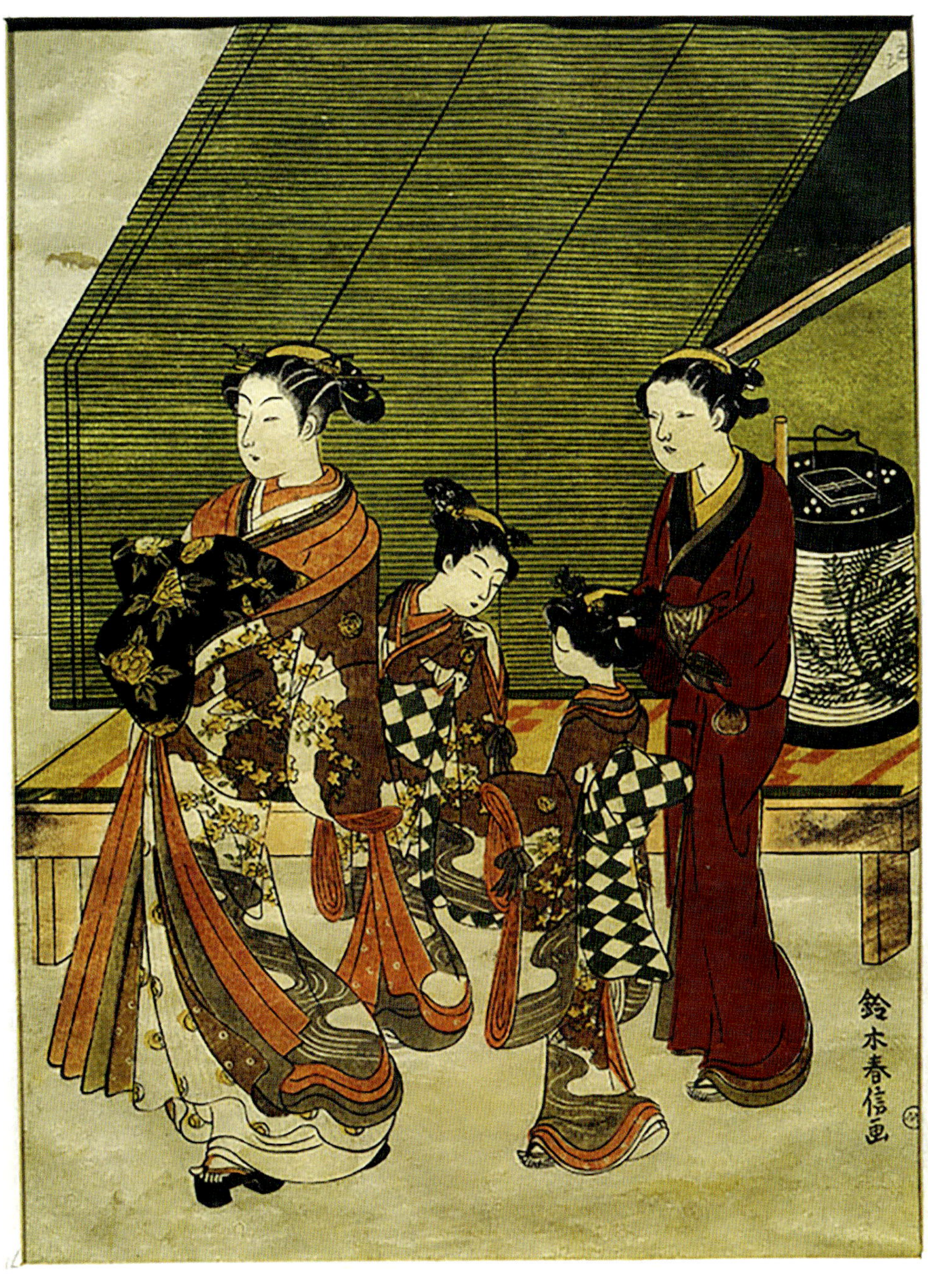

Suzuki Harunobu, 1724–70. *Parading Courtesans with Attendants*, 1760. Colour woodcut, an example of a *nishiki-e* print.

He began to depict *bijin-ga*, or prints of beautiful women and quickly became very successful.

He experimented with scale and prints of single portraits of women, rather than in groups, women engaged in their everyday business, bathing, arranging their hair, or with children in a garden. His skill at sophisticated composition and use of different printing processes, such as mica powder and gold dust, added to the nuance of his prints.

He produced many albums, among them his well-known nature studies book *Gahon chūsen* on insects. His pillow book of erotic *shunga*, *E-hon Utamakura*, displays a sensuality of flowing composition, partially revealed skin and tactile cloth that is quite extraordinary.

In 1804 he made a major miscalculation by producing a triptych depicting the Shōgun Toyotomi Hideyoshi and his life at court, a subject that was forbidden according to the

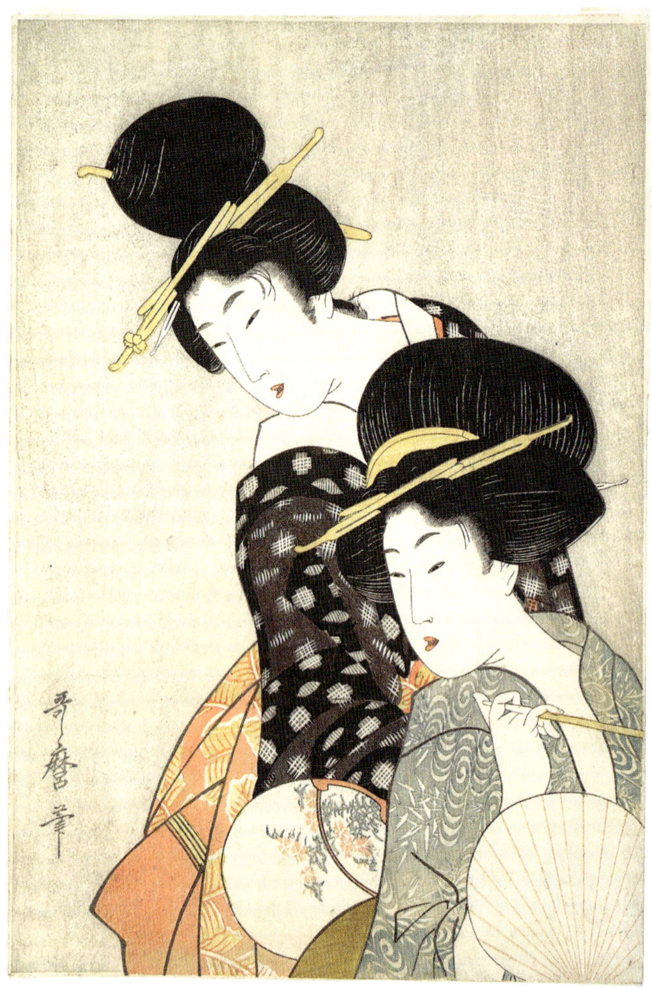

Kitagawa Utamaro, 1753–1806. *Two Women*, 1790. Colour woodcut (39.1 × 25.7cm).

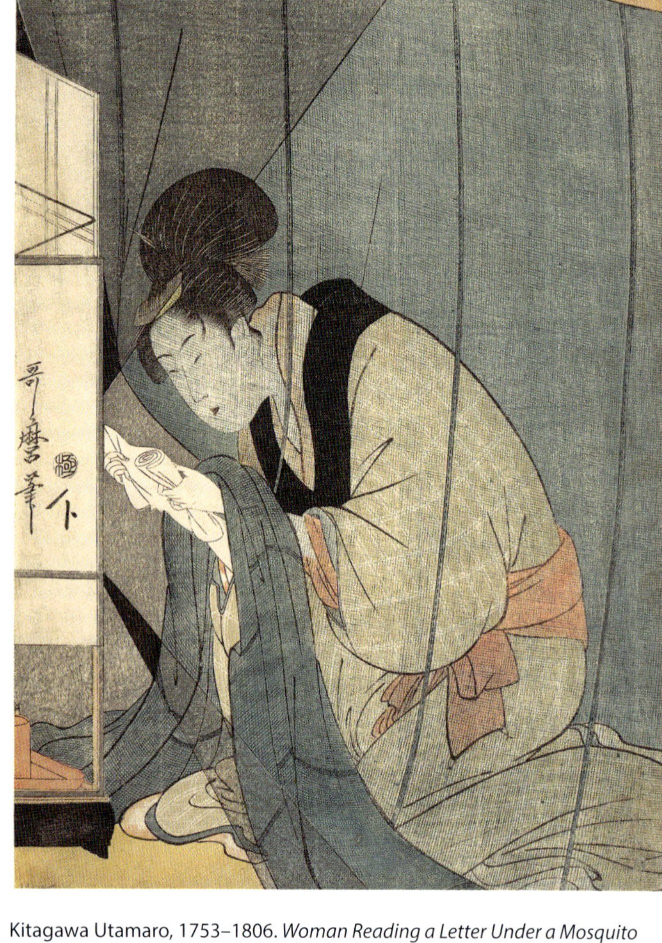

Kitagawa Utamaro, 1753–1806. *Woman Reading a Letter Under a Mosquito Net*, c.1798. The fine lines of the mosquito net are achieved by cutting all the horizontal lines on one block and all the vertical on another, then printing them in succession.

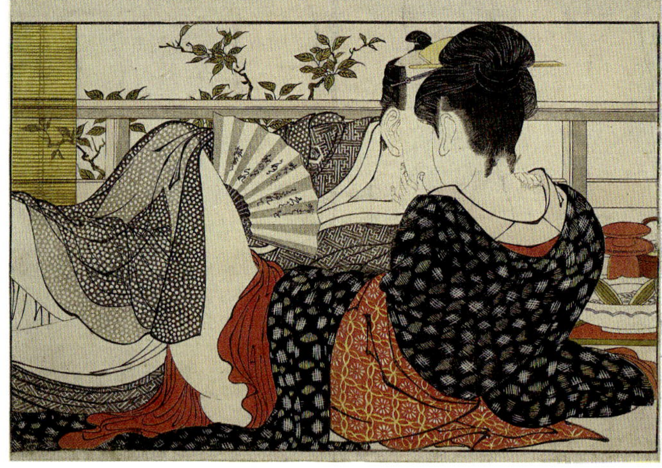

Kitagawa Utamaro, 1753–1806. *Uta makura/Poem of the Pillow*, 1788. *Shunga* or erotic print.

strict censorship of the day. He would have known this, but was perhaps overconfident due to his popularity and it was probably because of this popularity that Utamaro was placed under house arrest for 50 days in handcuffs, as an example to all who dared to insult the Shōgun.

His prints were among the first to become known in Europe – Toulouse-Lautrec was an admirer. In 1891 Edmond de Goncourt in Paris published a biography of both Utamaro and Hokusai. He called Utamaro 'le Watteau de là-bas', the 'Watteau from over there' because of both artists' predilection for the female form, based on direct observation of life 'as it was lived'. Tellingly de Goncourt can only praise Japanese artists by relating them to French artists; it has to be said that Utamaro was a great and important artist in his own right.

Kutsukawa Shunshō 1726–1793

Shunshō was a member of a samurai family and lived and worked in Edo. He is known mainly for his portraits of actors of the *kabuki* theatre and as the founder of the Katsukawa school; among his students were the artists Shunkō and Hokusai.

He became the leading master of the actor portrait, depicting large portrait heads, as well as the dressing room interiors, often using the narrow *hashira-e* format popularised by Masanobu. In his work he sought to bring portrait likenesses and expression to his actors' faces. The Katsukawa

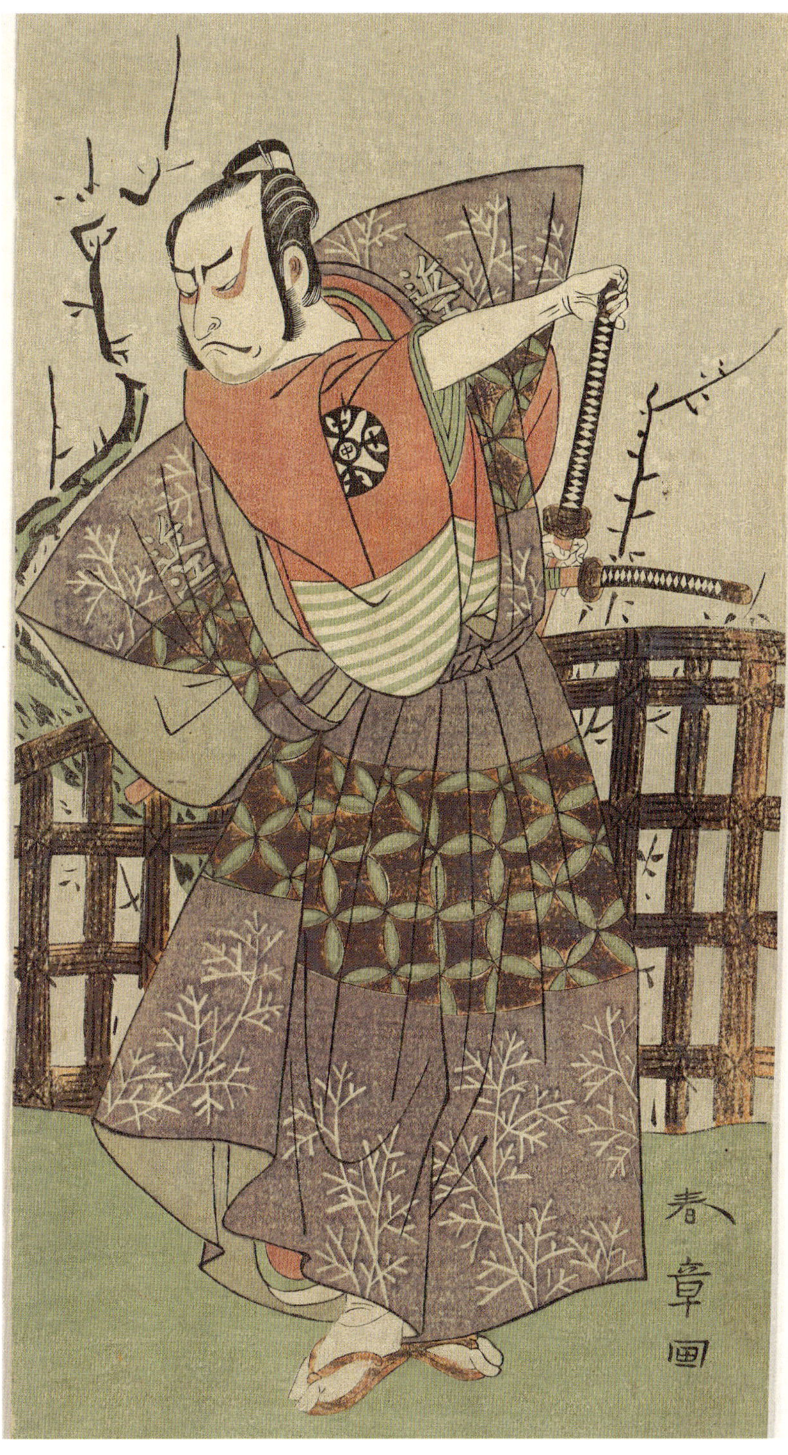

Katsukawa Shunshō, 1726–1792. *The First Nakamura Nakazo as a Samurai Dressed in Kamishimo*, 1775. Colour woodcut (31.8 × 14.3cm).

school taught the realistic observation from nature that was to become such a defining feature of Hokusai's work.

Kutsushika Hokusai 1760–1849

There is more information about Hokusai's life than any other *ukiyō-e* artist. This is partly due to the fact that he was so prolific, but also because many of his prints were still available when Japan's borders were opened to the West and eagerly collected by the leading Impressionists. The first biography of him was written in Japan by Iijima Hanjuro in 1890, followed in Paris by Edmund de Goncourt in 1896, cementing Hokusai's reputation in the West as one of the foremost Japanese artists. In Japan he had been almost considered a non-Japanese artist, because his style incorporated so many experimentations with both Chinese and Western perspectives.

Hokusai was born Kawamura Tokitaro on 12 October 1760 in Honjo, a working-class district in the suburbs of Edo. After the death of his father Kawamura Itiroyemon, he was adopted

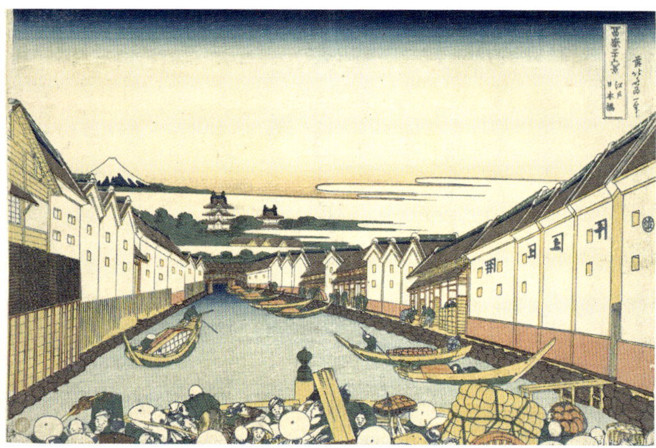

Katsushika Hokusai, 1760–1849. *Nihonbashi in Edo*, c.1830–2. This print shows Hokusai's use of perspective picked up from Dutch engravings.

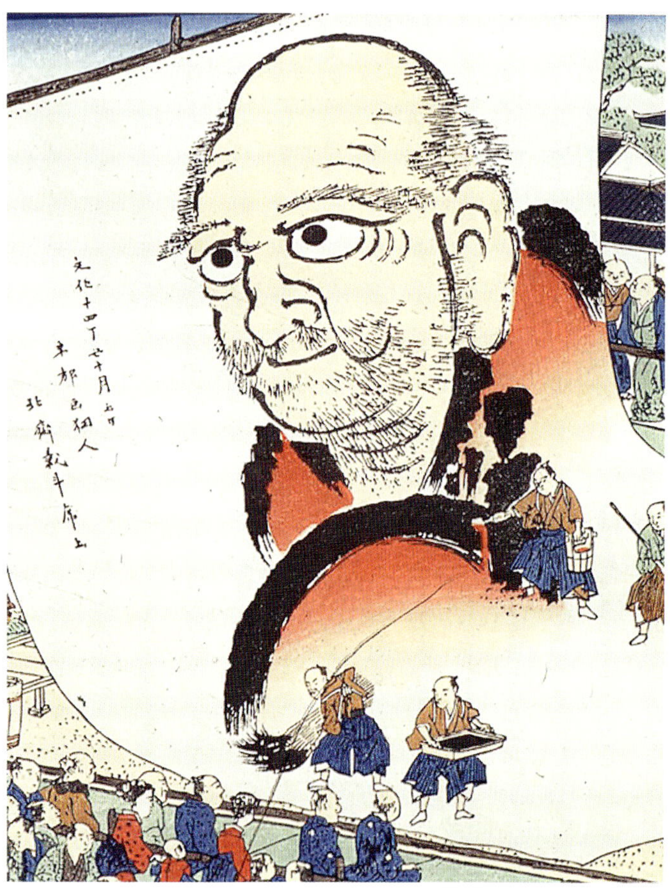

Contemporary print, unknown artist. *Hokusai Painting the Great Daruma Beside the Hongan–ji Nagoya Betsuin*, 1817.

by his uncle Nakajima Ise and changed his name to Tamekazu Nakajima. It would be the first of 30 name changes in his life-time. (It is thought that his mother had been a concubine, as

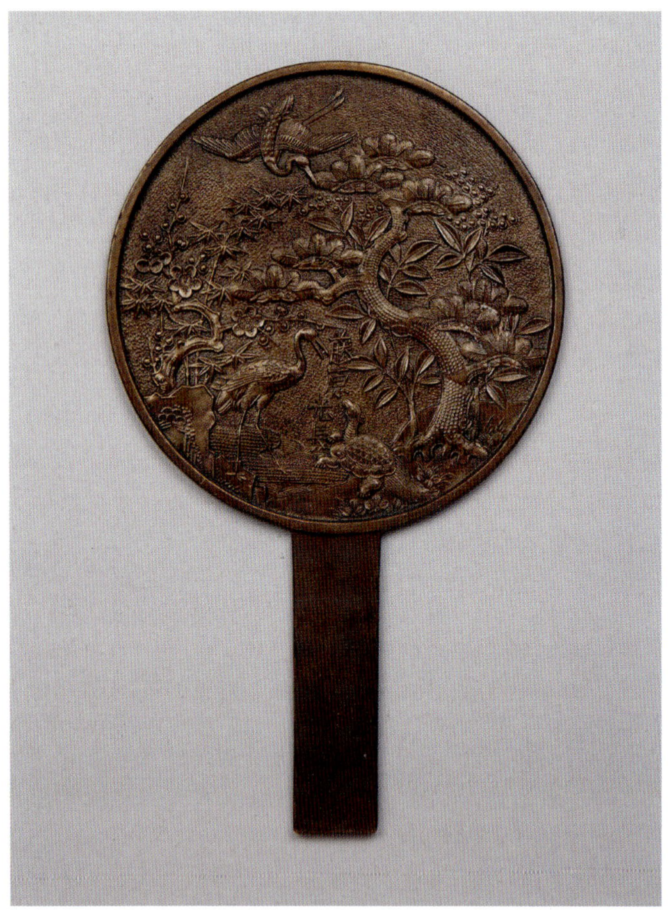

Nineteenth-century bronze mirror.

he was not accepted as his father's heir.) His uncle was the official mirror maker to the Shōgun Tokitaro and proved to be a formative influence on the young Hokusai. These exquisite mirrors were intricately decorated with ornate designs in relief on one side and highly polished bronze on the other. Mirrors played an important mystical part in religious and secular life in Japan, but the ancient traditional mirrors were being slowly superseded by the glass silver-backed imports from Holland.

Hokusai showed an early aptitude for drawing and painting, recording in later life, 'from the time I was six, I was in the habit of sketching things I saw around me'. By the age of 14 he had left his uncle's house, working first as a clerk, then in a lending library and finally gaining a place as an apprentice in the studio of Katsukawa Shunshō, changing his name to Katsukawa Shunrō and producing his first actor portraits.

He learnt the trade of *ukiyō-e* printmaking at this popular studio and became a very accomplished artist, staying at the Katsukawa school until 1785. He experimented with perspective and shading that he saw in the few Dutch engravings that circulated in Edo at that time. When Shunshō died, Hokusai the most talented artist at the studio should have been his successor – instead he was passed over for the more traditional artist Shunei. There was class snobbery involved in the choice; contemporaries described Hokusai as 'uncouth and dirty', he was disdained for his poor background and common accent.

In 1794 he joined the Tawaraya family, changing his name to Tawaraya Sori. They introduced him to book enthusiasts, who commissioned high-quality *surimono* (literally 'printed thing'), books and albums for the rich elite. He stayed for four years and then, unusually for a Japanese artist of the time, he became independent. To mark this change in his career, in 1798 he changed his name to Katsushika Hokusai. He had become very interested in Buddhist philosophy and iconography – the name Hokusai relates to the North Star and is linked in Buddhism to 'unshakeable conviction and purification'. The name 'Katsushika' relates to the district in Honjo where he was born.

There was a performative aspect to an artist's life in Edo, they were expected to produce calligraphy on demand and

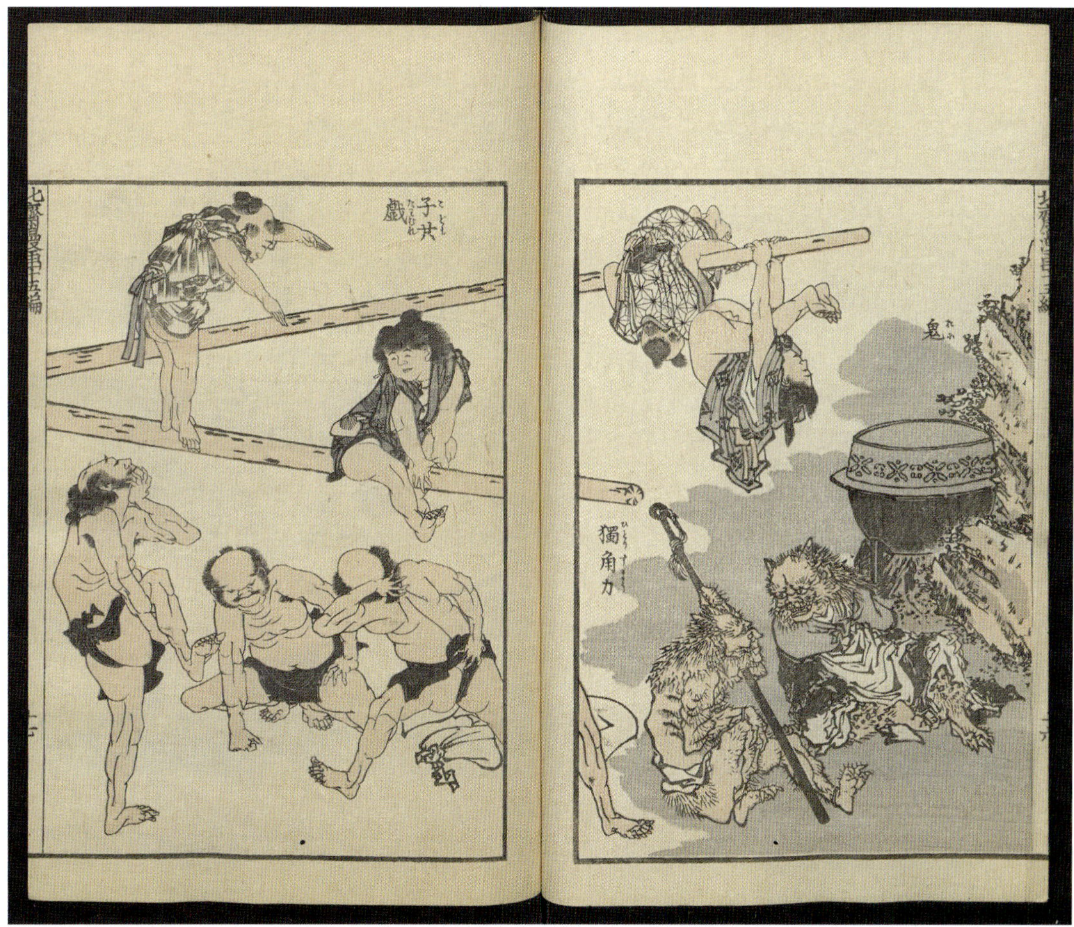

Katsushika Hokusai, 1760–1849. *Transmitting the Spirit, Revealing the Form of Things: Hokusai Sketchbooks*, 1878. Woodblock printed book (23.2 × 15.2cm).

perform artworks at parties. Hokusai was a born showman; he called himself Gakyojin Hokusai, 'the Madman of Art'. One example of this was a painting he made of 'Doruma the Zen Patriarch', which measured a vast 240 square metres and was hoisted high above the rooftops for the crowds to see. Another story told was of a painting competition between Hokusai and a more traditional painter, set up by the Shōgun Ionadi in Nagoya. Hokusai outclassed his more conservative rival's sycophantic portrait of the Shōgun by a characteristically bravura

ŌI HOKUSAI

There has been much recent speculation about whether some prints attributed to Hokusai may in fact be by Ōi. There are only ten works that are definitely attributed to her, but it would have been good for business to sign all of her prints and paintings with her father's brand name 'Hokusai'. She is thought to have lived with her father until his death, and it is generally supposed that she died in 1857. There is a *manga* series by Hinako Sugiura about her life and an anime film called *Miss Hokusai*, directed by Keiichi Hara and released in 2015.

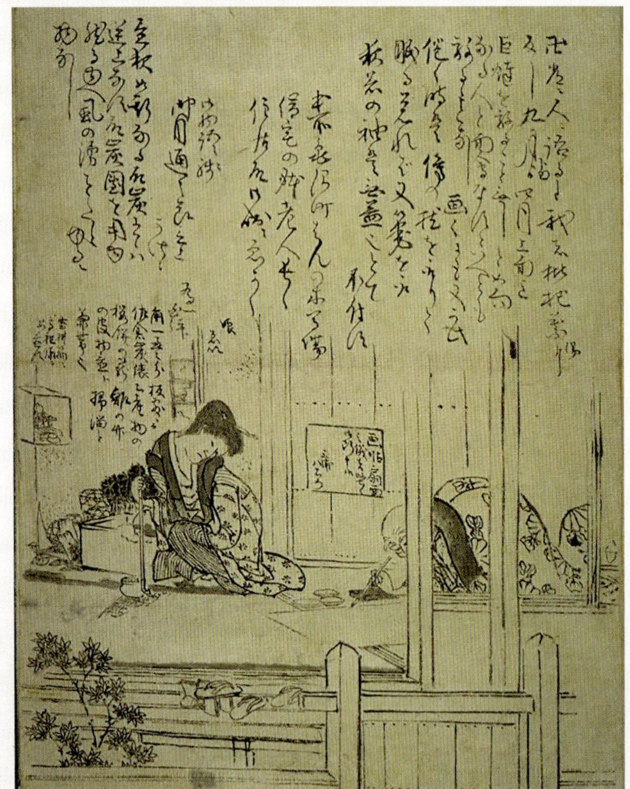

Tsukyuki Kōshō. *Hokusai and Ōi in their Lodgings*, c.1840.

performance. He unrolled a long piece of paper, then took a broom, dipped it into blue pigment and painted a broad cursive line down its length, then poured red pigment into a tray and encouraged live chickens to walk through the ink, sending them scurrying down the blue, leaving their red footprints behind. The blue cursive line represented the Tatsuta river and the red chicken footprints were the autumn maple *momiji* leaves floating in the water. He won the competition.

Between 1798 and 1805 he produced portraits of women and colour illustrations for picture and poetry books such as 'Songs from Itako', 'Famous Views of the Eastern Capital', and 'Mountains upon Mountains'. During this period, he also designed three-dimensional diorama, board games and paper lanterns. He took up Chinese painting and illustrating, leading to the creation in 1814 of his first set of *manga* (which translates literally as 'whimsical pictures') books that ran to 15 volumes. These books were seen as valuable visual resources in studios, as they covered acute drawings of a wide variety of everyday Japanese life, mythology, and close observations of birds, animals and plants.

Aged 60, he changed his name to 'Itsu' or 'One again' – 60 is seen as an important and auspicious age in China and Japan, as according to the Chinese zodiac it is the fifth cycle of 12. By the late 1820s, he produced many landscape colour print series including 'Reflections of Poets', 'One Hundred Nurse's Tales' and 'Around Trip past the Waterfalls'.

Hokusai was never the head of a studio and often led a precarious freelance life, spent in relative poverty. He changed his name 30 times, at each turning point of his career, ending with *'Gakyō-rōjin'* meaning 'Old man mad about Painting'. He moved house 93 times (allegedly moving studio when it became too dirty), he was married twice, and had two sons and three daughters. His daughter Ōi (from his second wife Koto) was an artist in her own right and unusually for a woman, it is thought she worked with him in his studio for around 25 years.

The year of 1820 was very hard for Hokusai. His second wife died, he was himself in bad health and he discovered that his grandson had lost all of his money. His grief and sudden poverty propelled him to make his most famous work, when he was in his 70s. From 1830–36 Hokusai created 'Thirty-Six Views of Mount Fuji', and four years later in three volumes, 'One Hundred Views of Mount Fuji'. The publisher Nishimuraya Yohachi advertised 'Thirty-Six Views of Mount Fuji' rather deprecatingly as 'one view per sheet issued in succession, printed in blue'. They form part of his *meisho-e* or famous

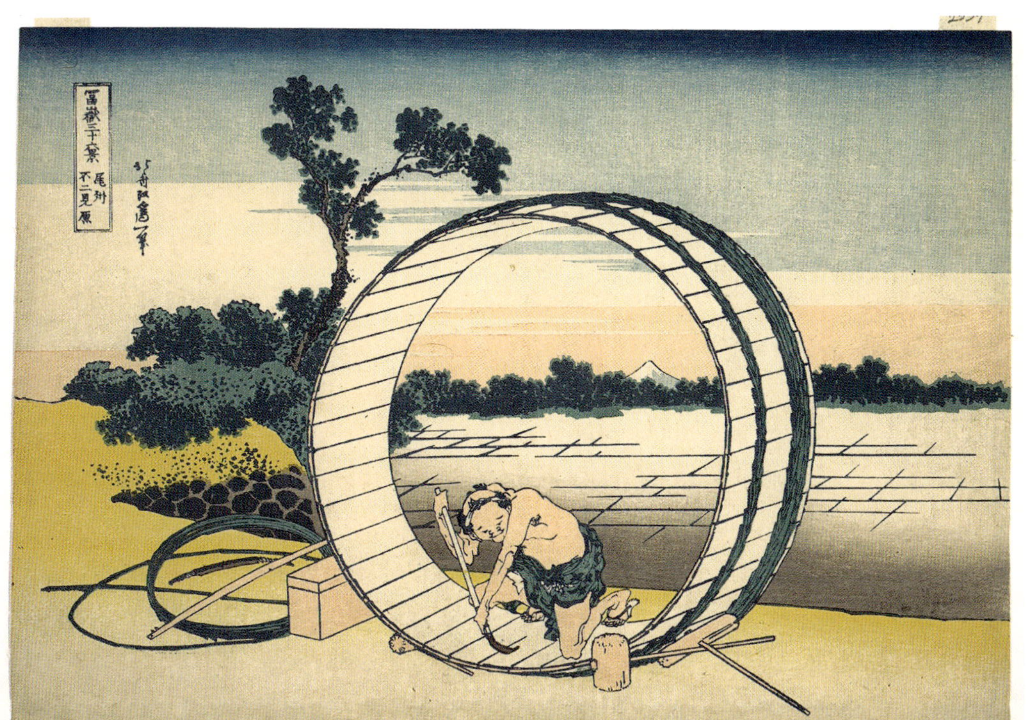

Katsushika Hokusai, 1760–1849. *Fujimigahara in Owari Province,* from the series 'Thirty-six Views of Mount Fuji', c.1830–2. Colour woodblock print (25.4 × 38.1cm).

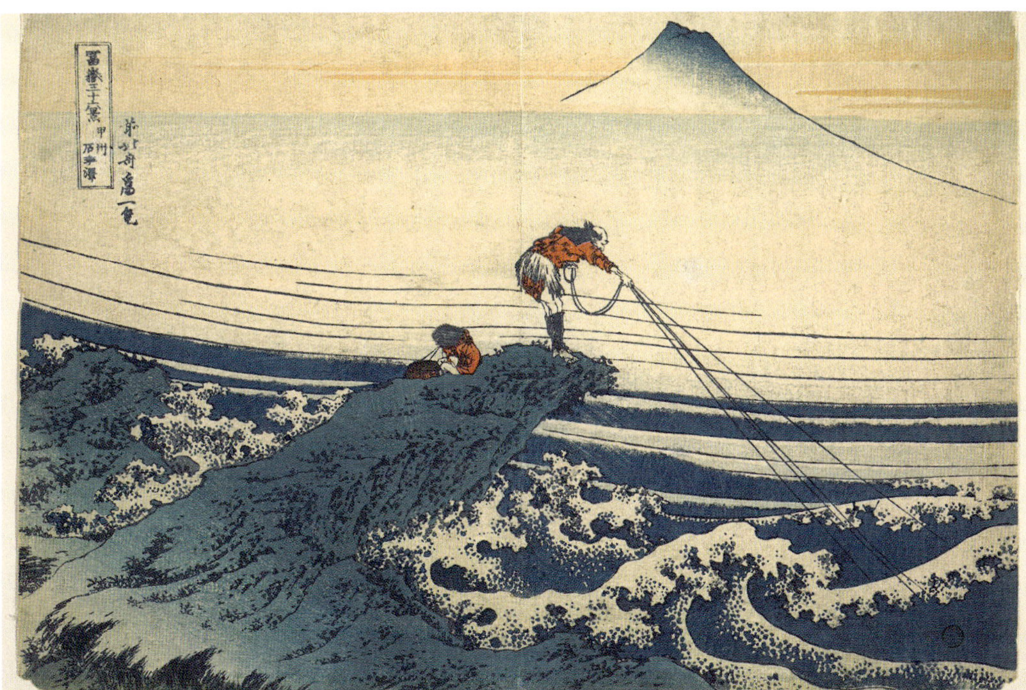

Katsushika Hokusai, 1760– 1849. *View of Mount Fuji from Kajikazawa,* from the series 'Thirty-six views of Mount Fuji', c.1830–2. Colour woodblock print (25.4 × 38.1cm).

place series. They proved to be incredibly popular; thousands of copies were sold and Hokusai was commissioned to make ten more prints. More than just a pleasing landscape view, Mount Fuji was traditionally venerated as a holy place and Hokusai followed the Nichiren School of Buddhism, who believed that the secret of eternal life was placed at its peak. The mountain is an eternal, ever present, enduring presence throughout the series, often showing people performing everyday tasks, with

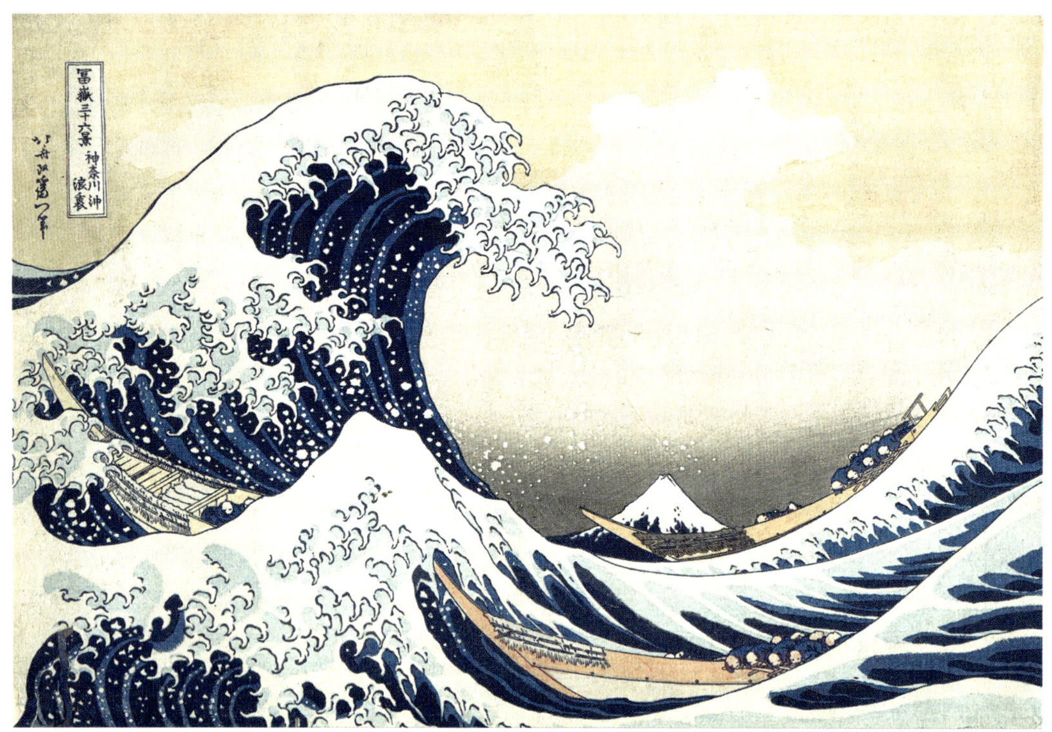

Katsushika Hokusai, 1760–1849. *Under the Wave off Kanagawa,* also known as *The Great Wave,* from the series 'Thirty-Six views of Mount Fuji', c.1830–2. Colour woodblock print (25.4 × 38.1cm).

the mountain quietly present. There are many underlying religious symbolic references in the work, such as the Zen broken circle *ēnso* signifying enlightenment and the infinite, with the triangle of Mount Fuji symbolising the fixed law of nature. The series show the use of innovative compositions and viewpoints, elemental forces of nature, different perspectives, and a new colour – Prussian Blue – that had just arrived in Japan from Europe. These prints are seen as the high point in his prodigious career.

Under the Great Wave off Kanagawa, popularly shortened to *The Great Wave*, is now one of the most reproduced prints in the world and even features on the Japanese passport. A rare early print recently sold at Christie's in New York for a record $2.8 million. It is seen as Hokusai's signature piece and has come to be regarded as symbolic of Japan's artistic heritage. Many theories surround the subject matter: does it foretell the imminent arrival of the Western powers threatening to engulf Japan like the boats in the print, is it a personal expression of the grief that he suffered with the loss of his wife and sudden poverty, or a composition that shows pictorially the central force and serenity of Mount Fuji and by extension the Buddhist faith, in the midst of nature's extremities?

In 1839, there was a terrible fire in his studio and many works of art were destroyed. Even so he is thought to have produced 30,000 works over the course of his lifetime including paintings, sketches, woodblock prints, as well as illustrations for 500 books. He wrote 'nothing I produced before the age of 70 is worthy of note... by the time I'm 80 I will have made some real progress... when I am a 110 everything I do be it a dot or a line, will be alive'. When he died in 1849 aged 88, his last words were said to have been 'If only heaven will give me just another ten years... just another five, then I could become a real painter.'

Utagawa Hiroshige 1797–1858

Hiroshige is considered to be the last of the great *ukiyō-e* masters. He was born Andō Tokutarō in Edo, the son of a fireman and apprenticed to the *ukiyō-e* master Toyohiro at the age of 14. A year later in 1812, he adopted the name Utagawa Hiroshige. When Toyohiro died in 1828, he took over the studio and called himself Toyohiro II, an example of the classic career trajectory of the Japanese artist of his day. He studied the traditional *Kanō* style of painting, with its adherence to Chinese landscapes and the more realistic style of *Shijō*, where direct observation is allied to an inner spirit and playfulness. He transferred his attention to the production of sublime landscape prints, popularised as a new genre by Hokusai and Eisen before him. Hiroshige had worked as an official in a government mission to the Emperor's Imperial residence in Kyoto, which proved to be a valuable resource to him.

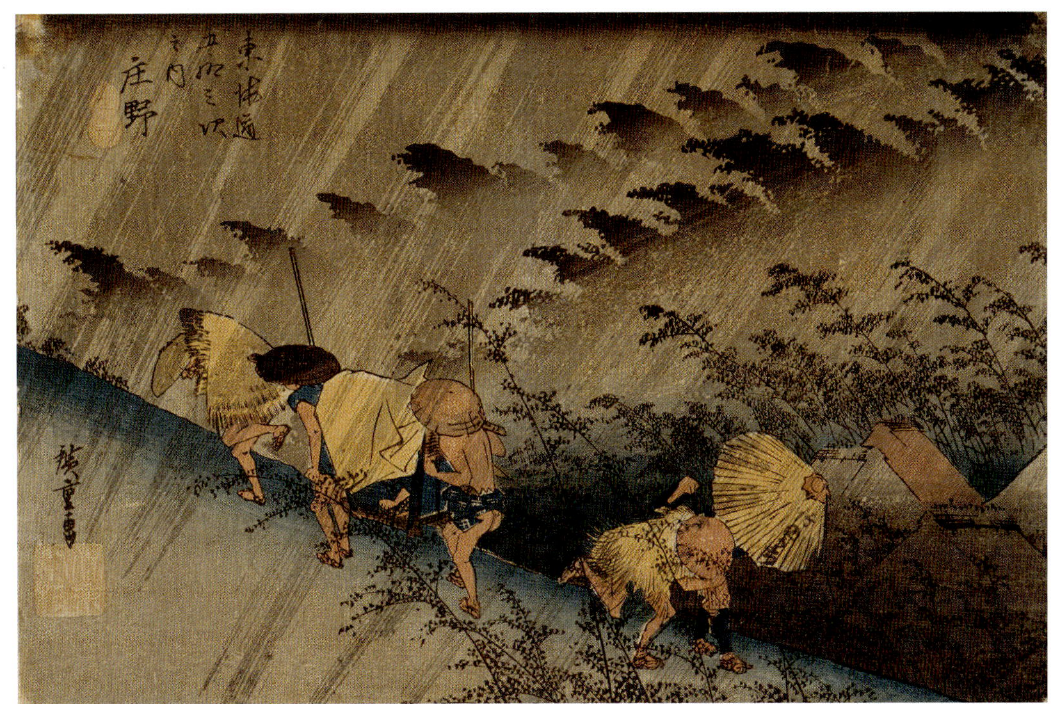

Andō Hiroshige, 1797–1858.
Shōno: Driving Rain, from the
series 'Fifty-Three Stations of
the Tōkaidō', c.1833–4. Colour
woodblock print (22.07 × 33.5cm).

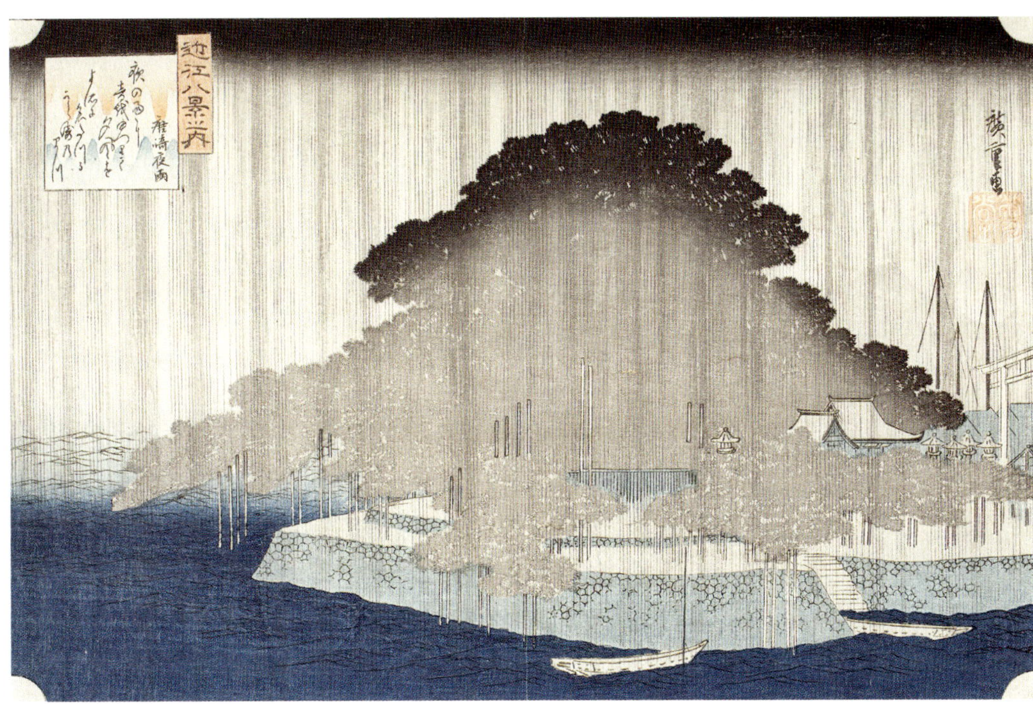

Andō Hiroshige, 1797–1858. *Night
Rain at Karasaki*, from the series
'Eight Views of Ōmi', 1835–6.
Colour woodblock print (22.54
× 35.08cm).

In 1833–4, his series 'Fifty-Three Stations on the Tōkaidō' brought him public recognition and attention. Japanese people were able to travel more than ever before and these prints of the great Imperial route between Edo and Kyoto were bought as mementos of this new-found freedom.

He continued to travel and work on landscape series from his own observations: 'Famous Places in Kyoto', 'Eight Views of Lake Biwa', 'Famous Places in Naniwa', 'Eight Views of Kanazawa', 'Sixty-Nine Stations on the Kisokaidō' and 'One Hundred Famous Views of Edo' to name a few in a career that

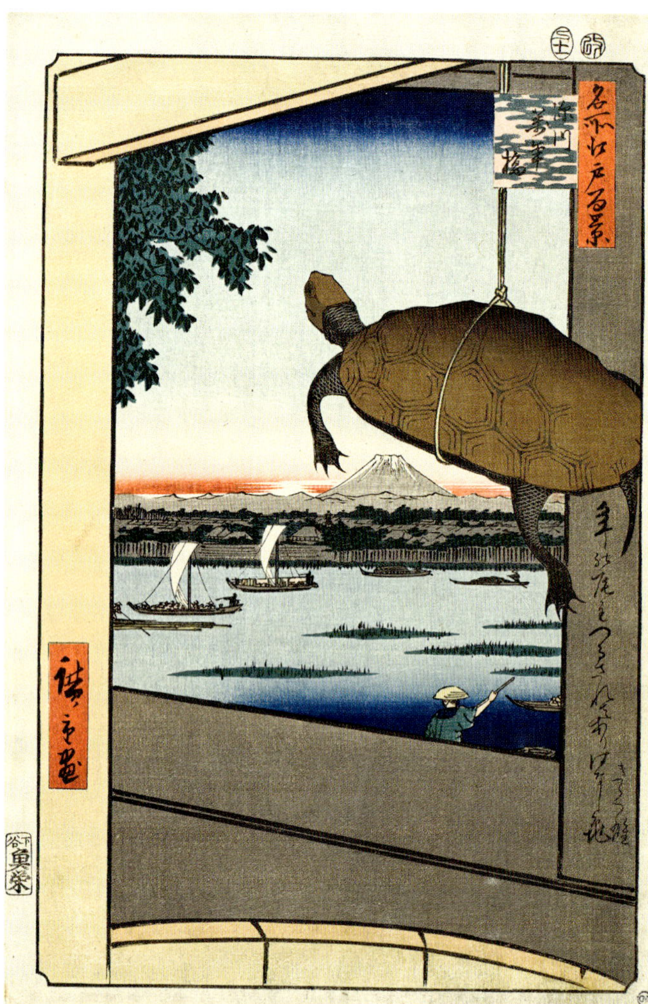

Andō Hiroshige, 1797–1858. *Mannen Bridge, Fukagawa,* from the series 'One Hundred Famous Views of Edo', 1857. Colour woodblock print (33.97 × 24.7cm).

produced more than 5,400 woodblock prints. His landscapes are beautifully realised images of nature in all seasons and weathers, with delicately graduated colours using the *bokashi* technique.

His compositions often include the extreme cropping of a large foreground figure or object adding a sense of distance and space with the background. In the print *Mannen Bridge*, in a wry observation the background is seen through the foreground of a suspended turtle.

Hiroshige's prints were shown at the Paris Expositions Universelles of 1855, 1867 and 1878 and had a huge impact on the Impressionists and Post Impressionists, particularly Van Gogh who painted a copy of the print called *Flowering Plum Tree (after Hiroshige)* in 1887.

BLACK SHIPS

In 1853 American 'Black Ships' appeared in Tokyo Bay, so called because of the plumes of black smoke issuing from

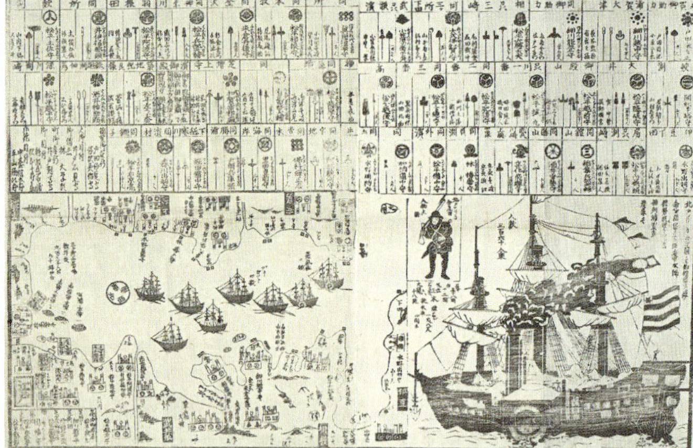

Unknown author. Japanese print from 1854 describing Commodore Perry's 'Black Ships', probably showing the flagship paddle steamer USS *Mississippi*. So called 'Black Ships' due to the black smoke issuing from their funnels.

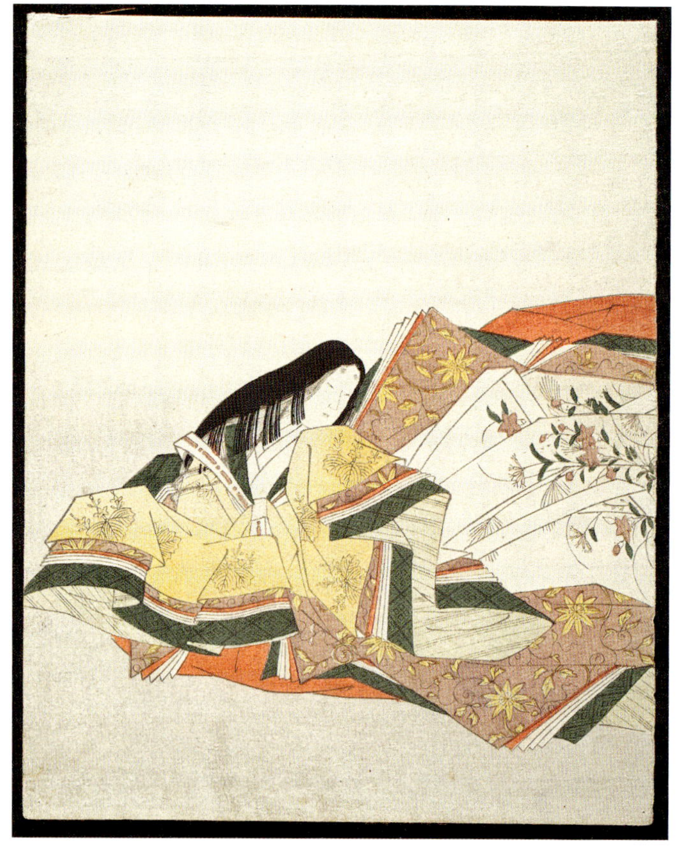

Chōbunsai Eishi, 1756–1829. From the book *The Thirty-six Immortal Women Poets,* 1801. Colour woodblock print (15.24 × 18.57). Delicate colours made from indigenous plants such as safflowers.

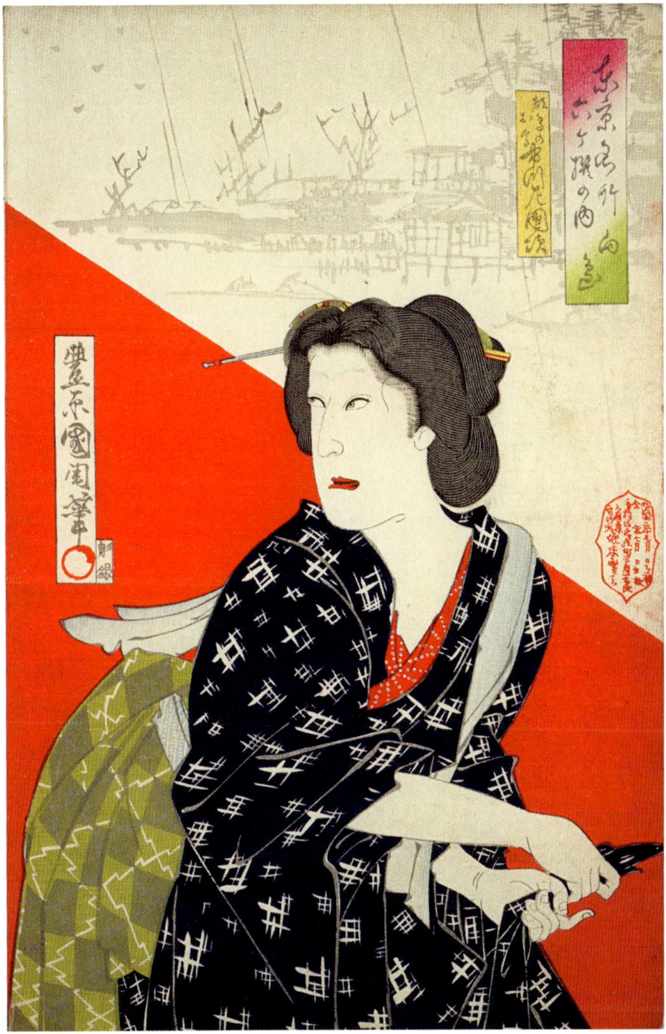

Toyohara Kunichika, 1835–1900. Woodblock print by Utagawa family, 1889. Strong, vibrant colours showing the use of imported aniline dyes from Europe.

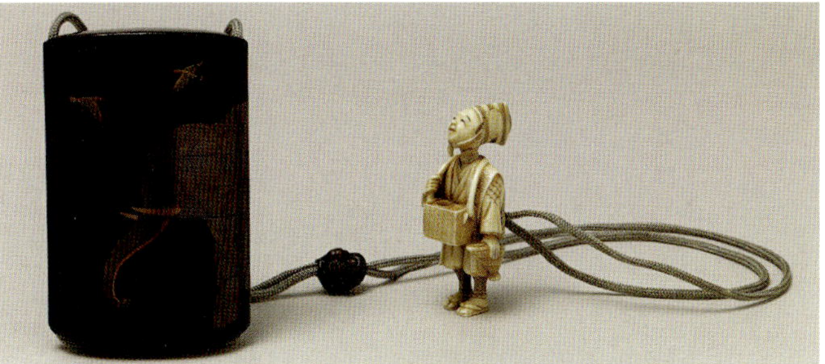

Netsuke. Nineteenth century, ivory. *Netsuke* were decorative toggles usually finely carved out of wood or ivory that hung from the wearer's belt. Highly sought-after in nineteenth-century Paris.

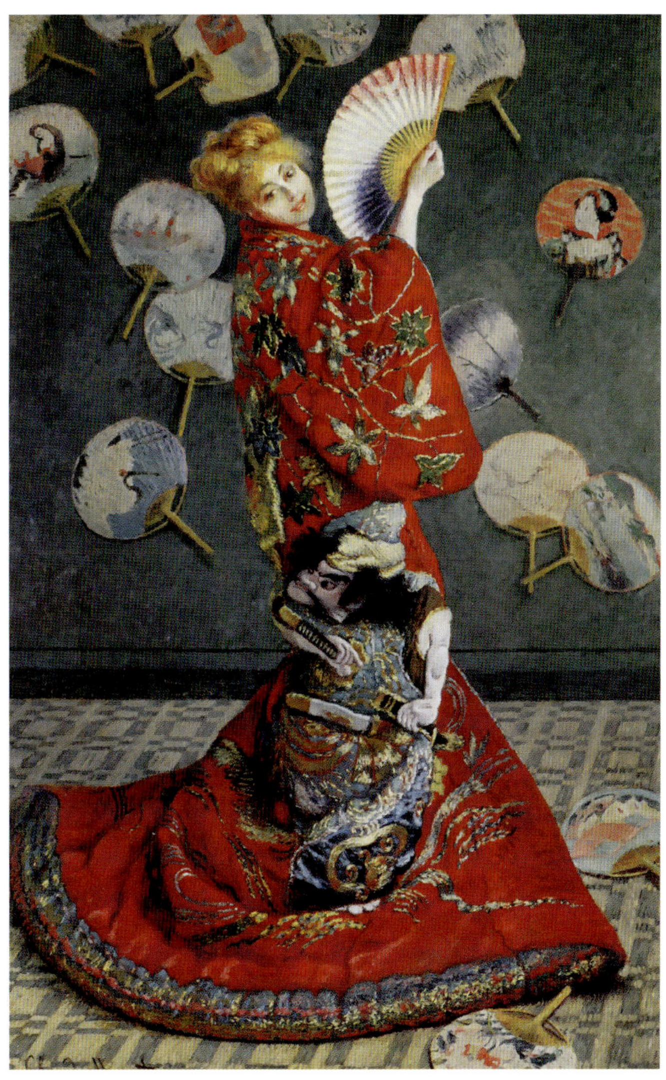

Claude Monet, 1840–1926. *Madame Monet Wearing a Kimono,* 1875. Oil on canvas (231 × 142.3cm). An example of *japonaiserie,* Monet is using a Japanese kimono in his work but not investigating Japanese art. This would change later on with his famous Japanese garden and paintings of waterlilies at Giverney.

their funnels. It signalled the end of Japan's isolation; in 1854 the ships returned in force under the command of Commodore Matthew Perry who threatened to fire on Japan's wooden cities, unless the Japanese opened their ports to Western trade.

Japan was forced to sign an unfavourable trade deal in 1858, euphemistically titled 'Treaties of Friendship and Commerce' with the USA, UK, France, Holland and Russia. Increased contact with the outside world brought a flood of new imports and new technologies. Mokuhanga quickly fell out of favour to Western lithography and photography, garish aniline dyes replaced the more delicate indigenous natural colours, and the quality of *ukiyō-e* prints at first sharply declined.

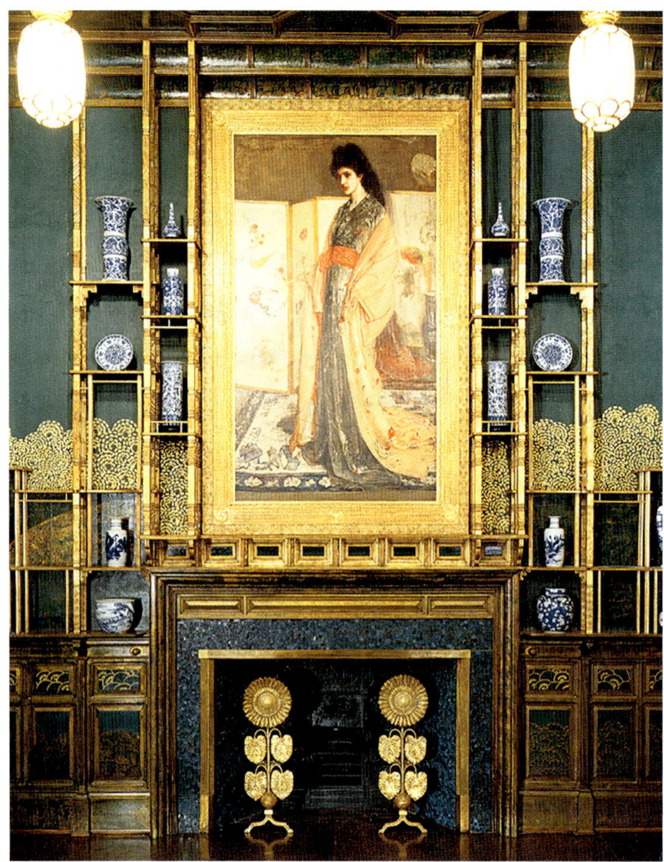

James Abbott McNeill Whistler, 1834–1903. *The Princess from the Land of Porcelain,* 1864. The painting is shown hanging in the 'Peacock Room' at the Freer Gallery of Art. Note how the model is wearing a kimono like a dressing gown, and the mixing of Chinese and Japanese artefacts.

JAPONAISERIE, JAPONISME

Immediately after the opening of Japan to the outside world, the fashion for all things Japanese spread quickly around the world. In Paris, particularly, there was a craze for Japanese kimonos, fans, netsuke, screens, ceramics and prints. Two new words were coined: 'Japonaiserie', a neologism invented by the poet Baudelaire to define the fashion for Japanese objects and 'Japonisme' invented by the critic Philippe Burty to define the impact of Japanese aesthetics on Western art. There is an apocryphal story that *ukiyo-e* prints first arrived in Europe as protective wrappings for ceramics – whether this is true or not, they soon began to be sought in their own right.

Hayashi Tadamasa had first come to Paris as a salesman and interpreter for the Kiryo Crafts and Trading Company, supplying Japanese manufactured goods to the Paris World's Fair of 1878. He was the primary source for Edmond de Goncourt's

biographies of Utamaro and Hokusai. De Goncourt, however, never went to Japan, so much of the information about their lives came from Tadamasa. He stayed on in Paris and set up as an art dealer and within 11 years had sold 156,467 *ukiyo-e* prints. It is ironic that many of the masterpieces of *ukiyo-e* had to be bought back by Japan later when it was understood how valuable they had become in the West.

JAPANESE INFLUENCE ON FRENCH ART

Today, over-familiarity with Impressionist paintings in big block-buster exhibitions and museums makes it easy to forget that France in the 1880s had recently been a revolutionary country and the Impressionists were considered radicals. Artists such as Manet, Monet, Degas, Mary Cassatt, Toulouse-Lautrec and Van Gogh were all hugely influenced by the asymmetrical compositions, bright colours and flowing lines of the Japanese *ukiyo-e* masters. But more than this, like

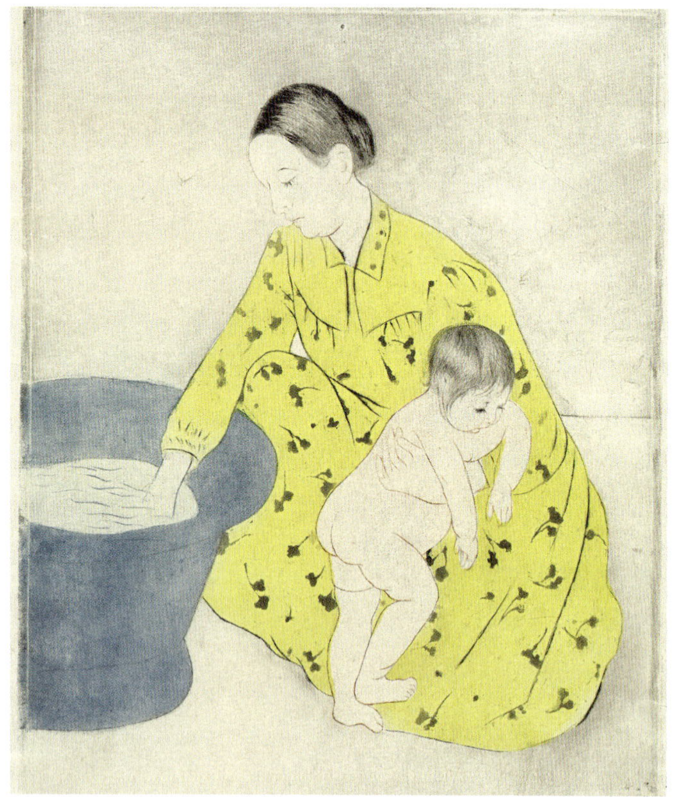

Mary Cassatt, 1844–1926. *The Bath*, 1891. Colour drypoint, soft ground etching and aquatint on wove paper (36.7 × 27.5cm).

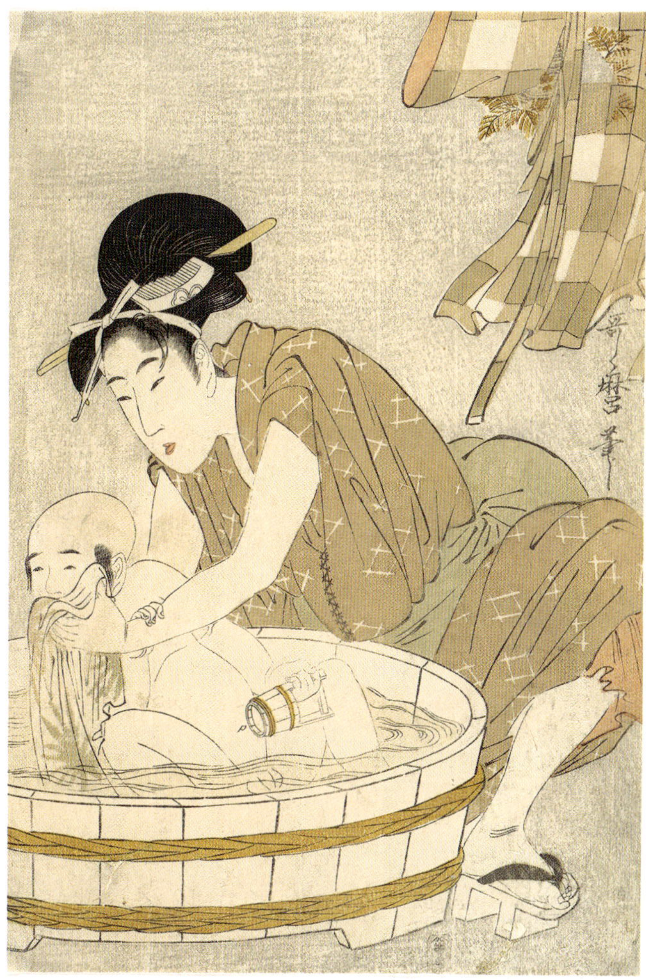

Kitagawa Utamaro, 1753–1806. *Woman Washing a Baby in a Tub,* 1801.
Colour woodblock print (37.3 × 25.1cm).

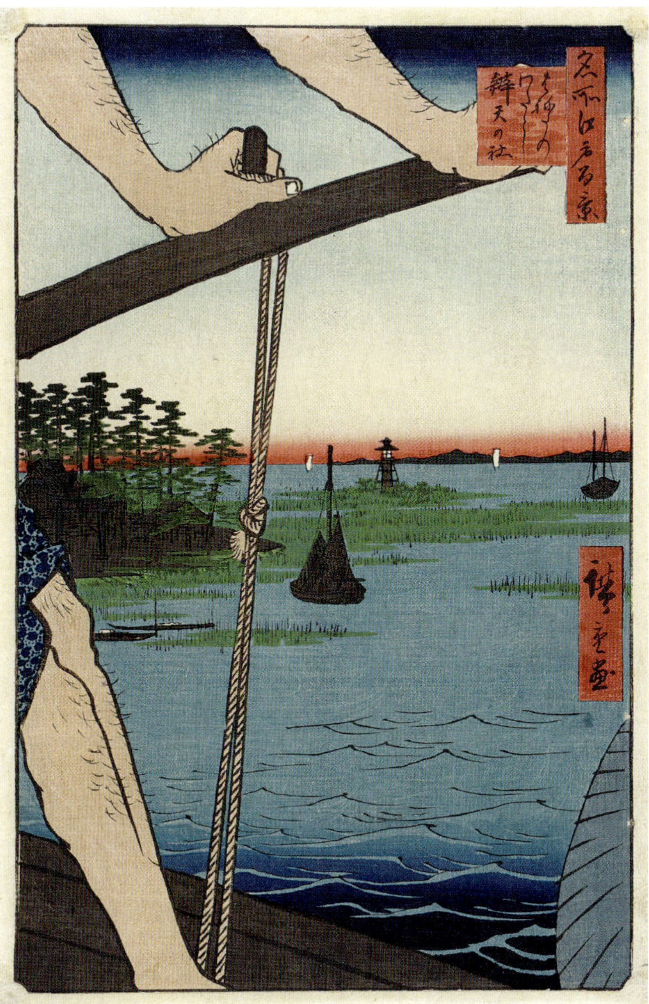

Andō Hiroshige, 1797–1858. *Haneda Ferry and Benten shrine,* from the series
'One hundred Famous Views of Edo', 1858. Colour woodblock print (33.97
× 22.54cm).

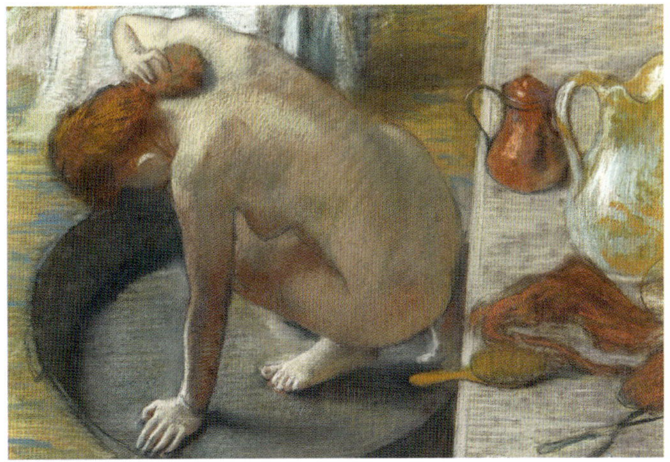

Edgar Degas, 1834–1917. *Le Tub*, 1886. Oil pastel on paper (60 × 83cm).

the merchants of Edo a century before, they were looking for
a subject matter that reflected their world. The *ukiyō-e* prints
of the demi-monde of Edo in the eighteenth century served
as inspiration for the paintings of the demi-monde of Paris in
the nineteenth. Most Impressionist and Post-Impressionist
painters were able to afford the *ukiyō-e* prints flooding into
Paris and collected them eagerly. Monet had 231 prints mostly
by Hiroshige, Hokusai and Utamaro. Degas owned 42 prints,
Hiroshige landscapes, Hokusai and Kiyonaga and Van Gogh
had 43 Hiroshige prints.

Edgar Degas' pastel drawing *The Tub* of 1886 caused a furore
when it was shown. It was not the nudity, the naked female form

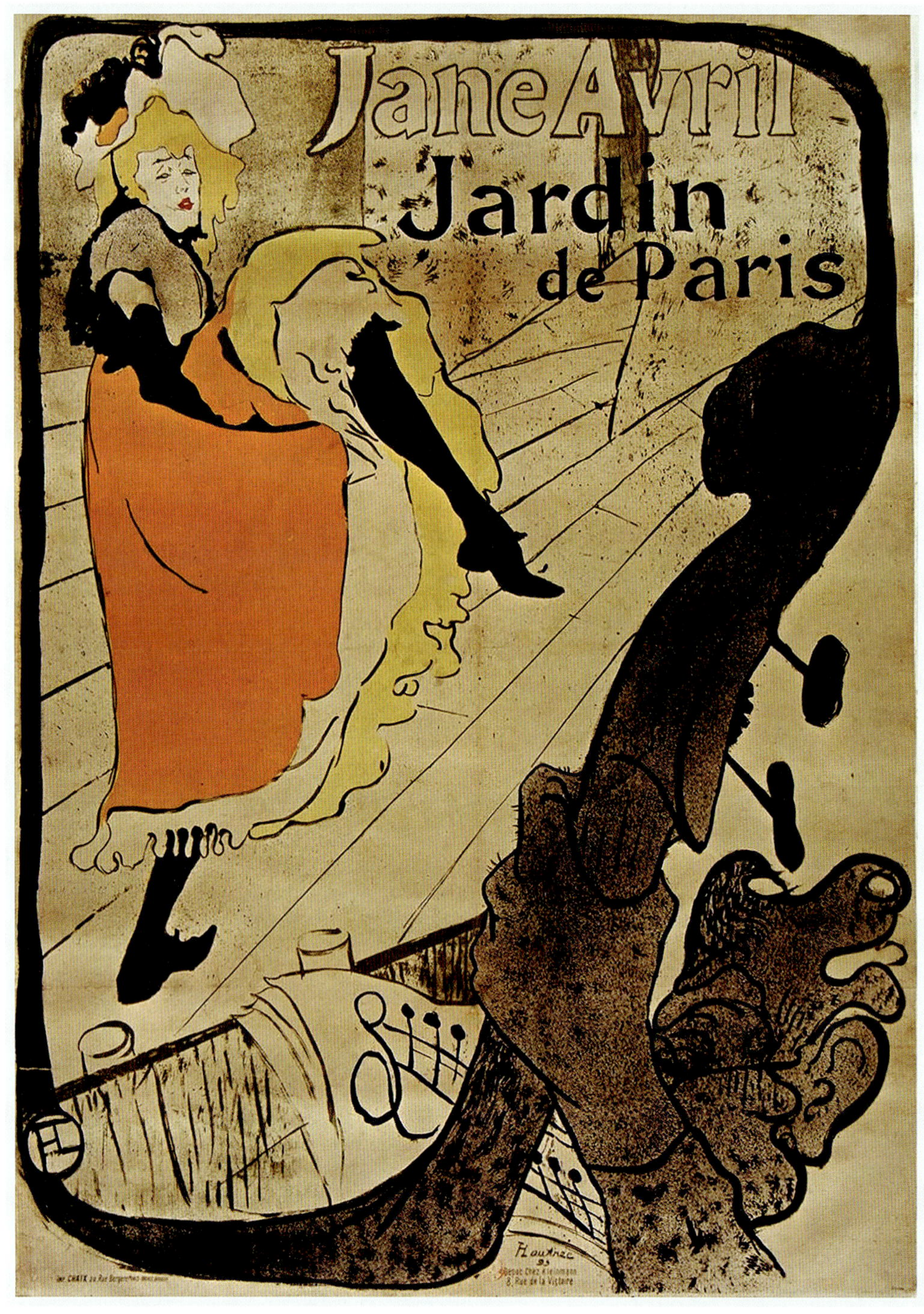

Henri de Toulouse-Lautrec, 1864–1901. Jane Avril poster, 1893. Colour lithograph (128.2 × 92.8cm).

is after all a canon of Western art, but rather the context that caused the disapproval. The woman depicted is in a modern domestic setting, in a tin bath; she is of the demi-monde.

Mary Cassatt's etching *The Bath* (1891) is a domestic scene and a direct lift from Utamaro's print of 1801, with the wash tub similarly placed off the picture plane. The outlines of the mother echo the cursive Japanese print – she is even wearing a gingko-patterned dress.

In Henri de Toulouse Lautrec's poster *Jane Avril* (1893), a sense of depth is created by using a strong foreground, with the cut-off figure of the bass player. This is heavily influenced by Hiroshige's *Ferry at Haneda*, part of his 'One Hundred Views

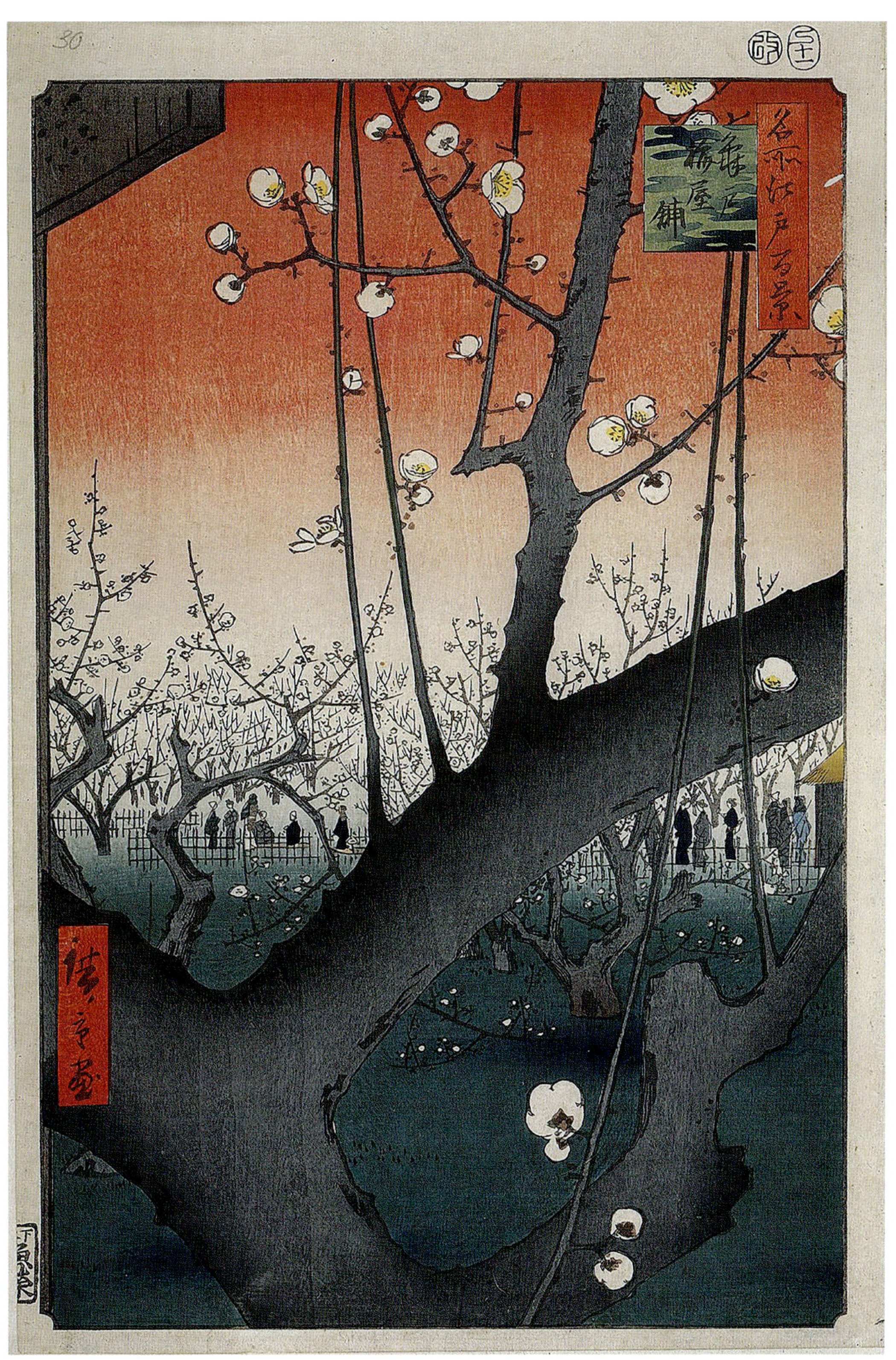

Andō Hiroshige, 1797–1858. *Plum Park in Kameido,* from the series 'One hundred Famous Views of Edo', 1857. Colour woodblock print (37 × 25cm).

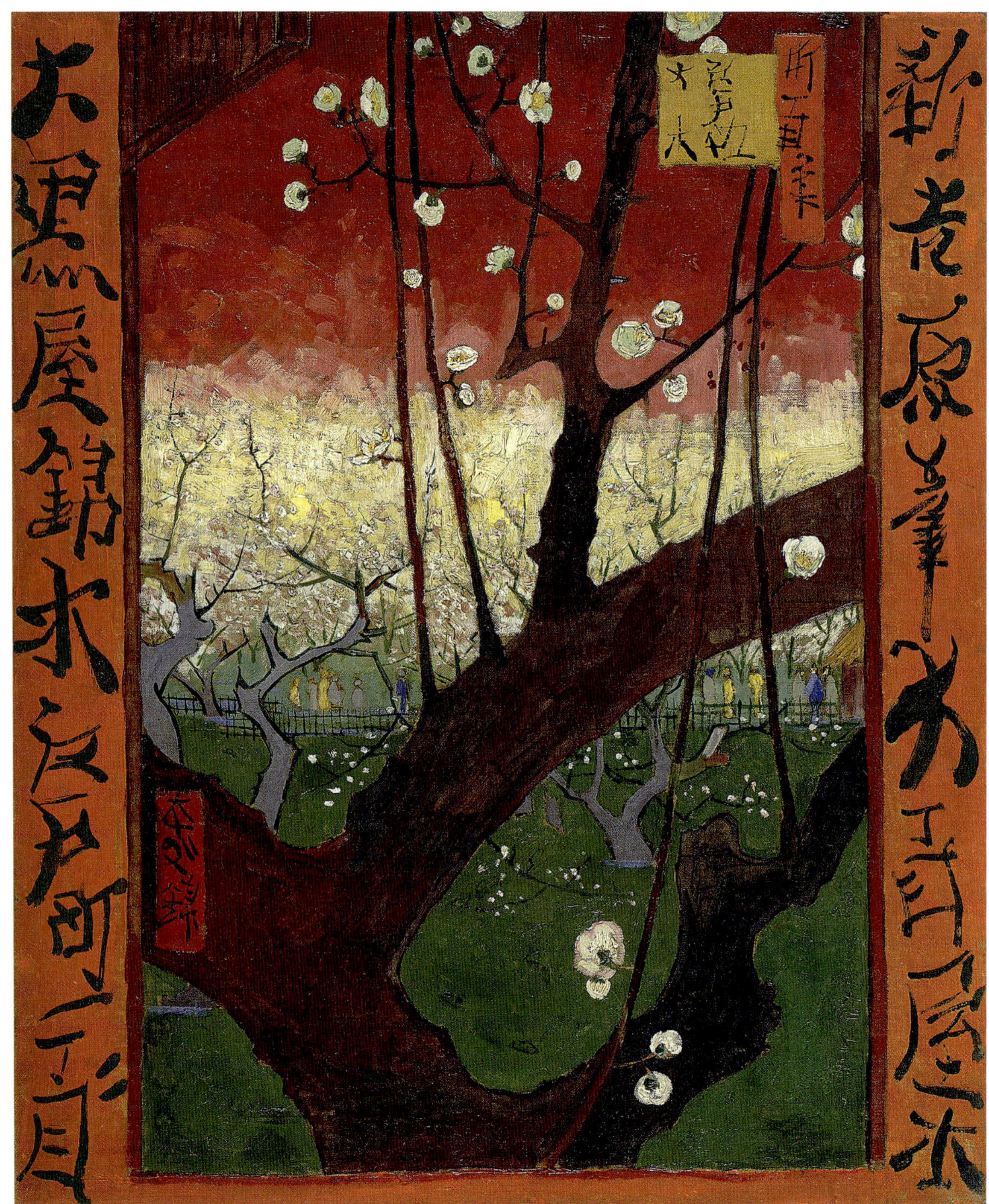

Vincent van Gogh, 1853–1890. *Flowering Plum Tree (after Hiroshige)*, 1887. Oil on canvas (55 × 46cm).

of Edo', 1856–8, the legs and arms of the ferryman vignetting the view beyond.

Vincent Van Gogh copied directly from the Hiroshige prints that he owned. Van Gogh's painting *Kameido Gardens* of 1887 is a direct copy of Hiroshige's print of the same name from 1856. In Van Gogh's painting he added decorative side panels with Japanese calligraphy that has been translated as 'Welcome to the brothel'. It is uncertain whether he knew this, or just lifted decorative calligraphy without knowing what it meant. It was the formal qualities of the prints, the bright colours, asymmetrical compositions and subject matter that delighted the Impressionists and they artistically appropriated from them freely.

MEJI ERA 1868–1912

After 1868 the influx of foreigners to Japan brought about the downfall of the Tokogawa Shōgunate that had been in power for 250 peaceful years. The Meji era began, with the restoration of the emperor to political power and a move of the Imperial court from Kyōto to Edo. Edo changed its name to Tokyo (Eastern capital), ushering in the new regime.

It was the beginning of a period of almost unbelievable intensive growth and expansion in Japan. Students were sent out across the world to gain knowledge of best practice, known as the Iwakura Mission, bringing back important information for the construction of railways, telegraph networks, education reforms and reforms of the military.

By the beginning of the twentieth century, a country that had been in many respects still feudal in 1854 had astonishingly in 50 years achieved the same level of industrial development as the other major powers of the day.

SOCIAL CHANGE

The Mokuhanga prints that were made after 1868 reflect some of the drastic social changes that were taking place; how to be

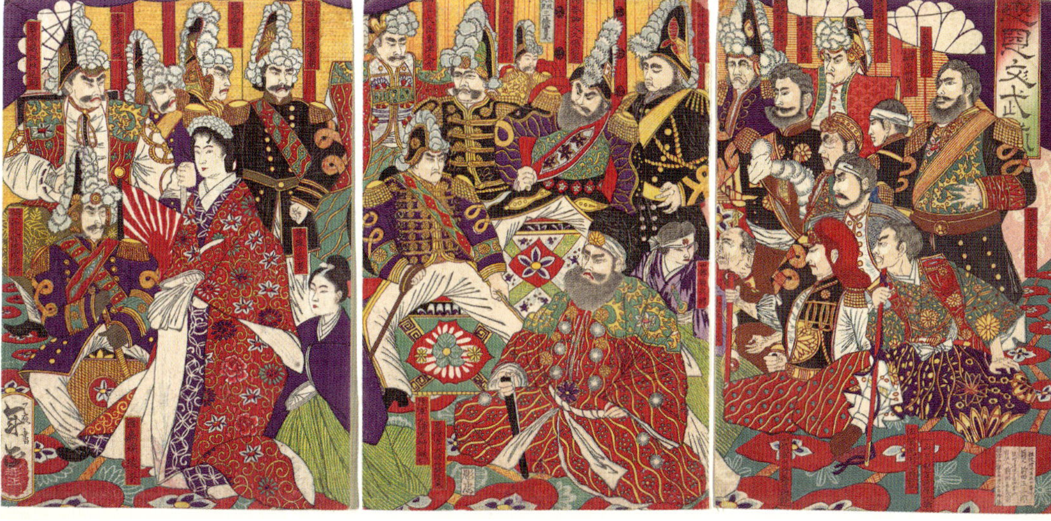

Toshimasa (active nineteenth century). *Civil and Military Officers*, 1877. Triptych of colour woodblock prints, each print *oban* size (34 × 23.5cm). Mixture of traditional Japanese dress and Western style military uniforms.

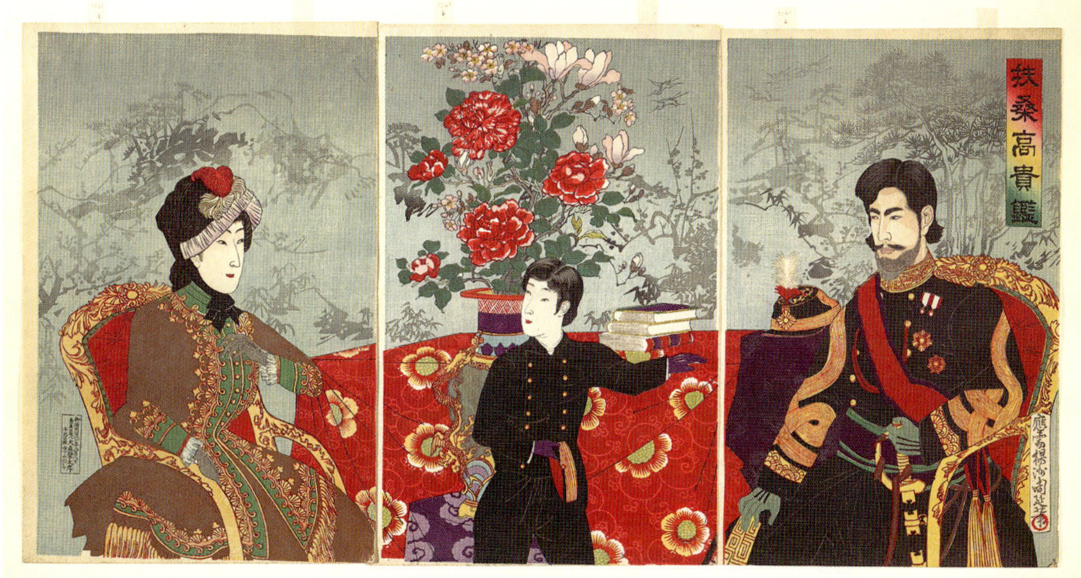

Yōshō Chikanobu, 1838–1912. *A Mirror of Japan's Nobility: The Emperor Meiji, His Wife and Prince Haru*, 1887. Triptych of colour woodblock prints (37.5 × 75.2cm).Not only a portrait of the Emperor, but also his family in contemporary Western-style clothing, depicted using the traditional *ukiyō-e* woodcut and triptych format.

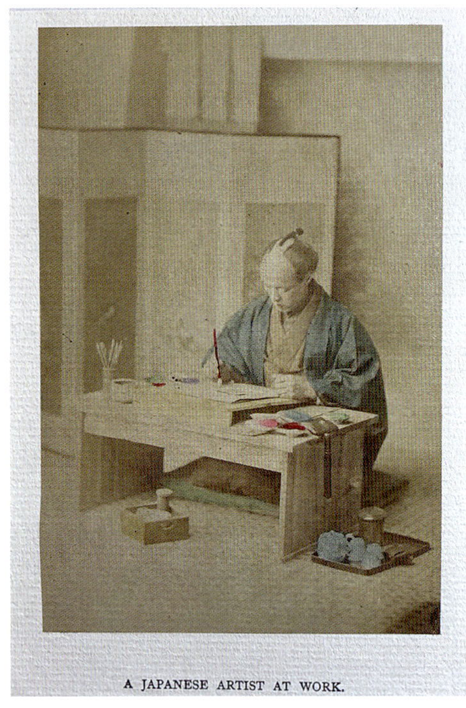

Unknown artist and photographer. Late nineteenth-century photograph of Japanese artist at work, hand tinted.

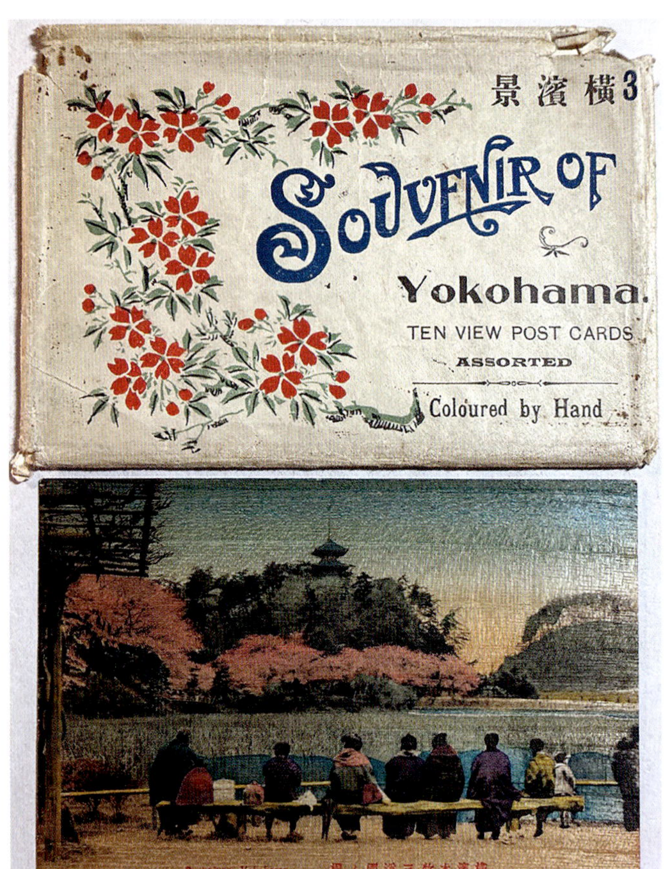

Unknown artist and photographer. Early twentieth-century postcard, views of Yokohama. Photograph, hand tinted on wood.

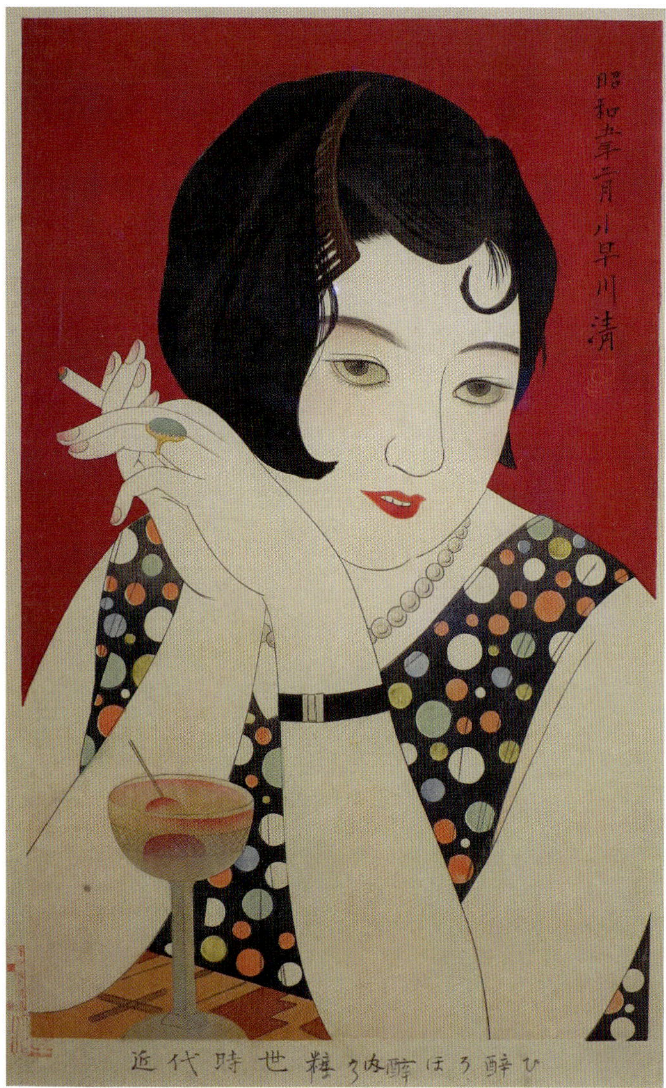

Kobayakawa Kiyoshi, 1897–1948. *Tipsy*, 1930. Colour woodblock print (43 × 27cm).

both modern and Japanese at the same time and maintain a coherent national identity.

New media competed with Mokuhanga, even though Mokuhanga prints were still cheaper and quicker to produce. There was a demand for the new modern technological imports (ironically the photographic postcards were coloured in by hand harking back to the *tan-e* prints of the eighteenth century).

The prints still reflected popular culture and showed the changing social mores, where women especially began to experience more liberated lives, and unprecedented freedoms.

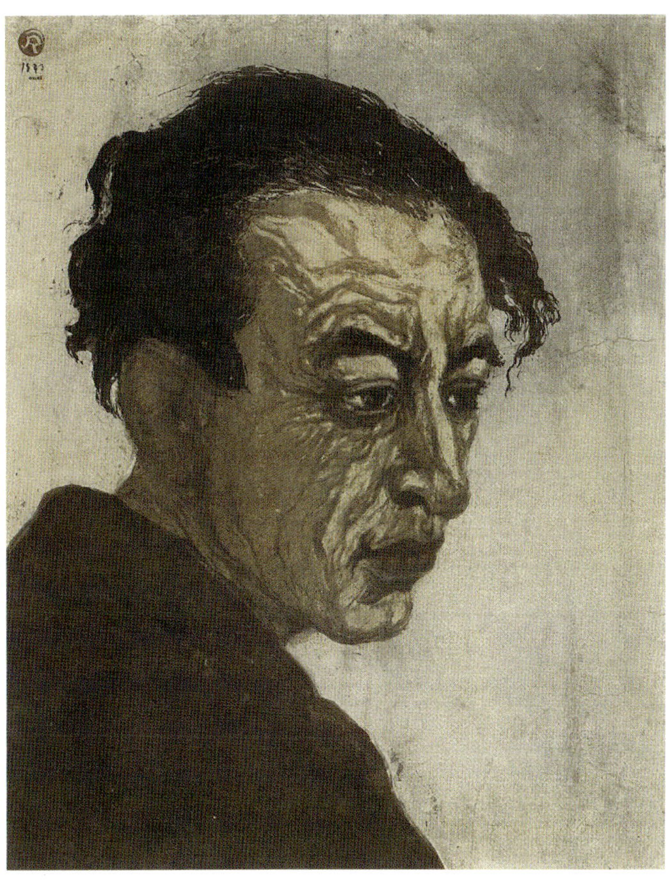

Kōshirō Onchi, 1891–1955. *Portrait of Hagiwara Sakutarō,* 1943. Colour woodblock print.

SŌSAKUHANGA 1918 CREATIVE PRINT MOVEMENT

By the beginning of the twentieth century, a new movement developed in Japan, influenced by the Western preference for original prints made directly by the artist. It was called *Sōsakuhanga*, or Creative Print Movement. Artists opted to design, cut and print their own work. They were influenced by artists they had met in Russia and France, and brought a wholly new individualistic approach. Koshiro Onchi was considered to be the founder of the *Sōsakuhanga* movement; he went on to create the first abstract prints in Japan and later turned to photography.

Kanae Yamamoto experimented with different print styles, borrowing from wood engraving techniques as well as Post-Impressionist paintings.

Shiko Munakata (1903–1975) gained recognition in the West, through winning the Grand Prix at the 1956 Venice Biennale. He had started his art career as a painter, very much influenced by

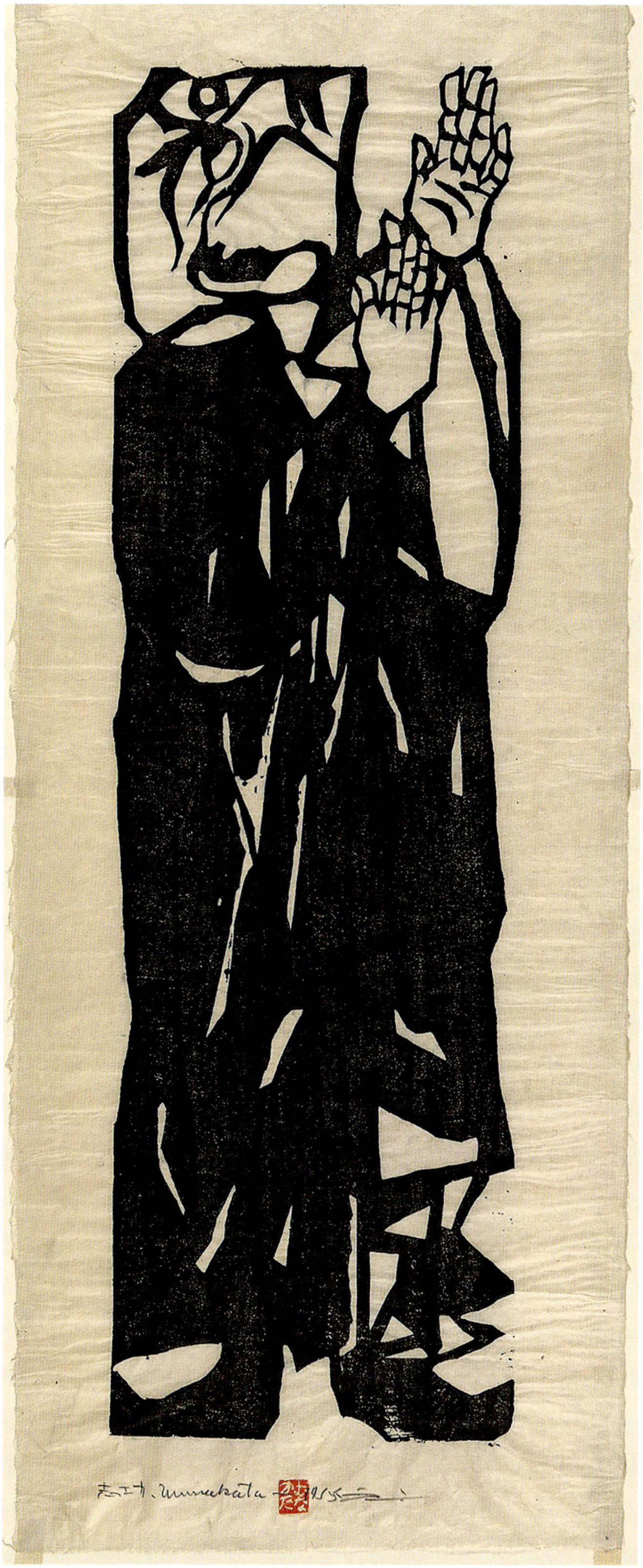

Shiko Munakata, 1903–1975. *Upali,* from the series 'Two Bodhisattva and Ten Great Disciples of Sakyamuni', 1955. Magnolia woodblock print and *sumi* ink.

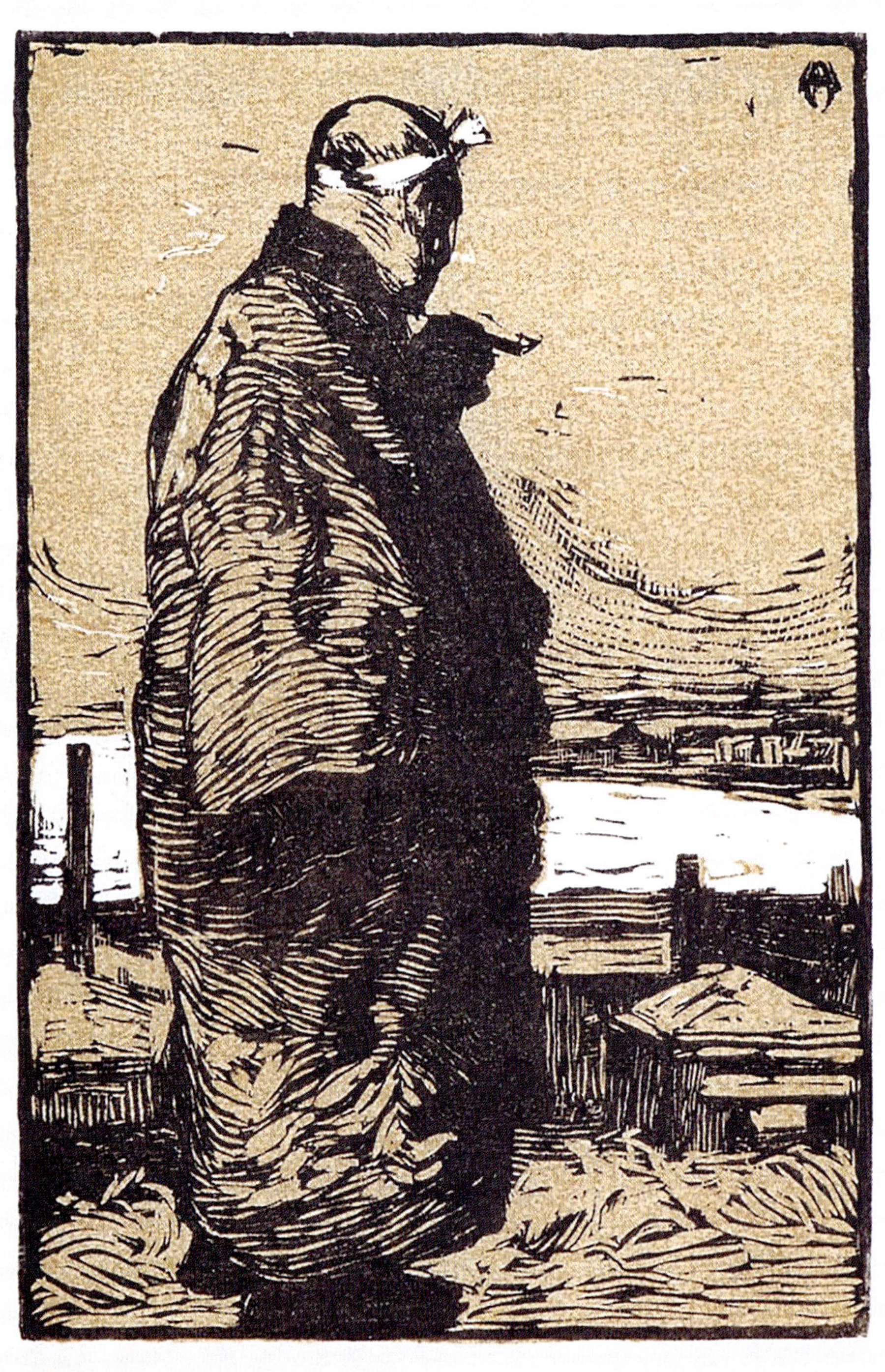

Kanae Yamamoto, 1882–1946. *Gyōfu (Fisherman)*, 1904. Colour woodblock print. Thought to be the first *sōsakuhanga* print.

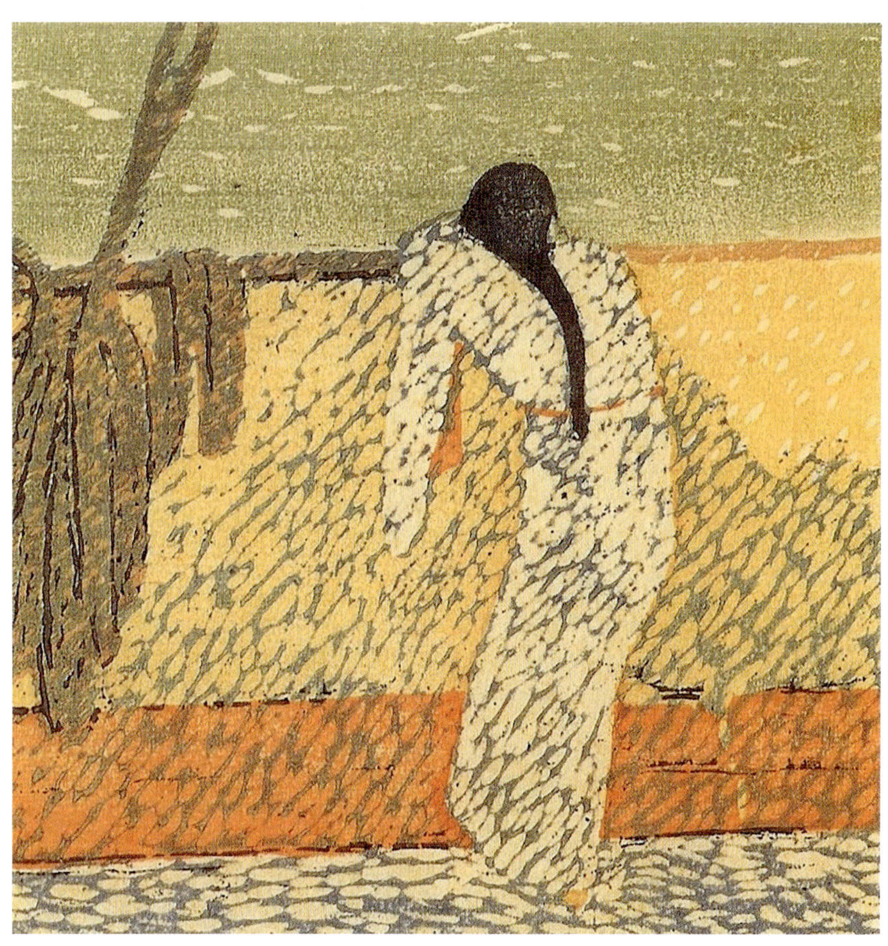

Kanae Yamamoto, 1882–1946. *On the Deck,* 1912. Colour woodblock print (85.4 × 86.9cm).

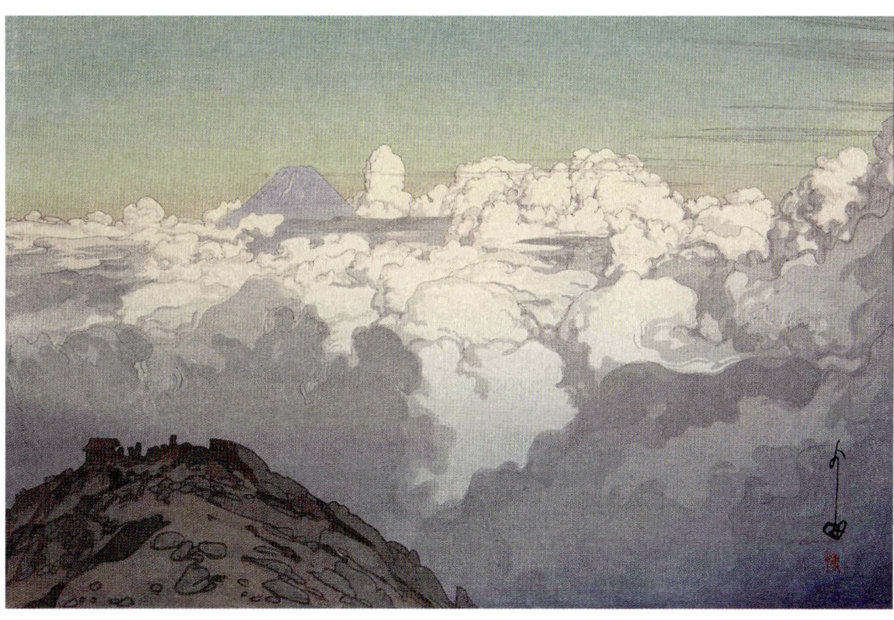

Hiroshi Yoshida, 1876–1950. *View from Komagatake,* 1928. Colour woodblock print (28 × 41cm).

Van Gogh, another example of the East-West cross fertilisation of ideas. He had very poor eyesight, however, and was unable to view his paintings from a distance. He began making woodcuts, looking back to Japanese Folk Arts and Buddhist imagery for his inspiration and founding the *Mingei*, or Folk Movement. His prints were cut quickly, printed using *sumi* ink onto thin paper that was often hand-coloured from behind.

SHINHANGA

Alongside the *Sōsakuhanga* Movement and counter to it was the *Shinhanga* Movement, which continued the long-established tradition of the *hanmoto* system from the *ukiyō-e* period. The strict hierarchies of publisher, artist, master carver and printer continued. The subject matter tended to be nostalgic scenes of old Japan.

Hiroshi Yoshida was an influential *shinhanga* printmaker, but even in his views you can see the modern city emerging.

The Yoshida family has produced four generations of print-makers, including Ayomi Yoshida who works on beautiful large installations in New York today. Reprints also continued to be made of the popular prints from the 'golden era' of *ukiyō-e* prints (1765–1868), many destined for the export market. By the middle of the twentieth century, however, Mokuhanga was considered to be old fashioned in Japan, even thought of as inappropriate for contemporary expression.

MOKUHANGA TECHNIQUE IN THE WEST

The transformative effect that Mokuhanga had sparked off in the late nineteenth century in Paris, which had so inspired the Impressionists and electrified their compositions, did not however extend to the technique itself. They copied the subject matter, the asymmetrical compositions, the flowing lines of the prints, but the technique with its specialist papers, wood

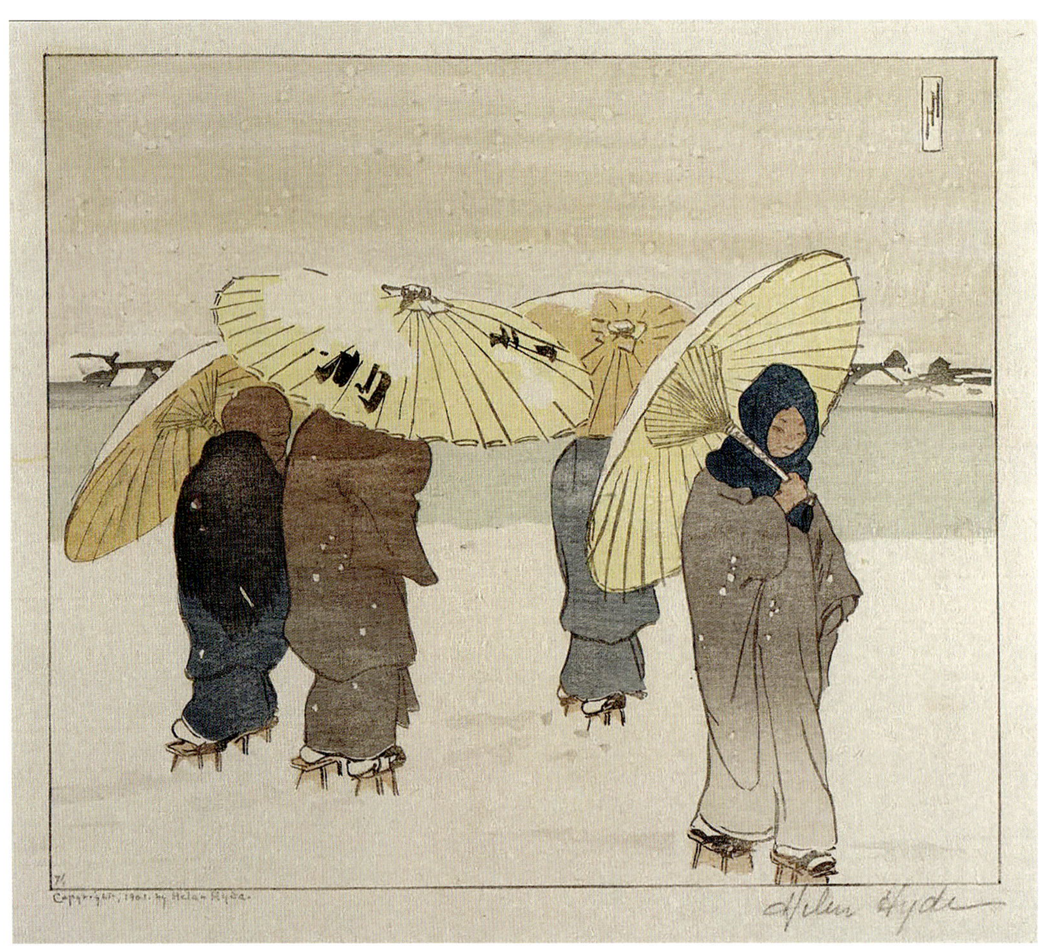

Helen Hyde, 1868–1919.
A Snowy Day, 1901. Colour woodblock print.

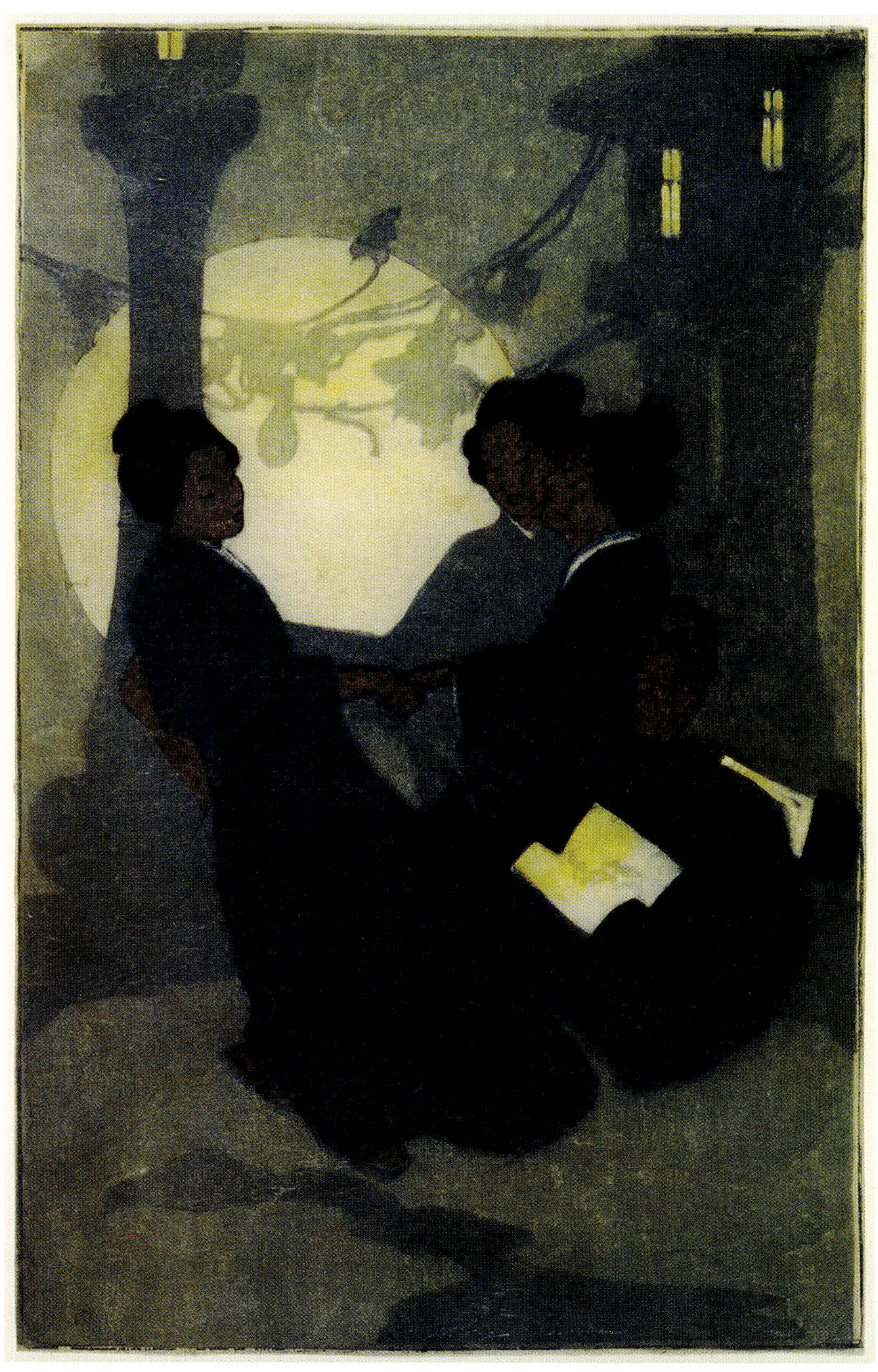

Bertha Lum, 1869–1954. *Fox Women (Kitsune in Human Form)*, 1908. Colour woodblock print.

and expert craftsmen was by and large unknown in the West. This was partly due to difficulties with travel, language and obtaining specialist Japanese materials, but also it has to be said quite a bit of Western arrogance.

There were a few early pioneers who travelled to Japan to learn the technique. The American artist Helen Hyde, influenced by Mary Cassatt's work, lived in Japan from 1903–13 and trained with Emil Orlik to learn the process of making colour blocks.

Bertha Lum, married to a corporate lawyer, spent her honeymoon in Japan in 1907 and worked, using a translator, with the block cutter Igami Bonkutsu in Yokohama and then with the artist Nishimura Kamkichi. Both of these women brought their new-found skills back to West Coast America, where interest in the prints grew.

It is also easy to see the Japanese influence in Art movements such as Art Nouveau with its abstraction of natural forms into calligraphic motifs and the later minimalism and flat colours of Art Deco.

After the Second World War, Tokyo was under occupation by the US from 1945–1952. American soldiers stationed in Japan contributed to the spread of *ukiyō-e* prints by sending them to their families back home. Interest in Japanese aesthetics of elegant, pared-down form allied to expert craftsmanship became global, influencing architecture, design, ceramics, furniture and the explosion of Scandinavian and Finnish glassware of the 1950s.

CROWN POINT PRESS

The resurgence of interest in Mokuhanga in the West began in the 1980s, with the Crown Point Press, based in San Francisco under the inspirational Kathan Brown. Brown had the idea of taking American artists and their work to Japan, to work on original prints with the Japanese master-printer Tadoshi Toda in Kyoto. He was the first Japanese master printer to work with artists from the West in this way. The portfolios of work made with Toda met with huge acclaim back in the US. Seventeen artists took part in the programme over a decade, including, Helen Frankenthaler, Jose Maria Sicilia and Richard Diebenkorn, producing an exciting cross-fertilisation of cultures. The prints promoted new directions and inspired more Western artists to look to Japan. It also inspired Japanese artists to look at their own Mokuhanga tradition afresh. Japanese master printers such as Hiroki Morinoue, Tetsuya Noda and Takuji

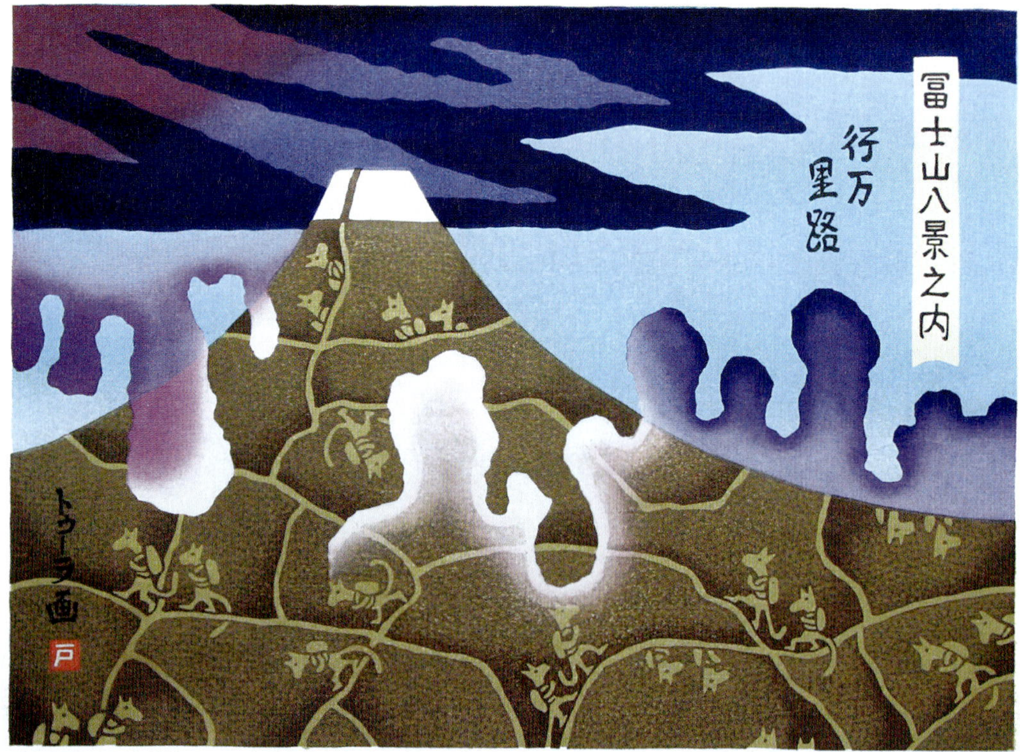

Tuula Moilanen, *Many Routes to the Top*, 2015. Colour woodblock print (38 × 25cm).

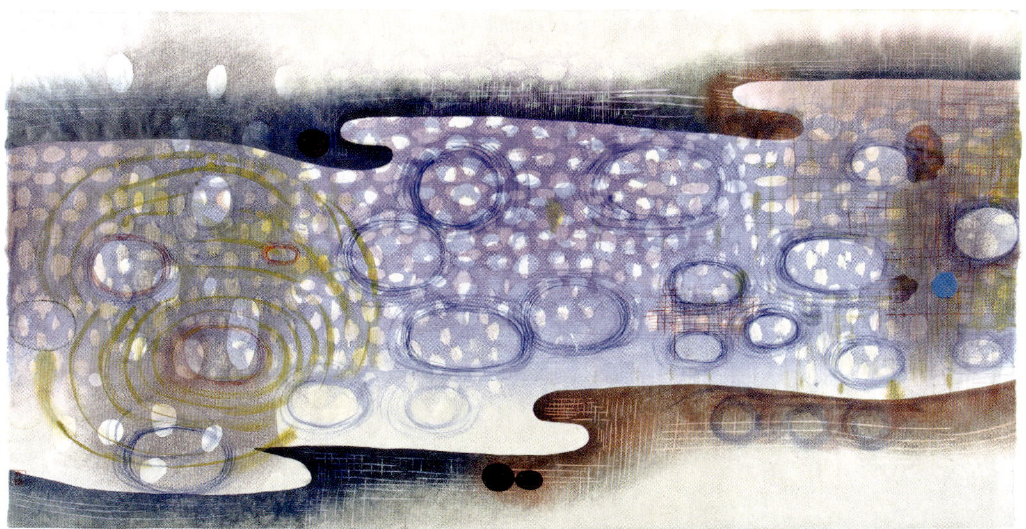

Karen Kunc, *Dawn*, 2011. Colour woodblock print, wax, on Okawara paper (48.6 × 96.6cm).

Hamanaka all developed international followings in the West, particularly in the US.

AKIRA KUROSAKI 1937–2019

Akira Kurosaki was head of Printmaking at Kyoto Seika University from 1987. He was a hugely influential artist of technical virtuosity and a wonderful teacher, disseminating his knowledge of Mokuhanga and papermaking to many Western artists who travelled to Kyoto to train with him. Artists such as Karen Kunc and April Vollmer from the US, Tuula Moilanen from Finland and Rebecca Salter from the UK. Through their respective teaching practices, his teaching has passed on to a wider world. I never met him, sadly he died in 2019, but I had the great good fortune to work with Tuula Moilanen in Finland where I learned new skills taught to her originally by him. I like this continuum of practice.

MI-LAB MOKUHANGA INNOVATION LABORATORY

In 1997 Keiko Kadota set up MI-Lab in the Nagasawa Art Park. She was following Kathan Brown's example, inviting Western artists to learn the traditional Mokuhanga technique, with the aim of introducing Mokuhanga as a creative practice internationally. She was alarmed by the disappearance of Mokuhanga from Japanese Art Schools and worried that many of the traditional papermakers and craftsmen had no one from the younger generation to follow the tradition. In 2011, after an earthquake in Nagasawa, she was forced to relocate to Fujikawaguchiko, in the foothills of Mount Fuji in the Yamanashi Prefecture. Her methodology was simple: to engage professional Mokuhanga Japanese *sensei* and with the aid of a translator, to teach Mokuhanga in its traditional form to Western artists in an immersive environment. Students' work was showcased at the CfSHE Gallery in Tokyo. Her students, myself included, have taken this knowledge back home and disseminated Mokuhanga through teaching, lectures, publications and exhibitions. I have seen Mokuhanga gaining traction in the West as a technique, partly due to its environmentally friendly ethos, but also the wonderful way that nuanced prints can be made from the paradoxical certainties of the woodcut and the subtleties of watercolour.

Keiko was also instrumental in forging links between Japanese and Western artists, networking through triennial International Mokuhanga Print Conferences, starting in Kyoto in 2011, Tokyo 2014 and Hawaii 2017. I attended the last conference in Nara in 2021 (unfortunately online due to Covid), presenting a paper, exhibiting one of my prints in Nara and participating in the many lectures and discussions. I was struck by the worldwide reach of Mokuhanga, the sense of community and generosity of spirit, sharing ideas, ways of making, best practice and outright enthusiasm. For a technique that is rooted in Japanese history, it is evolving globally all the time, in new directions and contemporary artistic practice.

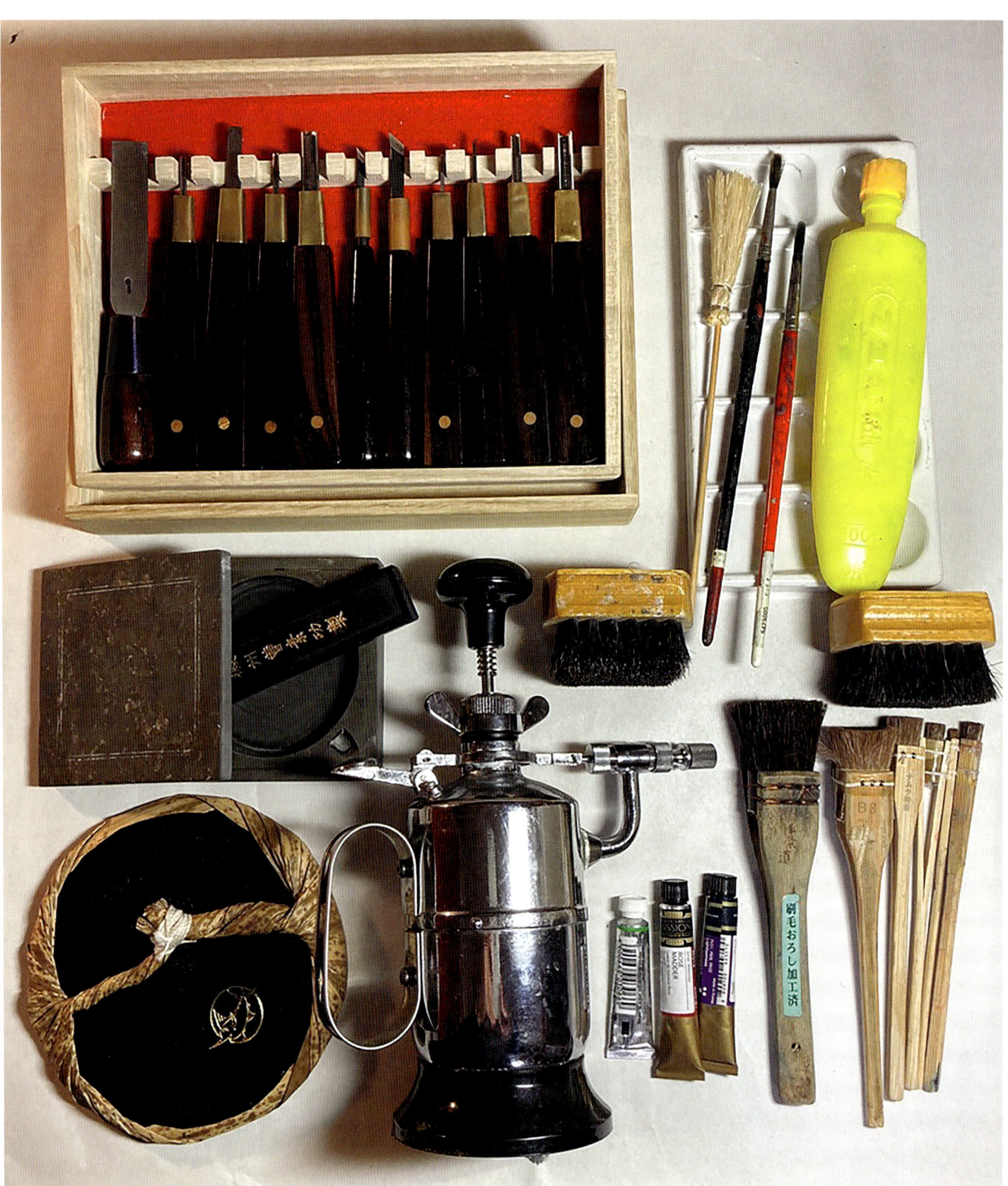

Chapter 2

MATERIALS AND EQUIPMENT

Mokuhanga is a completely non-toxic process; the woodcuts are printed by hand using watercolour pigments and *nori* (made from rice flour). There is no need for presses and no inky surfaces to clean. The process can be practised in the home, without taking up much space and it does not require expensive specialised equipment.

TOOLS

It has to be said that the best tools for Japanese woodcut are Japanese. For a professional Japanese woodcut artist, it is important for the outcome of your work to buy the best tools that you can afford. The best tools are expensive, but for those just beginning there are cheaper alternatives and with a modest outlay you can buy a decent set to get started, then as you become more familiar with your own requirements you can upgrade the tools that you use most often, or add different-sized tools to your tool set.

The best-quality Japanese woodblock cutting tools have handmade blades that are formed in the same way as samurai swords; they are made to last a lifetime, the high-carbon steel is laminated with softer steel to give a layered cutting edge that is both strong and flexible. The wooden handles are traditionally made from ebony or cherrywood and are hinged to reveal the entire blade which can be moved up or down to suit the individual artist.

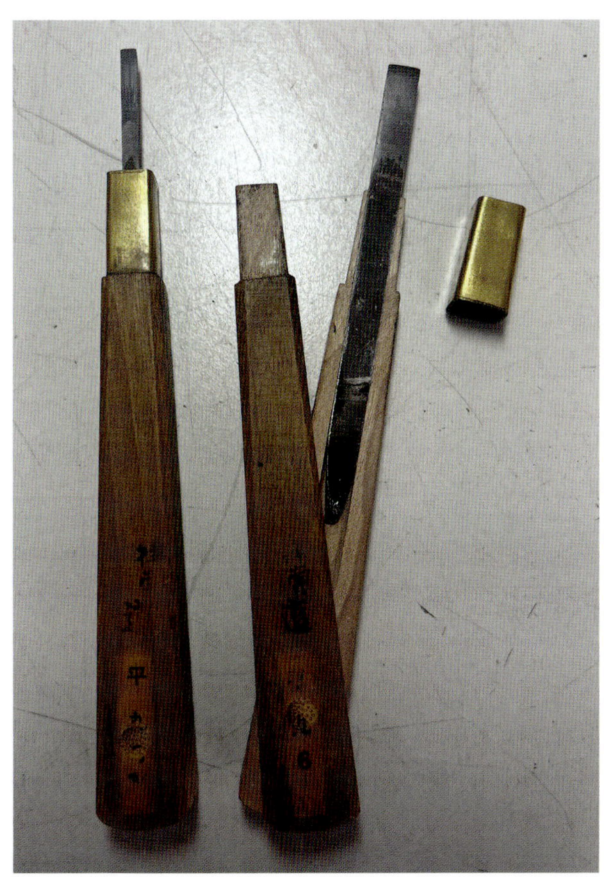

Showing how the brass collar slips off and the wooden handle hinges open to reveal the blade of the tool. This allows the user to move the blade up or down according to their preference.

◄ Showing some of the author's materials including cutting tools, *hakobi*, *te bake*, nori, palette, *maru bake*, pigments, water spray diffuser, *baren* and *sumi* stick in its own mixing palette.

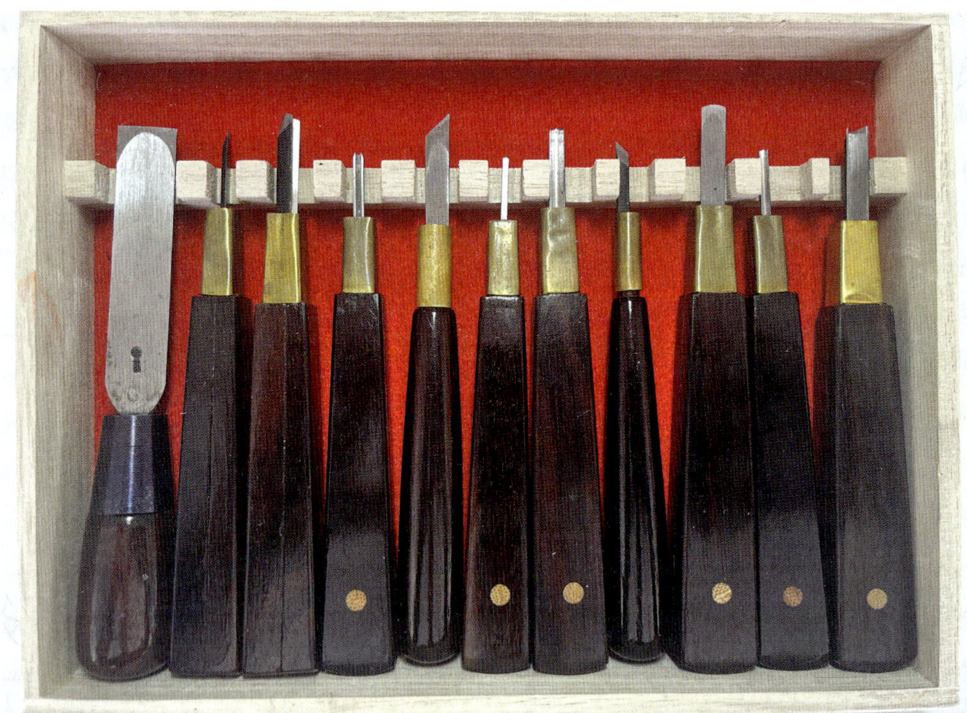

The author's tools. A beautiful toolset from Japan with ebony handles comprising a *kentōnommi*, two *hangitō*, three *marutō* and *hiratō* and two *sankakutō*.

Needless to say, good-quality tools are expensive to buy as a set, but you can introduce one or two better quality tools to supplement a cheaper set of tools, as you invest in the process. There are cheaper sets of tools available that are ideal for the beginner – the blades are of an inferior quality but properly looked after they should last a while and are a good starting point.

The tool names can be confusing as different centres for Japanese woodcut developed independently of each other and so one tool can have at least two names. To help identify the tools I have first given the Western equivalent name, followed by the name I was taught at MI-Lab in Japanese and its alternative Japanese name in brackets.

It is also worth noting that lino tools will not be suitable for woodcut – however, woodcut tools can be used for linocut.

The Essential Tools

These four tools are essential for making Japanese woodcuts. They all come in different sizes so I have noted the basic-size tool for your initial tool set.

The Knife, *Hangitō* (Hangi-Block, Tō-Knife, also known as *Kiridashi*)

The *hangitō* is the most important cutting tool in Japanese printmaking. It is also the one for which there is no Western counterpart. It is used for outlining the image area and when mastered allows for a greater flexibility and subtlety in the wrist movement. This can be seen in the exquisite cursive cut lines of traditional Japanese prints.

Hangitō come in different sizes and there are also left-handed tools available. Most professional carvers have a number of different sized *hangitō* with different blade sizes to deal with different print requirements. A basic *hangitō* to buy would be 6mm but smaller blades are really useful too.

V-Shaped Gouge, *Sankakutō*

This tool is very much the staple in Western woodcarving but was not known in Japan until its introduction in the mid nineteenth century. It is a very useful tool, especially for the beginner who may find the *hangitō* difficult to handle at first. It can also be used for texture cutting and as an outline tool, as it cuts a V-shaped trench in one stroke where the *hangitō* requires two strokes. It does, however, lack the subtlety and fluidity of the *hangitō* as practised by a more experienced practitioner. A basic tool would be 3mm.

Round Gouge, *Marutō* (*Komasuki*)

The *marutō* is a semi-circular gouge that is used for clearing away areas. Larger *marutō* are used to clear away further away

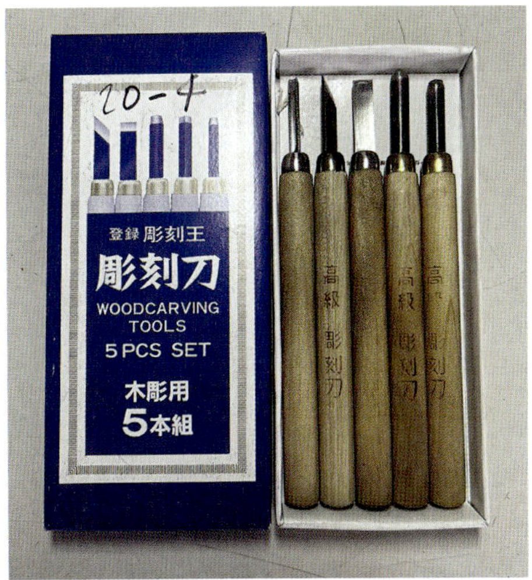

Economy set of woodcutting tools; an inexpensive ideal starter set for beginners to the technique.

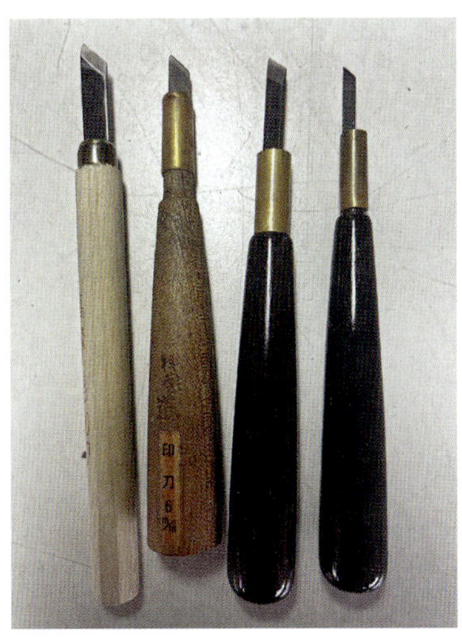

Range of different-sized *hangitō*. Note the very sharp point. The tool is bevelled on one side and flat on the other.

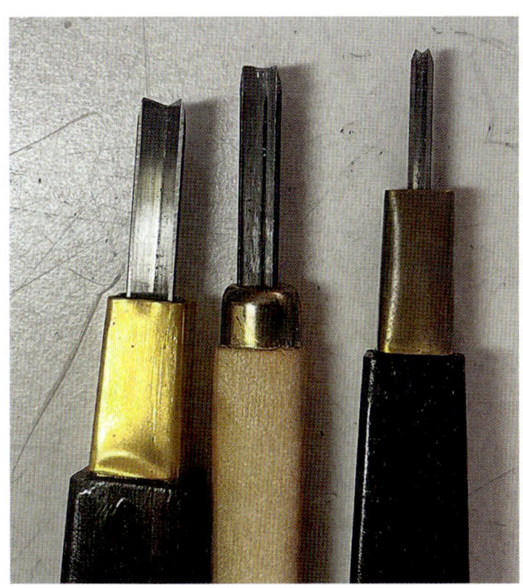

Range of *sankakutō* or V-shaped tools. These are not part of the traditional Japanese woodcarver's toolkit, but a mainstay of Western woodcuts.

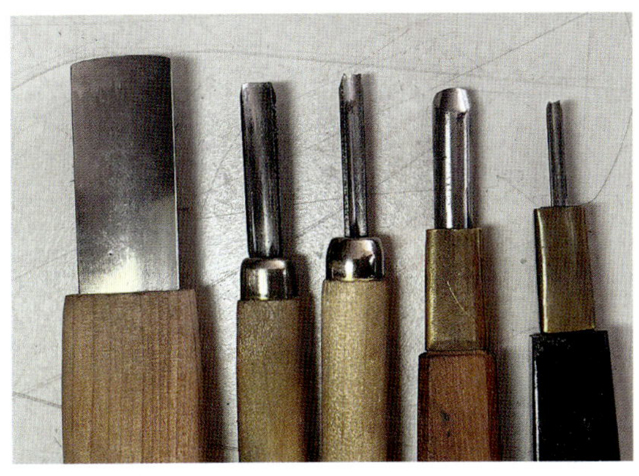

Larger number of the *marutō* or gouges in different sizes. It is a very useful tool for clearing and mark-making. The tool on the left is for clearing large areas.

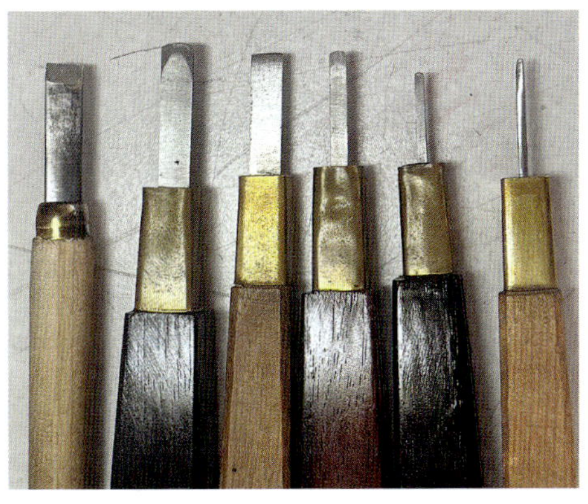

The *hiratō* or chisel has a bevel on one side and is flat on the other. The more expensive tools have curved sides that make it easier to clear close to the cut line.

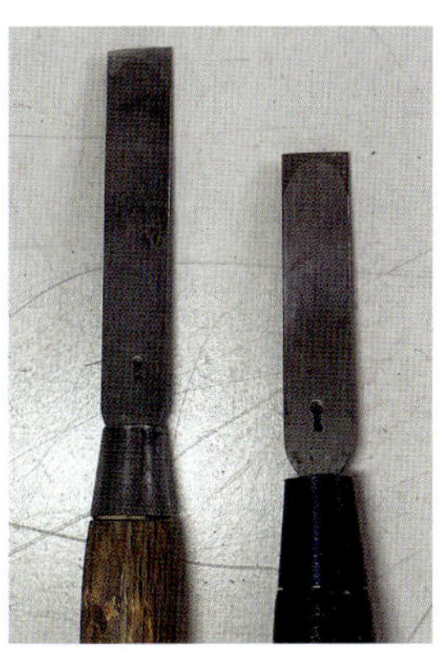

The *kentōnommi*, or registration chisel. This tool is always kept super sharp and is only used for making *kentō* registration notches.

from the printing area and smaller *marutō* closer to the outline cut of the *hangitō*. It can also be used for texture and carving soft lines. A basic tool would be 4.5mm but larger tools such as the 12mm *marunomi* make light work of clearing larger areas.

Chisel, *Hiratō* (*Aisuki*)

The *hiratō* is a flat-bladed chisel with a bevel on one side. In professional quality sets the tip is slightly curved, in economy sets the tip is straight. It is an important tool with many uses: to clear away the pre-cut *hangitō* line, to smooth down unwanted ridges thrown up by the *marutō*, to soften the edge of the cleared area to prevent the printing paper embossing and in more advanced cutting to make a graduated chamfer called *itabokashi*, and so on. The basic tool size is 4.5mm blade width.

Chisel, *Kentōnomi*

In addition to your essential tools the final chisel in your set is the *kentōnomi*. This is a flat-bladed chisel with a straight edge. It has a shorter blade and handle than Western chisels and is used to cut the all-important *kentō* – the registration notches in the woodblock itself where the printing paper is laid. A standard size would be a 15mm blade.

Looking After Your Tools

It is very important to keep your tools sharp and in good shape – a blunt tool is more dangerous than a sharp one because the extra pressure required to make a cut can cause the tool to slip in an unpredictable way. A blunt tool can still give you a nasty cut. A sharp tool is responsive to your touch and will cut the wood cleanly. When I met master printmaker Tuula Moilanen in Finland the first thing she wanted to see was not my work but my tools. How I looked after my tools, whether they were sharp or blunt, could tell her what kind of printmaker I was and how seriously I took my work.

You can test whether a tool needs sharpening by taking a practice piece of wood and making a trial cut against the wood-grain. If the line you have cut is frayed along its edges then your tool needs sharpening. The tool will also feel sluggish in the wood. Another tell-tale sign that your tool needs sharpening is by testing it against your thumbnail; a blunt tool will slip, a sharp tool will not move.

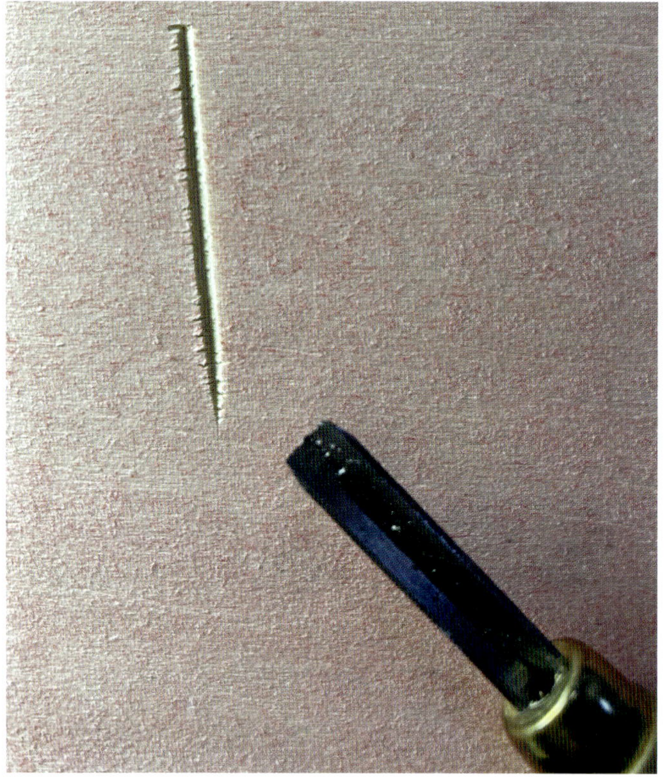
Close-up showing the frayed edge of a cut line indicating that this tool is in need of sharpening.

Honing Tools

I hone my tools often to keep them in good condition. It is easy to do and good for the beginner as it means that you will not have to use the sharpening stones so often.

Honing Pad

My honing pad is home-made and works well for me. It consists of a piece of leather glued with PVA on to a thick piece of grey board, suede-side up. The cardboard does need to be thick so that the surface stays flat when you are honing. Students of mine have gone to charity shops to source old leather belts or handbags for their honing pads. The leather should not be too thin.

Honing Paste

Purpose-made honing paste contains tiny particles that abrade the surface of the blade. A cheaper alternative to honing paste is cream bathroom cleanser, such as Cif, that performs in the same way. The honing paste or cleanser is placed at the top of the leather pad. Only a small amount of cleanser needs to be picked up with the tip of the tool. After the bevel angle of the blade is found (so that there is no gap between the tool tip and the leather) the tool is pulled downwards keeping the tool's blade pressed lightly into the suede. The action is in a downward direction only as pushing the tool upwards will damage the suede.

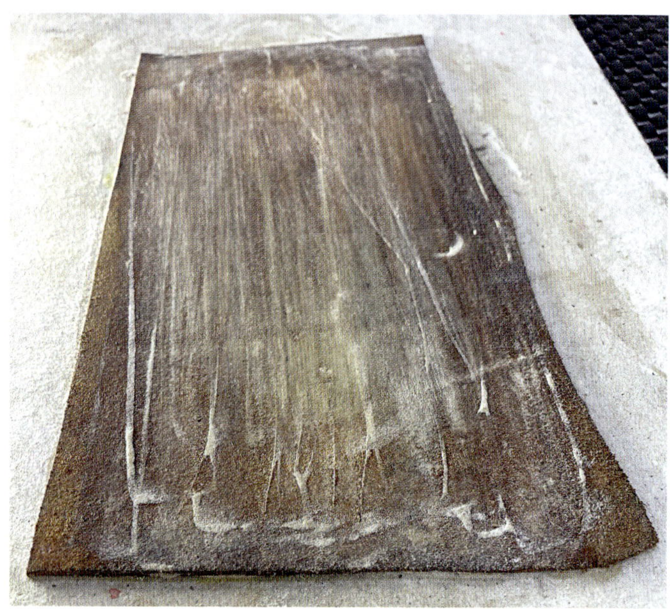
Honing pad. It is a good idea to place the honing pad on a non-slip mat while you are honing the tool, to prevent slippages.

Each tool has its own honing action but they are not difficult to master:

Test your tools after honing to see if there has been an improvement. Honing is good for the day-to-day upkeep of tools but if more remedial work is required, you will need to use sharpening stones.

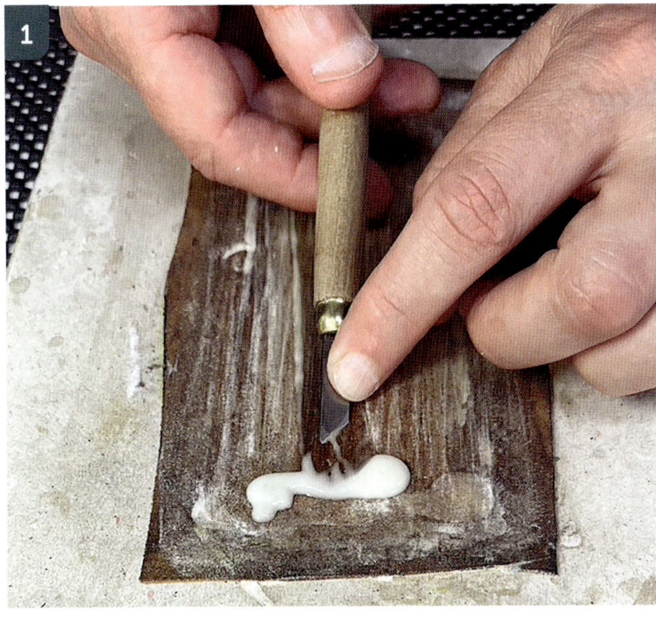

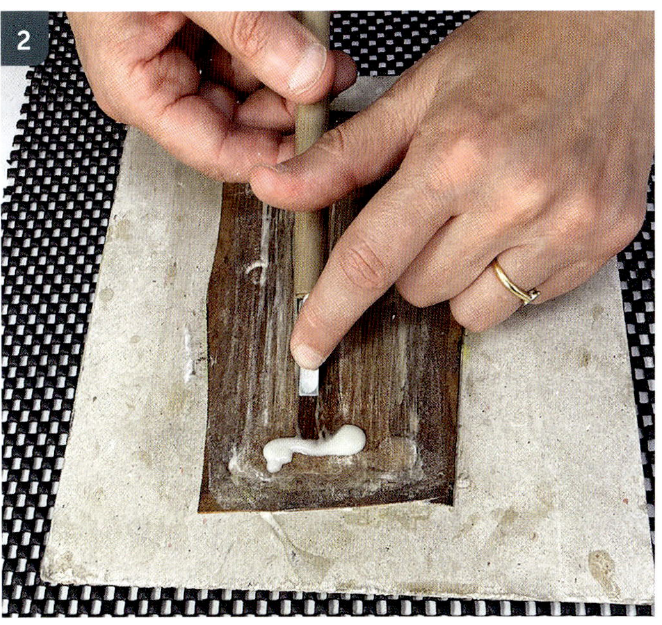

Hangitō: When honing, protect the sharp tip of the blade by not adding pressure on the tip. I am right-handed so I hold the handle lightly in my right hand, find the bevel angle of the blade and with my left index finger hold the blade in place away from the tool's tip. The tool is pulled towards the body, there is no need to use force, just the pressure of your finger keeping the bevel in contact with the leather is sufficient.

Hiratō: This tool is the simplest to hone. Find the bevel so that there are no gaps between the tool and the leather and pull downwards.

Marutō: Honing the *marutō* can be split into three stages; finding the bevel in the middle and pulling down, then turn the tool to the left, then right. Keep the number of strokes the same for each action. Ensure the sharp corners of the tool do not dig into the honing pad and become blunted.

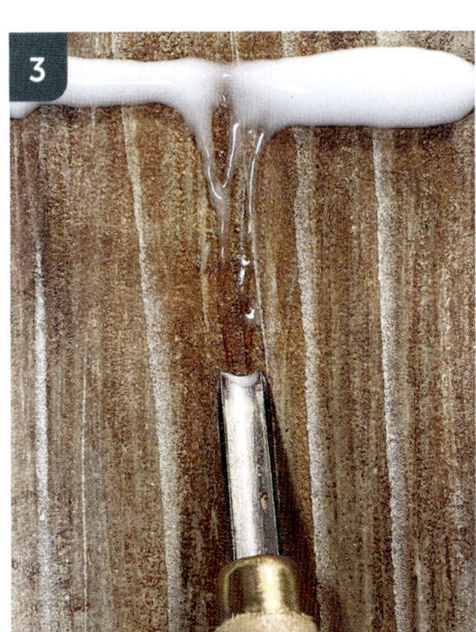

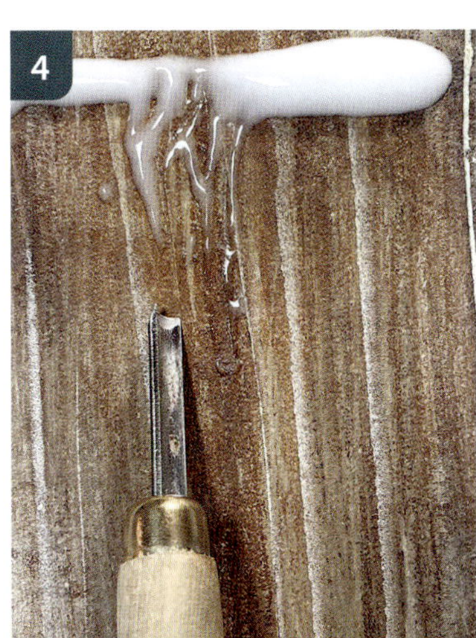

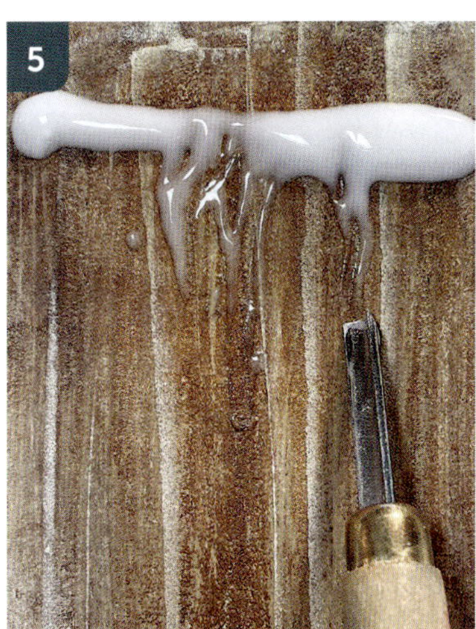

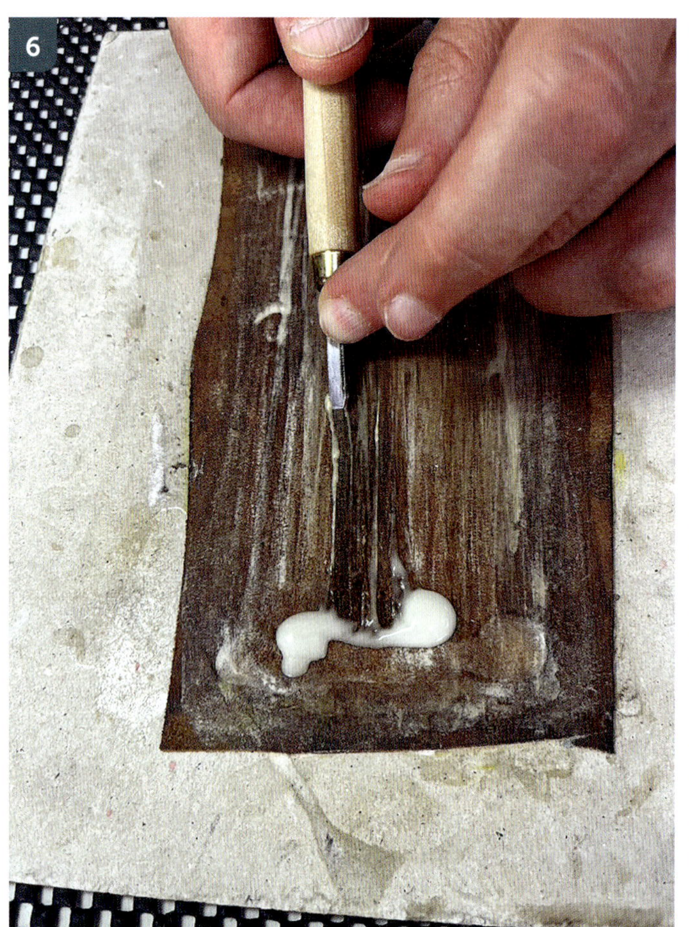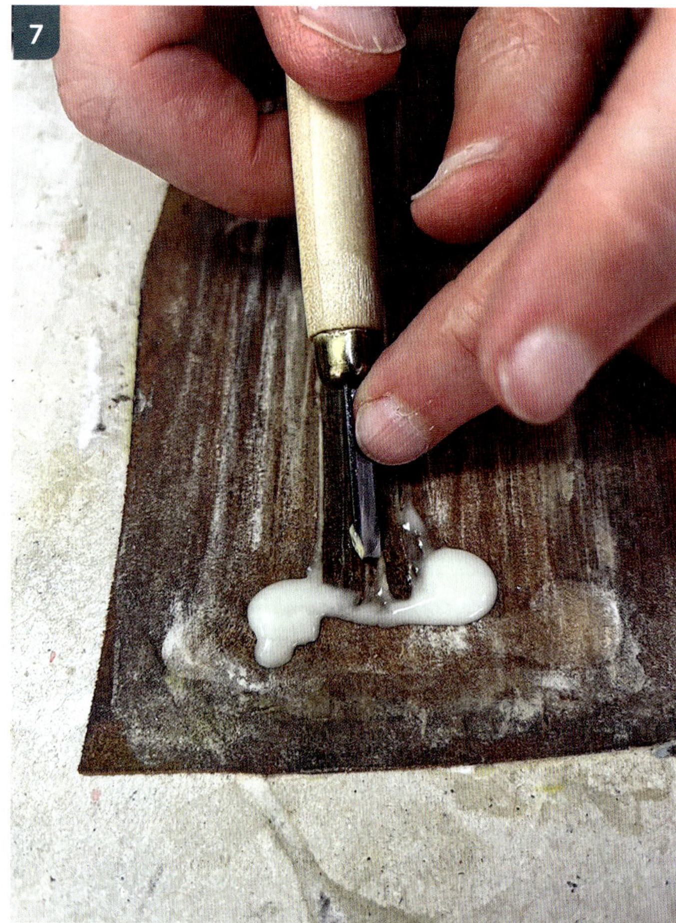

Sankakutō: This is honed by finding the bevel on one side and pulling down the honing pad and then repeating on the other side, keeping the number of strokes the same for each side.

Sharpening Stones

There are a variety of sharpening stones that are used for Moku-hanga – mostly these are whetstones or waterstones where water and not oil is the lubricant. Students frequently ask me how often I sharpen my tools, and my answer is always that it depends on how much cutting you have been doing. I tend to hone my tools regularly after a long session of cutting and sharpen them maybe once a month. I use my *hangitō* and *hiratō* more often than the others and so they get the most attention.

Traditionally naturally occurring stones in Japan called *toishi* were used as whetstones, but these are becoming scarcer to source and are consequently expensive to buy. In the man-made stones the granular grit is suspended in a ceramic block. The stones come in three different grades from coarse to fine. Care should be taken with these ceramic blocks, especially when handling them while wet as they break easily when accidentally dropped.

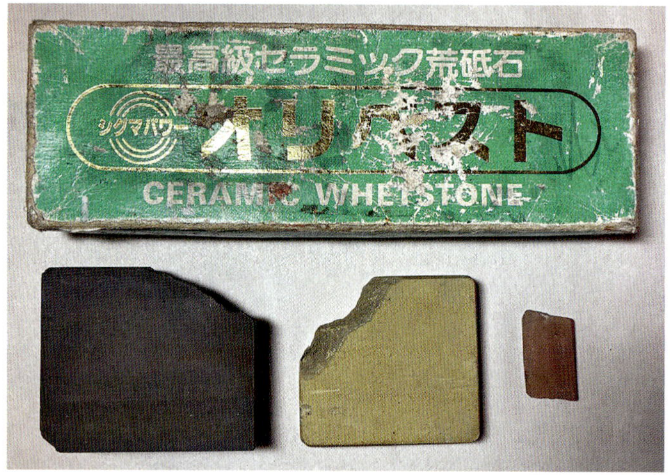

My ceramic waterstones have been well used and as you can see, they are highly friable and liable to break if handled clumsily when wet. The grey stone on the left is the *chūto* or medium grade, the yellow is the *shiageto* or polishing stone, the red is the slipstone, sometimes called the Arkansas stone.

For reworking a badly damaged blade the coarsest stone called *arato* is used. Mostly, however, my tools just need a small amount of work to redefine the edge and so I start sharpening my tool with the medium stone called *chūto*. The last stone used is called *shiageto* and here the blade is polished and the burr removed from the flat side of the *hangitō* or *hiratō*.

Also used are slipstones for clearing away the metal burr thrown up by the whetstone on the *marutō* and *sankakutō*.

There are also stones that have diamond dust embedded into the ceramic; these stones are for the professional, as not only are they expensive but also you can unwittingly alter your blade irrevocably very quickly indeed.

After prolonged use the whetstone may develop a dip on the surface, where the sharpening has taken place. To rectify this, you can use a second stone of the same kind and rub the two together, until the surface is level again.

There are also stones with ready-made grooves designed to fit the shape of the *marutō* and *sankakutō* that make the sharpening of these tools a simple matter of fitting them into the appropriate groove and moving the tool backwards and forwards. I have found that it is, however, sometimes too easy to get the angle of the tool wrong and change the bevel.

Process of sharpening the tools

The waterstones are soaked in water before use for at least ten minutes. Placing them on a non-slip mat is a good idea to stop them moving when sharpening. A slurry develops on the surface of the stone as the sharpening continues – this can be washed off as you progress.

If the stone becomes dry, spray some water on the surface or leave it in a bowl of water for a few minutes. Water is the necessary lubricant for the sharpening process.

Before beginning to sharpen your tool, it is a good idea to use an indelible felt-tip pen to colour in the bevel of your tool. After you start sharpening you can lift the tool and examine the bevel; areas of visible felt-tip show where you are not sharpening evenly. This is especially important when sharpening the *marutō*.

Each tool will be held at a different angle to find the angle where the bevel and the stone meet, ensuring that there is no gap between the tool and the stone. If you leave a gap between the tool and the stone and start sharpening you will be changing the angle of your original bevel, which is to be avoided. It is also important to remember that this is not a question of force or pressure as the rubbing contact with the stone is enough to sharpen the tool. Hold the handle of your tool lightly in your

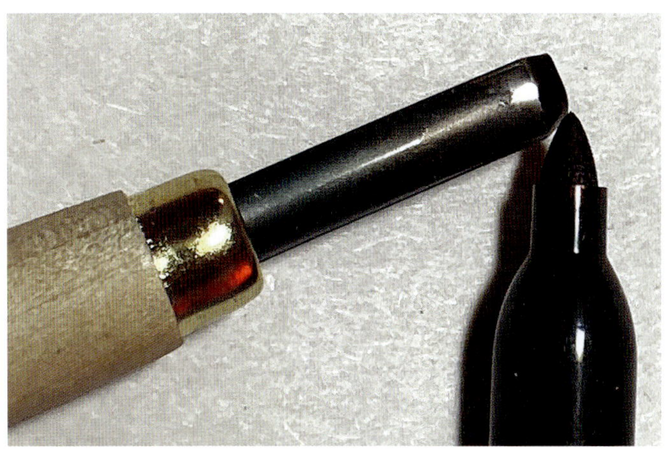

Marking the bevel of the *marato* with a black waterproof felt pen.

right hand (or left if you are left-handed) and find the contact point where the bevel meets the stone.

Hangitō

Start with the grey *chūto* or middle-grade waterstone. The point of the *hangitō* is vulnerable and must be protected from damage by inaccurate sharpening. As before with the honing, you will want to use the index finger of your non-dominant hand to keep the tool at a right angle to the stone and away from the point.

When you are satisfied move the tool up and down the stone. With your finger in place it can be difficult to see what you are doing and so with practice you will be able to tell through listening whether the tool is sharpening correctly. When it is incorrect the sound will change, becoming a more rasping sound instead of a steady rhythmic hiss.

Your hands will be able to keep the connection with the stone and you can check periodically whether the felt-tip colour has rubbed off the bevel evenly.

Then switch to the *shiageto* or polishing stone, turn the tool over so the flat side of the tool is resting flat on the stone and rub up and down to remove the metal burr thrown up by the sharpening of the bevel. Polish the bevel carefully by holding it to the stone as before and rubbing until your tool is shiny. You can also finish with a spell of honing.

Remember to clean and dry your tools carefully with a soft cloth after sharpening. Tools should never be put away damp, the economy tools have an iron quotient that turns to rust quickly if the tools are left in a box to dry. If the tools are not used for any length of time it is a good precaution to add a slick of vegetable oil to the blade – traditionally and ideally it would be camelia oil as it does not oxidise, deterring rust.

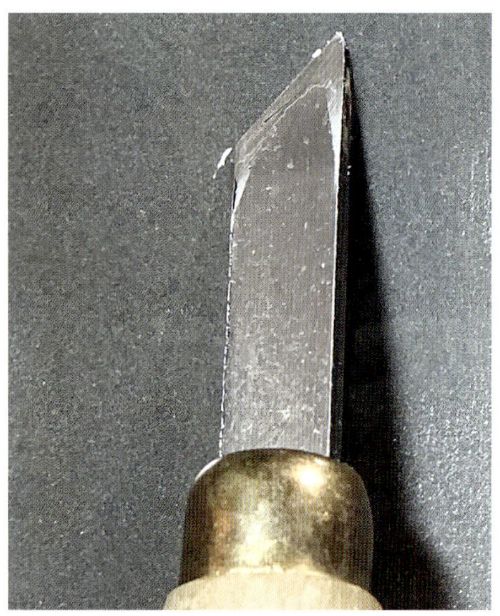

For the *hangitō*, care must be taken not to blunt the sharp tip of the tool.

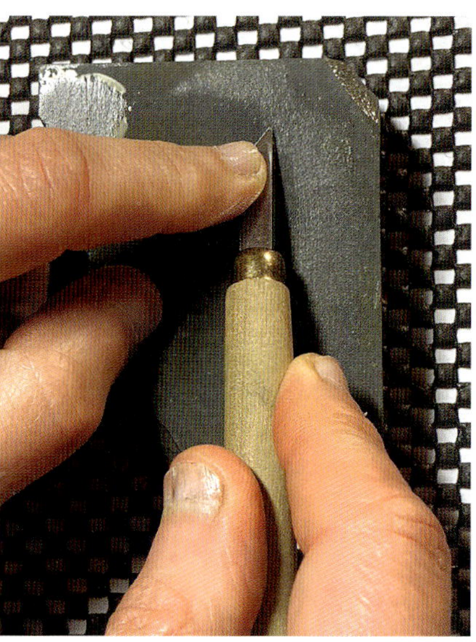

Move the tool up and down the waterstone.

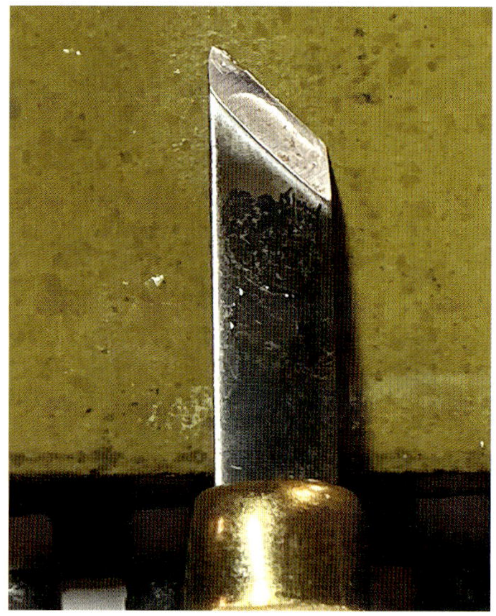

Finish by polishing the burr off on the flat side of the tool.

Hiratō

The chisel or *hiratō* is the easiest tool to sharpen – however, economy tools have straight edges and it is important not to blunt these, so watch those edges as you move the tool up and down the stone. The more expensive tools have slightly rounded edges that require a zig-zag motion across the stone. Finish with polishing, honing, cleaning and drying your tool as before.

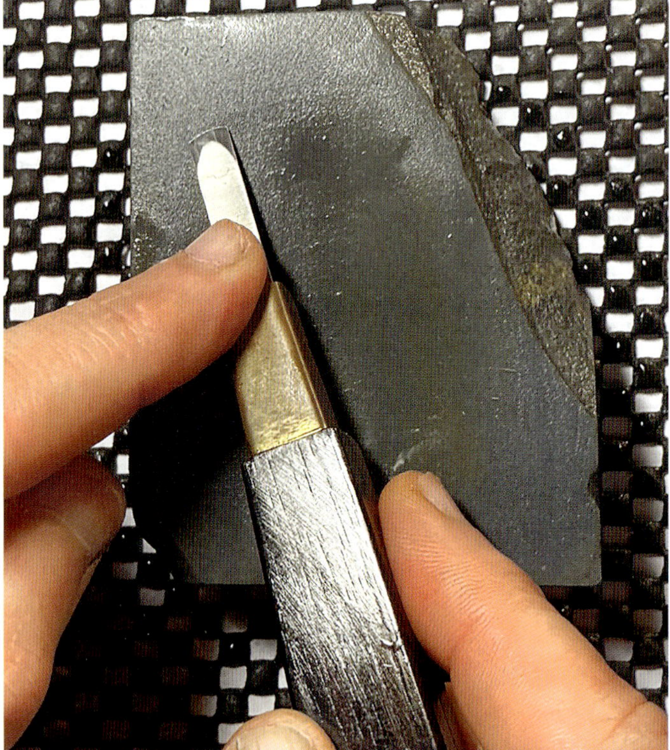

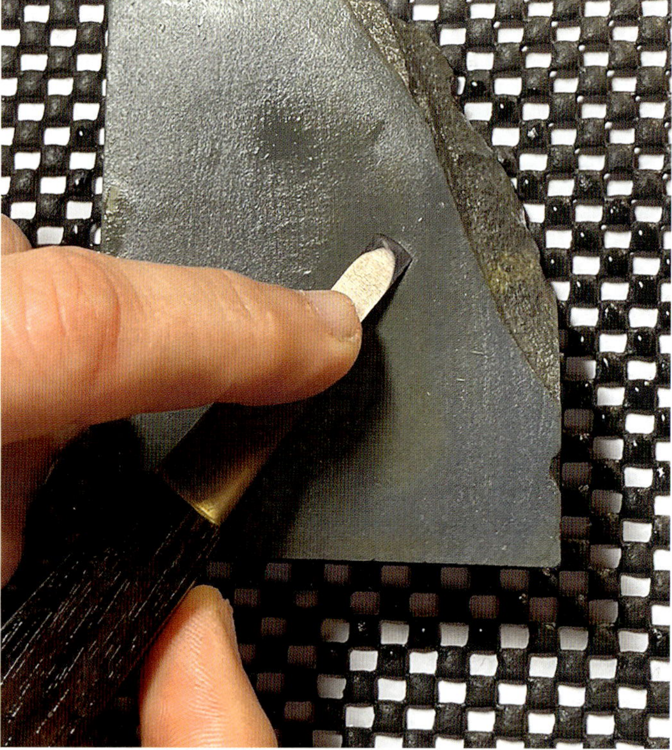

For a *hiratō* with rounded sides, a zig-zag action is required.

Marutō

For the beginner, sharpening with the *marutō* on a sharpening stone can be difficult to accomplish as it involves a fluid figure of eight pattern and a flexible turn of the wrist. The figure of eight ensures that all areas of the tool are sharpened evenly but I prefer a different method. I roll the tool along my thumb as I sweep the tool along the waterstone – this requires some practice as at the end of each sweep the tool is swivelled up to the right and then across the width of the waterstone to the left swivelling up again. Beware too of the upper points of the 'u', not to rub them blunt.

It is important to draw the black marker pen over the bevel area of this tool before beginning. As I am right-handed my hand has a natural bias and I find the tell-tale signs that my sharpening is not even easy to gauge by looking at the areas of black marker still visible on the tool.

To clear the burr on the *marutō* use the round side of the slipstone. Polish the bevel side on the *shiageto* stone. Hone, clean and dry as before.

Sankakutō

Care must be taken with the *sankakutō* to ensure that the fold of the 'v' does not get worn down more on one side than the other.

The best way to do this is by counting the strokes of the tool up and down the stone on one side and then repeating on the other side.

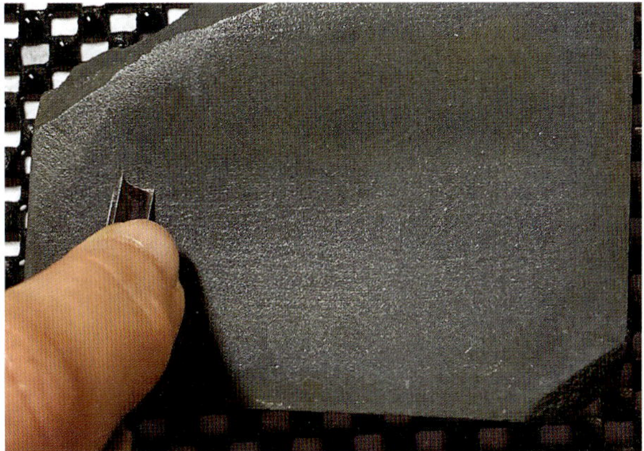

For the *marutō* I roll the tool along my thumb as I sweep the tool from side to side, swivelling it up to the right and then up to the left, using the width of the waterstone.

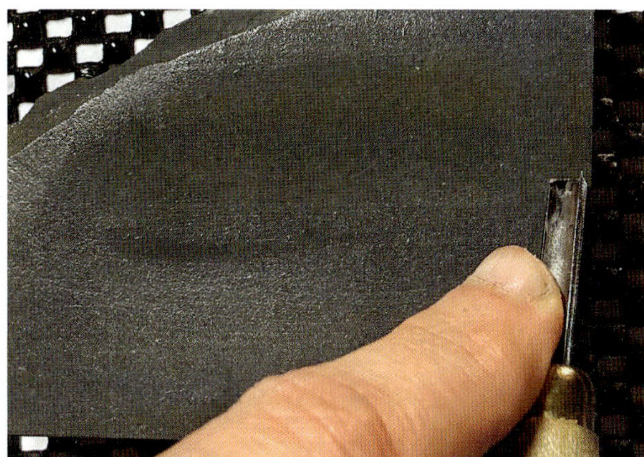

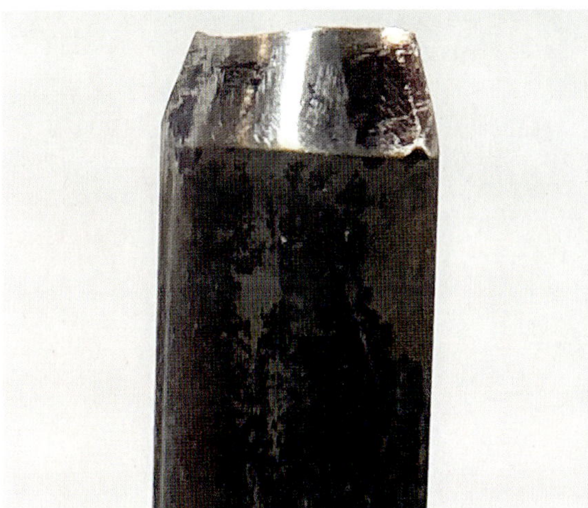

The black marker pen should be rubbed cleanly away; the presence of visible black marker pen shows that my tool has not been sharpened evenly.

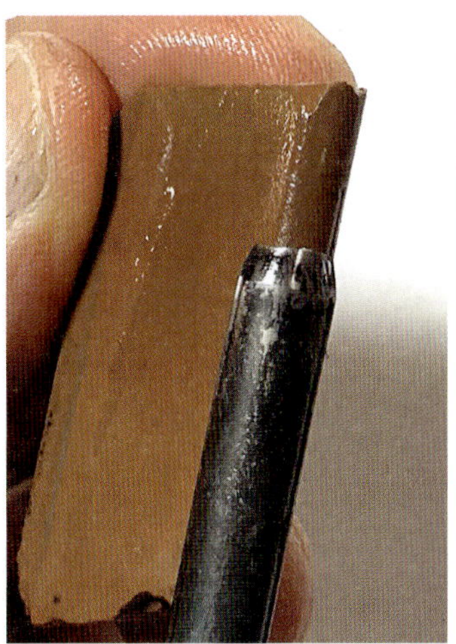

The *marutō* is finished off with the rounded end of a slipstone, removing the burr from the inside of the tool.

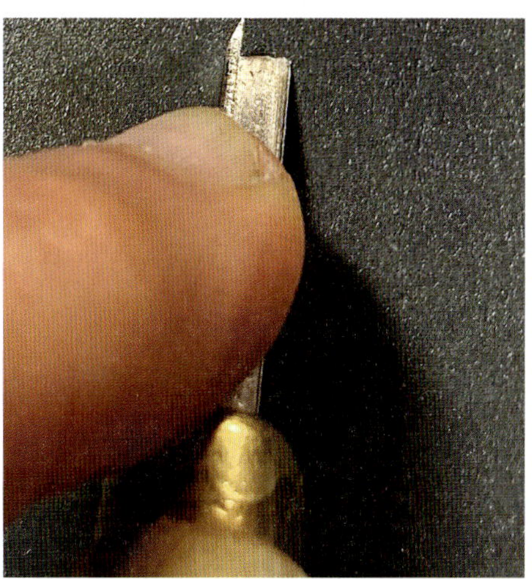

The *sankakutō* is sharpened on both sides of the central 'V' fold, counting the number of strokes to ensure even sharpening.

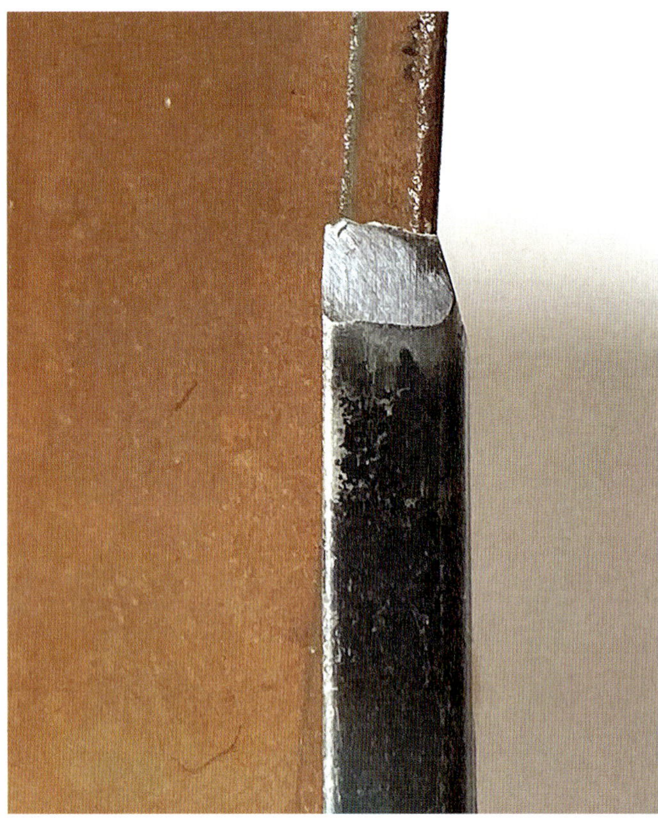

The tool is polished with the narrow side of the slipstone.

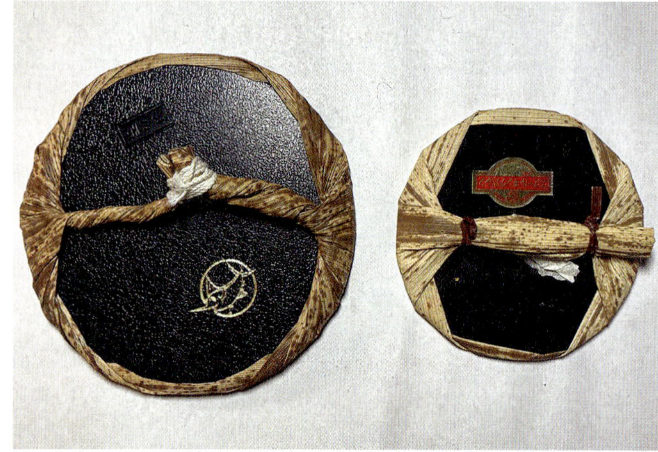

The example on the left is a good-quality *baren,* with a broad surface for even printing; the one on the right is an economy *baren* and much smaller.

Hon Baren

A top-quality *Hon baren* made by the master *baren* maker Hidehiko Gotou will be expensive to buy, but will last a lifetime, although the bamboo sheath will have to be re-covered after prolonged use. It is a good idea to keep a soft cloth pad impregnated with camelia oil (substitute – olive oil) next to

For clearing the burr use the pointed side of the slipstone and rub the inside of the 'v' outwards. Hone, clean and dry your tool to finish.

BAREN

The economy *baren* for beginners is a simple device made up of a cardboard disc approximately 14cm in diameter, wrapped in a bamboo sheath held in place with ties. It is used to hand-press the back of the print, the pressure allowing the pigment to transfer from the block to the paper. The broad surface area of the *baren* allows for an even printing. The student-quality *baren* is completely fine to use to begin with, but any progress with the Mokuhanga technique will involve upgrading your *baren*. The *baren* is an essential component in Mokuhanga, and unlike a printing press is highly portable.

Traditionally the *baren* would have been made by the printers themselves, but now they are either mass produced or handmade by specialists.

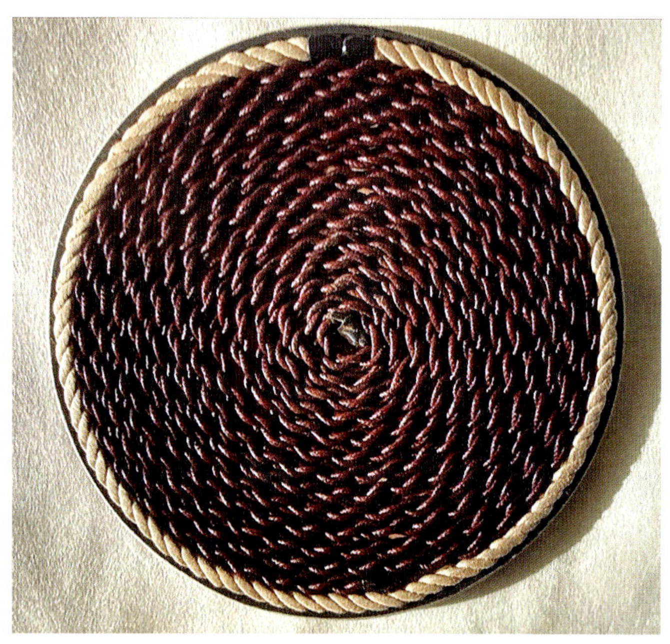

Image showing the twisted cord spirals of the *shirataki* or bamboo sheath. An eight-strand spiral will be good for printing fine details, a 16-strand spiral is for printing requiring heavier pressure. The multiple bumps formed by the twisting of the spiral coil are what give the *baren* its importance as a printing tool.

your woodblock when printing and from time to time rub oil into the *baren* to keep it supple and prevent splits from occurring. The *Hon* or 'true' *baren* is made of three parts: the backing *ategawa* is made of approximately 50 sheets of thin *washi* paper layers brushed with natural waterproof persimmon tannin, finishing with a layer of thin silk coated in eight layers of *urushi* lacquer. The *shin* or *baren* core is made from a coil of twisted white bamboo sheath *shirataki* tied into a spiral.

There are grades of *baren* based on the number of twists of fibre that have gone into the making of the *shin*. *Baren* profiles can also be graded into rough, average and smooth; several different *baren* can be used on the same print to achieve different effects.

A basic *baren* is made from a coil of eight strands known as *yakko*, but there are 12-strand *jyuniko* and 16-strand *jyurokko* as well. The 12-strand *baren* has a circular cross section, so it seldom leaves any tell-tale *baren* marks or *suji* on the print. The 16-strand *baren* gives a strong pressure, ideal for printing *tsubushi* or a totally flat colour surface.

A traditional *baren* needs to be looked after by keeping it lightly oiled, away from damp areas and out of direct sunlight or sources of heat.

Alternative *Baren*

It can be difficult to master the art of re-covering your *baren* when the sheath splits, and expensive to send it back to Japan to be re-covered in the traditional manner. It was because of this issue that alternative *baren* were designed and manufactured that do not rely on the bamboo sheath.

The Kurosaki *Baren*

This *baren* was designed by the master printer and teacher Akira Kurosaki. It is made of a plastic disc with a dimpled surface. To avoid *baren* marks coming out on your print it is important to have a sheet of protective paper between the *baren* and the printing paper when rubbing down. It is not as smooth as a bamboo-sheathed *baren* but it has the advantage in that it does not wear out and is relatively inexpensive to buy.

The *hon baren* is a thing of beauty, expertly handcrafted. The outer *baren* skin is called the *baren kawa*.

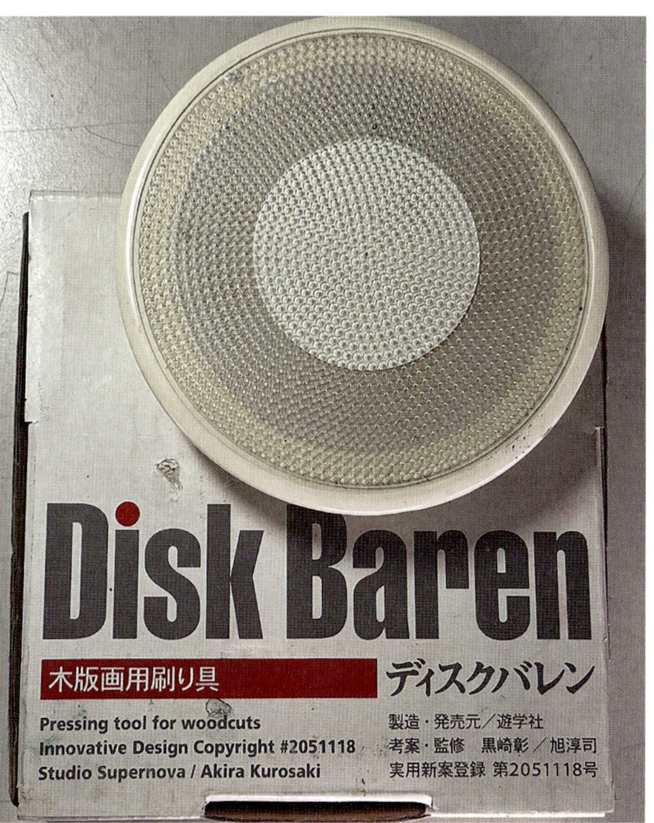

The Kurosaki *baren* made of washable plastic and a dimpled surface.

The Kean Delrin Ball *Baren*

Devised by Roslyn Kean with the help of her engineering partner, these *baren* are made by suspending ball bearings in a circular plate and attaching this to a leather backing. They are handmade with a slightly convex surface and internal materials that allow both cushioning and rotation of the balls. The Delrin housing for the balls is made from high-grade solvent-resistant plastic and the ball bearings are stainless steel. The ball bearings enable the *baren* to slide over the printing paper. They are expensive to buy but very hard wearing. The tiny steel balls give the equivalent of a 16-strand traditional *hon baren* and are suitable for heavy printing. Care needs to be taken to ensure these *baren* do not get damp.

Home-made *Baren*

It is possible to handprint linocuts with oil-based inks using a wooden spoon, the curved surface of the spoon allowing the ink to be transferred without leaving a pressure line.

For Mokuhanga prints however the small surface area of a spoon is inadequate for transferring watercolour pigments evenly onto the printing paper. To make a handmade *baren* it is best to look at the traditional *baren* and copy its attributes. For the disc, thin cardboard, laminated sheets or plastic could be

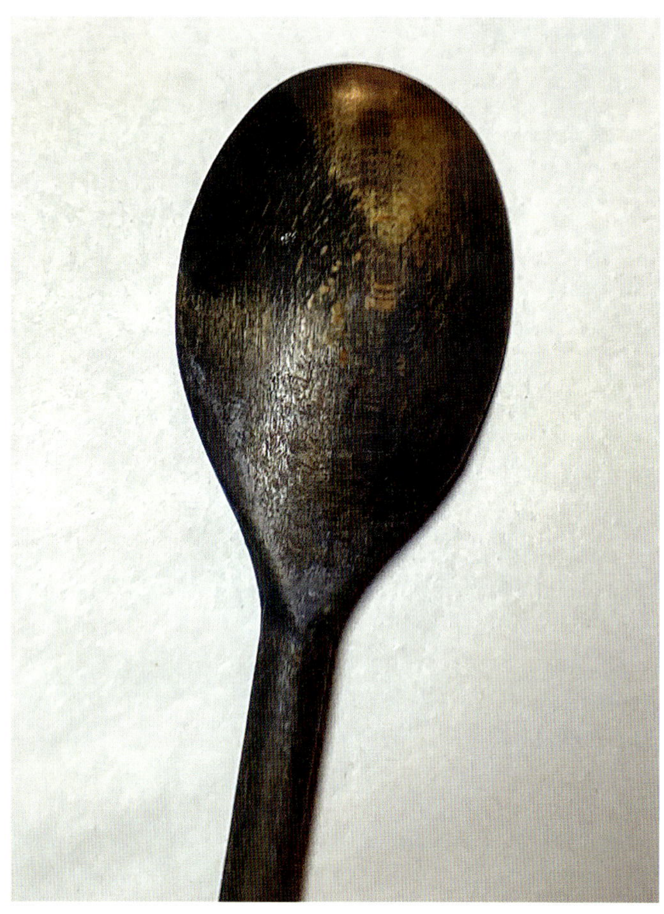

This is my wooden spoon that has seen some extensive use – see how the wood has been rubbed down to a smooth surface.

used. For the *shin*, a coil made from twine, or a small ball chain would simulate the effect of the ball-bearing *baren*. Using cloth as an alternative to the bamboo sheath or even tights stretched over the disc can work. It would of course be important to test out the performance of these *baren* before printing.

BRUSHES

There are a range of different brushes used in Mokuhanga. Each brush has evolved over time designed to suit specific requirements in the process from dampening *washi* paper to brushing colour into the blocks. Japanese brush makers still make their brushes in the traditional way and the care and attention employed is a pleasure to see and the brushes delightful to use, and with due care last a long time. Brushes play an important role in the Mokuhanga process, absorbing a quantity of liquid and brushing a smooth coverage of colour

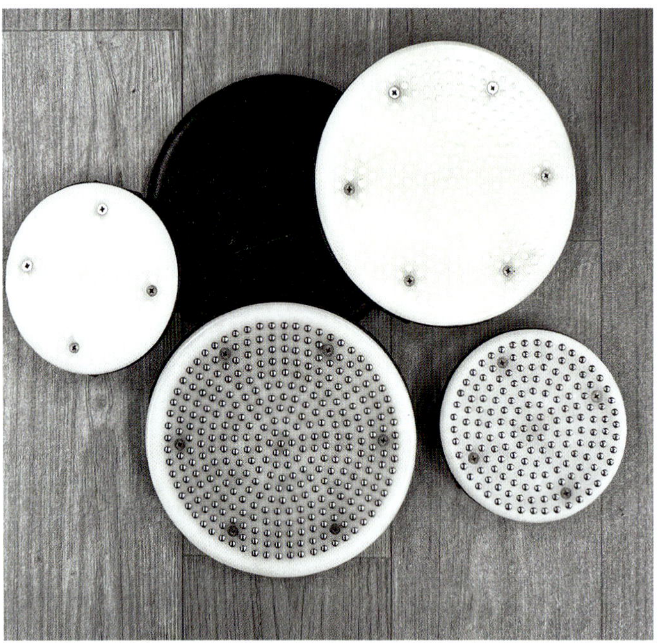

The Kean Delrin Ball Bearing *baren*. This *baren* exerts a strong pressure on the back of the paper and so it is advisable to use a protective piece of cartridge paper between the paper and the *baren*. More suitable for printing with thicker than thinner papers.

without streaks appearing on the block. It is a good idea to keep a separate brush for each colour of your print.

Types of Brushes

Print brush *Te Bake* (*Edo Hake, Hanga Bake*)

This Japanese brush is the oldest form of printing brush and has many different names. It is used to brush the *nori* and the pigment into the woodgrain. It is made from tight bundles of mane or tail hair from a live horse bound together and either sewn into a split wooden handle or bound with copper wire. The hairs are very densely packed together and if the brush is properly cared for, it should not shed hairs when used. Deer and hog hair are also used but horse tail hair is the most common form. They come in varying sizes according to the size of the area for printing from very small for printing single fine lines, to the size of a large makeup brush. Using a small elastic band to keep the bristles together can help when a small brush is unavailable, although as this can damage the bristles I tend to simply hold them with my fingers when printing.

If a *hake* is unavailable it is possible to use a stencil brush, although the hard bristles of the stencil brush often leave lines on the block. For finer cut relief lines, it is possible to customise a small Western paintbrush by trimming the bristles near the metal ferrule leaving a small, stiff brush, though these brushes do not tend to last very long.

Round brush *Marubake*

Marubake were imported to Japan during the Meji period (1866–1912) and evolved from clothes and shoe brushes. It is used for brushing pigment into larger printing areas. It has bristles made from small bundles of horse tail hair pulled through drilled holes secured with thin wire. After the exposed wires are flattened the lid is nailed into place, not glued, so that the brush is able to breathe through the air holes. The bristles are trimmed and bevelled to keep the pigment angled inwards rather than splaying outwards onto 'clean' areas of the woodblock. It is also possible to rub the bristles on a hot plate to singe the edges of the brush; here great care must be taken to ensure an even bevelling. On professional quality brushes the ends are also split

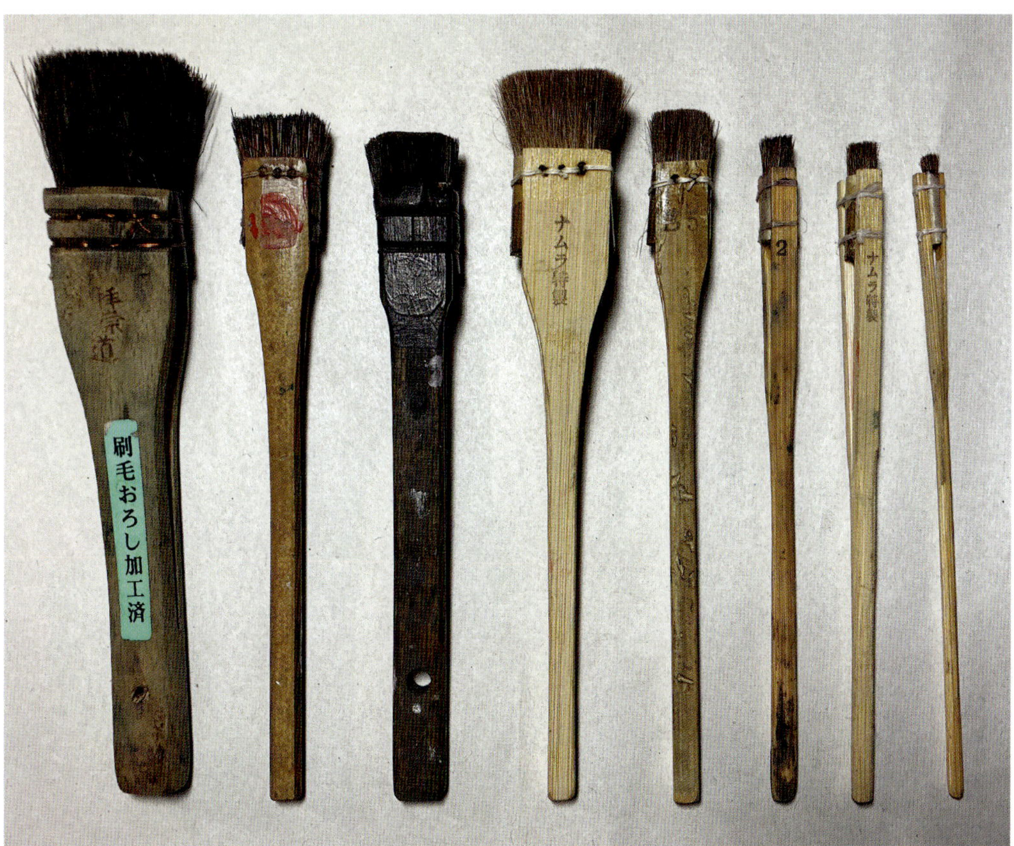

A range of my *te bake*. The tightly packed bristles are made from horse tail, hog and deer hair. The brush third from the left has been professionally shaped with sharkskin so that the bristles do not splay out.

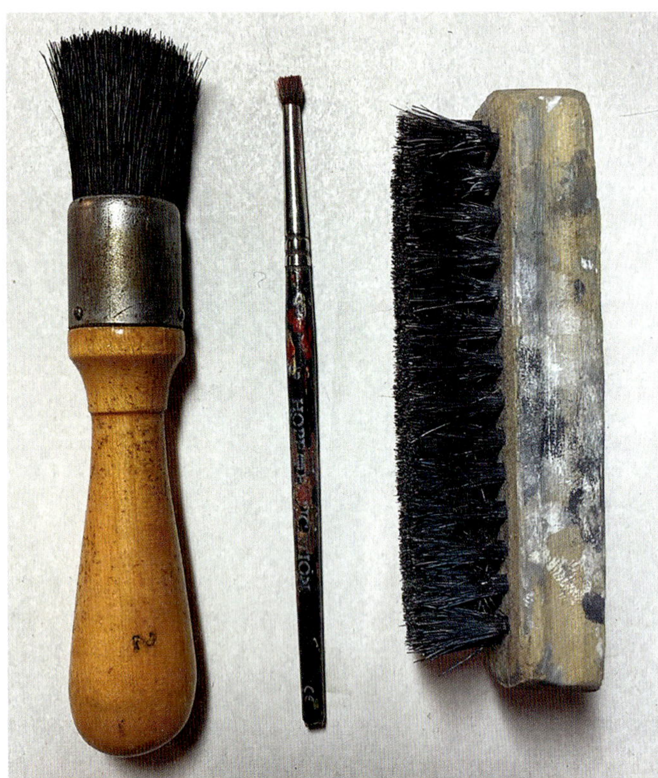

Left: A stencil brush instead of a *te bake*. Centre: For the smallest *te bake* used for printing details, I find that a cut-down, old Western paintbrush works really well. Right: A shoe brush can be used for brushing pigment into larger areas.

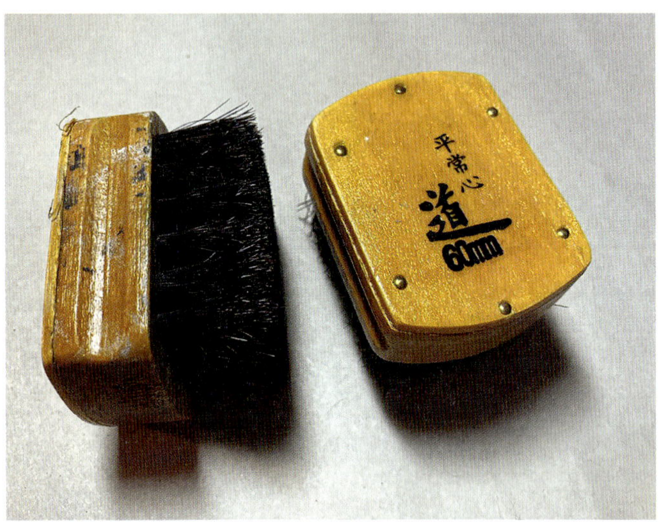

Marubake or round brush. In the late nineteenth century they began to be called *burashi*, from the English word 'brush'. The brushes are made entirely by hand, the bristles are tightly bound and pulled through drilled holes and secured with wire.

to improve the take up of pigment, by rubbing the brush on an Angel sharkskin, its fine placoid scales acting like sandpaper.

Carrying brush *Hakobi* (*Tokibō*)

These are called 'carrying brushes', for carrying the pigment from the palette to the woodblock. The *hake* and *marubake* are not used because they would absorb too much pigment flooding the woodgrain; using a *hakobi* means that the amount of pigment going onto the block can be controlled. Traditionally they are made by using the left-over pieces of bamboo sheath from *baren*-making, tied with string on to a wooden handle.

It is also common to use Western paintbrushes for the purpose, the wooden handles often cut shorter for ease of use.

Water Brush *Mizubake* and Sizing Brush *Dōsabake*

The *mizubake* is a broad, soft-haired brush used to brush water onto the printing paper. The brush is often made from white goat hair or sheep's hair and is densely packed so that it can take up a large quantity of water without replenishing. This makes for an even dampening of the paper using fewer strokes.

It can also be used for painting size, called *dōsabake*, onto the printing paper. Sizing the paper with *dōsa*, a mixture of animal glue and alum, controls the absorbency of the paper and prevents 'bleeding' of the pigment. If a *mizubake* is unavailable a wallpaper or decorator's brush is a good substitute.

A wire brush that you might use for cleaning suede can be used on the block to bring up the wood grain. It brushes out the softer wood leaving the harder grain in relief. Care must be taken to work evenly over the block and exert enough pressure to bring up the grain but not so much that the wood is scratched.

Care of Brushes

It is very important to look after your brushes to preserve their lifespan. After printing, the brushes must be washed carefully. It is important to avoid allowing the water to flow over the wooden handle – if the wooden handle gets wet it can warp and this causes a loosening of the bindings holding the bristles together. Holding the handle sideways to the stream of water from the tap allows the colour to wash out of the brush, then pressing lightly against the palm of your other hand, the colour is encouraged to fade away. When the water runs clear, run the brush over a cake of non-scented natural soap and then rinse the soap from the bristles. The soap prevents mould and unpleasant odours from developing.

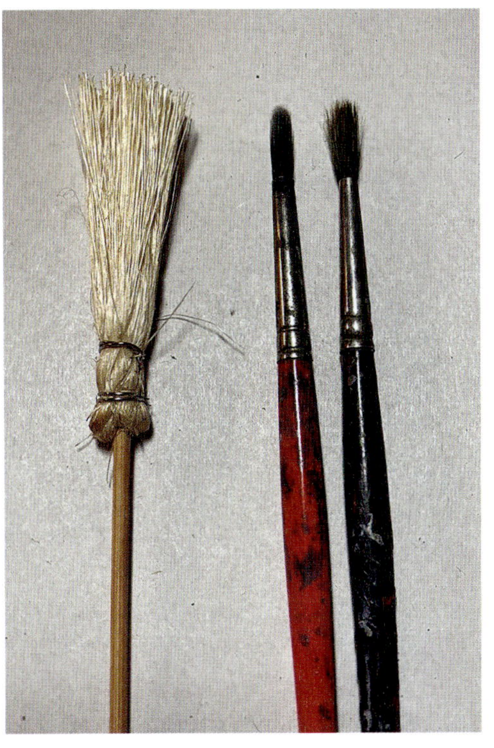

Hakobi or carrying brushes, for bringing the pigment to the block. The brush on the left is a traditional one, made from finely cut bamboo sheath. The Western brushes' handles are often shortened so that they balance in the palette without tipping.

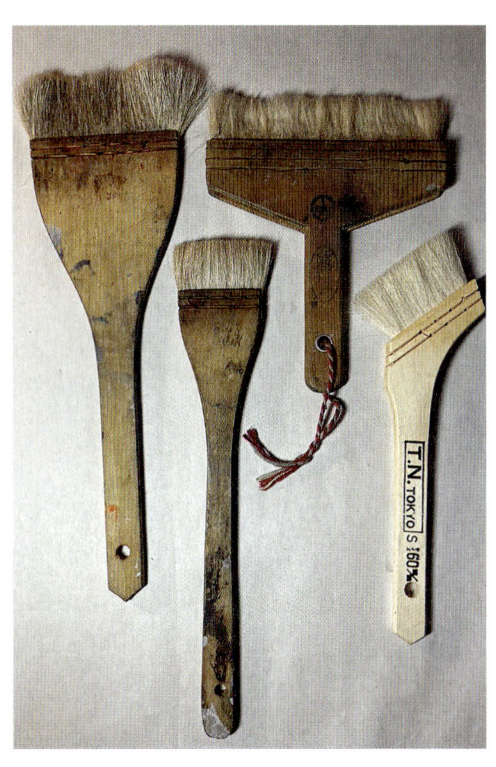

A range of different sizes and shapes of *mizu bake*, or water brushes. These brushes absorb a lot of water and so are ideal for dampening paper. If no alternative can be found, a soft decorator's brush will do.

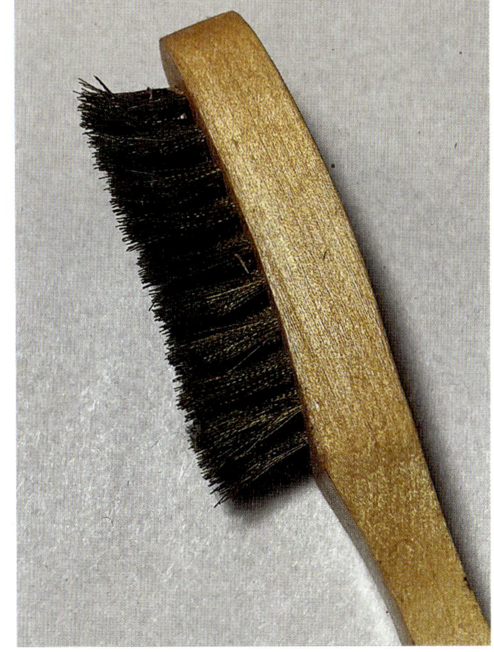

A wire brush (used for cleaning suede) can be used to bring up the woodgrain of the block by lightly brushing the surface.

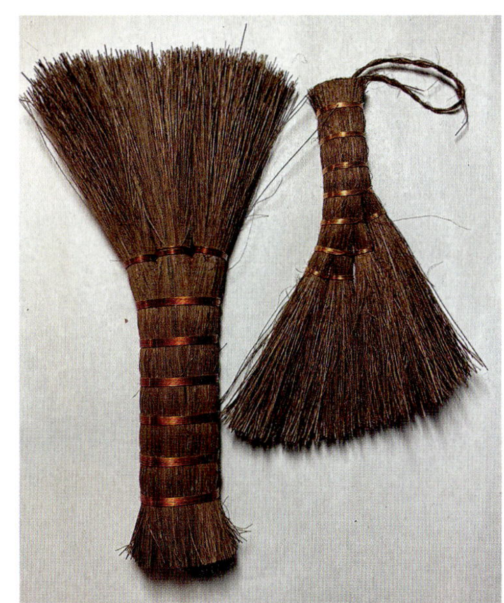

These delightful, hard to resist whisks are used to brush the wood chippings from the block as you work. Not essential but rather lovely.

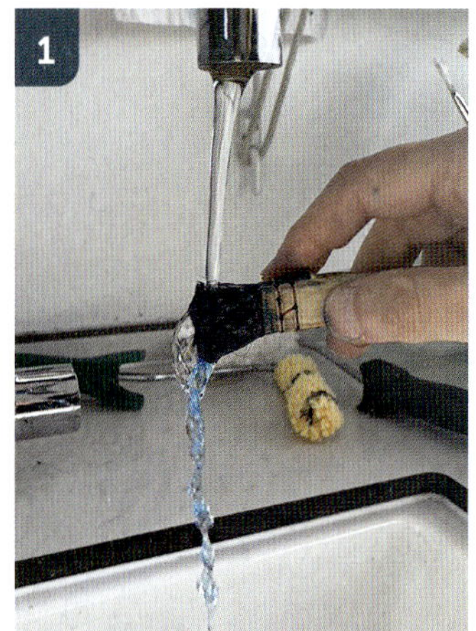

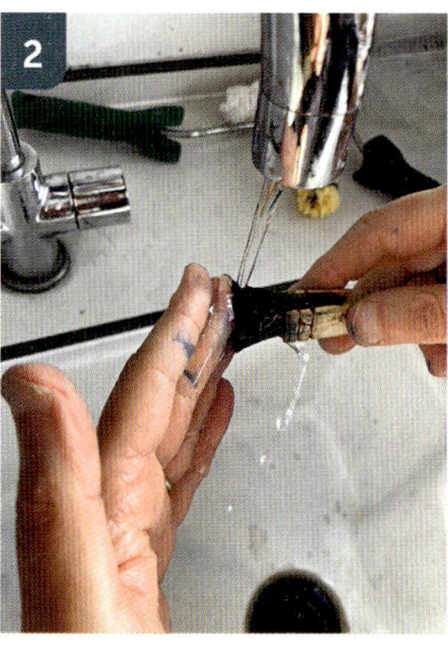

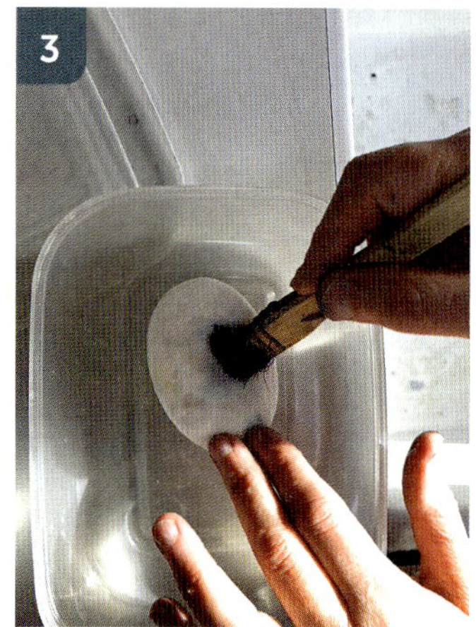

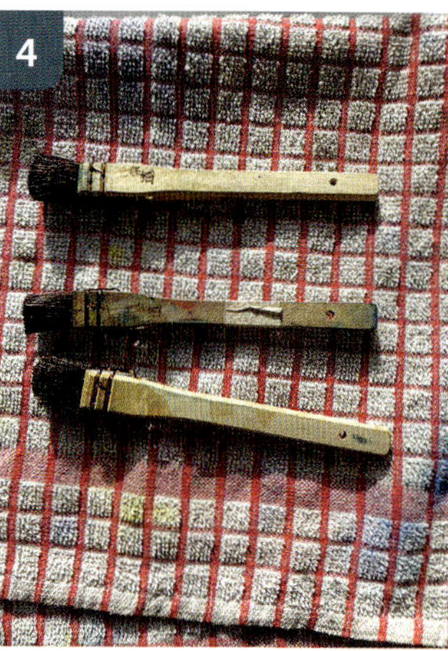

1. Hold the brush sideways into a stream of water from the tap, avoiding getting the wooden handle wet.

2. Press and swizzle the brush into your hand lightly, to encourage the pigment to be released.

3. When the water runs clear, pick up some non-scented soap with the brush. Swizzle the soap into the bristles. Then rinse all the soap out.

4. Ideally hang your brushes from the hole in the handle or at least leave them on a tea towel to dry naturally.

Apart from the *marubake* all Japanese brushes have a hole drilled into the handle; this is so that they can be hung with the bristles hanging downwards to dry. A small eyelet can be screwed into the *marubake* so that it too can be hung to dry. It must not be left to dry with the bristles facing upwards, as the water will drain into the lid and cause cracks to appear.

NORI

Nori paste is very important to the Japanese woodblock printing process. It is a kind of rice-starch glue made from cooked rice flour (often confused with the word for seaweed that sounds the same, but is spelt differently in *kanji*). It is water soluble, so

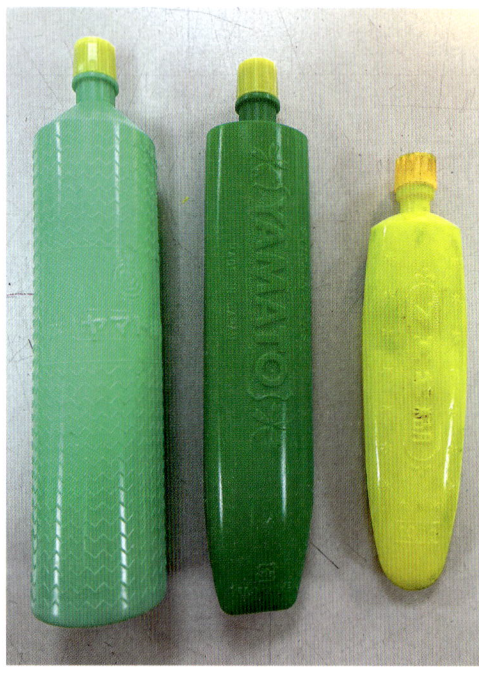

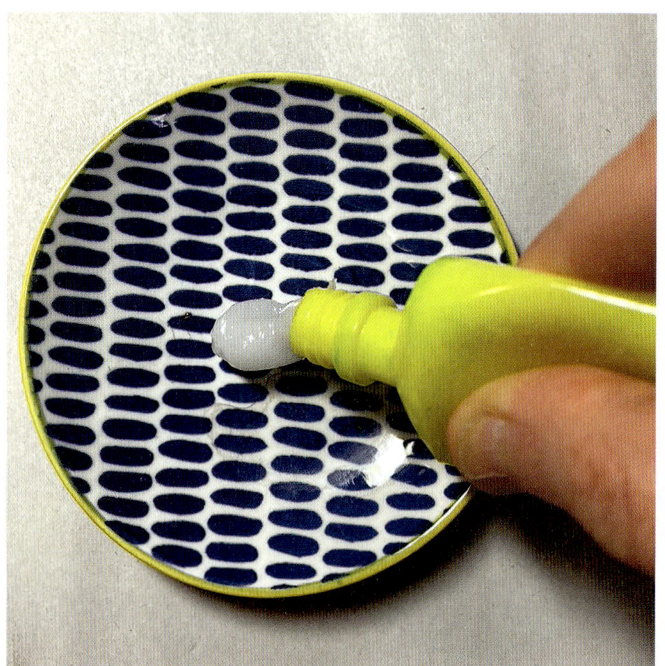

Nori paste.

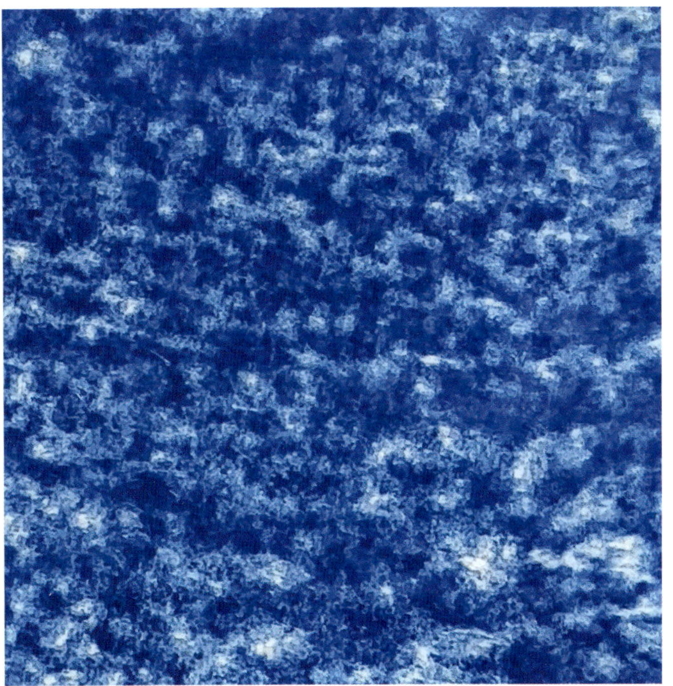

Speckled effect.

Finger painting effect.

RECIPE FOR *NORI*

Traditionally *nori* would have been made by soaking, cooking and straining rice. Nowadays rice flour is used. Only small quantities of *nori* are required for printing; more is needed if a *hanshita* is being pasted down.

On the hob:

You will need a small saucepan. Put it on a digital scale, set to zero. Add 4g (1 teaspoon) rice flour, then water (approx. 9 teaspoons) to make it up to 50g. Whisk smooth. Cook on a medium heat stirring constantly. When it begins to thicken take off the heat and cool, stirring occasionally. Takes about ten minutes to make. Ratio flour to water 1:9

Microwave:

Weigh out 1 teaspoon rice flour and 9 teaspoons water in a small microwaveable container, stir well. Set the microwave for a few seconds at a time stirring in between. Start with 20 seconds, then ten seconds, then five seconds until the mixture has begun to boil slightly. Stir once or twice as it cools.

The problem with making your own *nori* is that it does not keep very well, only a few days in the refrigerator. There are however ready-made, inexpensive *nori* tubes that are easy to obtain in Japanese or Chinese supermarkets as well as art shops. These contain a preservative extending the useful life of the *nori* and when the cap is sealed, the *nori* does not dry out.

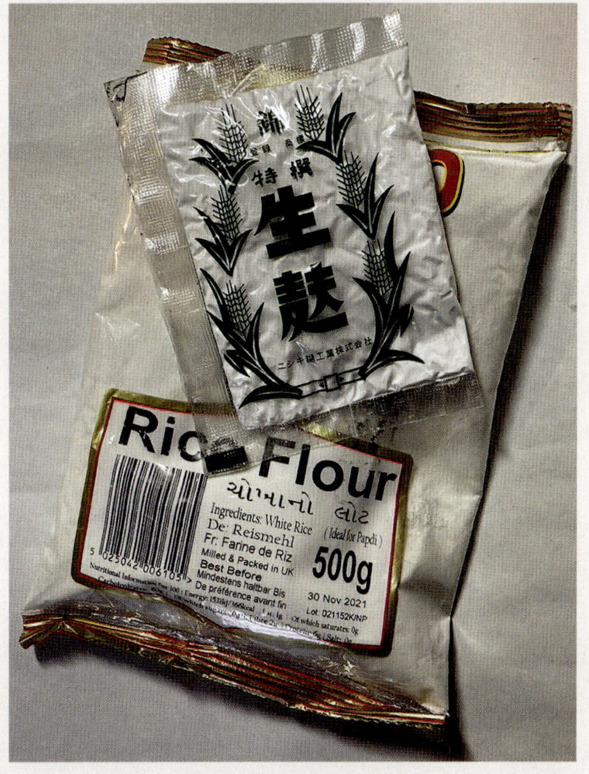

Rice flour.

for instance when used as a glue for joining papers, the papers can be separated simply by dampening the *nori*. It is archival and acid free too.

In the traditional *hanmoto* system the artist would send an original drawing to the studio and this would be pasted face down, called *hanshita*, onto the woodblock using *nori*. The original brush line drawing would still be visible through the thin paper allowing the master carver to cut to the artist's exact brush line.

Nori is also used during the printing process itself. A small amount of diluted *nori* is dotted onto the woodblock and brushed into the wood; this is repeated for each printing until the build-up of *nori* in the woodgrain is sufficient to leave it out – usually after six printings. The addition of *nori* acts as an extender for the pigment, thickening it slightly and resulting in a more even print. It also helps to hold the paper in place during printing. The extra water in the *nori* extends the drying time of the pigment on the paper. Without *nori*, there is often a speckled effect called *gomazuri* (seasame printing); too much *nori* and the brush lines will show on the print like finger painting.

WATER PIGMENT

Ukiyō-e Colours

One of the differences between Mokuhanga and Western printing processes is the use of watercolour pigments instead

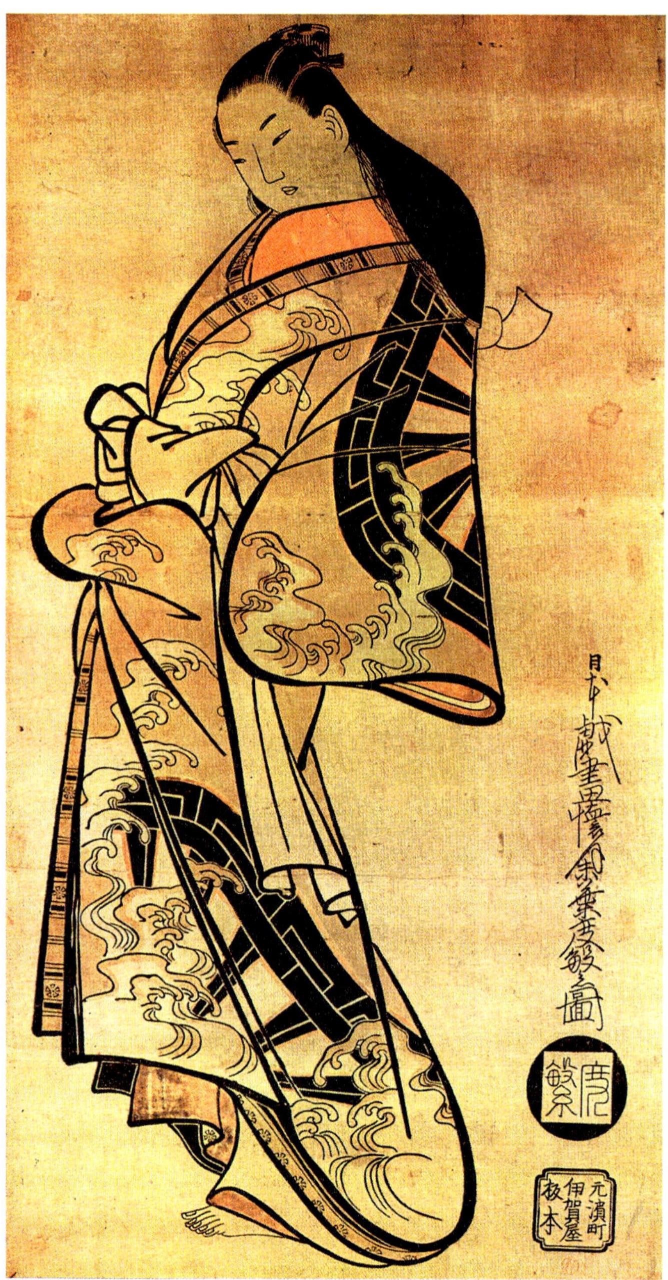

Kaigetsudō Dohan, c.1710. *Bijin* (Beauty). *Sumizuri-e* black printed lines, *tan* red coloured in by hand.

of oil-based inks. *Ukiyō-e* prints of the Edo period (1603–1868 CE) look like they are painted with watercolours – indeed, amongst the first prints sold by the popular publishers were black and white images that were painstakingly coloured in using an orange-red watercolour called *tan-e*.

It was the invention of the *kentō* registration system, attributed to the artist Suzuki Harunobu, that gave the freedom to use multiple colour separations, to build up exciting colourful

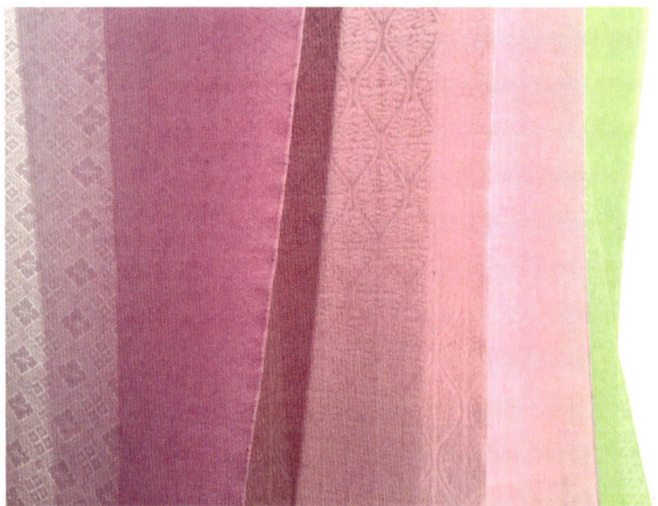

Dyed silk in shades of pink and pale green that were among the acceptable colour combinations for aristocratic ladies of the Heian period.

prints in large quantities. The colours used were made from indigenous plants and minerals, creating beautiful delicate hues. The plants used for dying, pigments and medicine were often sold in the same shop.

Colour was an important cultural and class signifier in the garments worn by the aristocracy of the Heian Period (794–1185 CE). The most formal kimono, the *juni-hitoe*, was made of 12 layers, cut so that each layer's colour would be offset at the collar, neckline and hem. A noble woman of the period would remain hidden from the outside world, but the colour combinations or *kasane* that she had selected in the hem of her kimono would communicate her taste and elegance. This refined sensibility, *miyabi*, influenced subsequent centuries and continues to be referenced in contemporary culture.

ORIGINS OF COLOURS USED IN TRADITIONAL *UKIYŌ-E* PRINTS

Colour	Mineral or Plant Origin
Red	*Akane*, Madder
Crimson red	*Benibana, beni/enji*, safflower
Darker red	*Suō*, sappanwood
Orange/red	*Tan*, red oxide of lead
Pink	*Benigara*, used for skin tone colour made from red oxide of iron
Vermillion	*Shu*, mercuric sulphide
Deep rich blue	*Tade-ai*, Japanese indigo from Polygonum tinctorium plant
Lighter blue colour	*Hanada*, raw leaves of indigo
Prussian blue	*Berō-ai*, introduced to Japan in 1820s from China and Europe
Green	*Rokushō*, coarsely ground malachite
Grey	*Yasha*, Japanese alder
Purple	*Shikon*, (Lithospermum root) Gromwell
Yellow	*Kariyasu, yamamomo*, bayberry
White	*Gofun*, ground oyster/clam shells
Gold and silver	*Unmo*, mica powders

These colours in a traditional studio would be mixed by the printer for each print, the colours having been personally approved by the artist.

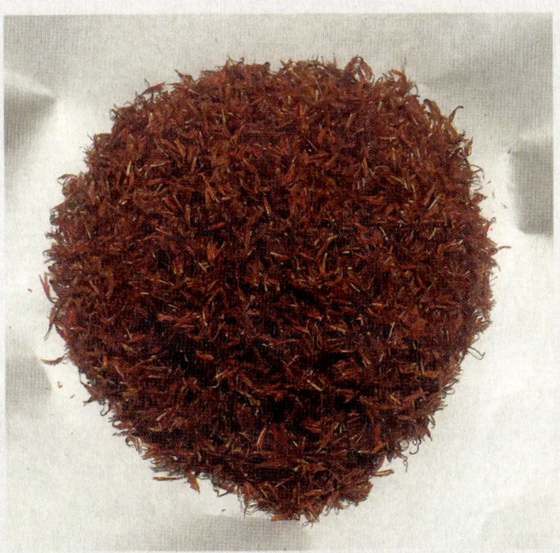

Dried safflower for dyeing.

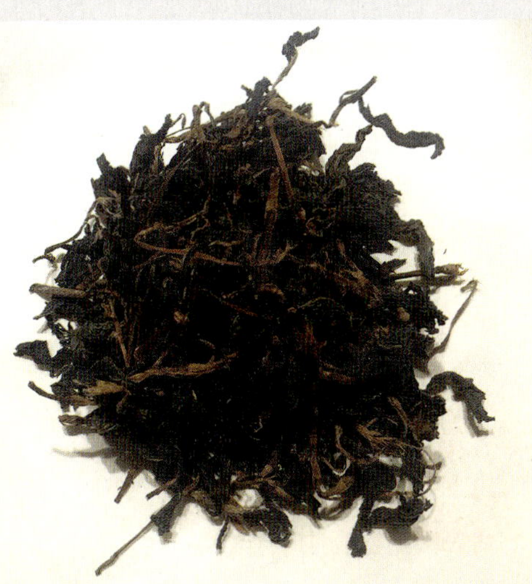

Dried indigo leaves for dyeing.

Making Your Own Colours

To make your own colours, it is possible to use powdered pigments available from Artists' Colourmen shops and grind the powder with gum Arabic, a binding solution made from the resin of the acacia tree, using a glass muller. Glycerine, honey and oil of clove can be added as preservatives. Proportionally the amount of gum Arabic used is one-fifth of the quantity of pigment. The muller is used in a figure of eight pattern to blend and grind the powder to a fine, even texture for up to 30 minutes. Water can then be added to the mixture to achieve the right consistency for printing. It can also be stored ready for future use. It is a good method to use if large quantities of pigment are needed for an edition run.

There are colours that can be obtained by boiling barks, spices and plants, reducing over the heat until the resultant liquid is a concentrated colour. After straining, the coloured water can be mixed with *nori* to thicken it and then used to print as normal. Experiments can be made with adding vinegar or bicarbonate of soda to the solution. These colours tend to be a bit more 'fugitive', that is they have a limited colour fastness.

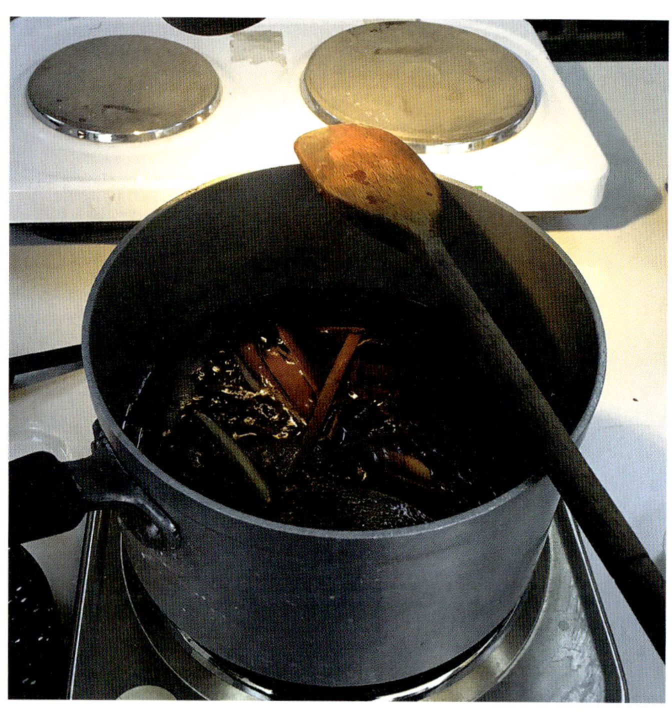

Simmering sticks of willow to release the colour.

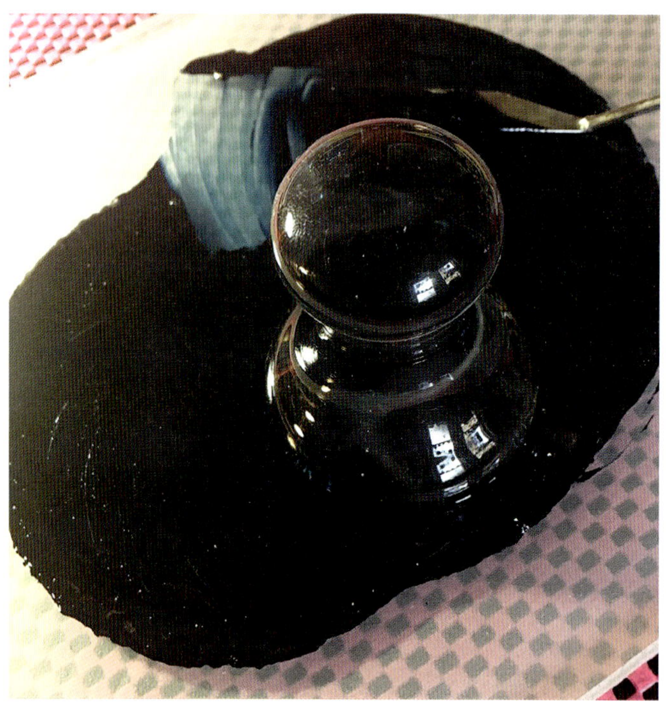

Grinding dry pigment, gum Arabic and honey together, using a glass muller, to make printable ink.

COLOURS MADE FROM NATURAL INGREDIENTS

Colour	Ingredients
Golden yellow	Turmeric
Pale lilac/purple	Red cabbage
Vivid pink	Hibiscus
Green	Red cabbage with bicarbonate of soda
Purple	Red cabbage with vinegar
Orange/brown	Onion
Brown	Red onion
Warm brown	Willow bark

Water-Based Pigments

By far the easiest way of obtaining colours for Mokuhanga prints is by using tubes of ready-made watercolour pigments. There is a difference, however, between Japanese watercolour pigments such as 'Holbein' and Western pigments. Japanese pigments do not contain ox gall, an additive that is used to improve the flow of the pigment and acts as a dispersant in

Western watercolours. As this is not necessarily required or desired for Mokuhanga, it is missing from Japanese pigments and the colours are consequently more vibrant. Tubes are best to use because it is possible to calibrate exactly how much water you add to the pigment, to achieve the desired consistency for printing. Pans of watercolour are also not used as the hues tend to be less intense and more water is necessary to release the colour, interfering with the printing process. Watercolour and gouache can be used but it is important to bear in mind that gouache is a heavier pigment than watercolour and it is mixed with white, making it opaque. If used it should be for the final printing, after the watercolour layers.

Acrylic is a water-based paint, but it should never be used for Japanese woodcuts as it dries quickly, is opaque and has a plastic component that seals the woodgrain of the woodblock. Water-based printing inks are designed to be used with a roller and are also not really suitable.

SUMI

Sumi literally means 'ink' in Japanese. It is an ink that produces the most beautiful lustrous black (there are now other *sumi* colours available but black is the traditional colour). It was used

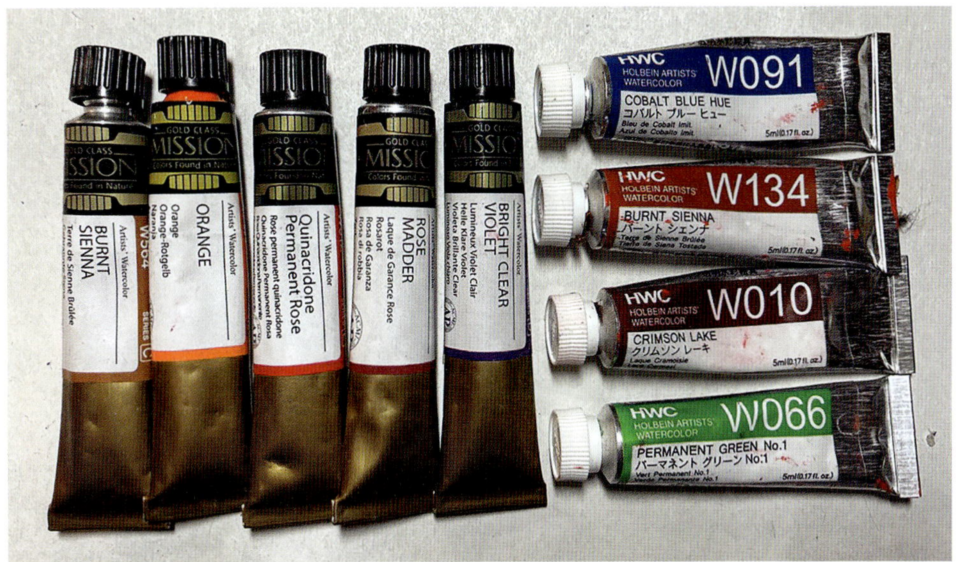

Some of my tubes of watercolour pigment.

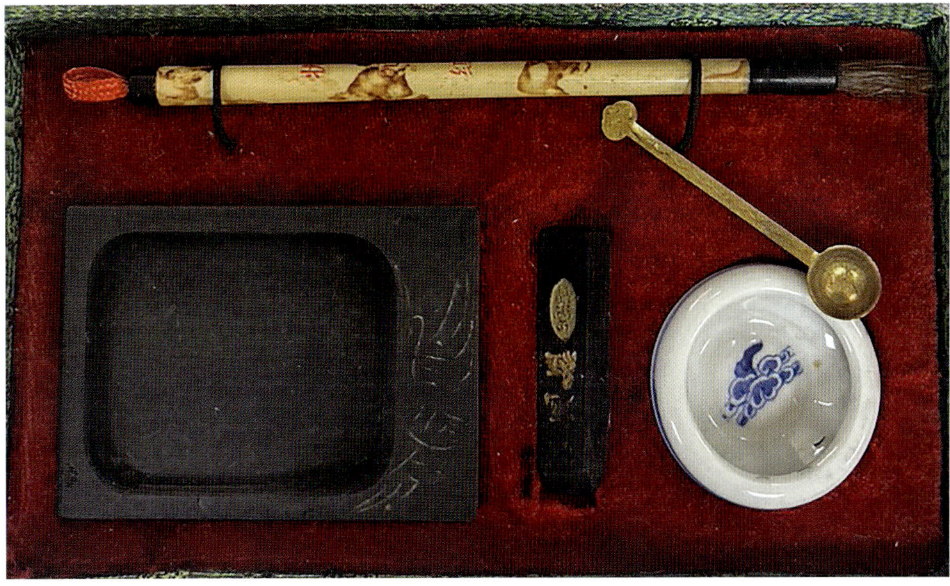

Delightful tiny *sumi* box containing inkstone, spoon for adding water, *sumi* stick and calligraphy brush.

throughout East Asia for calligraphy and printing. The earliest recorded use of *sumi* ink dates back to the second century BCE in China. In Japan, *sumi* ink sticks began to be produced from 710 CE at Nara, the Imperial capital in the eighth century, and they are still being made there today. *Sumi* ink is made of soot, collagen, perfumes and oils.

The oldest method of soot collection is from burnt pine called *Shoenboku*. *Sumi* ink made from pine soot has a slightly bluish tinge. Pine branches or roots are burnt in tall chimneys – the best-quality soot is collected furthest away from the flame source.

The other method of traditional soot collection is called *Yuenboku (*Lamp Black) made from the accumulated soot produced on the lid of a clay pot from a lighted wick. It produces a brownish-black ink that dries with a slightly shiny surface. The traditional methods are still in use today.

Manufacture of *Sumi*

Binder or animal glue called *nikawa* is heated until it is liquid and then mixed with the soot. Then perfumes are added such as camphor and musk and also oils such as sesame, soy or camelia and up to 27 different ingredients. It is possible to tell the difference between an expensive and inexpensive *sumi* ink by the smell: cheaper versions use fish oil instead of the more fragrant expensive *sumi*.

The mixture is kneaded together while warm and in modern times beaten with a hammer on a heated anvil to keep the *sumi* malleable. The warm ink mixture is rolled into a cylinder and pressed into a mould, forming solid sticks. When cooled the ink sticks are trimmed and dried from between six months to up to two years.

The sticks are embellished with intricate designs pressed into the surface and placed in decorative boxes; they are highly prized as gifts.

Using a *Sumi* Ink Stick

To make a liquid ink using a *sumi* stick for either calligraphy or printing requires a bit of application. First a small amount of water is placed onto an inkstone or *suzuri,* then the ink stick is rubbed against the inkstone releasing the *sumi,* more water is added in incremental amounts, while continuing to rub with

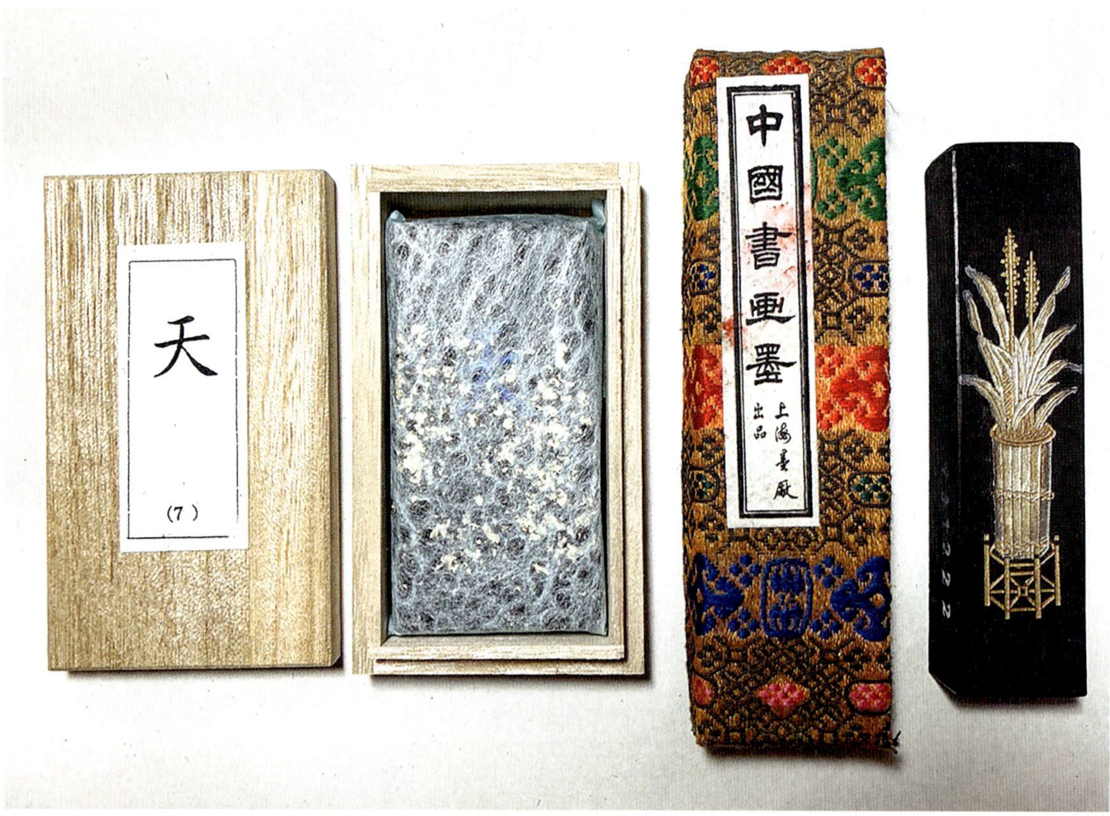

Sumi sticks wrapped in beautiful packaging.

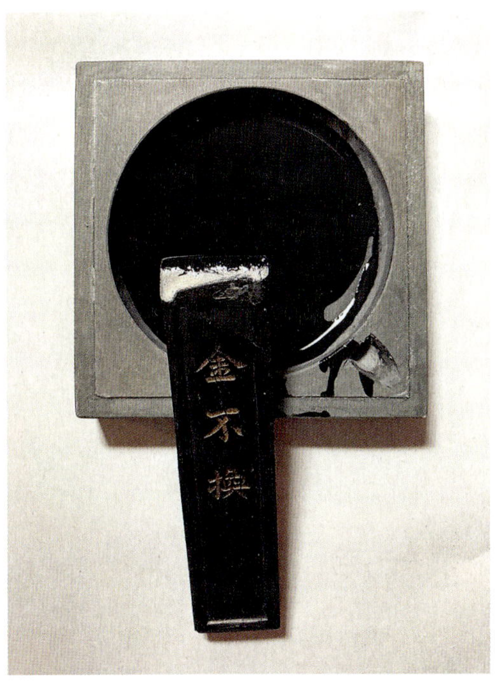

Rubbing the *sumi* stick in the inkstone, with a small amount of water.

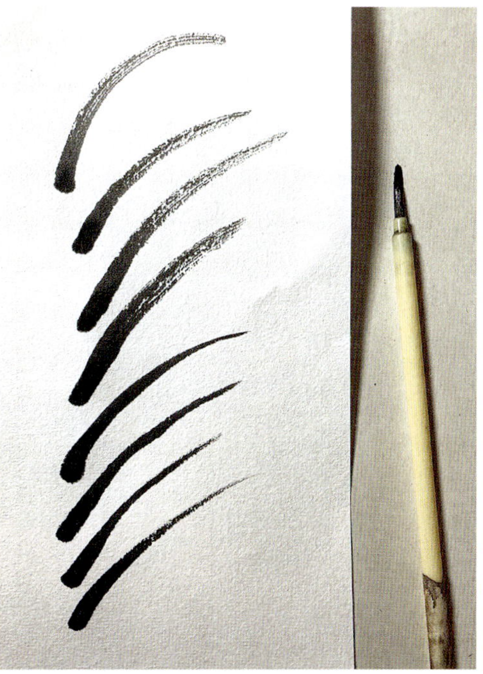

Testing the blackness of the ink to get the right shade of black.

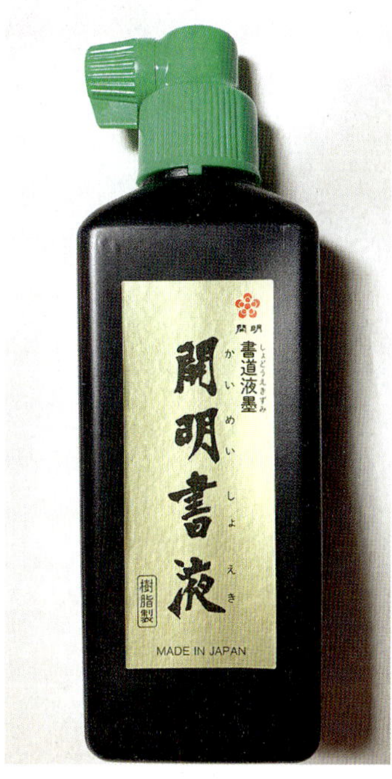

Ready-made liquid *sumi,* or *bokuju.*

the *sumi* stick, until the required amount of ink is produced of the correct shade of black.

The ink would then be decanted into a lotus leaf palette ready for dipping in the calligraphy brush, or for printing.

For printing, leftover sticks were also used. They were soaked in water for three or four days breaking down the ink-stick pieces, then ground smooth with a mortar. *Sumi* made in this way is called *tsukesumi*; it produces a strong black but can be a little coarse for printing fine detailed work. For areas of printing such as hair, a glossy black was achieved by adding a small amount of *nikawa* or binder to the ink.

In 1898 a more practical liquid *sumi* was invented by a Japanese company called Kaimei. This is called *bokuju*. It is ready for use, relatively inexpensive, produces a very strong black and can be diluted through all the shades of grey. The Chinese also make *bokuju*. It is important to get the right *sumi* ink as there are cheap modern alternatives using synthetic resin mixed with carbon black that is more like thin paint than the traditional rich *sumi* ink. Look for the brand Kaimei or *bokuju*.

WOOD

Cherrywood

The prints made by the *ukiyō-e* artists of the Edo period in Japan would have been mostly made from wild mountain cherrywood woodblocks, *yamazakura* (Prunus serrulate). The trees were grown on the mountains near the sea on the Izu peninsula near Tokyo. This wood was chosen for its plentiful supply, its fine, even woodgrain (which is highly cohesive and does not splinter) and for the fact that due to its hardness, up

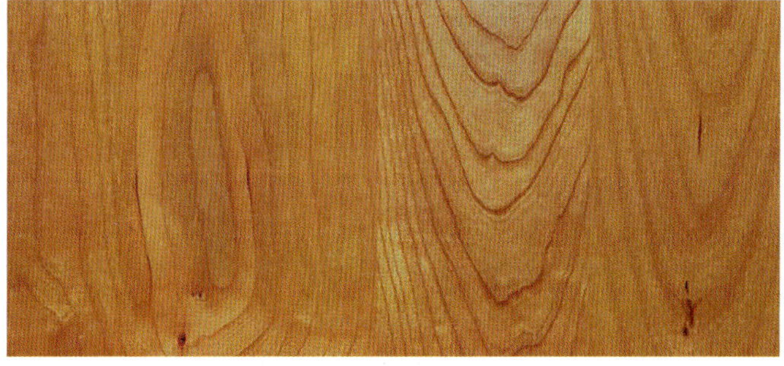

The warm tone of cherrywood.

to 10,000 impressions could be made before the carved edges of the woodcut began to erode. The hardness of the wood meant that chisels and mallets were used for the incredibly fine detailed cut blocks. The carver would begin with a thick piece of cherrywood approximately 3.5cm (1¼ in) and carve the block on both sides. After extensive print runs when the lines began to erode, the surface of the block would be planed down and the image recut. In this way a popular artist such as Utamaro would have prints sold for as long as there was a market to buy them.

The blocks were cut from the side grain of the tree trunk, down the wood grain, leaving intact the xylem tubes of the wood that transport water from the roots of the tree to its branches. This is important, as water absorption is a crucial factor in Mokuhanga printing. Blocks cut from the same tree were highly prized for their uniformity, harder parts of the wood being reserved for the all-important keyblock or outline block. The straight grain also made the wood less likely to warp when wet.

There is a lengthy process of seasoning the wood; two years before it is roughly cut into planks, several more years before the wood can be seen to be of a sufficiently high quality to be made into printable blocks. The surface would be prepared by planing carefully in different directions, grinding with a whetstone and rubbing with *tokusa* (rush leaves used for scouring pots).

The appearance of woodgrain in the print was not a desired effect in *ukiyō-e* prints and straight woodgrain was preferred to irregular patterns, making cutting easier and the blocks less prone to warping. Contemporary artists however often show woodgrain in their prints to great effect.

Supplies of *yamazakura* are dwindling now due to a diminished market and timber felling practices. As a result, the cherrywood woodblocks are expensive to buy. It is for this reason that block-makers today often supply cherrywood that is faced on both sides over a plywood inner layer. Contemporary artists have no need to print thousands of impressions or deal with the hardness of cherrywood and so other woods tend to be used more often today.

Other Types of Wood used in Japanese Woodcut

Magnolia *Hō*

Magnolia obovate, called *hō*. It is a surprisingly lightweight wood, much softer than cherrywood to cut, with an even texture.

Boxwood *Tsuge*

Boxwood grows very slowly so the woodgrain is consequently very close together. This makes the wood especially good for fine cutting, essential for areas such as the hairline in *ukiyō-e* prints (coincidentally *tsuge* is used to make combs). The boxwood cut areas would be inserted into the main woodblock.

Showing the cut lines for side grain blocks from a cherrywood tree trunk.

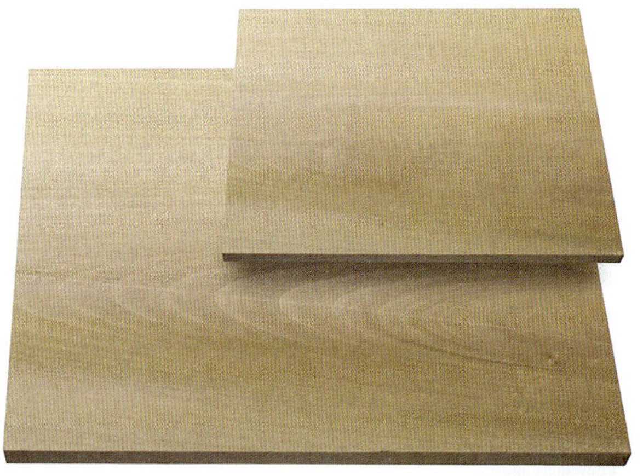

Magnolia.

Katsura

Cercidiphyllum japonicum or *katsura* has a coarser texture than *hō* but it has an even straight grain and again is easy to cut. It holds fine lines very well and when printed exhibits very little shrinkage. However, *Katsura* and *hō* can be difficult to source in the West and often come in small-sized blocks limiting their application.

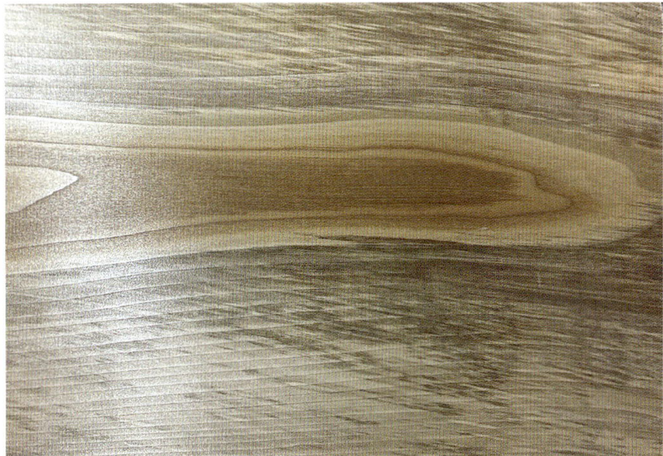

Katsura with a lovely woodgrain.

Shina **Plywood**

Tilia japonica or *shina* is the wood that is used most often by contemporary artists. It is called basswood in the United States and has similar qualities to lime wood, indeed it smells of old churches. It has a fine grain, even texture and is soft and easy to cut. When buying *shina* it is a good idea to buy a block with a thicker face of *shina* over the plywood so that you are cutting *shina* for your woodcut and not cutting too much into the ply. Economy *shina* plywood means exactly that; sometimes there are visible joins with the economy blocks. It is best to avoid these areas if possible as they can appear as an unwanted line in your finished print.

Shina is a delight to carve, however; it does not splinter, rarely chips and can be sourced in the West in blocks of up to around 60 × 90cm in size (approximately A1). As it is a relatively soft wood it does not hold fine lines as well as *katsura* but with good-quality sharp tools, a fine relief line can be maintained.

If the surface of the woodblock feels rough to the touch, some Mokuhanga practitioners use a fine-grade sandpaper to smooth the face of the block prior to cutting. There is some disagreement about the efficacy of this as the sandpaper can raise a nap that means that the watercolour pigment does not print cleanly.

Birch

Birch wood is more readily available. It is harder to cut than *shina* resulting in tools requiring frequent honing and sharpening sessions. It also tends to splinter. It does however, offer a more pronounced woodgrain for printing and could be included for that purpose.

MDF/Chipboard/Hardboard

These woods are not really recommended for Japanese woodcut. Not only are they hard on cutting tools, requiring frequent

Shina plywood also known as Asian ply or Japanese ply.

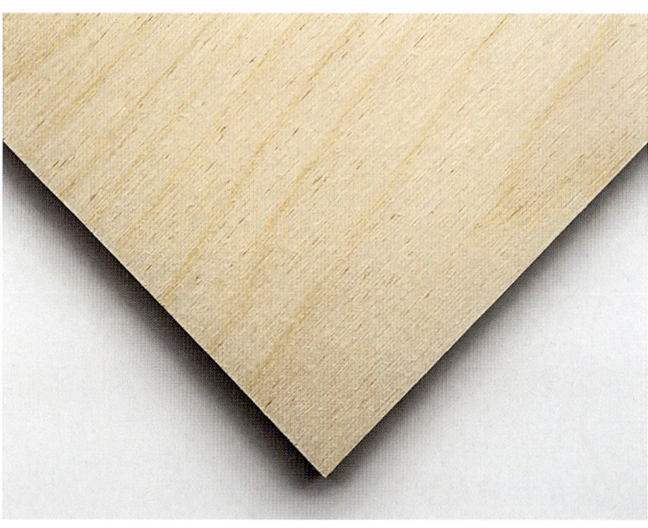

Birch lends itself to printing woodgrain.

tool sharpening, but because of their lack of character they have little to offer the finished print.

Care of Woodblocks

Blocks should be dried flat and then stored vertically, wrapped in a protective layer of newspaper or the more traditional cloth. Care should be taken that the blocks do not get damaged or damp and are away from sources of heat and light.

If a block has warped through repeated dampening and incorrect storage, it can be dampened again and left under a weight until dry and flat.

If there is no colour change in your printing it is fine to leave the colour to dry in the block. This keeps the woodgrain open and when water is applied prior to the next printing, the pigment in the woodgrain is reactivated. Excessive scrubbing of the colour from the woodblock can easily damage vulnerable fine lines.

PAPER

Japanese paper is called *washi*. 'Wa' denotes Japan and '*shi*' paper. Just the name *washi* however can refer to any paper that is manufactured in Japan, but for Mokuhanga it is the handmade *washi* that is used. This paper has evolved over time to suit specifically the requirements of Japanese woodcut and is the best paper to use. Paper was brought to Japan from China by Korean Buddhist monks in 610 – as a correlation paper only came to the West in 1100, nearly 500 years later, when the Moors brought it along the Silk Road into Spain.

Types of Fibre Used in *Washi*

It is often mistakenly referred to as rice paper, but it has nothing to do with rice; instead the most commonly used fibre is from the inner bark of paper mulberry Broussonetia papyrifera, called *kōzo* in Japanese. It is used most often because it is easy to cultivate and the long *kōzo* fibres when formed into thin translucent paper are remarkably strong even when wet.

Another fibre used is *Mitsumata* Edgeworthia chrysantha, which has shorter fibres than *kōzo* and can only be

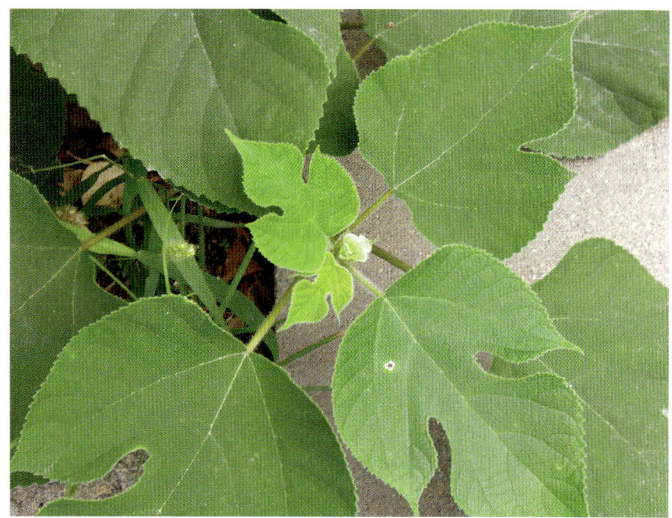

Kozo or paper mulberry shoots.

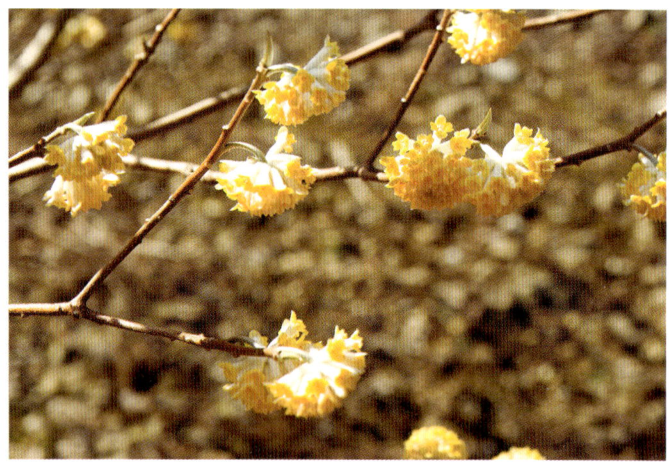

Mitsumata blossom growing along London's Embankment.

harvested every three years. It is often used joined with *kōzo* and has a warm tone with a high degree of absorbency. It used to be used for Japanese banknotes. I have seen its pretty yellow flowers in spring growing on the Thames Embankment in London.

The last of the main fibres used for Mokuhanga is *Gampi* Wikstroemia Sikokiana. *Gampi* grows in the wild and is resistant to cultivation. It forms a crisp, smooth surface with a beautiful sheen. It is often used for book conservation as it can be made into very thin, fine sheets of paper that are nevertheless very strong. It is a highly prized paper but due to its resistance to cultivation it is the most expensive to buy.

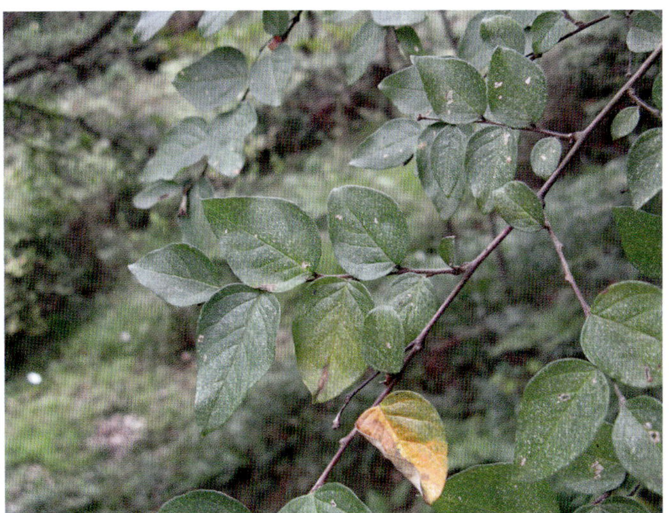

Gampi growing in mountain regions.

Paper Associations

The moist temperate climate of Japan is ideal for growing paper fibre and each region developed their own techniques to suit their indigenous plants. Many of the papermakers in Japan are family concerns that group together to form associations. So *Tosa* denotes paper that is made in Shikoku, *Awagami* is from Awa, *Mino* from the Gifu Prefecture and *Echizen* from Kyoto. The Echizen Paper Association represents around 70 paper producers such as Yamaguchi and Iwano. The famous *ukiyō-e* prints from the Edo period were made with *hoshō* style paper from Echizen. Paper has been made in the Echizen area for 1,500 years.

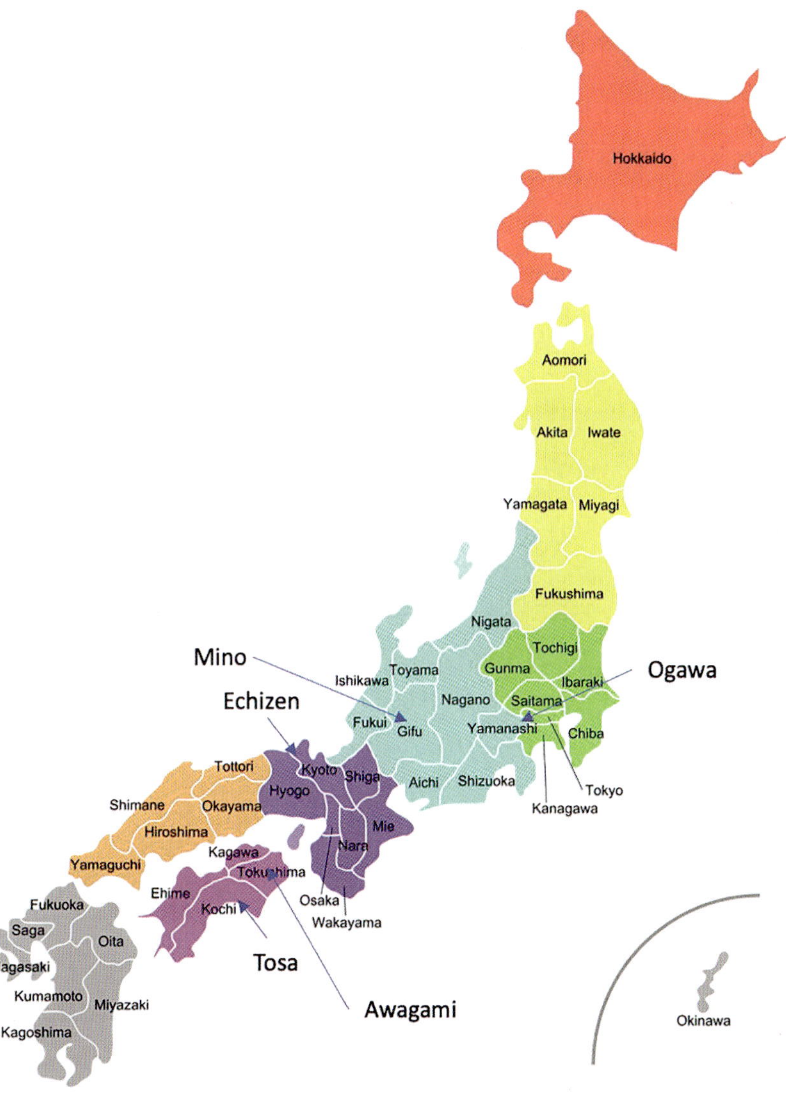

Map showing where some of Japan's paper associations are located.

Washi

Washi comes in many different weights, textures and colours. The heavier the weight of the paper, the better it is suited for printing multiple layers of colour.

Different varieties of *washi* paper from translucent thin tissue paper to heavy cartridge paper weight.

Paper has a grain direction which can be ascertained by a simple test: lightly bend the paper first along the long side and then the short side. You will find that one direction will 'give' more than the other and this denotes the paper grain direction. When printing large woodblocks, it is better to align the paper grain direction and the wood grain direction for ease of printing.

The special characteristics of *washi* are that the *kozō* fibres are hand beaten, not cut, so the fibres remain long, forming a dimensionally stable paper that keeps its shape even when wet, an essential consideration for Mokuhanga. Even with the pressure of the *baren* and the additional moisture absorbed from the pigments and dampened woodblock, the paper does not get distorted. This sophisticated paper means that multi-colour prints can be made from multiple blocks using a paper that is able to withstand repeated dampening, without losing registration. In the West paper historically was made from fabric, cotton rag, hemp and linen rag. It is said that the collection of rags for paper production led to the spread of the plague. Now paper in the West is often made mixed with soft wood pulp from the fastest growing trees such as spruce, pine and birch that have very short fibres with nothing like the

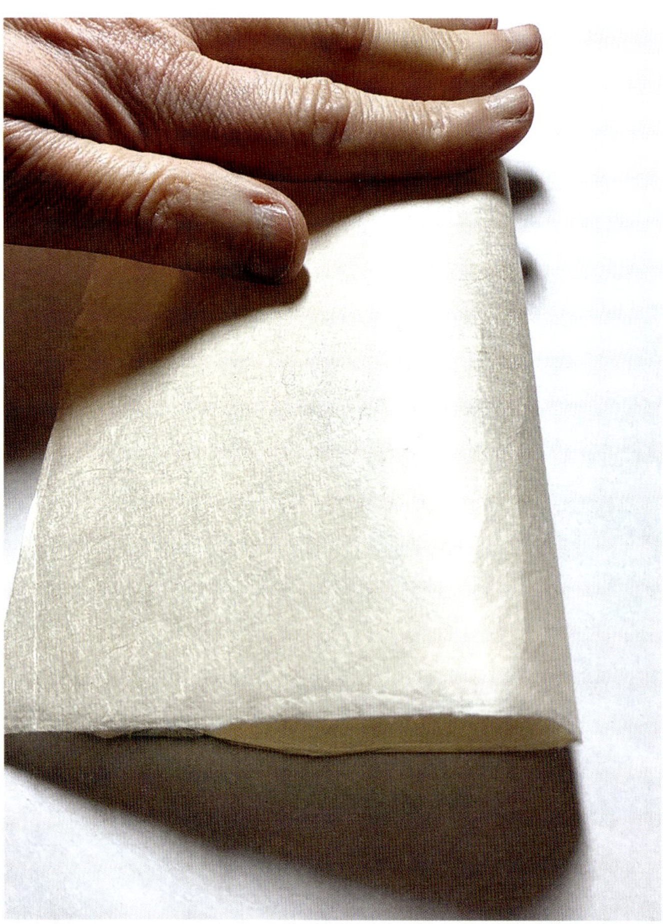

Testing the paper grain direction, where there is more 'give', that denotes the paper grain direction.

strength of handmade Japanese *washi*. China and Korea also make their own *kōzo* paper – however, due to the differences in climate with Japan, their *kōzo* fibres do not grow as long and consequently their paper is not as strong as *washi*.

Paper Production

Traditional handmade papermaking is hard and painstaking work – indeed, there was an old adage warning parents never to let their daughters marry papermakers. Added to this was the cold, as papermaking used to take place in the winter months when there was less farm work; now it can take place all year around.

Stages of *Washi* Production

The *kōzo* shoots are harvested from the parent stumps in the autumn. The bundled sticks are steamed to make it easier to strip the outer bark, revealing the inner white bark *shirokawa* that is used for the papermaking.

Cleaning (Chiriyori)

The bark is rinsed of impurities traditionally in a flowing stream. In Kyoto where the Echizen Paper Association is based, the water is very pure and ideal for papermaking. Quick rinsing may leave impurities in the fibres and produces a paper that is light green or brownish in colour. Thorough rinsing results in off-white fibres that are left to naturally bleach in the sun or on the snow. The fibres are then softened in a soda ash solution and again checked for impurities, a job that was often given to the older women as it meant sitting down but was, nevertheless, back breaking work as it meant bending over with hands in freezing cold water for long periods of time.

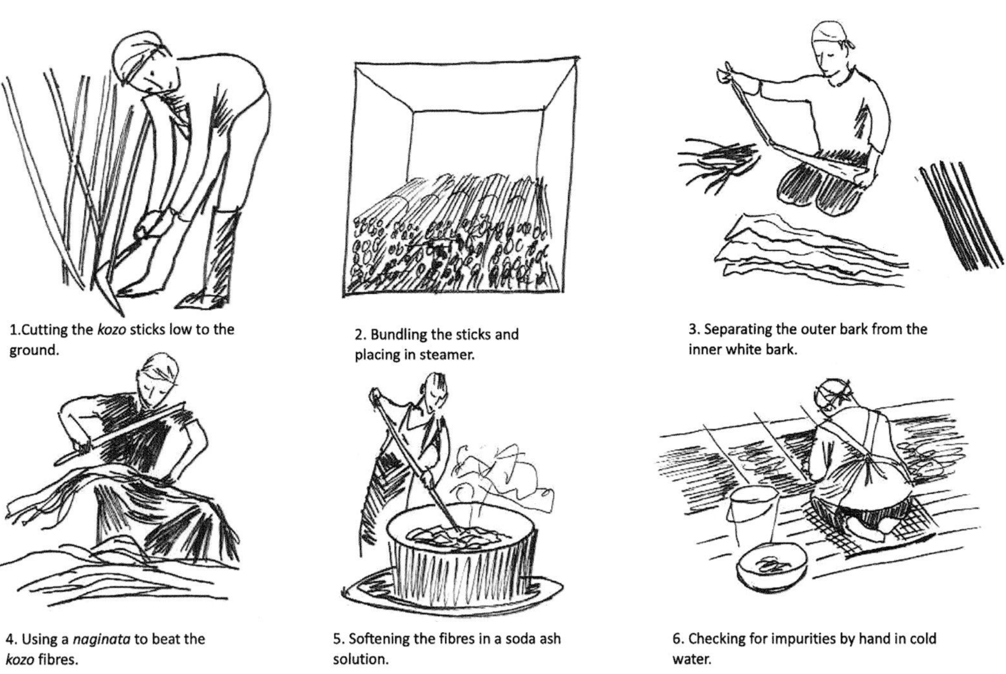

Showing the different stages in traditional papermaking pre-production.

Beating (Kokai)

The fibres are then beaten so they are separated but not broken. Traditionally this would be done by hand with a wooden stick called a *naginata* for a few hours, but often now the same can be accomplished with an automated stamper in half an hour.

Dispersing agent (Neri)

Finally, making the paper itself. The fibres are placed in a wooden vat of water *maguwa*. To the water is added *neri*, a viscous substance from the *tororo aoi* (Abelmoschus maniiot) root that when added to the water allows the fibres to be suspended evenly and not clump together. The amount of *neri* used depends on the weather, the type of paper being made and is based on the knowledge and experience of the papermaker.

Sheeting (Kamisuki)

The papermaker stands at the paper vat and scoops up a slurry of paper fibres in a mould called a *sugeta*. The *keta* is the wooden frame and the *su* is a flexible screen of super fine bamboo woven together with silk threads. The fibres are held on the bamboo and the water drains through the slats. You can see the marks of the bamboo on some sheets of paper if you look carefully.

For the manufacture of super-fine *gampi* sheets these textured marks are avoided by the simple expedient of laying a piece of sheer gauze onto the bamboo slats before papermaking. Using a technique called the *nagashi-zuki* or flowing method, the printmaker washes the fibres up the *sugeta* in a rocking motion that is incredibly skilful and ensures an even coverage of fibre over the whole surface. Layers of paper fibre are built up by scooping the *sugeta* again and again into the paper vat. When the printmaker is satisfied he has the correct thickness for the paper, he separates the *su* from the *keta* and lays the thin layer of paper fibre onto the post or *shito* of freshly made paper. The paper doesn't stick to the layer below because of those long *kōzo* fibres and the presence of *neri*. (In the West

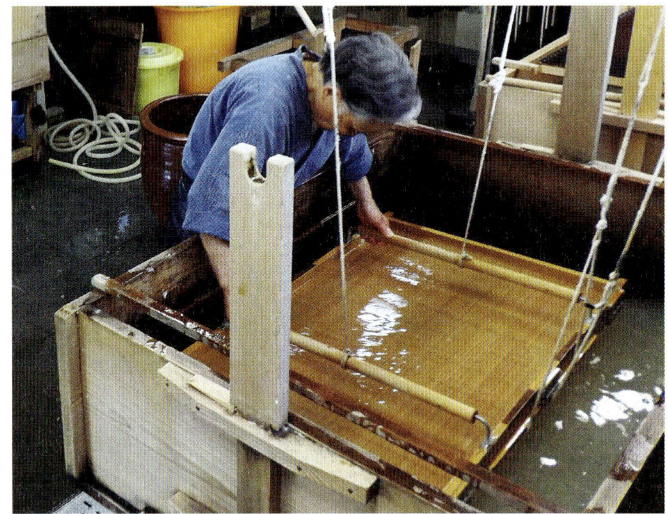
The papermaker at work scooping paper fibre onto the paper mould or *sugeta*.

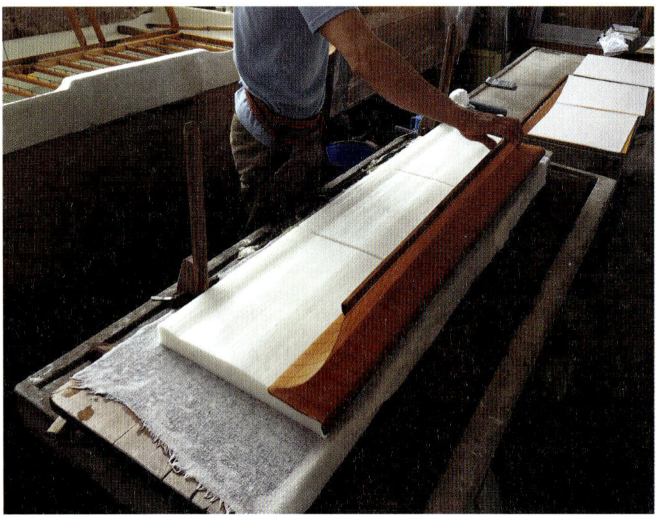
Post or *shito* stack of freshly made paper.

paper is couched with an interleaving blotting sheet or felt to prevent the sheets from sticking together.)

Drying (Kanso)

When a sufficient quantity of paper has been made the *shito* is left overnight to drain. Later a weighted board is placed on top of the *shito* to drain out the excess water. Then the individual moist sheets are peeled from the stack and brushed using a soft *mizu* brush onto wooden boards, traditionally made of cypress or ginkgo, to dry in the sun for one to three hours. It is a testament to the strength of the paper that you can see images of papermakers

bunching the wet paper up with one hand as they smooth it down with a brush in the other. (Western paper is not treated this way, and would tear easily.) It is more common now to brush the paper onto heated stainless-steel sheets to dry quickly.

Identifying the printing side of the paper

There is a definite front and back to the paper that can be identified by feeling with your hand. The side that was face down on the bamboo slats as the paper was being formed is also the side that is brushed face down onto the drying substrate. When the paper is dry, this side is smoother than the back where the paper fibres have been lifted by the brushing. The smooth side is the printing side for Mokuhanga.

Sizing

Japanese paper is receptive to water pigment; the pigment effectively dyes the paper and does not sit on the surface as

Tell-tale laid lines and rough texture of the back of the paper.

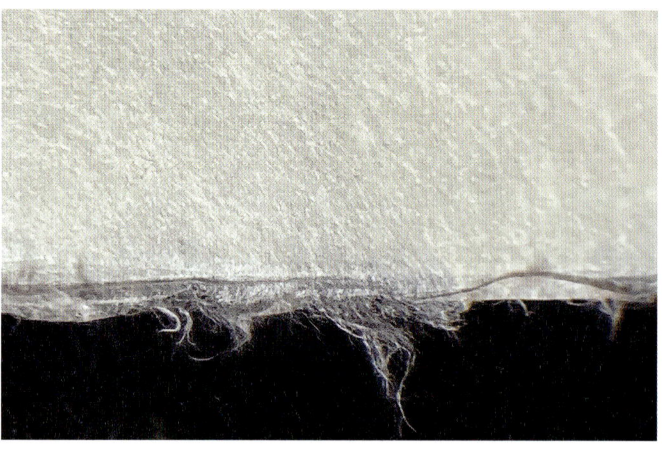
Smooth side of the front or printing side of the paper.

25g (1oz) Japanese *nikawa* or 5 sheets of gelatine

1 tsp alum

1 pint water

Melt the gelatine over a low heat with a small amount of water. Do not overheat. Add the alum until the mixture turns transparent. If necessary strain through muslin in case of impurities. Note that size does not keep and needs to be made fresh for each application. Brushing the size to the paper should be undertaken with a broad brush *dōsabake* in even strokes with the grain of the paper and hung to dry.

oil-based inks would do. To control the spread of the pigment the smooth side of the printing paper is brushed lightly with size called *dosa*. This is an animal glue *nikawa* mixed with alum that controls the absorbency of the paper. Some artists like to play with the absorbency of the paper with their prints and prefer to do their sizing themselves.

Buying Paper

Buying *washi* paper from the West can be problematical because the paper names are often inconsistent. Paper names tend to refer to the region where it was made, the paper fibre, the style of papermaking or some other characteristic. In Japan it is possible for the artist to establish a relationship with a tried and trusted papermaker but that can be harder to do from the West.

Things to Look for in a Paper

Handmade

Handmade paper can be identified by its four deckle edges *mimitsuki* (though it is interesting to note that deckle edges can be simulated with a serrated ruler). Handmade paper is generally considered to be better equipped to deal with multiple printings than machine-made paper. Deckle edges in the West denote a handmade paper and are given some prominence to show this – however, in Japan where the paper is mostly handmade anyway, this has not always been seen as so important.

Price

Price is often a guide to a 'good' paper, but a very expensive paper may not be ideal for the print that you have in mind. If you have spent a lot of money on the paper sometimes that can be an inhibiting factor when it comes to printing. Here are some of the things to look out for when buying paper:

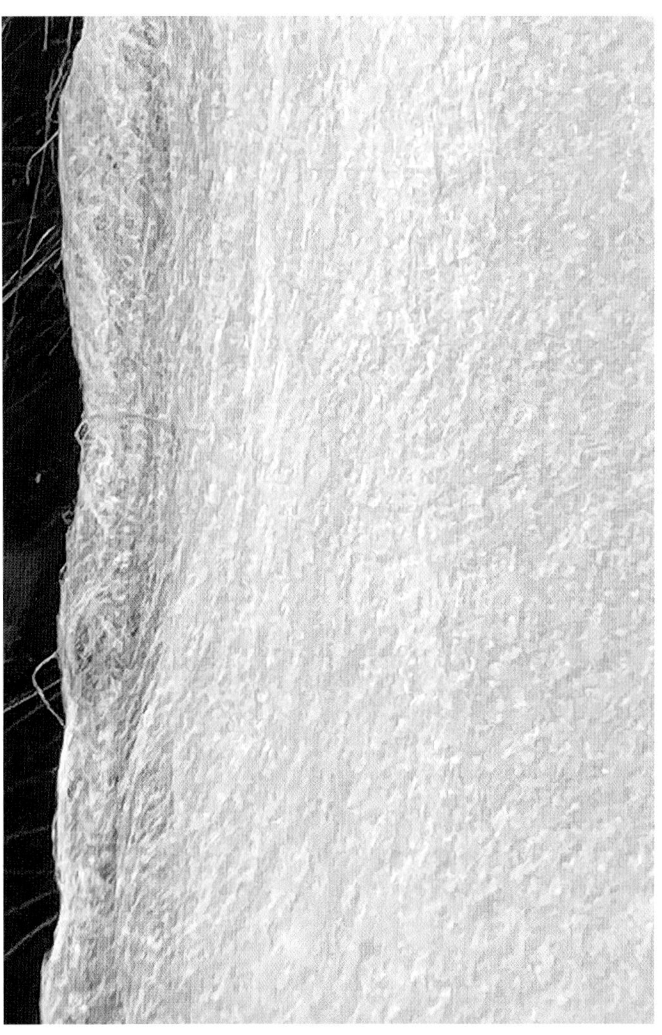

Ragged appearance of deckle edge denoting a handmade paper.

Kōzo

Look for a paper that has a high percentage of *kōzo* fibre. The paper seller should be able to tell you this. There is a paper called *Kizuki* that is 100 per cent *kōzo* fibre but it is consequently rather expensive.

Bleaching

Don't go for an overly bleached paper as this probably means that the paper has been chemically treated resulting in a weaker, inferior paper.

Shin

Shin as a prefix generally denotes that the paper is machine made; again handmade paper tends to be stronger but machine-made paper is cheaper and good for proofing.

Sizing

Look for a paper that is lightly sized. *Dōsa or Dōsabiki* is an animal-based glue that is brushed onto the paper usually on one side only. It is used to add toughness and limit the absorbency of the pigment. To test whether a paper is sized or not, try licking a corner of the paper – if it is absorbed immediately your paper is unsized.

Origins

Papers from Thailand, Korea and China don't tend to be as strong as Japanese papers due to the different climatic conditions. The more tropical climate of Thailand for instance causes the *kōzo* to grow quickly but the shoots are spindlier and often have difficult-to-eradicate resinous spots that end up in the final paper. Thai *kōzo* is often just used for machine-made paper.

Supplier

The best advice would be to buy your paper from a reputable paper shop who will have a relationship with the papermakers in Japan.

Feel of the paper

If you can, handle the paper before you buy it. It is best to ask for permission before you do this as the paper shop will not be able to sell a marked paper. Most paper shops have samples for this purpose. You can tell a lot from handling the paper: firstly, its overall quality including its weight or thickness. Paper that is too thin will not take multiple printings; too thick and you may struggle to get a good hand-printed impression without using a specialist *baren*. Check out the colour in natural light; is it suitable for the colours that you have in mind? Feel the

If you are making a single-colour print, you can use a lightweight paper. But for multiple colours involving many different colour separations it is advisable to go for a heavier-weight paper. Here are some papers that I have tried and can recommend:

Lightweight 18–29gsm

> *Ino shi*
>
> *Gampi*
>
> *Kawanaka*
>
> *Tosa washi*
>
> *Kōzo*

Middleweight 36gsm–45gsm

> *Kitikata*
>
> *Atsukoshi*
>
> *Hosokawa*
>
> *Shoji* – machine made and handmade, comes in sheets and rolls

Heavyweight 70–90gsm

> *Bunkoshi*
>
> *Inbe*
>
> *Hoshō* – sheet, pad, rolls (*Hoshō* sheet is a better-quality paper than the *hoshō* pad)

texture – ideally it should be lightly sized which will present as a slightly smooth surface, too smooth and it is oversized and will not absorb the pigment. Buying online will not give you the same haptic information.

Especially for large prints, ensure that you have paper that fits your woodblock as not all papers are made in the large sizes. Most of the *ukiyō-e* prints of the Edo period were not large, mostly approximating to A3 in size (29.7 × 42cm). Some artists start their print design with the actual paper, letting its size, translucency and colour dictate the print itself. Or you could buy your paper in a roll and cut down for exactly the size you need.

Thinking Ahead

Lastly, if you are printing an edition, it is advisable to buy the quantity that you need as supply can be difficult and handmade papers can differ in colour and quality from one batch to the next. Sadly, also too many papermakers are finding that their children are not willing to take over the family business and

JAPAN TO UK PAPER SIZE COMPARISON

Japanese Size	Dimensions in mm	UK Size	Dimensions in mm
BO	1000 × 1414	AO	841 × 1189
B1	707 × 1000	A1	594 × 841
B2	500 × 707	A2	420 × 594
B3	353 × 500	A3	297 × 420
B4	250 × 353	A4	210 × 297
B5	176 × 250	A5	148 × 210
B6	125 × 176	A6	148 × 210

consequently there are fewer skilled papermakers in Japan than there were even ten years ago, so you may find that your favourite paper has been discontinued. Happily, by using *washi* paper and keeping a steady flow of demand from the West it may be possible to keep the remaining incredible Japanese papermakers going for many years to come.

GETTING STARTED CHECKLIST

1. Woodblocks *shina* plywood
2. Original master drawing on copy paper
3. Tracing paper
4. Carbon paper
5. Non-slip mat
6. Carving tools
7. Sharpening stones
8. Honing pad + bathroom cleanser or honing paste
9. Printing paper
10. Newsprint
11. Water bottle with fine spray
12. Zip lock bags
13. Watercolour pigments in tubes
14. *Sumi* ink
15. Western brushes
16. Japanese brushes
17. Bamboo *baren*
18. *Nori* paste, *nori* pots, chopstick
19. Pipette
20. Baking sheet
21. Non-perfumed soap
22. Pencils, metal ruler, waterpots, masking tape, pencils, coloured pencils

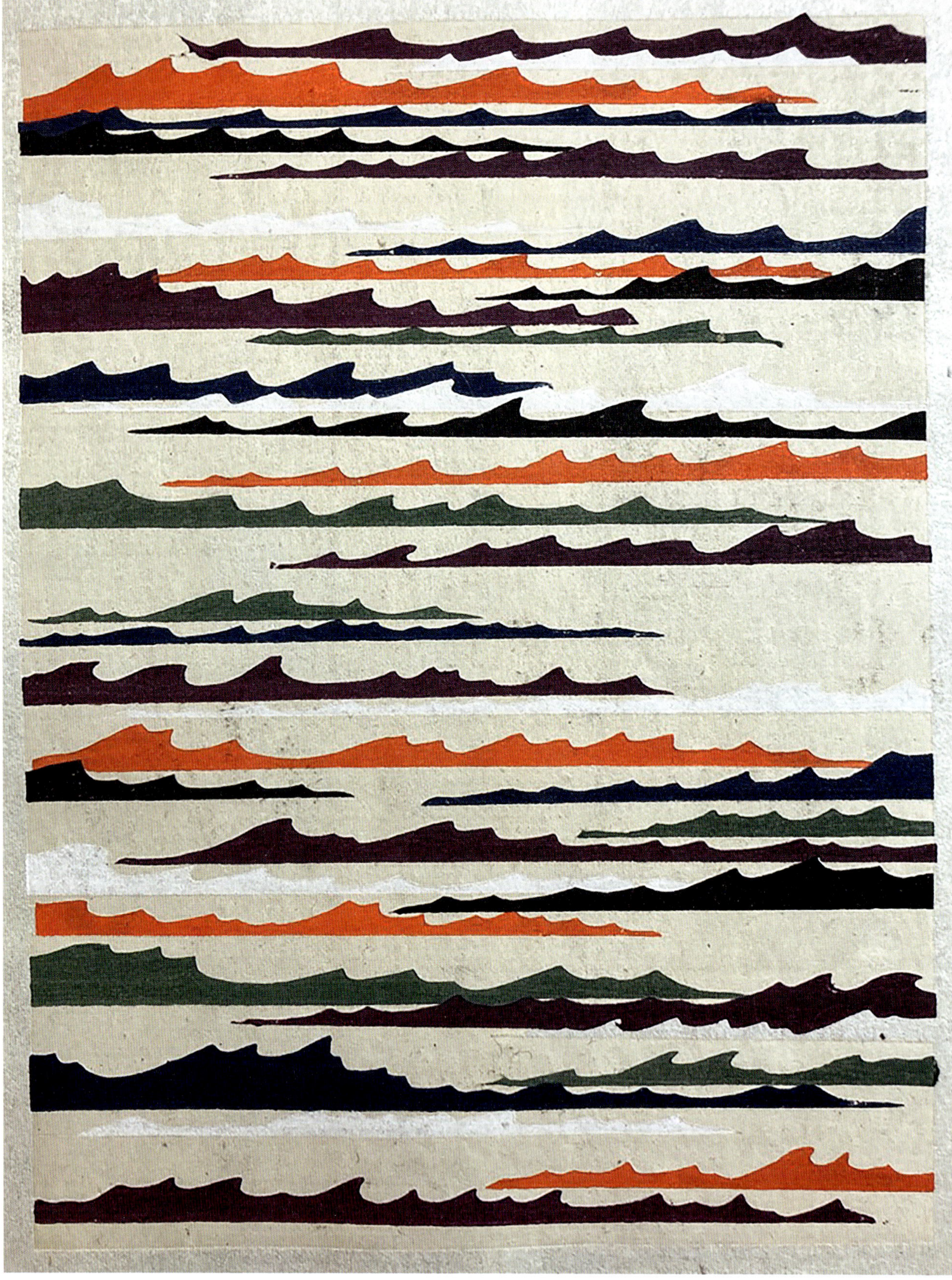

Chapter 3

DESIGN

esigning for print requires some important considerations. This chapter begins with initial starting points for a simple three-colour print, from master drawing through to making colour separations, marking up and transferring the image to the woodblock ready for cutting. Images from some of my students' prints have been included to stimulate inspiration as well as showcasing outcomes that can be expected at the beginning stages of learning the technique.

Before beginning your design, it is important to organise your work space. It does not have to be a large, fully equipped studio, in fact traditionally Japanese artists worked in very modest domestic spaces. Often, I use my dining-room table; it has an easy to wipe down Formica surface that makes it ideal to work on. I tend to only use larger studio spaces when I need to print large work. Wherever you set up, it is important to have a stable flat table to work on and to protect your back, a chair that is neither too high nor too low. An angle poise lamp will give a good directional light.

In Hiroshige's print of the late eighteenth century, you can see how strikingly modern the asymmetrical composition seems to us. The subject of the print is unusually in the background. The foreground is a domestic scene with discarded cloth, rice bowl, hairpins and cat. Parts of the composition are fragmented, the viewer looking at an image that is disappearing beyond the picture plane.

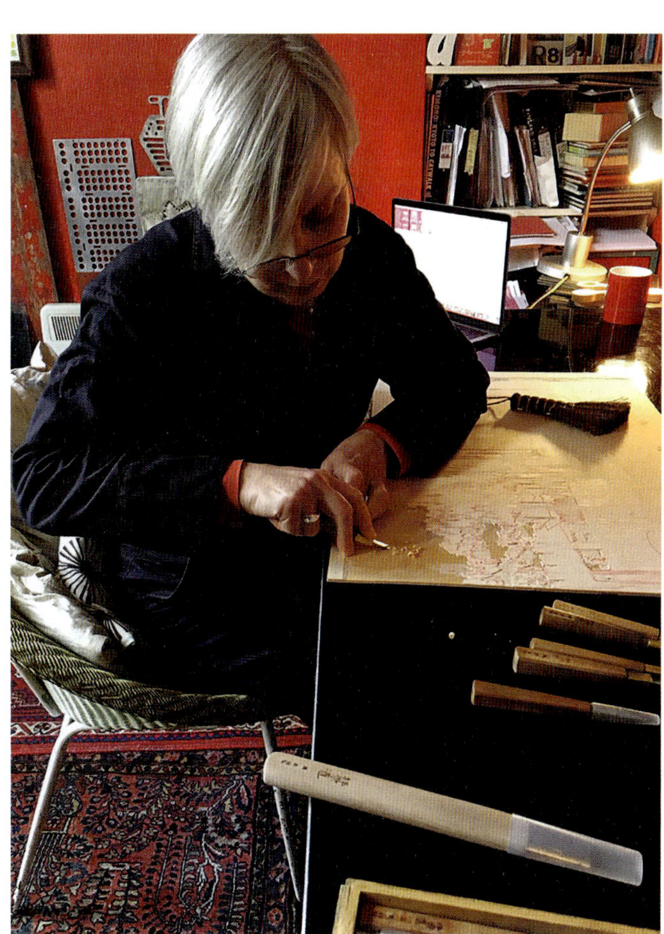

Author at work on dining room table.

◀ Artist unknown. Colour woodcut print from author's print collection.

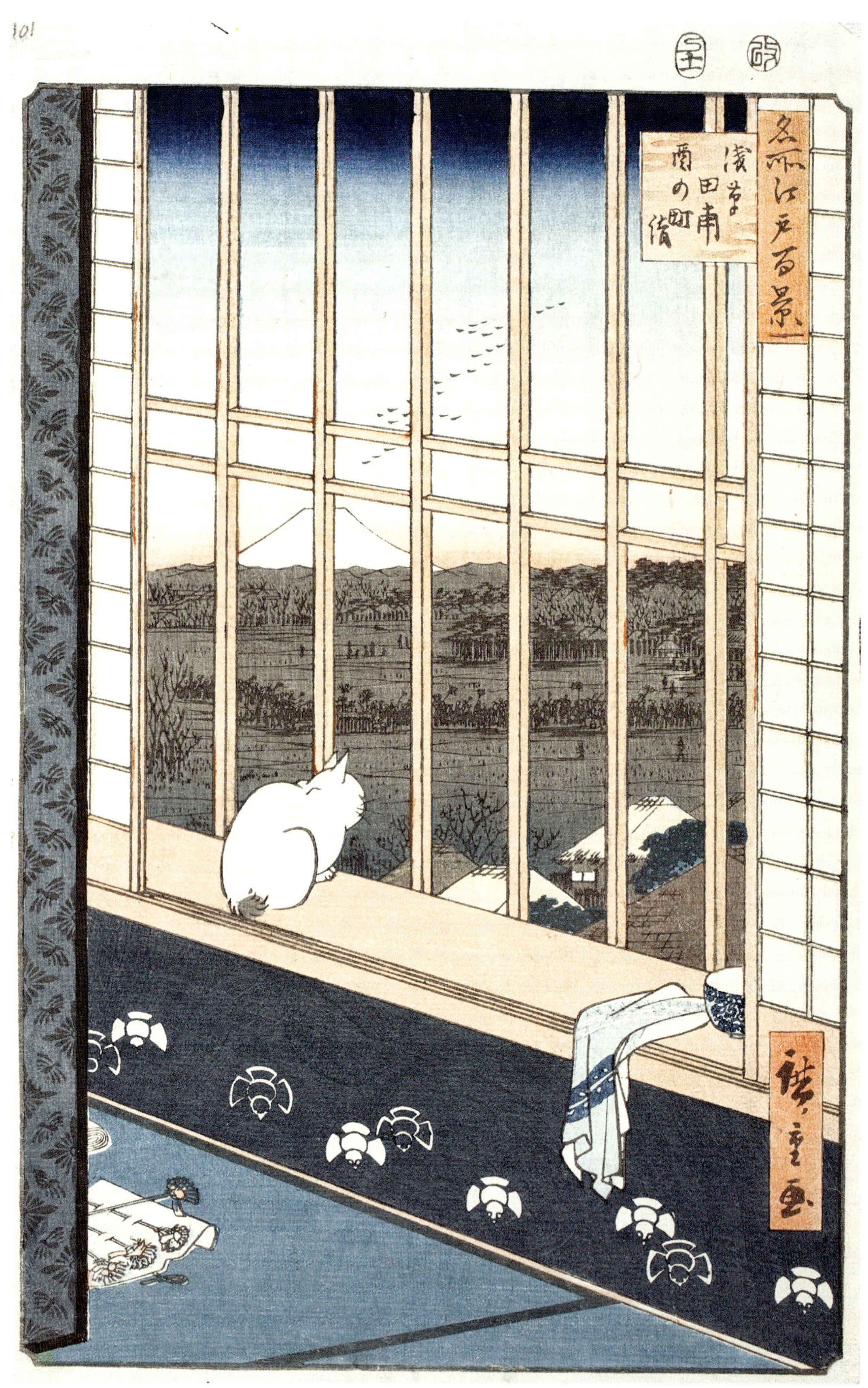

Utagawa Hiroshige, 1797–1858. *Asakusa Rice Fields and Festival Torinomachi*, 1857. Colour woodblock print (33.5 × 22.23cm).

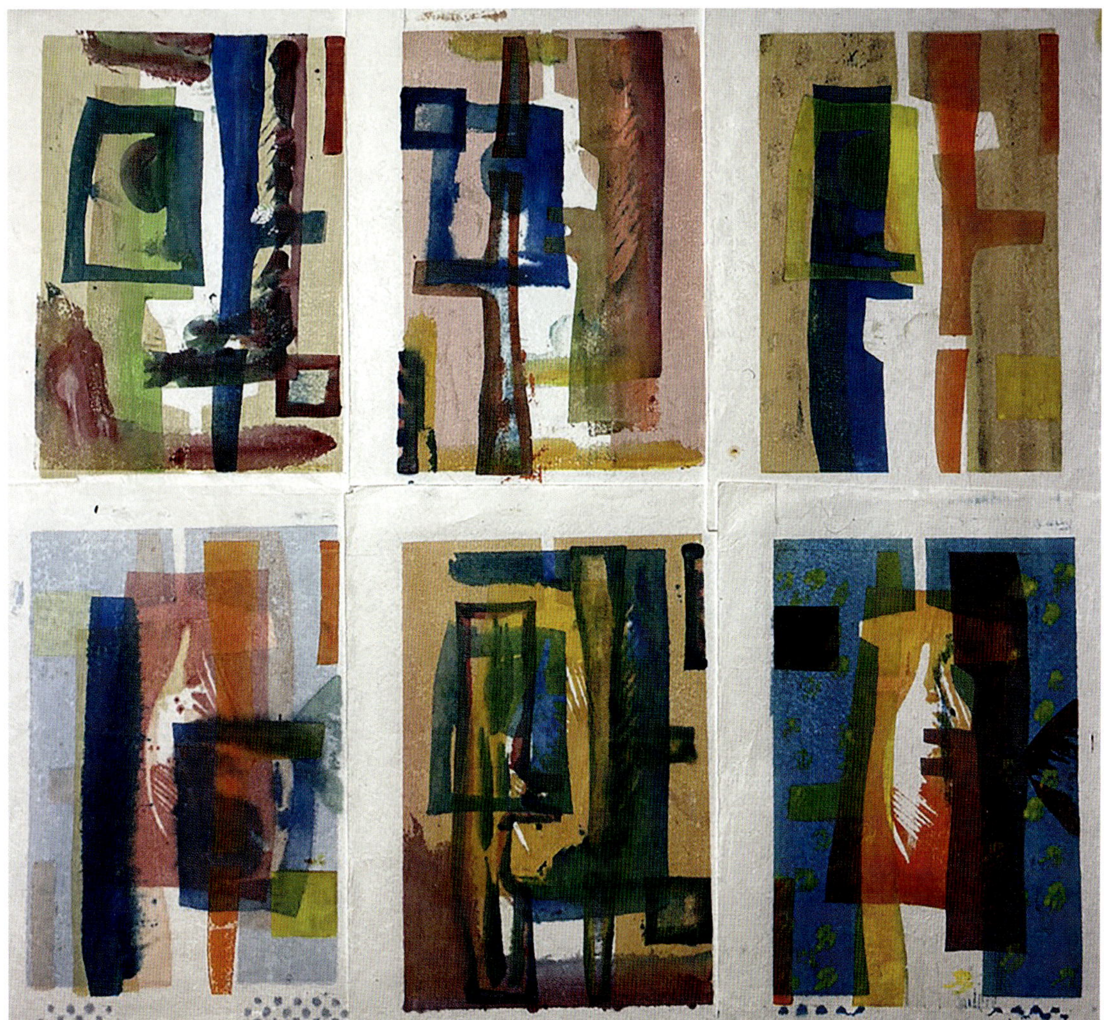

Series of prints made from simple shapes based on a sketchbook drawing. The 2cm all-round paper margin meant that the blocks could be printed upside-down too, creating new perspectives.

Making multiplate colour Japanese woodcut prints is a delightful process, but a good grounding in the basics of the technique is important. I have had complete beginners come to my class with a postcard of a print by Hokusai or Hiroshige, expecting to make a miraculous facsimile print. It is far better to start small and modest and build a repertoire of skills and understanding of this incredibly nuanced printing process.

To that end it is a good idea to start with a simple drawing, without fine lines, but including broad areas of colour. Simplification will ensure that your first experience of cutting and printing a Japanese woodcut will be an enjoyable one. Inspiration can come from many diverse sources – sketchbook

MATERIALS FOR DESIGN STAGE

1. Copy paper
2. Sharp pencil
3. Eraser
4. Biro
5. Metal ruler and set square
6. Tracing paper
7. Carbon paper
8. Dilute red watercolour and flat brush
9. *Shina* woodblock (in this example I used a woodblock measuring 225 × 300mm)

Printmaking involves quite a bit of process and this can be daunting to the new student. To introduce the technique in a manageable way, I often start my courses by asking my students to draw a simple shape no larger than 6 x 6cm, then cut it out with the tools and print it. Seeing the whole process through in a non-outcome way will help to set realistic goals for designing a multi-colour print and build experiential knowledge for later.

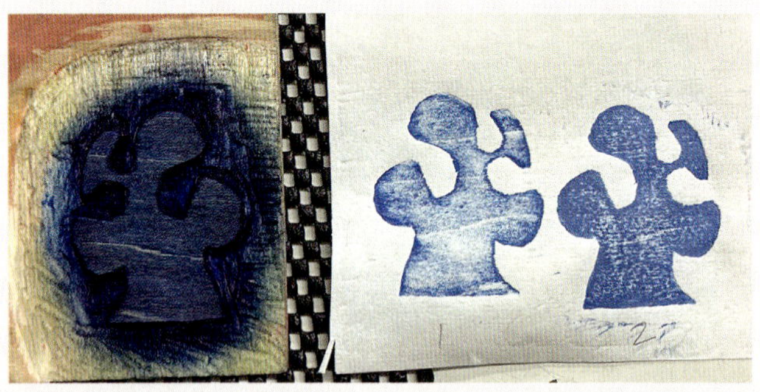

Practice piece for beginning cutting and printing. Invaluable for learning how to achieve different effects, without stress.

drawings, photographs, or even just playing with interlocking shapes. Whatever the source of your image it is important to remember that you will be working in a new medium – wood – so rather than imposing your design on the material, it is a better approach to allow the wood to dictate the kind of image you choose.

MASTER DRAWING

The first stage for making a multi-colour print is the master drawing. The idea for your print may be a small scribble in a sketchbook, but when it comes to designing your print it is important to make a master drawing that will have all the essential drawing decisions worked out and will ideally be coloured in, to make it easier for making colour separations. It is there to refer back to, as it shows the intention of your image and avoids any confusion later.

1. With a ruler draw an accurately measured box 10.5 × 15cm.
2. Look at how your image fits inside this box avoiding important details that are too close to the edge.

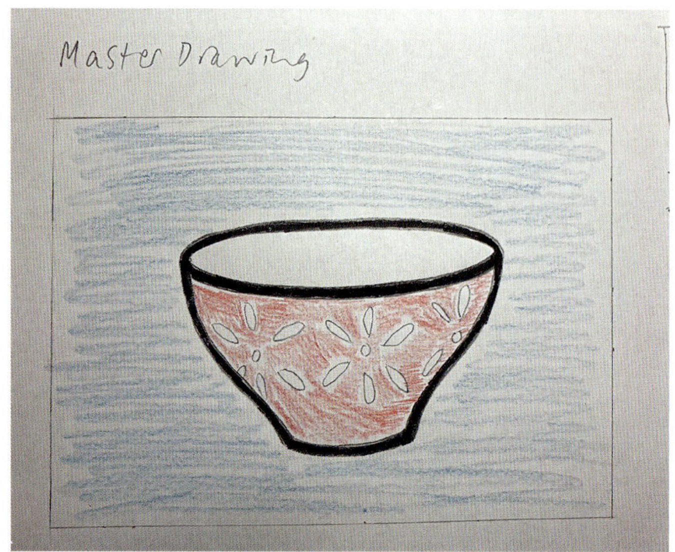

Master drawing on copy paper, in pencil, with all the colours indicated. Avoid fine line cutting as a beginner; outlines can be drawn with a Sharpie felt tip on your paper to give you the width of line to aim for, rather than a thin pencil or pen line.

3. Pay attention to the spaces between shapes (called negative spaces) as they help the flow of your composition.
4. Finish off lines where colours meet, so that it is obvious when you come to cutting where the divisions lie.

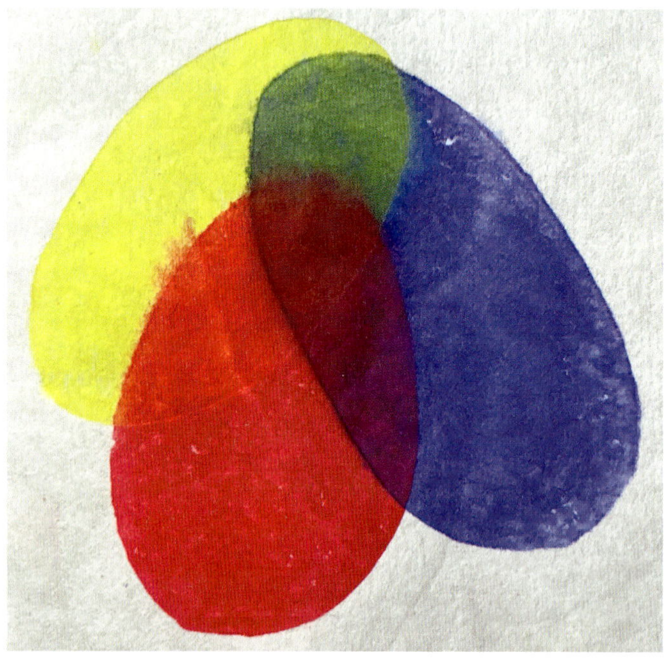

Example print showing how overlapping yellow, red and blue can give green, orange and purple colours.

Be aware of the potential of colour combination overlaps, to optimise the number of separations that you will need. In this way using the primary colours of red, yellow and blue will produce orange, green and purple when overlapped. Be aware however that some blues, like Phthalo blue, will not make purple when mixed with Vermillion red due to the presence of yellow in the pigment. Ultramarine and magenta make a good purple.

Lastly, keep it simple, try to avoid the common mistake of attempting an initial print that is too ambitious; it can leave you discouraged when it does not meet your anticipated outcome.

THUMBNAIL SEPARATIONS

When your master drawing is complete it is time to work out your colour separations. To make a multi-colour print each colour has its own separate block cut out. The colours are printed in turn, from lightest to darkest, one on top of the other to make the final print. For the thumbnail separations I draw small squares for each colour to be printed and refer back to the master drawing to look at the shape of the colour area.

I find that it also helps mentally to see the issues that may lie ahead. Overlapping colours need to be carefully drawn, ensuring that all areas of the overlap are covered and lines completed.

WOODGRAIN

It is important at this stage to look ahead to the woodblock itself and determine the orientation of your separation on the block. All woodblocks have a woodgrain direction that can be clearly seen by the growth rings visible on the surface. It is easier to cut with the woodgrain if you can, as cutting against the woodgrain involves more careful attention to prevent fine lines from splitting. If your image is of trees in a forest for example, you would align your tree trunk separation with the woodgrain that runs in the same vertical direction on your woodblock.

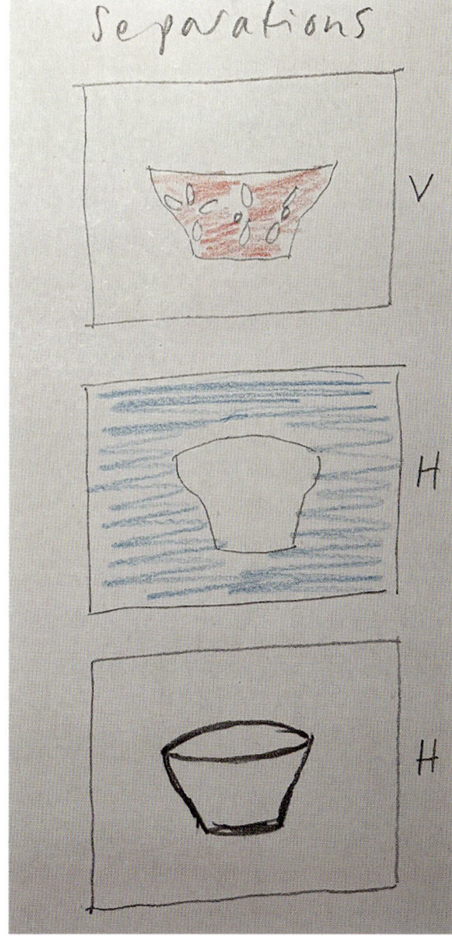

Thumbnail colour separations showing how each separation will look on the woodblock. Highly recommended, especially when your composition requires many overlapping colours.

In this photograph you can clearly see that the woodgrain direction is running vertically from top to bottom. Cutting with the woodgrain is easier than against the grain.

Look at your completed thumbnails and ascertain whether most of the cut lines are vertical or horizontal and annotate your thumbnails with a 'V' or an 'H'.

I have found that time taken for the thumbnail separations is never wasted; it is an invaluable preparation tool.

TRACING

At the tracing stage of your design it is possible to re-evaluate and tidy up your master drawing; for instance, make the curve of the line tighter or clarify any blurred lines. Tape your tracing to your master drawing securely with masking tape and re-draw your image box, re-measuring with a ruler in case there are any measurement discrepancies in the master drawing. The tracing is the drawing that you will use to transfer your separations to the block itself. Keep your pencil sharp – a blunt pencil will give an ambiguous thicker line. If you have many overlapping colours, it is a good idea to colour in your tracing too. When you come to cut the wood the image will be reversed so it is always useful to have a picture reference that can be viewed from both sides. Mark the top of the front of your tracing 'R' for right side – that is the image as it will be when printed. Do not as one of my students did mark 'T' for top, as when the tracing is turned over, it looks the same!

After flipping your tracing over, write 'kentō' in the bottom right corner if you are right-handed, or bottom left if you are left-handed. Writing *kentō* the right way around will ensure that you will not mistake the front and back of your tracing and ensures that the *kentō* registration corner is always in the same corner for each of the separations.

MARKING UP THE WOODBLOCK

Before beginning to mark up the woodblock it can be a good idea to tint your block with a light watercolour wash on both sides.

Shina is a very pale wood and tinting the block does two things; it makes the cut lines easier to see and it prepares the woodblock for printing by opening up the woodgrain. Allow the block to dry completely before marking it up.

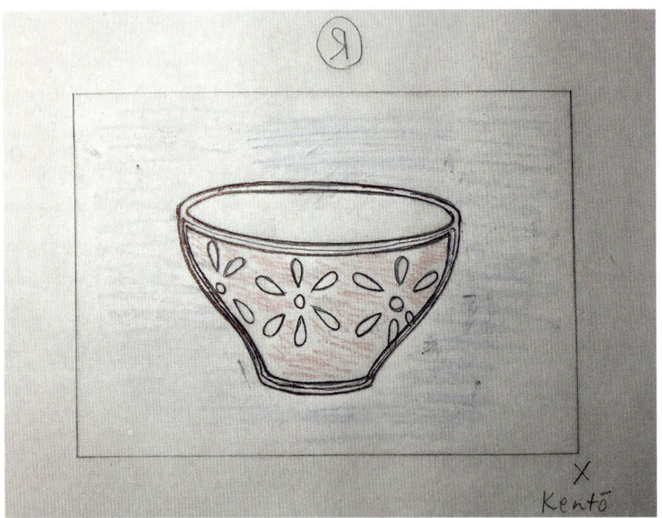

The 'R' denoting the right side of the image is back to front, showing that this is the flipped tracing ready for transfer to the woodblock. The 'X' for the *kentō* corner is clearly marked.

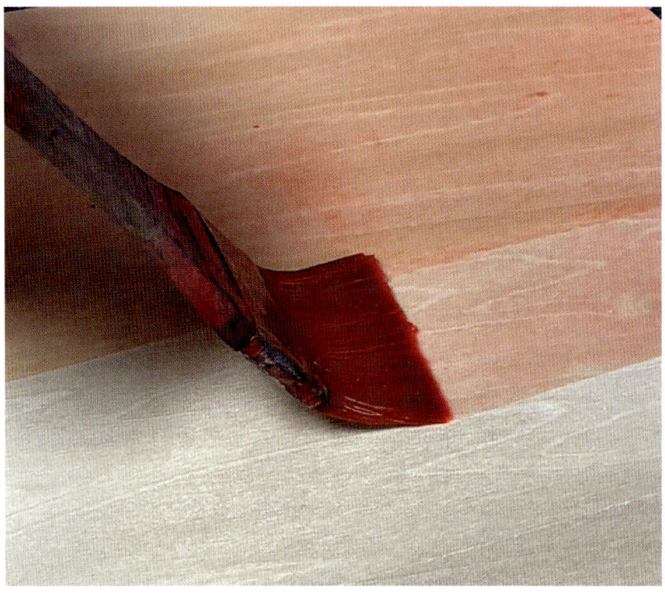

Tinting the pale *shina* plywood on both sides, with a dilute watercolour wash, using a broad flat brush.

MEASUREMENTS

In my classes we use *shina* plywood measuring 225 × 300mm.

It is possible to get four separations, using both sides of the woodblock.

Image size 10.5 × 15cm

Gutter 11.5 × 16cm

Registration 12.5 × 17cm

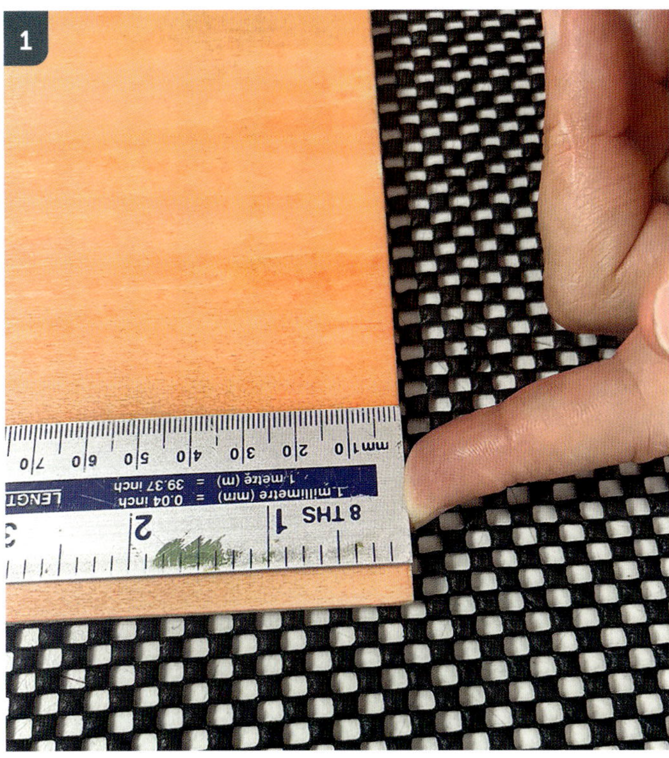

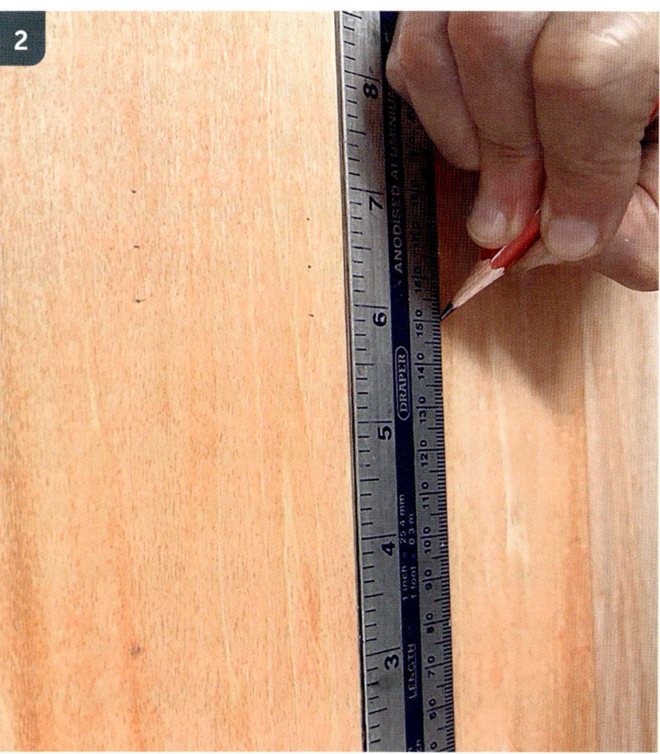

1. The printing paper will overlap the block, the image box will go right up to the edge of the woodblock, so there is little wastage. Using a metal ruler, line up the ruler with the edge of the block. Use a sharp pencil – a blunt pencil will make a wider line that could change the accuracy of your registration.

2. Using a ruler line up the edge of your woodblock and mark with a pencil dot for image, gutter and registration, without moving the ruler. Then make three more spaced-out measurements.

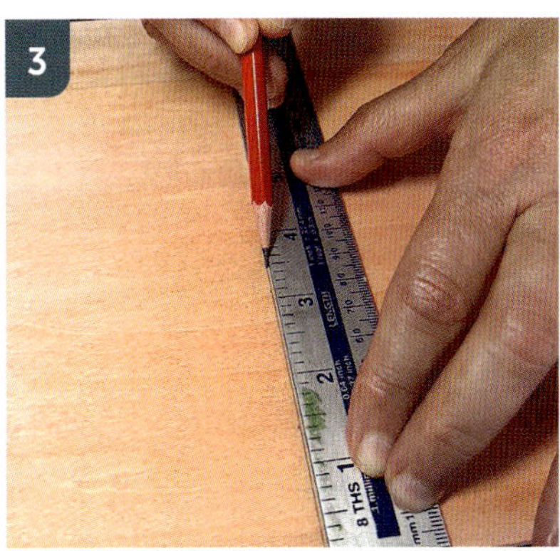

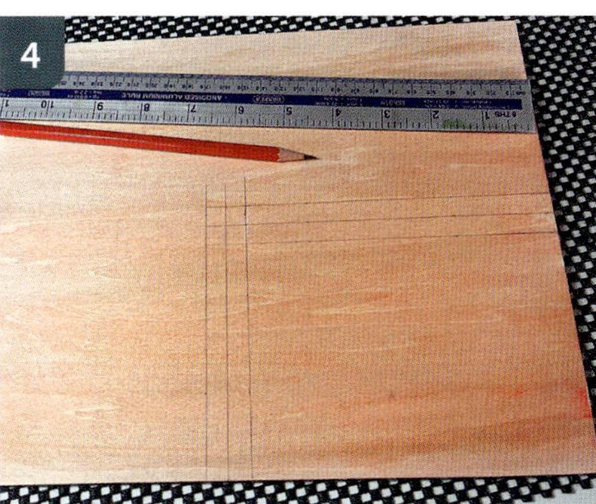

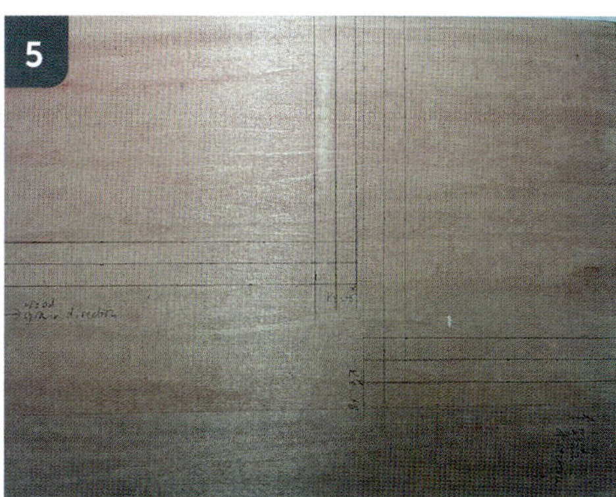

3. Line up the dots and draw a line. You will have three lines for image, gutter and registration spaced 1cm apart. Note that each separation will need to be transferred according to the wood grain direction.

4. Showing all the lines in place, ready for the first separation image transfer.

5. It is important to ensure that the *kentō* corner is in the same orientation for each separation, for ease of printing later. The 'X' that you have marked for the *kentō* corner on your tracing is invaluable as a guide for placement.

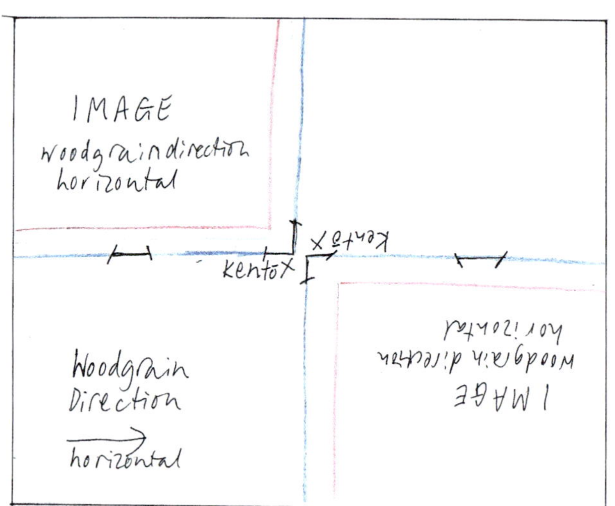

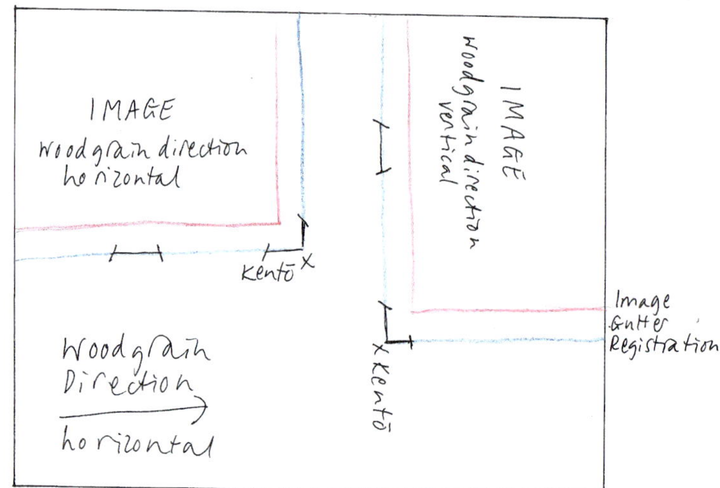

Diagrams showing different image orientations and *kentō* placements.

TRANSFERRING THE IMAGE TO THE WOODBLOCK

When the image boxes have been drawn up, the tracing needs to be flipped for transfer onto the block, so that when printed your image will be the right way around. Line up your flipped tracing box with the image box drawn on the woodblock – in the correct orientation, it should fit exactly. If it doesn't, now is the time to check your measurements!

Slide in carbon paper shiny-side down. Sometimes it is difficult to see the tracing lines, so if you put a piece of paper between the tracing and the carbon paper you will be able to see the lines clearly.

Use a biro to trace each separation. A biro will give a hard, clean line, and you can easily see where you have already traced. There is no need to press hard.

Label the colour for your separations on the woodblock, in pencil, outside the registration area. This helps later on to identify separations when printing.

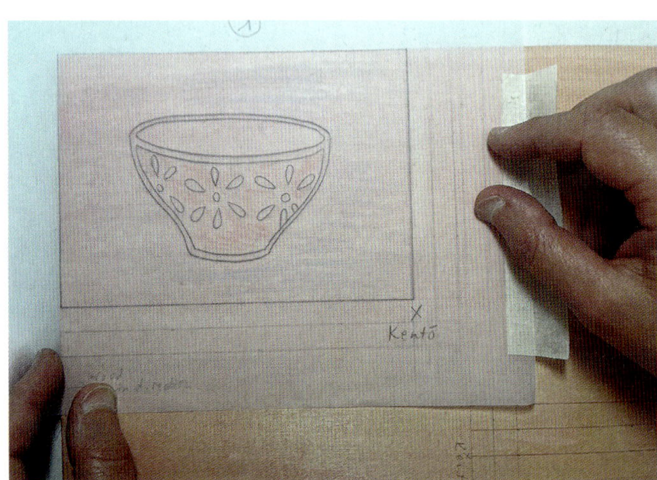

Lining up the flipped tracing box with the image box drawn on the woodblock, making sure they match exactly. Tape your tracing down with masking tape, on one side only.

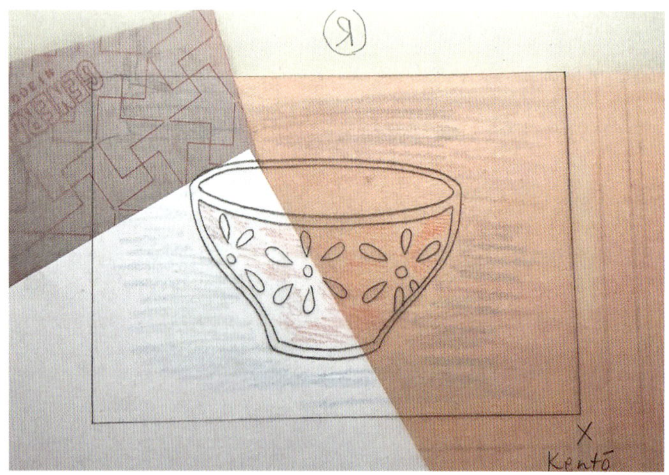

Showing how much easier it is to see your lines, when a sheet of paper is slipped in between the carbon paper and the tracing.

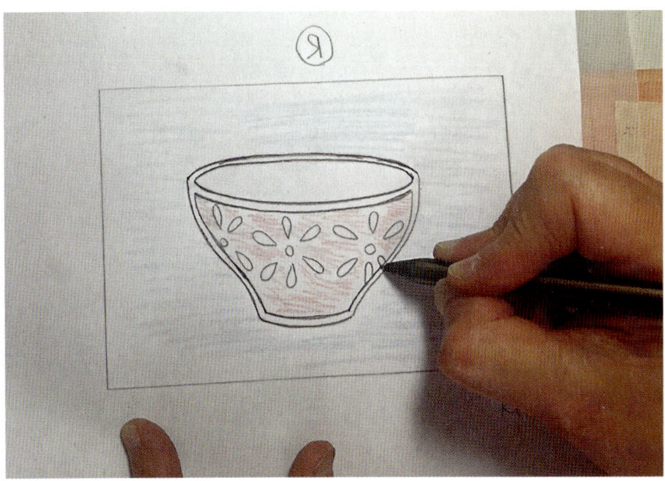

Trace down only the lines that relate to the colour separation. In this case I am drawing only the black outlines for my black separation.

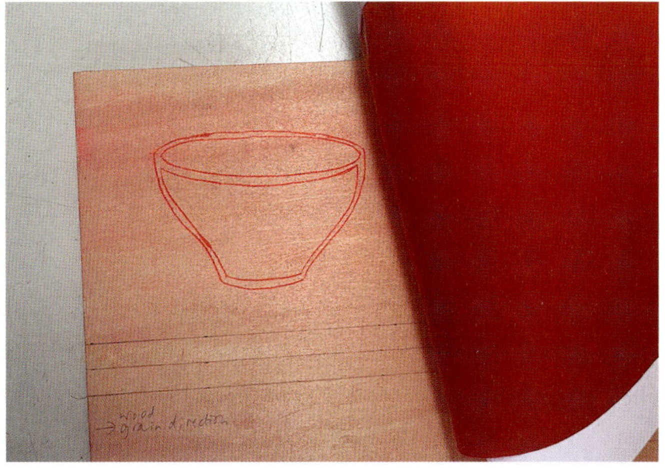

The carbon lines traced onto the woodblock. Carbon lines are indelible but don't appear on the print. Never mark the woodblock with biro or pen as this will come out on your finished print.

ISLANDS AND GUTTERS

When your separations have been transferred to the woodblock it is good to take some time before cutting to mark your block to show areas to cut and areas to leave. Please note that you must only use pencil, never biro, to write on your block, as biro ink may well appear on your finished print.

It is not necessary to cut the entire woodblock, if the area to be printed is small. A simple rule is to leave a gutter around your printing, the width of a finger.

If the area between shapes is a large one, I use 'islands'. These are areas of uncut woodblock that are left un-inked when printing and act as a sort of clean shelf, so that the damp printing paper can rest on the surface and not dip

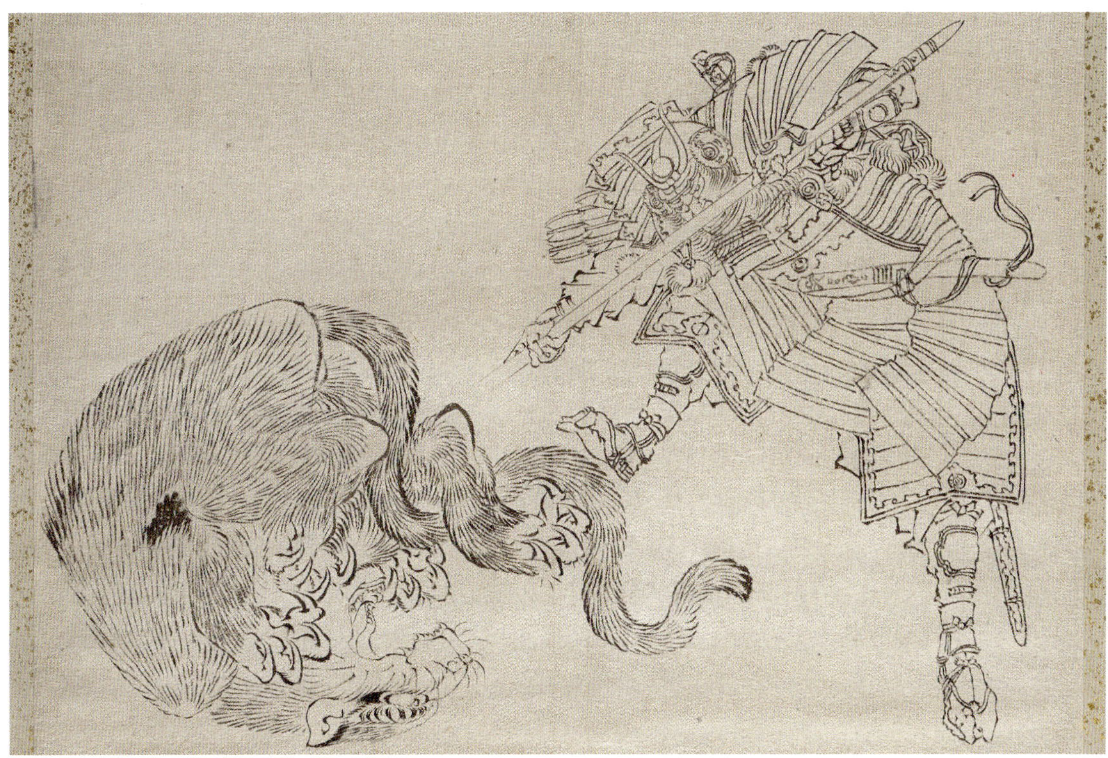

Katsushika Hokusai, 1760–1849. *Album of Sketches by Katsushika Hokusai and his Disciples*, nineteenth century. Album of 97 leaves, ink and colour on paper (39.4 × 26.7cm).

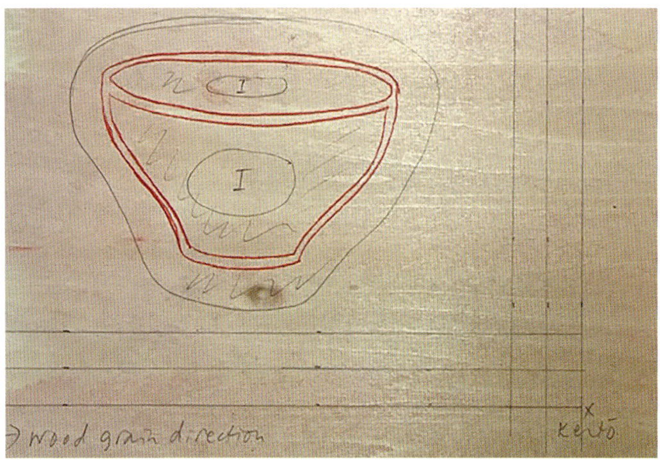

I use pencil to mark areas that are to be cut out. I label 'I' for Island areas that are not inked up when printing.

down into a large cleared area. If allowed to dip into a large cleared area the paper will pick up unwanted random lines called 'chatter'.

ALTERNATIVE METHODS OF TRANSFERRING THE IMAGE TO THE WOODBLOCK

Hanshita

The traditional method for transferring the image to the woodblock in the *ukiyō-e* prints of the Edo period is called *hanshita*, literally meaning 'picture down'. The artist would be commissioned by the publisher to create an image and he would produce a drawing using *sumi* ink on fine *mino* paper. This drawing would be sent to the print studio and actually pasted face down onto the cherrywood block. The keyline *sumiban* or outline block would be cut through the fine paper to the exact brush lines of the artist's drawing, but the drawing itself would be lost in the process. The British Museum's exhibition 'The Book of Everything' showcased Hokusai's drawings that he made for a book that was never in fact published and the exhibited drawings were therefore rare survivors of the book production process.

I use *hanshita* in my prints, as I find working directly from a drawing without tracing and copying gives me a freer expressive line to cut to. When I have cut my first block, I print it and use the print as a *hanshita* for the second separation and so on. This allows me to respond more directly to the wood, rather than working all the details of my print beforehand and losing some of the serendipity to be found when cutting.

Citrasolv

Another method of transferring your image to the woodblock is by using 'Citrasolv'. It is an environmentally friendly cleaning product. Your image needs to be photocopied on a toner photocopier, not a laser printer. The images that work best have strong contrasts of light and dark; subtle tonal images work less well.

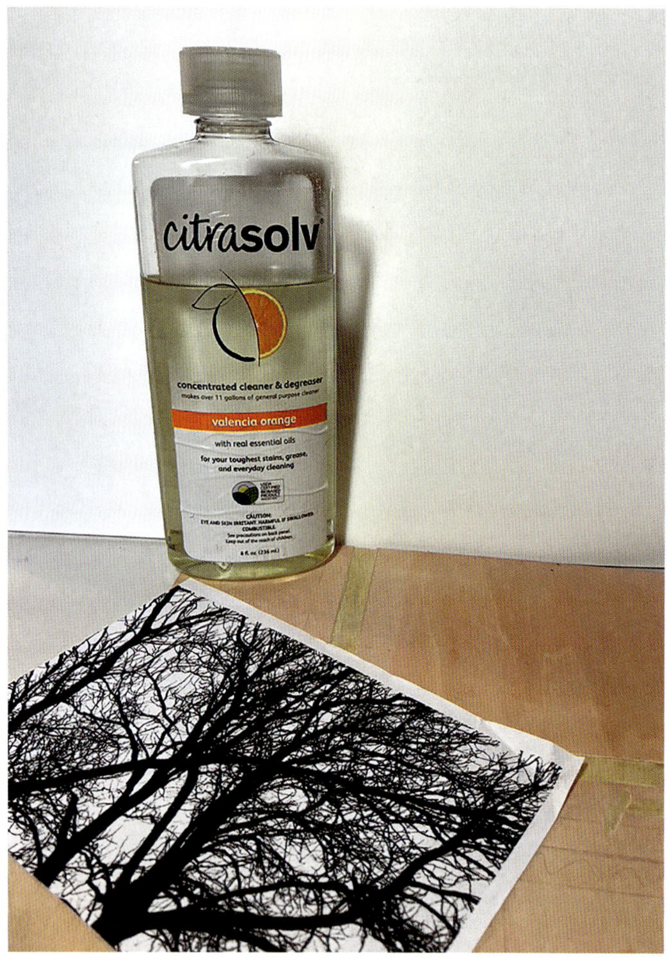

Citrasolv and photocopy ready for use.

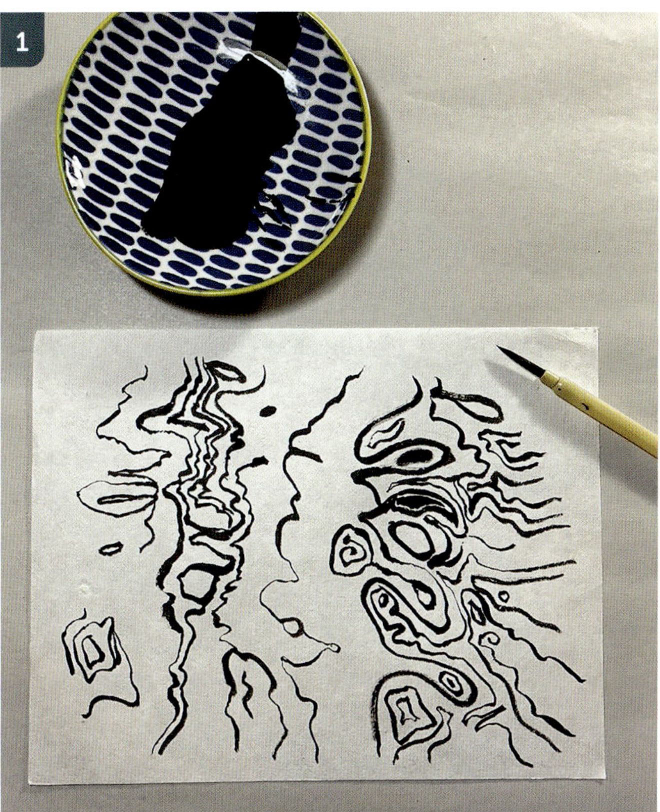

1. For the best results I use *sumi* ink and make a brush line drawing onto *washi* paper. *Washi* paper is formed of layers of paper fibres and making a *hanshita* with a thicker paper like *hoshō* means that those layers need to be peeled away to reveal the topmost layer where the line drawing sits. Traditionally a thin paper such as *minogami* would have been used.

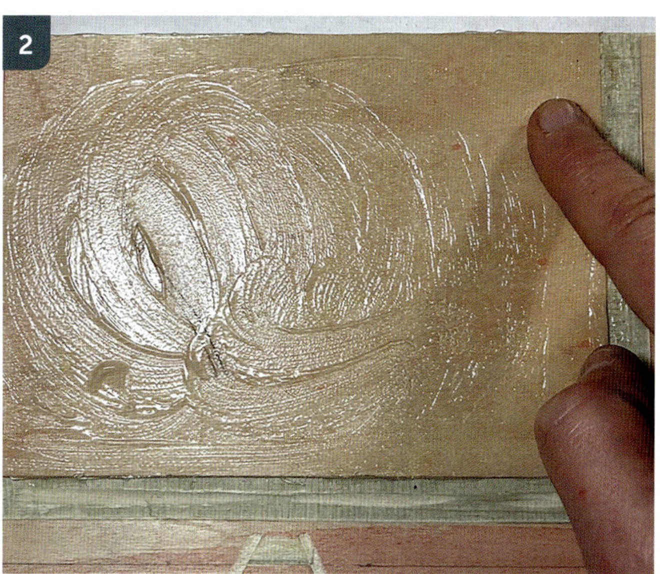

3. Using the palm of your hand, key the surface to present a more ruffled appearance – this ensures a good adhesion with the paper.

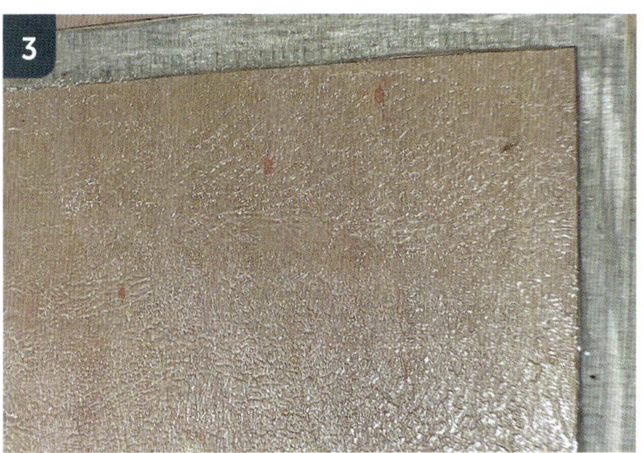

2. It is important to ensure that the paper is cut to size, the woodblock marked up and the *kentō* registration notches cut. Undiluted *nori* is spread evenly from the middle of the image area to the edges, taking care that the entire area is covered.

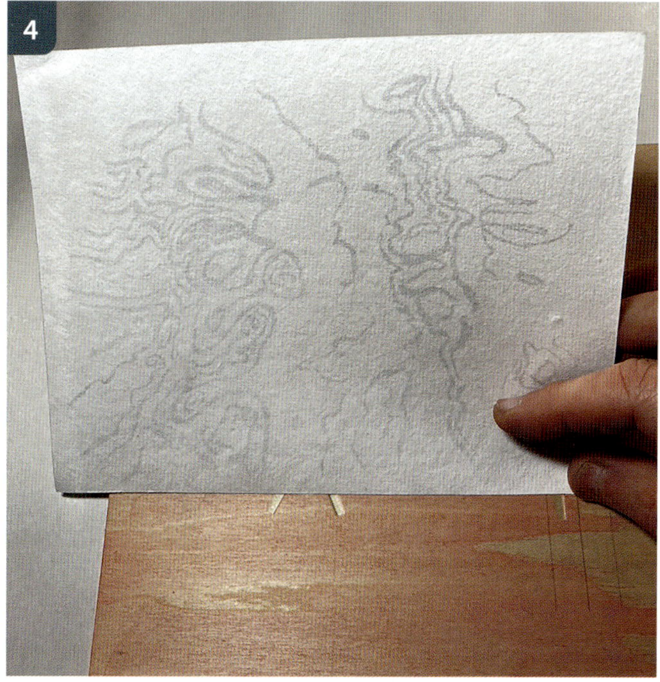

4. The drawing is then carefully placed in the *kentō* notches face down.

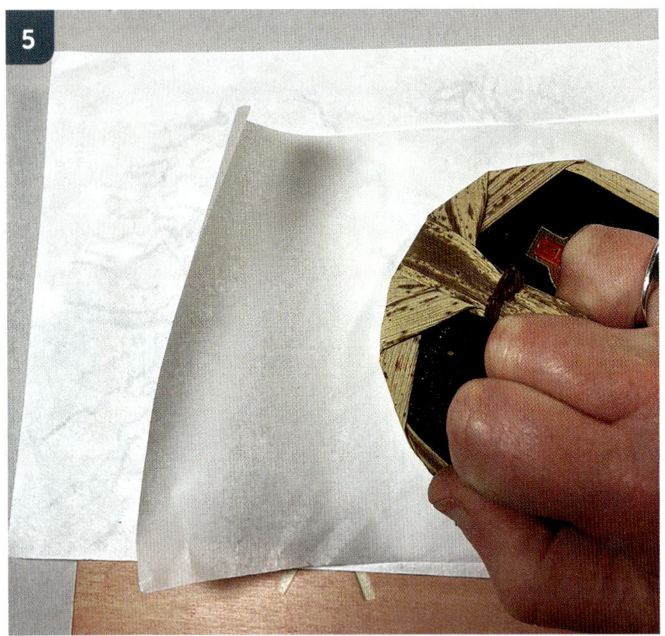

5. Using a sheet of baking paper between the paper and the *baren,* gently rub down from the centre of the image to the edges, taking care that the paper does not slide out of registration due to too heavy pressure with the *baren*.

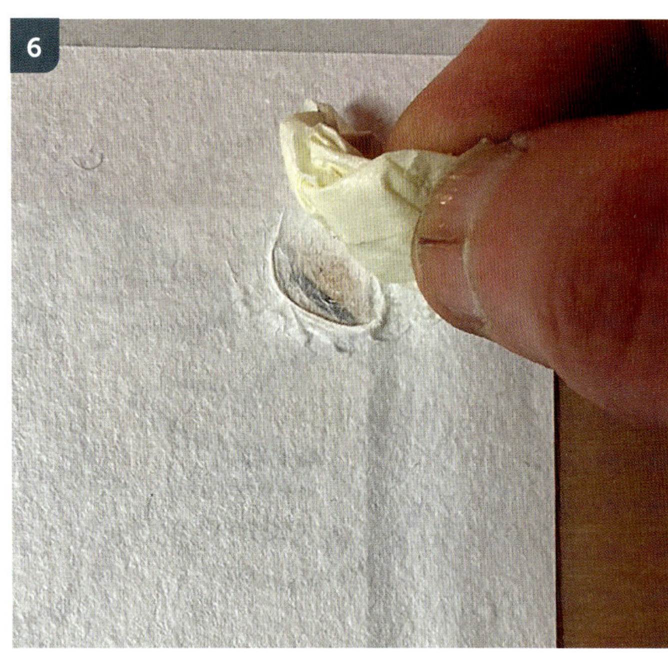

6. The waiting time depends on the size of your *hanshita*. If the image is small around ten minutes may be sufficient. If the paper is still cool to the touch, it is still too wet to begin the peeling process. Wait till the paper feels warmer under your palm, but is not bone dry. Often the hard bit is waiting for the paper to be ready! Trial an area away from your design rubbing with a balled-up piece of masking tape. If the paper comes away revealing the wood, it is not ready.

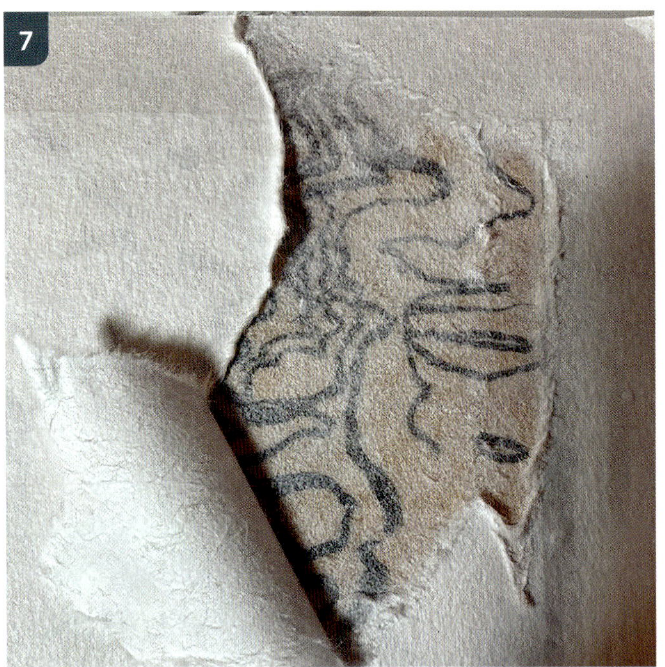

7. Peeling away the excess paper revealing the line drawing. You can use a soft eraser but I find that the balled-up masking tape is gentler. Note that edges dry quicker than the centre, so be cautious and don't be tempted to rip the paper off in one go.

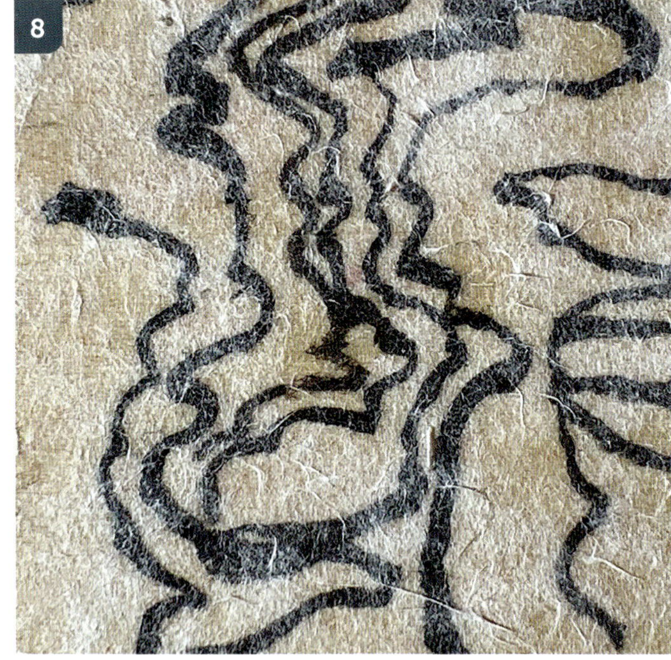

8. Close-up showing the film of paper and original line drawing, ready for cutting. The extra *nori* is an advantage when cutting fine lines, as it stops the wood from splitting. When you have finished cutting your design out, the *hanshita* remaining on the surface of the woodblock is washed away, using either your hand or a soft sponge.

STEP-BY-STEP CITRASOLV TRANSFER METHOD

I have had no difficulty printing with water-based pigments after making a Citrasolv transfer, however due to the blackness of the photocopied line, it tends to show up as a grey line if you are printing a light colour, it works best for a black line.

1. Place the photocopy face down on the woodblock and tape along one edge.

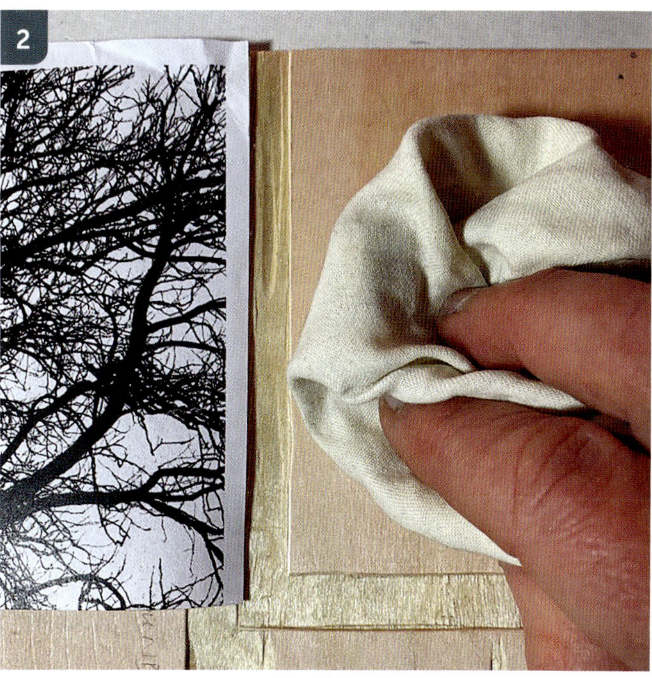

2. Fold the photocopy back and out of the way. Using a soft cloth, apply Citrasolv to the image area, working into the edges. You should be able to see the wood darken slightly as the Citrasolv is absorbed.

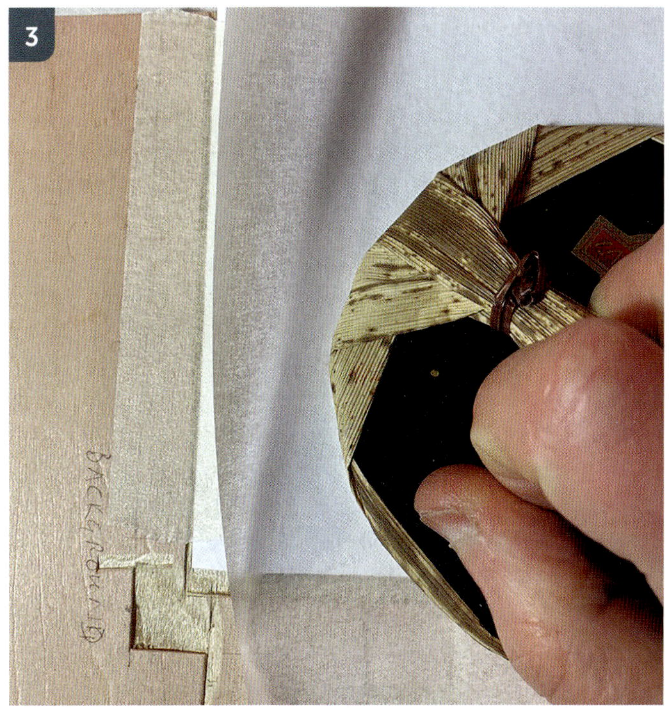

3. Use a baking sheet to protect your *baren* from the oil and rub down firmly. Check that the image is coming through and if it is faint, apply more pressure with the baren.

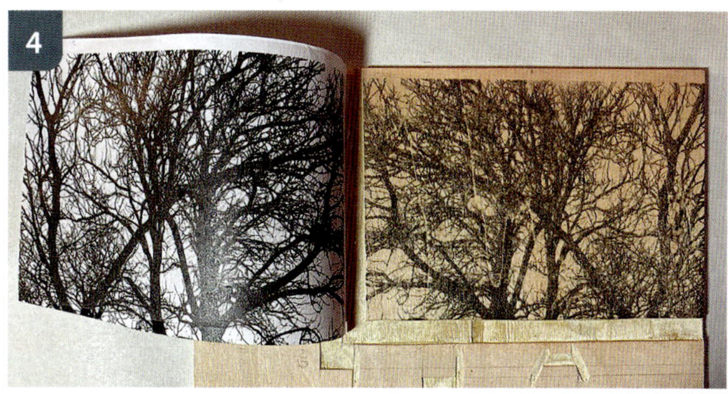

4. The photocopied image will appear on the woodblock ready for cutting.

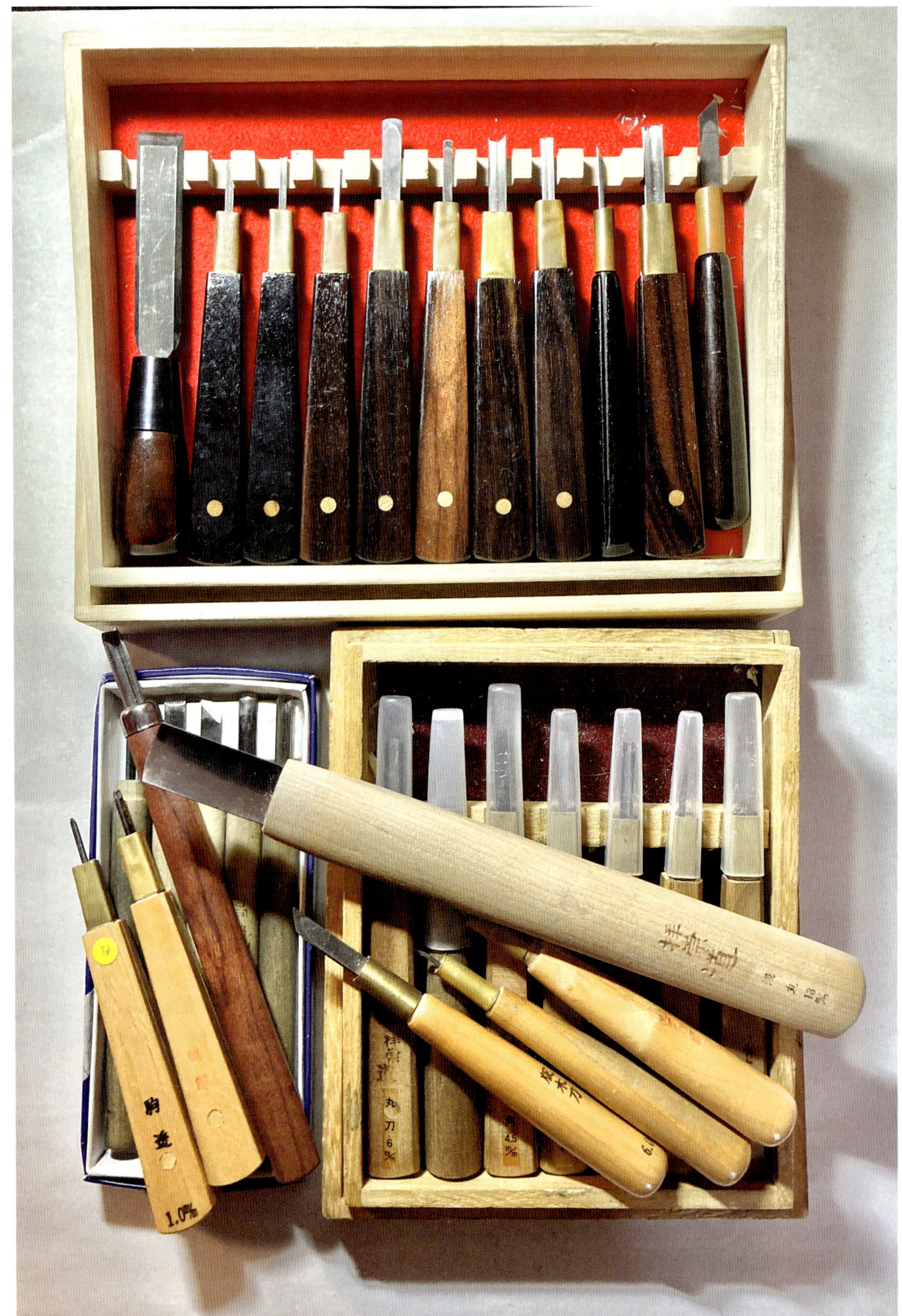

CUTTING

The cutting tools for Mokuhanga have similarities and differences to those used in Western relief processes. In this chapter each tool will be shown with their different handholds and mark-making purposes for both the beginner and more advanced Mokuhanga artist. The *kentō nommi* or chisel is fundamental to the accurate registration of multiple blocks to make a colour print; different ways of making the *kentō* will also be shown.

BEFORE YOU START

Before beginning cutting it is very important to establish the sharpness of your tools. I always hone my tools before beginning a lengthy session of cutting and if necessary I also sharpen them with waterstones if they have really lost their edge. I have outlined both sharpening and honing in Chapter 2, 'Materials and Equipment'. A sharp tool is much less dangerous than an unpredictable blunt tool. It is best to test the tool on a spare piece of wood against the grain. If the tool needs sharpening the cut line will have frayed edges, and it will feel hard to push through the wood. I have also heard of artists testing the edge of their tool against their fingernail – if it sticks then it is sharp if it slips then it needs sharpening. Personally, I prefer to test the tool in the wood that I am using.

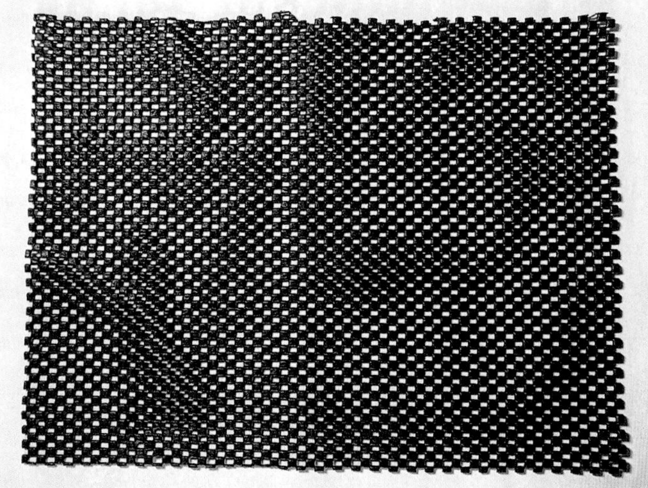
Non-slip mat.

When cutting, I put a square of non-slip mat under my woodblock.

I use my non-dominant hand to rest on the woodblock, the pressure downwards prevents the block from moving. The mats come in rolls from discount stores and are readily available and cheap to buy. They are invaluable and replace the old-fashioned clunky bench hooks that limited the way the woodblock could be turned and cut.

◀ The author's cutting tools.

THE KNIFE *HANGITŌ (HANGI-BLOCK, TŌ-KNIFE,* ALSO KNOWN AS *KIRIDASHI)*

The *hangitō* is the most important tool in Mokuhanga print-making and is used primarily for outlining shapes or delineating lines in relief. It is also a tool that has no Western counterpart and as such requires some practice to familiarise yourself with it. In the West the V-tool takes the same function, but after using the *hangitō* for many years now I prefer the flexibility it offers, freeing the wrist to make flowing cutting movements. It is shaped like a knife with a flat side and a bevelled side coming to an exceedingly sharp point – it is the point of the tool that does the cutting.

Beginner's Method

At my residency in MI-Lab I was taught by Japanese *sensei* or teachers. I was shown two different angles of holding the *hangitō*; the first, the beginner's way, requires the tool to be held vertically at a 90-degree angle and pulled towards you. This approach is easy to understand and control.

It is held upright like a dagger with the thumb on top with the index finger of your other hand supporting and steadying the tool in the opposite direction. This incidentally keeps your non-dominant hand out of danger of being cut – an important consideration. This hand also rests on the woodblock ensuring the downward pressure essential for keeping the woodblock stationery on the non-slip mat.

The tip should be positioned furthest away from you with the bevel side next to the image area to be kept. The bevel side of the tool makes a slanting cut next to the image that provides more stability to the raised line to be printed than a straight cut down would do. The tool is pulled towards you – never pushed away.

Common Errors

- The tip of the tool is very fine – making it vulnerable to snapping.
- A common mistake is pressing the tool into the wood too heavily making it difficult to pull the tool through the wood.
- It is also a mistake to press too lightly as the cleared areas will not be defined and will pick up ink in the printing stage. The tool might also move unexpectedly quickly if pressed too lightly.
- The tool should run smoothly through the wood, with the tip gliding below the surface.
- When cutting a curve it is important to do it in stages, taking the *hangitō* out of the line when your wrist and

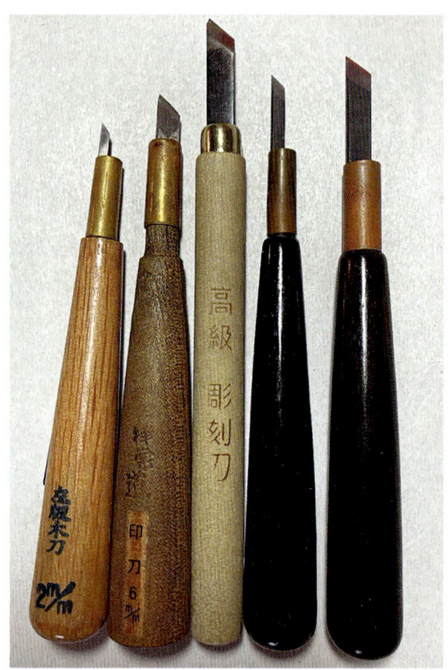

Selection of different sizes of *hangitō*.

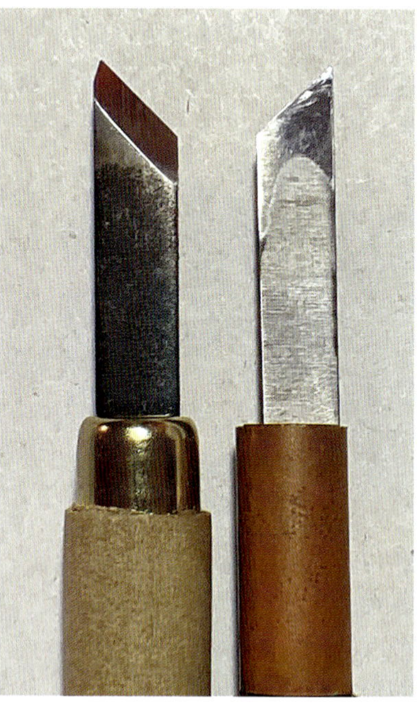

Showing the bevelled and flat side of the tool.

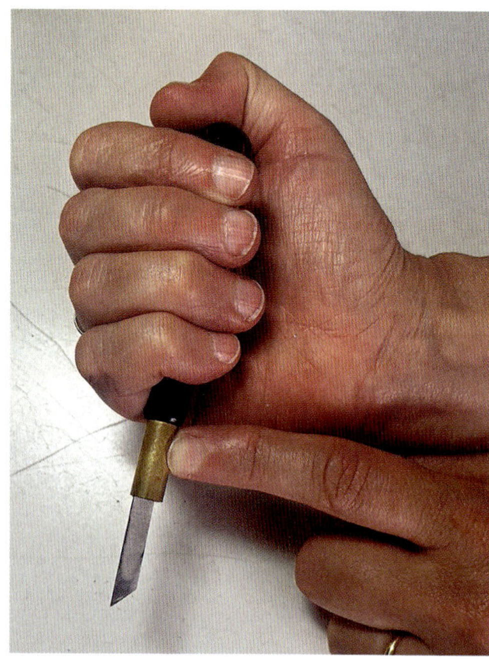

My handhold for using the tool.

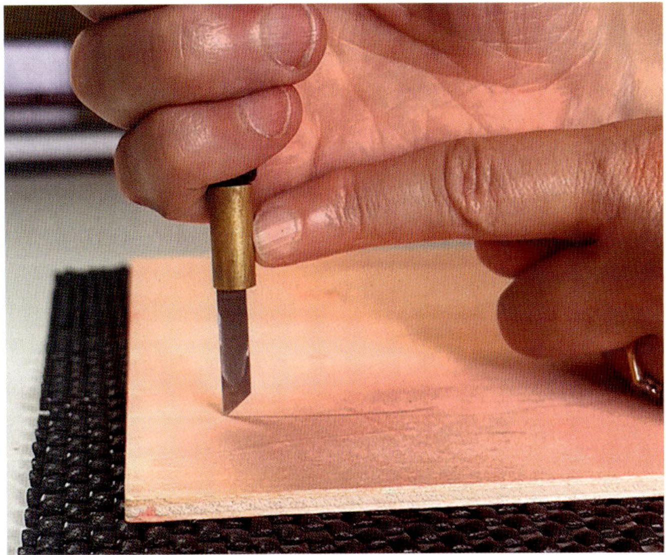

The tool is pulled towards you.

elbow start twisting sideways and moving the block so that the curve is angled towards you before you reinsert the *hangitō* to carry on. Leaving the tool in the curve line as you attempt to cut could twist the tip of the tool and result in it snapping off. It has happened only once in my years as a tutor, but it's good practice to avoid risking it.

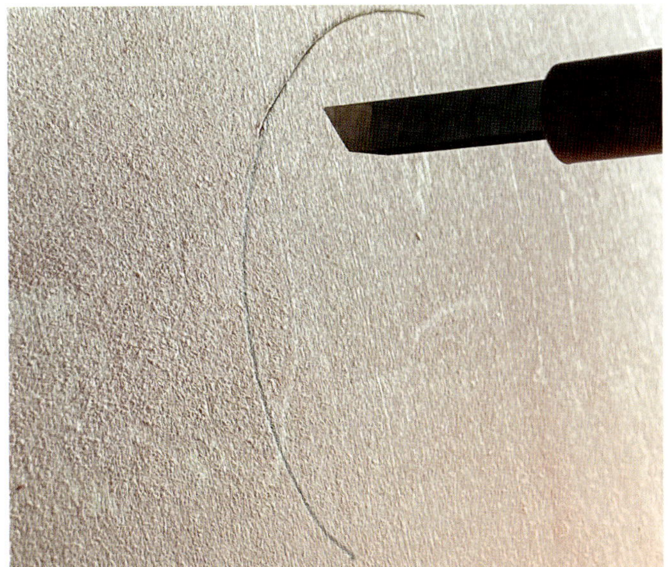

Cutting a curve in instalments.

Advanced Method

The more advanced hold for the *hangitō* requires the tool to be held at a 45-degree angle, (instead of upright as in the beginner's hold) with the bevel to the line. This has the advantage

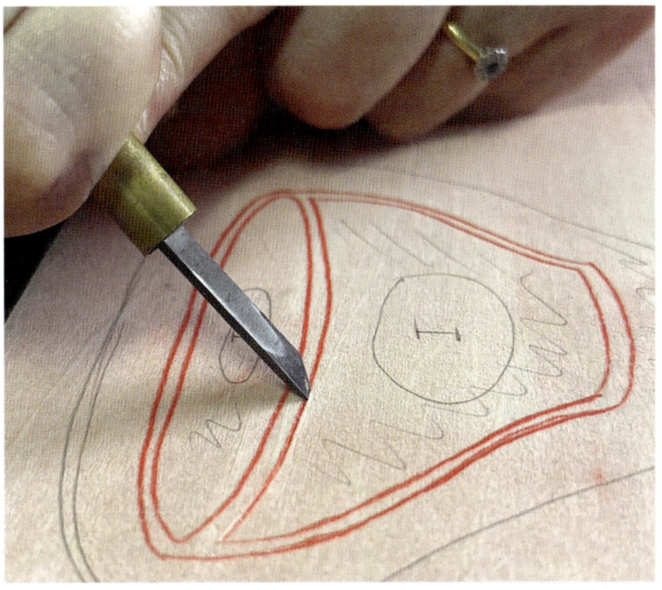

Advanced method of cutting at a 45-degree angle away from the line.

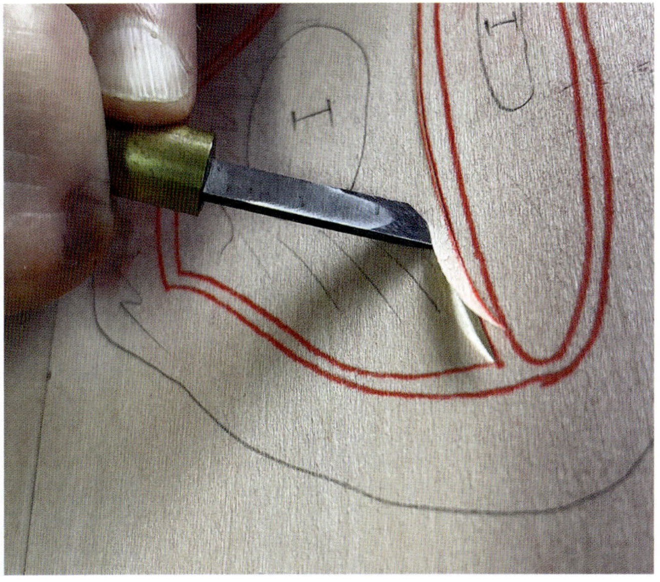

The return cut, lifting a section of wood up to the cut line, creating a trench.

of cutting a wider slope providing a more secure base to your image area, allowing for finer lines to be cut.

Turning the block and repeating the cut coming from the other way will release a fine trench from where you can clear away without worrying about losing your fine details. As you become more proficient it is possible to cut one way with the tool and turn your wrist to cut the other way without turning the woodblock. This is very useful when cutting larger blocks as they are cumbersome to move around.

Be mindful of undercutting your line however; this happens when your clearing cut is too close to the edge of the pre-cut line and the sharp tip of the tool undercuts and lifts off your fine line. To avoid it happening ensure that your clearing cut is at least 3mm away from your initial cut line, the width of the *hangitō*'s tip.

Once mastered this technique allows for a greater cutting freedom as the tool flows through the wood beautifully and is akin to drawing with a brush. It is however better to start with the beginner's hand hold and only progress to the more advanced as you gain in confidence.

ROUND GOUGE, *MARUTŌ* (*KOMASUKI*)

The *marutō* is a tool used primarily, though not exclusively, for clearing areas of your design that will be un-inked. It has a rounded end with a bevel on the underside. It is held with the

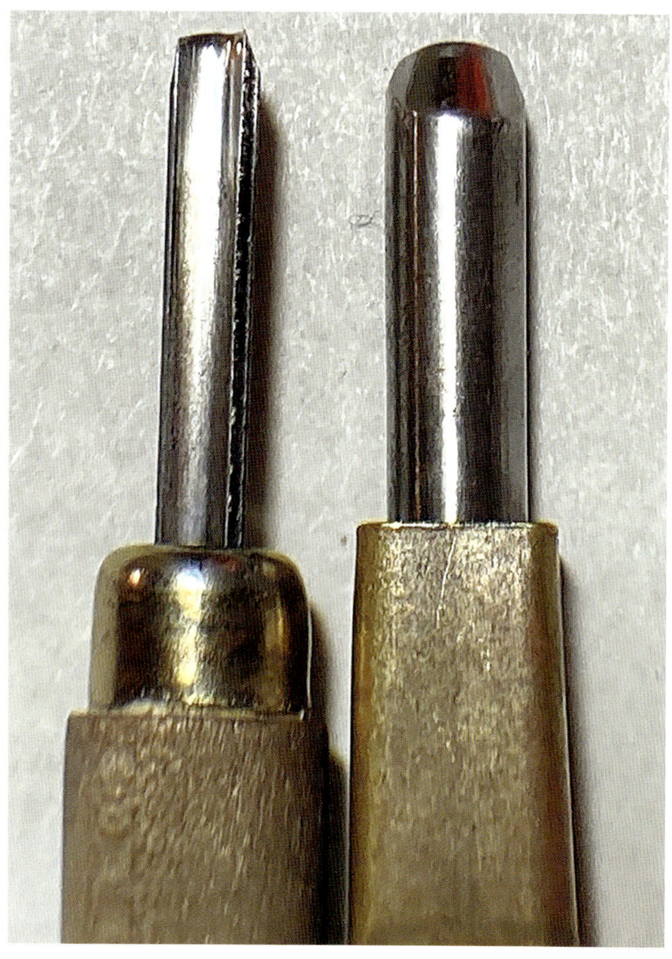

Showing the round bevelled base of the tool and the scoop of the top.

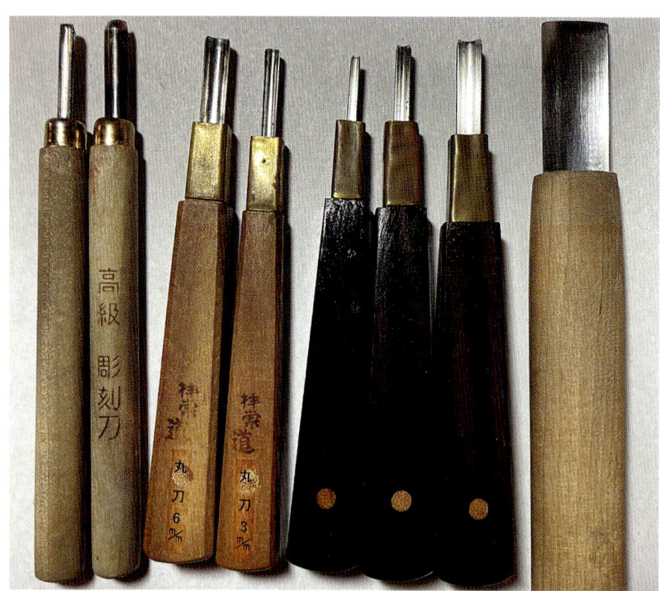

Selection of different sizes of *marutō*.

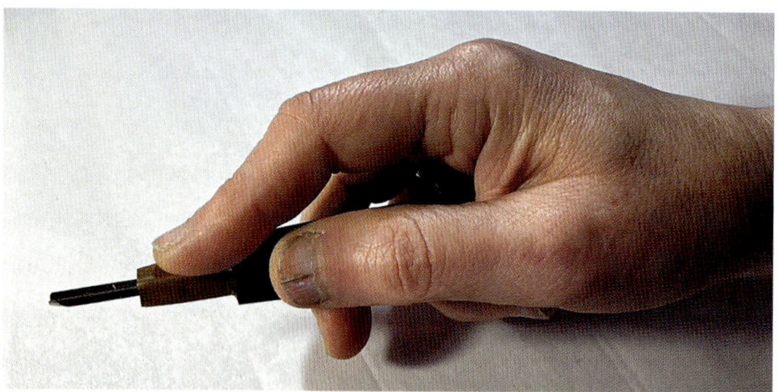

My handhold for using the tool.

handle end pressed into the palm of your hand, your fingers are wrapped around the handle leaving the index finger on top of the metal shaft. The non-dominant hand's index finger rests against the tool as a support, again staying out of harm's way when cutting.

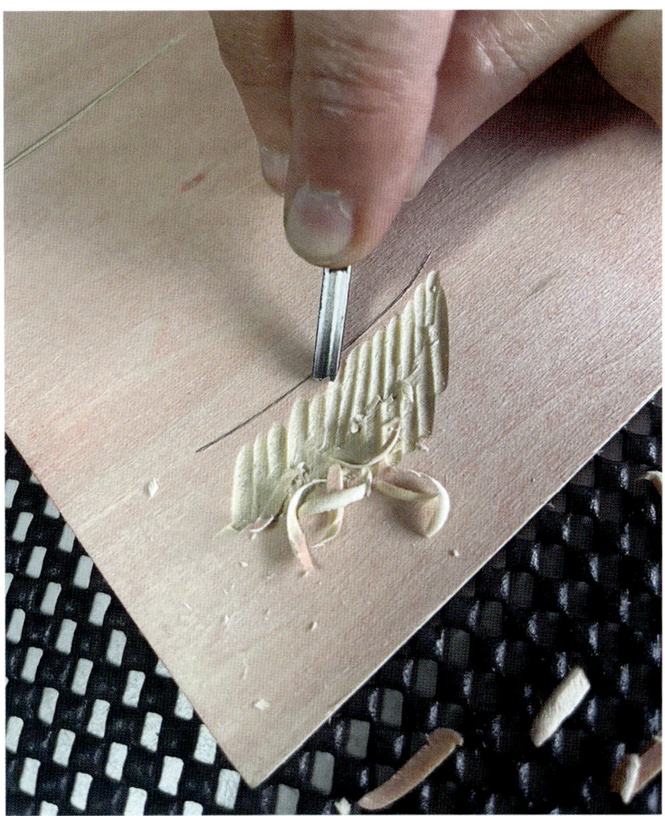

Using the tool to clear obliquely away from the cut line, in overlapping rows.

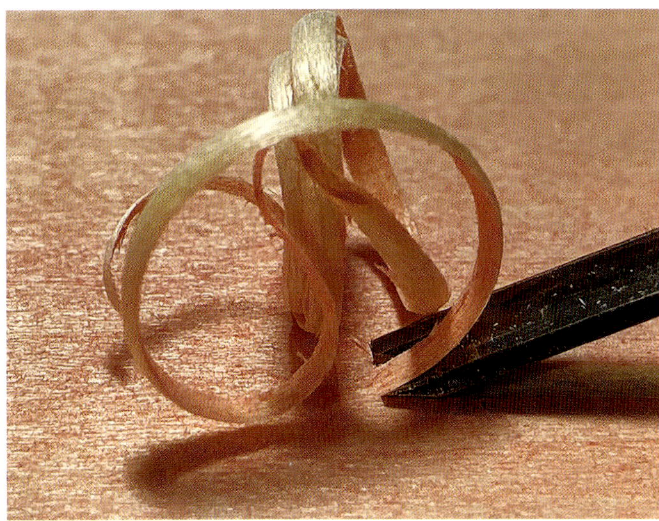

Testing the correct pressure and depth required to achieve an even line by cutting a spiral of wood.

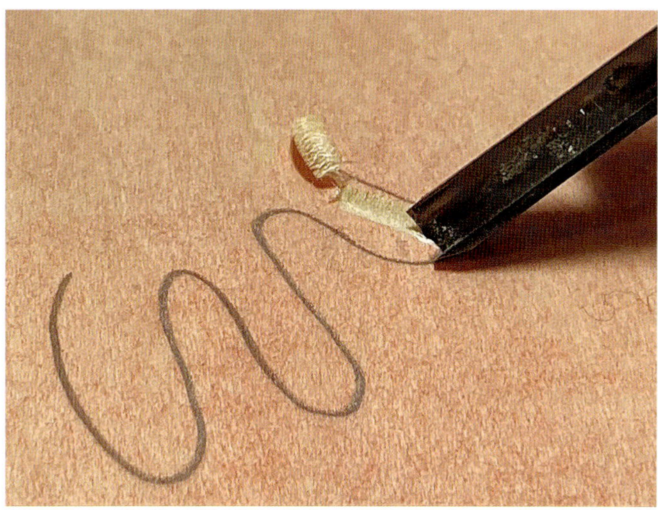

Using the round end of the tool to cut out a round shape in your design.

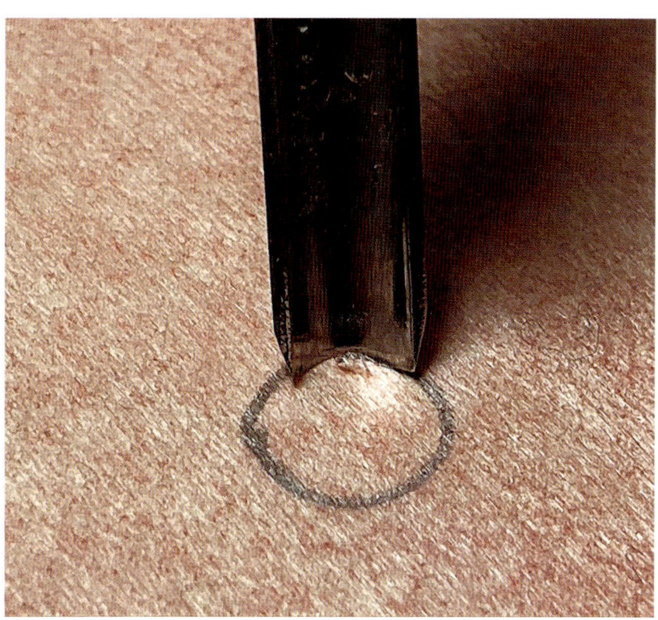

Using the tool like an apple corer to cut holes.

Once the fine lines have been cut with the *hangitō*, the *marutō* is used to clear away from the line. This is done with overlapping cuts away from the cut line, leaving a 3mm gap of uncut wood next to the line.

Due to the rounded shape of the *marutō* it is not advisable to go too close to the *hangitō* line as it could nick the edges. In the economy toolset that I use with my students there are two *marutō*, one larger than the other. The larger tool I use to clear wider areas and the smaller I use to bring the clearing areas closer to the *hangitō* pre-cut line.

I have found that students of mine who are familiar with linocut cutting use a dipping action with the tool as a consequence of clearing lino. The correct pressure however to use for

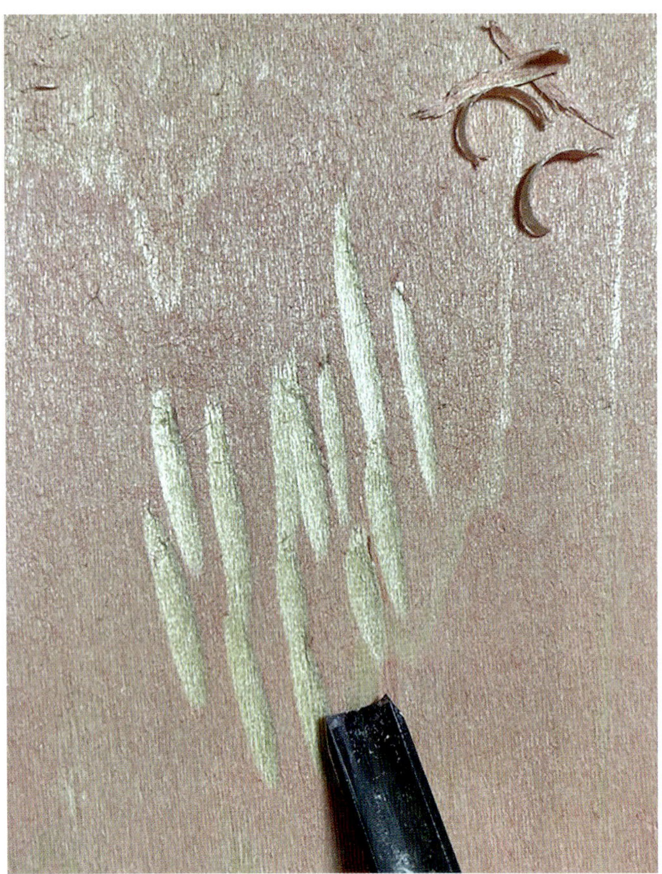

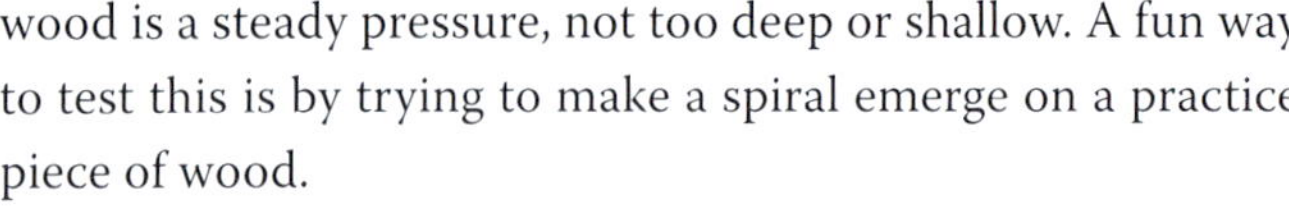
Playing with the tool's textural mark-making possibilities.

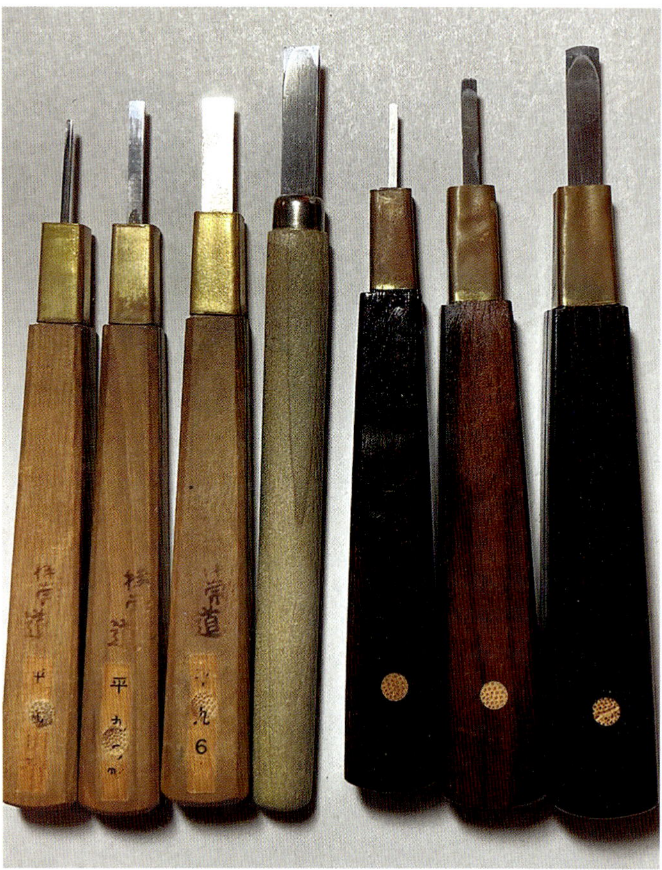
Selection of different sizes of *hiratō*.

wood is a steady pressure, not too deep or shallow. A fun way to test this is by trying to make a spiral emerge on a practice piece of wood.

The rounded end of the *marutō* can also be used for clearing rounded shapes that can be difficult to negotiate for the beginner using the *hangitō*.

Holes can be made by turning the tool.

Textures can also be created.

CHISEL, *HIRATŌ (AISUKI)*

The *hiratō* is shaped like a chisel with a flat side and a bevelled side. The bevel always faces downwards; if you attempt to cut with the bevel upwards the tool will rip the wood. The hand-hold is the same as the *marutō* with the end of the wooden handle pressed into the palm of your hand, your fingers wrapping around the handle leaving your index finger on top. Your non-dominant hand's index finger comes in to support as before

with the hand resting on the wood adding downward pressure so that the block does not move on the non-slip mat.

I have found the *hiratō* to be a very versatile tool. For beginners, after the *marutō* has cleared away from the *hangitō* pre-cut line, the *hiratō* is used to clear away the final area of wood, revealing the clean cut line. To do this only the corner of the *hiratō* is used, positioning the tool approximately 1mm away from the cut line (this is important as the tool is sharp and can easily nick the line if care is not taken).

With a little practice you will be able to feel the correct angle to hold your tool; when you do there is a 'sweet spot' where the wood will peel away from the cut line easily.

The *hiratō* is also used to flatten ridges left by the *marutō*.

Used on its side with one side in the cleared area and the other on the sharp edge of a cut line it is also possible using less pressure to gently smooth the edge of the line. This is done to prevent or limit the appearance of unwanted embossing on your print, particularly on island or gutter areas.

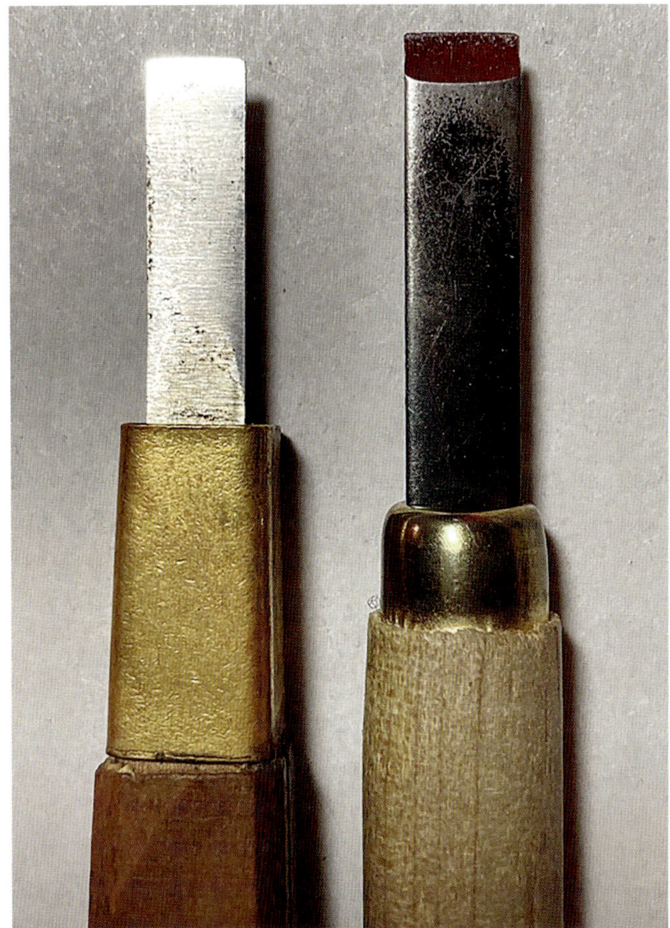

The front of the tool is flat, the base bevelled. Bevelled side down when cutting.

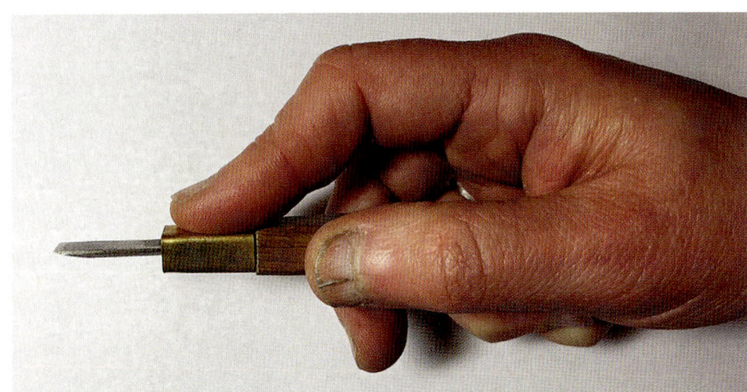

My handhold for the tool.

I have found with practice that the *hiratō* is very useful for cutting in a more intuitive way, making shallow cuts just shaving the surface of the wood to leave a graduated surface that prints as a tone. This is called *ita bokashi*.

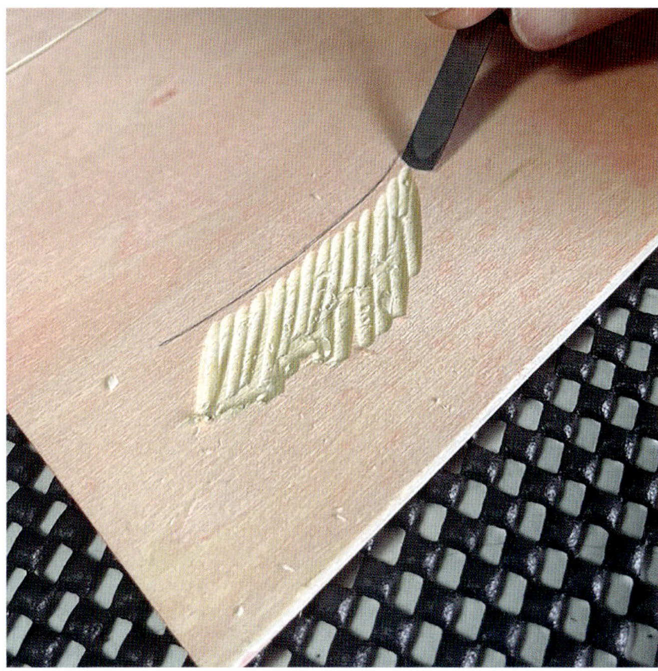

Position the *hiratō* approximately 1mm away from the cut line, dig down until you feel the wood lift.

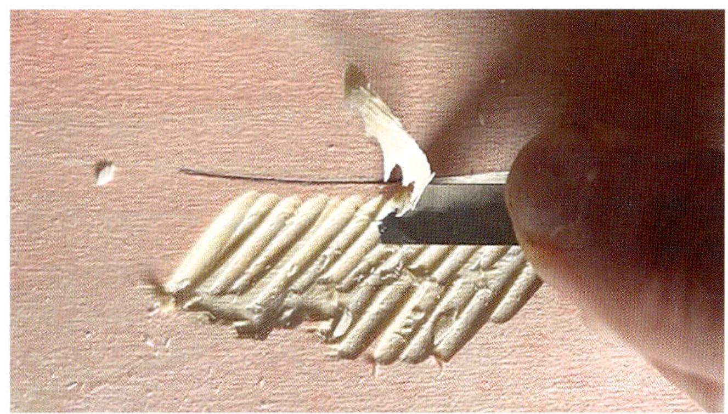

Run the tool up the line, lifting the wood up to the pre-cut line.

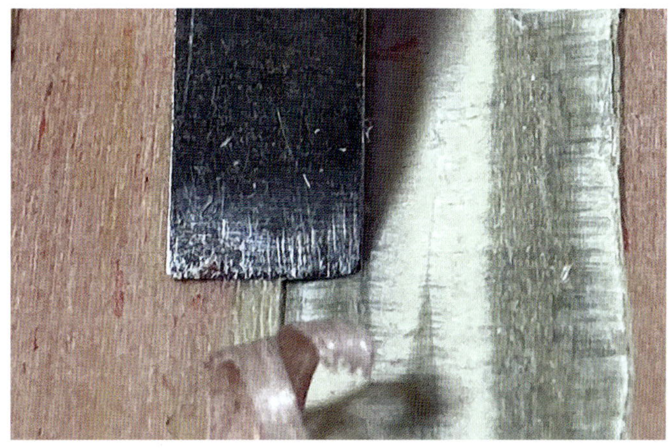

Using the tool on its side, gently shave the edge of the gutter line.

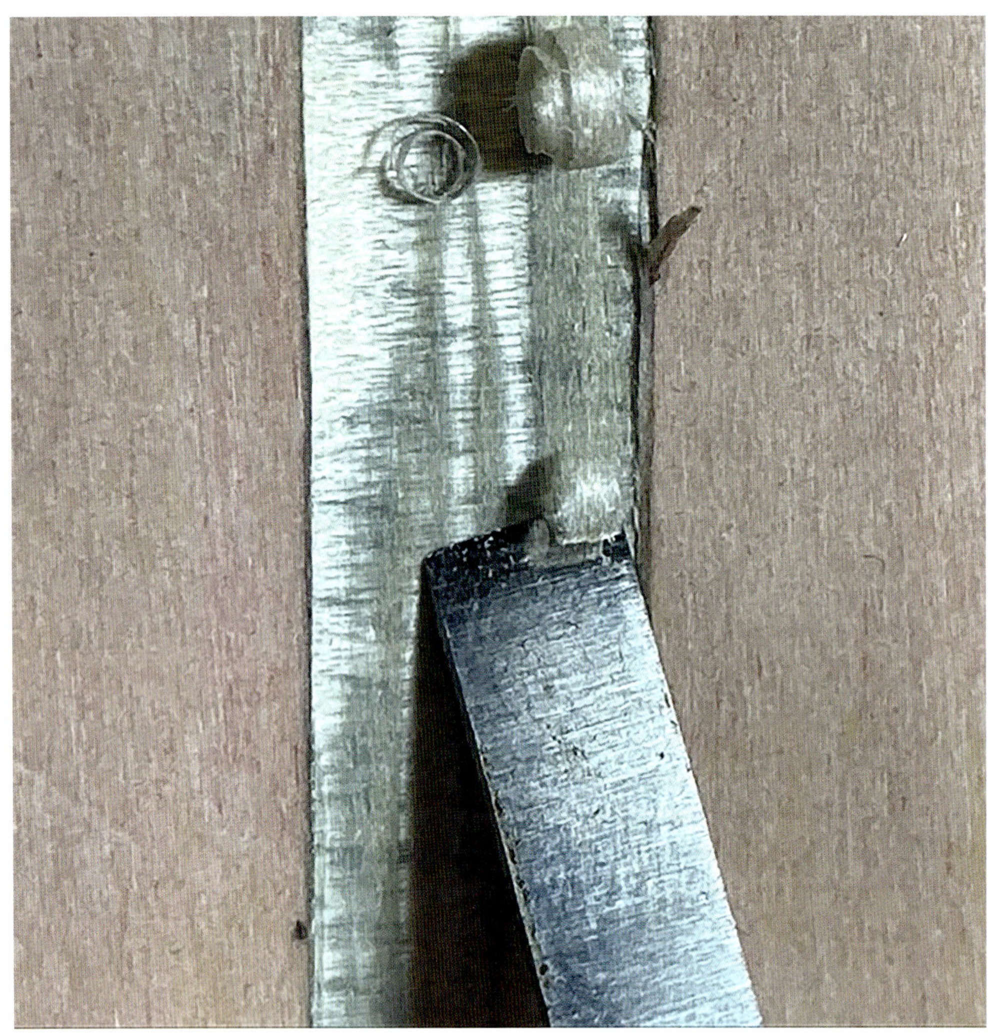

Using the tool bevel side down to flatten the ridges formed by the *marutō* clearing areas.

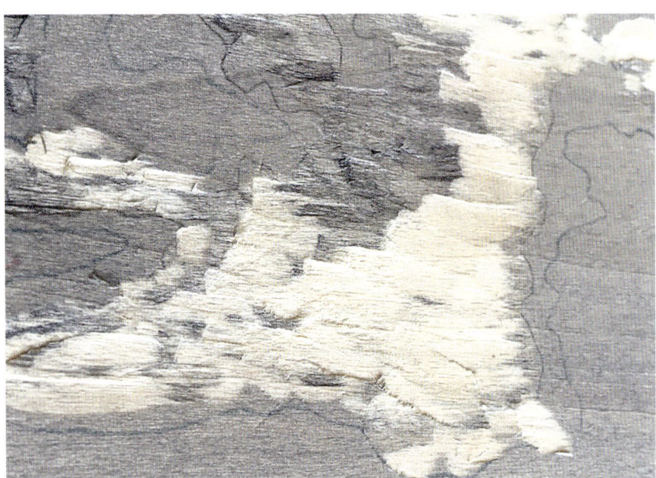

Showing a block that has been cut with shallow areas of *ita bokashi*.

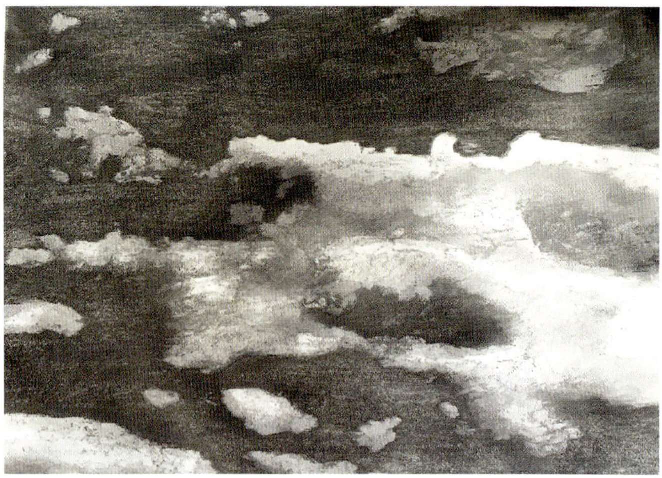

Above Us. Reduction Japanese woodcut. Copyright Carol Wilhide Justin.

It can be used to soften the edge of an area that will be printed as a graduated tone or *bokashi,* or to describe soft subjects such as clouds. This print of mine called *Above Us* is a reduction print (*see* Chapter 6) almost exclusively cut using the *hiratō.*

V-TOOL, *SANKAKUTŌ*

The V-tool or *sankakutō* was not introduced to Japan until the late nineteenth century with the import of Western technologies and tools. It is a handy tool to have however, especially

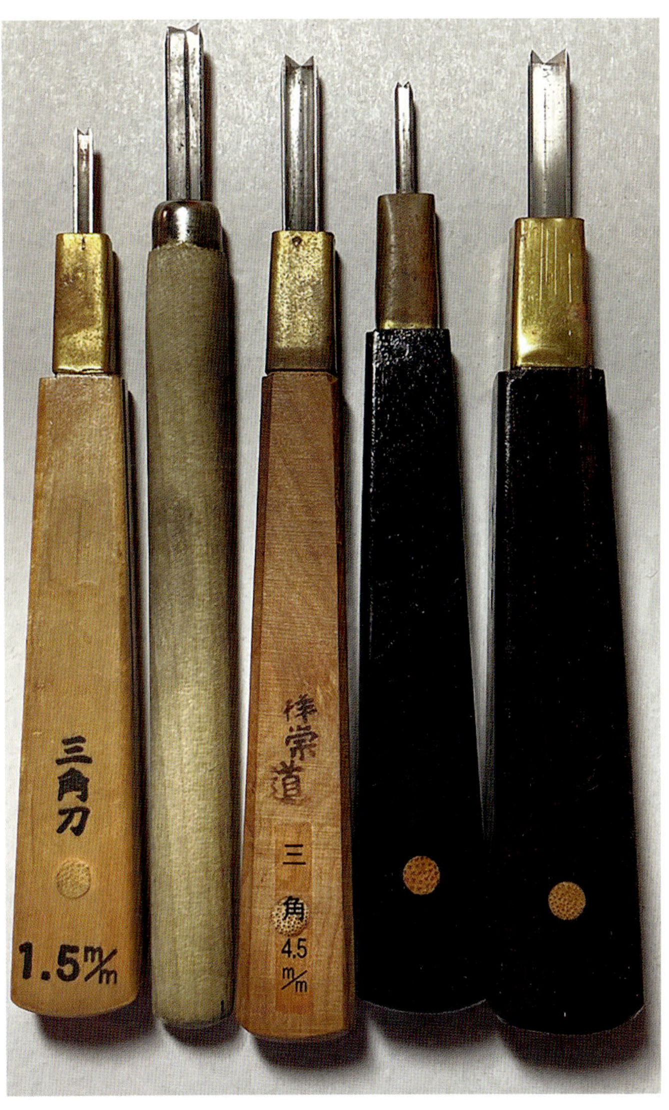

Selection of different size *sankakutō*.

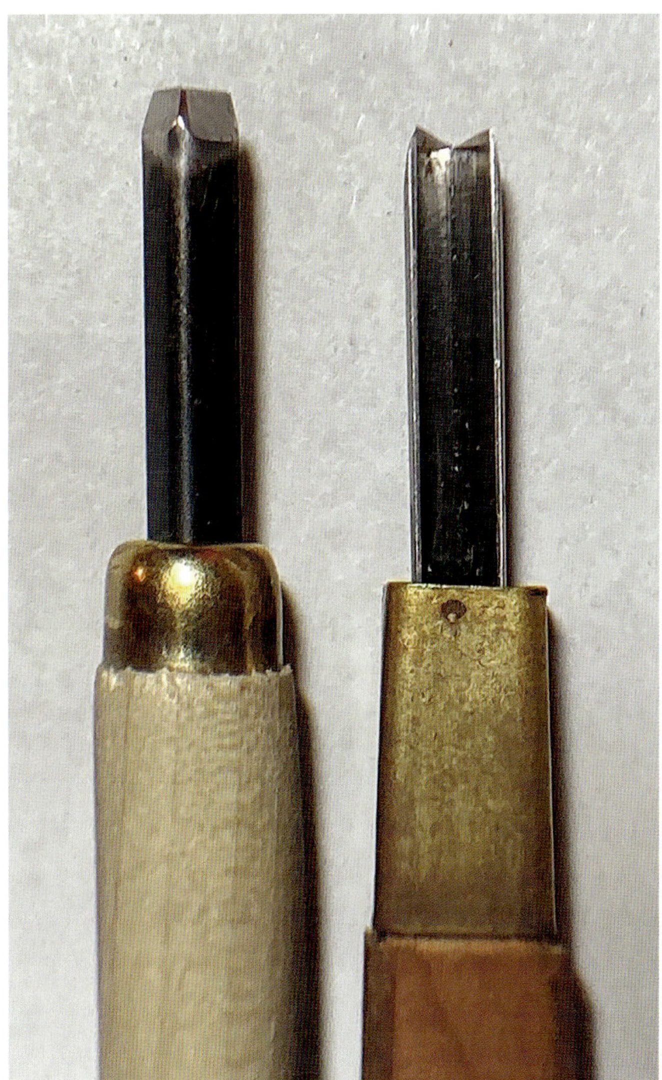

Showing the front of the tool and the bevelled back; note the fold is straight.

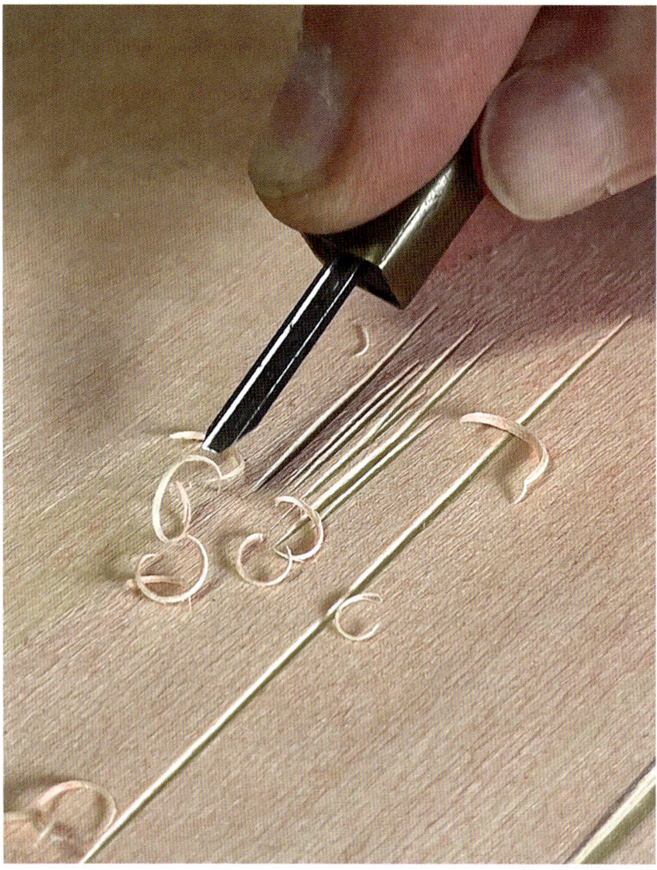

Cutting a line with the tool – it is also useful for textured areas.

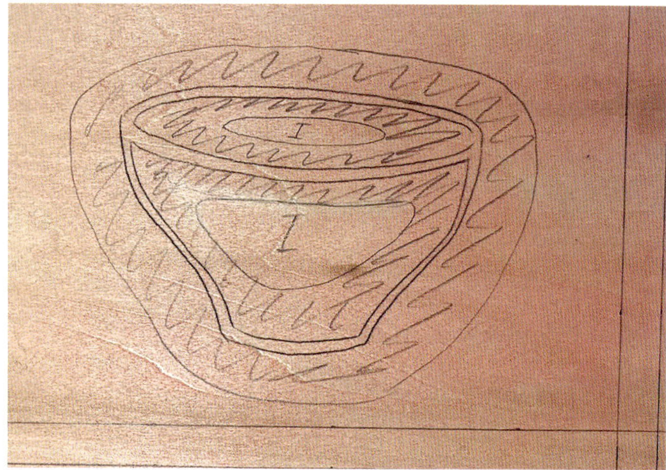

Identify areas to be cleared before starting to cut.

HOW TO COUNTER A SPLIT

Particularly vulnerable to splitting are the sharp tips of a pointed shape. A way of countering this is by extending the cut line beyond the shape, making an 'X'. The line including the extension is cut with the *hangitō* and cleared as before with first the *marutō* and then the *hiratō*. The 'X' cut takes the pressure away from the tip of the point leaving it crisp and unlikely to split even when cut against the woodgrain.

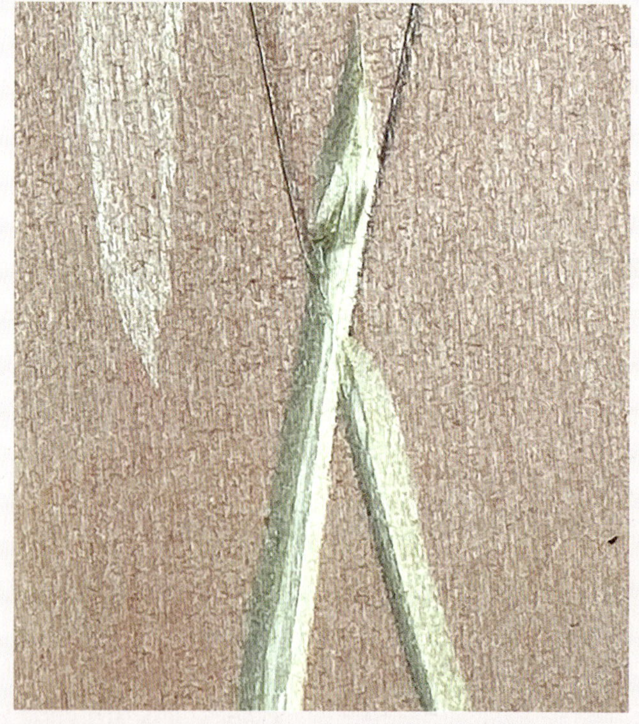

Showing how to avoid losing the tip of a sharp, pointed shape.

for beginners who may find the *hangitō* difficult to use at first. When I was making linocuts, it was the tool I used most often to cut lines. It has the same handhold as the *marutō* and *hiratō*. I now seldom use it because after I began to use the *hangitō* properly, I found that there is an increased flexibility in the wrist movement with the Japanese tool, allowing for a more responsive cutting technique.

CUTTING ISSUES

It is important to take care when using the tools, they are sharp! Apart from the *hangitō* that is pulled towards you, *all the tools cut away from you*. By using the non-slip mat you can place the woodblock at the correct angle to cut away from yourself. By using your non-dominant hand to support the tool and press down on the block your hand will never be in the cutting line. Most problems with cutting I have found have been from either using the tools incorrectly or having tools that are too blunt.

Before starting I make sure that I have identified areas to be cleared by marking them in pencil on the block. I cannot tell you how often I have been grateful for this extra bit of planning.

If you do make a mistake and you are determined to reattach the cut piece there are wood glues on the market, but I have yet to find an entirely satisfactory one that can deal with the rigors of multiple dampening and pressure rubbing without leaving a tell-tale trace on the print. Avoid any water-based glues like PVA as they will loosen with repeated dampening of the block. Ensure that the wood is completely level with the surrounding area by using a fine-gauge sandpaper to lightly level the surface.

Alternatively, you can re-evaluate your design, or live with a broken line, which can sometimes be a surprising asset to the finished result.

GRAPHITE RUBBING/CARBON WITH *BAREN*

To test your cutting and to get some idea of how it might print, I use newsprint paper and a stick of graphite to make a rubbing. The graphite should be used on its side and not like a pencil; this simulates printing with the flat surface of the *baren*. The resulting image will not be the same way around as your finished print, but you can turn the paper over and hold it up to a light source to see your image the way it will be printed.

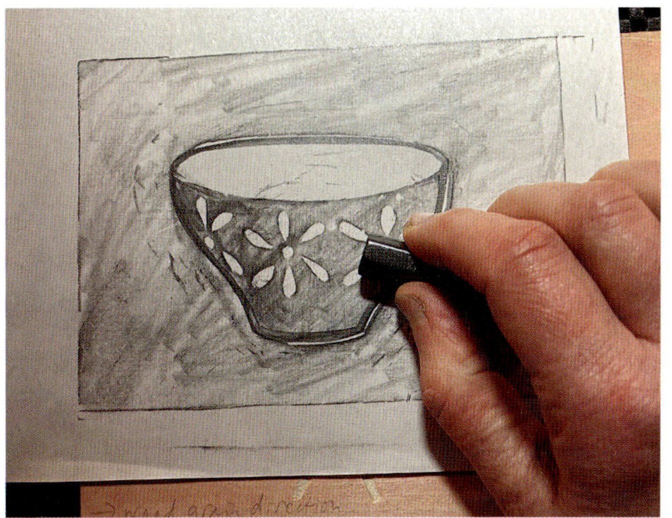

Using a graphite stick sideways on, take a rubbing of your cut area.

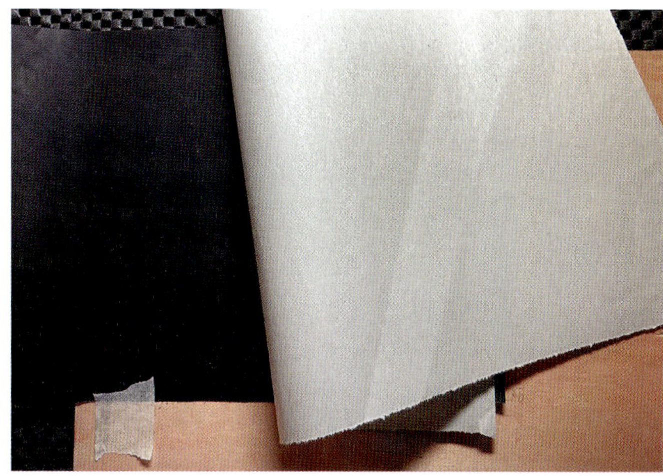

Using carbon paper to see how your cutting is going, tape the newsprint down, slide the carbon paper in shiny side up.

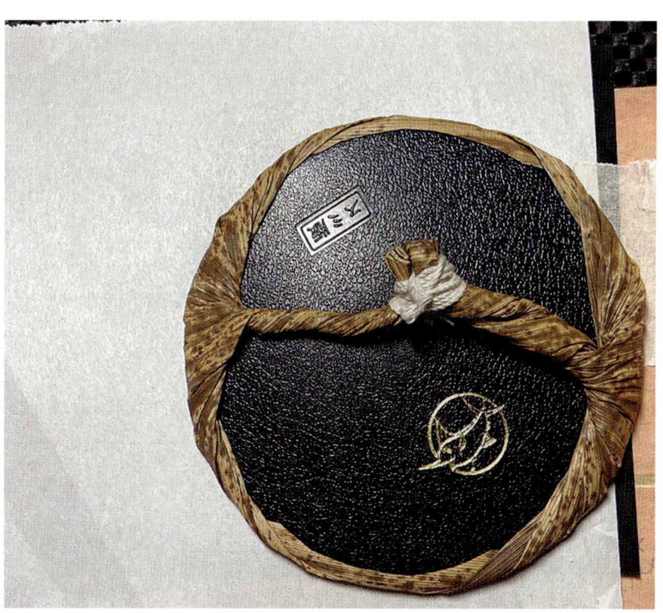

Rub down firmly with the *baren*.

It is useful to see how much 'chatter' or unwanted marks from cleared areas still need to be flattened before printing.

Another method for testing your cutting is by using carbon paper. The carbon paper is taped *shiny side up* on the cut woodblock.

The newsprint is taped on top of the carbon paper and using a *baren* the surface is rubbed; the carbon paper will print on to the newsprint revealing areas that need attention.

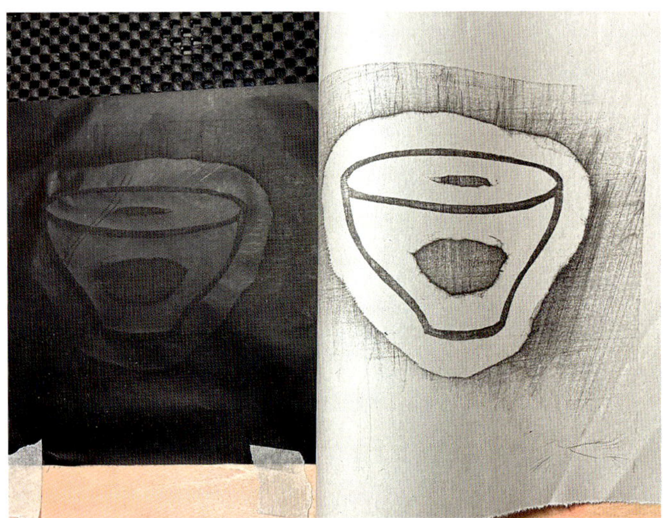

The image of your cutting transferred onto the newsprint paper.

KENTŌ REGISTRATION

Prior to the invention of the *kentō* registration, to achieve a colour print the printer would make a black and white print from the keyline block and then the print would be painstakingly coloured in by hand with watercolour *tan-e* (*see* Chapter 1). The prints were popular but slow to produce and demand soon outstripped supply. The publishers of the prints were looking for an inexpensive solution to make colour prints.

The *kentō* registration method is elegant and simple, and it is unique to Japan; it is one of the fundamental components of Mokuhanga and revolutionised the way that colour prints could be made. Its implementation can be dated back to 1765 when the artist Suzuki Harunobu devised a way of cutting notches directly into the woodblock, each colour separation having its own set of *kentō* registration cuts. When printing, the paper slides into the two registration cuts placed horizontally and vertically, so that each colour layer registers exactly with the one before.

The corner *kentō* or *kagi* has a slight dip where the corner of the printing paper is held, positioning the paper accurately. The second *kentō*, the *hikitsuke*, is cut along the middle of the long straight edge and supports the paper, as if on a shelf. The *kentō* would be cut by the master carver so there were no issues with accuracy in *ukiyō-e* printing. The registration was integral to the block allowing for greater flexibility when printing. *Kentō* registration paved the way for the production of multi-coloured prints comprising 30 or more different colour separations called *nashiki-e* or brocade pictures because they were so colourful, like brocade cloth. These proved to be very popular and the ease of registration meant that many more prints could be produced and sold cheaply. At the height of *ukiyō-e* popularity, a studio would employ a production line of printers who could produce on average around 200 prints a day, each print comprising 20 or more colour separations.

HOW TO CUT A KENTŌ

Method 1

After you have drawn up your design on tracing paper and flipped it ready to be transferred to your block, position the *kentō* corner by marking an 'x' on the right side if you are right-handed, left if left-handed. The *kentō* should be in the same place for each of your separations, so that if there are any discrepancies with the cutting of your printing paper your separations will still be accurately registered (it is also useful to have your dominant hand's thumb in control of the placement of the printing paper). *Kentō* are normally cut last after the cutting of the separations. Sometimes it is useful to make a temporary registration with masking tape on the woodblock if printing proofs are taken prior to cutting the *kentō*.

I use a *kentō nommi*, a 15mm-wide chisel with a bevel on one side, a short shaft and very sharp thin cutting edge. This tool needs to be kept in good condition and only used for the cutting of *kentō*. On older traditional *kentō nommi* the top of the

Showing the printing paper lined up in the *kentō* registration notches.

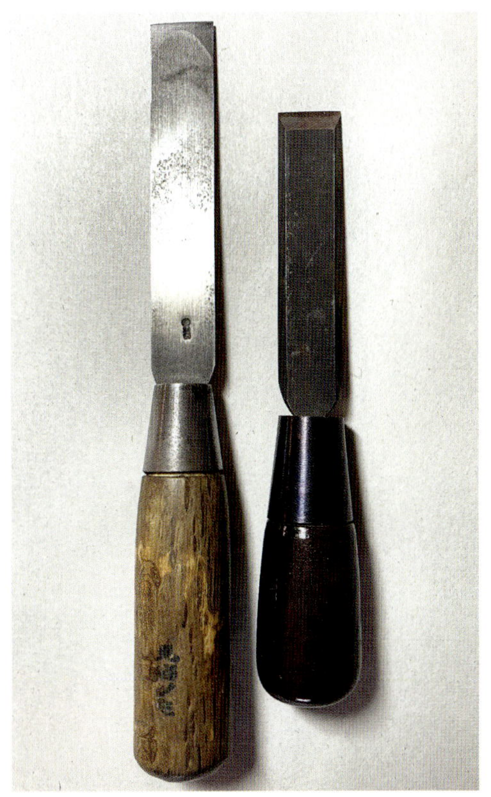

Kentō nommi or chisels with a super fine, sharp cutting edge and short, thin shaft. Bevelled on one side.

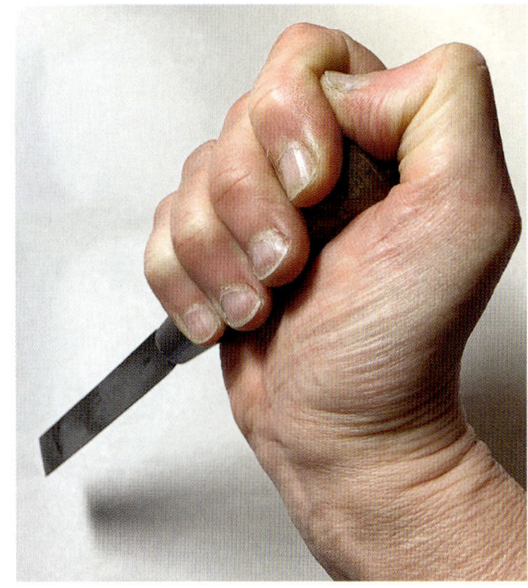

Initial handhold with the thumb on top of the tool for greater support.

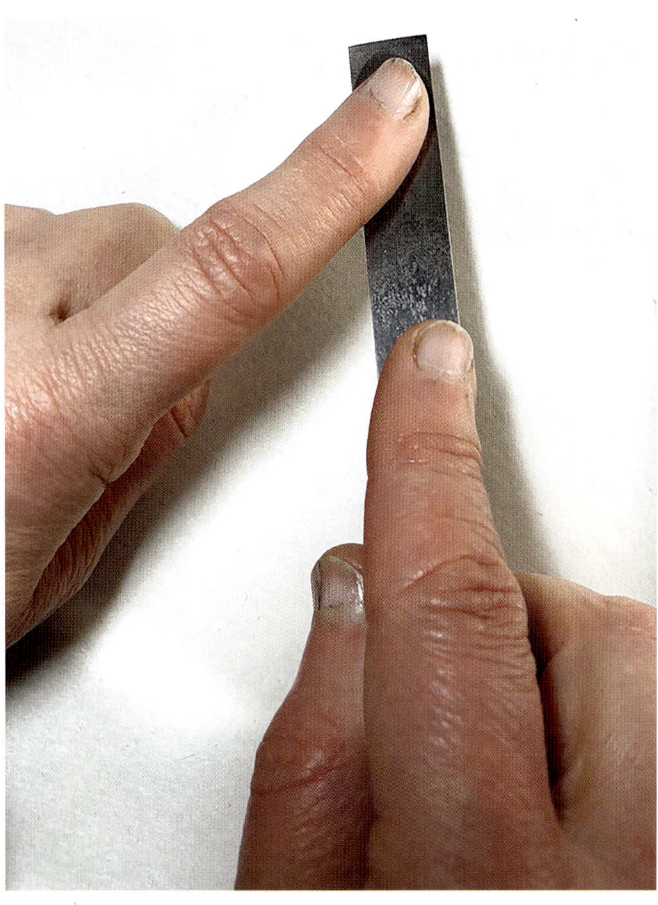

Handhold when cutting with the tool. Note that the index finger of the left hand presses down on the tool, giving added weight to the cut and also keeping the hand out of harm's way.

handle would be surmounted with metal to protect the wooden handle from splitting as a mallet would be used to make cuts in the hard cherrywood blocks that were used for *ukiyo-e* prints.

The first *kentō* is the *kagi* or corner *kentō*. You want a straight cut down so the tool must be positioned with the flat side to the registration line. If you cut with the bevel side you will be cutting an angle into your registration and your paper will not be sitting right up against the line.

I lay my left hand flat on the board with my thumb out making an L-shape. Resting the tool on my thumb with the flat side down allows me to see the line clearly and line up the tool accurately, instead of trying to eyeball the line from above.

Once the line has been lined up, press the tool into the wood so that it does not move out of alignment as you bring it into the upright 90-degree position. Again, if you attempt to cut and the tool is not upright, you will be cutting at an angle.

With both hands on top of the handle, rock the tool from side to side, not up and down as this makes the cut bigger. You should be able to see the cut easily; you can also run your fingernail along it to assess whether you have made a deep enough cut. There will be a difference cutting with the grain and against it. The depth of the cut should be equivalent to

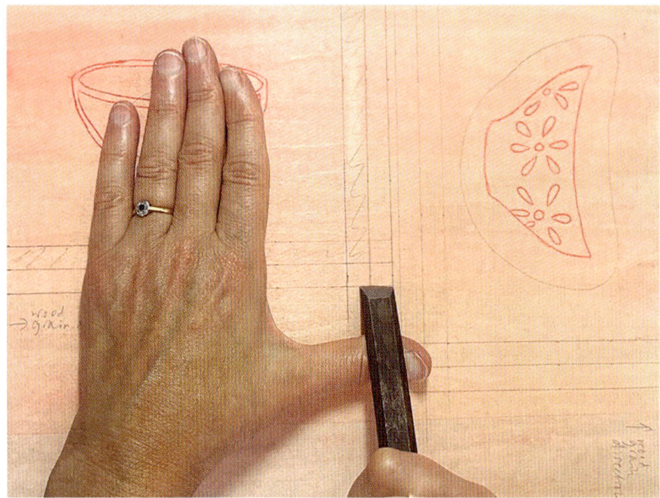

Making an L-shape with the left hand, the tool rests on the thumb, enabling a steady base so that the tool can be lined up accurately. The flat side of the tool is facing the line.

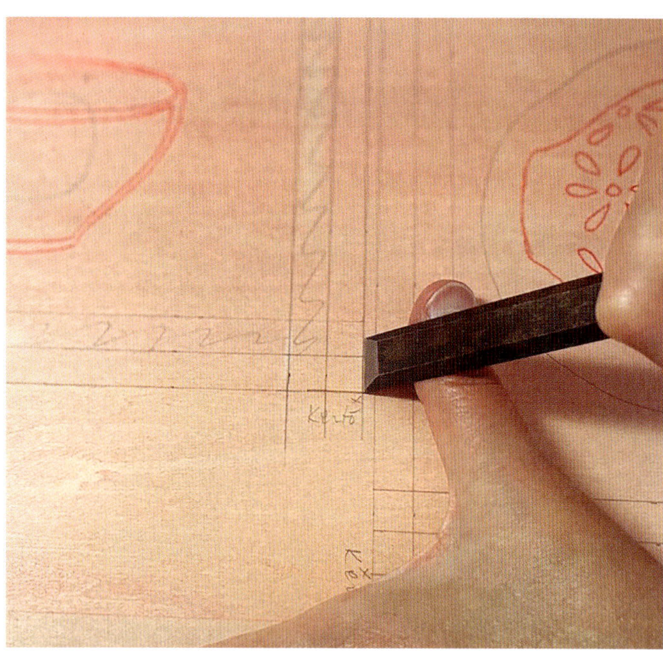

Cutting the other side of the corner or *kagi kentō* to form an L.

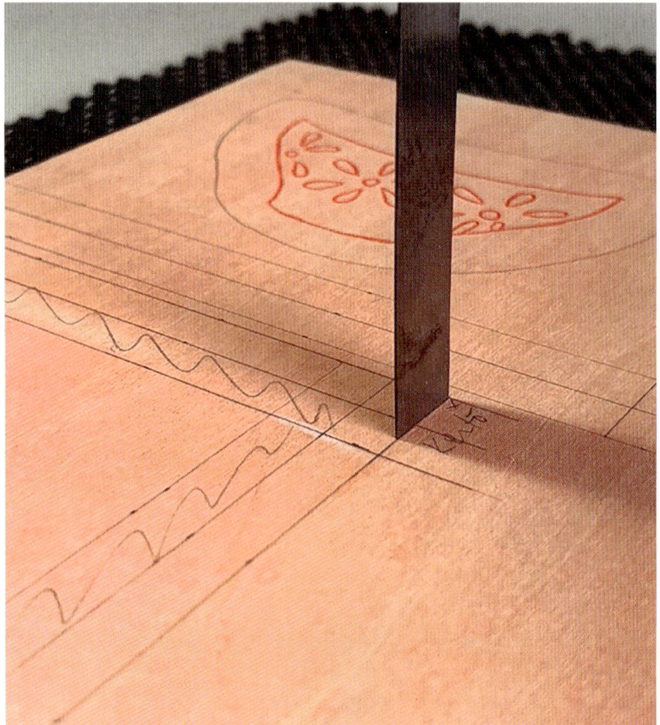

Bringing the tool upright to 90 degrees, the tool is pressed down firmly, with both hands on top, rocking from side to side.

approximately three times your paper's depth. In the same way, cut the other side of the *kagi Kentō*.

At the end of the cut line position your tool with the bevel turned and straddling the line half on one side, half on the other. Cut as before with your tool upright, hands on top rocking from

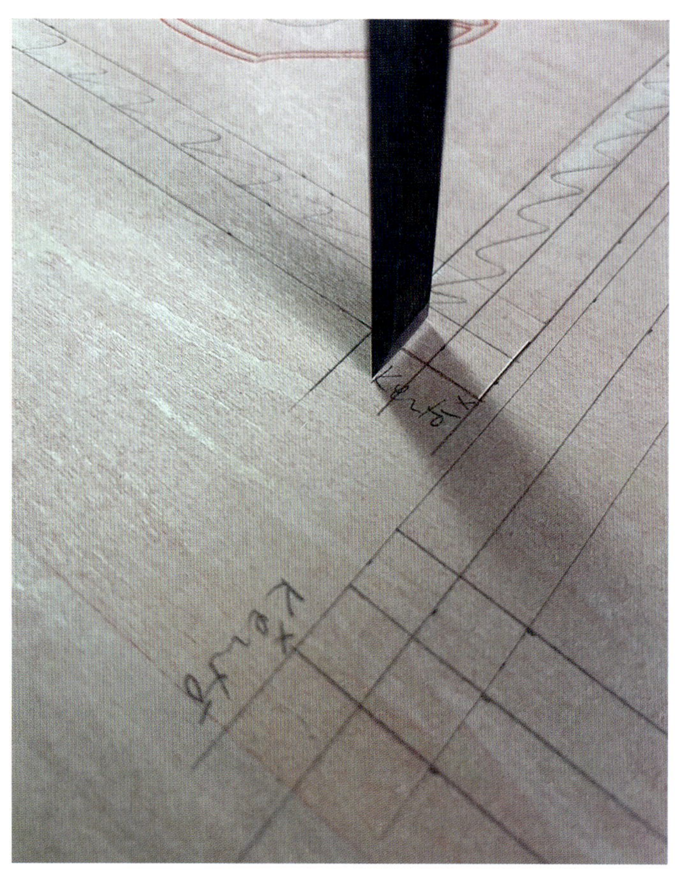

Cutting the finger slots at the end of the cut line, straddling the registration line.

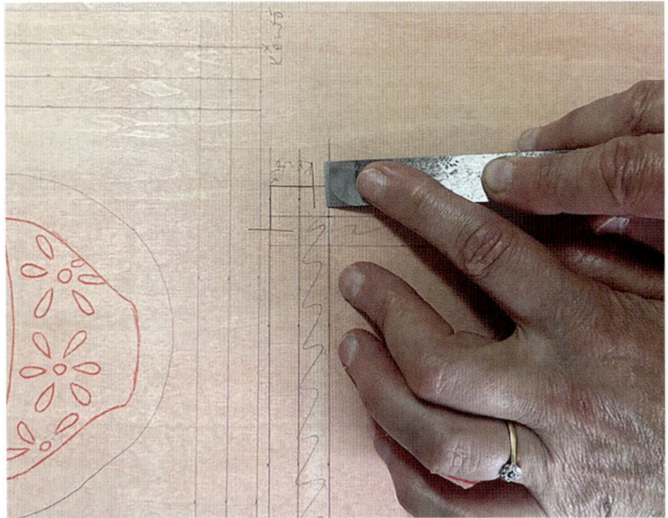

Lining up the tool with the line, pull back and make a shallow cut for the finger notches.

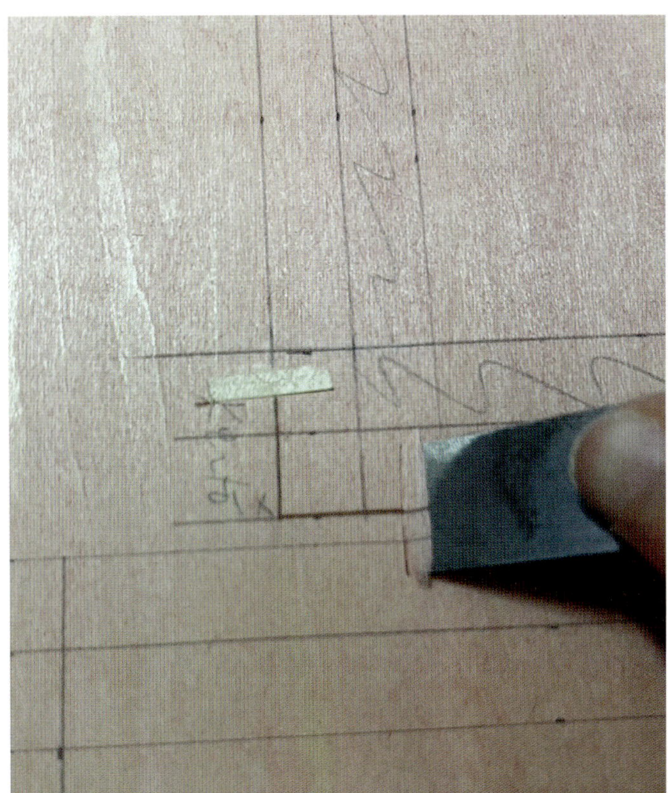

Cutting the other finger notch.

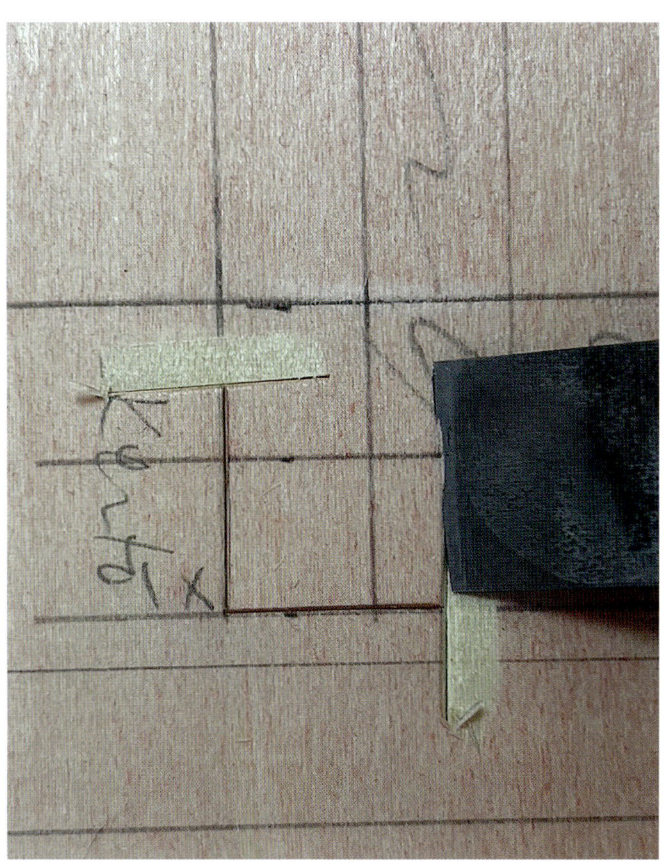

Lining up the tool approximately 1mm away from the cut line to cut out the corner *kentō*.

side to side. When you begin to print, the block is damp and so is the paper and sometimes the paper can get stuck in the *kentō* – these cuts are designed to use your fingernail to lift the paper out.

To cut out the notches the *kentō nommi* is positioned with the bevel down. The tool is held in the hand with the end of the handle wedged into the palm. The index finger of the non-dominant hand is resting on the metal shaft providing downward pressure, ensuring the tool does not slip and incidentally keeping it from harm's way.

I begin with the finger notches. I line up the tool with the cut line, pull back a little way and angling my tool to approximately 30 degrees, I make a shallow cut. One finger notch will be cut with the grain and makes a satisfying clunk when it clears, the other notch is against the woodgrain and is a bit untidier.

When cutting out the main notch the tool is angled to approximately 45 degrees and positioned so that the side nearest the registration line is at least 1mm away.

This is to protect the line from accidental nicks from the very sharp tool. I find cutting *kentō* standing up to be beneficial as you can slightly lean your weight behind the tool to make the cutting easier. It is important to cut steadily to make a flat

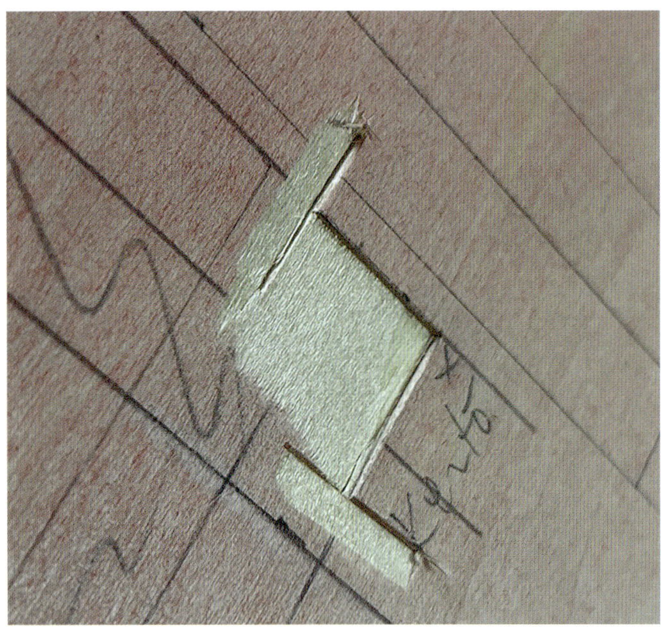

Steady pressure with the tool to cut out the square of wood forming the *kagi kentō*.

cut, not rock the tool from side to side, or lift the tool as you encounter resistance – all-natural reactions, but to be avoided.

Cut the other side of the *kentō* in the same way. To finish or if there are any areas remaining you can clear from a different direction. Ideally the immediate corner should be slightly deeper as this allows the damp printing paper to stay in place.

Halfway along the longest edge of your design is the second and final *kentō*; this is called the *hikitsuki kentō*. If your separations are close together on your board use your judgement about its placement. Not too near the *kagi kentō* or your paper could potentially not lie straight. Ideally the *hikitsuke* should be positioned towards the farther end of the block (but not too close to the edge) so that the printing paper can be held taut before placing into the registration notches.

To begin, line up your *kentō nommi* on the line with the flat side facing the line as before.

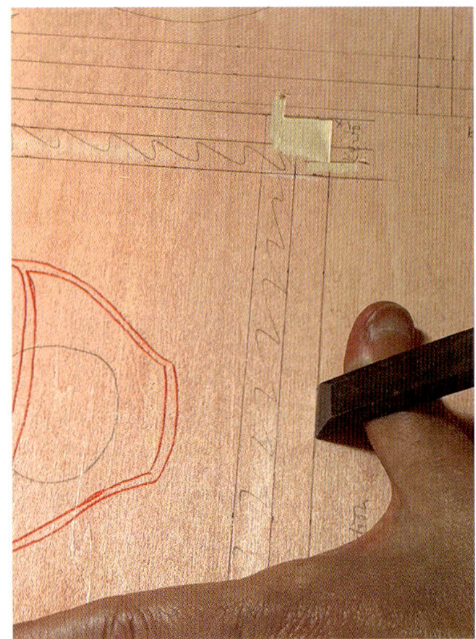

Line the tool up towards the middle of your registration line for your *hikitsuke kentō*, making sure that the flat side is facing the line. Bring your tool upright as before to make the cut.

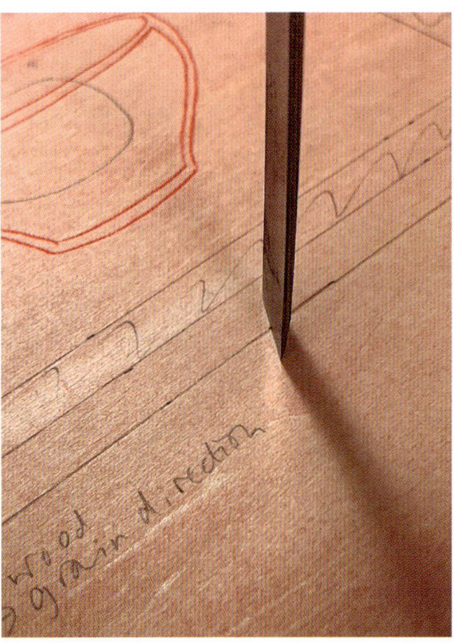

Make finger notch cuts on either side of the line, slanting inwards like a mountain slope.

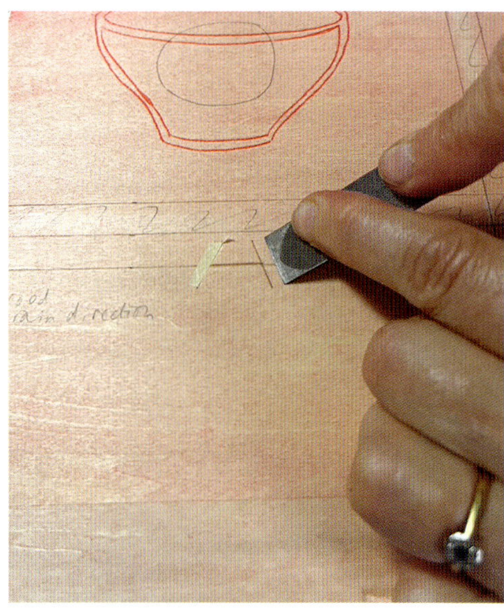

Begin by cutting out the finger notches.

Bring the tool upright, both hands on top and rock from side to side. Turning the tool so that the bevel faces the cut line, angle the tool and make two cuts either side of the cut line to make a mountain shape for the shoulder cuts.

Cut the shallower finger notches.

Cut a single notch for the final cut making a sort of shelf for the printing paper to rest on.

Finished *kentō*.

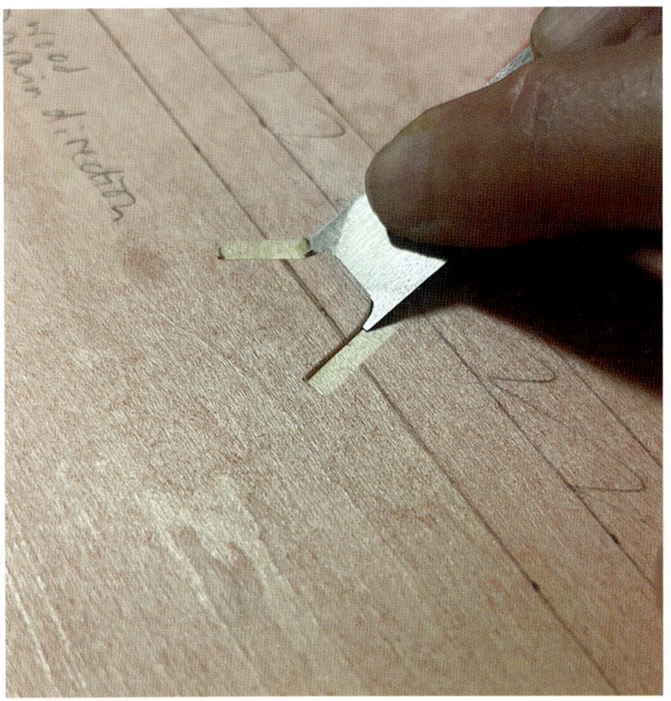

Clear from inside the registration area up to the cut line to make your *hikitsuke kentō*.

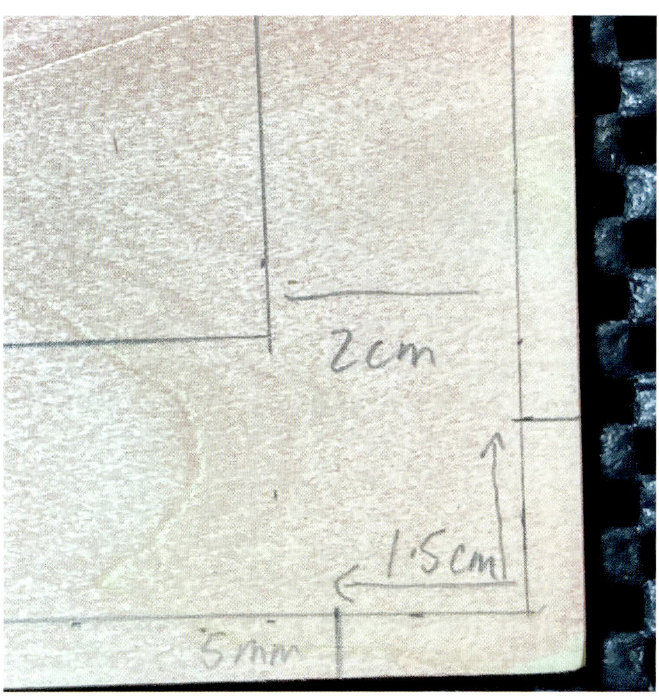

Alternative *kentō,* marked up on the woodblock.

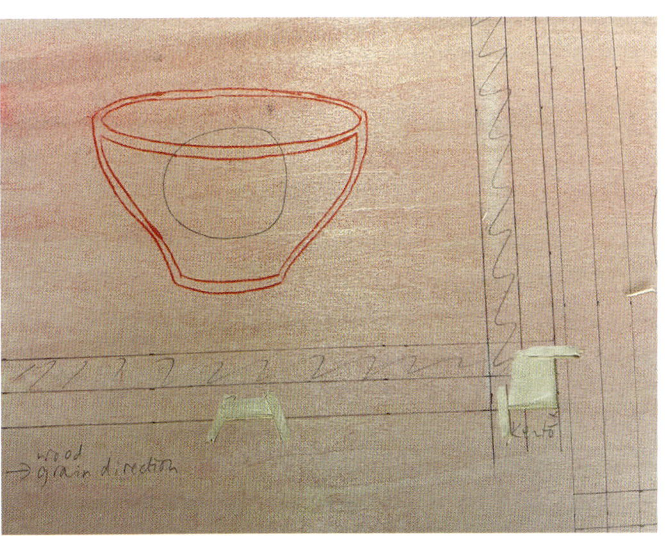

The cut *kentō*.

Repeat the process for all your colour separations.

The *kentō nommi* is not a cheap tool to buy and it can be difficult to source outside of Japan. It is the best tool to use in my experience but it is also possible to use the *hiratō*, the flat chisel, and the *hangitō*, making sure that the initial cut line with the *hangitō* is with the flat side to the registration line.

Method 2

There are alternative ways of cutting the *kentō* registration but the principles of the registration notches integral to the woodblock remain the same. In this method the *kentō* are cut along the edge of the woodblock, but it is important to take care to ensure

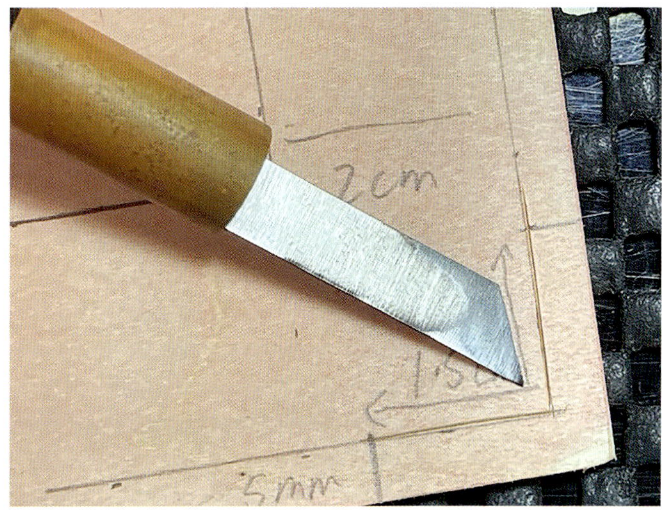

Using the flat side of the *hangitō* cut an outline around the L-shaped registration.

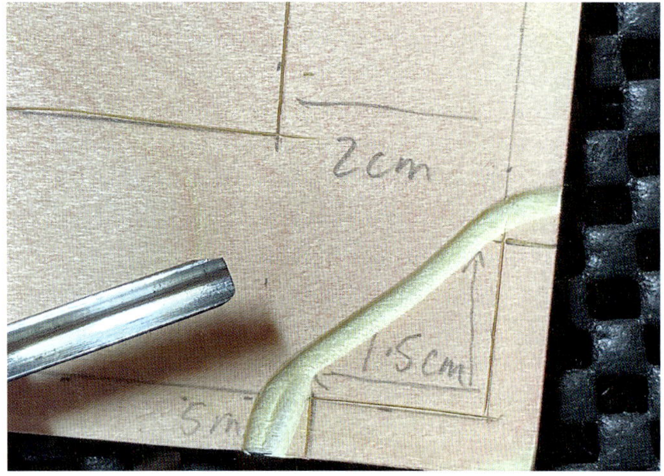

The *marutō* cuts a groove.

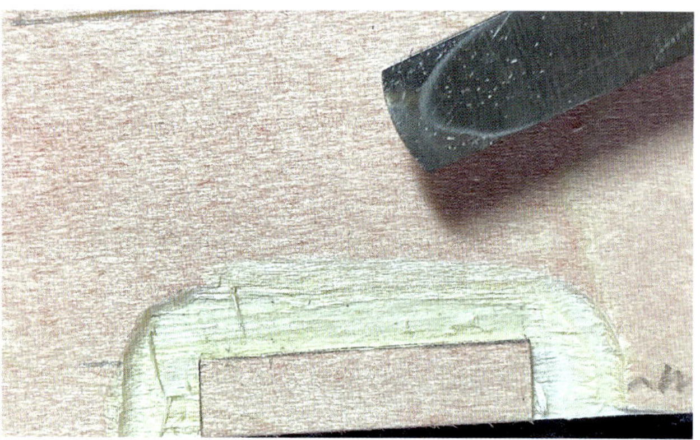

Clearing away with the *hiratō*.

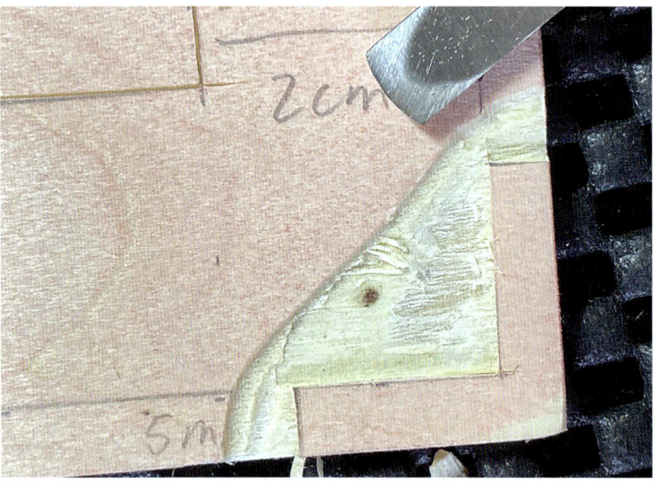

The *hiratō* clears away up to the cut line. Care is needed not to lose the raised registration area as it is on the edge of the board.

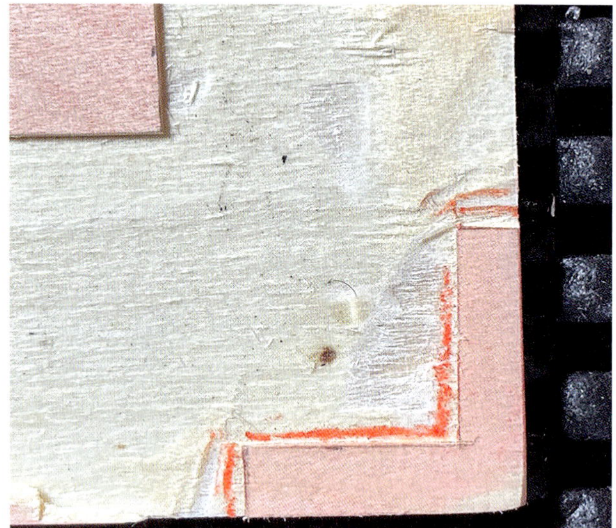

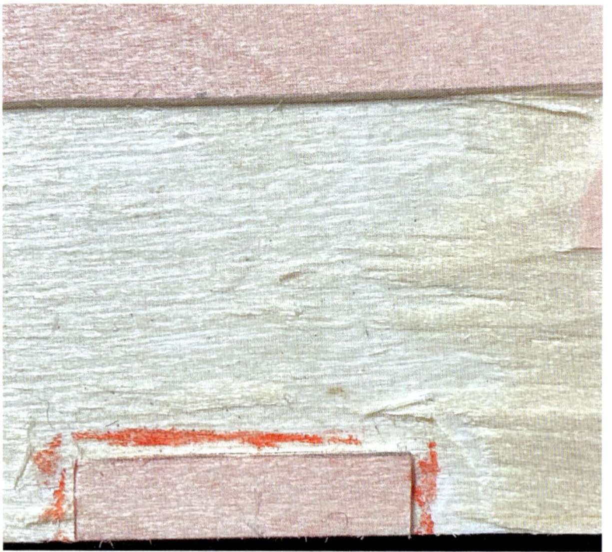

Cutting the outline of the *hikitsuke kentō* with the flat side of the *hangitō*. Using the *marutō* to cut a groove around the area.

Marking the registrations with a colour pencil.

that the cuts are made at least 5mm from the edge otherwise the surface veneer of the plywood is vulnerable to splitting.

Mark up 2cm for the paper gutter and 5mm from the edge of the corner of the block and 1.5cm horizontally and vertically to form the L-shape of the *kagi*, or corner *kentō*.

Cut the registration edges with either the *kentō nommi*, a scalpel, Stanley knife or the *hangitō* with the tool turned so that the flat side is nearest the line, so that a straight cut down is made. Finish off the ends too.

Use the *marutō* or gouge to cut a rough groove around the *kentō* area.

Use the *hiratō* to clear away revealing a clean cut *kagi Kentō*.

For the *hikitsuke,* a simple cut along the registration line then cut a groove with the *marutō* around the shape.

Clearing with the *hiratō*, leaving a raised rectangle of wood where the printing paper rests.

Clear the wood around both of the *kentō* areas and up to the image area. It is useful to mark the *kentō* with a coloured pencil to avoid removing it by accident.

Method 3: *Kentōban*

A useful tool for the registration of mainly larger blocks is an accurately cut L-shaped length of wood the same depth as your woodblock called a *kentōban*. In Japan, Keiko Kadota called it the 'stupid' *kentō*, as it is not a traditional tool. The printing woodblock slots into the L-shape and holds it in position – it is best to do this on a non-slip mat. In this way your image can go right to the edge of your woodblock.

Kentō registration notches can be cut into the *kentōban* itself too, so that the printing paper can be positioned accurately, and separations registered, effectively giving a margin and increasing the size of your finished print.

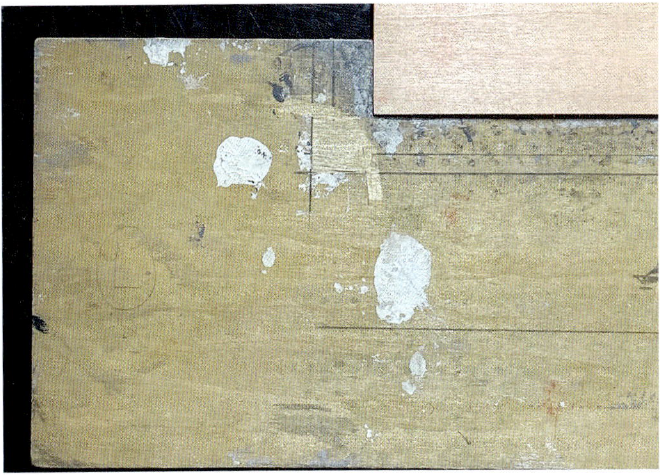

Kentōban or floating *kentō* with woodblock slotted into L-shaped cut-out.

Showing printing paper slotted into *kentō* notches cut into the *kentōban*.

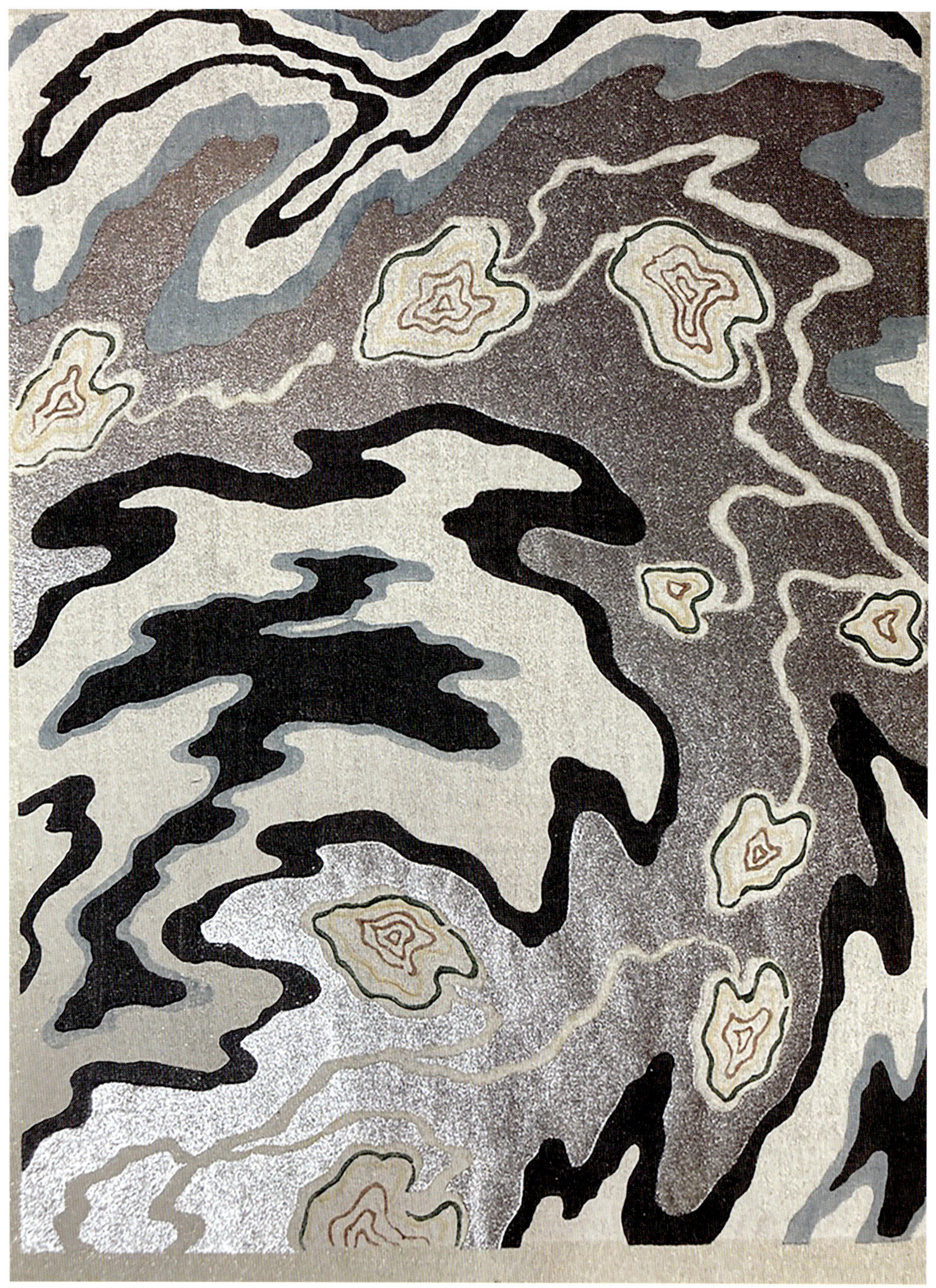

Chapter 5

PRINTING

The secret of Japanese woodcut printing is mainly to do with the control and use of water. The ideal day to print is on a rainy day as the moisture in the atmosphere affects and improves the printing. This chapter looks at setting up ready for printing for those learning the technique for the first time and at different methods of achieving specific printing effects for the more advanced, including printing larger woodblocks.

Where Mokuhanga and Western press-based printmaking most markedly diverge is in the printing process itself. There is a

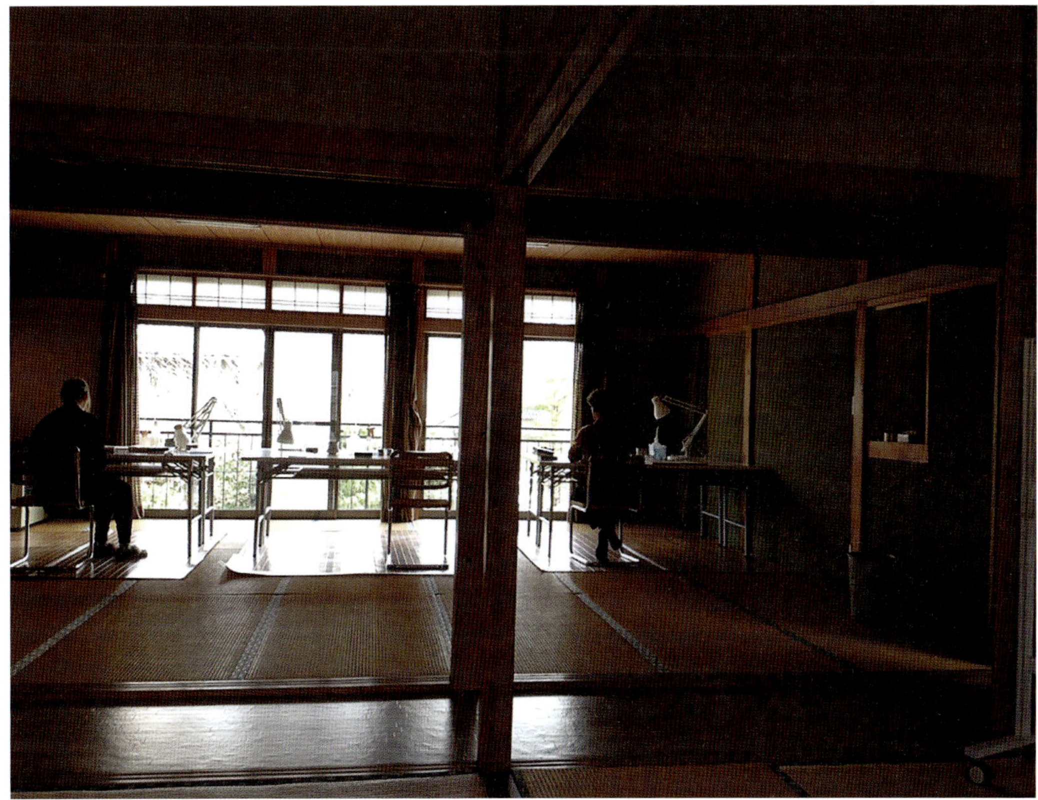

The printmaking studio at MI-Lab in Fujikawaguchiko, Japan. This clean space with *tatami* mats was a very calm, restful place. The only sound was the soft scratching of woodcutting. Out of the window to the right was the view of Mount Fuji.

◀ Unknown artist. Japanese woodblock print, part of author's print collection.

deceptive simplicity to printing Mokuhanga; there are no messy oily inks to deal with and clear away, there is no expensive, heavy press to service or press blankets to keep clean.

Printing linocut blocks, for example, typically involves using a roller or brayer to add a thin even layer of oil-based ink to the surface of the block, placing the block onto the bed of the press between registration marks, laying the paper on top and rolling the block and paper through a metal roller. After rolling through the press, the ink has transferred to the paper and the print is pulled from the block.

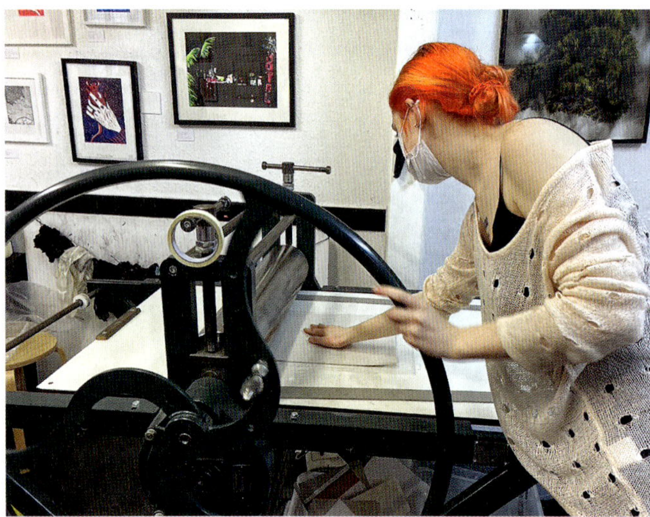

A Western relief printmaking studio press in action.

In one of my classes, a student once set the roller in motion, crossed the room to collect some forgotten item, only to return when the roller had completed its rotation. Bad practice, certainly, but one that serves to emphasise the point that the artist is no longer part of the printing process. Effectively, this has been surrendered to the machine.

Of the five senses, the most crucially the overlooked is arguably the sense of touch. The feel of the wood grain, the exact amount of pressure you need to exert with the tools to achieve a cursive line, the tactile nuance of different *washi* papers, the press of the baren: all these become haptic memories. To become proficient at Mokuhanga it is essential to empathise with the materials. I am frequently asked how much water do I add to the *nori*? How wet is too wet? My answer is always that it is a matter of experience. More than any other printmaking process that I have ever encountered, Mokuhanga is a holistic technique where every element is relevant – even the weather plays a significant role. It is wonderful to see my Mokuhanga students reawaken suppressed senses and re-establish individual control over the printing process.

To print a Japanese woodcut, you begin with dampening the woodblock. Watercolour pigments and *nori* are then brushed into the woodgrain of the block and an impression is made by placing damp printing paper into the *kentō* registration notches and rubbing the back of the paper with a *baren.* Even though the process is easy to understand it would take a lifetime to learn its many, many variables.

CHECKLIST FOR PRINTING

- Newsprint paper
- Zip lock bag (big enough to take your paper comfortably) or sheet of strong plastic
- Printing paper cut to size
- Two waterpots
- Pipette
- Palette
- Watercolour pigments in tubes not pans
- Western brushes
- Japanese *te bake* and *maru bake*
- *Nori* diluted in a sealable pot
- Chopstick
- Baking sheet
- *Baren*

PREPARATION

Printing Paper

The deckle or ragged edge of handmade paper has been a very attractive feature in Western printmaking and books since the seventeenth century. Originally, when papers were imported from Asia with a deckle edge they were trimmed by the bookbinders as it was seen as a defect. Later with the production of machined paper, a deckle edge became a mark of the handmade and now there are even artificially made deckle edges on machine-made paper – an imitation of imperfection to fool the purchaser into thinking that they are buying a handmade, quality paper.

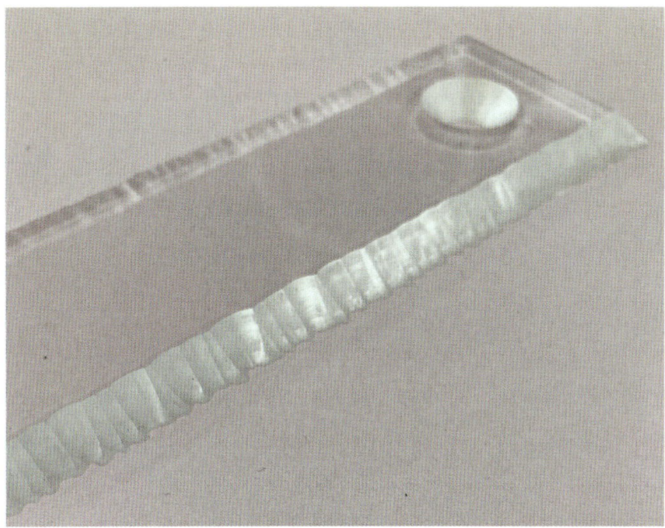

A Perspex ruler with jagged serrations; when a paper is torn along this edge it simulates a handmade deckle edge.

For Mokuhanga the deckle is cut away so that the clean edge can slot easily into the *kentō* registration notches. It is worth noting that in Japan during the *ukiyo-e* period all the paper was handmade and so a deckle edge denoting a handmade paper was not seen as exceptional.

If you wish to retain the deckle edge it is possible to use *nori* to paste a folded piece of paper to the front and back of your printing paper positioned away from the deckle edge, ensuring that the folded pieces of paper line up with both *kagi* and *hikitsuke kentō* on the woodblock. The straight edge of the folded paper can slot into the *kentō* notches when printing, and be removed when printing is complete by dissolving the *nori* using a damp, soft sponge.

Cutting your Printing Papers

Line up your set square with the bottom edge of the paper, then when you place your metal ruler alongside, you can be

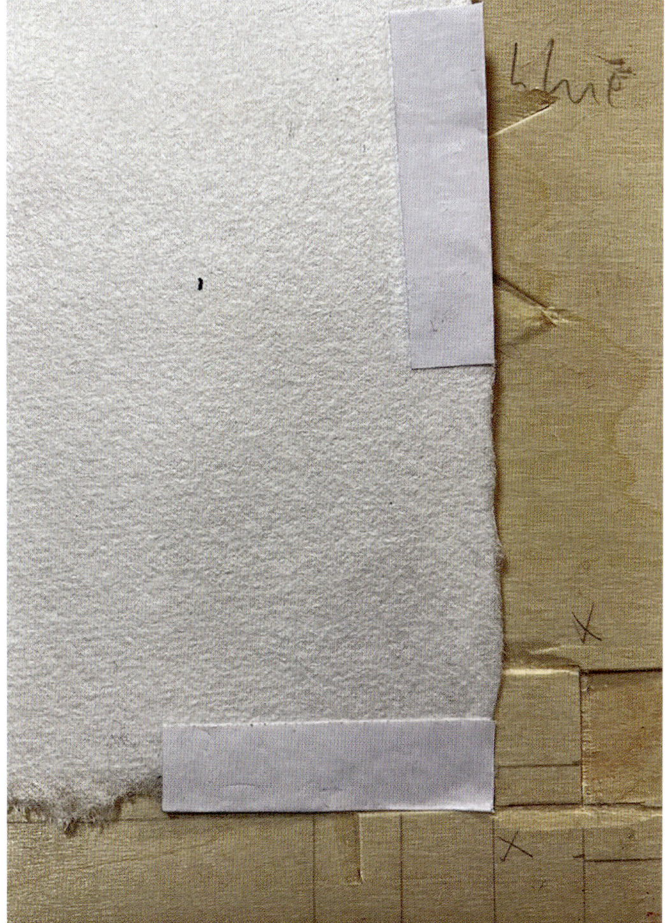

Using *nori* paste to glue removeable paper tabs to register deckle-edged paper in the *kentō* notches.

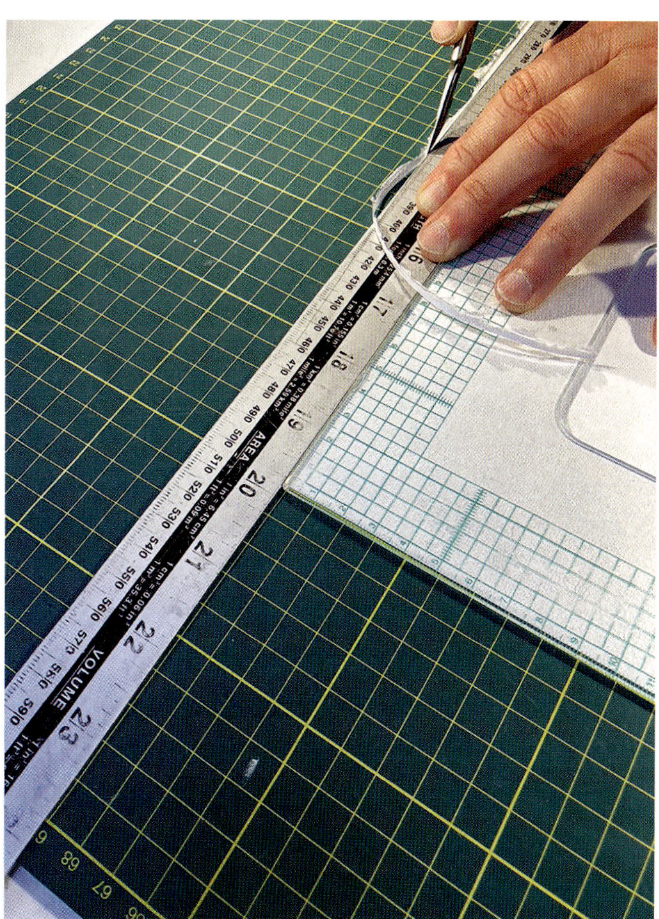

Use a set-square to ensure that when you cut your deckle edge it is at a right angle.

The back of the printing paper is the rough side. You can see it, and also feel it by touch.

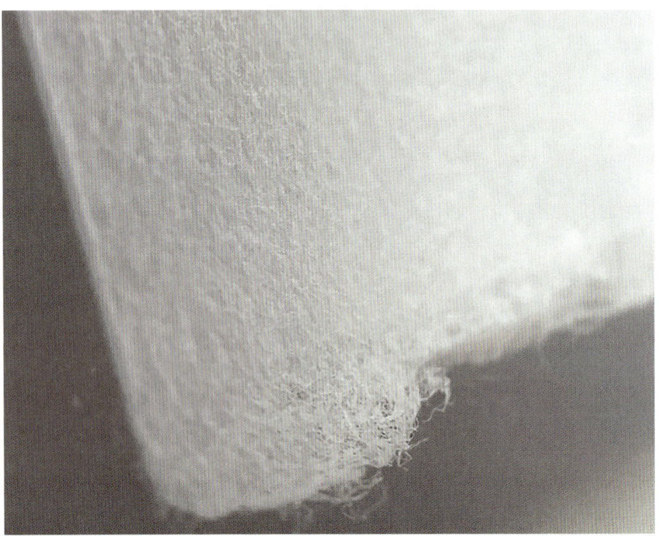

The smooth, printing side of the paper.

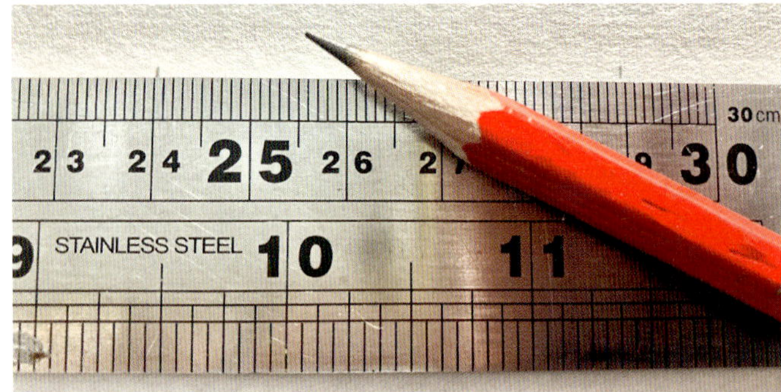

Showing three pencil dots along the ruler's edge.

confident that when you cut with a scalpel, the paper will be all-square. I have found that some of the handmade papers have slightly variable sizes and are not necessarily of equal length.

There are two sides to the printing paper; the smooth side is the printing side. Turn your paper over to mark it up on the back, so that the pencil lines will not show up on the finished print. The smoothness is due to the presence of a light amount of size or *dosa*, a kind of glue that allows the pigment to effectively dye the paper but not bleed sideways.

There will be an equal margin around the print image on all sides (at least 2cm for smaller prints, a wider margin for larger). As your image is cut right into the corner of your woodblock two sides of the paper will overhang the block leaving the other two sides to slot into the *kentō* registration notches. If for example the image measures 10.5 × 15cm, the paper will measure 14.5 × 19cm.

I use a long ruler and measure all the widths and then the lengths. I mark the paper with three parallel dots so that when I lay the ruler down to cut all I need to do is join the dots. Use a metal ruler not a plastic one as it is very easy to cut notches into the plastic leading to an inaccurate or bumpy cut line.

Ensure that you have a cutting board underneath and always use a fresh blade in your scalpel – a blunt scalpel will tear not cut the paper. When you have lined up your ruler against the measured dots it is most important that the hand holding the ruler down is well away from the cutting edge. For cutting using a long ruler, I cut just past the hand holding the ruler and then 'walk' the hand down the ruler and carry on cutting. It is important to keep the ruler in place during this process. Hold the scalpel at approximately a 45-degree angle and cut.

When all the papers have been cut, on the wrong side (the rough side of the paper) mark an 'X' in the corner that corresponds with the *kentō*. This really helps when printing; firstly, to tell the back from the front of the print and also to identify the orientation of the print, useful in the early stages of printing separations.

Damp Pack

The paper needs to be dampened prior to printing, it is important to note that the paper is just damp and not wet. Some Mokuhanga artists do this by spraying the back of the paper and brushing the water evenly across with a *mizu bake* or water brush, each piece of paper stacked on top of the next and placed in a zip lock bag. The main issue I have with this method is

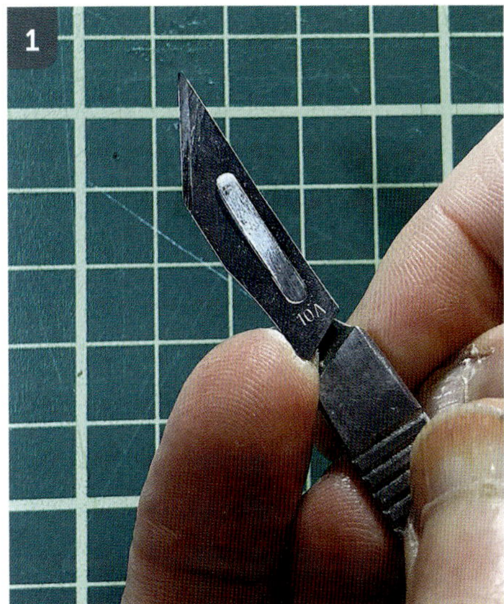

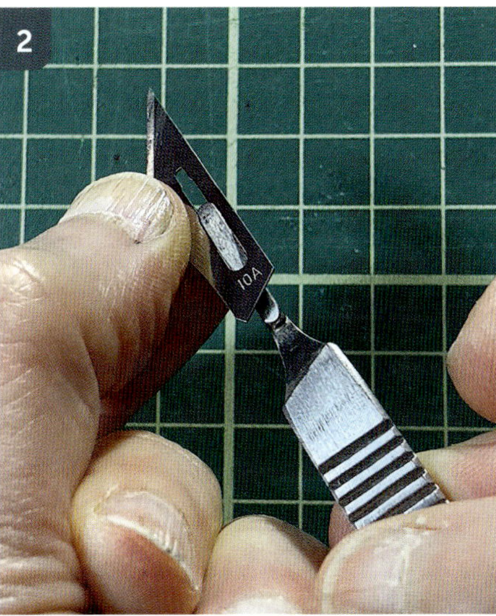

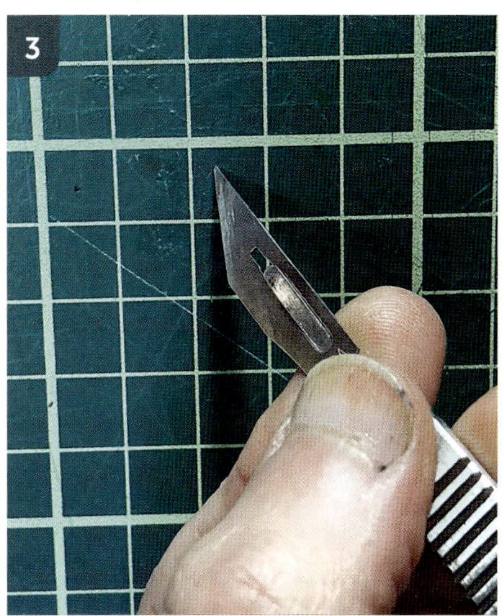

1. Hold the scalpel securely in your right hand, lever the blade out of the raised holder with your left index fingernail – without too much force as it could snap.

Keeping your hand away from the cutting blade slide the blade down and off, with your left hand.

Taking a fresh blade, slide it on to the raised holder. Hold securely in place as you press it into the cutting board. It will snap into place.

inadvertently over-saturating the paper with water making the watercolour pigment liable to bleed on the print. The papers on either end of the stack are also more inclined to dry out and the papers in the middle to be too wet.

Another method for dampening the paper is to make a damp pack. This is made from newsprint paper; it could be from a newspaper but do ensure that if so it is at least two weeks old so that the printers' ink has dried completely and will not transfer onto your pristine paper. The number of sheets needed for the damp pack is dependent on how many printing papers you are intending to use. There should ideally be two blank sheets between each printing paper so that it absorbs water from above and below.

Starting at the back of the 'book' of newsprint, begin by brushing with the *mizu bake* from the top to the bottom of the 'page'. Take care to cover the newsprint with water, leaving no dry areas. The *mizu bake* made from either goat or sheep hair is ideally suited for the job as the densely packed brush picks up enough water to 'paint' an entire 'page' without refilling and the soft hairs leave no trace. A wallpaper brush would also work but make sure that the bristles are not too coarse.

Leave a 'page' undampened between each dampened page, which allows the water to percolate through making for an even

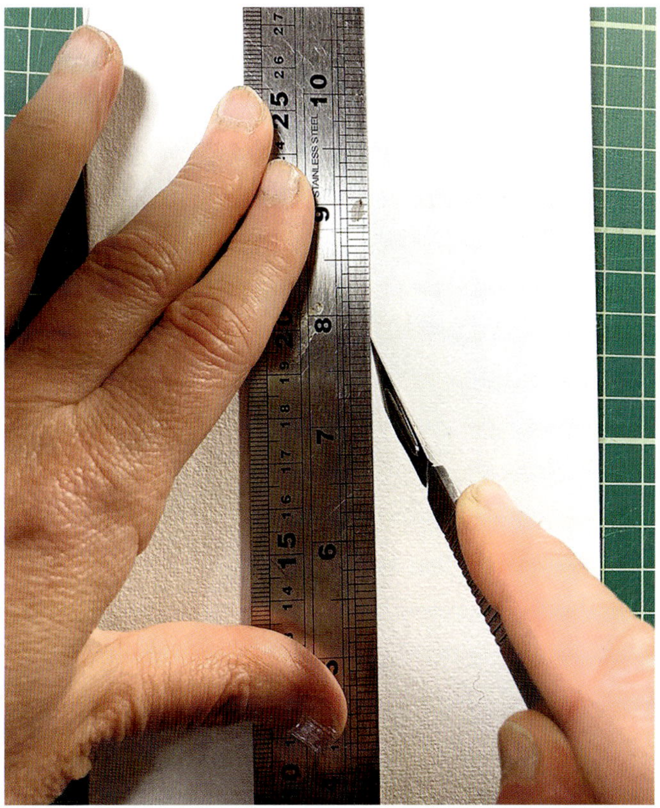

Showing the position of your left hand away from the edge of the ruler. The scalpel blade is at a 45-degree angle and cut against the metal ruler.

dampness. The next 'page' is dampened from the bottom up, the following one top down. This is because the initial brush with the *mizu bake* is full of water and by alternating the starting points, the water in the damp pack becomes more evenly distributed.

The damp pack is stored in a sealed zip lock bag until all of the sheets are evenly damp – this may take 30 minutes or more. The longer you allow the damp pack to soak up the water evenly the better it will be for your printing papers. I have left mine overnight so that I am ready to print first thing in the morning. But in very warm weather this is not advisable as mould can develop.

When inserting your papers into the damp pack start at the back and if you can, put two printing papers next to each other. Avoid putting printing papers in the 'covers' of your damp pack as these areas dry out the quickest.

Place them with the 'X'-marked *kentō* corner uppermost and next to the open end of the damp pack. This simple placement ensures that you never print on the wrong side of the paper and your papers are in the same alignment and orientation.

Leave one or two pages and then insert the next papers and so on. This allows the printing papers to soak up water from both sides. Do not be tempted to overfill your damp pack as it will dry out quickly and result in poorly dampened paper. When you are finished, put the damp pack back into the zip lock bag with the open end of the damp pack nearest the zip for ease of access when printing.

If your paper is thick then it will need to be dampened for a longer time than a thin paper. For an midweight paper such as *hoshō*, I leave it in the damp pack for at least 30 minutes. It is possible to leave papers overnight if they are thicker, thin papers (less than 30gsm) need only five minutes, if that. The paper should feel cool to the touch, it should not be too floppy – if it is then you have too much water in the paper, which can be rectified by putting the paper between dry sheets of newspaper or blotting paper to soak up the excess. There should be no visible water on the surface; if there is it needs to be gently brushed off with a soft brush. If there are visible drier patches on your printing paper these will print differently to the rest, so put the paper back into the damp pack until it has achieved a more even dampness.

In warm weather it is a good idea to regularly monitor the dampness of the damp pack and the printing papers, and if required spray water onto the newsprint when it seems to be drying out too quickly. Any papers not used during the

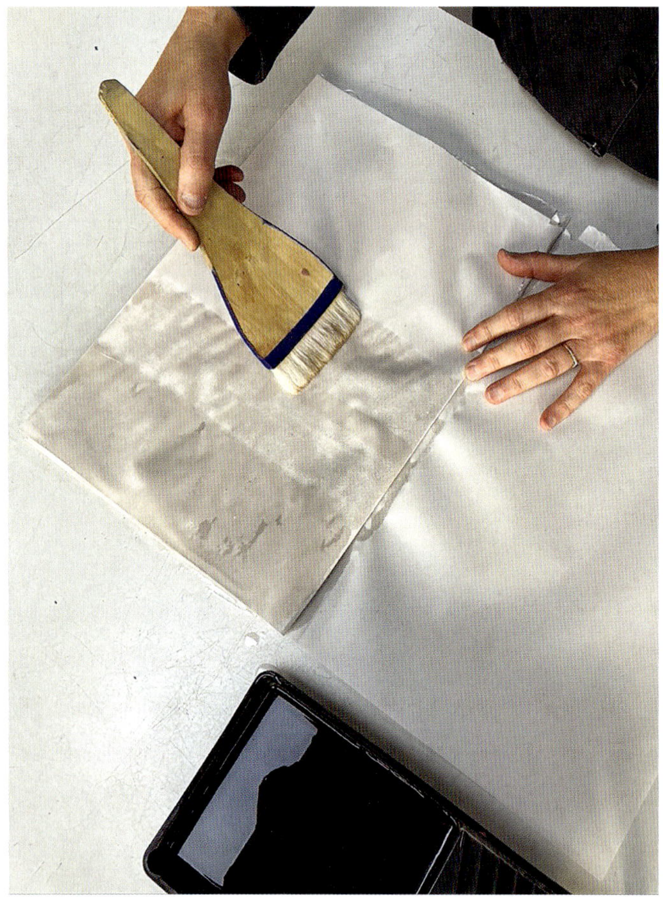

Painting water onto newsprint to make a damp pack for your printing papers.

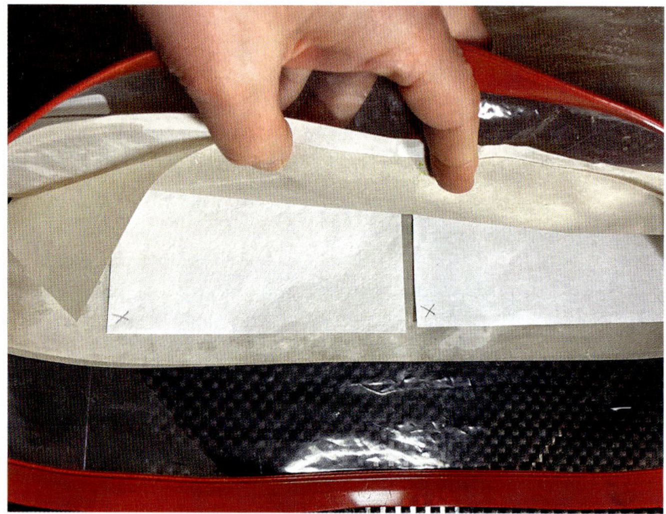

Alignment of printing papers showing *kentō* corners right way around ready for printing.

printing can be taken out of the damp pack, allowed to dry and re-dampened for a subsequent printing session.

Mixing *Nori*

Nori is a key component of the Mokuhanga printing process. It is made from cooked rice flour to form a paste. Its purpose is to provide an even surface for the pigment when printing; it also contributes water to the process lengthening the time available before the block dries.

Squeeze a small amount of *nori* about half a finger's length into a pot with a sealable lid. Using a pipette, add a small amount of water.

Taking a chopstick (because the *nori* would get stuck in a brush's bristles) stir the paste until there are no lumps. Do not be tempted to add a larger amount of water because this will result in a too-watery *nori* that cannot be used.

Add a small amount of water at a time (like making a white sauce), stir the paste until the *nori* drops off the end of the stick willingly. Then seal the pot so that the *nori* stays the right consistency and does not thicken before printing.

As I have said before, the secret to Mokuhanga is the control of water. If you want to use a thicker pigment then your *nori* needs to be more dilute; similarly if you are using a pale, dilute pigment then your *nori* needs to be correspondingly thicker to keep the balance of water in the woodblock.

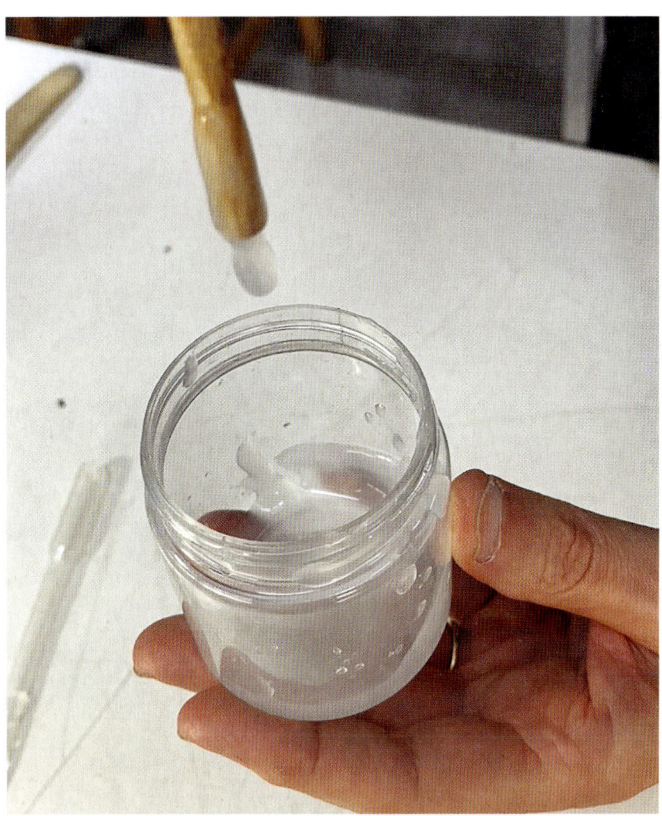

Water is mixed with the *nori*, with a chopstick. The right consistency is achieved when the *nori* drops willingly off the chopstick.

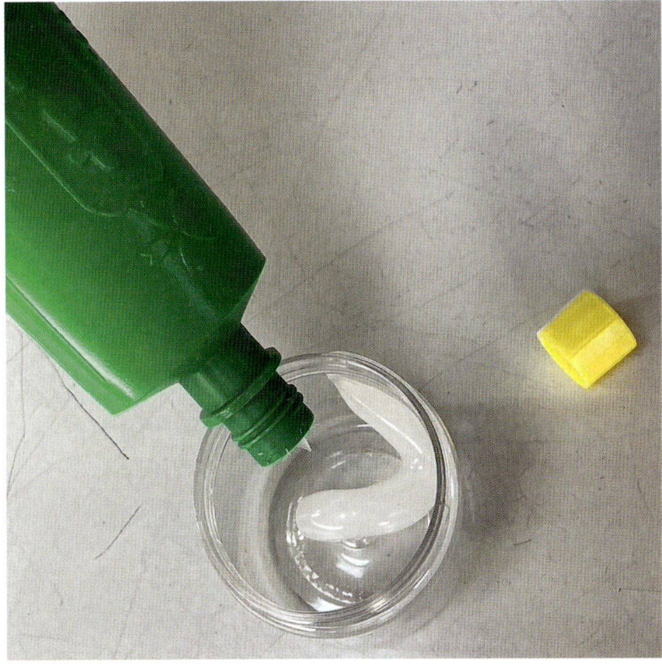

Nori squeezed into a sealable glass container.

Setting Up Your Print Area

Traditionally printing would be done by a production line of printers in a print workshop completing on average up to 200 finished prints a day. The printer would sit on a cushion on the floor and work on a low table called a *suridai that* slanted away from him. This inclination is important as it eased the position of the lumbar spine during printing and also prevented the wrists from becoming too tired. In front of the printer would be the *maebako*, a shelf holding the moistened sheets ready for printing, and to his left the *yokoita*, a low table covered in moisture-resistant wood where the fresh prints were laid. On the right would be the *yokobako*, a set of drawers containing tools, brushes, *barens* and pigment bowls. Everything would be laid out within easy reach taking up very little space.

For my classes I ask students to set up their printing area in a way that allows for easy movement when printing with everything needed to hand. The process requires the control of water and there should be a fluidity to the printing too, to ensure that the paper, pigment and block do not dry out before a print has been pulled.

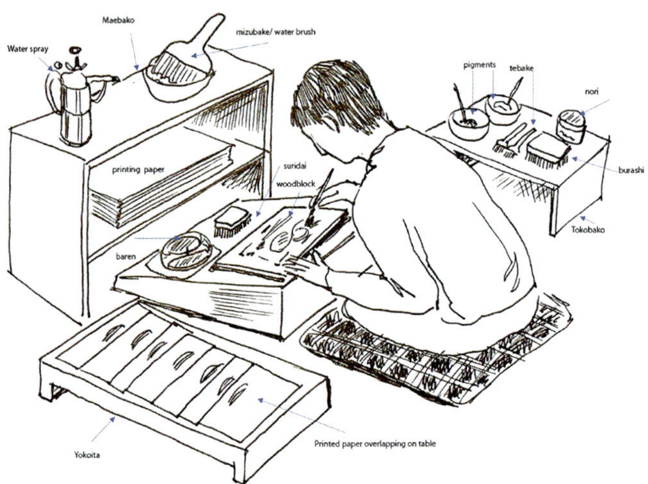

Drawing showing a traditional printer's set-up. (Copyright Carol Wilhide Justin.)

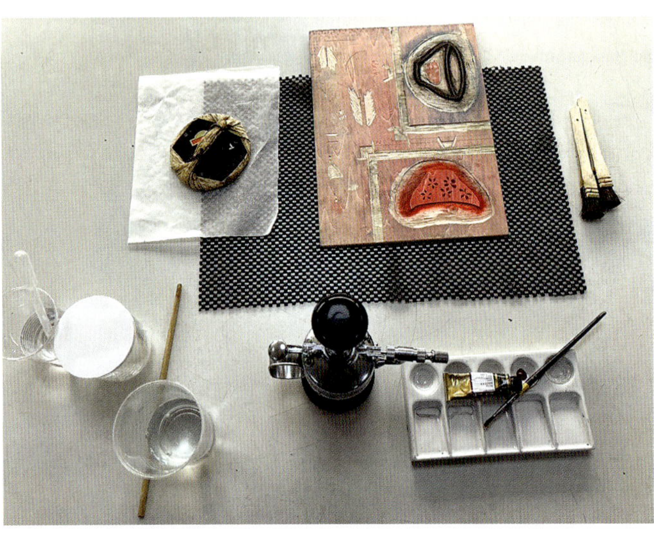

Setting up your print area.

I have become tired with paintbrushes loaded with pigment slipping off the edge of the palette, messing up the table and potentially ruining the print. I have devised a very simple paintbrush holder device that works very well. I begin by folding a piece of stiffish card, and then with a pair of scissors make V-shaped cuts into the closed fold. Opening it out, I now have notches so that I can keep my brushes propped up. Easy to unfold flat and store too.

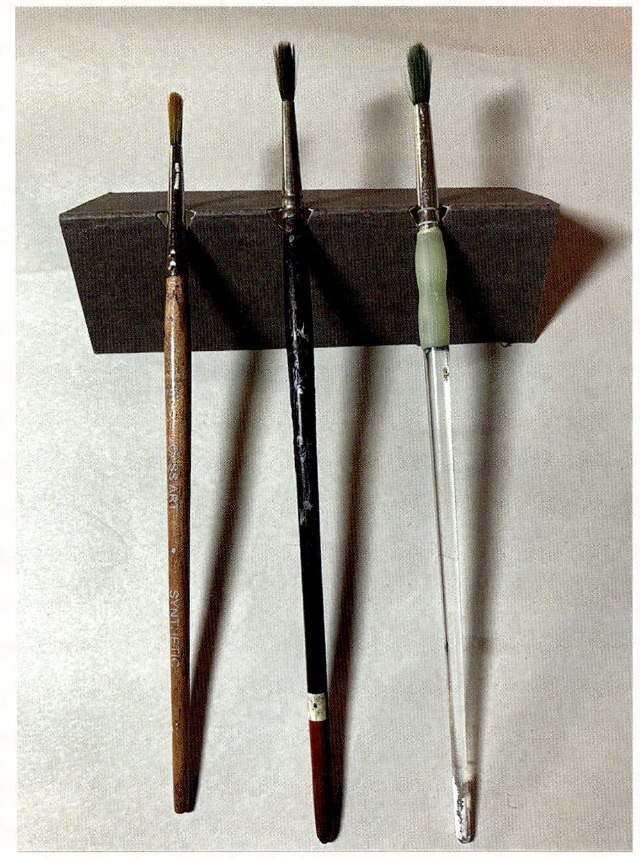

My handy solution to a perennial problem.

PRINTING PROCESS IN STEPS

1. Make your damp pack, allow time for water to percolate through the pages, at least 30 minutes.
2. Cut your printing paper and mark the *kentō* corner with an 'X'.
3. Interleave your printing papers in the damp pack and leave for at least 30 minutes.
4. Ensure gutters are smoothed on your woodblock and rubbings taken to identify 'chatter' to be removed.
5. Dilute *nori* to the consistency of single cream; seal the pot after mixing.
6. Set up your print area, clear any wood chippings.
7. Spray the separation area on the woodblock you are about to print; allow the water to sink into the woodgrain before beginning.

You can use an inexpensive water spray bottle from your local discount shop – however the water droplets are often large and do not absorb evenly into the woodblock. Finest of all is a water spray from Japan, a 'Dahlia sprayer' used for misting plants. The water is pumped up and comes out in fine droplets.

8. Generally, you would begin with the lightest colour and work towards the darkest.

9. Squeeze watercolour pigment from a tube into the palette, mix colour with water again use the pipette so that you can calibrate the amount of water used.

10. When the water is no longer visible on the surface of the woodblock, dot on *nori* with a chopstick and brush well in with a *te bake* or *marubake* until there is just a sheen on the surface and no visible streaks of *nori*. Do not apply too much *nori* especially if you have fine cutting, as it will clog in between the cut lines and pick up pigment.

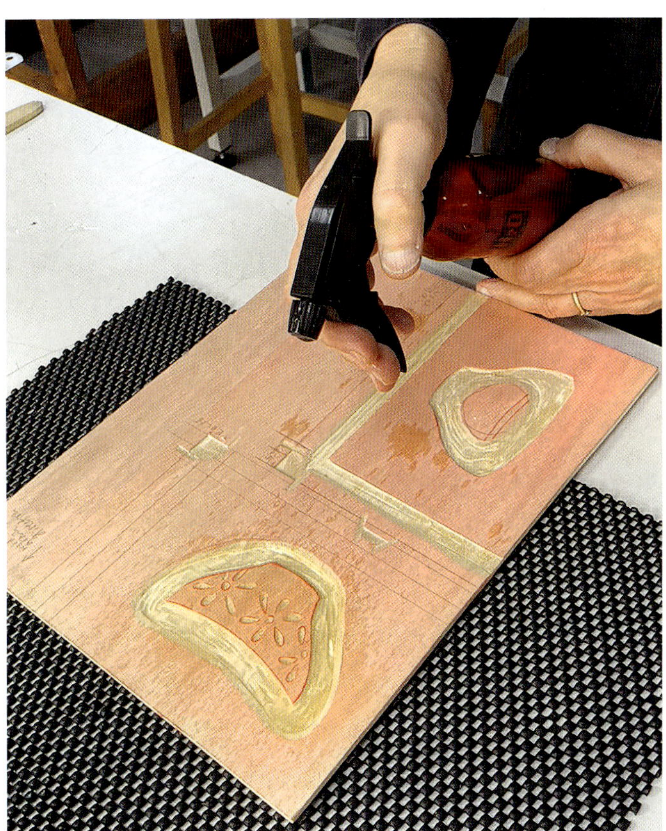
Spray with water just the area that you are about to print, and allow some minutes to let the wood absorb the water.

11. Using a *hakobi* or a Western brush, dot the pigment onto the woodblock and brush in with the *te bake* or *marubake* in a circular motion to ensure all areas are covered.

12. Repeat until three layers have been added; finish with brushing in a single direction.

13. Remove printing paper from damp pack.

14. Ensure corner marked with an 'X' matches the *kentō* corner.

15. Using a scissor action with your hands, place first the *kagi* corner into the notch keeping it in place with your thumb then holding the paper away from the inked image, slot the long edge of the paper into the *hikitsuke kentō*.

16. Allow the paper to drop – do not be tempted to touch the paper with your fingers as this leaves a finger-shaped mark on the print. The dampness of the block and paper plus the *nori* will keep your paper in position while you use the *baren*.

17. Place a sheet of baking paper on top as a protective layer between the paper and the *baren*.

18. Hold your *baren* with the loop tucked between your middle fingers and press lightly with a zig-zag motion to allow the paper to adhere to the block.

    Increase the pressure for specific areas if required and finish with rubbing the *baren* along the woodgrain or in a single direction.

    It is possible to take a peek at the print before lifting it completely from the block if you first hold the paper in position with the *baren*.

19. Lift the paper on the block to a halfway point while you weight the paper still in contact with the block. After identifying any specific areas that might need further attention, you can place the paper back down on the block and continue rubbing with the *baren*.

20. Return the print to the damp pack ready for the next colour or to overprint for a more intense printing. It is possible to print a new colour immediately, but for better results I allow the print to dry and then re-dampen to apply the next colour, so that the pigment is fully embedded in the paper.

21. Repeat the process – water, *nori,* colour – and return to the damp pack until you have finished printing, then you can leave your print out to dry.

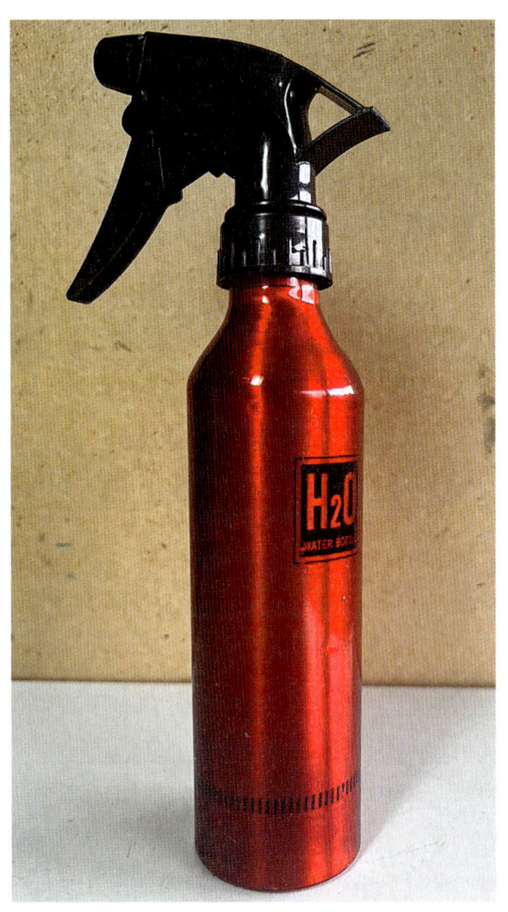

A cheap water spray from a discount store.

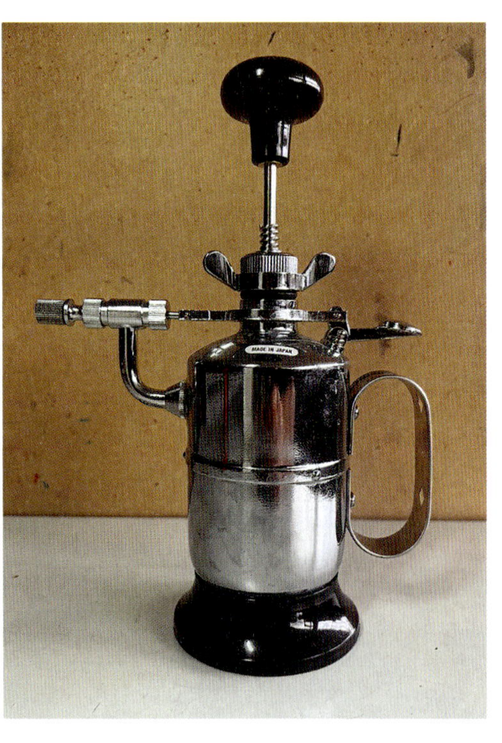

An expensive Japanese mister that is pumped up and sprays fine droplets.

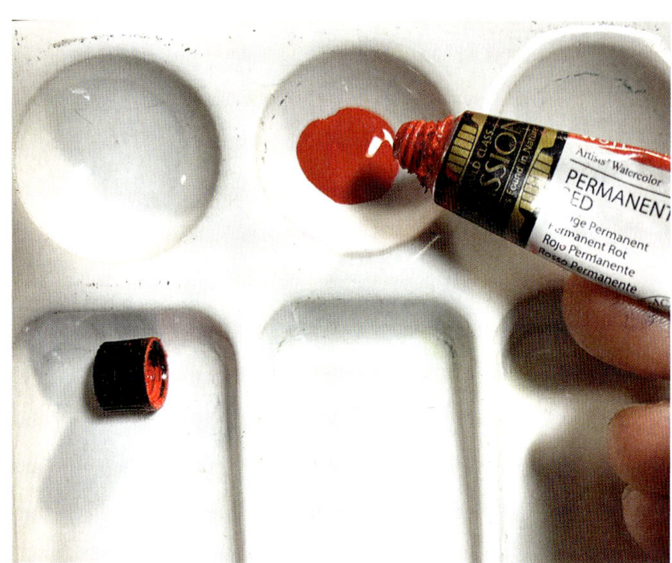

Ideally a ceramic palette is used for mixing tube watercolours, as it does not stain.

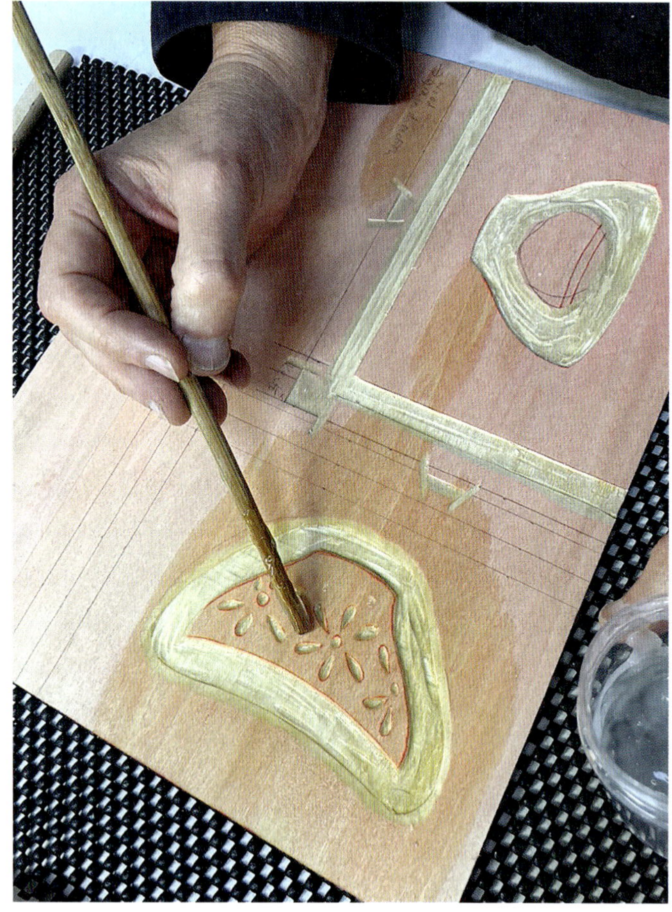

Dotting on *nori* with a chopstick.

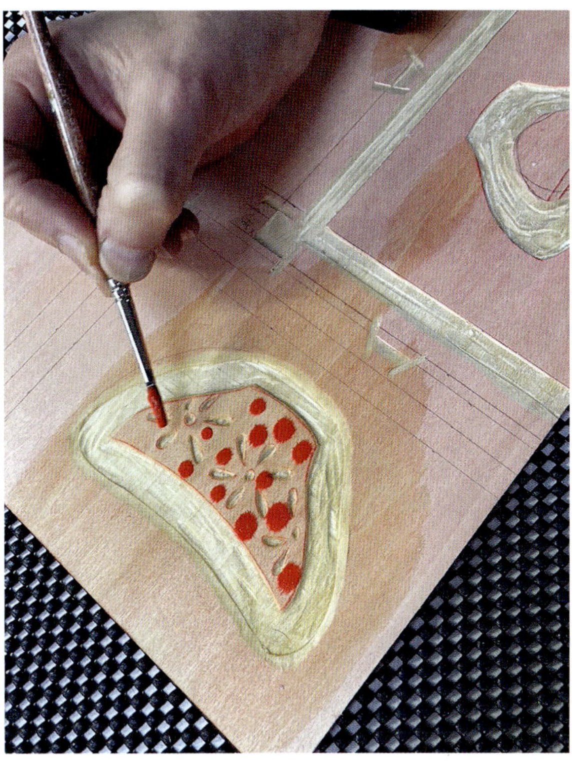

Dotting diluted pigment with a Western brush.

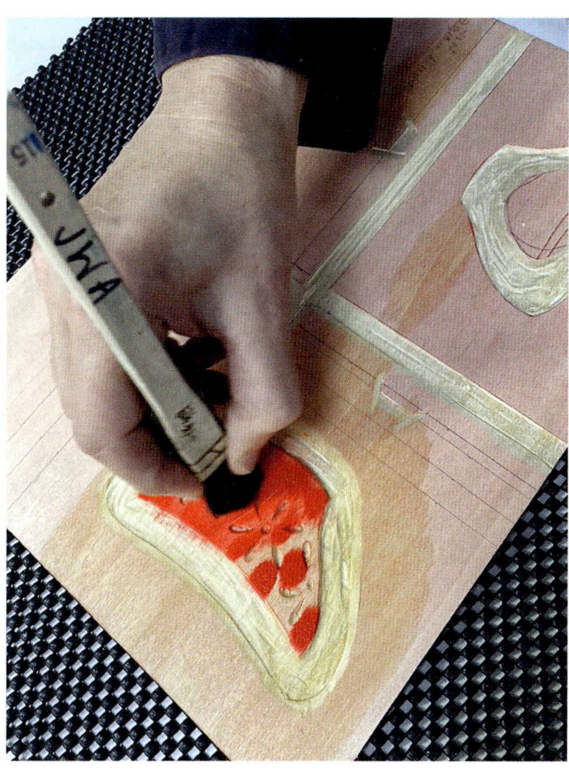

Brushing the colour into the woodgrain with a *te bake*.

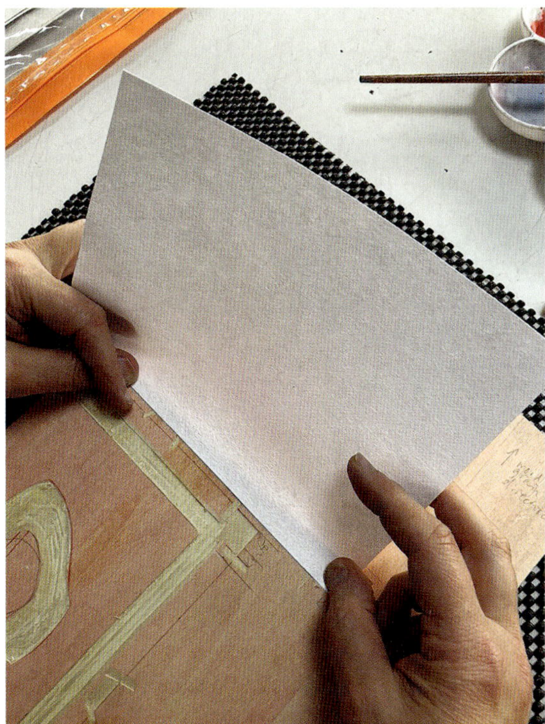

Place the printing paper into the *kentō* notches, allow it to fall down onto the woodblock.

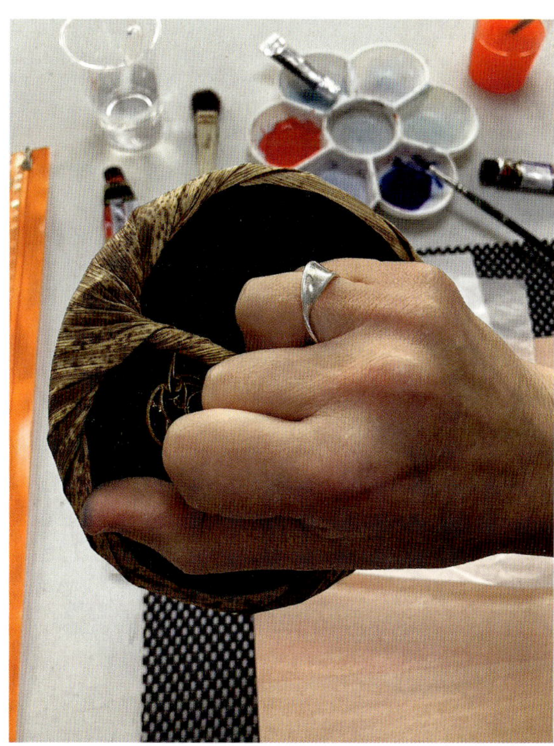

Correct handhold for a *baren*, so that the hand pressure comes from the middle of the *baren* and not the edge.

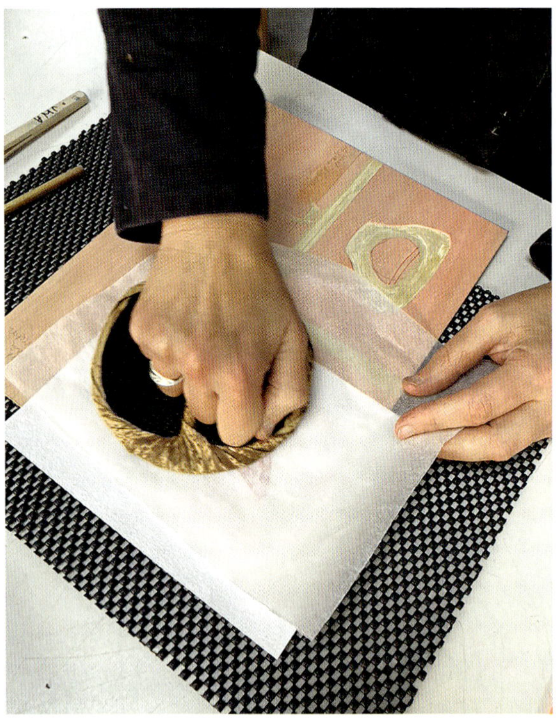

Use a piece of baking sheet on top of your print as protection and rub in a circular way with the *baren*.

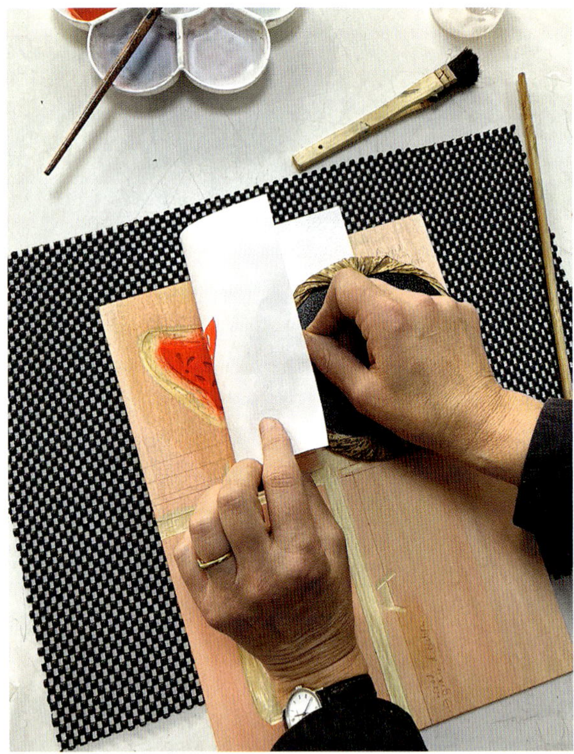

Use your *baren* as a weight to keep your printing paper in place while you take a peek at the print in progress.

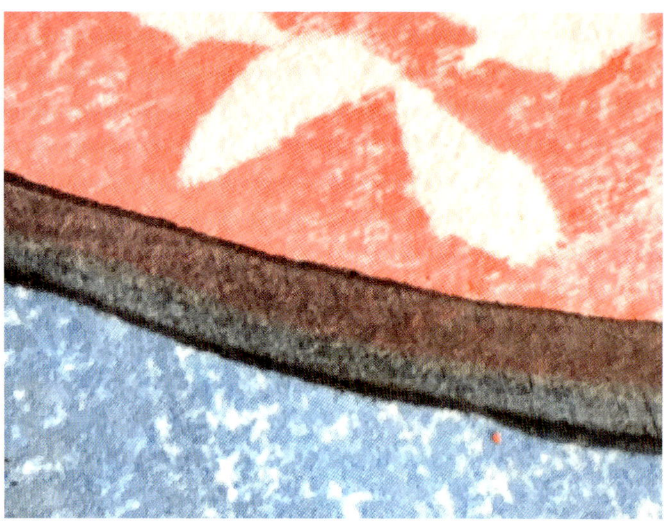

Outlined edges of the black line indicate over-inking.

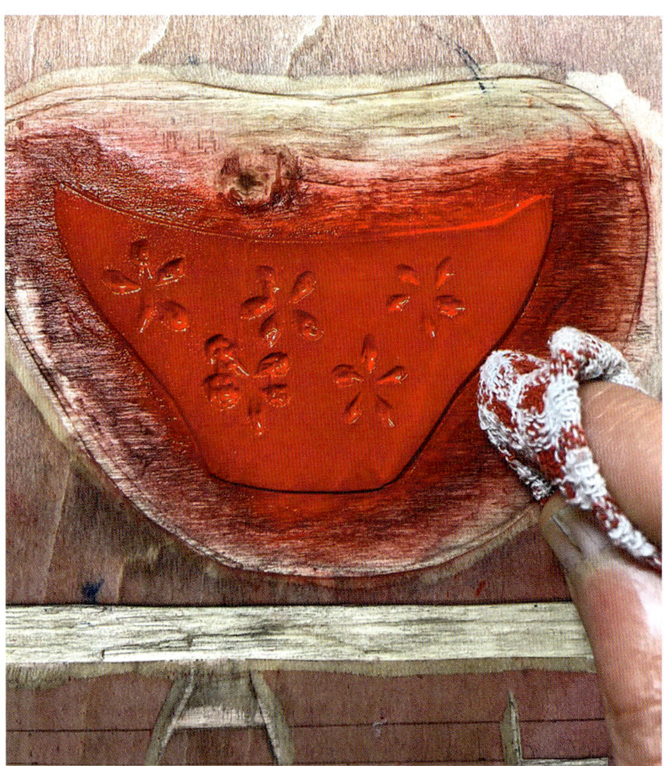

Using a clean cotton rag to wipe excess ink from image edges.

The pigment is absorbed into the paper fibres, dyeing them like fabric; it does not sit on the surface as it would with oil-based inks. This means that the papers can be stacked on top of each other without leaving a mark. It also means that any hand-painted corrections will show up as a significantly darker area, so this is best avoided.

ISSUES WITH PRINTING

Beginners to the technique often over-ink the block. If a block is over-inked there are tell-tale darker lines around the image areas. This is where the ink pressed into the paper with the *baren* goes to the point of least resistance – the cleared areas of the block, particularly on fine line printing. To resolve this, immediately after printing take a piece of clean newsprint or tissue paper and lightly with the flat of your hand smooth the paper to lift the excess pigment.

Before printing use a cotton-based cigarette filter or cloth to pick up any excess pigment that may have collected along the edge of your image. Keep a clean cotton rag handy while printing. It is best not to use paper towel or paper-based cloths as the paper fibres can get caught in the wood and these will pick up pigment too.

Similarly, beginners to the technique often under-ink the block. Typically, the first print from a new block will be fainter than subsequent printings as the woodblock requires time to absorb pigment and *nori* before a more even print is achieved.

Troubleshooting

Name	Image	Description	Possible Causes	How to Correct	How to Avoid
Ketsuochi		Pigment picking up in unwanted areas	1. Poor carving of the woodblock 2. Paper is too damp	Carefully wipe the block with a clean cloth prior to printing Reduce moisture using blotting paper or clean newsprint	Leave 'islands' of uncarved, un-pigmented areas of woodblock for the paper to rest on so it doesn't dip into cleared areas Graphite rubbings to identify problem areas before printing
Goma (literally *sesame seeds*)		Often appears with the first impression, looks grainy	1. Too little *nori* 2. Paper is too dry 3. Block is too dry 4. Too little pressure with the *baren*	Print again on top of grainy image Moisten paper and block Apply more pressure with the *baren*	Make several trial proofs on newsprint paper to condition the woodblock, building up the amount of *nori* and pigment in the woodgrain
Mura		Uneven and weak impression	1. Uneven pigment layer 2. Pigment too dry 3. Paper too wet 4. Uneven woodblock surface 5. Unevenly sized paper	Reprint the layer Watch the moisture levels in your pigment and paper	Use a better-quality woodblock and paper Some artists advocate sanding the woodblock but this often causes more problems than it solves as the sandpaper raises a nap that absorbs ink, leaving a furry impression

	Symptom	Causes	Remedy	Prevention
Tamari	Clogged details Fine cut areas filling with pigment	1. Too much *nori* 2. Too much pigment 3. Too heavy *baren* pressure 4. Overly sized paper	Clean the woodblock with a clean cloth Lift the excess pigment from your print with a clean piece of newsprint or tissue paper. For small, specific over-inked areas use a cotton cigarette filter to wipe away the excess Use less *nori*, pigment Apply less pressure with the *baren*	Identify overly sized paper – if water is not absorbed quickly the paper is too hard to use for Mokuhanga Take care when printing, remember how much *nori* and pigment you have used and decrease the amount as the woodblock becomes saturated with repeated printings
Hekomi	White marks	1. Uneven paper dampening 2. Dents in the woodblock 3. Woodchips left on the block 4. Bristles from inking brush on surface of block 5. Inadvertent fingerprints	Smooth 'gutter' and 'island' areas to prevent embossment Use a brush to clean your printing area and brush your woodblock to clear wood chippings Use the *baren* to rub with specific pressure over problem areas	Ensure damp pack is evenly dampened before putting in printing papers. Do not over stack and leave at least one sheet between pages so paper absorbs from both sides To avoid dents occurring store your woodblocks carefully wrapped in newspaper before printing Use a non-slip mat to protect the underside of your board

The use of trial proofs on copy paper or newsprint will condition the woodblock ready for an edition of prints on your precious *washi* paper and solve many of the teething problems encountered when starting printing.

Give yourself enough time to print, with a calm, clean place to work in; do not be in a hurry and rush. The printing process is a continual conversation and evaluation between yourself and the block and paper. Over time you will be able to read the signs and develop a repertoire of problem-solving answers for issues that arise. When I was in Japan my *sensei* said that you have to 'think inside the wood' and although I didn't fully appreciate it at the time, I now understand that to print effectively you have to be aware of the condition of the block, paper, pigment and *nori* consistency at all times. This only comes from practice, and evaluating both successes and failures.

DRYING PRINTS

The best way to dry your prints is slowly. Place the still slightly moist finished prints between cardboard sheets with a weight on top. Allow to dry over a few days.

Alternatively, you can stretch your print as you would prepare a sheet of watercolour paper for painting, by attaching gummed tape to the edges. Do this on the reverse of the print.

In Japan I was taught an unorthodox method that also works well. Take your still-damp print and place it face down on a clean sheet of Perspex or glass. Working clockwise, stick Sellotape around the edges of the back of your print ensuring that there is at least 5mm of tape on the print. If your print is a large one, it is a good precaution to use a double layer of tape to prevent the print from pulling out of the Sellotape.

Using the back end of your wooden *te bake*, rub the tape so that there are no air bubbles and the tape is adhering to the paper and the Perspex. There is a subtle difference before and after rubbing the tape.

The paper will stretch flat but wait until the paper is warm rather than cool to the touch before removing the tape. If it is still cool, it is still damp and will not dry flat if you remove the tape at this point.

Remove the tape in an anti-clockwise direction and pull away from the print. The tape will remove the topmost layer of the paper but as this is on the back of the print it will not be visible.

If your prints have already dried and are not as flat as you would like, it is possible to slightly dampen them with a water spray on the back and then continue with any of the techniques outlined.

STORAGE

Storing Prints

It is best to store your prints flat between sheets of acid-free paper, ideally in a plan chest, or in portfolios that can protect the paper from dampness or damage. Rolling large prints may be problematic as it can cause cracks and folds to appear. If this happens I have found that simple wrinkles can be ironed flat using a moderately hot iron and placing the print between two sheets of clean newsprint paper. For more stubborn folds it is better to re-dampen the back of the print and re-stretch as outlined before. If space is an issue and rolling large prints is the only option, take time to store them carefully between sheets of acid-free tissue paper and roll as loosely as possible.

Storage and Maintenance of Blocks

I tend not to wash my blocks after printing unless I am changing the printing colour. Please note that black *sumi* ink once used will not be effectively washed out of the woodgrain and will add grey to any colour that you use subsequently. If it is a light colour on a fresh woodblock and only a few prints have been pulled, it is possible to change the colour completely by using a damp cloth to rub the colour out of the woodgrain. There is often a little transference of the previous colour for a couple of prints until the new colour settles in the woodgrain.

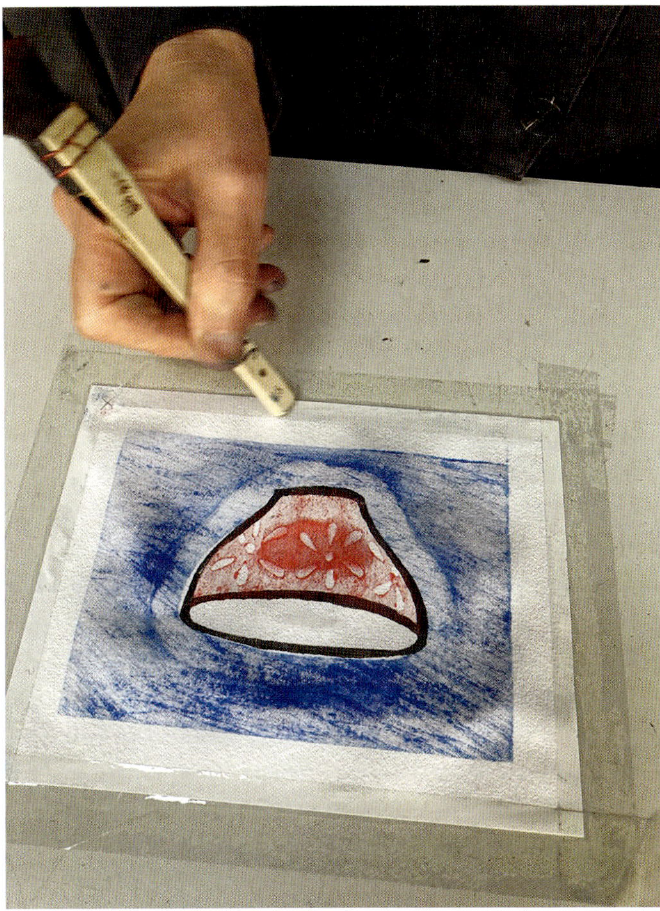

Using Sellotape to flatten prints.

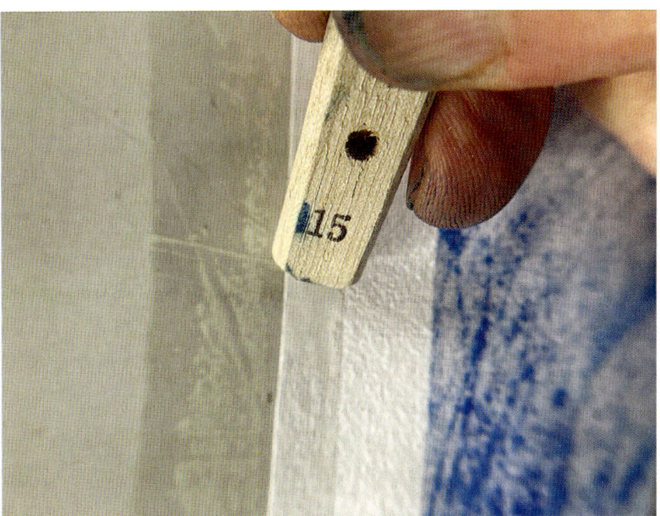

Ensuring a good adhesion by rubbing the Sellotape with the back of a wooden brush.

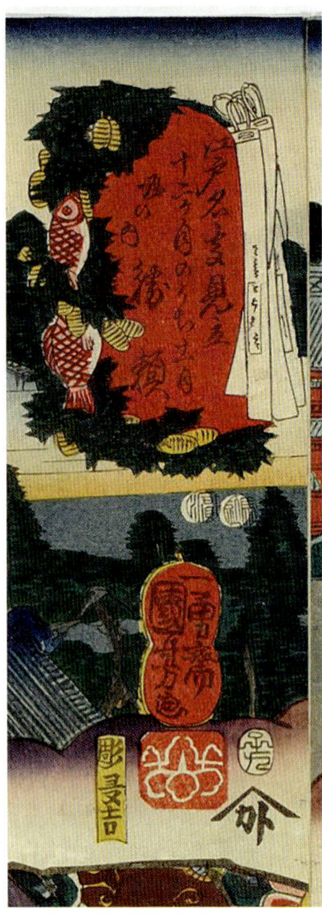

Markings on an *ukiyō-e* print.

Not washing the pigment out of the woodblock does two things: it keeps the woodgrain open and means that for subsequent printings the pigment is reactivated easily with the renewed application of water.

Sometimes woodblocks get warped if for instance there are large cut-out areas on one side or both sides of the block. If this happens dampen your block slightly, put between protective cardboards and weight it, covering the whole woodblock area until it becomes flat again.

Traditionally woodblocks would be wrapped in cloth and stored – I tend to use newspaper. It is important to protect them from anything that might scratch or dent the surface as this will appear on any further prints that you might wish to do.

I store my blocks upright like books on a shelf, which enables me to access them easily. It is an idea to write the name of the print on the edge of the woodblock for ease of identification. Do not use tape or anything sticky on the wood as this will gum up the woodgrain and be difficult to remove without the use of solvents.

EDITIONING MARKS

Ukiyō-e prints were not editioned. The popular prints were made in their thousands and they were seen as ephemera and not fine art. The writing integral to the *ukiyō-e* print shows the title of the work, the name of the commissioned artist (not the master carver or printer) and the censor's stamp of approval that also helpfully gives the year it was made.

Thick boards made from cherrywood blocks were used for the woodcarving. Blocks of popular *ukiyō-e* artists would be a valuable commodity to a publisher and would be printed, the blocks re-planed, reprinted, sold to other publishers and so on as long as there was a willing market to buy the prints.

At the beginning of the twentieth century with the increased interest and respect for *ukiyō-e* prints, some editioning marks began to appear showing the names of the master carver, printer and sometimes the copyright owner.

Editioning marks really only began to be used in the West when prints started to be sold as a fine art commodity in the nineteenth century. They came about mainly to show the distinction between editions of artists' original handmade prints and mechanical photographic reproductions. The printing matrix degrades over time and there is a natural end to the life of the woodblock or plate. Rarity is valued in the art market and so a low edition of prints is more potentially commercial than a high or unlimited edition.

Contemporary Mokuhanga prints can be difficult to edition given that there are so many variables to keep constant: fluctuating dampness levels, condition of the block, how much pigment and *nori* has been absorbed into the woodgrain, even atmospheric conditions can play havoc with a print run and so on. I tend to make a small edition of ten or less.

The conventions for numbering a limited-edition print is well established in the West. Prints are hand-signed with a pencil (never a pen for paper conservation purposes). On the left-hand side, the total number of prints is written as a fraction below the actual print's number in that edition, so 1/10 denotes the first print pulled from an edition of ten prints made.

Sometimes galleries require 'V/P' or 'Variable print' to be written on Mokuhanga prints to show that there might be a variation in the edition. 'A/P' signifies 'Artist proof' and are prints, usually ten, allocated to the artist extra to the edition.

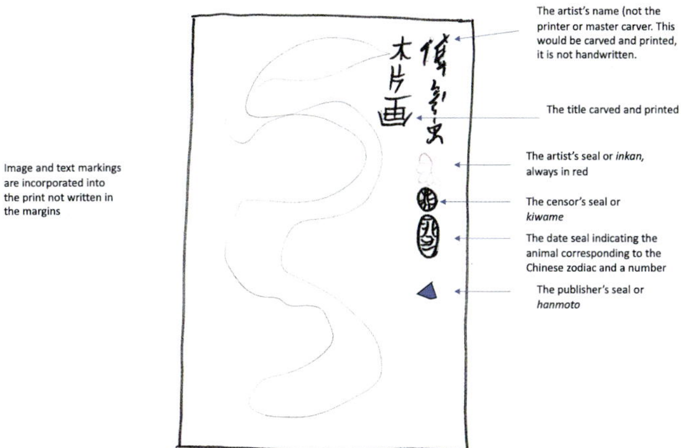

Writing and symbols printed directly on the print.

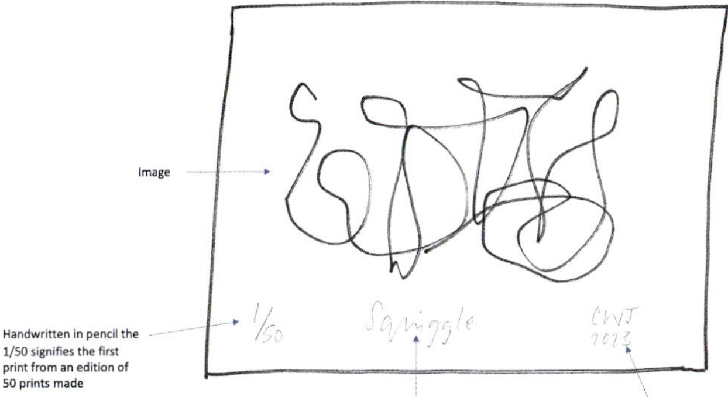

Western tradition of the artist signing their print by hand, even if they did not actually print it themselves.

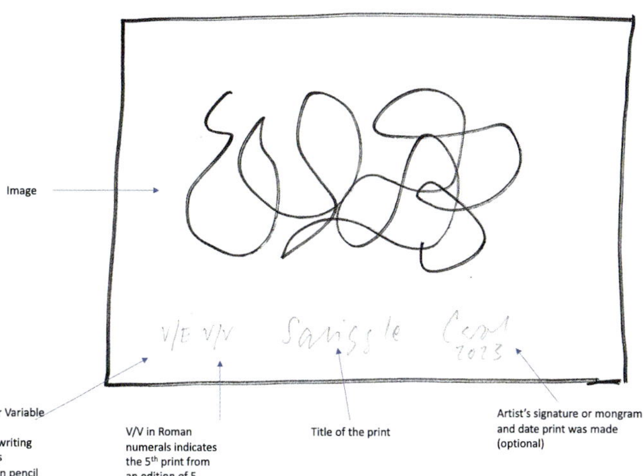

Some galleries insist on my Mokuhanga prints being labelled as 'Variable Edition'.

The title is written in the middle and the artist's name on the right; the date is optional.

I have often cut my prints to the image edge without a margin of white paper. This is in keeping with traditional *ukiyō-e* prints and because of this I sign my print on the back. This has caused some confusion for framers who despite all the work visible on the front of the paper have gone with the Western established print tradition of signing on the front and on two occasions have framed my work back to front!

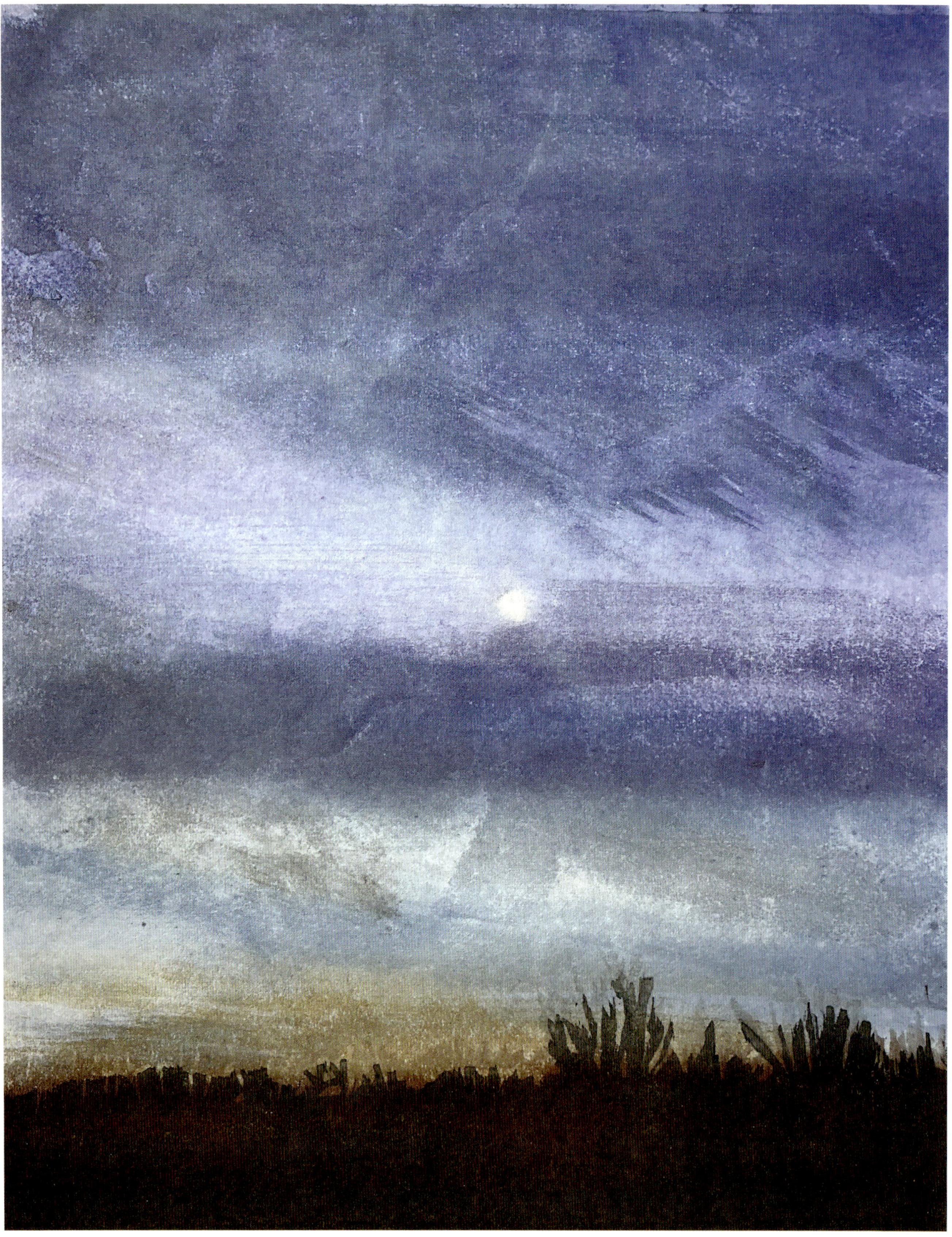

Chapter 6

ADVANCED TRADITIONAL PRINTING TECHNIQUES

t is not difficult to understand basic Mokuhanga printing but it takes a lifetime to learn and to be able to employ the infinite variety of nuanced printing that makes Mokuhanga such a special and unique printmaking process. This chapter looks at some of the traditional printing effects and how to achieve them.

I recommend practising basic Mokuhanga printing over time before moving on to more advanced techniques. When I was on my residency in Japan we were often impatient to learn the next stage, but it was emphasised over and again that the 'slow reveal' was a better learning method, with lots of repetition to embed the process. It took me a good long time to fully appreciate the control of water that is at the heart of the technique: how damp the woodblock is, how damp the paper, how much water has been added to the *nori* in relation to the amount of water added to the pigment, even how humid the surrounding atmosphere is. We were told to 'think inside the block' – an odd exhortation to me at the time but one that now I remember always when printing – to be aware of the condition of the block and all the elements when printing as they change all the time.

Betazuri: Overprinting to achieve a more solid colour.

PRINTING EFFECTS

Betazuri

This is a really useful technique to employ as it makes a flat saturated colour of uniform tone.

Method

Apply *nori* and watercolour fairly generously onto a dampened block and brush in with a *te bake* to spread the pigment over the printing area. The direction of the brush should be against the woodgrain and the pressure should be light and even.

Elizabeth Myers, *February Twilight*, 2021. Japanese woodblock print using *bokashi* and stencilling *kappazuri*.

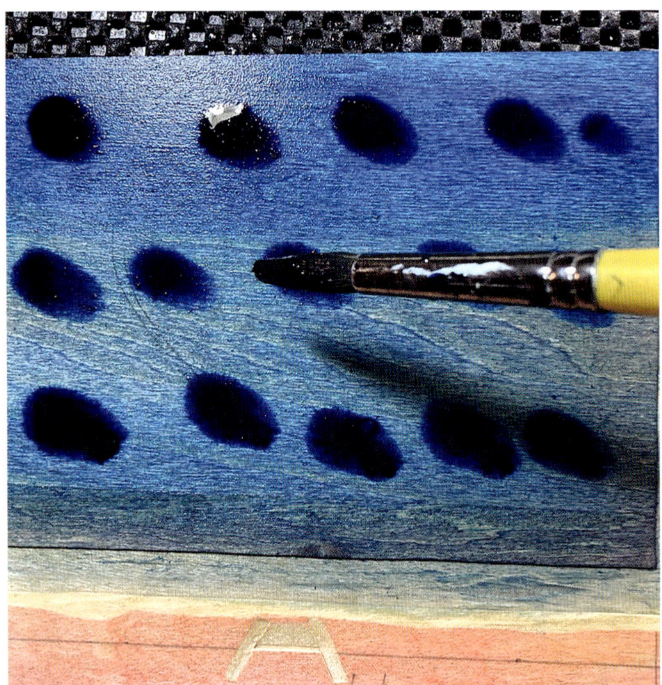

Dotting the pigment onto the woodblock.

Gomazuri: Speckled effect.

When printing, pay close attention to the positioning of the printing paper in the *kentō* registration and use a high pressure with the *baren* to bring up the pigment. I have found it important to work fairly quickly as there is a tendency for the paper to stick to the block.

Betazuri is best achieved by over-printing on the same area to deepen the intensity of colour. The master printer Akira Kurosaki employed this method to great effect overprinting five or six times to gain the saturation of colour he wanted.

Gomazuri

Gomazuri is named after *goma* or sesame seeds as it leaves a grainy impression on the print. *Gomazuri* is often seen as an unwanted effect and appears often on the first proofs of beginners to the technique, but it can be quite challenging to employ it for specific textured areas, even for more advanced practitioners.

Method

For this effect the block and paper will need to be quite damp. No *nori* or very little should be used, and only a light pressure with the *baren*. Different *baren* types will also produce different effects; a plastic *baren* often works quite well for *gomazuri*.

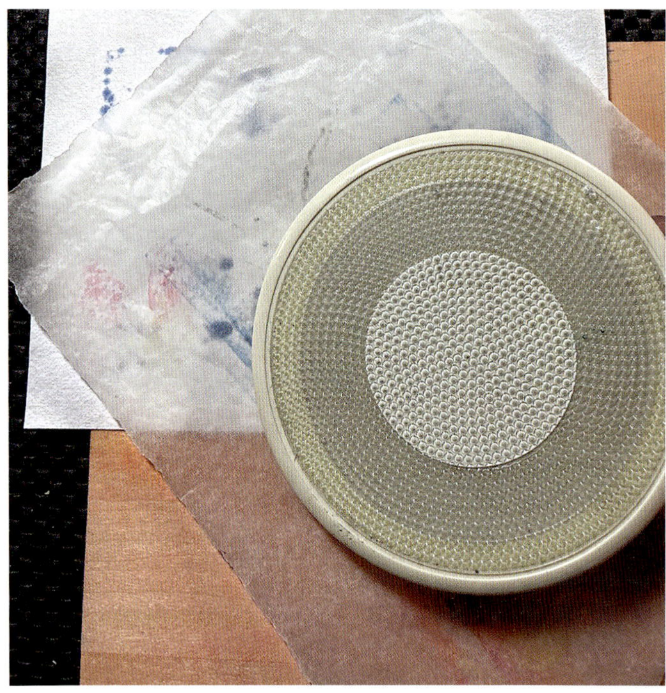

Using the Kurosaki *baren*.

Mokume-zuri

Mokume-zuri is for employed for transferring woodgrain on to the print. This technique was seldom used by the *ukiyō-e* printers, firstly because they used fine-grained cherrywood that does

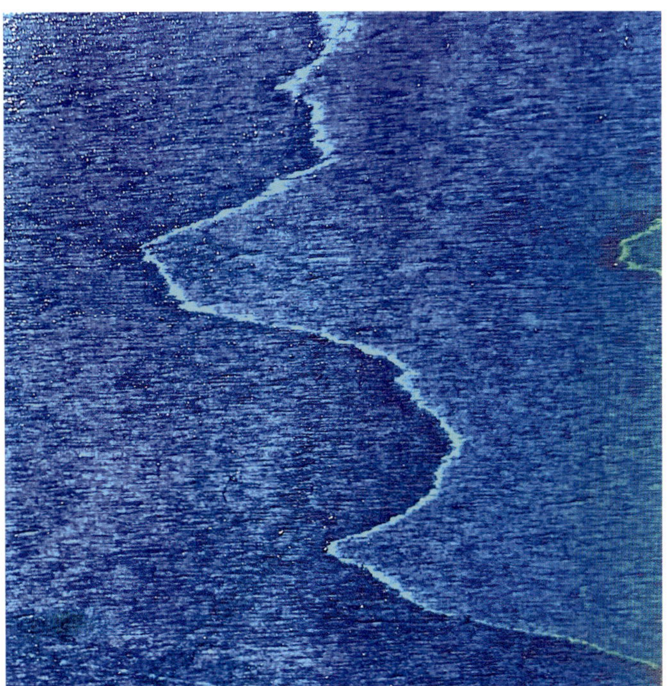

Mokume-zuri: Bringing up the woodgrain.

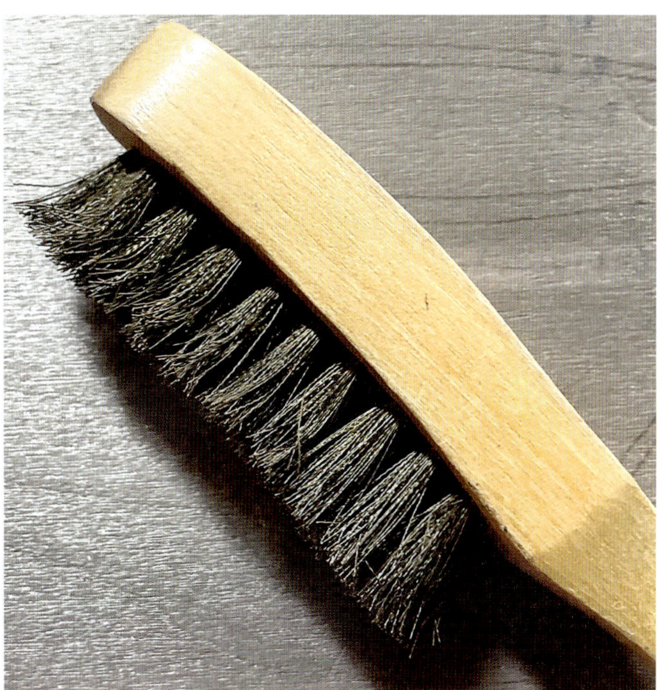

Wire suede brush.

not produce a very defined woodgrain and secondly because the prints were ideally designed to emulate watercolours.

The *shina* plywood that I use does not have a very pronounced woodgrain. Sometimes you will get a block that will print a woodgrain but it is quite subtle. Some artists scorch the block or you can use a wire brush along the grain to encourage the harder grain to stand in relief but I would recommend using a different wood such as pine, birch, cedar or even driftwood as an insert for your design.

Method

This technique works best with only a small amount of colour, a little *nori* and with the block relatively dry. When applying the pigment with the *te bake*, brush against the woodgrain. A strong pressure with the *baren* will bring the pigment up into the paper fibres.

Bokashi

There are many different kinds of *bokashi* or graduated printing in Mokuhanga. Shading to give a three-dimensional aspect to a form was not really the intention of *bokashi* as seen in *ukiyō-e* prints; instead it was the stylised graduation of the sky or sea from dark to light that was most often used to give a wonderful suggestion of space and depth. *Bokashi* once mastered can lift a print from a flat surface to a nuanced, delicate, graduated watercolour effect.

Ichimonji Bokashi

This is the most commonly used *bokashi* in *ukiyō-e* prints to express the sky. The graduation is formed on the very edge of the woodblock image from a dark blue or Prussian blue to a fade out.

Method

Use a brush loaded with water or a dampened cloth and draw it in a straight line along the top edge of the image area of the woodblock from left to right.

Dot on enough colour with a pigment-carrying brush. Then using a *te bake* brush that is as broad as the area to be printed, pick up the pigment from left to right along the upper part of the waterline. Do not be tempted to go back over your *bokashi*. Print and if required add a deeper blue at the topmost edge.

A variation to pulling the brush in a straight line is moving the brush in an irregular way to give an uneven edge to the graduation. This is often used to suggest the edge of a rain cloud or an oncoming storm. It is called *Ichimonjimura Bokashi*.

Ichimonji Bokashi: Graduated narrow colour, often used for depicting sky.

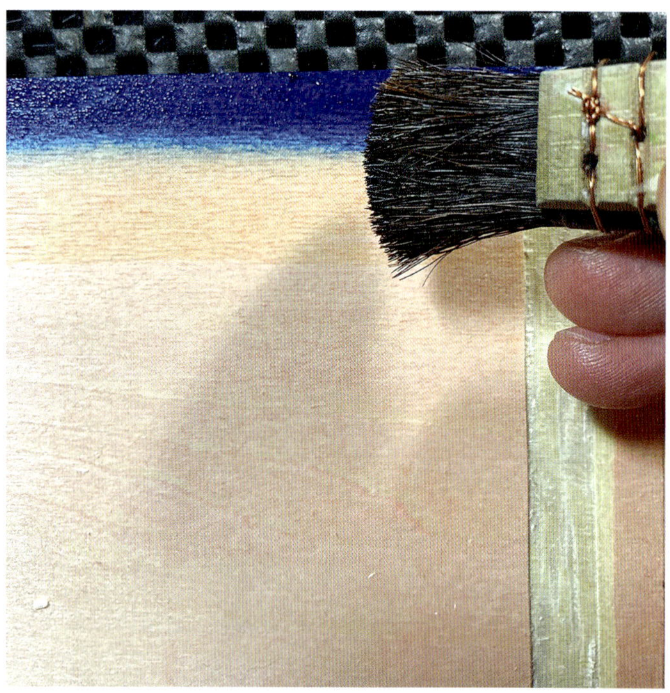

Using a *te bake* to brush the pigment from right to left.

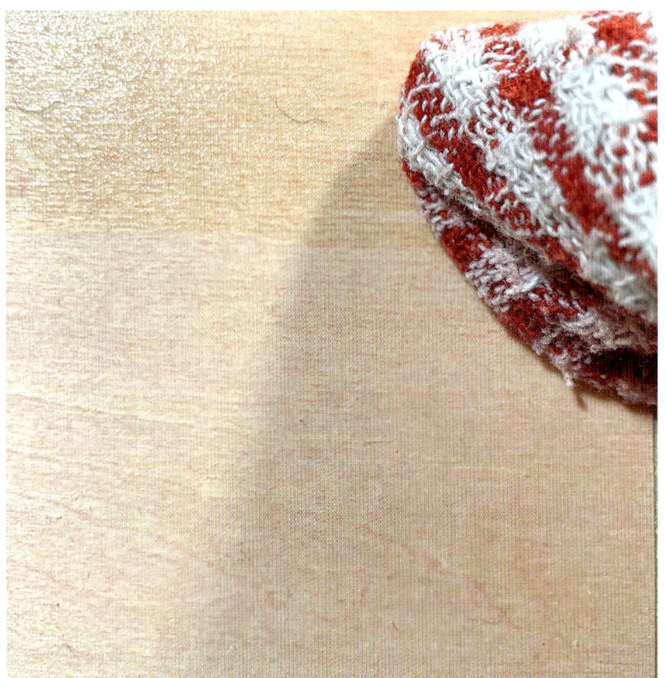

Dampening the print area with a cloth.

Fuki Bokashi: Graduated colour over a larger area.

Fuki Bokashi, also called Ōbokashi

This technique is similar to *Ichimonji Bokashi* but the graduation is broader. I tend to use this on a print that already has a pale background colour as it tends to blend better.

Method

Prepare your shades of pigment in your palette before starting from lightest to darkest and test that they blend well together without any too obvious jumps in colour. The first and palest colour laid will appear as a background colour for the second and so on. It is a good idea to brush a large area for your first colour and then add the second graduation on top and so on. The overlaid colours will be affected by the colours that are beneath.

Make a water line with a brush or dampened cloth where you want your graduation to end. Dot on pigment with small dots of *nori* at the top of your graduation area.

Identify one side of the *te bake* with a small piece of masking tape so that one end of the brush is loaded with colour and the other kept just damp. I hold my brush with the masking tape end angled up and away from the pigment as the pigment is picked up with the other. As the brush moves down the block the angle of the brush is levelled out until the damp end touches the waterline making a soft graduation. Too much pigment at the waterline will result in a solid line instead of a subtle fade.

If your graduation area is large it is a good idea to print at this stage and then repeat the process bringing your waterline up the board, reapplying pigment and brushing it from left to right down to the redrawn waterline.

If required finish with an *ichimonji bokashi* at the top edge. It is important to take care that the graduation does not look stripey, so ensure an even brushing of the pigment and well blended colours. Only use a light pressure with the *baren*.

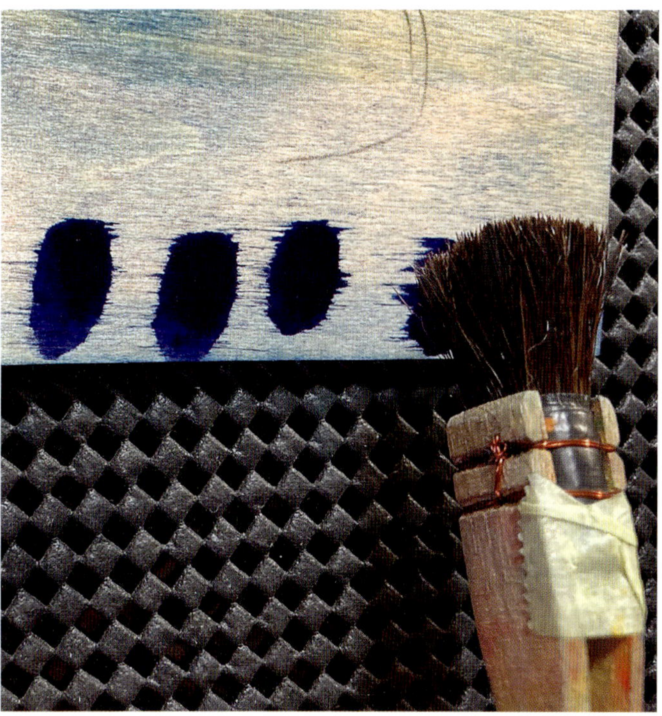

Preparing to brush the colour in.

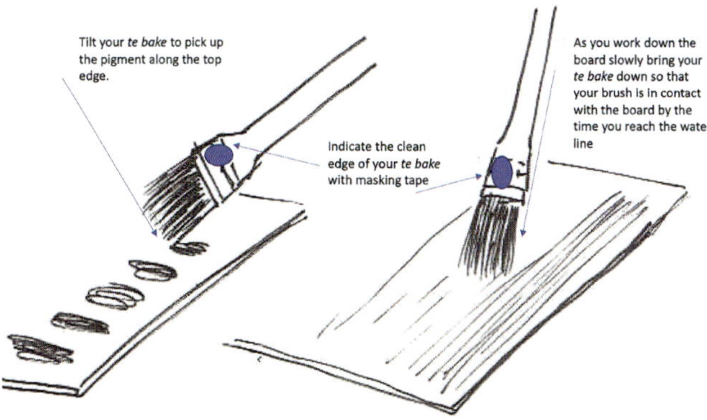

Drawing to show the angle of the *te bake* when printing.

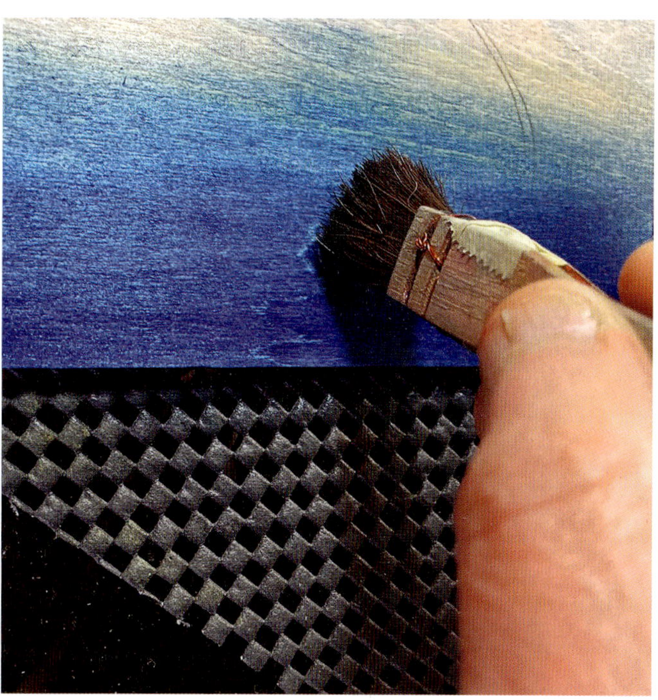

Finish with a slightly darker *Ichimonji bokashi* at the top.

Tsukeawase Bokashi

This technique is for creating a graduation of two colours meeting.

Method

If the area attempted is small, it is possible to work quickly and make the *tsukeawase bokashi* in one go by dotting pigment at one side of the image area and dotting the second pigment on the opposite side with *nori*. Use separate brushes for the different colours.

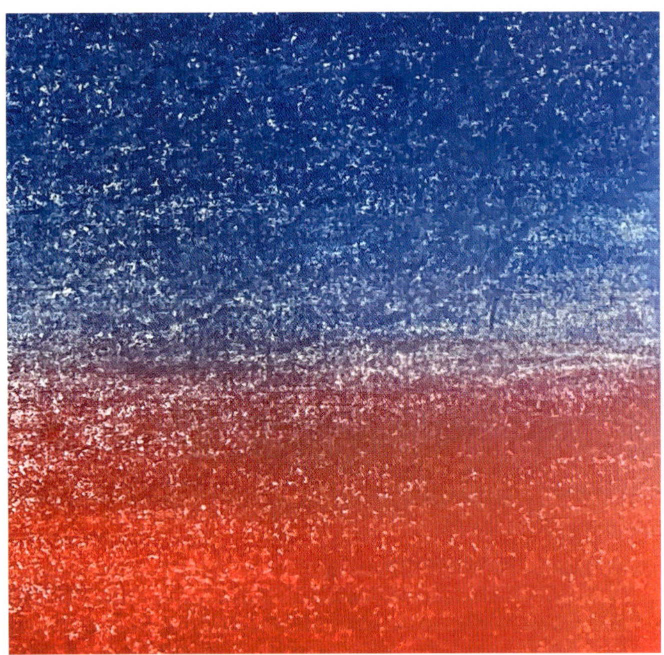

Tsukawase bokashi: Using two different graduated colours meeting in the middle.

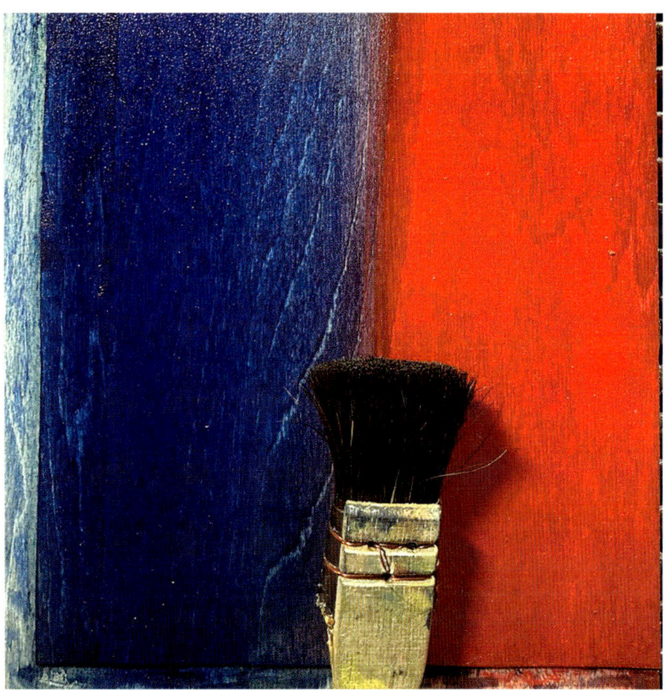

Separate clean *te bake* to blend the two colours together.

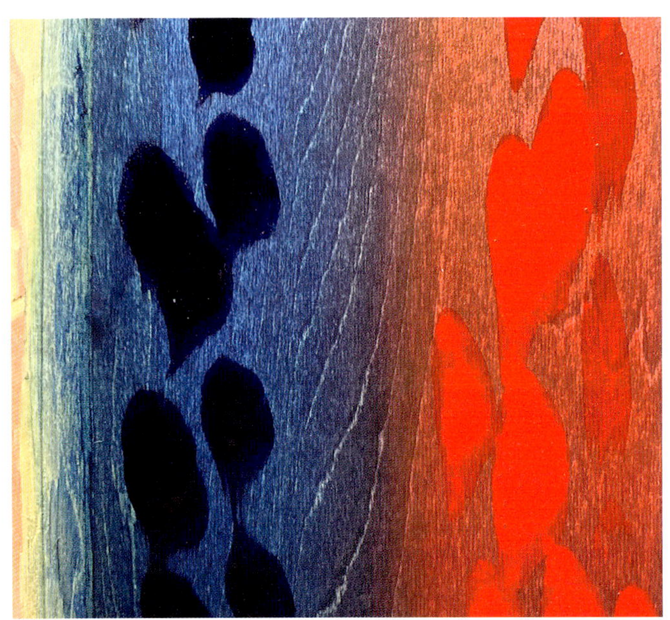

Two different pigments dotted on either side of the board.

Brush evenly on both sides until they meet, then with a third brush blend the meeting graduation. On a larger graduation area, it is better to print the two colours separately and where the colours overlap, the brush blends the two colours together. It is usual to start with the lightest colour and blend the darker into it.

Atenashi Bokashi

Shadows were not a feature of *ukiyō-e* prints as a rule but subtle graduations of tone such as the halo effect around the sun or moon or a deepening shade on a mountain, for example, adds a subtle intensity. *Atenashi bokashi* is used for small areas of graduation. If an edition of prints is required it is a good idea to first mark with carbon paper on your block the area that you wish your graduation to cover so that it can be replicated. It is a technique more like a monoprint, as you paint with a brush freeform onto the block and there is no cut line to determine the edge.

Method

Lightly dampen the area to be printed with a wet cloth. With a brush loaded with pigment, draw the area and allow the pigment to seep into the water. With a clean and dry *te bake* gently brush the edges of the colour creating a soft graduation.

Atenashi Bokashi: Freeform graduated colour.

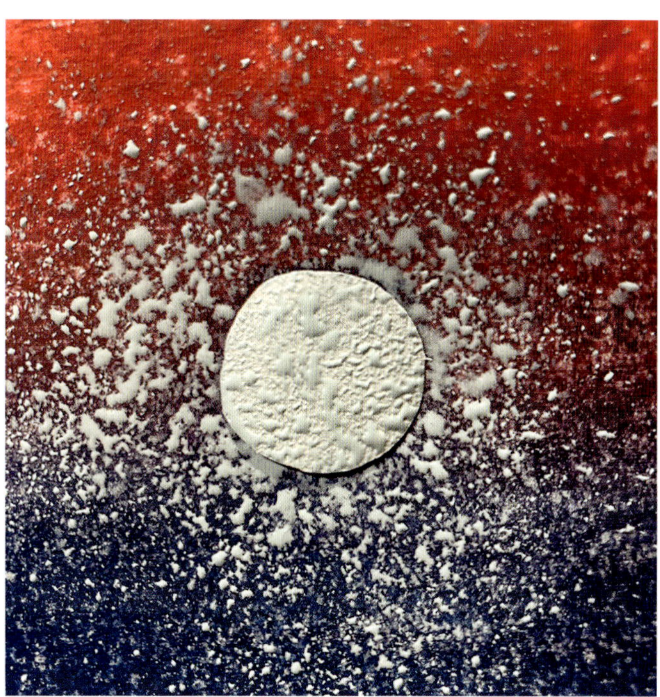

Fukibokashi: Flicking pigment using a toothbrush.

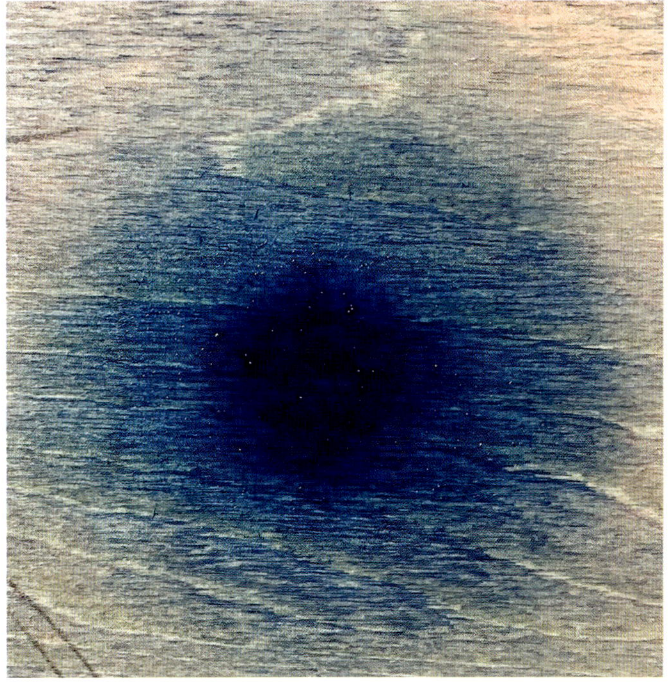

Inked block ready for printing.

Fukibokashi

This is a fun technique using a paper stencil as a mask. Textured effects can be achieved by flicking pigment using a toothbrush loaded with colour.

Method

It is a good idea to cut your paper stencil so that the edges fit into your *kentō* registration exactly. Your woodblock should be quite dry for this effect, so that the dots of colour do not absorb too quickly into the paper.

Ensure that the paper for your stencil is not too thick because you will not get a good outline edge, or too thin because the application of water will cause the edges to curl and is unsuitable for repeated printings.

Experiment beforehand with the consistency of the pigment to get it just right; too watery and the pigment will collect in puddles, too thick and the pigment might make large clumps. Do protect the other areas of your print and any unprinted papers from paint spatter.

Itabokashi

The most common *bokashi* is achieved through brushing pigment onto the block using water as a graduation tool, but *bokashi* can also be effected by carving a graduation in the wood itself. I have used *itabokashi* in my prints to create different cut levels of printing that take the colour in different ways. I also use my fingers to gently press the paper in specific areas to pick up colour that would be missed by the *baren*.

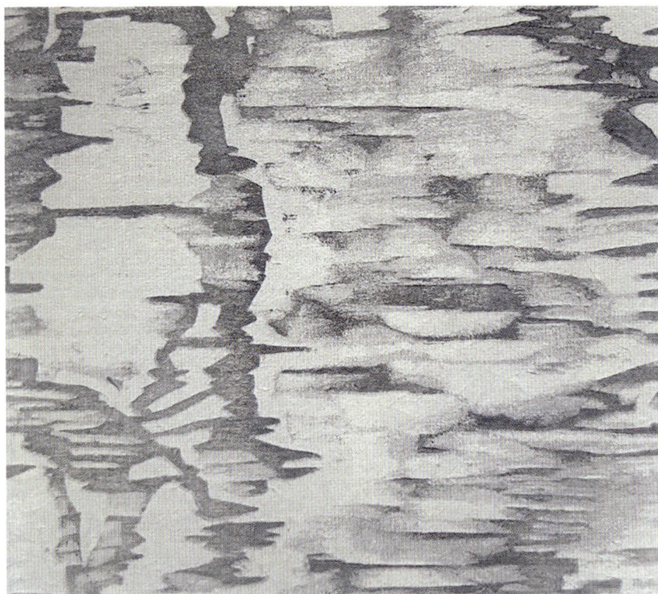

Itabokashi: Textured tones achieved through cutting.

Method

Use the *hiratō* to gently shave the wood from the surface. The tool needs to be very sharp and responsive. Feel the surface and carefully cut in smooth, easy strokes of the tool. There should be no ripples of wood but rather a gentle slope from the surface to the cleared level of the block.

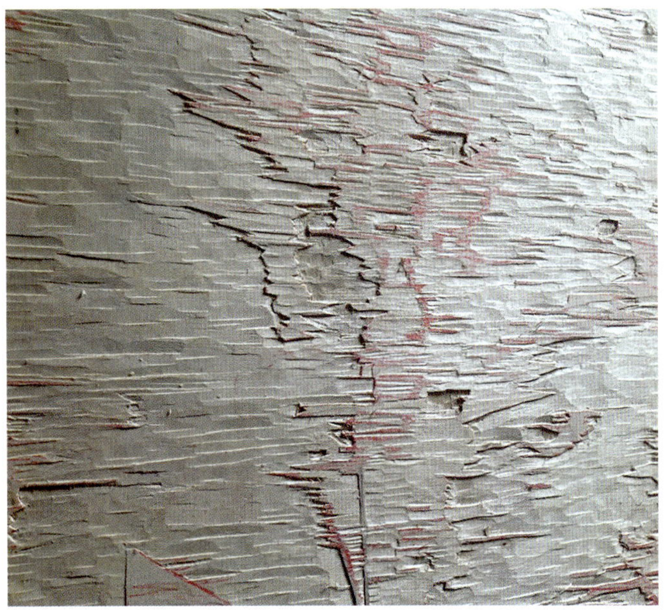

Appearance of the woodblock, the wood is cut at different levels.

Karazuri

This technique is for making an embossing or raised surface without colour. In *ukiyō-e* prints it was used to great effect for describing the subtle textures of kimonos.

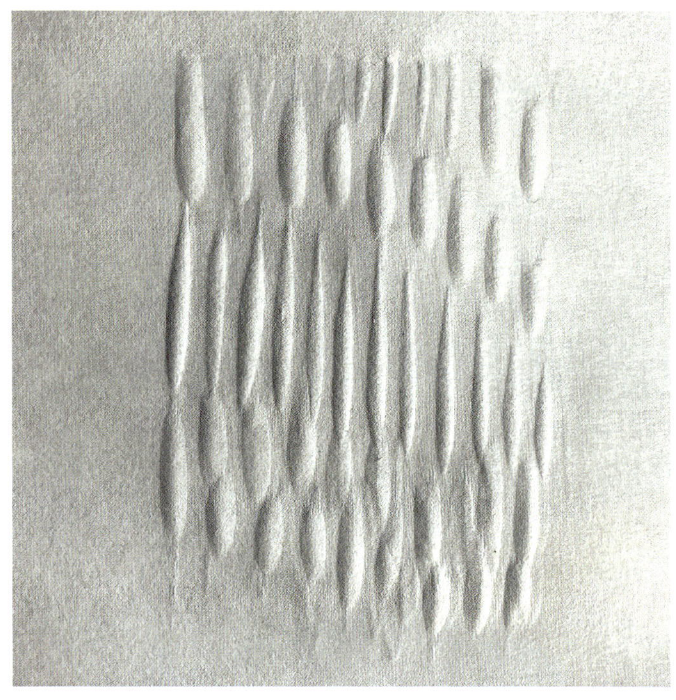

Karazuri: Embossing cut lines.

Method

It is always printed last from a specially cut block made for the purpose. If it is printed first, subsequent printings will soften the emboss and can also cause white marks to appear. It can be printed over colour areas or show a texture in the paper itself. Embossing works better with dampened, slightly heavy paper – care should be taken to ensure that the paper stays damp throughout or the paper might slip (as there is no *nori* to provide adhesion). Strong pressure with the *baren* is required. It is also important when drying your prints not to over-weight them as you will lose the emboss.

It is also possible to glue a textured cloth or coil of string to your block and try an emboss that way. I find however that the cut emboss is much more reliable given that the woodblock needs to be kept damp when printing and most glues do not respond well to repeated dampening.

The embossing used to suggest the musculature of *sumo* wrestlers is called *kimedashi* and involves thick, damp paper being pushed down into the larger cut *bokashi* areas using a cloth, an eraser or even the printer's elbow or heel.

Takuzuri

This is an ancient technique originating in China during the Han dynasty (220 BCE–206 CE) and is one of the earliest recorded types of printing; stone rubbings. In Japan, it started in the sixteenth century as a way for scholars to record images and text on old monuments and iron bells. It is a lovely way to make a delicate, textured effect on your print.

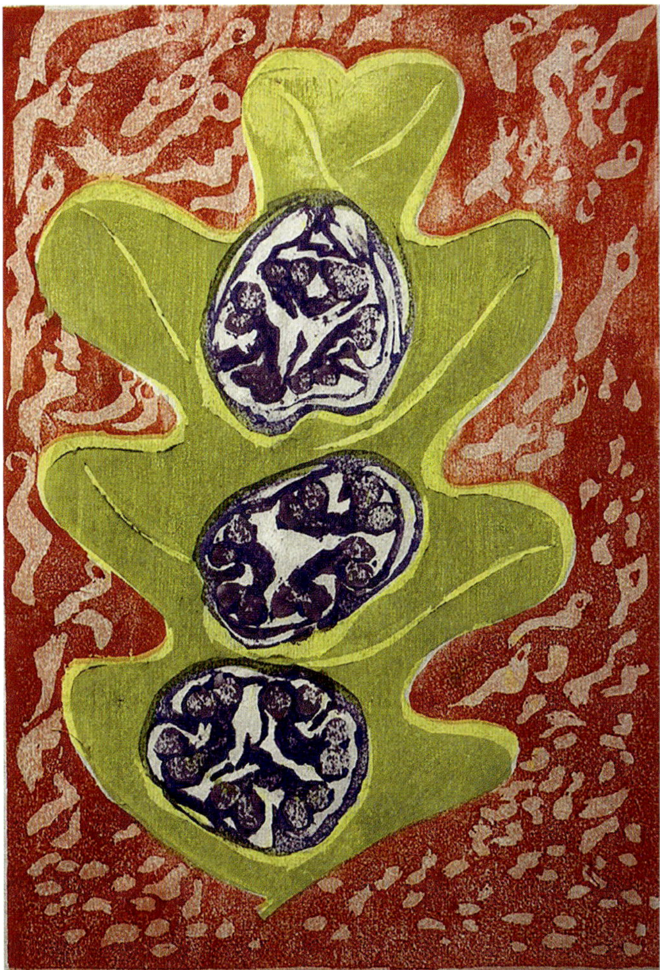

Elizabeth Myers, *Talisman*. Japanese woodcut employing *takazuri* and *urazuri*.

Method

A dampened sheet of paper is laid onto an un-inked block. Note that the block is reversed as in Elizabeth Myers' print, so that the textured area will appear in the right place.

The paper is gently pushed into the areas that have been cut out, with a soft cloth rolled into a ball. The paper will take on the memory of the object/texture underneath and as it dries it will retain the shape.

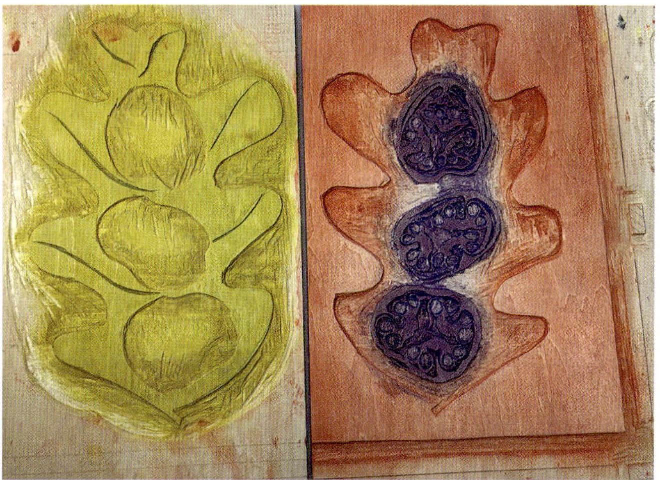

Showing the woodblock for *Talisman*. Note that the blue separation is reversed.

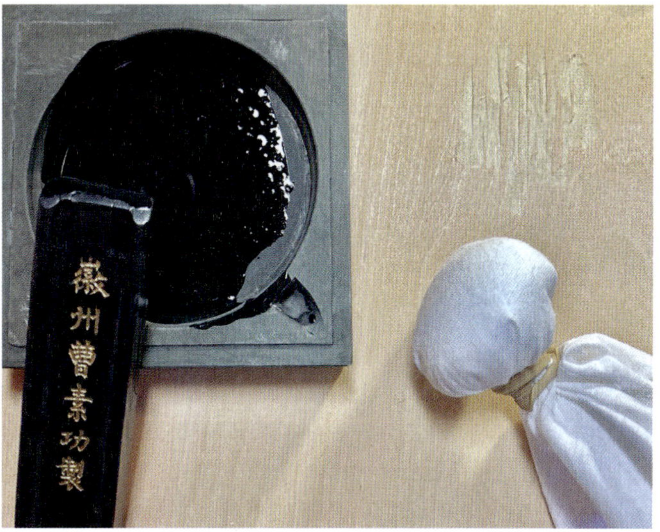

A *tanpo* for applying *sumi* ink.

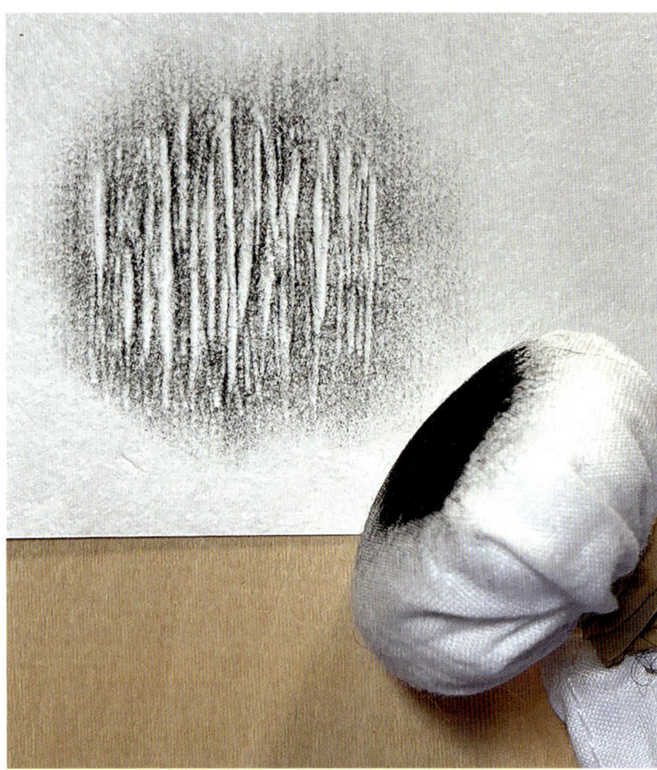
Soft textured print over embossed surface.

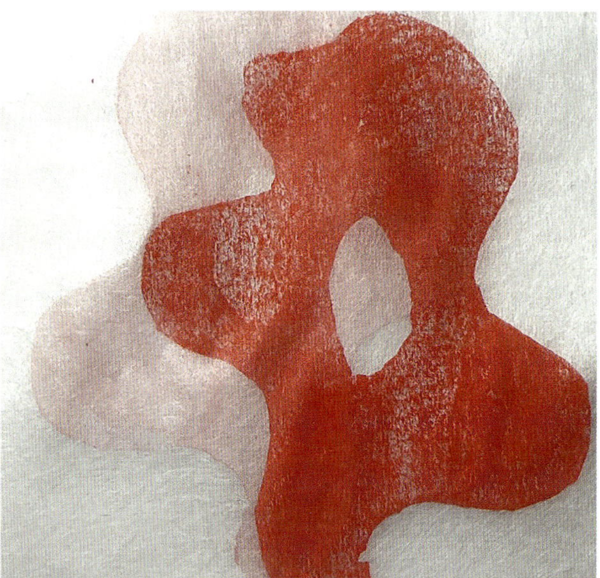
Urazuri: Red printed on the back of the paper shows up as pink on the front.

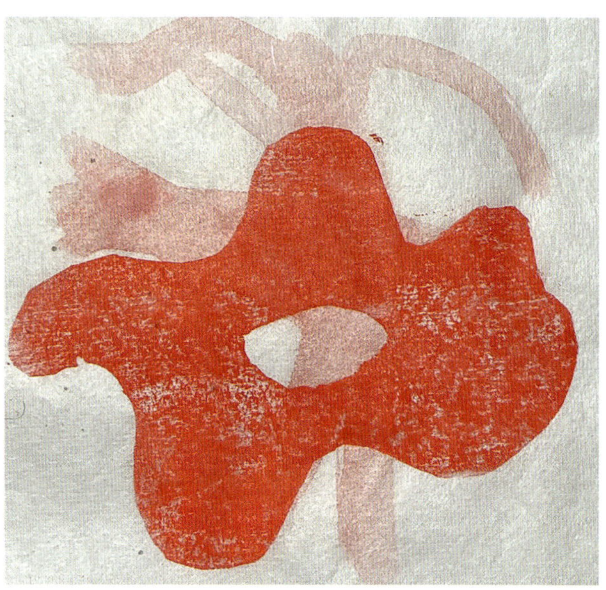
Freeform brush painting on the back of print showing through.

Sumi ink is picked up onto a *tanpo*, a cloth wrapped around cotton wool and gently patted onto the paper, revealing the textures beneath. Too much ink and the paper will absorb the pigment and the effect will be lost. Similarly, too much water in the pigment will cause the ink to 'bleed' in the paper. Too much pressure with the *tanpo* and the raised areas will flatten. Before beginning, I test the effect on a spare piece of the same paper I am printing with, until I am happy with the way it looks.

Urazuri

This technique involves printing from the back of the paper so that the effect from the front is of a soft colour showing through. Shikō Munakata employed this technique to great effect, often hand-painting colours on the back of a black and white print.

Method

This method involves specially cutting a block without reversing the image. Larger areas work better than fine cut lines. The printing paper is placed on to the inked block face up because you will be printing the back of the paper. It is a good idea to correctly identify and lightly mark in pencil the front and back of your paper it saves on any confusion. The best paper to use is a lightly or unsized *kōzo* paper to allow the pigment to permeate through. Use a lot of pigment and water but no *nori*. Strong pressure with the *baren* also helps to push the colour through the paper.

Kirazuri

This technique involves the use of a fine crystalline mica powder to make a shimmering area on the print. It was often

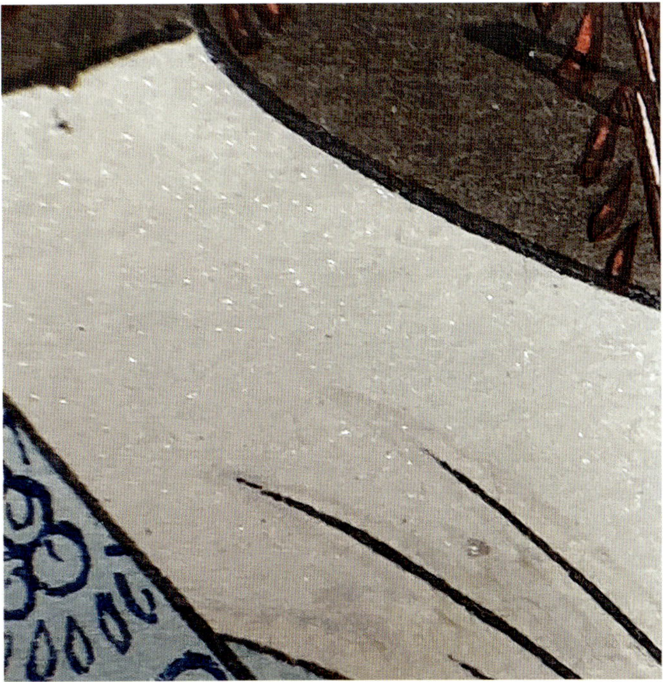

Kirazuri: Use of fine mica powder for shimmer effect.

Julie George, *Afternoon Light*. Japanese woodcut.

used in *ukiyō-e* prints of actors as a background effect. In the low light of the traditional Japanese house, the prints would catch the light and softly scintillate.

Method

Sometimes the print would have an initial darker grey background so that the sparkle of the mica would show up better. *Nori* is brushed onto the designated area of the block and printed on its own onto the printing paper. Mica powder is sprinkled on while it is still wet – best to do this onto newspaper or in a tray to keep the powder from your working area. Mica is a fine powder and dangerous to inhale, therefore it is a good idea to wear a mask. Excess mica can be carefully shaken off but wait until the *nori* has dried completely before gently brushing the surface of the print.

Use of Paper as Another Colour

Washi paper comes in many different colours, from an antique fawn to pale green depending on how long the *kōzo* fibres were left to naturally bleach in the sun. This paper colour can act as a beautifully soft extra colour when overprinting. The areas that are printed with pigment will react in a different way to overprinting than the clear areas of unprinted paper.

Mixed Cutting and Printing

In her print *The Bathers II*, Judith Elisabeth de Haan makes use of different woods that produce a more defined grain when printed. She also experiments with colour by monoprinting the pigment directly onto the block without cutting.

In Pat Rougeau's print *World within Worlds*, she used elm wood for printing. The woodgrain of the wood itself was the inspiration for the print.

Monoprinting

In this print the woodblock has not been cut at all; after brushing the pigment onto the surface, the marks are made by drawing with the back of a paintbrush. To edition such a print would require drawing onto the block with carbon paper so that the lines could be replicated. More often this is a one-off print, not part of an edition.

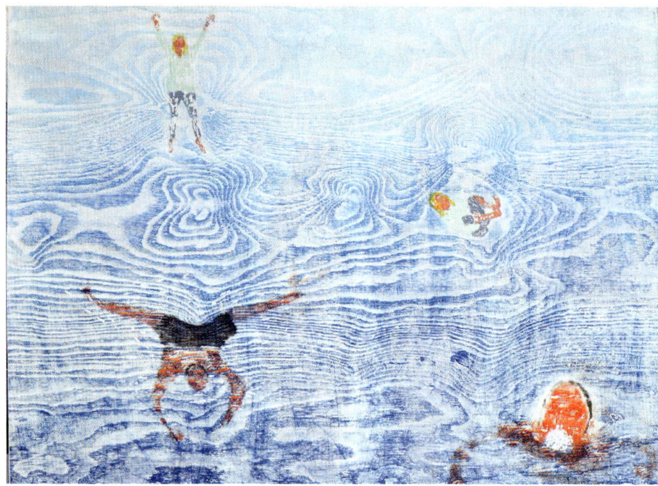

Judith Elisabeth de Haan, *The Bathers II*. Japanese woodcut.

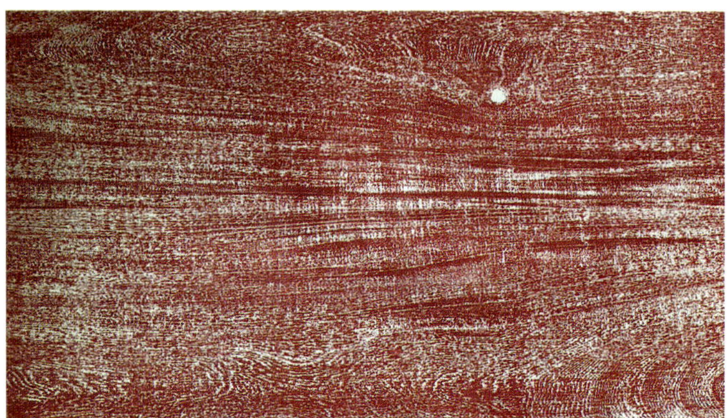

Pat Rougeau, *World within Worlds*. Japanese woodcut on elm wood.

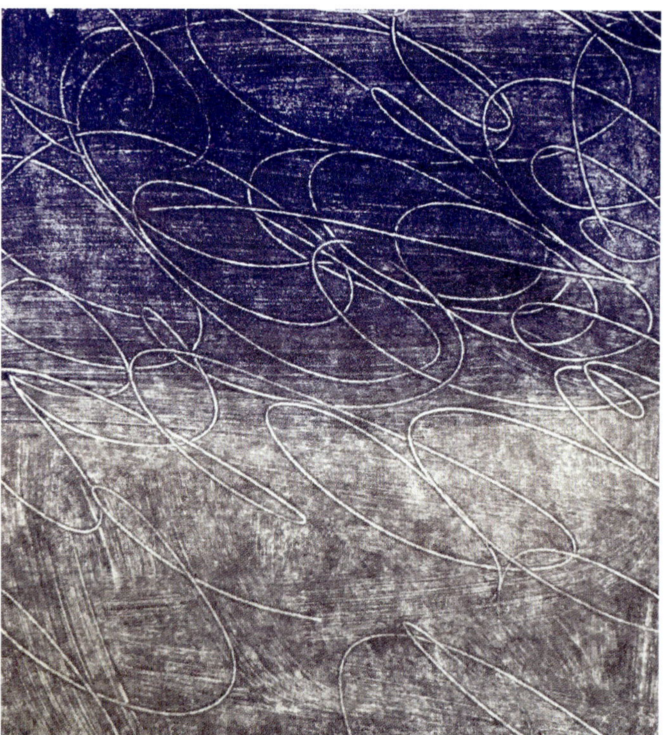

Sue Rowling. Japanese woodcut using monoprint/monotype effects.

OTHER ADVANCED PRINTING TECHNIQUES

Reduction

Reduction printing is made by cutting and printing each successive colour of your print using just one block. Starting with the lightest colour, the entire edition of your print needs to be made from the outset. Then you cut away the areas where the first colour will appear and print the second colour over the entire edition and so on, until the last colour is the only part remaining on your block. The block will be destroyed in the process of making the print.

There are advantages and disadvantages to the technique. The first advantage is economy; instead of using multiple separations on multiple blocks, only one is used. The main disadvantage is that there is no going back and recutting where a mistake has occurred.

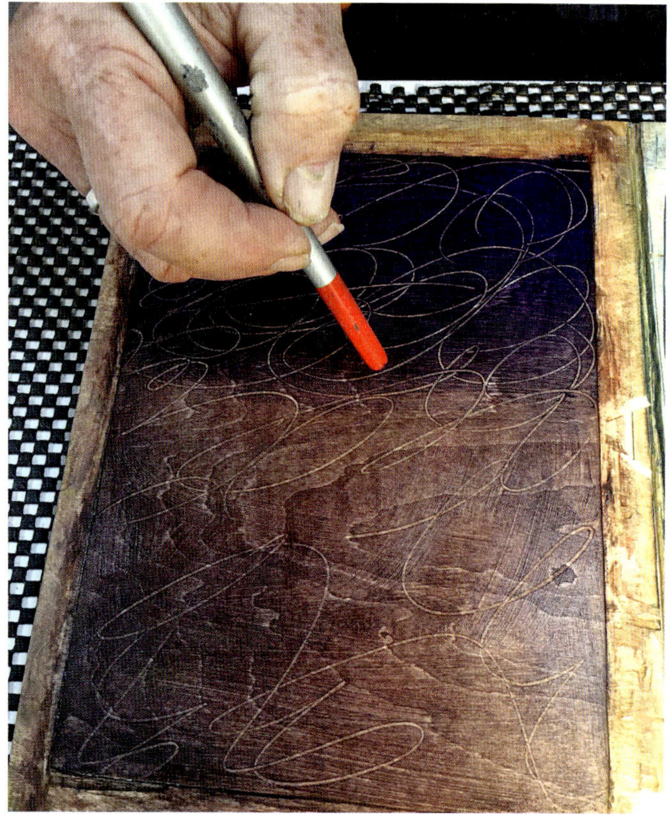

Sue Rowling. Drawing with the back of a paintbrush.

Blue layer printed, areas to remain blue cut away, yellow printed to make green.

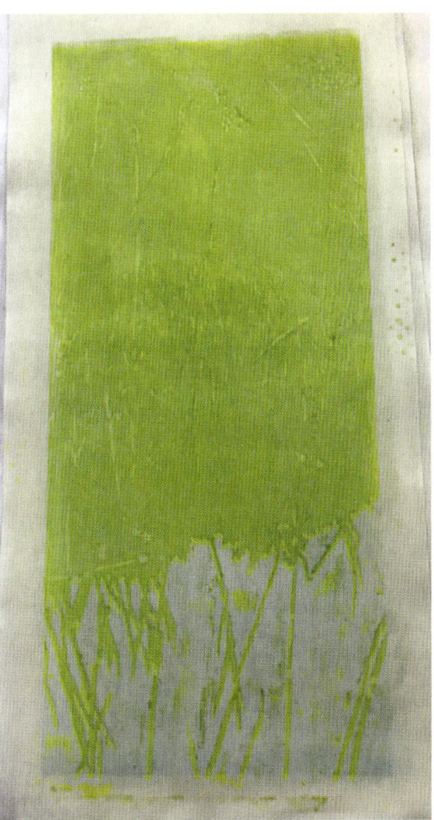

Showing the print developing.

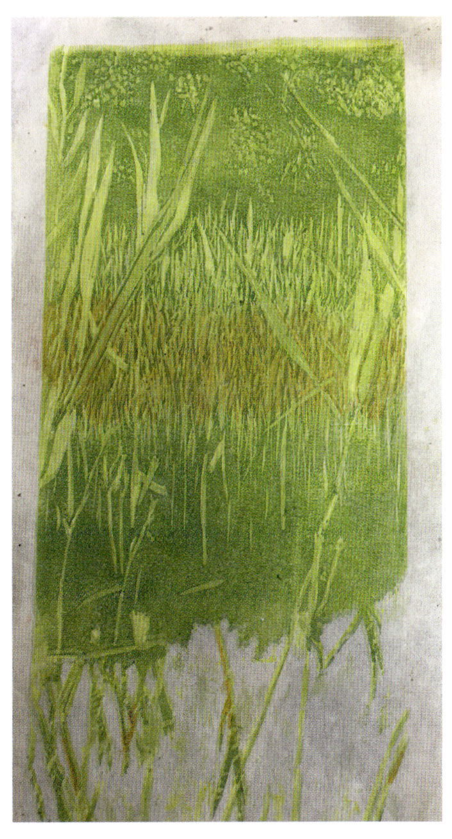

More definition.

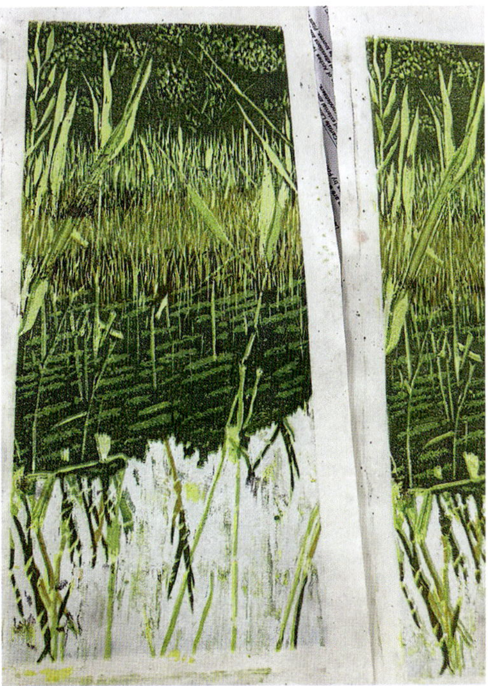

Last dark layer.

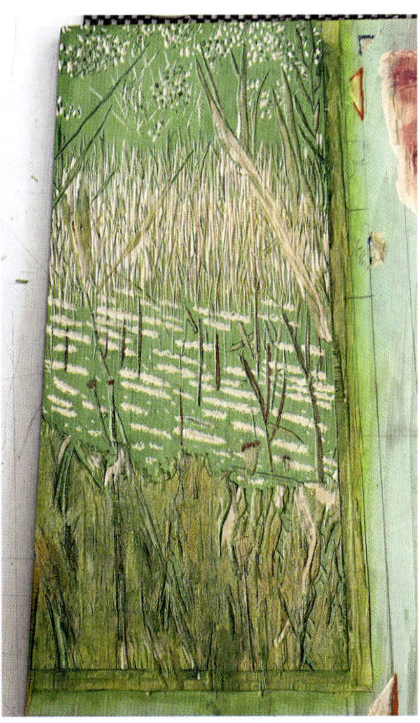

Showing the woodcut before the last printing with most areas cut away.

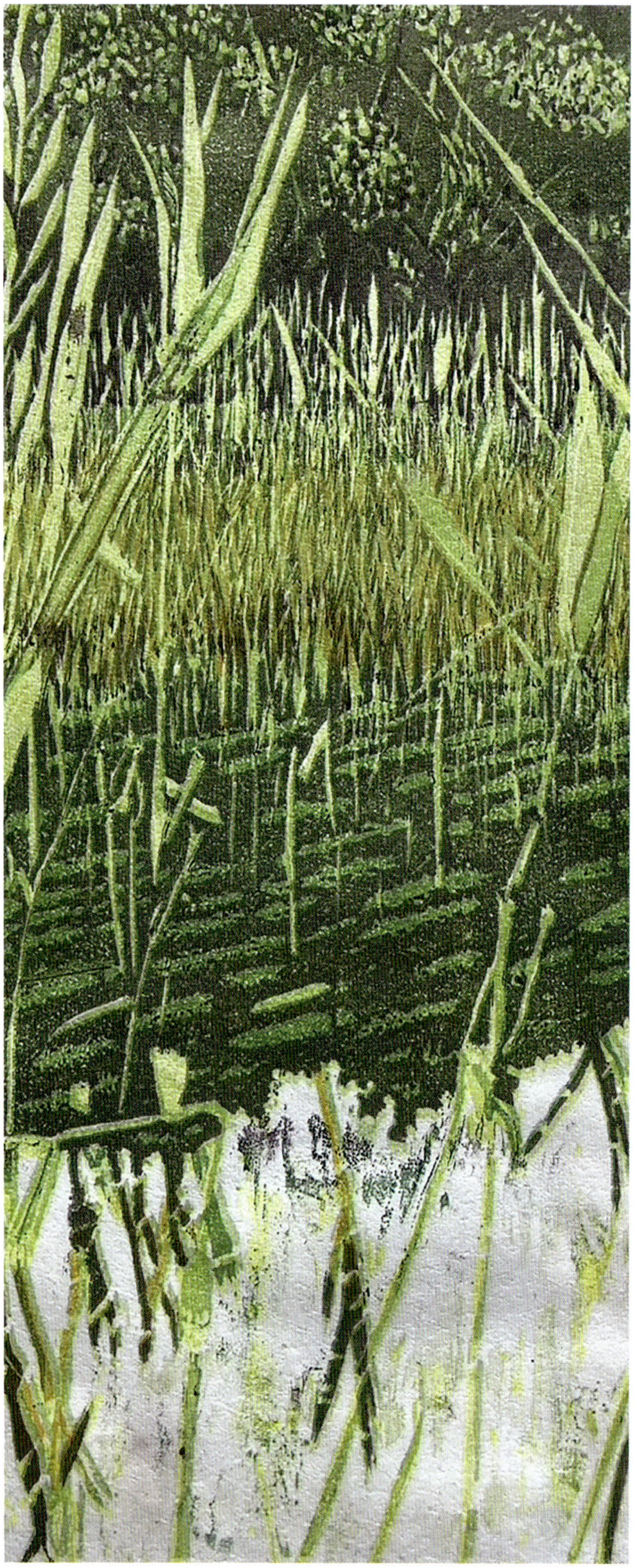

There is however a lot to be said for this method. For me, it is like a conversation between myself and the woodblock, where I respond directly to the print and the material. Wood is an organic material and has idiosyncrasies of its own, unlike the uniform lino. It is good when cutting to allow the wood to take its own course; in this way a print may take a different direction than the one initially conceived. It is also a considered and slow process, there is a rhythm to be found in cutting and printing and then allowing the block to dry out naturally while you evaluate the print ready for cutting and printing the following day. Too often I have students make a finished drawing, make separations and then cut them, having already a precise notion of what the finished print will look like. All very well but making a reduction print means that you can evaluate your image according to the print you have just made, altering direction as fresh possibilities present themselves. *Washi* paper is also ideal for printing multiple layers, though I would recommend a medium- to heavyweight paper and avoid the thinner papers. I printed ten layers of successive darker tones of grey to make my cloud print without distortion or damage to the paper using *hoshō* paper.

White Line Printing

White line printing is also known as Provincetown Printmaking as it developed in Provincetown, Massachusetts,

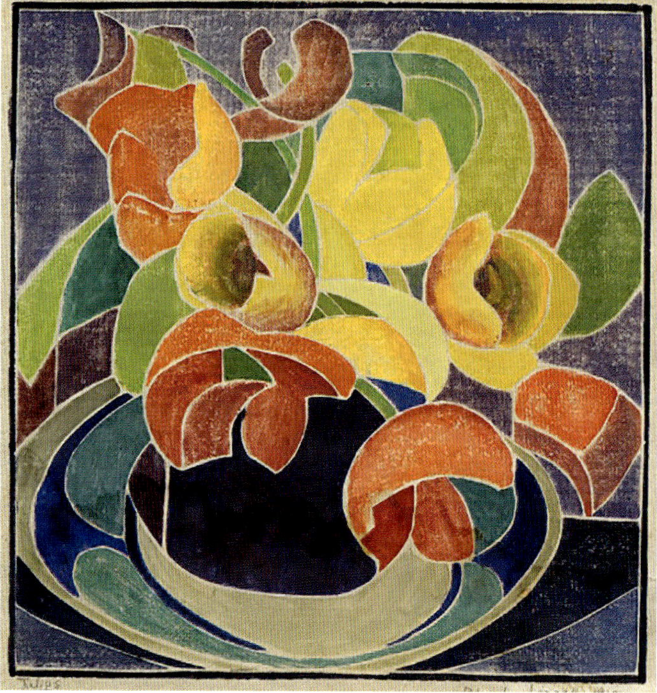

Blanche Lazzell, *Tulips,* 1920. White line woodcut print.

Valerie Johnson-Bell, *Reeds in a Scottish Loch*. Reduction Japanese woodcut.

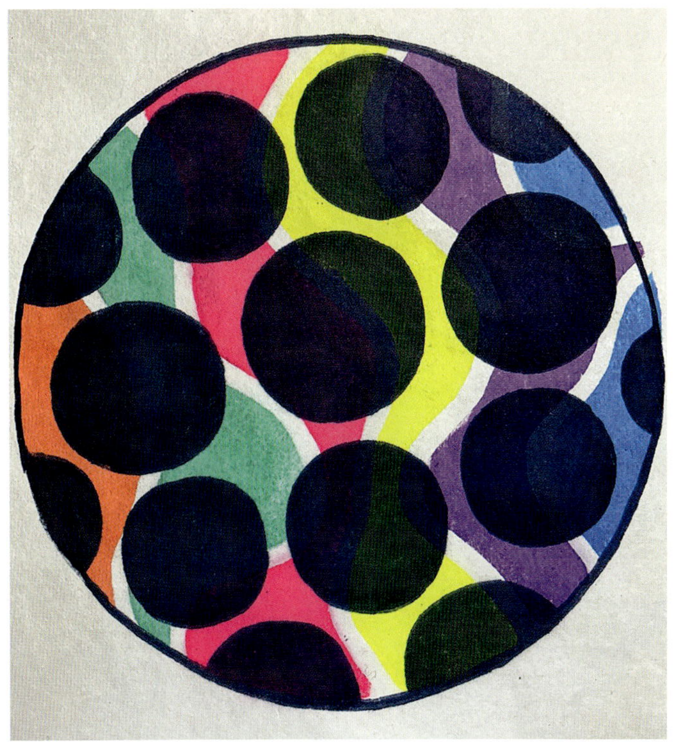

Mary Veronica Howard, *Stuckness*. White line Japanese woodcut with reduction.

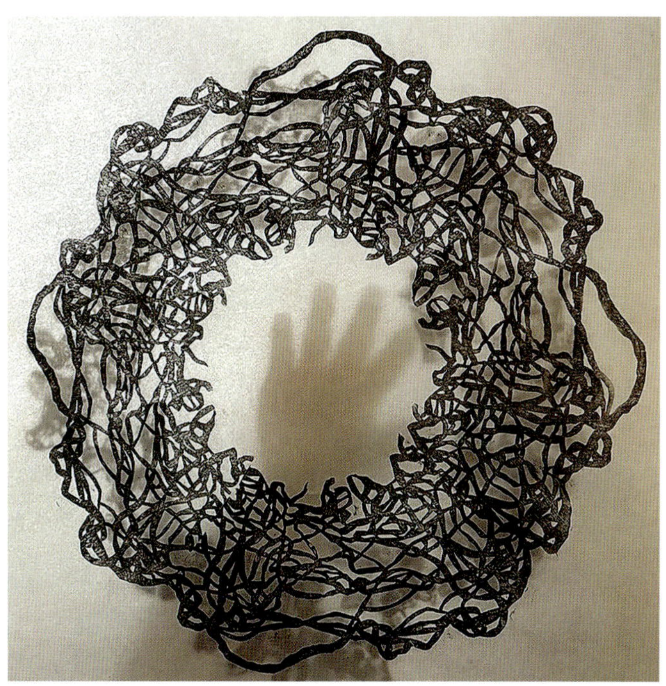

Carol Wilhide Justin, *Wisteria*. Japanese woodblock print on *kozo* paper.

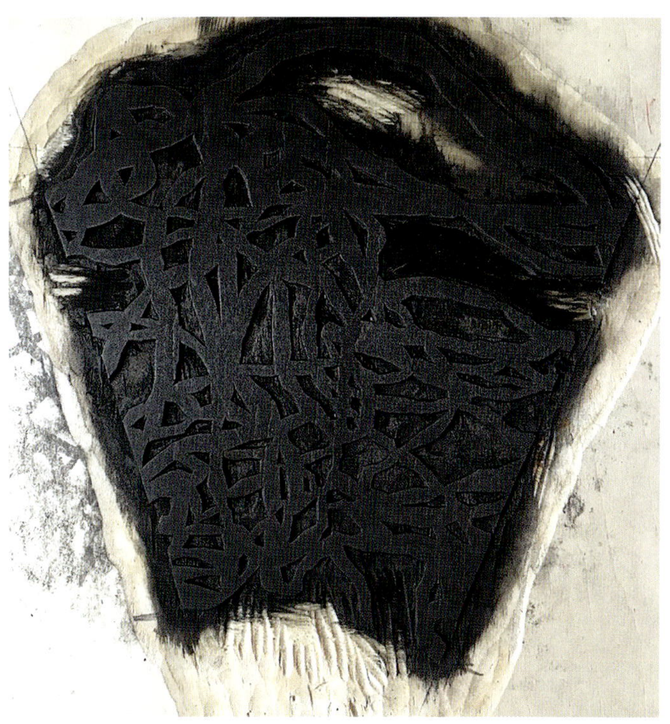

Woodblock for *Wisteria* #1.

USA in 1915. It began as an alternative to Japanese multiplate woodblock, using only one block to create colourful prints. The colours are separated by a cut white line enabling the printmaker to colour each area separately. With no access to specialised Japanese wood and tools, all the materials would have been those most readily to hand: craft knives instead of *hangi-tō*, soft pine instead of cherrywood and a wooden spoon instead of a *baren* to press the colour into the paper.

Repeat Pattern

This print *Wisteria* is made from just two small blocks that printed to make a circular wreath.

The two blocks were cut so that the tendrils link from side to side. Alternating the blocks meant that the repeat pattern was less obvious. Accurate block placement was very important so that the joins do not show.

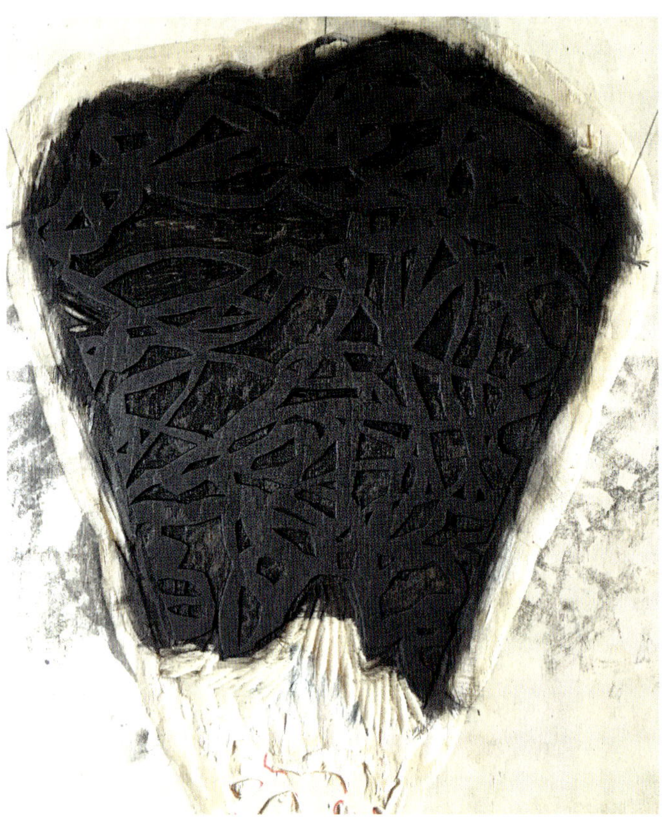

Woodblock for *Wisteria #2.*

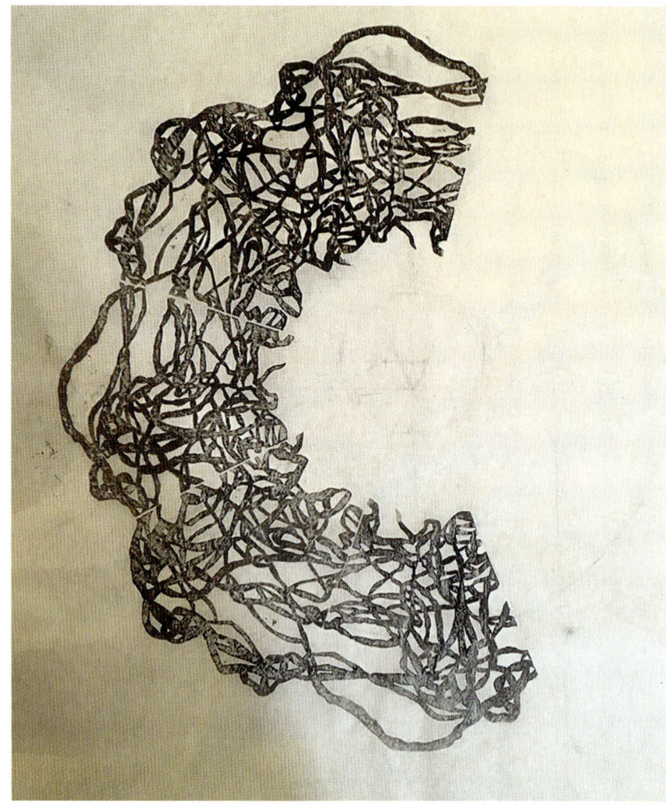

Newsprint proof showing how the print was made.

OTHER FORMATS

Scrolls *Ekimono*

Scrolls have been an important part of Japanese culture since the eighth century. Originally religious subjects were depicted, but during the Heian period (794–1185 CE) a more secular refined aesthetic developed at court that established a unique Japanese cultural identity.

Scrolls are traditionally read from right to left, the narrative unfolding in what seems to us a cinematic way. The scroll is simultaneously unwound with the left hand and wound up with the right.

Leporello/Concertina

The concertina format developed from scrolls. The prints are joined using wheat paste in such a way that the connection is hidden in the pleated folds of the concertina.

Books

Mokuhanga originated from popular book production. The prints for the books are made of a long sheet that when folded in half, forms two pages back-to-back.

The reverse of the print would be hidden from view and the short edge pages are bound together in a stab binding.

Note that a Japanese book would open from right to left.

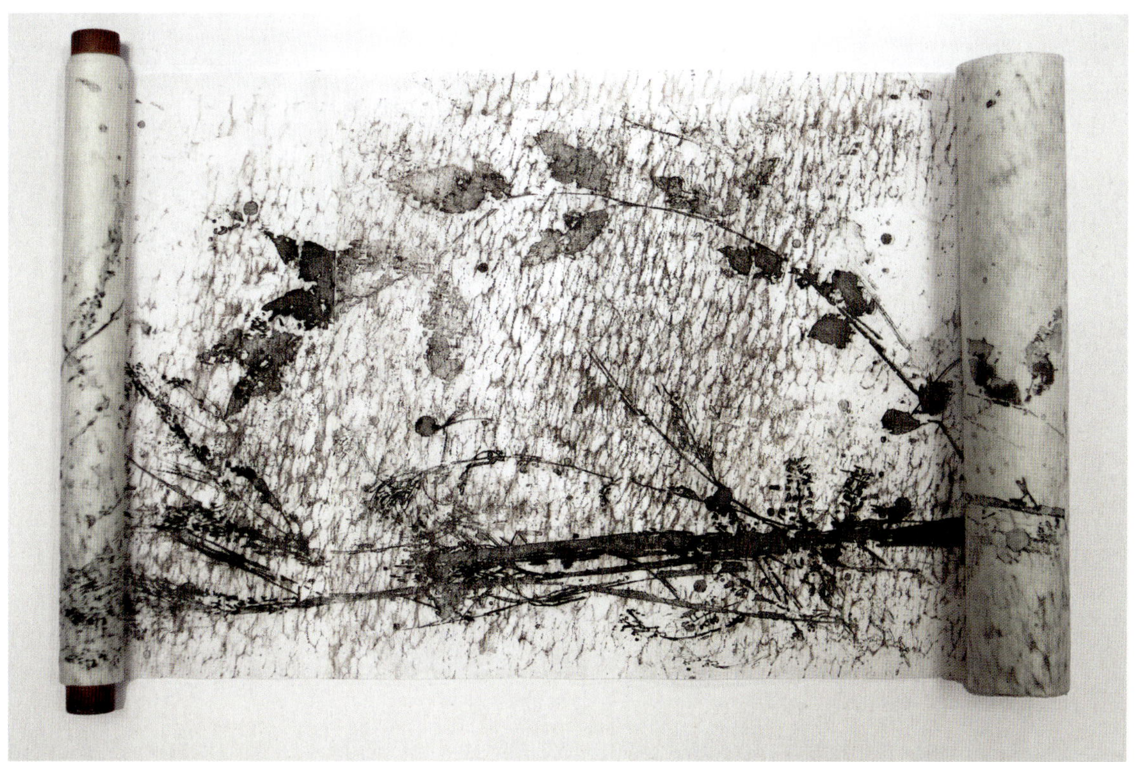

Inga Eicaite. *Pi.* Japanese woodcut scroll *ekimono*.

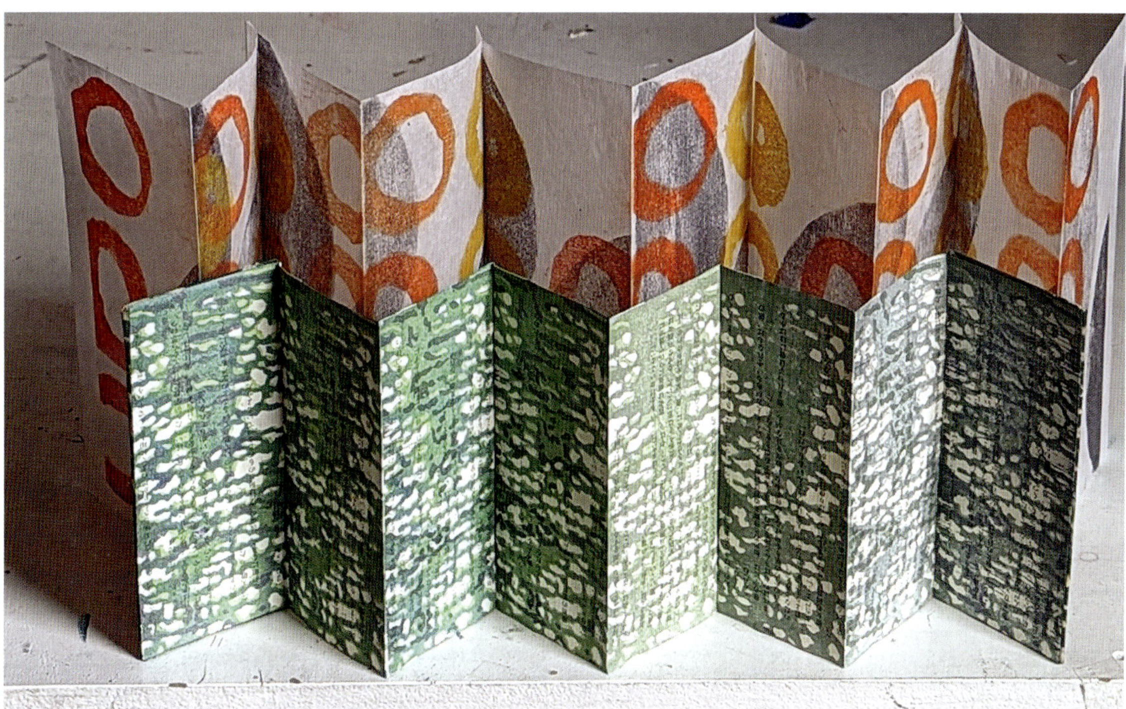

Margaret Cooter, *Moons and Tides*. Two Leporello Japanese woodcut books.

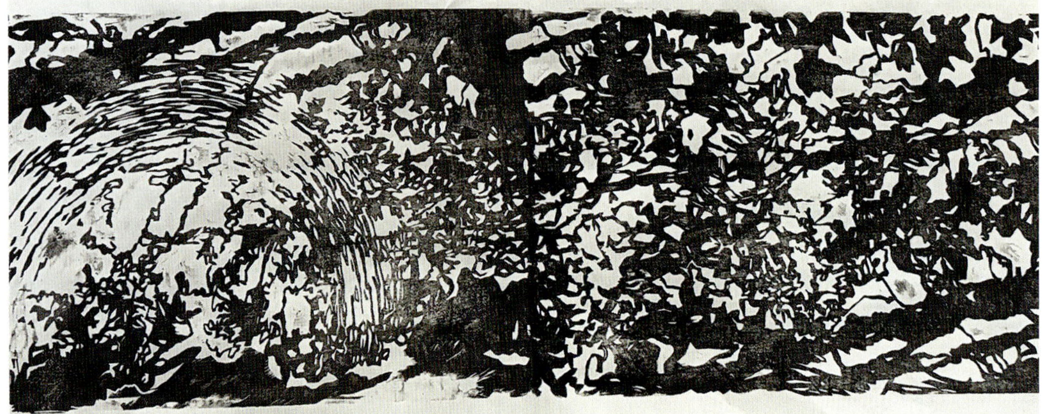

Two of my prints printed side by side, ready to be folded.

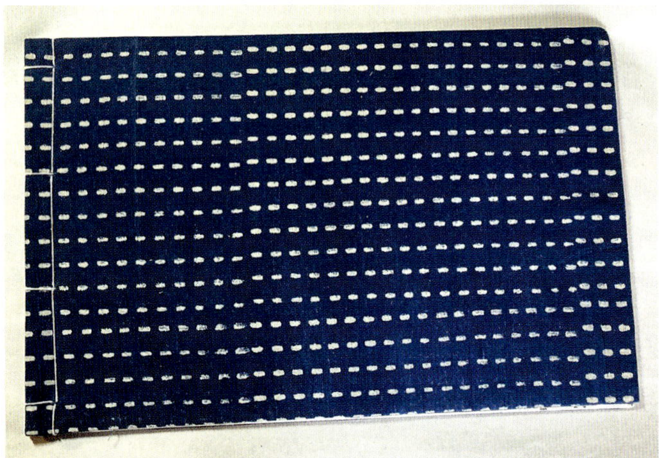

Stab binding.

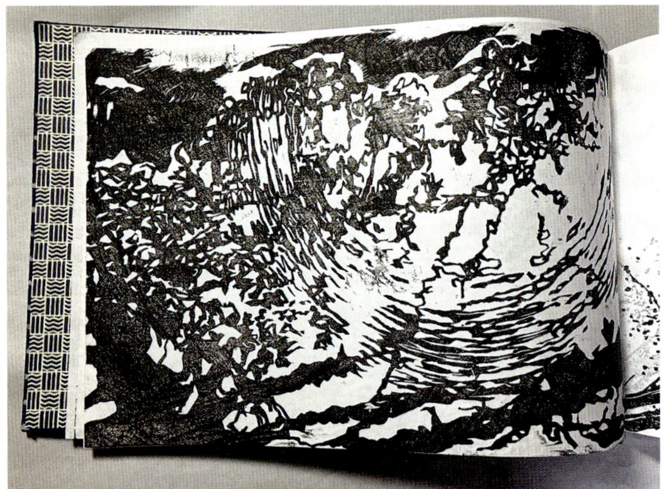

Folded print bound at the spine in a stab binding.

Using the woodblocks themselves as book covers

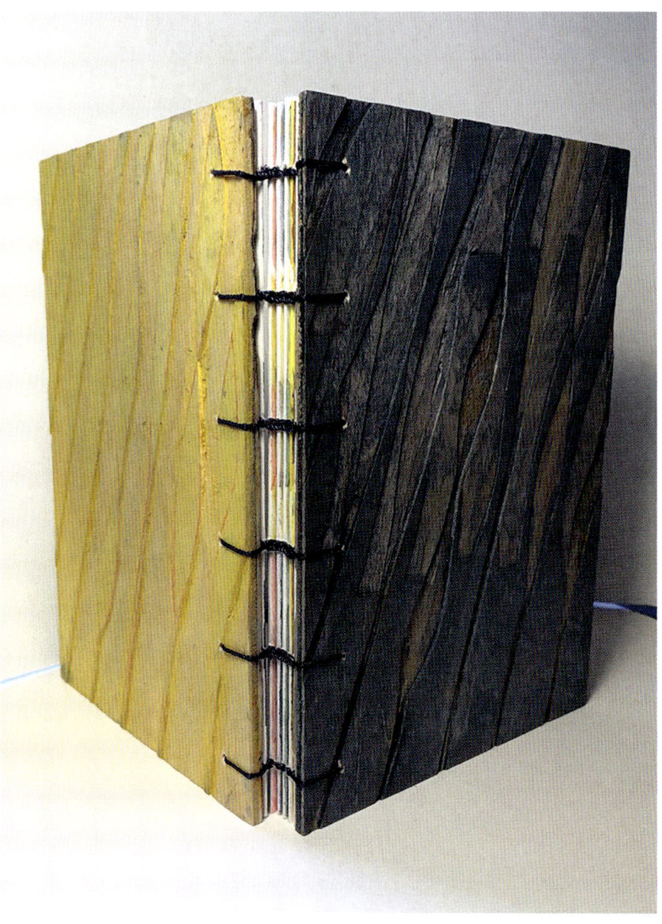

Using the woodblocks themselves as book covers, pages bound in a Coptic binding.

3D shapes

It is possible to have fun with 3D shapes by first printing in the flat, cutting the shape out and then using *nori* to paste the edges together.

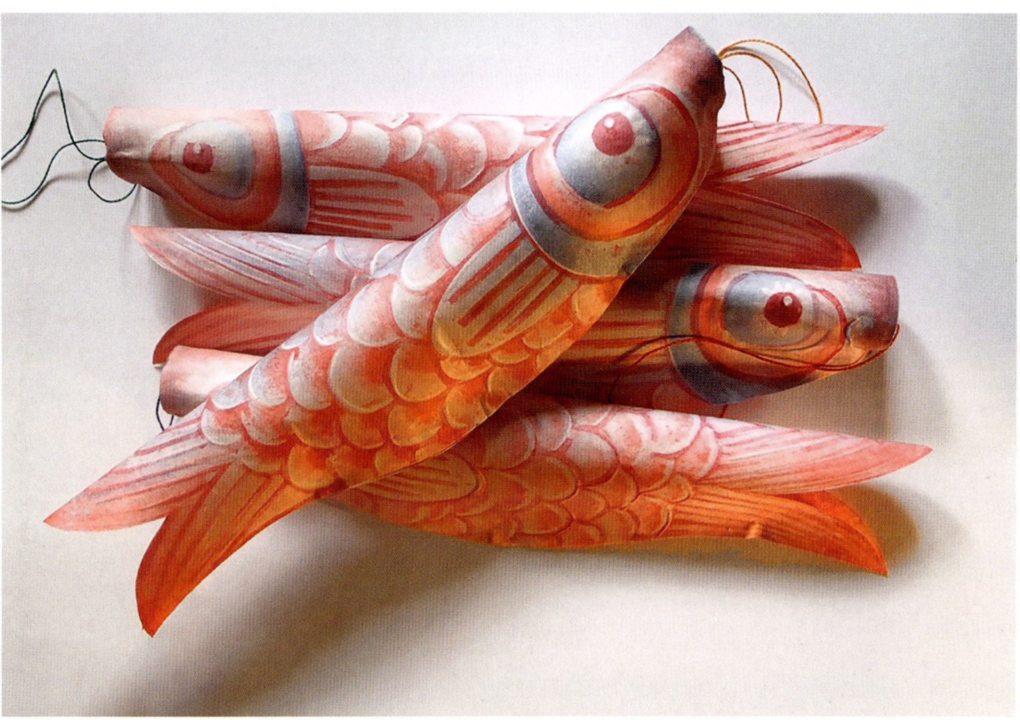

My *koinobori* Japanese woodcut fish kites made for 'Children's Day'.

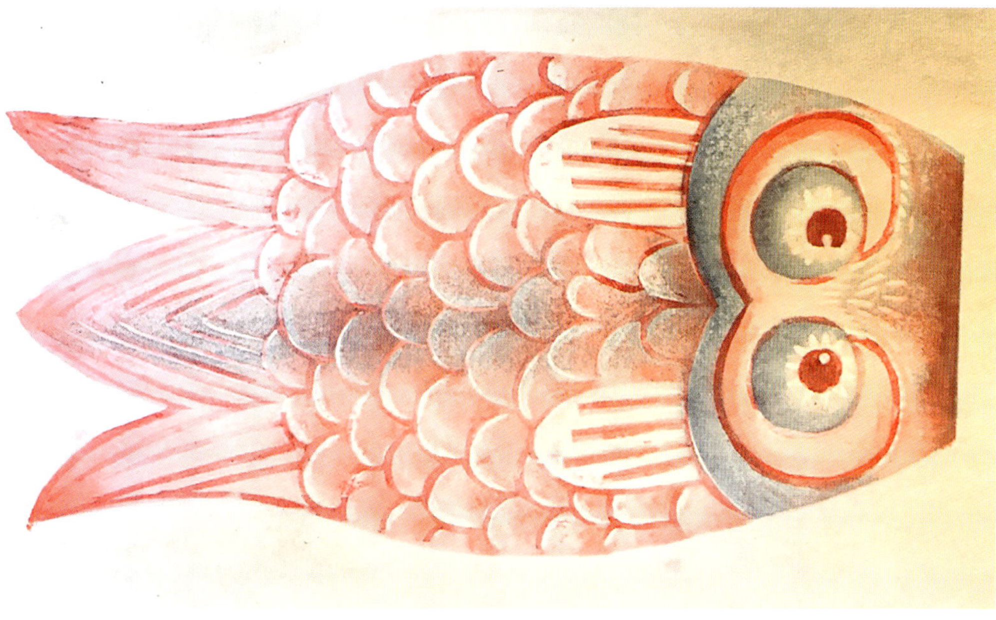

Showing the print before it was cut out.

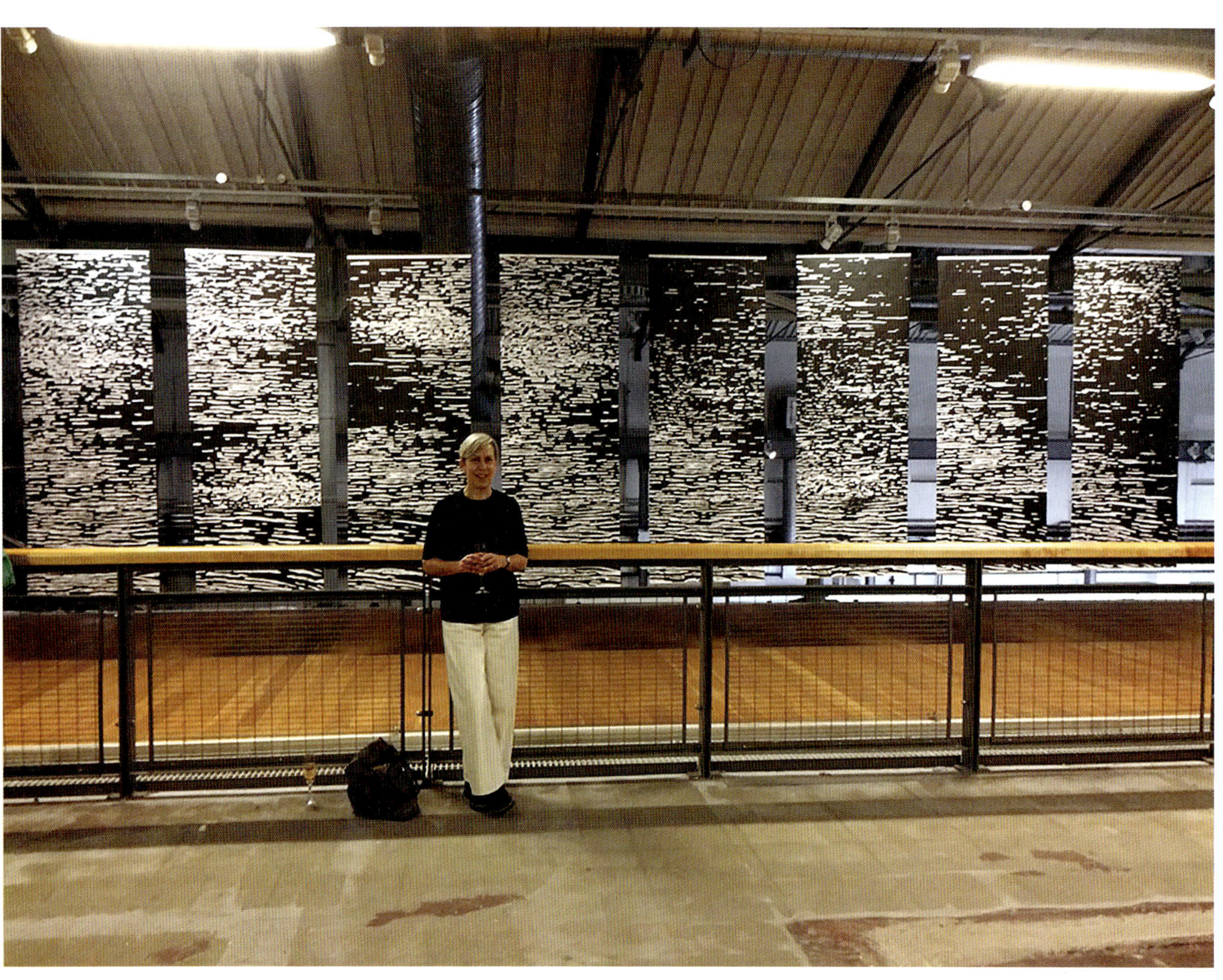

Chapter 7

PRINTING LARGE WORKS

Printing on a larger scale than book size requires some special planning and preparation. This chapter looks at some of the issues encountered and shows some strategies to deal with printing larger works that have helped me.

Most *ukiyō-e* prints were small in size, not usually larger than a book A3 (29.7 × 42cm). In part this was due to size constraints placed on the publishers by the censors, who were anxious that this very popular medium would not attract subversive elements.

However, the small size meant that many more prints could be quickly made. Printers sought ways to circumvent the authorities by making very tall prints or making prints that fit together in a diptych or triptych, where the individual prints met the criteria but the end result was much larger, pushing the boundaries of what was permitted. In contemporary Mokuhanga, although there are no size constraints due to censorship there are still some issues that need to be thought through before embarking on a large work.

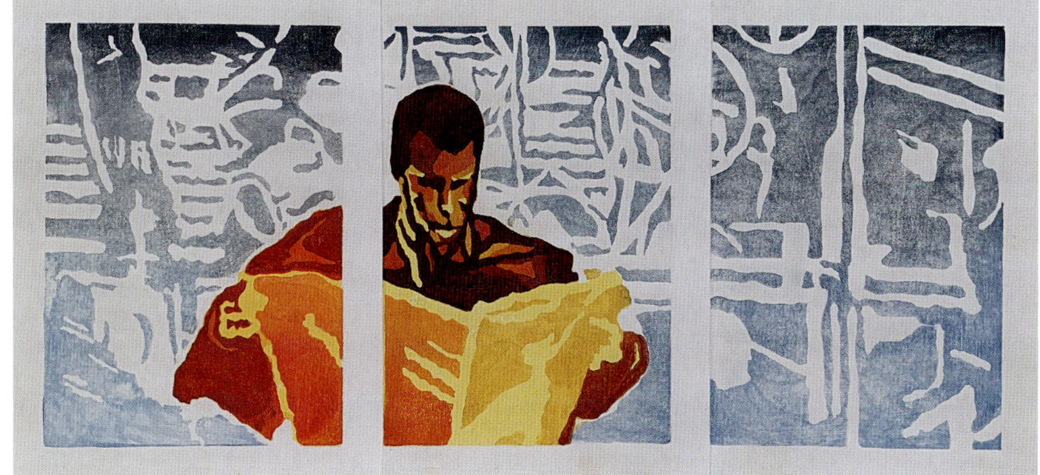

Sarah Ann Mitchell, *Media: Bladerunner.* White line triptych with reduction elements.

◁ My installation *Water* at Woolwich Contemporary Print Fair comprised eight A1-sized woodblocks printed in 32 different configurations, hand printed on *Shoji Baika* rolls.

PAPER

I have found that it is helpful to buy your paper before you even begin cutting your blocks. Handmade Japanese paper is often made in smaller sizes than Western papers and it can be disappointing to find after you have cut your blocks that your paper of choice is too small, or the selection limited. Alternatively, buying paper in rolls means that you can cut your printing paper to the size you want, but do remember to also check the width of the roll.

PRINTING LARGER WORKS

Method 1

My prints for my MA degree show at the Royal College were all A1 size (60 × 84cm). Each print was made of up of three blocks. Ideally the woodgrain direction of your block and the grain direction of your paper should align; in much the same way that

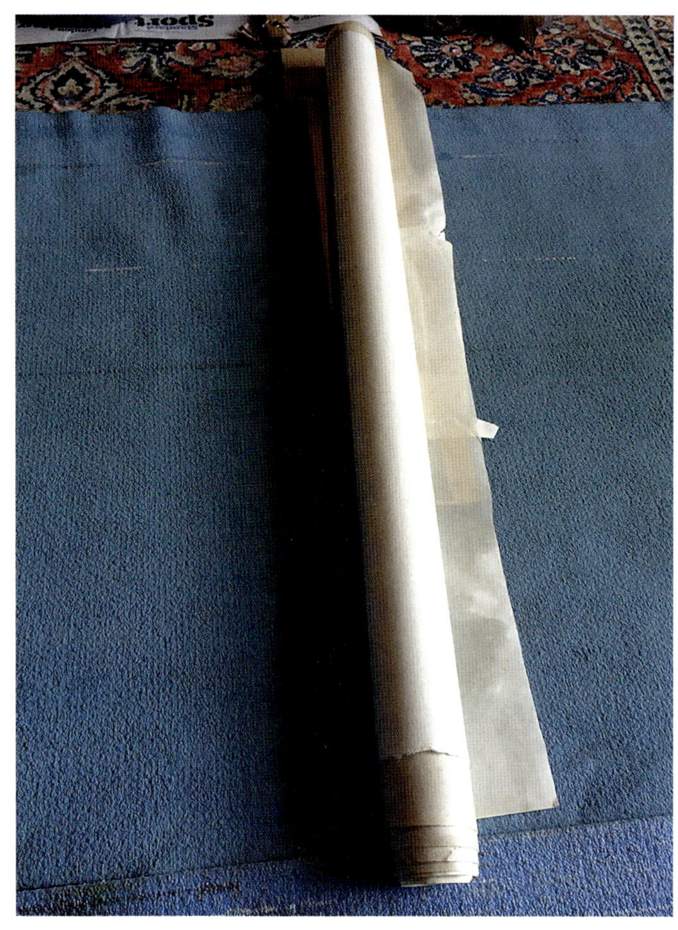

The roll with attached *kentōnban* just visible beneath.

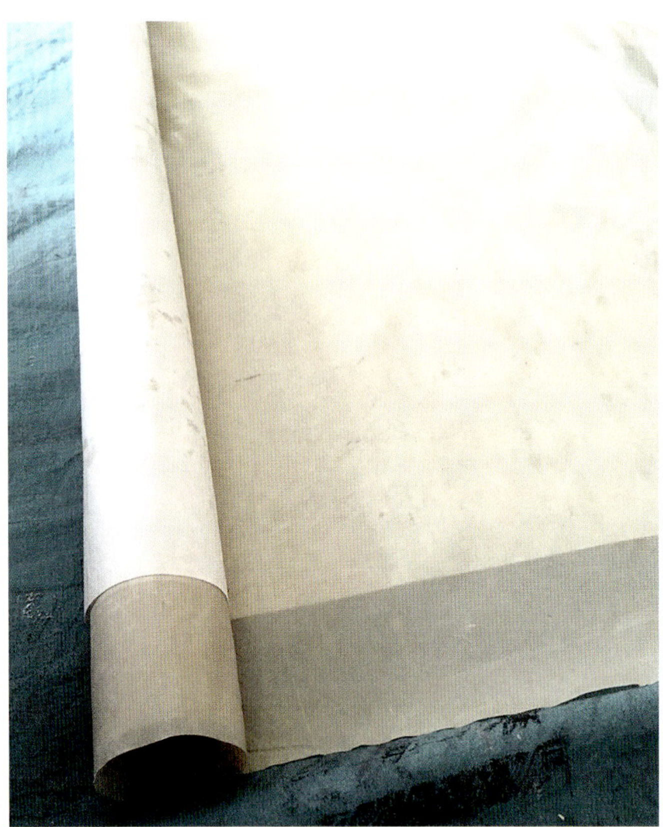

Rolling the printing paper and dampened newsprint together on a cardboard tube.

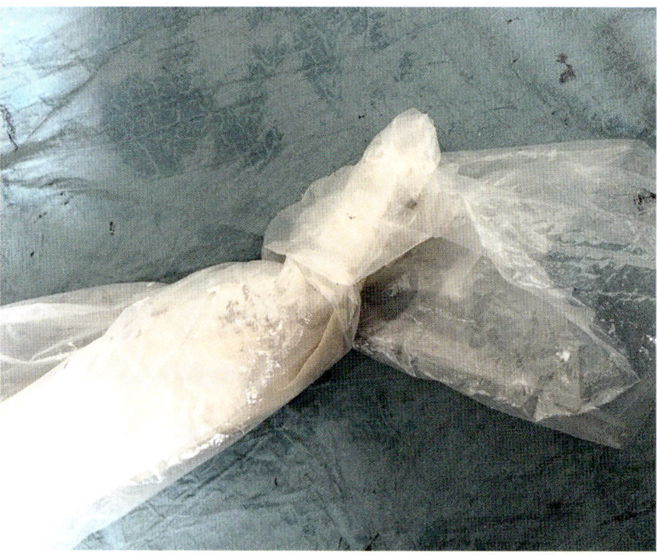

Wrapped in plastic. Poster bags are ideal for the purpose.

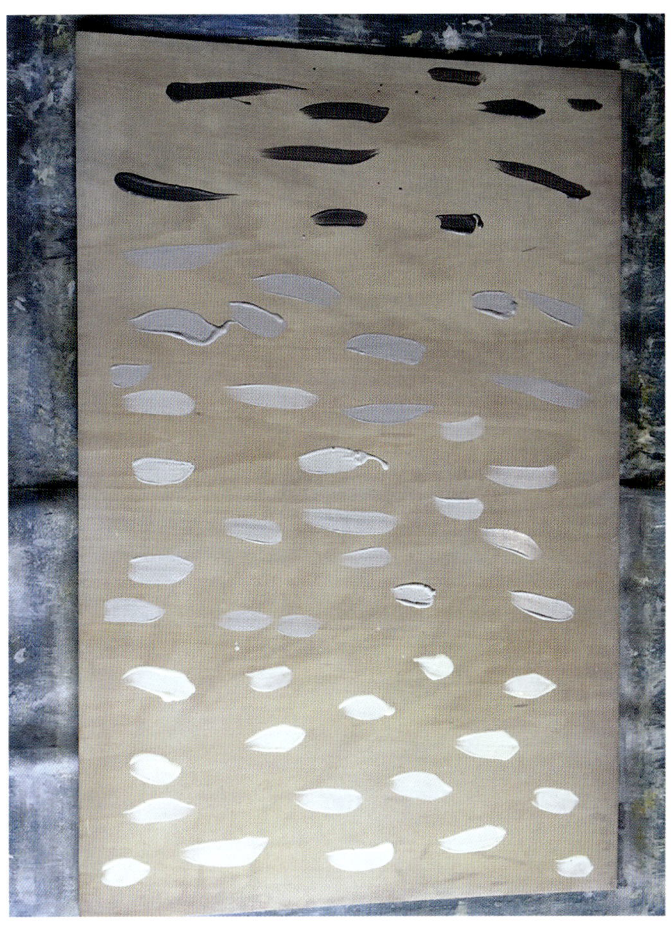

Pigment applied across the whole board in different colours to create a tonal graduation.

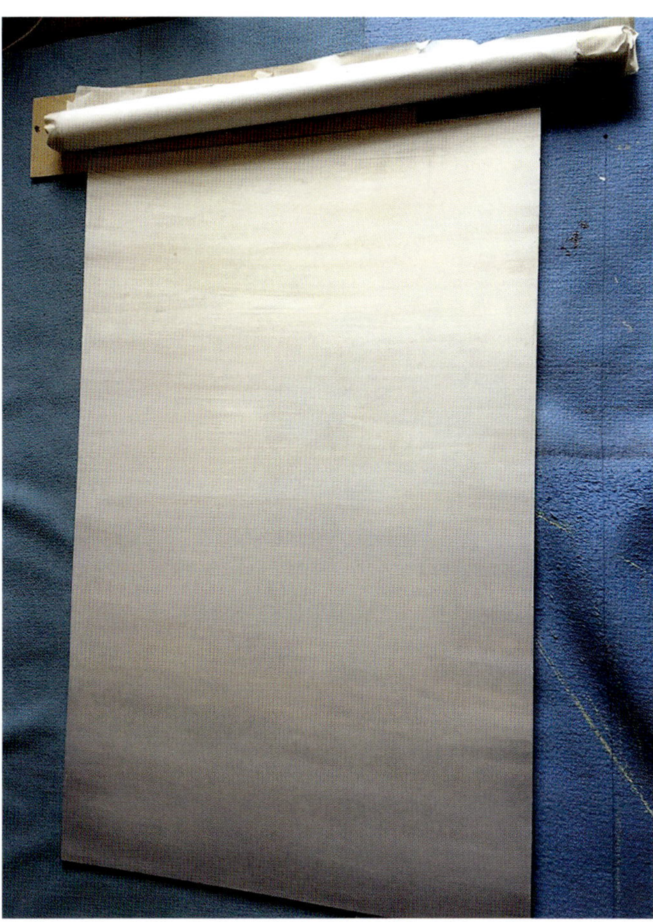

Showing the woodblock ready for printing

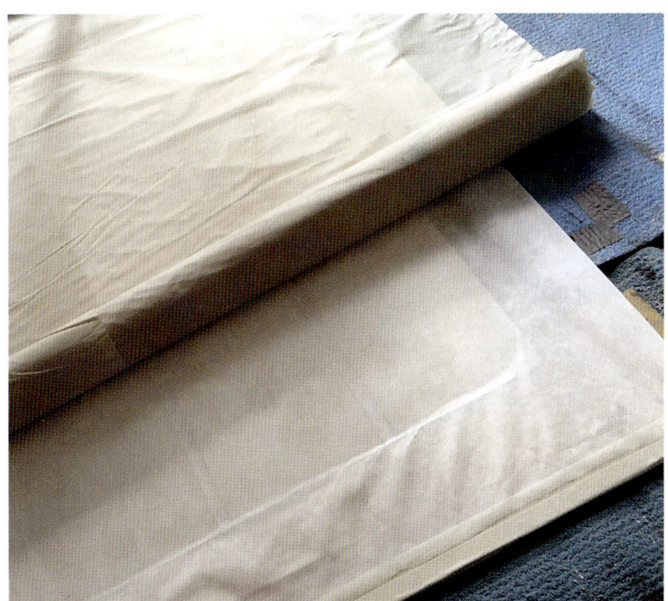

Unrolling the newsprint and printing paper, setting aside the damp newsprint for reuse.

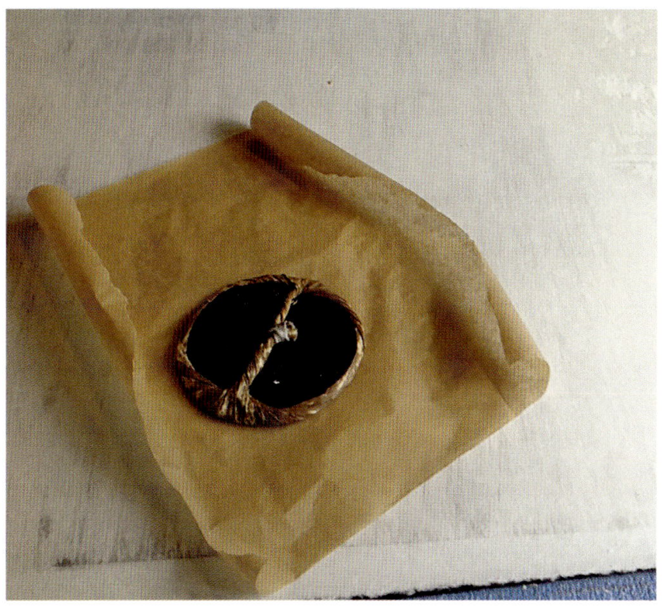

Using a baking sheet and rubbing down with the *baren*.

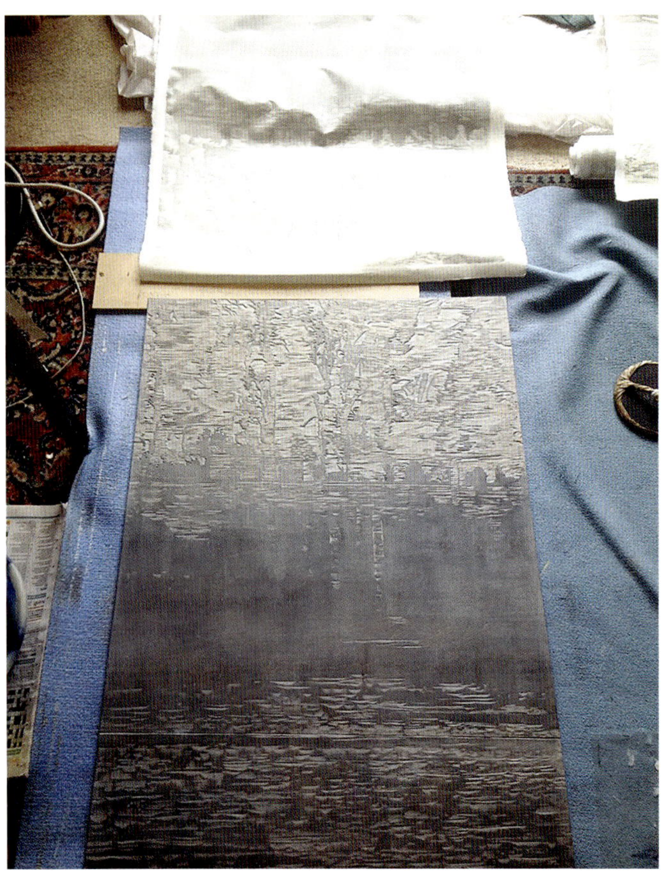

Showing a later stage in the printing, with the woodblock slotted into the *kentōban*.

cutting with the grain is easier than against the grain, printing with the grain is also smoother.

Working with large woodblocks I found it easier to work on the floor, setting my block on a yoga mat, to provide a bit of surface give when printing. Two problems quickly emerged; how to keep the paper evenly damp and how to register large, damp paper that was too floppy and unwieldy to place in the *kentō* registration by hand. To deal with the registration, I taped the printing paper smooth printing side down to the *kentōban*. To address the issue with paper moistness, I placed dampened newsprint on top of the printing paper and rolled both newsprint and printing paper onto a cardboard roll.

The roll with the attached *kentōban* was wrapped in plastic and left until the paper was evenly damp and ready for printing.

I prepared my pigments and *nori* as usual. After spraying my woodblock with water and allowing the water to be absorbed, I put the *nori* and pigment on together, so that the woodblock would not dry out too fast. Then I used a large *burashi* to brush the pigment and *nori* in.

When the inked block was ready for printing, I removed the roll of paper and *kentōban* and slotted the right-hand angle of the *kentōban* into the corner of the woodblock.

Then I used the *baren* and a protective baking sheet to rub down the block in a systematic way from top to bottom before the pigment had a chance to dry.

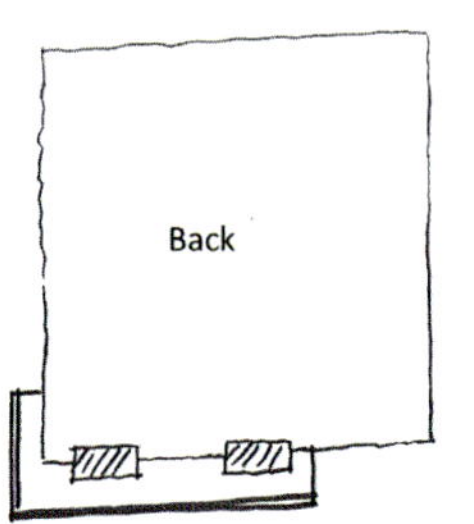

1. Place your printing paper, printing side down into your *kentō* notches on your *kentōban*. Secure in place with tape.

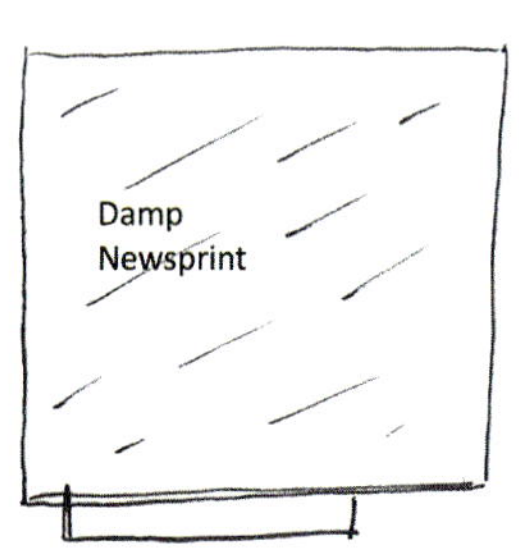

2. Lay damp newsprint on top ensuring that all the printing paper is covered generously..

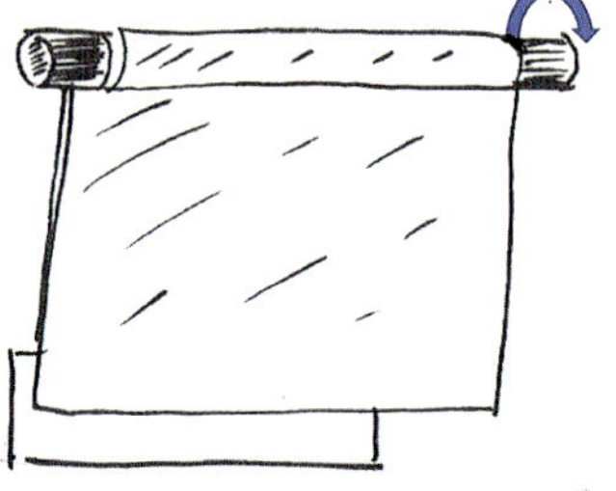

3. Starting at the top, roll the damp newsprint and the printing paper together around a cardboard tube.

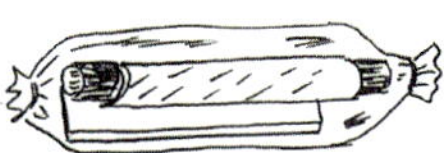

4. Wrap the *kentōban*, printing paper and newsprint in plastic, make sure that it is airtight. Leave at least 30 minutes, longer if the paper is thicker.

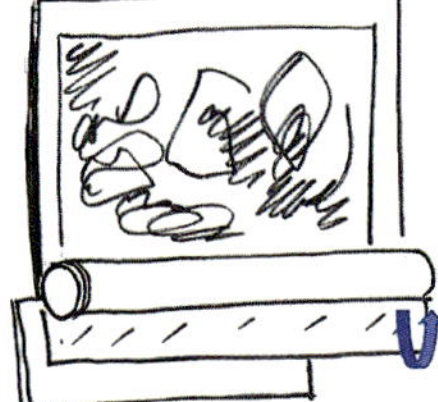

5. Ink up your woodblock. Remove *kentōban* from plastic, slot the woodblock into the *kentōban* and unroll printing paper and newsprint along inked woodblock from bottom to top.

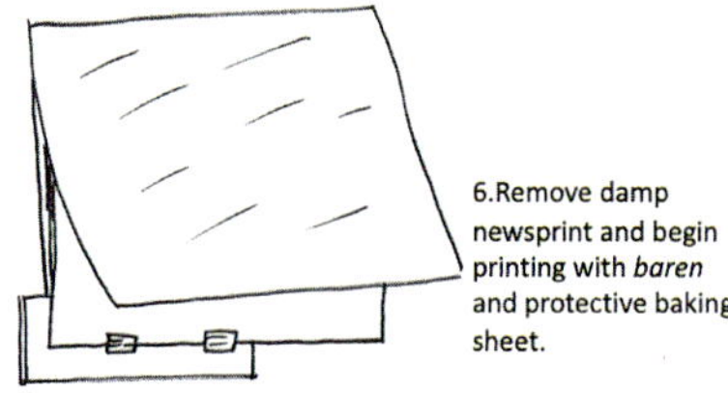

6. Remove damp newsprint and begin printing with *baren* and protective baking sheet.

Diagram showing the stages in printing using a cardboard tube and *kentōban*.

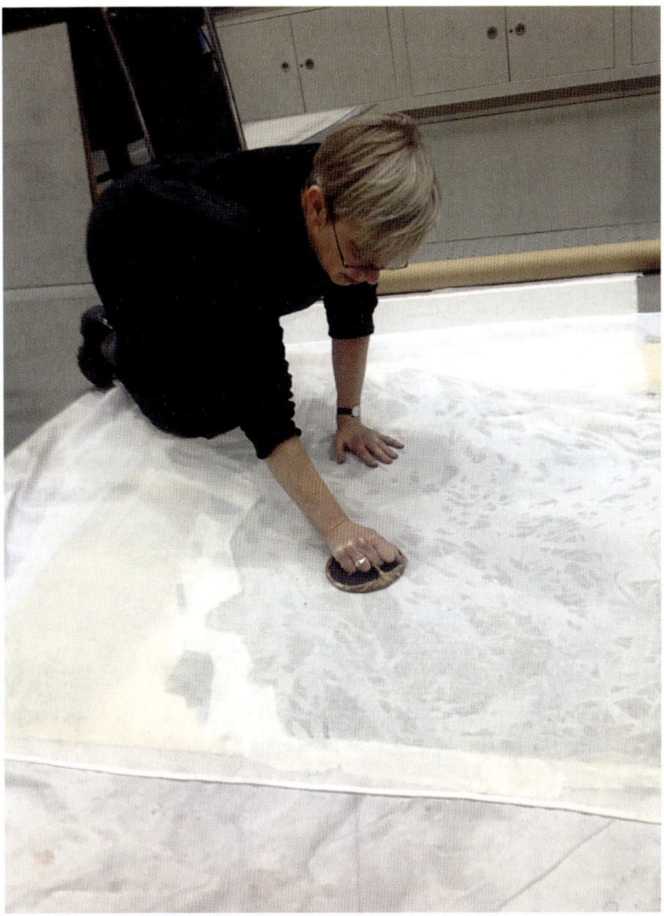

Printing a large woodblock.

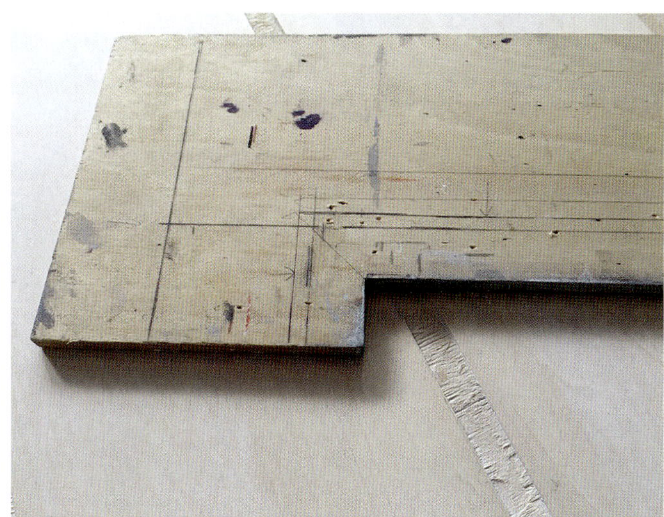

A *kentōban*.

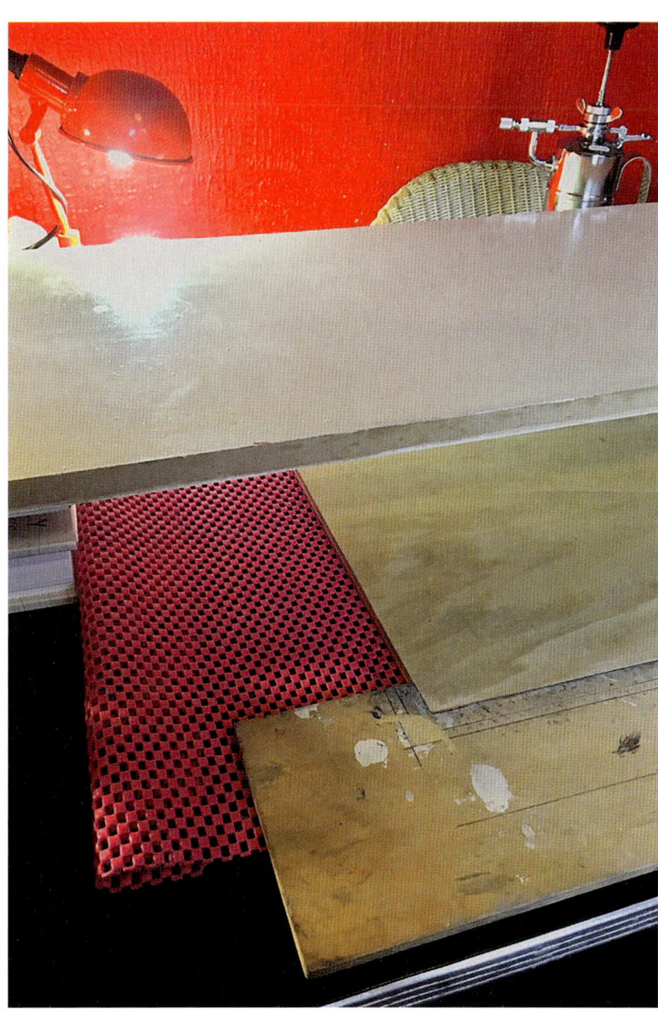

Showing the printing set-up, with *kentōban*, inked woodblock and bridge.

I found that printing from one day to the next could produce very different results; for instance, after one day of successful printing, the next day was a heatwave and everything had to be recalibrated, as the block, paper and pigment were all drying too quickly. More than any other printmaking I have come across, printing Mokuhanga is a holistic process that can be affected by the very atmosphere you are working in.

Working on a large woodblock is quite physical work and I found it important to allow myself enough time to print an edition and not attempt too much in one day. It is upsetting if under time pressure the print is misaligned on the last layer, not to mention the cost of wasted *washi* paper.

Method 2

Another method for printing larger works uses the traditional *kentō* registration that is cut into the woodblock itself. A *kentōban* can also be used if the image is cut right to the edge of the woodblock – I have cut *kentō* registration notches into

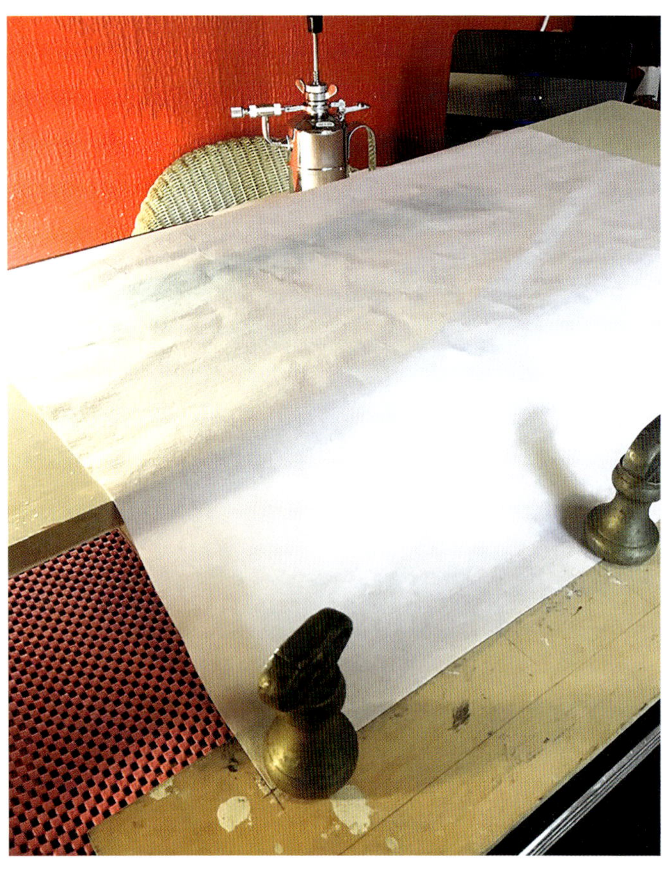

The printing paper resting on the bridge is weighted into the *kentō* notches.

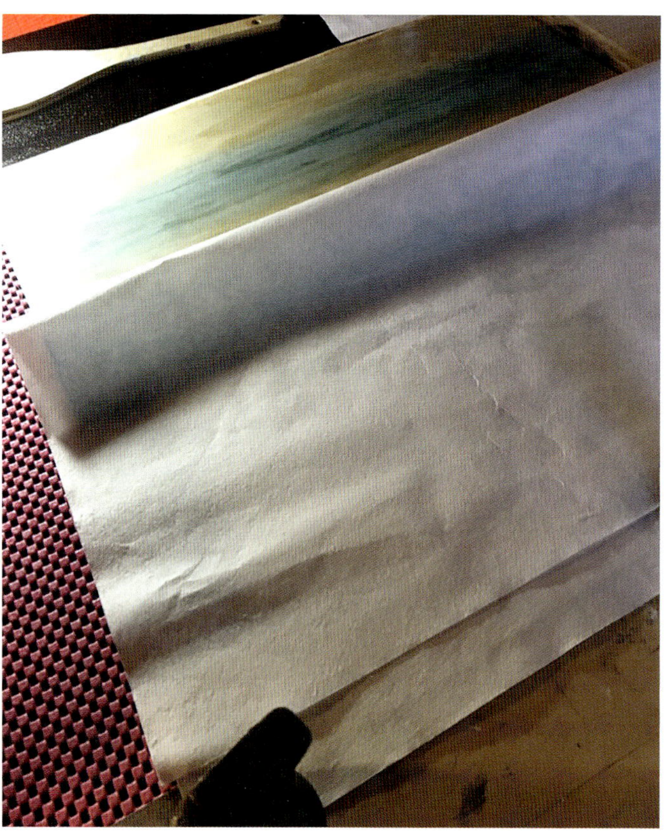

Lightly folding the printing paper widthways, placing in the *kentō,* weighting and then unfolding.

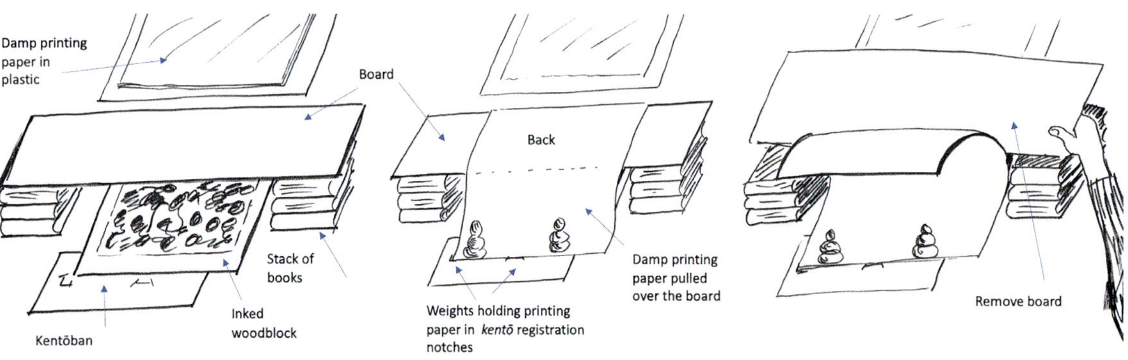

1.Slot the inked block into the *kentōban.* Ensure your stack of books are equal in height. Place a board ontop.

2. Pull a printing paper from the plastic over the top of the board and place corners into *kentō* notches. Weight the paper so that it does not move.

3. Carefully remove the board. The paper will flop down evenly across the inked woodblock. Move the weights and stacks of books. Using a protective baking sheet begin printing with a *baren.*

Diagrams to show the stages in printing using a bridge.

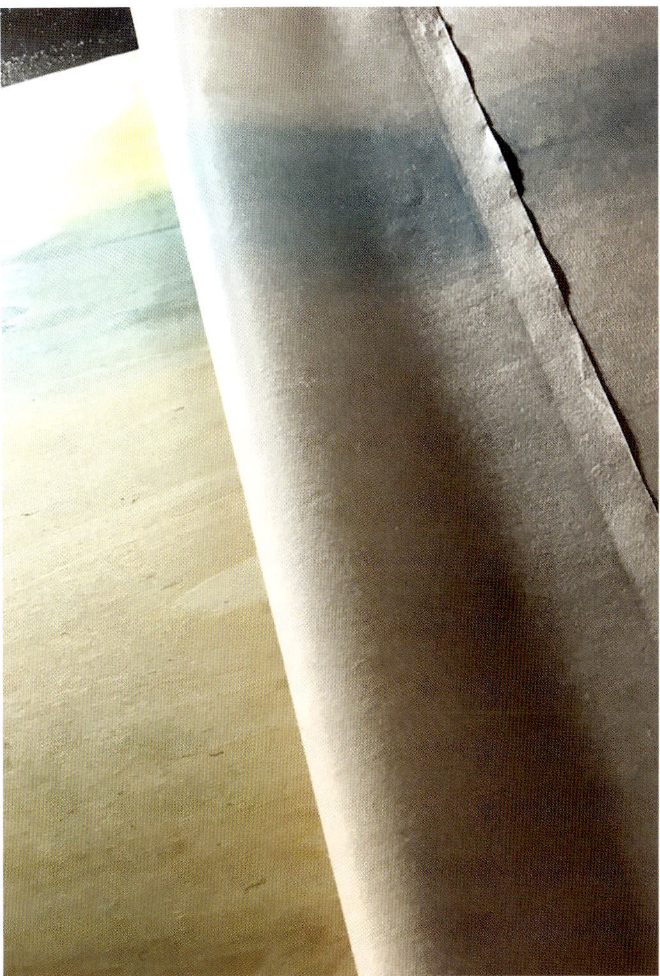
Lightly folding the printing paper lengthways to print half the board.

my *kentōban* to facilitate this method. It is advisable to anchor the *kentōban* to the table with tape to prevent slippages during printing, or to at least ensure that it is placed on a non-slip mat.

The paper is dampened between sheets of newsprint and wrapped in plastic until ready for printing. When the woodblock is inked ready for printing, it is placed between two stands. I have used two stacks of books, ensuring that they are of an even height and placed on a level surface, for example a tabletop. A flat board, large enough to accommodate the width of the paper you are using, is set on top of the two stacks of books, making a bridge over the inked woodblock.

The paper is taken out of the damp pack so that it rests, printing side down, on the board above the woodblock. The paper is gently pulled down so that the edge of the printing paper locates the *kentō* registration notches. I have found that using weights or rounded beach stones to hold the paper securely in place is a good idea to stop it from moving at this point.

Once the paper is in place, the board can be removed and your printing paper will fall softly onto the inked woodblock.

If the printing paper is very large it is sometimes easier to manipulate a damp printing paper that is gently folded widthways, as it is not so floppy. Ensure that you have folded it without creasing the paper and that the printing side is outermost. When the paper is placed into the *kentō* notches be sure to weight the edge before you flip the other half of the paper over.

When printing large areas time can be a critical factor; you do not want the woodblock to dry out before you have finished printing. If you carefully fold the paper lengthways and print one half and then fold over the paper and print the other, you can print quicker and achieve an even dampness.

CONTEMPORARY ARTISTS

n this chapter I want to showcase the range and scope of Mokuhanga and importantly its global reach as an artform. I was inspired when I saw April Vollmer's book *Japanese Woodblock Print Workshop* (2015) for the first time and it showed me some of the boundless possibilities of this process. In this chapter I will show some of the Mokuhanga artists from around the world who are working today. Each artist has written in their own words a short accompanying artist statement.

MARA COZZOLINO

Italy

I fell in love with the medium of Mokuhanga (water-based woodblock printing) in 2011 and have been working exclusively in the medium ever since. My prints changed with the medium I was using. The natural connection with the medium of Mokuhanga

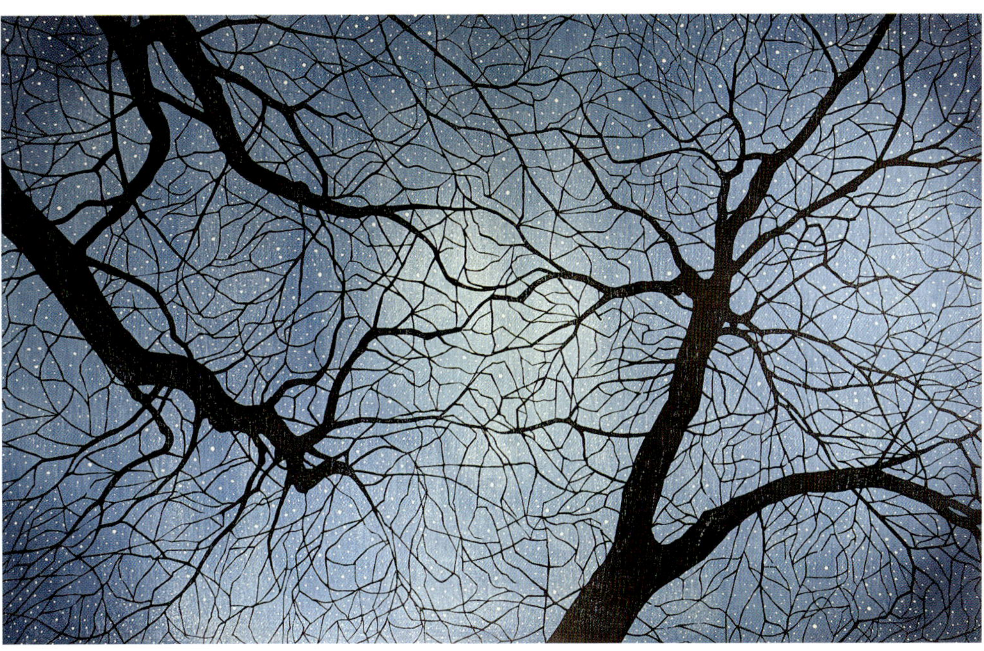

Mara Cozzolino, *Heaven and Earth*. Japanese woodcut.

Carol Wilhide Justin, *Not Yet* (65 × 90cm). Printed on *Bunkoshi* paper.

started to be reflected in my work, concentrating mostly on depicting nature, particularly the trees I have always been fond of since childhood. The idea of using wood, and paper made from wood (mulberry) and water to depict the trees and nature around me is particularly attractive. I also enjoy carving a lot as a process, so taking my time carving intricate branches is a meditative and enjoyable process. I tend to carve a few blocks for each print, but I then over-print each block several times to obtain a rich and intense colour.

SARA LEE

London, UK

My practice involves walking in and working from the land and invites the viewer to pause and question our profound relationship with landscape, especially at this time of ominous environmental change.

I was introduced to Mokuhanga by Rebecca Salter PRA and encouraged to find my own use of the traditional method within my practice – not always straightforward when using such a revered tradition.

I have been using techniques borrowed from the Mokuhanga tradition for 15 years now, feeling drawn to the subtle layering of colour it can provide and its 'low tech' hand-printed nature.

Unusually I often paint areas of colour directly onto the block, not always using a carved line but instead a drawn one.

I mostly use Lascaux gouache applied with brushes and have lately found that I don't always need to use nori. I now most often print using a contemporary baren (with ball bearings), using a good-quality traditional baren when needed.

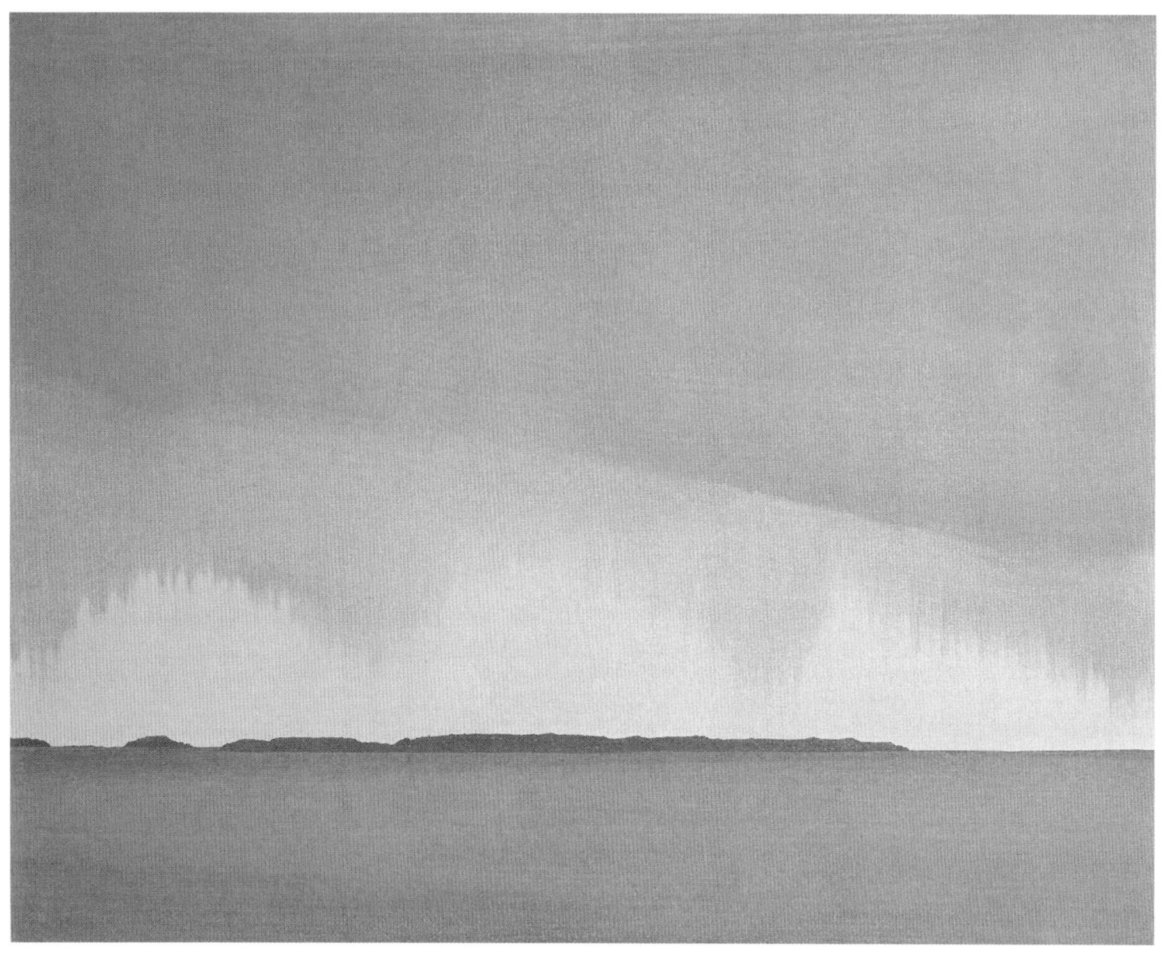

Sara Lee, *Imminence* (43 × 55cm). Japanese woodcut printed on *Shioji* paper.

LAURA BOSWELL

Kirkcudbright, Scotland UK

After learning the Mokuhanga technique in Japan as part of what was originally the Nagasawa Art Park Programme, now known as MI-Lab, I added Mokuhanga printing to my practice and made either Mokuhanga or linocut prints. I was captivated by Mokuhanga's flexibility as a printing method and went on to complete two public art projects for the National Health Service, *creating two sets of large-scale Mokuhanga prints for a health clinic and a hospice. More recently I have been combining Mokuhanga with linocut and mokulito (lithography on wood). Mokuhanga has also had a profound impact on my approach to printing the reduction linocuts which make up the largest proportion of my work. I now work with lino using the same transparent layering approach that I use when printing Mokuhanga. Conversely, lino printing has affected my Mokuhanga work and I often use graphic cutting and layering of woodblocks to build texture in my prints.*

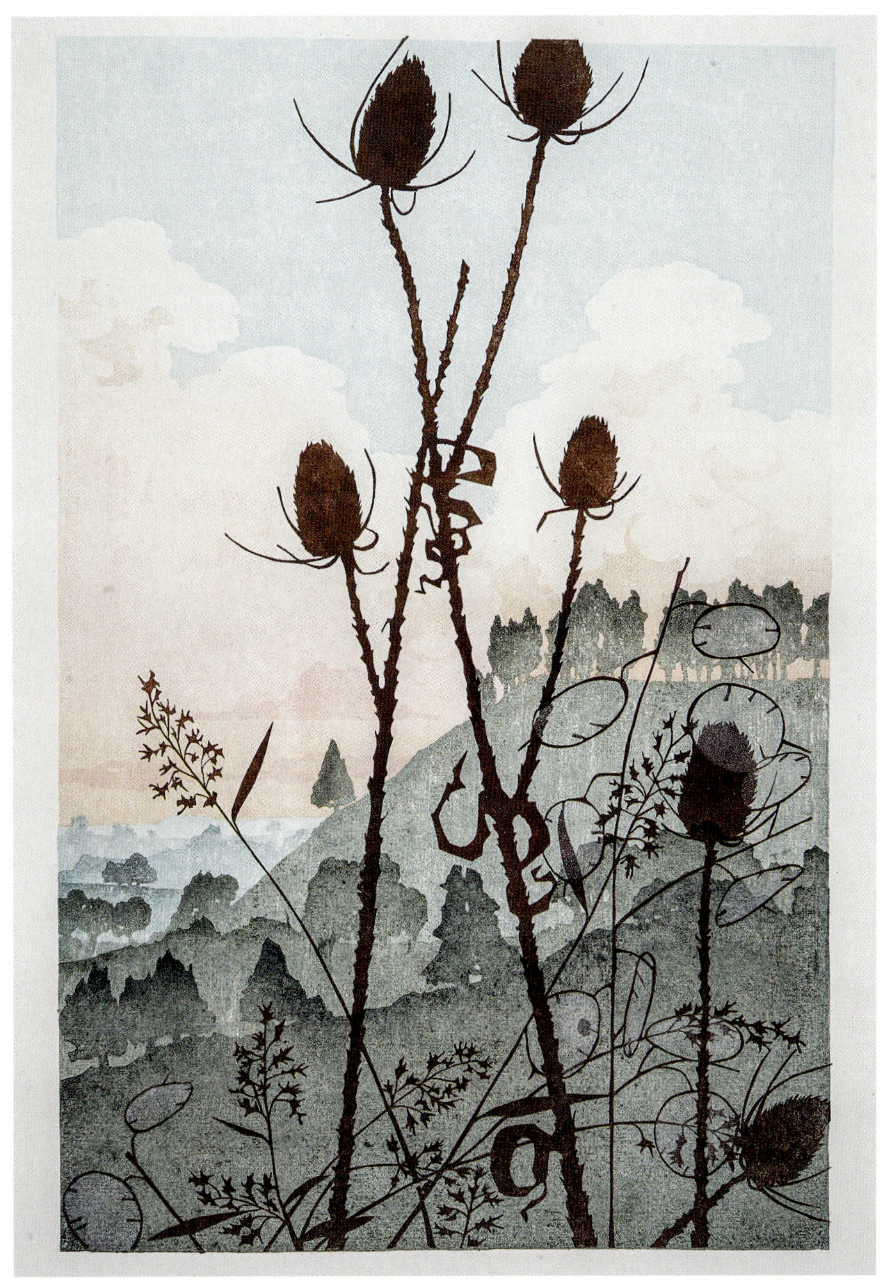

Laura Boswell, *Vale Teasels* (29.5 × 44.5cm). Japanese woodcut and linocut. Bamboo *washi*.

KEVIN FRANCES

New York, USA

Objects are spread across a table: books, bills, an almost empty cup of coffee, a note to self – 'the sun moves across the sky'.

My work is about the made-world, the world of objects, their cultural significance, what they can tell us about a person, that transformational moment when they transcend bland reality and become new and strange, and that shimmering edge in between those two states of mind.

These prints are all woodcuts made in the Japanese technique, with water-based inks and printed by hand. They are made with about 10 or 12 blocks usually. I am drawn to this technique because it offers an unusual degree of subtlety; the blocks are inked with stiff bristle brushes, allowing precise gradations of colour and transparent overlays.

Equally importantly, I value its stubbornness. Unlike say, screen printing, it resists perfect reproducibility, I'm always confounded and surprised.

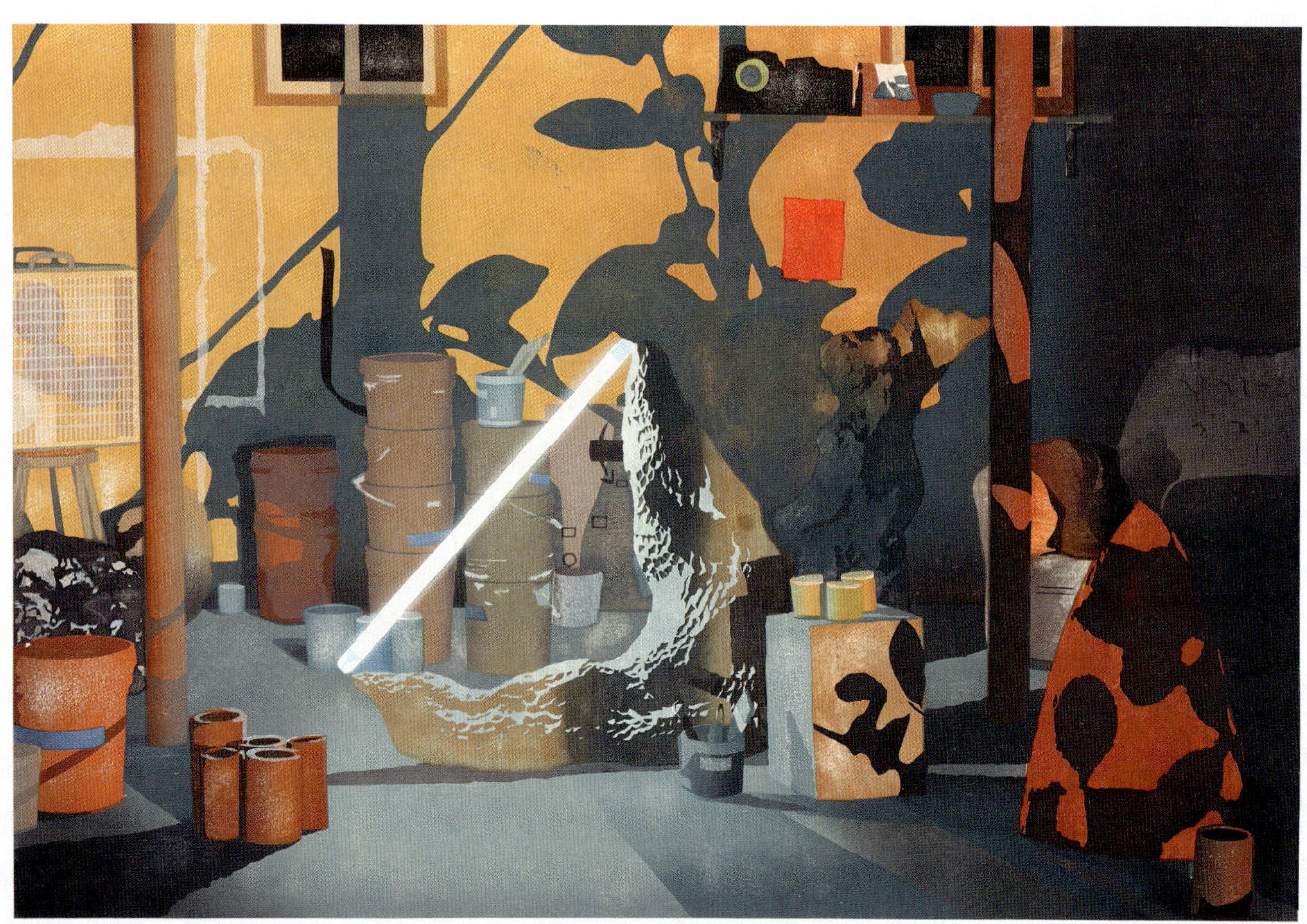

Kevin Frances, *In the Clearing* (20 × 30cm). Printed on *kōzo-shi*.

CAMERON BAILEY

New York, USA

Cameron Bailey is an artist and printmaker specialising in water-based woodblock printmaking. He studied painting at the Maryland Institute College of Art and began print-making in 2016. Primarily working in a multi-layer reduction technique, Cameron uses traditional Japanese printmaking tools and materials to create evocative landscapes and portraits.

'Much like a reduction print, memories are built with bits and pieces of moments, small seemingly unimportant details coalesce to form an image, an event, a snapshot of a place or feeling. When starting an image, I begin with a field of colour, a mood, atmosphere, time in space that affects everything coming after it. Out of this construction a memory emerges, imprinted.'

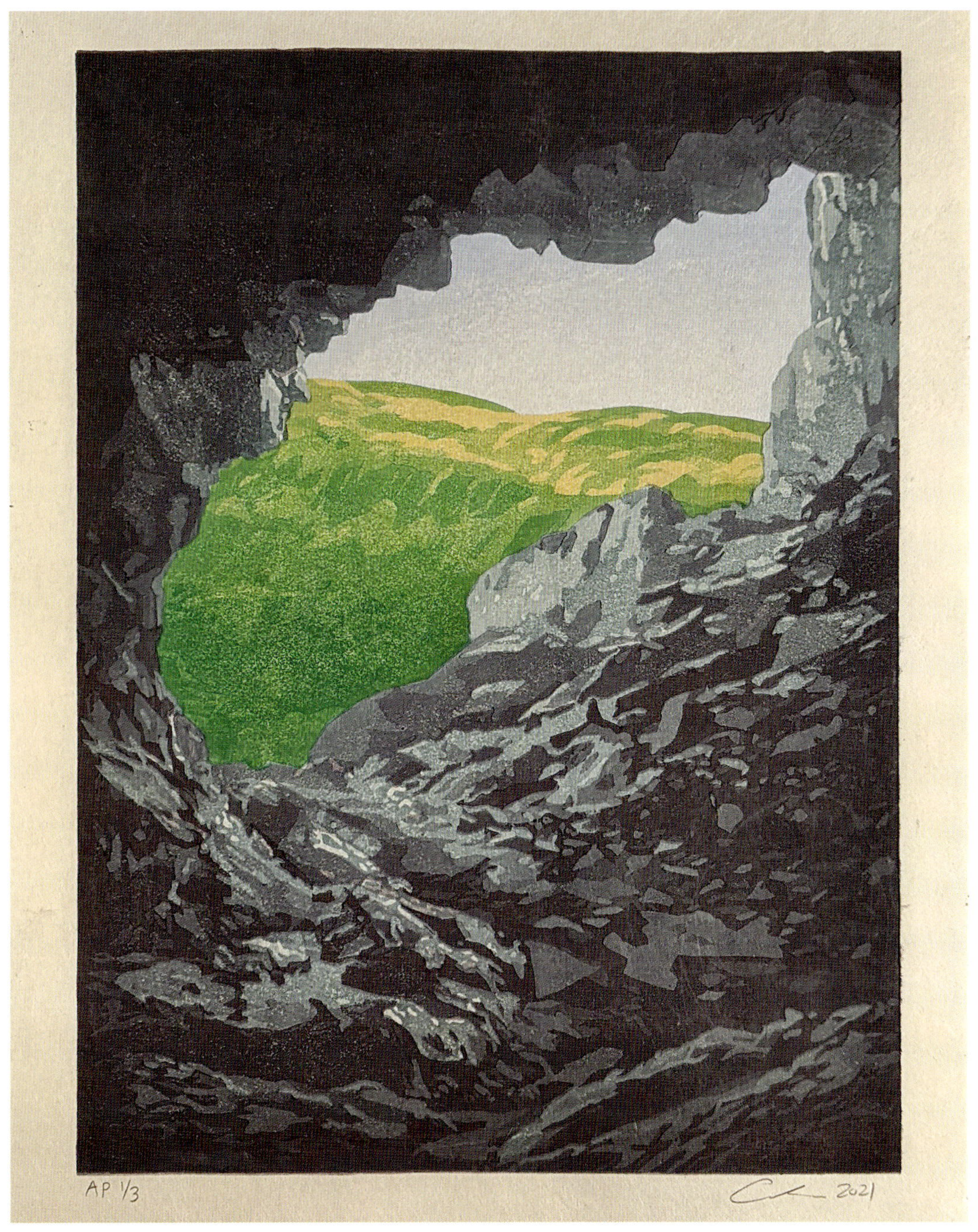

Cameron Bailey, *The Cave* (32 × 41cm). Reduction Japanese woodcut printed on *kōzoshi washi*.

ELISABET STRAND

Trondheim, Norway

Seas refers to the possibility of finding safe passages for the boat you are travelling in. Creating the series Seas, I wanted to explore the relation between the empty paper and the printed fields of the print, based on forms and atmosphere in nature. The archipelago off the coast of Nordland with its islands and skerries randomly scattered on the sea suggested the space and contained the sense I was looking for. The horizon out of reach makes you turn into a state of longing and belonging at the same time. I tried to catch the essence of the seascape, the elements of rock and water, sky and sea. My landscapes are also mirroring the Japanese stone gardens, but instead of stones resting on raked waves of sand, my islands are floating on paper.

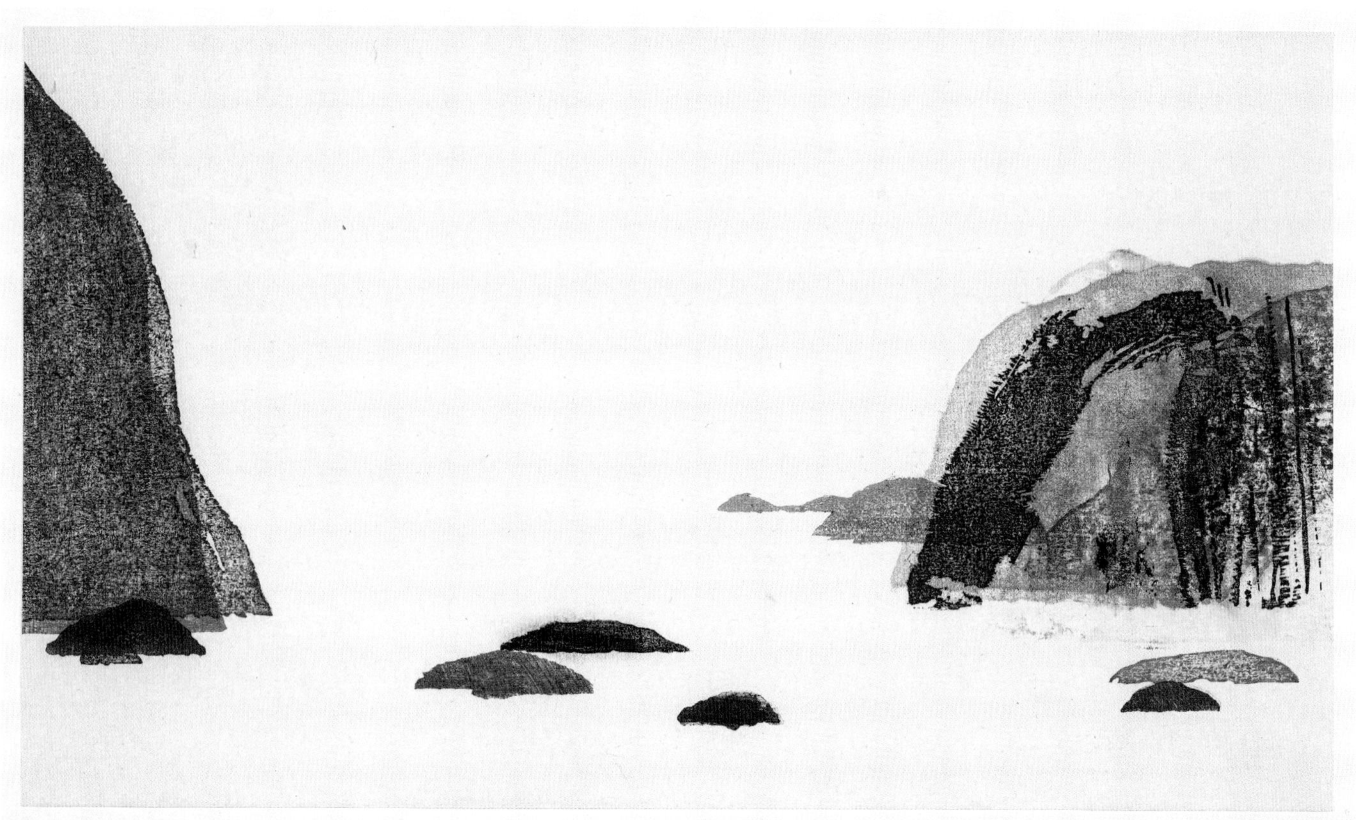

Elisabet Alsos Strand, *Seas II* (27 × 47 cm). Printed on 30 gsm Korean paper.

SYBILLE SCHLUMBOM

Aotearoa, New Zealand

My art explores belonging and dislocation. The process can result in a very narrative print or follow certain materials that spark an association leading to evocative, abstract pieces.

Currently I am exploring 'light' as the subject in my prints, playing with white ink, white paper, hints of colour and mica.

This means that any reproduction is unsatisfactory; it can only show a flat view on one aspect of the work. This makes it a very corporeal work, alive in paper, hibernating only in a digital representation.

This work was commissioned by the Print Council of Australia for the Print Commission 2022.

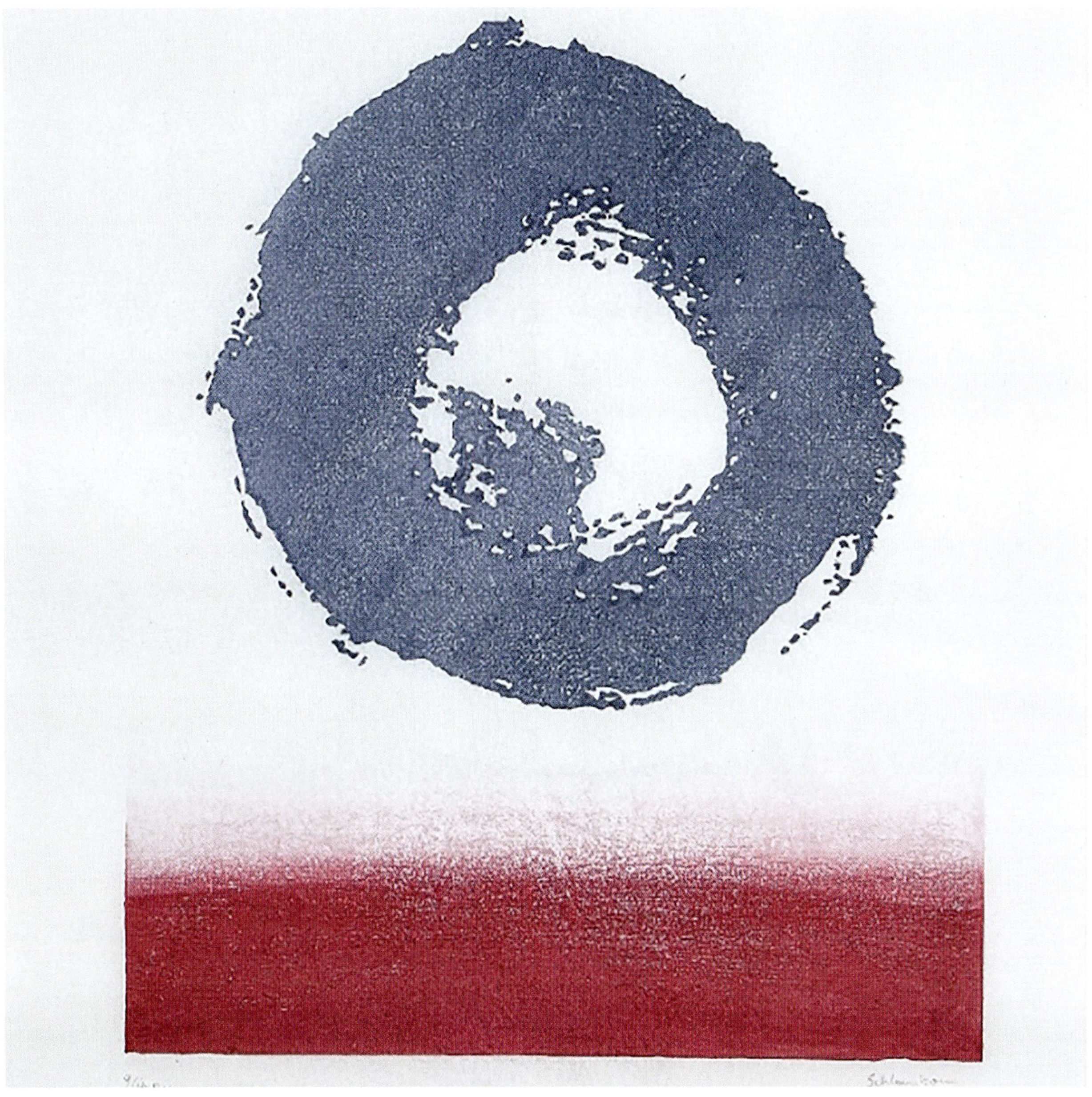

Sybille Schlumbom, *Circle of Kotahiyanga* (55 × 55cm). Printed on Thai *kōzo* paper. Commissioned by Creative Waikato, Unity through Creativity Project, University of Waikato Art Collection.

NATASHA NORMAN

Cape Town, South Africa

Woven Water is a work particular to my experience of learning to make Mokuhanga prints. At the time that I made this work, Mokuhanga materials were difficult to procure in South Africa. From the imported shina plywood I had saved I made two simple blocks that when overlaid with opposite bokashi gradients provided a complexity of shimmering colour in the most economical way. I wanted to make a work that spoke to the multiple nature of the medium as well as the shifting way that each hand-made print responds to pigment density, water and pressure. By weaving the prints together, I was able to create a work that speaks to all these ideas: interference patterns, multiplicity and repetition.

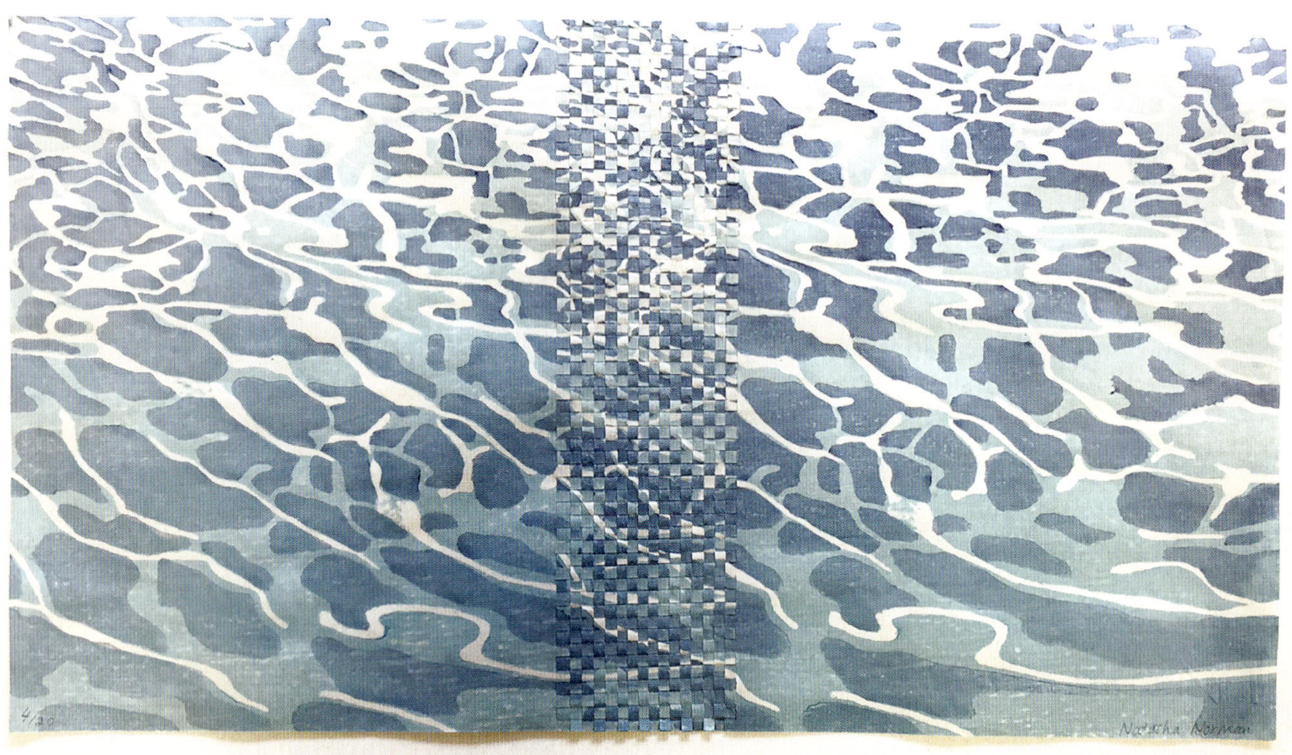

Natasha Norman, *Woven Water* (28 × 51cm). Japanese woodcut prints woven together.

SUSAN RUSHFORTH

Pittwater, Sydney, Australia

The woodblock print, Fireworks Over Ryogoku Bridge, 1856–8 by Utagawa Hiroshige hung in a house which I was living in back in the late 1980s. This print inspired me to research other traditional woodblock prints as well as Shiko Munakata and Akira Kurosaki's work. I decided to leave Australia and live in Japan to study the techniques of Mokuhanga.

I lived in Kyoto, Japan from 1990 to 1994 and studied under Tokuriki-San and then with Professor Akira Kurosaki as a Research Student at Seika University in Kyoto. I also studied sumi brushwork under Shotei Ibata-San.

It was at Seika University that I became interested in making paper using kōzo fibre and this followed with being awarded with a Faculty Research Grant from the University of NSW, Sydney to do research at the Hall of Awa Japanese Handmade Paper at Tokushima, Japan. Since returning to Australia I have continued to apply and extend the Mokuhanga.

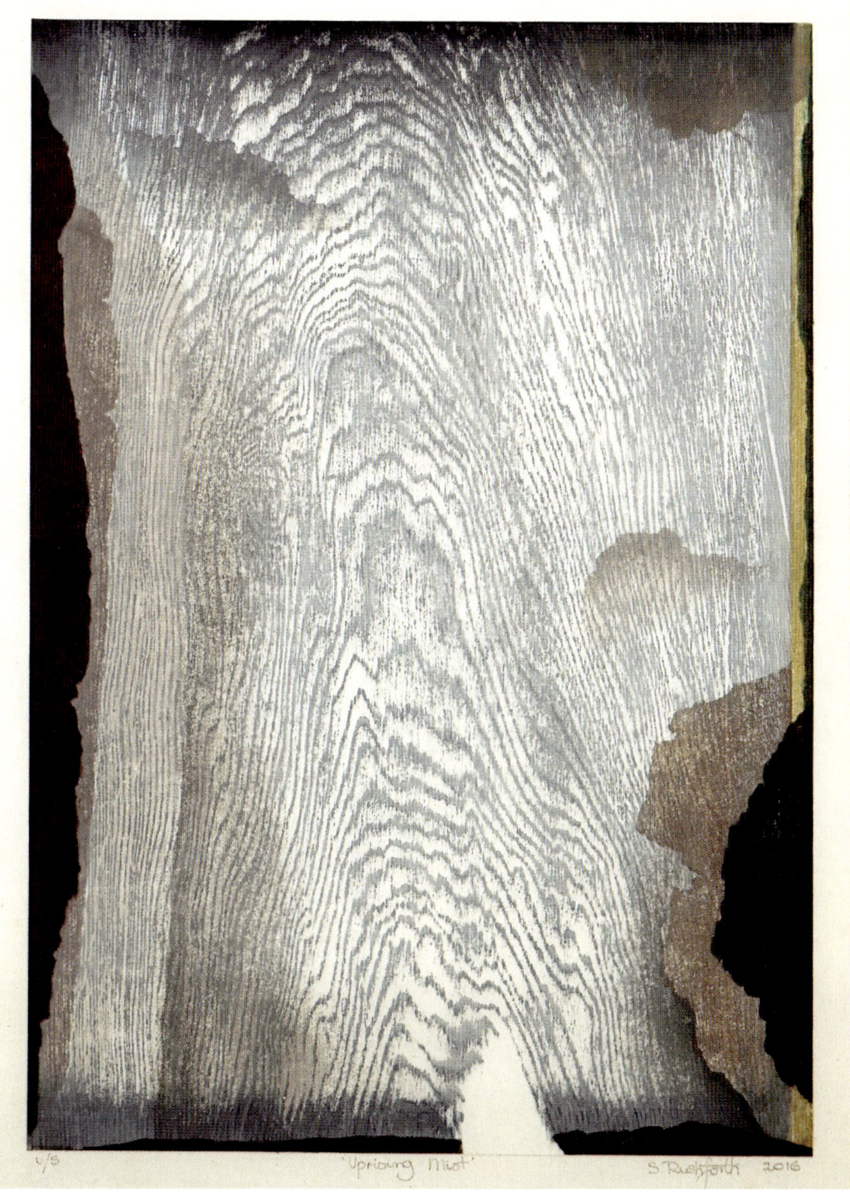

Susan Rushforth, *Uprising Mist* (28 × 37.5cm). Printed on *kōzo* paper.

ANNIE BISSETT

Providence, Rhode Island, USA

Over the nearly two decades that I've been working with Mokuhanga I've come to the conclusion that this ancient method is so versatile and flexible that any image can be made using it – it's simply a matter of figuring out how. I am an artist who is more topic-oriented than process-oriented, so I tend to shape my ways of working in service to the idea behind the print. Because of its versatility, Mokuhanga has so far never failed to allow me to create the images I'm after. Mokuhanga is difficult to master, requiring a lot of practice before one can control the outcomes, but it's fairly easy to begin experimenting with it. All one needs is wood, a cutting tool, watercolours, a brush or two, paper, and something with which to rub the paper against the inked block. I highly recommend giving it a try.

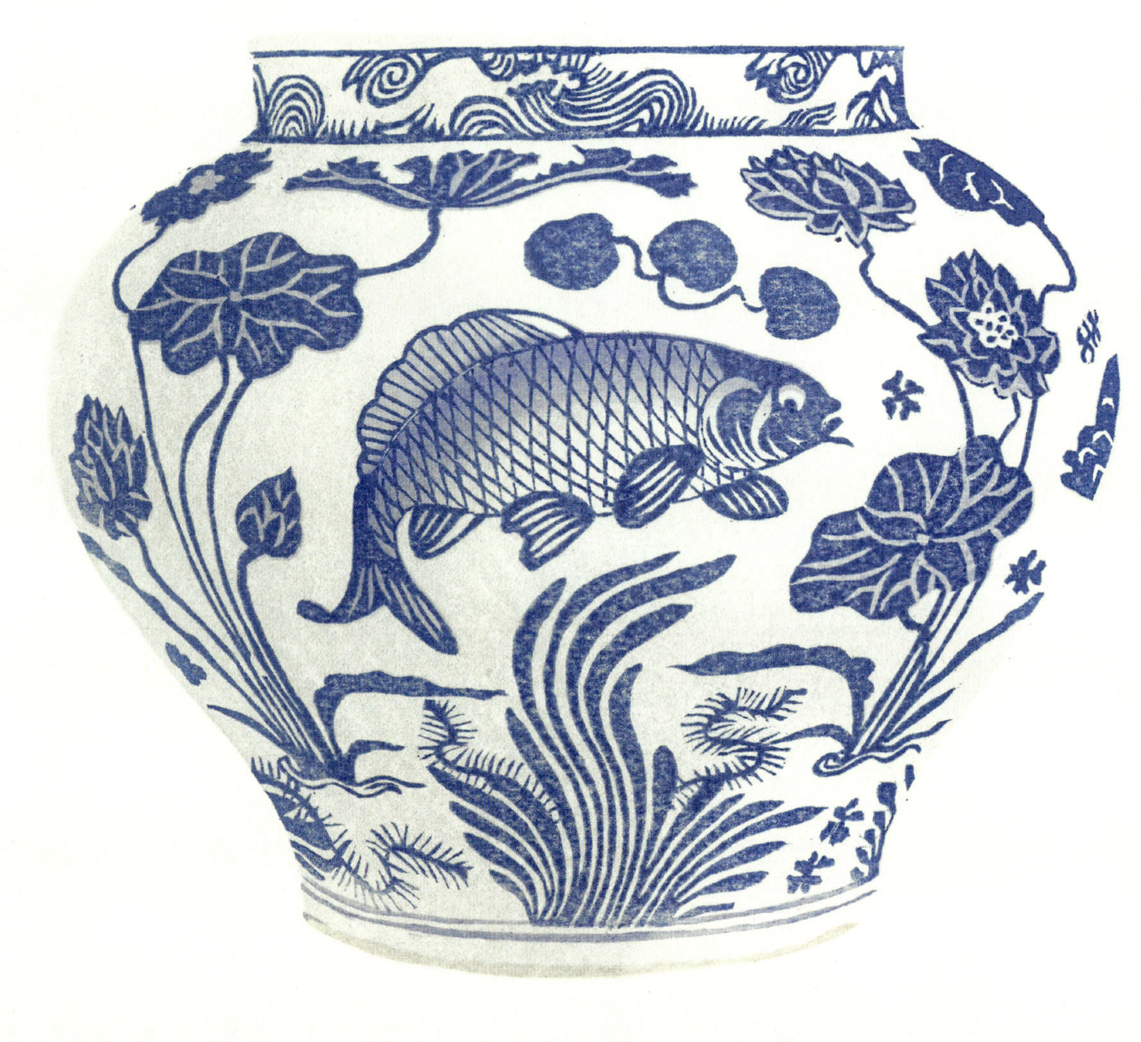

Annie Bissett, *Fish Pot* (33 × 33cm). Printed on Echizen *kōzo* paper. Photographed by Stephen Petegorsky.

NANA SHIOMI

London, UK

'Her Own Interpretation'

Take Classic Music, for example. The musicians have been using the same musical score for hundreds of years. The score is the same, but every musician presents us with a slightly different musical result. Take Four Tragedies of Shakespeare for another example. Every theatrical company shows us these plays with totally different impressions and atmospheres. In this way, a person has their interpretation, and through one's interpretation, the result of one's creation has been dramatically changed. Every time I make a piece of work, I am thrilled to see the audience's reaction and hear their interpretation of my work.

Hand-printed woodblock prints are delicate prints that are affected by the temperature and humidity of the day. The physical habits of the printer and the way they breathe can also change the result. It is important to hold the baren with the message I want to convey in work in mind.

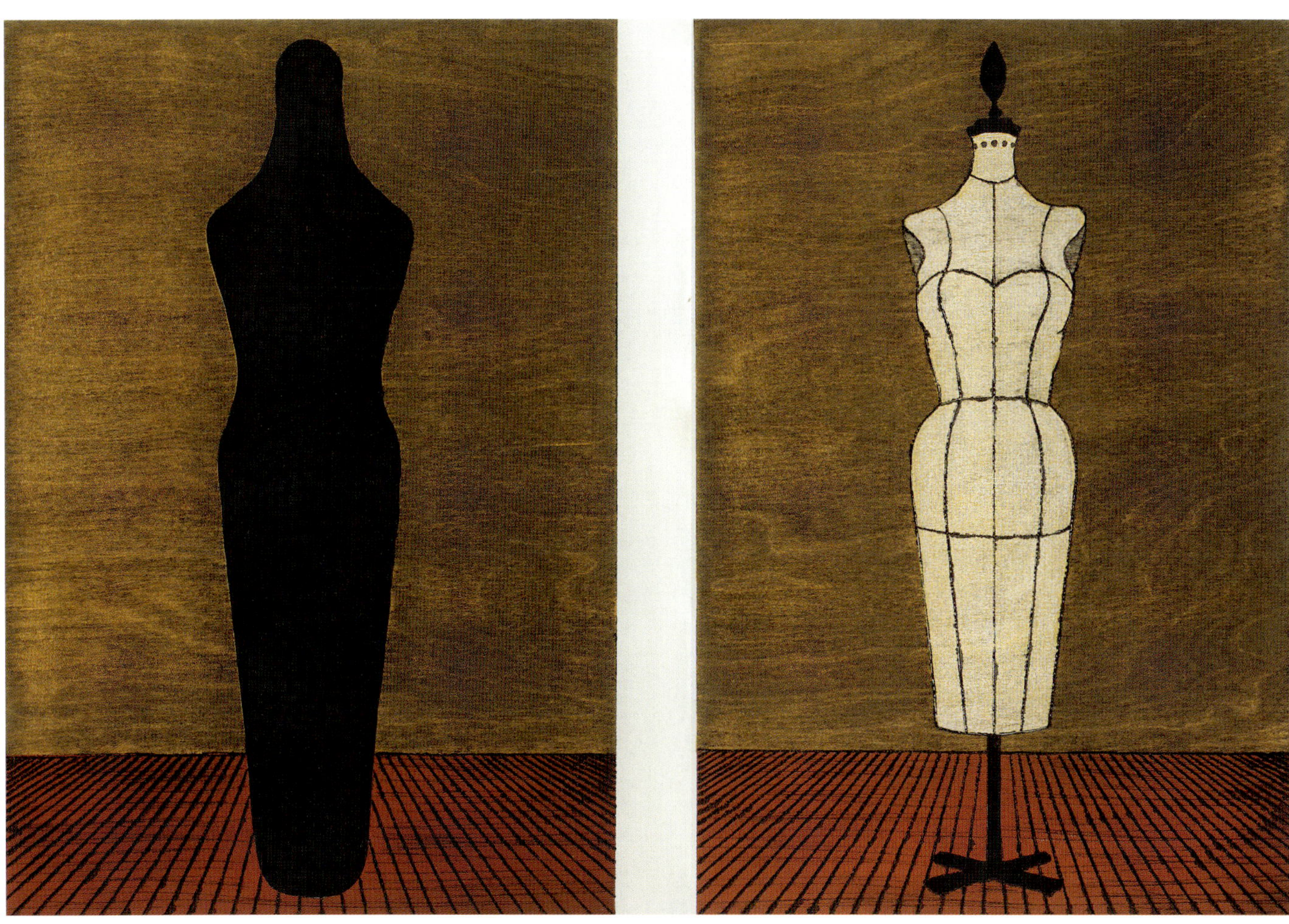

Nana Shiomi, *Her Own Interpretation* (60 × 89cm). Japanese woodcut with oil and water-based inks. Printed on *Han-kusa* paper.

WUON-GEAN HO

London, UK

I've been interested in adapting traditional Mokuhanga with local materials. The image was initially carved on a small block of vinyl, printed, then scanned to capture elements on the print where the ink was applied more lightly. Subsequently one block was laser-engraved with an enlarged version of the image, and the second hand-carved. The colour was printed on Somerset paper, which is a thick printing paper traditionally used for etching, chosen for its receptiveness to ink and ability to withstand being dampened in a wet paper pack. Printing such a large image took three hours and the paper had to be kept damp with regular misting and a plastic sheet on the back. I used traditional Mokuhanga technique with Holbein watercolours but substituted hydropropycellulose for the glue. I think the Mokuhanga technique helps convey the atmosphere of the early days of Covid lockdown.

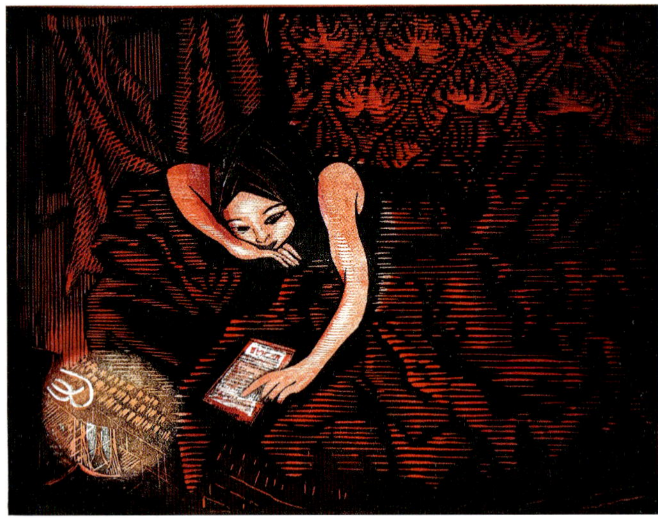

Wuon Geon Ho, *Horror Scroll 22* (40 × 60cm). Hybrid cutting first block on vinyl with laser technology and hand cutting second block. Printed on Somerset Satin paper.

FAITH STONE

Holualoa, Hawaii

My background is the study of traditional Tibetan Buddhist scroll 'Thangka' painting. I became interested in the form of Buddhist art that includes thangka woodblocks. I had the great fortune to begin studying Mokuhanga with Hiroki Morinoue in 2014. I had observed that the thangka woodblocks were becoming more and more rare. It was a dying artform. I thought to combine my Buddhist painting background with Mokuhanga woodblocks. I discovered that carving is probably my favourite part of the process. I felt this was an area where I could be of service, I could preserve the artform and I love carving them.

I attended the advanced Mokuhanga residency at MI-Lab in Kawaguchiko, Japan in 2018 and also learned so much from master carver Shoichi Kitamura in Kyoto.

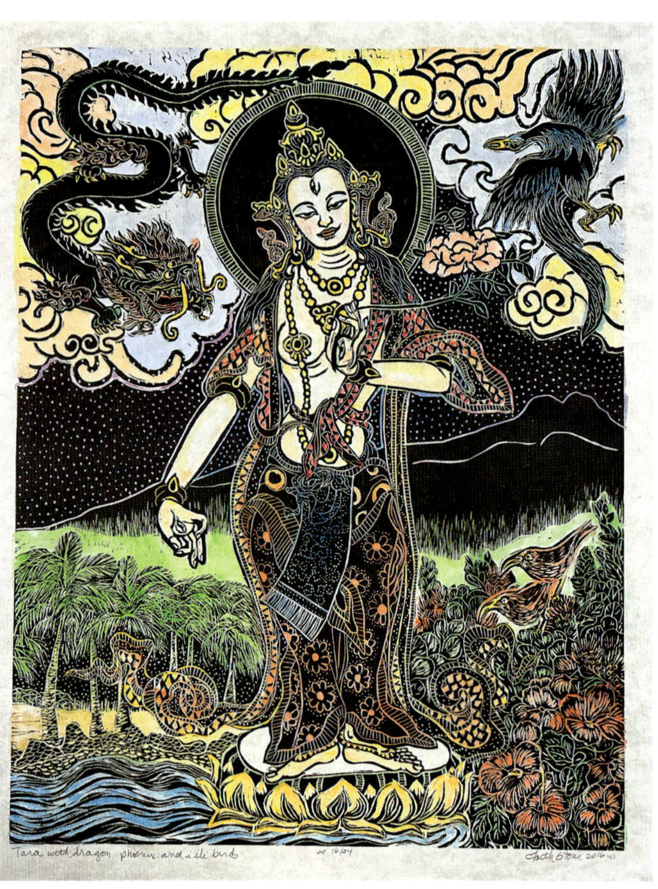

Faith Stone, *Tara with Dragon, Phoenix and I'ili birds* (81 × 66cm). Printed on *kōzo* paper.

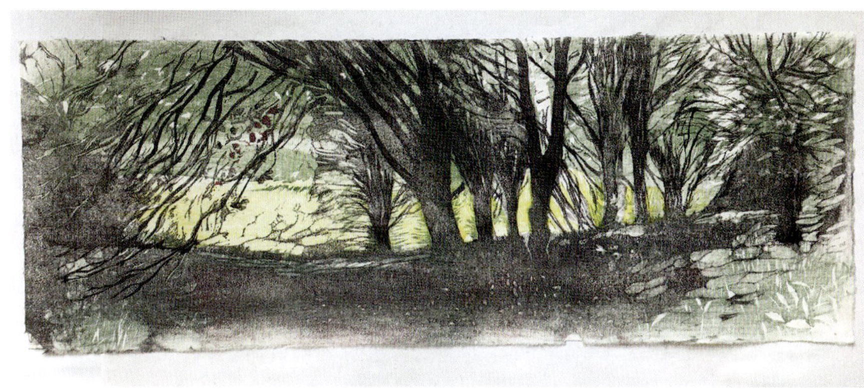

Rowan McOnegal, *Coppice Field* (75 × 27cm). Printed on *Hosokawa* paper.

ROWAN MCONEGAL

Herefordshire, UK

For many years I worked with photography and stained glass, loving working with light and the layering of colours. I felt drawn to work with more natural and environmentally safe materials. In 2016 I went to Japan for the MI- Lab residency. I enjoyed the physical process of woodblock printmaking – the indirectness that gives the print 'a secret and unintended beauty… (which) is why prints are mystifying'. There is a tension between the spontaneity and the elaborate processes involved. I relished the engagement with natural materials, the elemental qualities of wood, pigments, the beautiful handmade paper and hand printing with the bamboo baren, all contributing to the sensual and meditative experience of Mokuhanga.

I like to immerse myself in the landscape, to be contemplative, to surrender to the creative process, and to embody and not just document my experience.

LINDA J. BEEMAN

Owosso, Michigan, USA

I was Artist in Residence at Petrified Forest National Park in Holbrook, Arizona in 2019 and created the Erosion series. Erosion: Hoodoo shows desert formations caused by thousands of years of wind and water.

My work has long reflected the landscape I was born to in Michigan, its lakes and its wetlands. This was the first time I had been in a desert.

As an environmental artist I have tried to create a body of work that reveals the needs of conservation, protection and appreciation of our natural spaces. It is a joy to showcase the beauty, diverse ecology, geography and healing value of our world through my art.

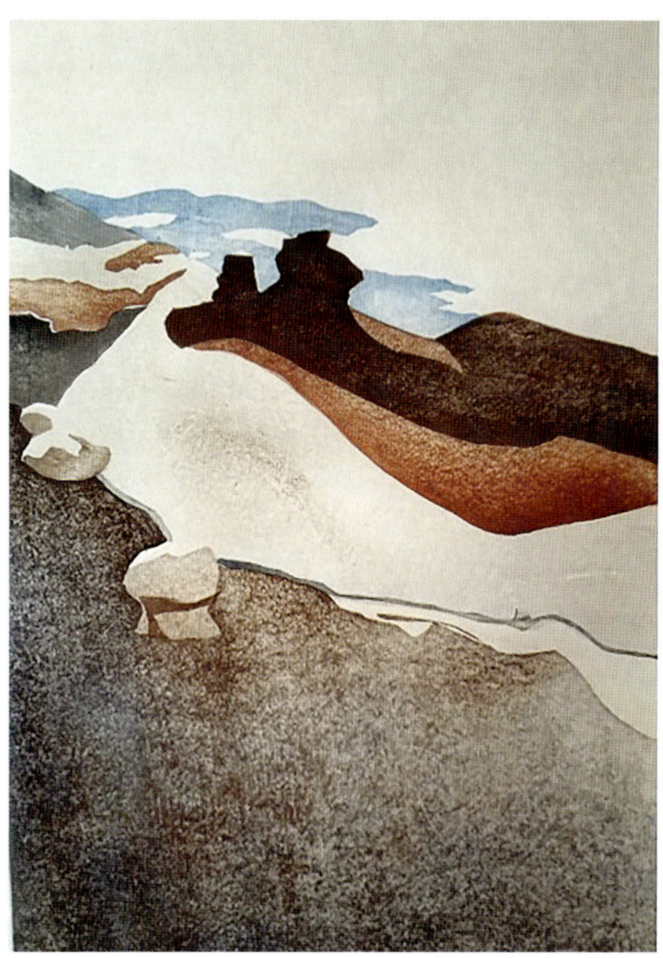

Linda Beeman, *Erosion: Hoodoo* (30 × 43cm). Printed on Japanese *washi* paper.

YOONMI NAM

Lawrence, Kansas, USA

In my work, I am interested in beauty, irony, inevitability, and the common and extraordinary way we structure our everyday surroundings. I find beauty in the man-made spaces and objects, both handmade and commercially mass-produced, that we surround ourselves with. It is especially true when these spaces and objects subtly suggest a contradicting sense of time that seems both temporary and eternal. There is truth and honesty in time, as all of us share the fate of impermanence. But the way we surround ourselves with collections of things and shelter ourselves within the structures we build, it is as if we feel a sense of permanence through these comforts.

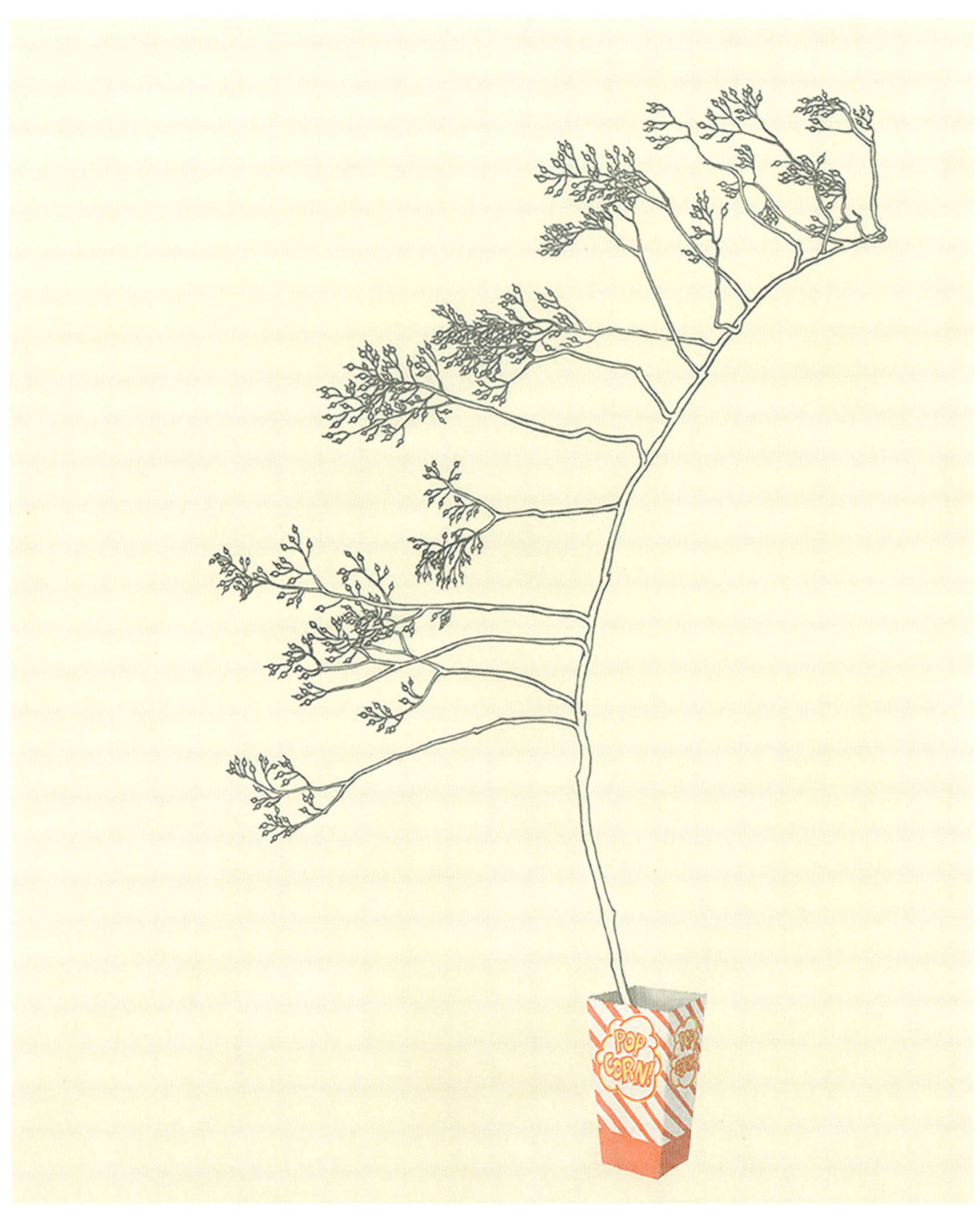

Yoonmi Nam, *Pop Corn!* (90 × 61cm). Printed on *Pansion* paper.

KAORU MORITA

Tokyo and Matsumoto, Japan

I love the warm feel and soft beauty that the wood has. In order to make the most of the beauty of wood, I would like to express a delicate expression using the entire woodblock.

A very shallow engraving will subtly affect the printing pressure and will be printed on paper. In addition, the strength and softness of the line changes depending on how the edges are carved, creating a relationship between the line and the surface.

If the woodblock is carved too much and it turns white, it will be difficult to correct it, so I make a woodblock while checking the feel of my hand and the printing.

I feel that spending time facing the woodblock in this way is necessary both for making the woodblock and for maturing the image of the work.

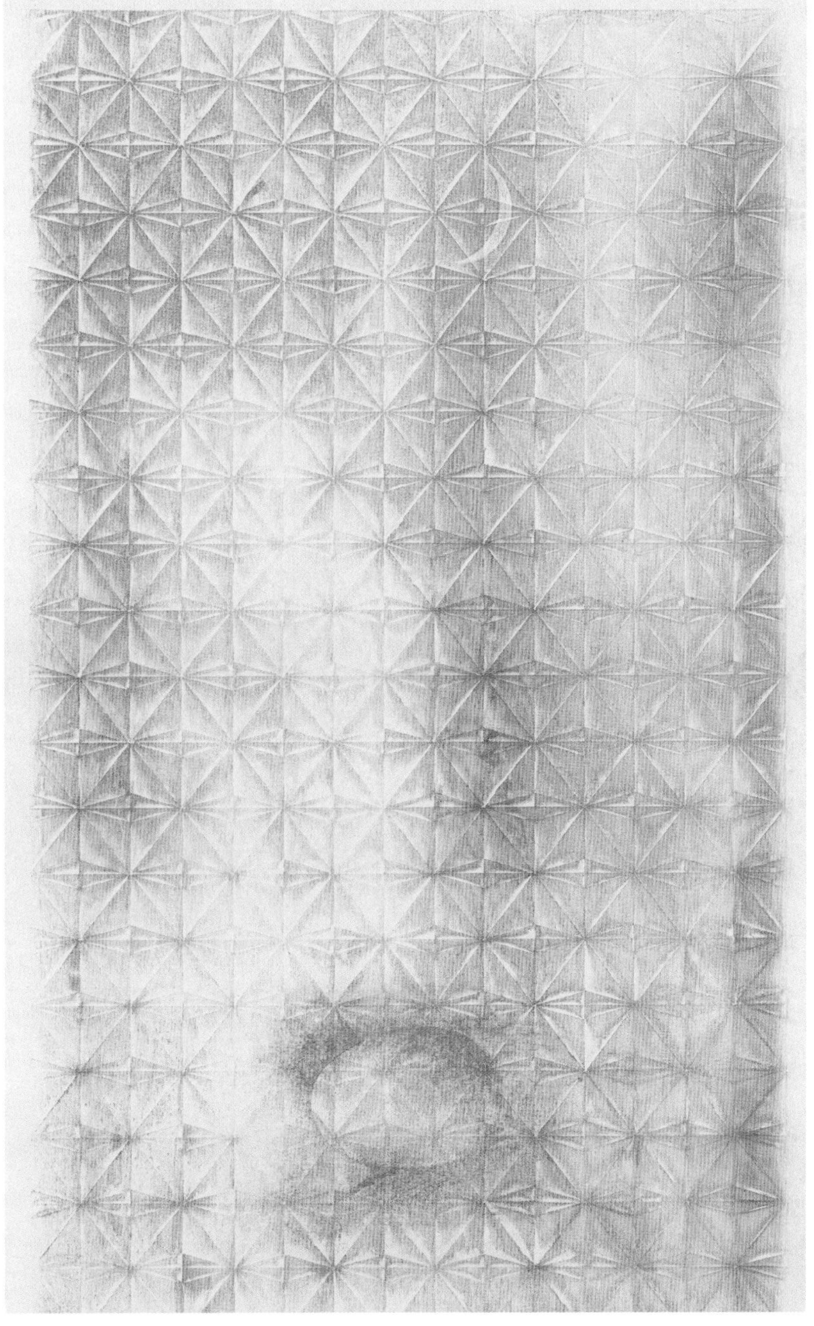

Kaoru Morita, *Light Through the Glass* (45 × 27cm). Printed on *Kihada washi*.

PAUL FURNEAUX

Edinburgh, Scotland, UK

The washi is very strong. I learned how to stretch dampened prints over panels. Taking this further I learned how to make byobu. It has been a difficult process but over time I have learned the techniques needed to move and handle washi in new ways.

The initial impulse to wrap a print around a form was born more out of frustration, a state of mind that paradoxically led to playfulness and experimentation. At first, I found or adapted objects that expressed their history or familiarity or simply occupied space in an interesting way. This developed further into making or enlarging forms which I felt could be clothed in Mokuhanga, not merely in a decorative way, but in a way that investigated the form itself, that enhanced it and the experience of that form. It was a conceptual shift, one that opened up areas both in the two-dimensional printed works and that fed into the three-dimensional ones.

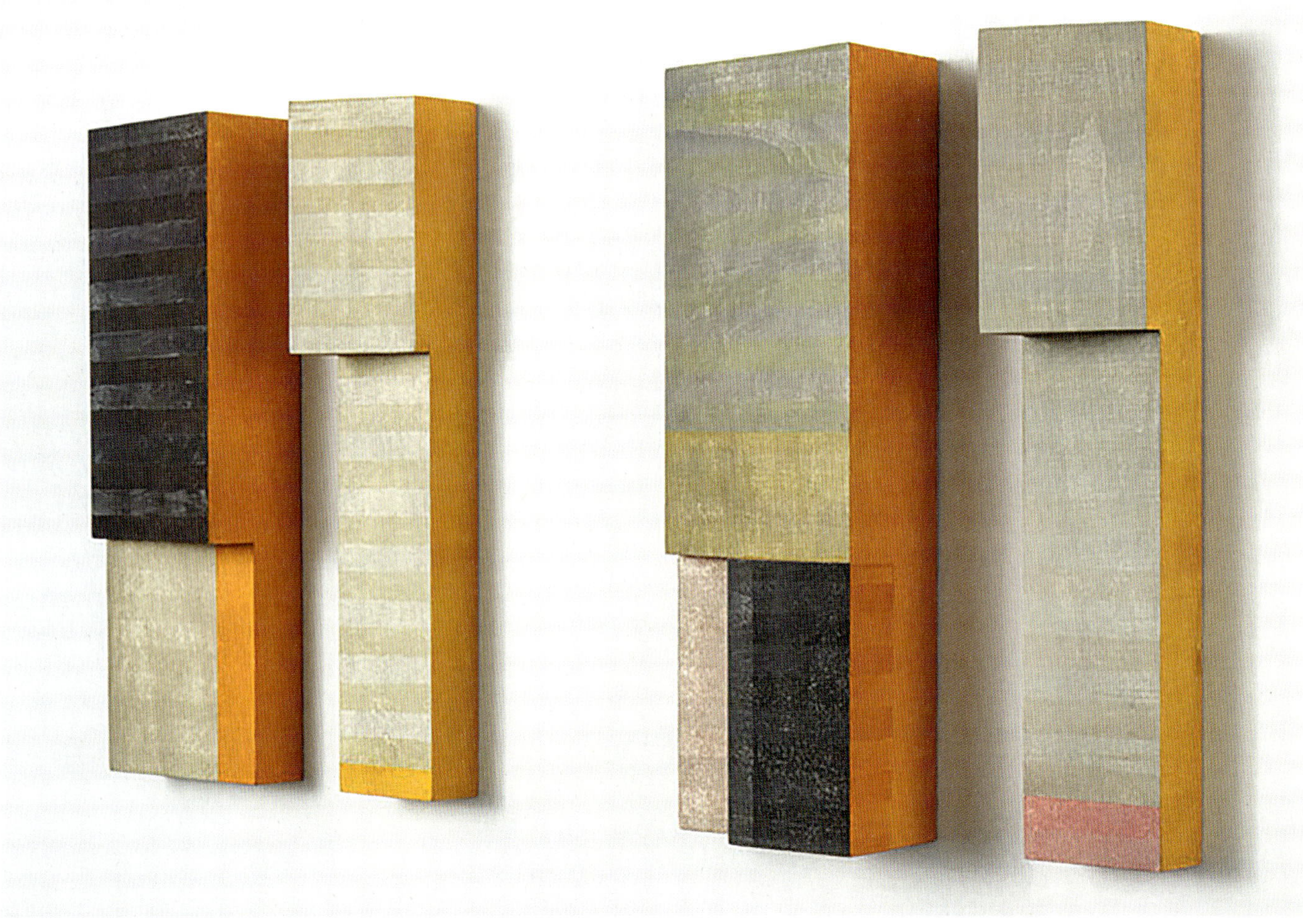

Paul Furneaux, *City Trees (View left)*. Japanese woodcut wrapped around 3D form.

TOMASZ KAWELCZYK

Poland

Bringing together contradictions definitely broadens the horizons of my creative explorations. In my artistic experiments, I make use of traditional aspects of printmaking techniques.

Rational 'Western' thinking meets 'Eastern' sensitivity and intuition. The spatial objects described herein contain both traditional elements of Japanese art, as well as my proprietary improvements of the woodcut printing technique, already functioning in the international contemporary printmaking community.

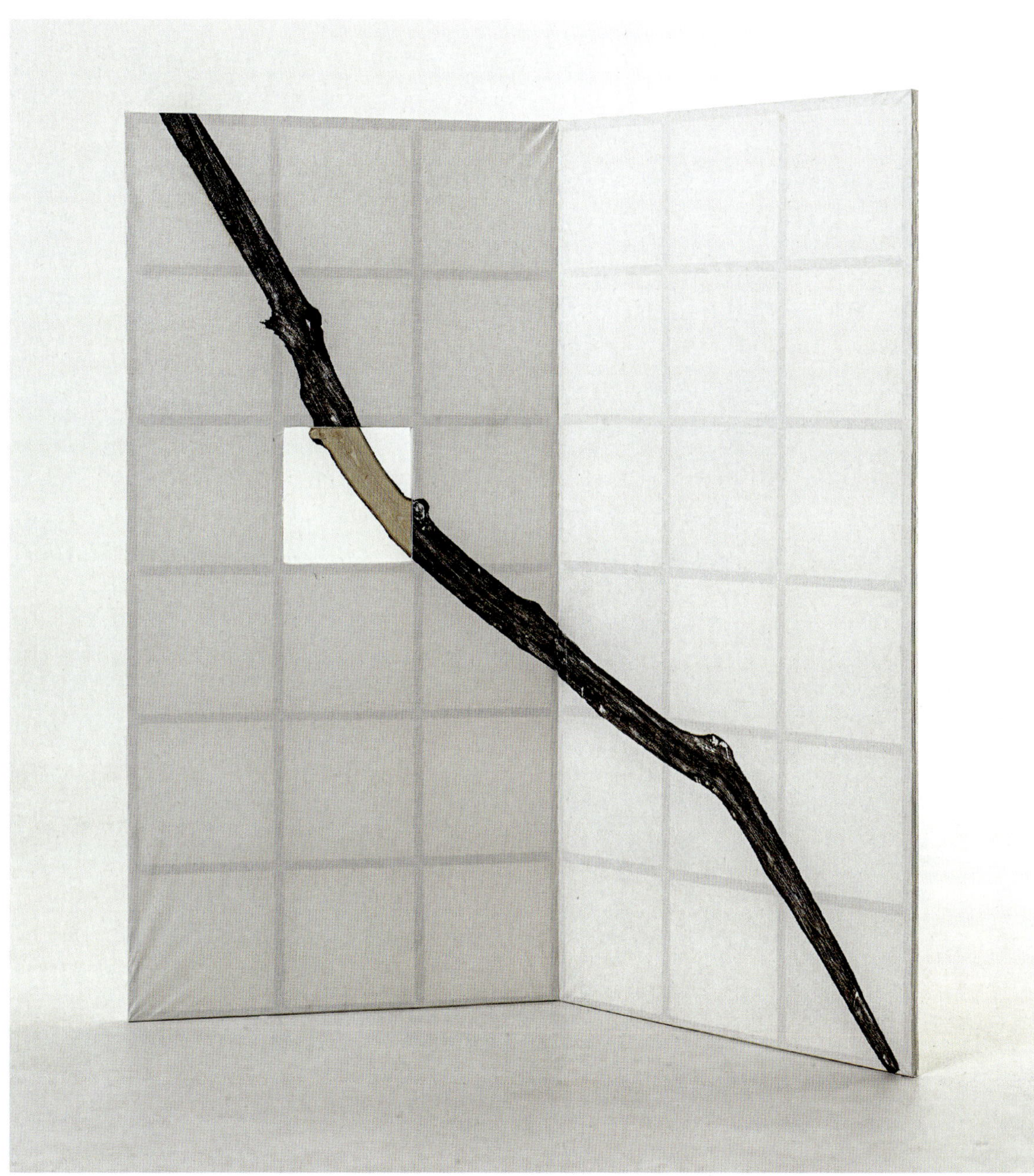

Tomasz Kawelczyk,
The Golden Bough
(front) (89 × 45cm).
Folded screen *hyōbu*,
Japanese woodcut
with wooden insert.
Photographed by
Michał Borowski.

JACQUELINE GRIBBIN

Australia

Shapes of the Rain is a response to monsoonal weather in the Northern Territory, Australia. The flooded land in the lower right-hand panel comes alive with deep colour after heavy rains. Superimposed on this image is the impact of droplets on water. The skies are full of voluminous clouds with squalls and impending storms hanging over the sea. Heavy, relentless rains and light, steady rains both form part of this season.

This subject aligns itself naturally with the adjustment, control and balance of water-based inks, water and glue on woodblocks in the technique of Mokuhanga, creating a natural symmetry.

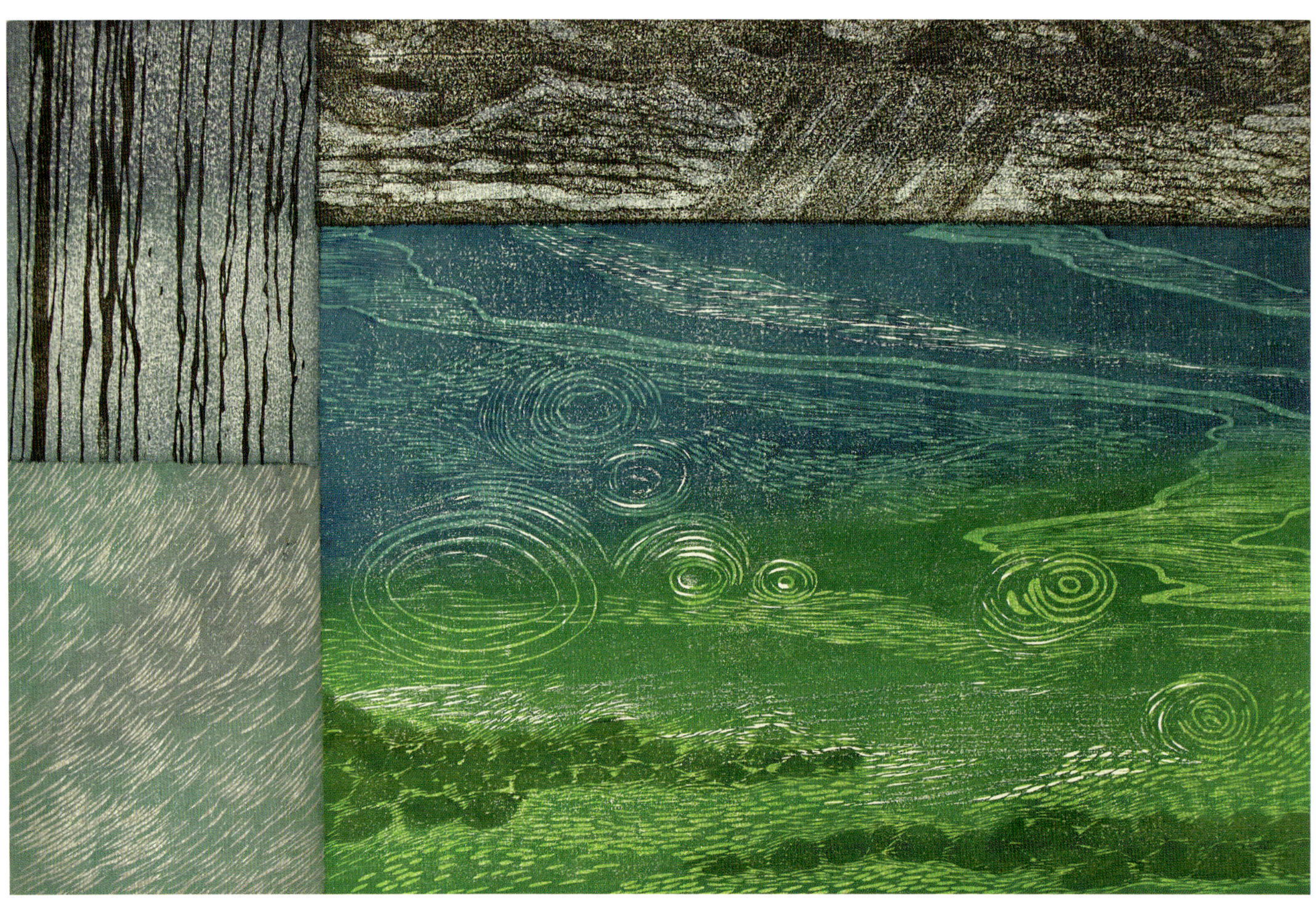

Jacquelin Gribbin, *Shapes of the Rain* (38 × 58 × 4.5cm). Printed on *Tosa washi*.

TERRY MCKENNA

Karuizawa, Japan

This print was created for the 2021 Summer Mokuhanga Fair Exhibition in Tokyo, and showcases both detailed carving and mokume (woodgrain), while using the Winter set of Holbein Irodori colours and specialty washi from Echizen provided for the project. The carving faithfully reproduces an original sumi ink brush drawing, copying the 'dry brush' and variations in thickness of the original brush marks. The mokume is brought out by two contrasting colours in the large background area and used a selected piece of shina plywood with suitable grain pattern. This is a different technique to brushing the wood with a wire brush, is much more demanding, but gives more beautiful, subtle results. I like to focus on both technically challenging carving and printing in a contemporary sosaku hanga technique, while producing my original imagery.

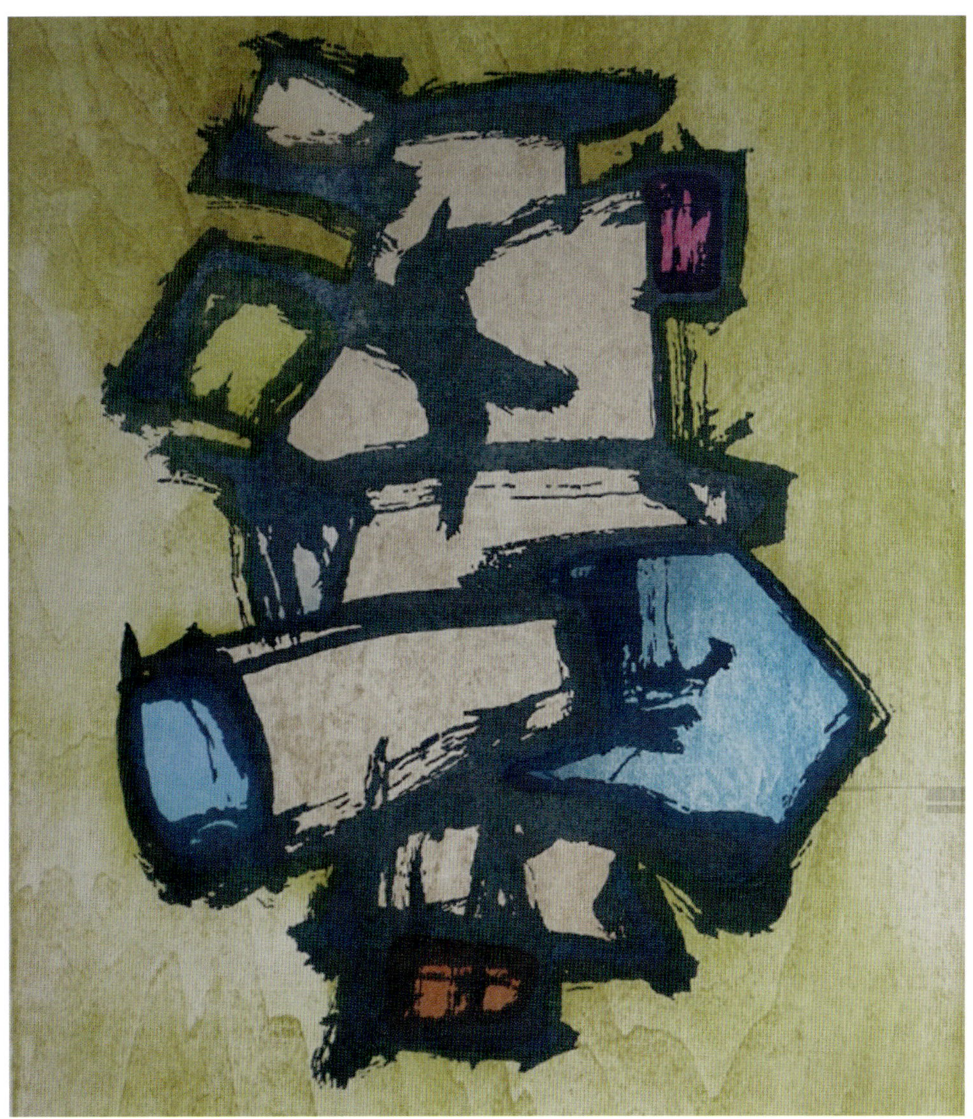

Terry McKenna, *Thought from Nowhere*
(43 × 60cm). Printed on *Udatsu kōzo* paper.

KAREN KUNC

Nebraska, USA

I draw from many sources: makeshift/manmade structures, patterns of decay and weathering, 'everyday science' images of graphs or maps from weather charts to DNA to galaxies. I see compelling images and design elements such as a sense of compression, and geometric versus organic that formally reflect such ideas as a rhythmic design.

My approach to making woodcut prints is an evolutionary process that mirrors such processes in nature and our own effects on the earth. I recognize human and natural destruction and benevolence as abstract symbols, especially in our time of climate change with unknown consequences. There is a poignancy to this landscape of newly vulnerable, or toxic, evolving worlds of microbes, gaseous pools, and clouds, distended yet elegant forms in an imaginary place, discovered in my studio investigations.

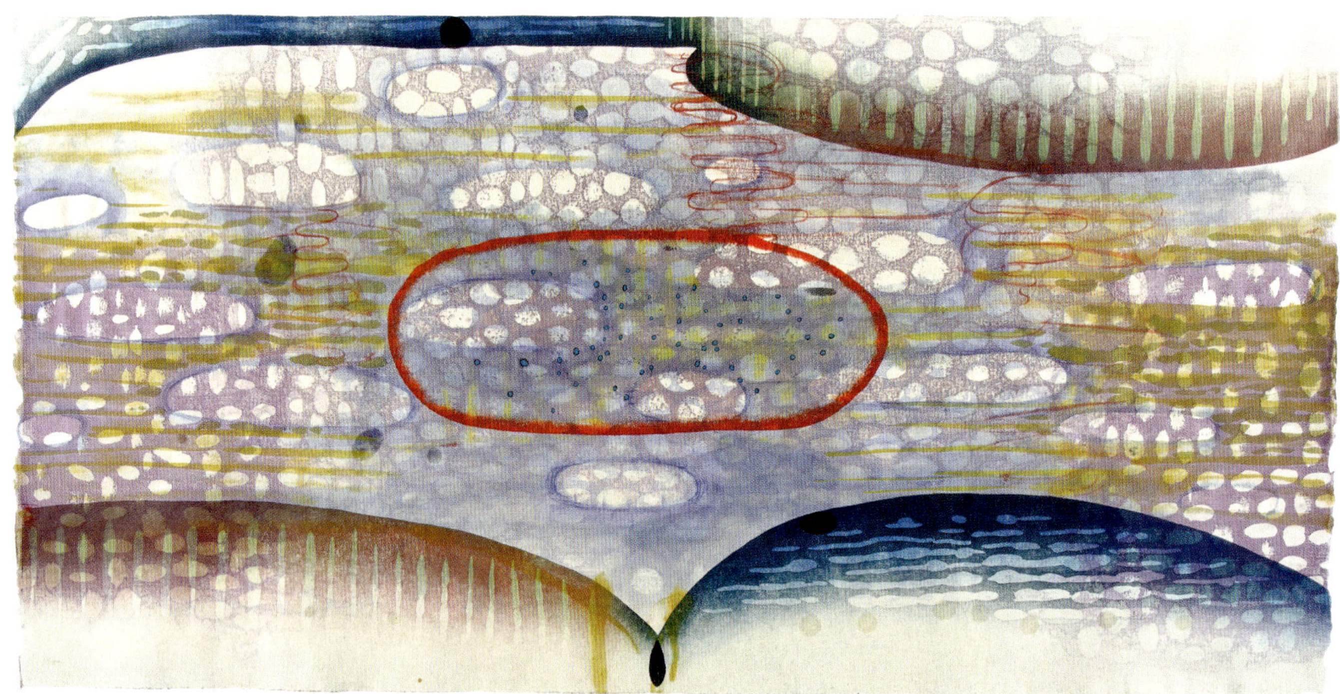

Karen Kunc, *Bay* (48 × 96.5cm). Japanese woodcut, wax printed on *Okawara* paper. Photographed by John Nollendorfs.

TAKUJI HAMANAKA

Brooklyn, New York USA

I have been investigating characteristic effects and materials found in printmaking and trans-place them in unfamiliar contexts or use them in an emphasized manner. One of the projects is to focus on typical printing application called 'Bokashi' that is a variation in lightness and darkness of single/multiple colours by hand applying a gradation of ink to moistened woodblock.

Using these prints in different colours as a starting point, I construct images by cutting them in various shapes and mount them on museum board to construct an image as one makes mosaic using sheets of stained glass.

I like to think that my work is a fusion of two ancient crafts and it is my hope that I contribute to expand the possibility of printmaking.

Takuji Hamanaka, *Sliced Stone* (81 × 63.5cm). Printed on *kōzo* paper, museum board.

MIA O

Tokyo, Japan

I used to observe landscape with a bird's eye view. However, I have changed my viewpoint so that I am now looking upwards towards the sun, which I believe has energised me to start producing circular prints.

I work within the mediums of painting and Mokuhanga printing quite freely, with no parameters. Personally, I feel challenged because the ways I approach both these mediums are in total opposition. However, I now realise that painting can influence Mokuhanga, and vice-versa. When I approach print-making, I don't want to simply replicate a drawing or painting. I want the print to be 'original' and to evolve naturally and organically. I enjoy the element of unpredictability within the print medium.

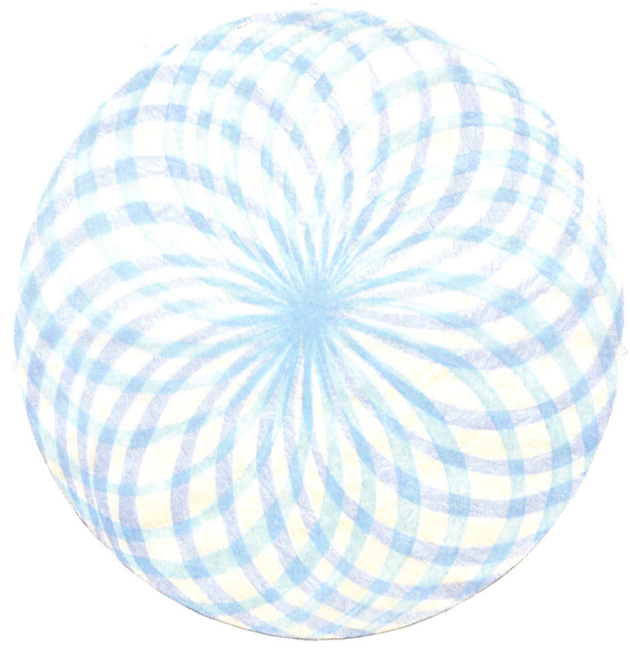

Mia O, *Untitled 2* (diameter 44cm). Layered Japanese woodcut with *Mino* and *Ogawa washi*.

TUULA MOILANEN

Helsinki, Finland

My works are based on old stories and mysteries of various origins. I also utilise travel adventures and other incidents in my life for sketching the images. Usually there is some humorous animal character in the picture. My alter ego at the moment is a female moose or a cat. I learned Japanese watercolour woodcut technique while living over 20 years in Kyoto. It is a printing method which offers a wide range of possibilities in expression. I enjoy the touch of wood and mixing bright and strong colours in the working process. Along with printmaking I also make artist books, using handmade Japanese papers and other natural materials in them. Binding my prints and paintings into books gives me a pleasurable sense of satisfaction. I hope to conceal many playful and positive feelings in my works for transferring them to people of all ages.

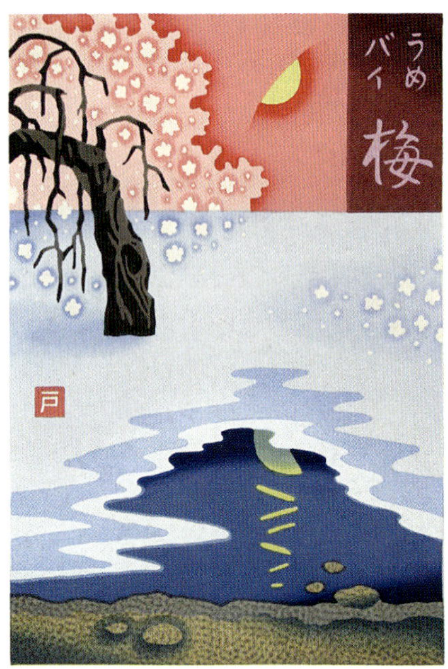
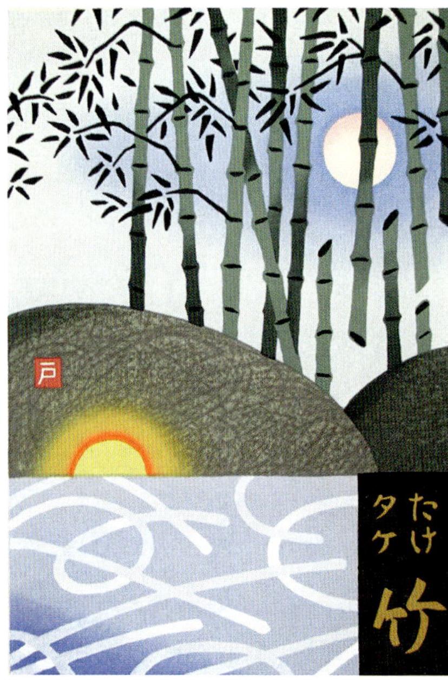
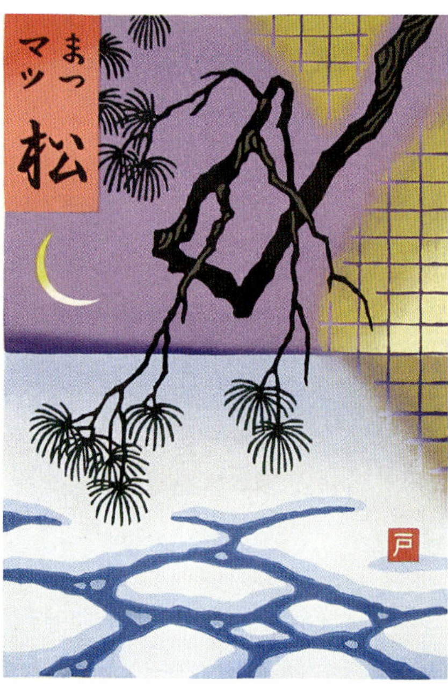

Tuula Moilanen, *Shochikubai Triptych* (each 36 × 25cm). Printed on *washi*.

LUCY MAY SCHOFIELD

Northumberland, UK

The Moon and the Sledgehammer is a collaborative print project between artists Guillaume Brisson-Darveau and Lucy May Schofield. The series is a visual and emotional correspondence between them as artists; a dialogue motivated by the desire to know more about one another and feeds from the experience of the present. From these playful exchanges a new vocabulary arises, specific to the meeting of two universes conversing to create one. This dialogue implies a particular attention to the others' sensibility whilst inviting them to redefine their own.

The 'phases' of prints explore the idea of what collaboration means to them as artists and how the two versatile print mediums of silkscreen and Mokuhanga form a bridge between their independent practices, as well as challenging perceptions of their limitations.

Fifteen collages combining silkscreen and Mokuhanga printing form the series. Japanese kōzo and gampi washi on Stonehenge paper, edition of six with two APs, 2016, printed at Kala Art Institute, California while artists in residence.

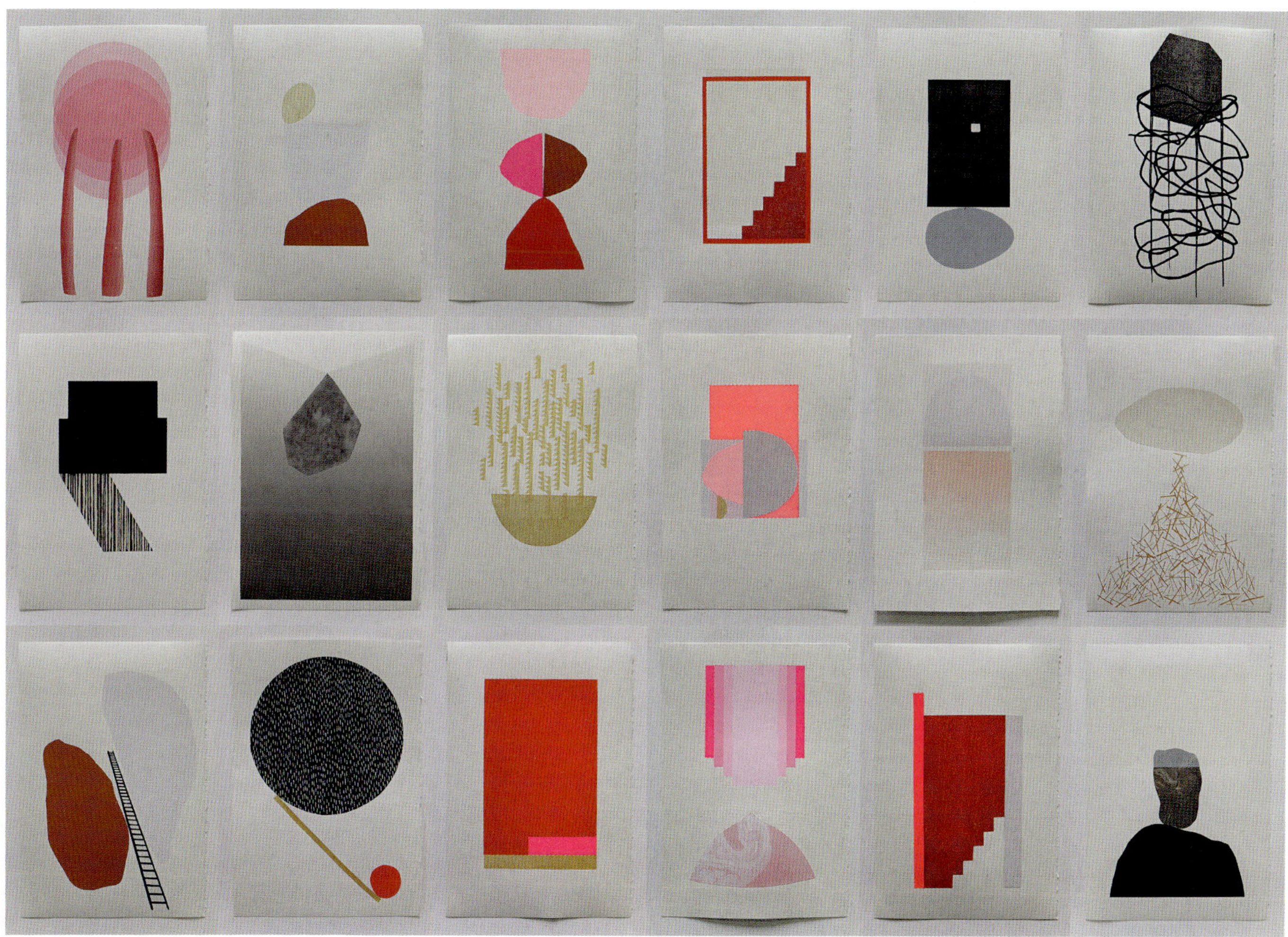

Lucy May Schofield, *The Moon and the Sledgehammer (phases 1–18)* (38 × 26.5cm). Collaborative print project with Guillaume Brisson-Darveau. Silkscreen and Japanese woodcut. *Kōzo* and *gampi washi* collaged on Stonehenge paper.

PATTY HUDAK

Vermont, USA

Relating print and natural matrices I explore cellular shapes that correspond to the energy permeating earthly systems. Using sumi ink, I print on both sides of the paper, adding aluminum pigment to the overlaying blocks.

The aluminum reflects light from the surface of the paper just as the dark sumi absorbs light. The duality of the surface represents the dualities of life and death, united by the porous medium of Mokuhanga.

The woodblock creates the mother form. I arrange the forms into a matrix of patterns, creating new hybrids. Repeating images discourage the sense of actual scale, and represent a feeling of expansion, such as when you are in a spectacle of nature or have the feeling of greatness extending beyond our known world. I consider the print as if it is a brushstroke, collaging pieces together to form an image.

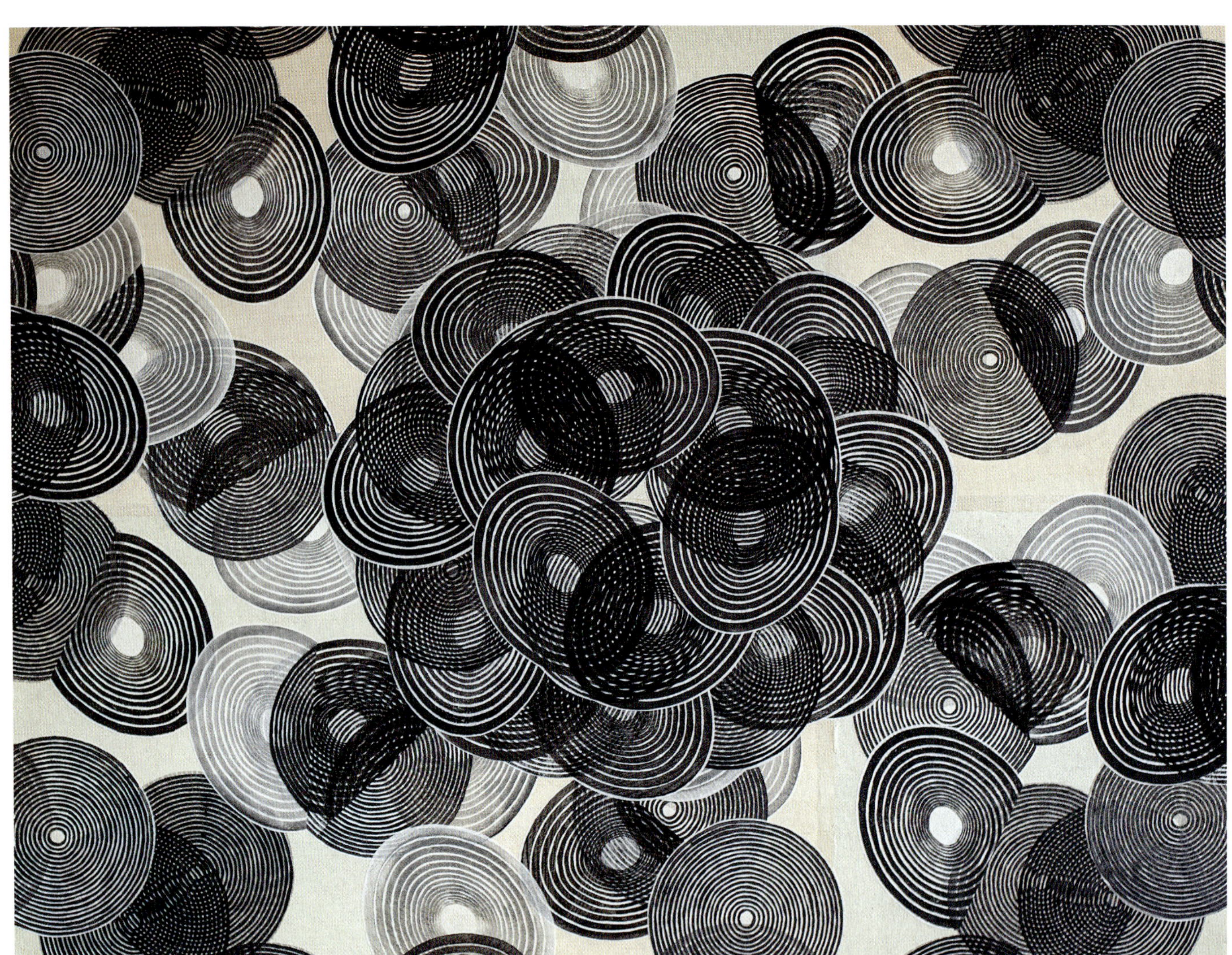

Patty Hudak, *Secret of the Flower* (91.5 × 122cm). Printed on *Kitakata* and handmade *kōzo,* mounted on wood.

ROSLYN KEAN

Sydney, Australia

When considering making a work for IMC Nara2021–Sumi Fusion I was immediately taken back in thought to my days living in Japan. The soft shadows of small lane ways and intimate courtyards with shoji screens filtering the light from within. The blend of aged timbers, concrete and new growth of bamboo shoots shimmering under streetlights.

The work reflects light and shade in nature and the experience of the silence of a space, with a minimalism and limited colour scheme to evoke a sereneness and contemplation within the landscape.

I enjoy the practice of very traditional seventeenth-century woodblock printing with numerous blocks to build a printed image and incorporate the decorative elements of gilding and mica powder which have been used for centuries.

My contemporary application of this ancient printing practice remains nontoxic and relies on all blocks to be hand printed with a selection of barens.

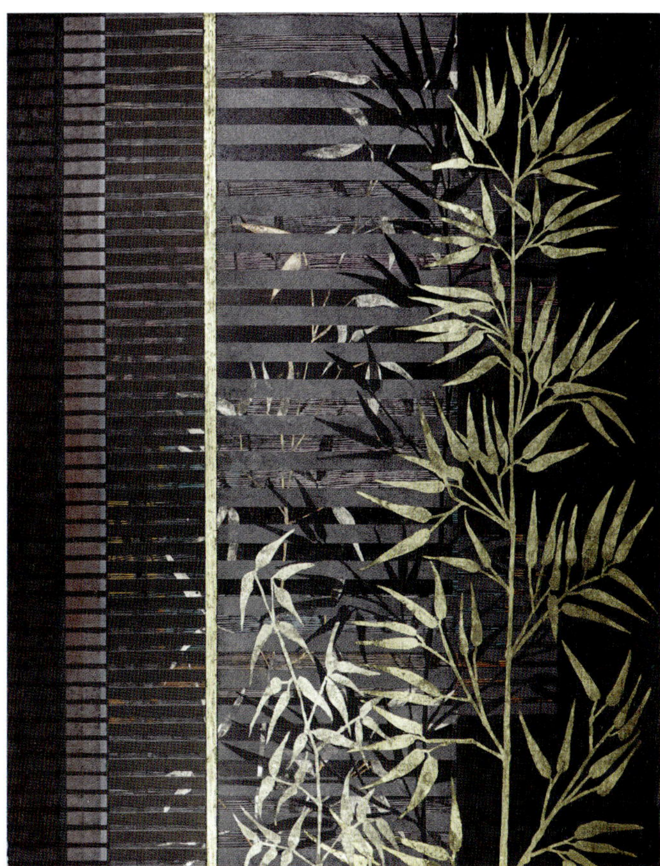

Roslyn Kean, *Courtyard Winter Shadows* (76 × 56cm). Printed on heavyweight *kōzo*.

REBECCA SALTER

London, UK

Obviously I knew about Japanese prints but until I went to live in Kyoto I had not had the opportunity to explore the technique. I studied with Professor Kurosaki Akira and then went on to research and document many of the remaining workshops in Japan for my two books on the subject.

In my own work I either print small editions myself or I work with the Satou Woodblock Workshop in Kyoto on larger editions. Their skills reflect the 'painterly' tradition of woodblock in Kyoto which can render the softness of watercolour in print.

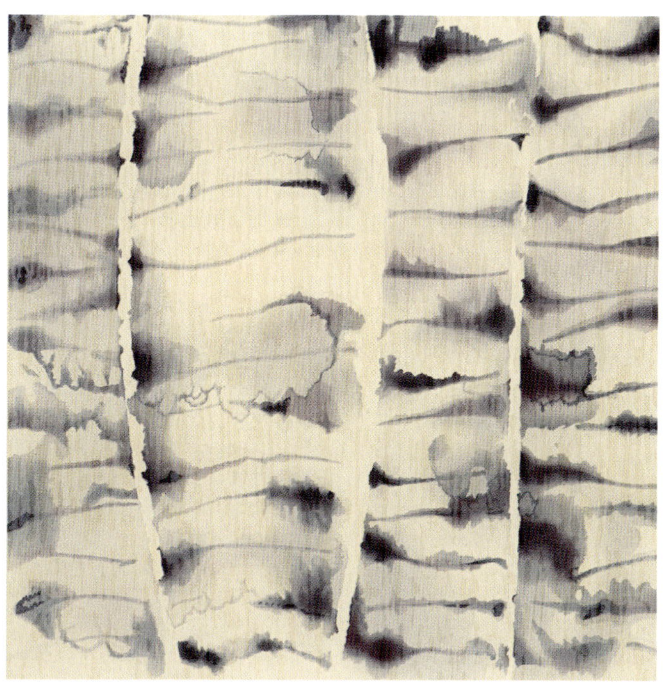

Rebecca Salter, *Weft 1* (28 × 46cm). Printed on *kōzo* paper.

HIDEHIKO GOTOU

Kanagawa Prefecture, Japan

The title of my work 'The Moon of Others' is derived from the Zen word 'Jita Ichijo'. It means to think of others as your own. It might be necessary to think of others in this time of uncertainty and chaos. How another person's moon appears to you?

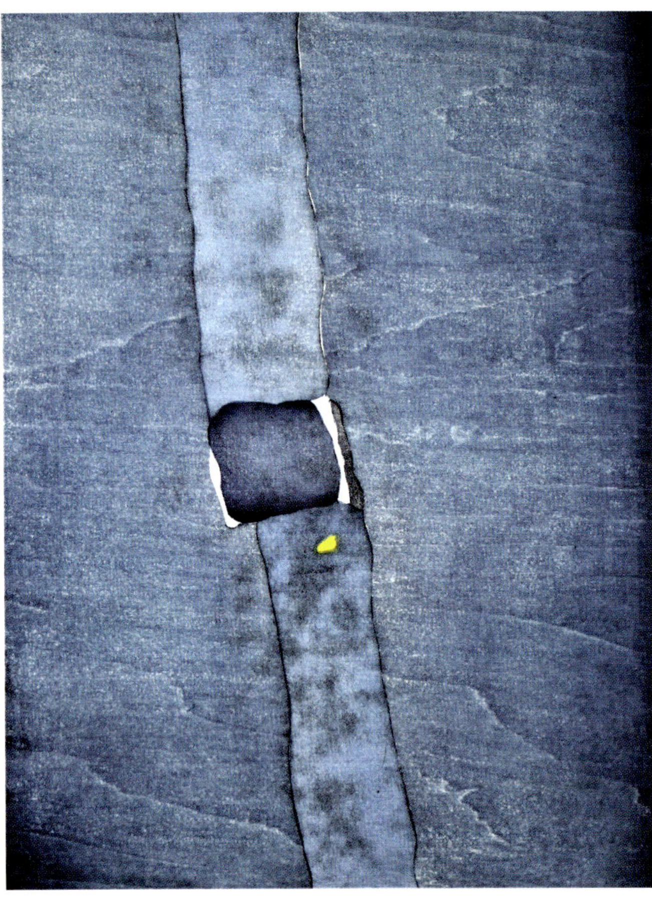

Hidehiko Gotou, *The Moon of Others* (33 × 25cm). Japanese woodcut on *washi*.

JANE FULTON SURI

Berkeley, California, USA

I started printmaking with lino in 2012. In Tokyo a few years later I had the good fortune to become a student of master woodblock carver Asaka Motoharu. I loved the discipline of the craft, the simple tools, the tactile connection with nature through wood, water, and materials made from local flora and fauna. Mokuhanga soon became the core of my art practice. It's a robust and delicate medium through which to explore the visual character of everyday visual experiences – reflections, luminosity, shadows, light filtering and framed by things around us. I'm enjoying the challenge of representing views from daily experiences that combine soft and hard, crisp and fuzzy, strong and subtle effects. Sometimes my works are presented as diptychs showing contrasting perspectives at single glance – perhaps aspect and ground shadow from inside a favorite tree in California, or lifted gaze from flat agricultural landscape to the misty height of Mt. Fuji.

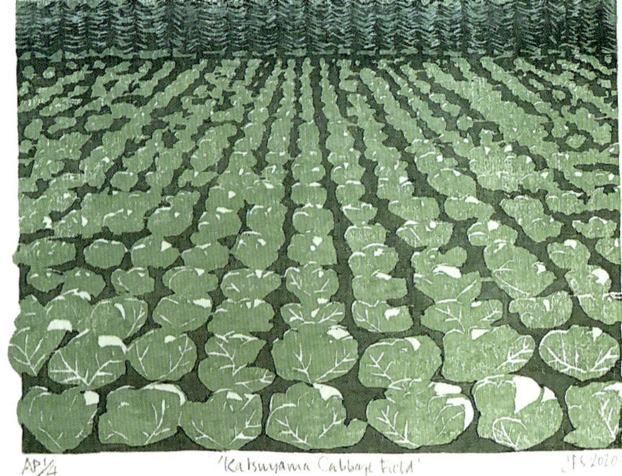

Jane Fulton Suri, *Katsuyama Cabbage Field* (18 × 25cm). Printed on *kōzo* extra thick paper.

ELIZABETH FORREST

Waterloo, Ontario, Canada

I was an experienced printmaker/print instructor when I went to Japan on a Canada Council grant in 1988 to study Mokuhanga with Akira Kurosaki. I felt encouraged to continue a serious practice in Mokuhanga after meeting a young papermaker who took over the old uchiyama paper facility in Nagano area and I continue to use her paper to date. Back to Canada I developed expertise in colour printing exploring various methods of application, while reusing the same woodblocks (Grid series 2000–2009). Then having an increased interest in representational imagery – I completed several works using the photographic qualities attainable with photo silkscreen contrasted with Mokuhanga's smooth, blended and mottled matt surfaces. Utilisation of digital technology has led to laser-cut blocks that invoke a screen motif. The screenlike imagery when printed using stencil masks or positives facilitates an immediacy of working where I can explore visual metaphors for all manner of 'screens' so prevalent in our shared environments.

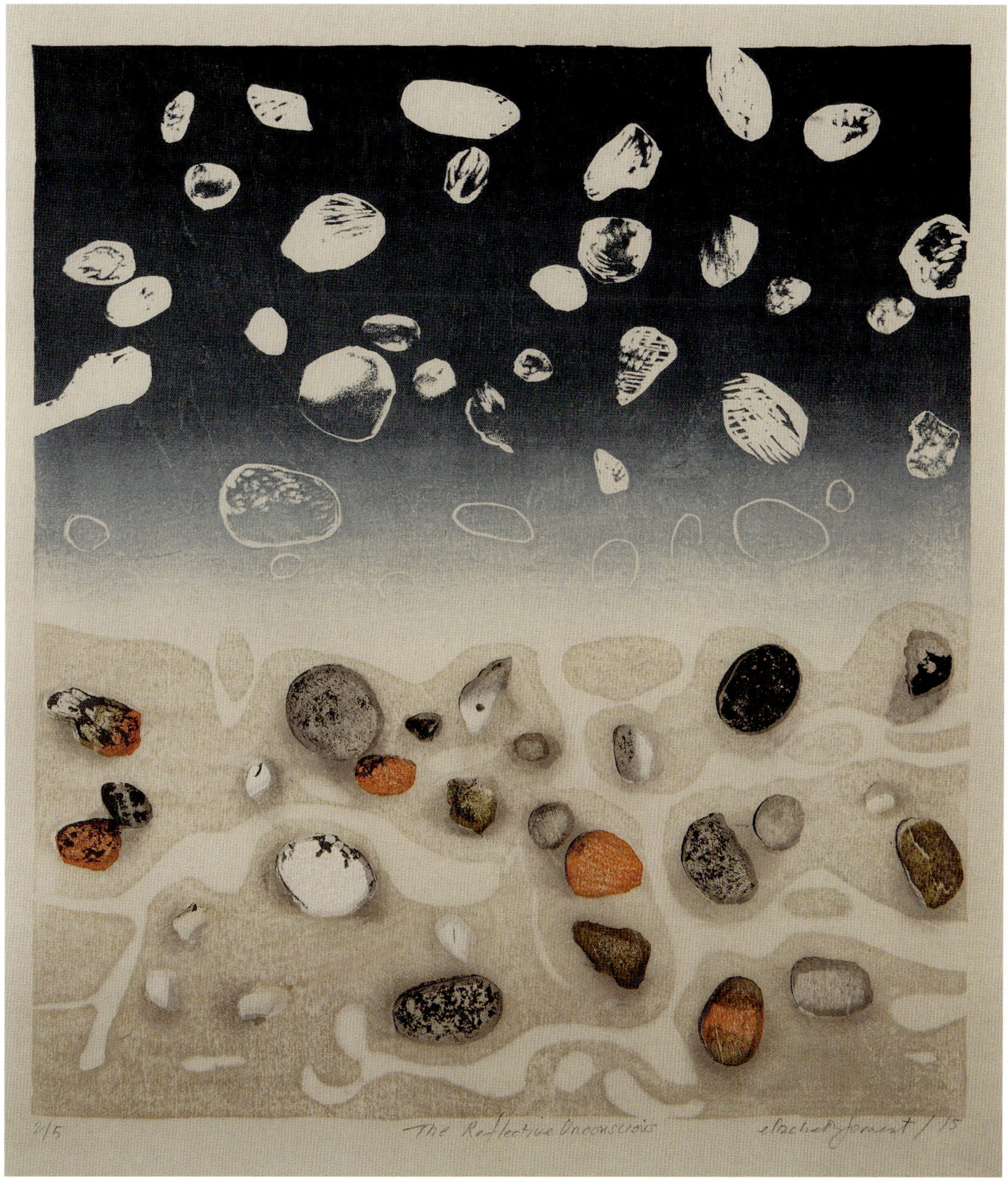

Elizabeth Forrest, *The Reflective Unconscious* (53 × 43.2cm). Japanese woodcut and photo screen. Printed on *Uchiyama washi*.

CAROL WILHIDE JUSTIN

London, UK

Time-consuming to produce, woodcuts are built up in a slow, exacting process, one layer at a time. In a world increasingly driven by the digital, my work celebrates the abiding value of the haptic and analogue.

I derive my inspiration from the natural world, the interplay of light and shade, and the mutability of time, movement, and memory. My woodcut prints seek to capture these fleeting moments of change. This is reflected in my subdued choice of colour.

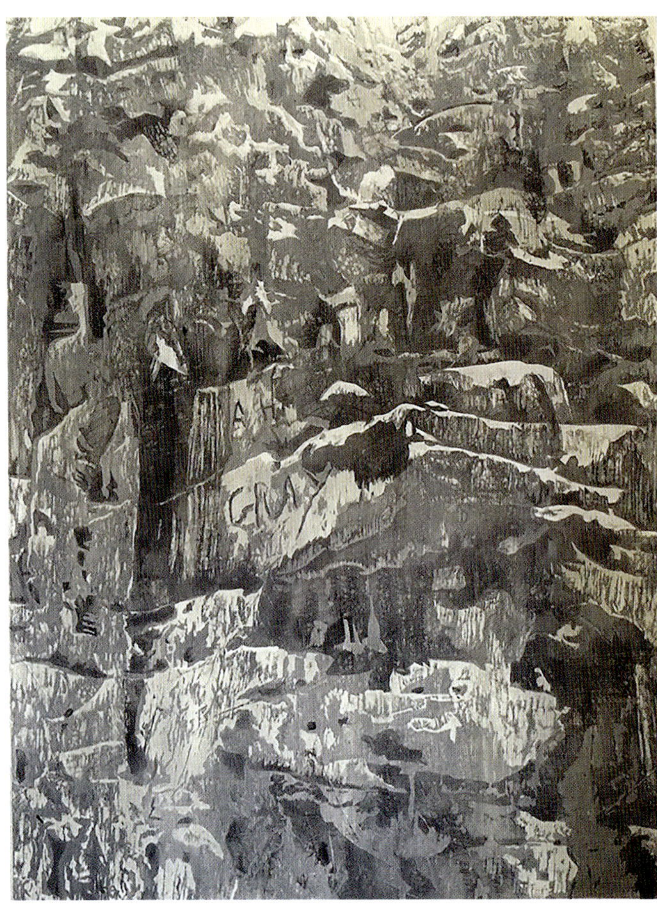

Carol Wilhide Justin, Gray. Japanese Woodcut on Bunkoshi paper (60 × 90cm).

APRIL VOLLMER

New York City, US

I first learned the pleasures of hand printmaking while studying etching for my MFA at Hunter College, NY, in the 1980s. Since then I've worked in many techniques, but Mokuhanga is the most flexible with the most satisfying tools and materials. Precise tools allow expressive cutting and good washi gives prints a present tense tactility.

These prints all include non-traditional Mokuhanga. Cupola is a woodcut of a chandelier printed on a digital image of a church ceiling on Gozen washi. Blue Torso is a digital, woodcut, and silkscreen print mounted on a shaped wood panel. Big Zova is untraditional in the way I printed two small blocks multiple times in a rotating pattern to create a kaleidoscopic effect. These are the same blocks I printed in smaller format for the cover of my book. Finally, Cranefly Moon is a simple two-colour Mokuhanga print, but the block with the rotating crane fly pattern was a laser-cut cherry block.

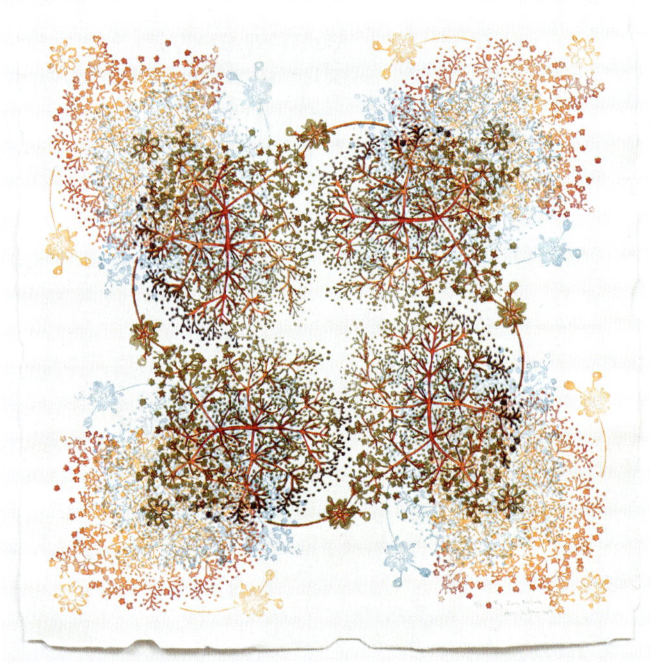

April Vollmer, *Big Zova* (66 × 66cm). Japanese woodcut on *Echizen washi*. Photographed by D. James Dee.

KATSUTOSHI YUASA

Kanagawa, Japan

My woodcut print is based on digital images, which I have taken with my digital camera. Woodcut print is the oldest printmaking technique. While especially Japan has a long tradition of woodcut print such as ukiyō-e (pictures of floating world), I think there contains many important questions regarding the origin of image-making and possibilities of renewed images. I use this traditional technique as a way of exposing images for adapting the subjective perception to the objective fiction. I would like to create a picture of light by hand-carving and printing like a photograph in the early days.

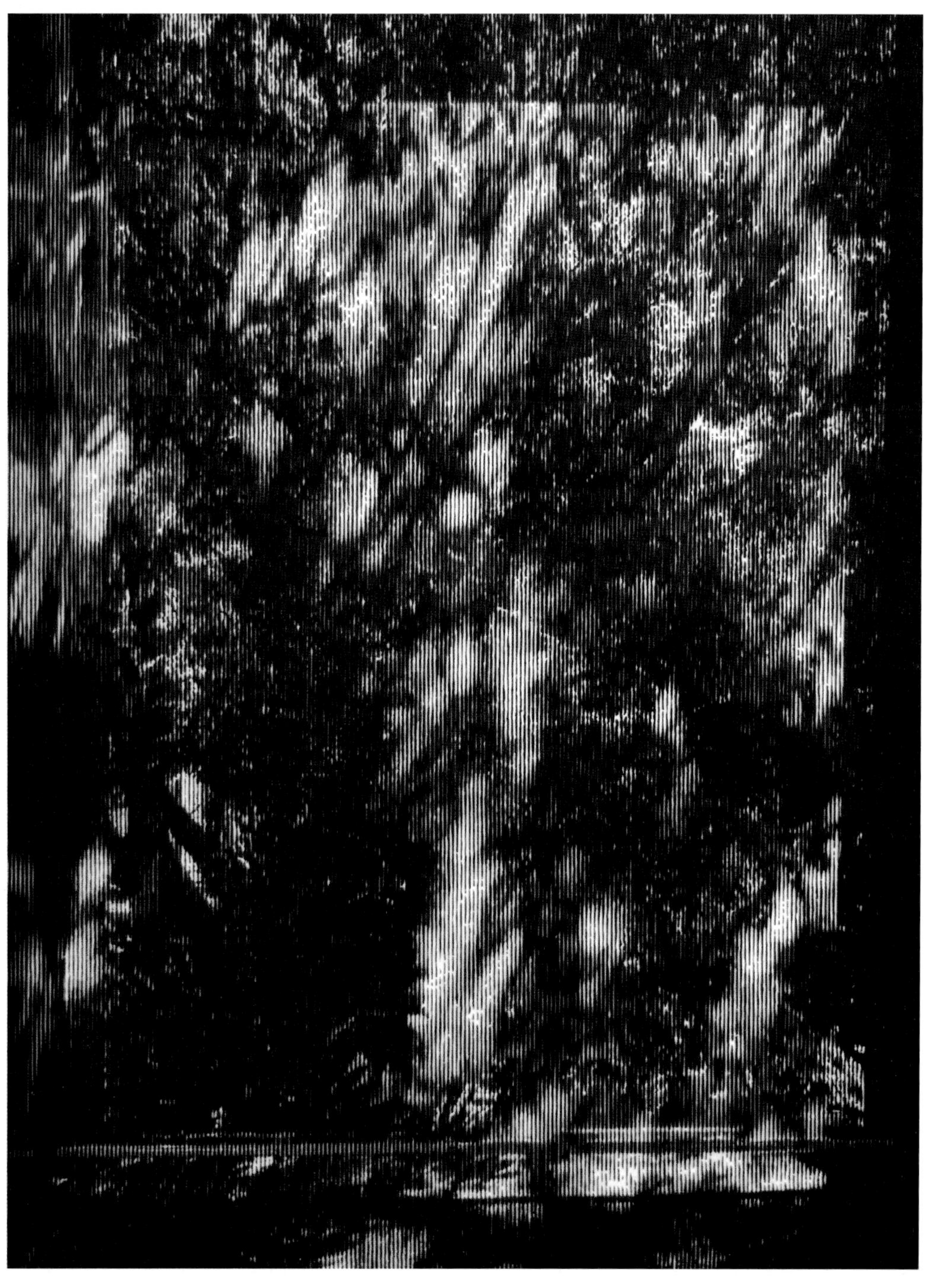

Katsutoshi Yuasa, *I Know Not What.*
Japanese woodcut.

GLOSSARY

Aniline – chemically produced bright dyes originally derived from coal tar

Anime – Japanese animation

Aratame – a stamp from the censor to show the print had been examined

Arato – coarse whetstone

Ategami – piece of paper, backing sheet, between *baren* and print during printing

Ategawa – *baren* backing

Atenashi bokashi – halo effect, typically to show the glow around the moon

Baren – printing tool made from a backing, an inner coil and a bamboo sheath

Betazuri – overprinting to make a more intense colour (also known as *tsubushi*)

Bokashi – printing a graduated fade

Bokujū – liquid *sumi* ink

Burashi – literally 'brush' made from horsetail hair used to brush pigment into the wood

Carbon paper – inked paper used to transfer image to the block

Chatter – unwanted raised areas on woodblock that pick up ink, also known as *ketsuochi*

Chiriyori – cleaning the fibres in papermaking

Copy paper – inexpensive paper as used in photocopiers

Cutting board – mats made from 'healable' rubber for cutting with a scalpel

Damp pack – 'book' made from dampened newsprint

Dōsa – size for paper made from animal glue to make the paper slightly less absorbent

Dōsabake – broad brush used for sizing

E-hon – Japanese picture book

E-nanushi – picture censor

Edition – number of prints made

Edo – former name for Tokyo. Edo era was 1603–1868

Embossing – blind printing leaving an un-inked raised surface

Ēnso – incomplete circle, symbolic in Zen Buddhism with togetherness, infinity

Formica – type of smooth laminate plastic surface for tables, counters

Fuki bokashi – broader stroke graduation line

Fune – vat used in papermaking

Gampi – type of fibre for papermaking

Gingko – tree native to China

Gofun – white pigment made from crushed shells

Gomazuri – 'Sesame seed' effect when printing

Hake – handled brush used to carry the pigment to the block

Hanga – a print

Hanga bake – printing brush

Hangitō/Kiridashi – sharp pointed, bevelled cutting tool

Hanmoto – commissioning publishers

Hanshira-e – 'pillar print', long thin prints joined at short edge

Hanshita – method of transferring image to block by pasting drawing face down

Hekomi – raised areas on a print that leave unwanted marks

Hiratō/Aisuki – chisel type tool

Hō – magnolia wood *Magnolia Obovata*

Hon baren – 'true' *baren* made by expert craftsmen, printing tool

Horishi – master carver

Hoshō – type of paper; most *ukiyō-e* prints were made using this type of paper

Ichimonji bokashi – thin graduated line at top of print, typically for sky

Iroita – colour blocks

Ita bokashi – cut graduation

Japonaiserie – fashion for Japanese objects in Paris, late nineteenth century

Japonisme – impact of Japanese aesthetics on Western art

Kabuki – a traditional form of popular theatre

kagi, hikitsuke – Registration notches for corner and straight *kentō*

Kakemono-e – unframed painting on paper or silk displayed as wall hanging

Kami – paper

Kamisuki – sheeting paper

Kano Academy – formal school training elite Japanese painters

Kanso – drying in papermaking

Karazuri – embossing

Kasane – colour

Katsura – type of wood from *Cercidiphyllum japonica*

Kawa – bamboo leaf cover for *baren*

Kentō – registration system

Kentōban – L-shaped piece of wood for registering larger woodblocks

Kentōnomi – chisel used for making registration notches

Keyblock – woodblock with outlines cut (also known as *sumiban*)

Kimedashi – embossed areas of print typically to show muscles

Kōshime – printing fine nets

Kotsuita – keyblock, also known as *sumiban*

Kōzo – paper mulberry fibre used in papermaking

Kurokawa – outer layer of stripped bark for making paper

Kurosaki baren – dimple surfaced plastic baren devised by Akira Kurosaki

Madake – species of bamboo leaf used for wrapping baren

Maebako – shelf in printer's

Maguwa – papermaking vat, also known as *fune*

Manga – Japanese comics or graphic novels

Marubake – handle-less round brush used to brush pigment into the woodgrain

Marutō/Komasuki – round-edge gouge tool

Matrix – the woodblock

Mawashi – circular action for rubbing down with the *baren*

Meisho-e – famous place pictures

Mica – fine crystalline powder used to add shimmer to print

Mimitsuke – deckle edges on handmade paper

Minogami – thin *kōzo* paper used for original drawing and pasted face down on the woodblock; *usumino* is a thin *minogami*

Miyabe – refined sensibility

Mizu bake – water brush used to dampen paper

Mokuhanga – Japanese term for Japanese woodcut, literally 'wood, carved block, picture'

Mokume-zuri – woodgrain

Nagashi-zuki – flowing method employed by printers to get an even coverage of paper fibres

Nagura – fine whetstone for levelling other stones

Neri – mucilage used in papermaking

Nikawa – animal glue/binder used to make size

Nishiki-e – literally 'brocade picture' describing early multicolour prints

Nori – rice paste

Proof – test of colours on copy paper or newsprint

Reduction – method of printing using one block, cutting and printing from lightest colour

Sakura – cherrywood

Sankakutō – V-shaped Western tool

Sensei – teacher

Set square – triangular ruler for ensuring square corners

Shin – prefix for a paper indicating it is machine made

Shin baren – core of baren made from twisted, coiled bamboo sheath

Shina – basswood plywood *Tilia japonica* used for woodblocks

Shinhanga – art movement continuing tradition of *hanmoto* system in the twentieth century

Shirataki – bamboo sheath used for making the *shin* coil in *baren* making

Shirokawa – inner white bark used for papermaking

Shita-e/hanshita – drawing on thin paper pasted down onto the block

Shito – post of finished wet paper in papermaking

Shunga – erotic prints

Sōsakuhanga – creative art movement from early twentieth century

Sugeta – *su* is the slatted bamboo, *keta* is wooden frame, together forming *sugeta*, used to make paper sheets

Sumi – Japanese black ink made from soot (*shoenboku* pine soot, *yuenboku* lamp soot)

Sumiban – keyline block

Suridai – printer's table angled down and away from printer

Surimono – literally 'printed thing', upmarket picture books

Surishi – printer

Suzuri – inkstone for rubbing *sumi* stick

Takuzuri – reverse block rubbing using ink applied with soft cloth, also known as *tanpo*

Tamari – unwanted dark edge on a print due to too much pigment

Tan-e – hand-coloured prints

Tanpo – soft cloth pad used to apply ink in *takuzuri*

Te bake – literally 'hand brush'

Toishi – whetstones

Tokusa – rush leaves used for scouring woodblock

Triptych, diptych, polyptych – prints formed with three, two or many prints together

Tsubushi – flat colour printing, also known as *betazuri*

Tsuge – boxwood

Tsukeawase – two colours printed as a bokashi, joining in the middle

Tsukesumi – sumi made from leftover sticks

Ukiyō-e – literally 'Pictures of the Floating World'

Urazuri – printing from the reverse, forcing colour through to the front

Urushi-e – literally 'lacquer' printing rich shiny black highlights

Washi – Japanese paper

White line – printing technique

Yakko, jyuniko, jyurokko – different strands of *baren* cord

Yamazakura – wild mountain cherrywood used for blocks

Yokoita – printer's low table for laying out prints

SUPPLIERS

UK

Intaglio Printmaker
9 Playhouse Court
62 Southwark Bridge Road
London SE1 0AS
020 7928 2633
www.intaglioprintmaker.com

Lawrence Art Supplies
208, 212 Portland Road
Hove BN3 5QT
www.lawrence.co.uk

Great Art
41-9 Kingsland Road
London E2 8AG
www.greatart.co.uk

Handprinted
22 Arun Business Park
Shripney Road
Bognor Regis PO22 9SX
www.handprinted.co.uk

Jacksons Art
1 Farleigh Place
London N16 7SX
www.jacksonsart.com

L. Cornelissen & Son
105 Great Russell Street
WC1B 3RY
www.cornelissen.com

Shepherds
30 Gillingham Street
London Sw1V 1HU
www.bookbinding.co.uk

John Purcell Paper
15 Rumsey Road
London SW9 0TR
www.johnpurcell.net

USA

McClain's Printmaking Supplies
15685 SW 116th Avenue PMB 202
King City
OR 97224-2695
www.imcclains.com

Hiromi Paper International
2525 Michigan Avenue
Bergamot Station G-9
Santa Monica
CA 90404
www.hiromipaper.com

Washi Arts
www.washiarts.com

Kremer Pigments Inc.
247 West 29th Street
New York, NY 10001
212-219-2394
www.kremerpigments.com

Daniel Smith
PO Box 84268
4150 First Avenue south
Seattle, WA 98124-5568
www.danielsmith.com

JAPAN

Awagami Paper Factory
www.awagami.com

Bumpodo
1-21-1 Jinbocho
Kanda
Chiyoda-ku
Tokyo 101-0051
www.bumpodo.co.jp

Ozu Washi
www.ozuwashi.net

Sekaido
www.sekaido.co.jp

Woodlike Matsumura
Kamishakuji 1-11-9

Nerima-ku
Tokyo 177-0044
www.woodlike.co.jp

AUSTRALIA

Melbourne Etching Supplies
33A St. David Street

Fitzroy 3065
www.mes.net.au

Roslyn Kean Ball Bearing Baren
ww.rozkean@bigpond.com

BIBLIOGRAPHY

Japanese Woodblock Technique
Azechi, Umetaro, *Japanese Woodblock Prints, Their Techniques and Appreciation* (Toto Shuppan Company Ltd., Tokyo, Japan, 1963)
Boswell, Laura, *Making Japanese Woodblock Prints* (The Crowood Press, 2019)
Laitinen, Kari, Moilanen, Tuula, Tanttu Antti, *The Art and Craft of Woodblock Printmaking* (Aalto ARTS Books, 1999)
McKenna, Terry, *Creative Print, Intermediate Mokuhanga* (Karuizawa Mokuhanga School, 2021)
Petit, Gaston, Arboleda, Amadio, *Evolving Techniques in Japanese Woodblock Prints* (Kodansha International Ltd., 1977)
Salter, Rebecca, *Japanese Woodblock Printing* (Bloomsbury 2013)
Tokuriki, Tomikichiro, *Woodblock Print Primer* (Japan Publications Inc., 1970)
Vollmer, April, *Japanese Woodblock Print Workshop* (Watson-Guptill Publications, Berkeley, 2015)

Japanese Prints
Baker, Stanley, Joan, *Japanese Art* (Thames and Hudson Inc., New York, 1984)
Fahr-Becker, Gabriele, *Japanese Prints* (Taschen, GmbH, 2002)
Ficke, Davison, Arthur, *Chats on Japanese Prints* (T. Fisher Unwin Ltd,1915)
Forman, Hájek, *Japanese Woodcuts Early Periods* (Spring Books, 1950)
Hillier, J., *Japanese Colour Prints* (Phaidon Press Ltd., Oxford, 1966)
Ives, Feller, Colta, *The Great Wave, The influence of Japanese Woodcuts on French Prints* (The Metropolitan Museum of Art, New York, 1974)

Statler, Oliver, *Modern Japanese Prints: An Art Reborn,* (Charles E. Tuttle Company Rutland, Vermont, Tokyo, Japan, 1959)
Tinios, Ellis, *Japanese Prints Ukiyo-e in Edo, 1700-1900* (The British Museum Press, 2010)

Japanese Artists
Allen, W., Laura, Brown, H., Kendall, Skibbe, M., Eugene, Welch, Matthew, Koichi, Yasunaga, *A Japanese Legacy, Four Generations of Yoshida family Artists* (The Minneapolis Institute of Arts, 2002)
Baatsch, Henri-Alexis, *Hokusai a Life in Drawing* (Thames & Hudson, London 2016)
Clark, Timothy, *Hokusai, beyond the Great Wave* (Thames & Hudson Ltd., London, The British Museum, 2018)
Clark, Timothy, *Hokusai, The Great Picture Book of Everything* (The British Museum Press, 2021)
Paget, Rhiannon, *Saitō Kiyoshi, Graphic Awakening* (The John & Mable Ringling Museum of Art and Scala Arts Publishers Inc., 2021)
Thompson, E., Sarah, *Hokusai's Lost Manga* (MFA Publications, Museum of Fine Arts, Boston, 2016)
Trede, Melanie, Bichler, Lorenz, *Hiroshige* (Taschen, GmbH, 2010)

Japanese History
Mason, P.,H.,R.,Caiger,G.,J., *A History of Japan* (Tuttle Publishing, 1997)
Reischauer, O., Edwin, Jansen, B., Marius, *The Japanese Today, Change and Continuity* (The Belknap Press of Harvard University Press, 1995)
Shimizu, Yoshiaki, *Japan, The Shaping of Daimyo Culture 1185-1868* (George Braziller Inc., Publishers, New York, National Gallery of Art, Washington, 1988)

Williams, John, R., *The Buddha in the Machine, Art, Technology, and the Meeting of East and West* (Yale University Press, 2014)

Japanese Arts and Culture
Frydman, Joshua, *The Japanese Myths* (Thames & Hudson, 2022)
Garis, de, Frederic *We Japanese* (Fujiya Hotel, Ltd., Japan, 1934)
Hearn, Lafcadio, *Out of the East, reveries and Studies in New Japan* (Cosimo, Inc., 2006, originally published in 1910)
Ishiguro, Kazuo, *An Artist of the Floating World* (Faber and Faber Ltd., 1986)
Jackson, Anna, *Kimono, Kyoyo to Catwalk* (V & A Publishing, 2020)
Leach, Bernard, *A Potter in Japan,* (Faber and Faber Ltd., London, 1960)
Menegazzo, Rossella, Piotti, Stefania, *Wa, The Essence of Japanese Design* (Phaidon Press, London, 2014)
Nakata, Yujiro, *The Art of Japanese Calligraphy* (John Weatherhill, Inc., New York and Heibonsha, Tokyo, 1973)
Ozeki, Ruth, *A Tale for the Time Being* (Canongate Books Ltd., 2013)
Röttgen, Uwe, Zetti, Katharina, *Craftland Japan* (Thames & Hudson, Ltd., London, 2020)
Shelton, Barrie, *Learning from the Japanese City, Looking East in Urban Design* (E and FN Spon, 1999)
Shikibu, Murasaki, *The Tale of Genji* (Martin Secker & Warburg Ltd., 1976, written in the 11th century)
Tanizaki, Junichirō, *In Praise of Shadows* (Jonathan Cape, 1991)
Yanagi, Sōetsu, *The Unknown Craftsman, A Japanese Insight into Beauty* (Kodansha, New York, 1972)

RESOURCES

Online resources

The Unfinished Print podcast with Andre Zadorozny, based in Toronto. Interviews with artists, gallery owners and collectors of Mokuhanga.
theunfinishedprint.libsyn.com/

David Bull
David Bull is Canadian born but has lived in Japan for a long time. Online tutorials, blogs and posts on all things related to Mokuhanga.
mokuhankan.com/

Annie Bissett artist blog
www.woodblockdreams.blogspot.com

Journals

Impressions: The Journal of the Japanese Art Society of America
www.japaneseartsoc.org/impressions/

Printmaking Today
www.cellopress.co.uk/

Galleries/Museums

Japan
Tokyo National Museum
www.tnm.jp/

Kamigata Ukiyō-e Museum, Osaka
osaka-info.jp/

UK
Victoria & Albert Museum
www.vam.ac.uk/

The British Museum
www.britishmuseum.org/

FitzWilliam Museum, Cambridge
www.fitzmuseum.cam.ac.uk/

Japan House
Japanese cultural showcase in London
www.japanhouselondon.uk/

Anastasia von Seibold
London dealer in Japanese Art at Cromwell Place,
London SW1
www.avsjapaneseart.com/

USA
The Metropolitan Museum of Art, New York
www.metmuseum.org/

Los Angeles County Museum of Art
www.lacma.org/

Ronin Gallery, New York
www.roningallery.com/education

Residencies/Classes

MI-Lab Residency
Artist in residency programme in Japan designed to teach Mokuhanga to international students
endeavor.or.jp/mi-lab/aboutus/

My Japanese Woodcut classes for Beginners, Intermediate and Advanced Students in London, UK and lectures for The Art Society:

Morley College
www.morleycollege.ac.uk/

The City Literary Institute
www.citylit.ac.uk/

The Art Academy
artacademy.ac.uk/

The Art Society
theartssociety.org/

Laura Boswell based in Kirkcudbright, Scotland
www.lauraboswell.co.uk

Zea Mays Printmaking, Florence, Massachusetts, USA
www.zeamaysprintmaking.com

Richard Steiner's Kyoto International Mokuhanga School, Kyoto, Japan
www.mokuhanga-school.net

Terry McKenna's Karuizawa Mokuhanga School, Nagano, Japan
www.mokuhanga-school.jp/

Conferences

Triennial International Mokuhanga Conference
mokuhanga.org/

International Print Conference IMPACT
cfpr.uwe.ac.uk/impact/impact-conference/

ARTISTS' DETAILS

Mara Cozzolino
www.instagram.com/mara_
cozzolino/
www.maracozzolino.com

Sara Lee
www.instagram.com/saraleeartist/
www.saraleeartist

Laura Boswell
www.instagram.com/
laura_boswell_printmaker/?hl=en
www.facebook.com/
LauraBoswellPrintmaker/
www.lauraboswell.co.uk/

Jane Fulton Suri
www.instagram.com/jfultonsuri

Cameron Bailey
www.instagram.com/cambaileyprints/
www.Cameronbaileyprints.com/

Elisabet Strand
www.elisabet.no/

Sybille Schlumbom
www.instagram.com/sybille_schlumbom/
www.sybille_schlumbom/

Natasha Norman
www.instagram.com/natashanormanart/
www.natashanorman.co.za/

Susan Rushforth
www.sydneyprintmakers/

Annie Bissett
www.instagram.com/anniebissettartist/
www.anniebissett.com/

Nana Shiomi
www.nanashiomi.com/

Wuon-Gean Ho
www.instagram.com/wuongean/?hl=en

Faith Stone
www.instagram.com/faithstoneart/
www.FaithStoneArt@etsy.com/

Rowan McOnegal
www.instagram.com/rowanmconegal/
www.rowanmconegal.co.uk

Linda J. Beeman
lindajbeeman.com

Yoonmi Nam
www.instagram.com/yoonmi_nam/
www.yoonminam.com/

Kaoru Morita
www.instagram.com/k.a.o.r.u.m/

Paul Furneaux
@Paul_furneaux
www.paulfurneaux.com

Jacqueline Gribbin
www.instagram.com/jacquelinefgribbin

Terry McKenna
www.instagram.com/mokuhangaschool/
www.mokuhanga-school.jp

Karen Kunc
www.karen-kunc.com
www.constellation-studios.net

Takuji Hamanaka
www.instagram.com/takujihanga/

Mia O
www.instagram.com/mia_o_pen/
www.mia-o.format.com/

Tuula Moilanen
www.instagram.com/tuulahelenamoi/

Lucy May Schofield
www.instagram.com/lucymayschofield/
www.lucymayschofield.com/

Patty Hudak
www.instagram.com/hudakpatty/
www.pattyhudak.com

Roslyn Kean
www.instagram.com/roslynkean/
www.roslynkean.com.au/

Rebecca Salter
www.instagram.com/rsalterra/
www.rebeccasalter.com/

Kevin Frances
www.kevinfrances.com

Elizabeth Forrest
www.elizabethforrest.ca
www.instagram.com/elizabethforrest.artist/

Carol Wilhide Justin
www.instagram.com/caroljustin1/
www.carolwilhide.com/

April Vollmer
www.aprilvollmer.com
www.facebook.com/april.vollmer
www.instagram.com/aprilvollmer_artist/

Katsutoshi Yuasa
www.katsutoshiyuasa@hotmail.com

IMAGE CREDITS

All images are the authors' own, with the exception of the following: page 9: McGill University Rare Books and Special collections, courtesy Ms Sarah Welch, CC BYSA 4.0; page 10 (top right): P-D Los Angeles County Museum of Art, gift of Chuck Bowdlear PhD and John Borozan MA (M.2000.105.99); page 12 (top): British Museum; page 12 (bottom right): Collection Los Angeles County Museum of Art; page 14: The Phil Berg Collection, Los Angeles County Museum of Art; page 15: Tokyo National Museum, photographer Emuseum; page 16 (left): British Museum; page 17: Brooklyn Museum; page 20 (top right): The Joan Elizabeth Tanney Bequest, Los Angeles County Museum of Art; page 21 (top): Los Angeles County Museum of Art; page 22: Henry L. Phillips Collection, Bequest of Henry L. Phillips, 1939, The Metropolitan Museum of Art, NY; page 23: Gift of Miss Bella Mabury, Los Angeles County Museum of Art; pages 24 and 25: Gift of Cole J. Younger, 1975, The Metropolitan Museum of Art, NY; page 26 (top): British Museum; page 26 (bottom): United States Library of Congress; page 28: Metropolitan Museum of New York, Henry L. Phillips Collection, Bequest of Henry L. Phillips, 1939; page 29: Metropolitan Museum of New York, Mary and Cheney Cowles Collection, gift of Mary and Cheney Cowles, 2018; page 30: United States Library of Congress; page 32 (top left): Metropolitan Museum of New York, The Howard Mansfield Collection, Purchase, Rogers Fund, 1936; page 32 (top right): Metropolitan Museum of New York, H.O. Havemeyer Collection, bequest of Mrs. H.O. Havemeyer, 1929; page 32 (bottom): British Museum; page 33: Metropolitan Museum of New York, purchase, Joseph Pulitzer Bequest, 1918; page 34 (left): Metropolitan Museum of New York, Museum Accession; page 34 (top right): Metropolitan Museum of New York, Rogers Fund, 1936; page 35: Metropolitan Museum of New York, Rogers Fund, 1932; page 36: National Diet Museum, Tokyo; page 37: Metropolitan Museum of New York, Rogers Fund; page 38: Metropolitan Museum of New York, H.O. Havemeyer Collection, bequest of Mrs. H.O. Havemeyer, 1929; page 39 (top): Los Angeles County Museum of Art, Mr and Mrs Allan C. Balch Collection (M.45.3.537); page 36 (bottom): Los Angeles County Museum of Art, gift of Dr Harvey Eagleson (M.66.35.7); page 40 (left): Los Angeles County Museum of Art, gift of Arthur and Fran Sherwood (M.2007.152.15); page 40 (bottom right): Los Angeles County Museum of Art, The Joan Elizabeth Tanney Bequest (M.2006.136.76); page 41 (top right): Netsuke (Japan); ivory; Gift of Anonymous Donor; 1952-164-37-a,b, Cooper Hewitt Collection; page 41 (bottom right): P-D Museum of Fine Arts, Boston; page 42 (left): PD-US National Endowment for the Humanities; page 42 (right): Rosenwald Collection, PD-National Gallery of Art, CC0; page 43 (top left): Metropolitan Museum of New York, H.O. Havemeyer Collection, bequest of Mrs. H.O. Havemeyer, 1929; page 43 (bottom left): P-D Musée d'Orsay, Paris; page 43 (right): Los Angeles County Museum of Art, Far Eastern Art Council Fund (AC1995.62.1); page 44: P-D gallica.bnf.fr/Bibliothèque nationale de France; page 45: De pruimenboomgaard te Kameido-Rijksmuseum RP-P-1956-743.jpeg Created: 1857date QS:P571,+1857-00-00T00:00:00Z/9; page 46: P-D Van Gogh Museum s0115V1962; page 47: Metropolitan Museum of New York, gift of Lincoln Kirstein, 1959; page 48 (right): P-D Honolulu Museum of Art accession 26926; page 49 (left): P-D National Museum of Modern Art, Tokyo; page 49 (right): Metropolitan Museum of New York, Kate S, Buckingham Endowment Reference Number 1979.622; page 50: P-D Yamamoto Kanae Memorial Museum; page 51 (top): P-D : Catalogue/Yamamoto Kanae; page 51 (bottom): P-D Tokyo Fuji Art Museum; page 52: P-D Smithsonian Museum of Art; page 53: P-D US Library of Congress's Prints and Photographs Division; page 54: © Tuula Moilanen; page 55 © Karen Kunc; page 92: P-D Los Angeles County Museum of Art, gift of Dr. Harvey Eagleson (M.66.35.8); page 99 (bottom): P-D Metropolitan Museum of Art, New York, Charles Stewart Smith Collection, gift of Mrs Charles Stewart Smith, Charles Stewart Smith Jr, and Howard Caswell Smith, in memory of Charles Stewart Smith, 1914; pages 142 and 151: © Elizabeth Myers; page 154 (top left): © Judith Elisabeth de Haan; page 154 (bottom left): © Pat Rougeau; page 154 (top and bottom right): © Sue Rowling; page 155 and 156 (left): © Valerie Johnson Bell; page 157 (left): © May Veronica Howard; page 159 (top): © Inga Eicaite; page 159 (bottom): © Margaret Cooter; page 163: © Sarah Ann Mitchell; page 171: © Mara Cozzolino; page 172: © Sara Lee; page 173: © Laura Boswell; page 174: © Kevin Frances; page 175: © Cameron Bailey; page 176 © Elisabet Strand; page 177: © Sybille Schumblom; page 178 © Natasha Norman; page 179: © Susan Rushforth; page 180: © Annie Bissett; page 181: © Nana Shiomi; page 182 (left): Wuon-Geon Ho; page 182: © Faith Stone; page 183 (top): © Rowan McOnegal; page 183 (bottom): © Linda J. Beeman; page 184: © Yoonmi Nam; page 185: © Kaoru Morita; page 186: © Paul Furneaux; page 187: © Tomasz Kawelczyk; page 188: © Jacqueline Gribbin; page 189: © Terry McKenna; page 190: © Karen Kunc; page 191 (left): © Takuji Hamanaka; page 191 (right): © Mia O; page 192: © Tuula Moilanen; page 193: © Lucy May Schofield; page 194: © Patty Hudak; page 195 (left): © Roslyn Kean; page 195 (right): Rebecca Salter; page 196 (left): © Hidehiko Gotou; page 196 (right): © Jane Fulton Suri; page 197: © Elizabeth Forrest; page 198 (right): © April Vollmer; page 199: © Katsutoshi Yuasa.

INDEX

Artists

Bailey, Cameron 175
Beeman, Linda J. 183
Bissett, Annie 180
Boswell, Laura 173
Cassatt, Mary 42
Cooter, Margaret 159
Cozzolino, Mara 171
De Haan, Elisabeth 154
De Toulouse-Lautrec, Henri 44
Degas, Edgar 43
Eicaite, Inga 159
Forrest, Elizabeth 197
Frances, Kevin 174
Fulton Suri, Jane 196
Furneaux, Paul, 186
George, Julie 153
Gotou, Hidehiko 66, 196
Gribbon, Jacqueline, 188
Hamanaka, Takuji 191
Harunobu, Suzuki 18, 20, 31
Hiroshige, Andō 21, 39–40, 43, 45, 92
Ho, Wuon-Gean 182
Hokusai, Katsushika 7, 28, 34–38, 99
Howard, Mary Veronica 157
Hudak, Patty 194
Hyde, Helen 52
Johnson-Bell, Val 155–156
Kawelczyk, Tomasz 187
Kean, Roslyn 68, 195
Kunc, Karen 55, 190
Kunisada, Utagawa 24–25, 26,
Kurosaki, Akira 55, 67
Lazzell, Blanche 156
Lee, Sara title verso, 172
Lum, Bertha 53
Masanobu, Okumura 30
McKenna, Terry 189
McOnegal, Rowan 183
Mitchell, Sarah Ann 163
Moilanen, Tuula 54, 192
Morita, Kaoru 185
Munakata, Shiko 49
Myers, Elizabeth 142
Nam, Yoonmi 184
Norman, Natasha 178
O, Mia 191
Onchi, Kōshirō 49
Rougeau, Pat 154
Rowling, Sue 154

Rushforth, Susan 179
Salter, Rebecca 195
Schlumbom, Sybille 177
Schofield, Lucy May 193
Sharaku, Tōshūsai 22
Shiomi, Nana 181
Shunshō, Kutsukawa 33
Stone, Faith 182
Strand, Elisabet 176
Tōyō, Sesshū 13–15
Utamaro, Kitagawa 23, 32, 43
Van Gogh, Vincent 46
Van Rijn, Rembrandt 16
Vollmer, April 171,
Wilhide Justin, Carol cover, inside
    cover, frontispiece, 93, 112, 157, 160,
    161, 162, 170, 198
Yamammoto, Kanae 50–51
Yoshida, Hiroshi 51
Yuasa, Katsutoshi 199

baren 66–68, 135, 144 (*see* printing)
books, making 16–18, 160
    leporello 158–159
    scrolls *ekimono* 158–159
brushes 69–70 (*see* Printing)
    care of brushes 70, 72
carving tools 57–66
    cutting 106–114
    hangi-tō 58, 64, 106–107
    hiratō 59, 64, 110–112
    honing tools 60–62
    kentōnommi 59, 117–128
    marutō 58, 65, 108–109
    sankakutō 58, 65–66, 113–114
    sharpening tools 63–66
drawing
    design 93
    master drawing 94
    thumbnails 95
ceramic
    Delftware 12
    porcelain 11, 12
editioning 140–141
graphite rubbing 115
keyblock 17, 25
nori 57, 72–74, 131, 166
    recipe 73
paper 82–89, 153, 164,
    cutting 126–128, 129

dampening 130
Japanese paper sizes 88
recommendations 88
sizing 87
pigments 74–77
printing
    checklist 126, 132–133
    drying 138–139
    issues with printing 137–138
    setting up 132
    step by step 134–136
printing techniques
    3-D 161
    betazuri 143–144
    bokashi 145–150
    gomazuri 144
    karazuri 150
    kirazuri 152–153
    large format 162–169
    mokumezuri 144–145
    monoprinting 153–154
    reduction 154–156
    repeat pattern 157–158
    takuzuri 151–152
    urazuri. 152
    white line 156–157
registration
    kentō 18, 20, 116–122
    kentōban 123, 135, 165–169
schools
    Crown Point Press 54
    Kano academy 13–16
    Katsukawa School 33
    MI-Lab 6, 7, 55, 125
    Shijo 38
sumi 77–79
transferring image
    carbon paper 98–99
    Citrasolv 100, 103
    hanshita 100–102 (see *Nori*)
wood
    marking up 97
    tinting 96
    types of wood 79–82
    woodgrain 95, 98, 144–145, 153–154
ukiyo-e 16–20, 24–25
    artists 29–40
    buying a print 26–29
    editioning 140
    prints in Europe 40–41, 42–46

First published in 2024 by
The Crowood Press Ltd
Ramsbury, Marlborough
Wiltshire SN8 2HR

enquiries@crowood.com
www.crowood.com

British Library Cataloguing-in-Publication Data
A catalogue record for this book is available from the British Library.

ISBN 978 0 7198 4318 1

Cover design: Sergey Tsvetkov
End paper: Carol Wilhide Justin
Tangled
Triptych Japanese woodcut using handmade pigments on magnolia wood
Frontispiece: Carol Wilhide Justin
In the Fold of the Sea
Folded Japanese woodcut
Contents image: Sara Lee
Abate
45 × 35 cm
Japanese Woodcut printed on *Shioji* paper

Typeset by Envisage IT
Printed and bound in India by Thomson Press (India) Ltd

ACKNOWLEDGEMENTS

I would like to thank the late Keiko Kadota for setting up MI-LAB and introducing me to Mokuhanga, and for having the vision to introduce the triennial International Mokuhanga Print Conference, instrumental in disseminating Mokuhanga to the rest of the world.

And a big thank you to the Mokuhanga artists from around the world who have generously allowed me to show images of their work in my book.

Also to my family for their wonderful support.

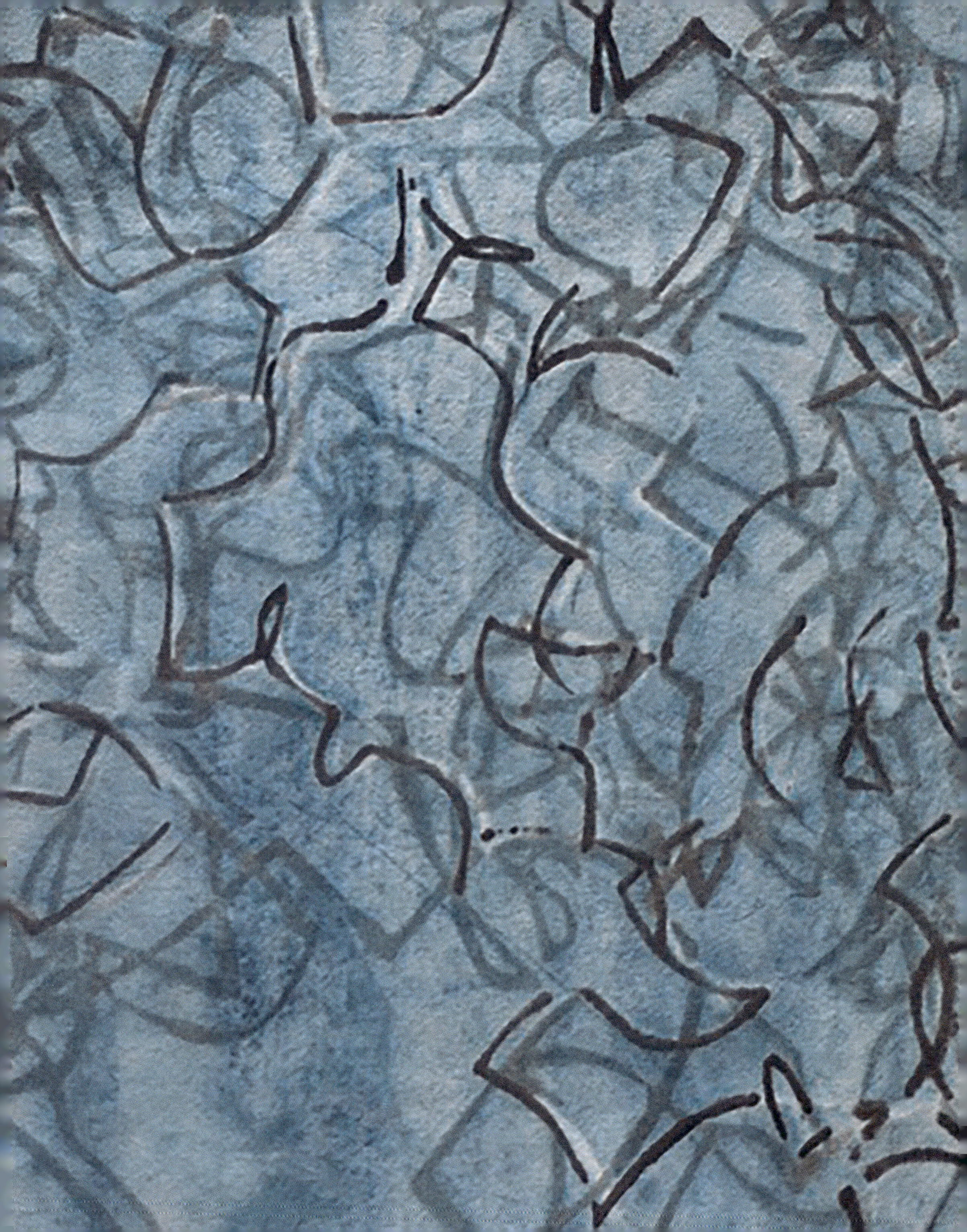

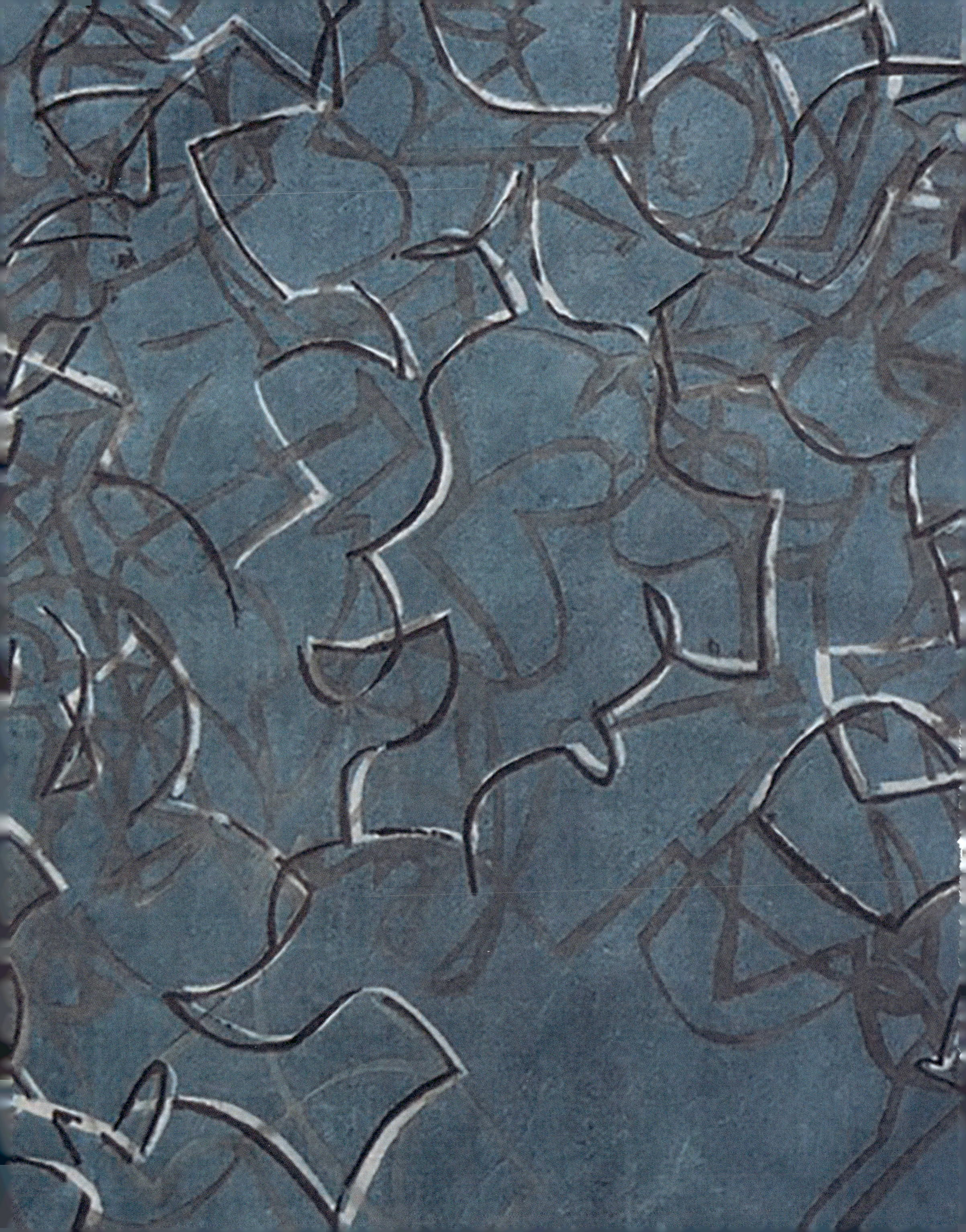